Tobias Aichele • Porsche 911

Tobias Aichele

PORSCHE 911

Forever young

Translation by: Peter Albrecht

Beeman Jorgensen

Dust jacket design: Johann Walentek. Photo by René Staud.

Photo sources: Title photo: René Staud
Contents: Tobias Aichele, Porsche archives, Christoph Bauer, Eberhard Strähle, gad Studios,
Karl Maria Hofer, Dieter Röscheisen, H.D. Seufert, René Staud Studios, Ulrich Upietz

Layout: Stefanie Götz.

Translation: Peter Albrecht

Technical Assistance: Howard Adams, Bill Block, William Fishback, George Hussey, Olaf Lang, Kirk Minster,
A. Everett Singer

Those who assisted materially in writing this book are mentioned in the introductory chapter ("The Challenge").

Dedicated to Prof. Dr. Ing. h.c. Ferry Porsche, on the occasion of his 85th birthday, September 19, 1994

ISBN 0-929758-11-0

Contents

Foreword

Forever Young

The 911, with its air-cooled six-cylinder boxer engine, was not an immediate success. Thirty years ago, at the 1963 Frankfurt auto show, many critical voices could be heard. To potential customers, the 911 seemed strange and unfamiliar. This did not worry me greatly; in such cases, I am of the opinion that if something is an immediate success, it will quickly fall out of fashion.

Furthermore, I was convinced of the validity of the 911 concept. In price, performance and design, it

represented a continuation of the 356 Carrera 2, but had a considerably more functional character. Indeed, this concept has proven itself; over the years, the 911 has emerged as our greatest success.

Continuous product development and pioneering engineering refinement have made the 911 immortal. After thirty years, we are presenting, and not without pride, the new Carrera generation at the Frankfurt IAA. With the new Carrera, we once again demonstrate the potential of the rear-engined sports car. Thanks to countless improvements, we have underscored our claim of leadership in sports car design. At the same time, in the new Carrera, we have once again created a car with personality, with which the customer will readily identify; a vehicle whose overall concept so captivates its driver that he treasures the features that define its strong character. For thirty years, this was the recipe for the 911's success, and will remain so for years to come.

I am most pleased that Tobias Aichele, in this book, has reconstructed the success story of the 911 in such fascinating detail.

Introduction

The Challenge

Anniversaries are usually retrospective celebrations of things long gone. In the case of only one sports car presently in production, this definition is incomplete – even on its thirtieth birthday. For this car, the anniversary is also an occasion to look ahead, and particularly to examine the car's future. Thirty years to the day after the introduction of the Porsche 911, the new Carrera generation, known internally as the Type 993, with great promise for the future, was presented at the Frankfurt International Automobile Show.

These anniversary celebrations were reason enough for me to fulfill a long-held desire to delve into the history of this legendary sports car, and to write a book about my discoveries.

How did this desire come about? There was no key event, but rather a perfectly normal childhood dream, the dream to someday drive a 911, and if possible to own one. The dream soon became a wish. After I had been infected by the automotive virus in my eighteenth year, and I quickly gathered experience with old cars, this wish became reality in 1985. I was still a student, so the sought-for 911 had to be inexpensive; naturally, only a restoration project could be considered. By coincidence, I discovered a quite acceptable car parked in front of a small work-shop. The owner greeted me with the following: "I'll tell you right off, you can't turn this one into a Turbo." I had no intention of doing that, but his spontaneous outburst made me curious. It was explained to me that the parts required for such a conversion would not fit, as this very old 911 had a shorter wheelbase. I also found the narrow wheels, with their peeling chrome, the wooden steering wheel and the wooden dashboard curious. These details were so foreign to a 911 that at first I thought somebody might have added these random parts independently. Further, I could hardly believe that this 911 had been built in early 1965, as claimed by the title.

I had just bought a car about which I knew nothing, for which hardly anyone could give me information, and for which – as I would learn during its restoration – few parts were available. At the time, the 911 was 22 years young. Out of necessity, I began to research its history, and discovered that the car was an authentic rarity; after a great deal of restoration work, it wound up in the Porsche Museum in Zuffenhausen. In the future, it would move under its own power only for various Porsche parades and photo sessions. To satisfy my 911 habit, this car was followed by a somewhat newer 911 T. Meanwhile, while working on two special publications (*All about the Porsche 911* and *All about Porsche*) for my longtime employer, Motor-Presse Stuttgart, I had the opportunity to thoroughly immerse myself in my favorite subject. In short, from the moment I bought that original 911, this car has occupied my personal life, as well as my career.

Yet I had doubts about my book project, as the question was raised time and again: aren't there enough books on the Porsche 911? Thorough research quickly led to a definitive answer: no. There are many books on Porsche, but I could not find an up-to-date, comprehensive work on the 911. A book that would tell me exactly, and under what conditions, the car was created and how prototypes led to the birth of the car. A book without sweeping generalizations, but rather with facts. A book in which the subjects are so clearly structured that the desired information can be found readily. And naturally this work must inform us about the people behind this unique sports car project, and what their assignments were. It was obvious that such a fascinating car could not possibly have been the product of only a few well-known personalities. Such a book did not yet exist. As I occupied myself with the body of Porsche literature, one thing became clear: many know a little, only a few know a great deal, but nobody knows everything that I wanted to know. Above all,

I wished to comprehend how this design could remain in production well past its thirtieth anniversary. That was the summer of 1992. As the anniversary was not that far in the future, I began to seek partners for the project.

First, I came across Jörg Austen, a dedicated engineer and lifelong Porsche man. As his retirement after 33 years at Porsche was imminent, he immediately agreed to provide technical specifications and to chronicle transmission development. But who would be willing to spend their free time poring over hundreds of pages of Porsche history, looking for errors and suggesting ways to make the presentation as clear as possible? For this task, I was able to enlist Stefan Weidenfeld, an expert in German literature who had gained his automotive experience at the magazine *auto motor und sport*. He became so engrossed in the subject that he authored the chapter on the development of the Fuchs alloy wheel. In particular, I was delighted that Porsche's long-serving vice president of research and development, Helmuth Bott († May 19, 1994), took time to examine the historical texts for content and accuracy. In hours-long sessions at his home in the Swabian town of Buttenhausen, he provided his personal insights and impressions, and gave me valuable background

An imposing lineup: these models trace the 30-year development of the 911.

information from the past. He gave freely of his valuable time, from which I learned a great deal. The curator of Porsche's archives, Klaus Parr, and his assistant Ursula Joop, often found themselves answering daily queries from me. With infinite patience, they unearthed many details and rare photos. Above all, they made available the countless files, long believed lost, containing correspondence between individual departments in the early 1960s, which gives this book an especially valuable perspective. For the individual special topics within the thirty-year success story of the 911, I have worked with the appropriate specialists. I had enthusiastic support, far beyond his normal area of expertise, from RS specialist and restorer Wilfried Holzenthal. For motor sports topics, I could call on the comprehensive knowledge of Ulrich Upietz. The engineers and the styling department in Weissach, as well as many employees in Ludwigsburg, including Olaf Lang, were happy to provide information and support. Motorbuch-Verlag and those of its employees who saw this project through must also be mentioned. No effort was spared to ensure that this book was absolutely current, even if this required unconventional production methods. I would also like to thank Porsche's public relations manager, Anton Hunger, whose trust and confidence in this project made it possible to obtain information on the new Carrera generation in a timely manner. I am equally grateful to every employee of the press department, whose commitment contributed to the realization of this book. The contributing photographers were also of critical importance. I would especially like to single out René Staud, who lent generous support to the project.

Then there are the Porsche employees, present at the creation, who gave freely of their time for interviews. In accord with the aim of this book, to reconstruct history on the basis of the recollections of many employees, these people will recognize themselves in the individual chapters. In all conversations, I made an especially valuable discovery: the spirit of Porsche lives, in each individual. This will undoubtedly encourage the company in its future endeavors.

10

From 356 to 911

Beginnings

"When we talk about the 911, we first have to consider the 356." This observation comes from Helmuth Bott. After more than 36 years at Porsche, the Swabian engineer, who served on Porsche's board of directors as chief of research and development until his retirement on September 30, 1988, knows the complete development history of the 911.

In the mid-1950s, no thought was being given to a successor for the 356; there was not yet pressure to develop a replacement. Quite the contrary, the 356 was just entering its prime. But Porsche's people were giving some thought to improving the product and the wish list of customers was discussed. Even in the 1950s a Porsche was an exclusive car, tailored to very specific customer demands and customer suggestions were taken very seriously. Often, these wishes included increased interior space in two respects: first for the rear-seat occupants, second for luggage. This desire also came from Porsche's own ranks. After all, several Porsche employees had two or three children, which could fit into a 356 only with great difficulty. Freimut, youngest son of Helmuth Bott, had to sit on the bulge over the transmission, as his two older sisters requisitioned the jump seats. Helmuth Bott underscores the importance of the Porsche car to his family at that time: "Even if a more practical four-door car was available, my children always wanted to ride in the Porsche."

The luggage space, too small and at best sufficient for two people, also drew criticism. The rear luggage rack was only a partial solution, as it brought with it several disadvantages including inadequate weather protection for the contents of the suitcases, the risk of theft, and restricted vehicle performance combined with higher fuel consumption.

In terms of the powerplant, the engineers were well aware that sooner or later the limits of the air-cooled four-cylinder engine would be reached. After all, the engine of the Volkswagen Beetle served as the basis for the first 356 models with 1100, 1300 and 1500 cc; until 1955, Porsche even used the VW crankcase. It was replaced for all models when displacement grew to 1500 and finally 1600 cc.

By the end of the decade, the pushrod engines of the 356 were approaching the limits of their power output; on the Autobahn, Porsche drivers had to make way for touring cars like the Mercedes 220 SE or the Jaguar Mk. II when the oil temperatures of their air-cooled engines soared. Helmuth Bott emphasizes that "With the 356, one drove with an eye on the oil temperature gauge." One must also recall that at Porsche, the racing engines were

Helmuth Bott: "When we talk about the 911, we first have to consider the 356."

Company head Ferry Porsche recognized that he would have to seek inspiration from outside the company, as in Komenda's mind there was no difference between the technical and styling aspects of body design; as an experienced engineer, he would tolerate no stylist at his side.

Ernst Bolt, one of the Porsche model makers of the very early years, recalls the first rumors to circulate among the employees: "The word came down that a man would come from America and make a new car." This man from America had already garnered a noteworthy reputation. His name was Count Albrecht Goertz, who, as an associate of the American design guru Raymond Loewy, had developed into a successful designer and made his mark with the BMW 507 sports car of 1955.

As of July 1957, Goertz would often travel to Stuttgart, to the spacious styling studio in the basement of Werk I, and begin to sketch. Other drawings were completed in his New York studio. He strictly followed Porsche's guidelines to design a fastback vehicle with increased interior space. But even with the concept sketches it was apparent that the Goertz design was too peculiar; too American; it was too far a reach from the 356. Nevertheless, the design was modelled in full scale in the Werk I model shop. Ferdinand Alexander Porsche laughingly recalls the frugal Swabian mentality of the firm: "As we had to pay for the design anyway, we figured we might as

always based on production engines. Even sports machines like the 550 Spyder were born of the four-cylinder boxer engines. The decision to build a six-cylinder was not made until the 1960s, after Ernst Fuhrmann finally reached the limits of the four-cylinder when, with enormous engineering effort, he was able to mobilize 130 horsepower.

But in the mid-1950s, numerous suggestions for the improvement of the 356 had not even been collected and written down. Moreover, Porsche was looking for a car which had not even been defined yet, a car which could confidently be expected to offer more space than a fastback. One gave more thought to a four-seat body based on the 356, to expand the model line upwards – possibly also with a more powerful engine, rather than a replacement for the successful four-cylinder. Today, Butzi Porsche confirms that "It had not even been decided that there would *be* a successor to the 356." Erwin Komenda, who had been responsible for Porsche sheet-metal technology and body design since 1931, had developed all Porsche bodies since the VW Beetle. Komenda adhered closely to one of his time-honored principles, that the external bodywork could be given enormous strength by means of strong curvature. Unfortunately this led to a somewhat plump and naturally, due to its larger wheelbase, heavier four-seat variant. In addition, Komenda's concepts no longer fulfilled modern design expectations.

Ferdinand Alexander Porsche: "It had not even been decided that there would *be* a successor to the 356."

Erwin Komenda, responsible for Porsche body engineering and styling since 1931, designed this four-seat experimental prototype in the early 1950s.

In 1959, Ferdinand Alexander Porsche based his design of the Type 754 T7 on the wheelbase of this Type 530 four-seater.

Count Albrecht Goertz designed this four-seat Porsche 356 successor in July, 1957.

Even the preliminary design showed that the car would be too unusual and too "American"...

...yet a full-scale, three-ton clay model was made.

well have a model of it too." Furthermore, drawings were never as conclusive as models. Thirty-six years later, Bolt recalls working with the American designer: "With Count Goertz, we were only allowed to put on Plasticine and sweep up the scrapings." A wooden model (today one would use polyurethane foam) was installed on a surface plate, primitive by today's standards. The three by six meter plate, which was leveled on jackscrews, was surrounded by a wooden framework (see illustration, p. 16). These wooden slats were precisely located by a height gauge and served as reference rails. While the side view of the Goertz model had stylistic leanings in the direction of the later 911, the front aspect in particular, with its quad headlights, was much too busy and seemed extremely American. The angular rear end with its abrubt cutoff and three taillights, also drew attention. Nevertheless, the design was not discarded. Quite the contrary, to permit an even more objective assessment of the Goertz design, which weighed all of three tons, a model with proper glazing was to be built. At the end of 1957, two Stuttgart plasterers were hired to make a female mold. The plaster mold consisted of five parts: both sides, the front, the rear, and the roof section. But before the plaster mold could be filled with fiberglass, the project was halted for two reasons: first, finances were limited, and second, Ferry Porsche recognized the design as, "A beautiful Goertz, but not a Porsche." The plaster mold was destroyed two years later.

Goertz was working on a second design in parallel, but only on one half of a body. The other half was styled by the Porsche model shop, under the leadership of Heinrich Klie. For a direct comparison, the two halves could be bolted together (see photo, p. 17). The styling studies were done under Project Number 695; To keep the project movable, its substructure consisted of a 356 body, split down the middle. Ernst Bolt recalls a remarkable technique: "If, while scraping the clay, we hit metal, a body and fender man was called in, and he lowered the metal skin with a hammer and torch."

Heinrich Klie, who had trained as a pastry chef, founded the Porsche model shop in 1951 and guided many ideas and suggestions through the initial design stage. Meanwhile, Ferry Porsche's eldest son, Ferdinand Alexander, known to all as "Butzi" and fresh out of the renowned Ulm College of Design, had also joined the firm, but was assigned to body design under Erwin Komenda. Ernst Bolt remembers that "Butzi wandered back and forth between the body department and the model department." His father, Ferry, is more specific: "Butzi soon showed a remarkable talent for styling." Suggestions from the young designer were gladly incorporated, but overall responsibility for the Goertz-Porsche cooperative project remained with Heinrich Klie. The half-

15

To compensate for uneven flooring, the three by six meter surface plate rested on jackscrews. The boards, through which freshly applied Plasticine is oozing, were located to an accuracy of one millimeter.

models (see illustrations) were considerably closer to the later 911 silhouette than the first Goertz creations. Particularly noteworthy are the arched glass headlight covers, formed as extensions of the front fenders, a feature which Butzi would later employ in the Porsche 904 racing prototype. Not only Porsche liked this solution: in the early 1960s, the Jaguar E-Type and the Alfa Duetto Spyder mounted their headlights behind glass.

On these concepts, the leader of the model department worked trim strips into the Plasticine models for the first time.

These aluminum shapes were formed by the wooden hammers of panel beaters. In a direct comparison, the Porsche design differed from the Goertz alternative in the permanent use of round lights. This development stage was also the first to take into consideration the admission of air into the engine compartment. Overall, however, the design came across as very awkward; its ham-shaped curves drew particular criticism.

In the late 1950s, engineers were frequent visitors in the model department. The old hands from Porsche's beginnings in Gmünd, engineers Walter Hüttisch, Karl Motzelt and Franz-Xaver Reimspiess,

16

These half-models of
the Type 695 rested on
356 platforms.

The left half of the Plasticine model was
developed by the Porsche model department
under Heinrich Klie; the right side is a Count
Goertz design.

For this design, the
Porsche designers
adopted the small
round taillights of the
Goertz proposal.

enjoyed a high degree of freedom. In addition, some designs were realized in the Reutter Body Works, located first in Stuttgart's Augustenstrasse and later behind Porsche's Werk I. Reutter had its own model shop and body shop, under the leadership of long-serving *Meister* Gottlob Sturm.

Fritz Plaschka, from whose drawing board most of the designs of the early 1960s had originated, was deeply involved. Designer Konrad Bamberg and convertible top specialist Gerhard Schröder presented their own creations. Porsche employees put their hearts and souls into the new project; all were highly motivated.

Meanwhile, several design variations were on hand. Although the need for a 356 successor was becoming increasingly acute, it was still not well defined. Some clung to the idea of a fastback four-seater. "I always maintained that a Porsche was not necessarily a fastback," recalls Butzi Porsche. "Also, I was of the opinion that the requirements of a four-seater and a fastback body were mutually exclusive," he adds. "But my father always wanted a fastback to underscore the relationship to the 356." In spite of

these contradictory sentiments, Ferdinand Alexander Porsche began his first interpretations under Type Number 754 T7, after he had nearly completed his design for Porsche's Formula 2 racer, the Type 718/2. He used the pair of four-seat experimental Type 530 prototypes, based on the 356, as his guide. For them, the minimum wheelbase required for a four-seater had been calculated at 2400 mm.

The production 356 had a wheelbase of 2100 mm. Butzi Porsche quickly went to work on a $1/7.5$ Plasticine model. Today, the leader of Porsche Design in Zell am See documents his working methods: "I recorded my ideas in rough sketches, in part so I could have better control of the lines, but then quickly translated everything to the model so that I could better visualize the shapes."

While Heinrich Klie still preferred to work in clay, which had to be moistened repeatedly during shaping, the young Porsche used Plasticine as a modelling material. The first Plasticine model was finished on October 9, 1959, and a modified version appeared six months later. This version was then realized in cast resin and given a fresh coat of blue

Design chief for chassis and engines Leopold Schmid (left), body design chief Erwin Komenda (center) and chief designer Karl Rabe, Ferry Porsche's longest serving co-worker.

The clay models shown here, in $1/10$ scale, resulted from a mid-1950s cooperative effort between Erwin Komenda and Heinrich Klie. The model shown above is strongly reminiscent of the Type 530; the version below appears more elegant.

The engineers were also thinking about a 356 successor. The rendering shown here, by Gerhard Schröder was modelled in 1/5 scale in the mid-1950s.

Ferdinand Alexander ("Butzi") Porsche made only rough sketches, then immediately translated them into clay models.

paint. The new study, widely discussed before the Christmas holidays, met with considerable approval. Work had already begun on a full-size display model. There was no longer any thought of a Christmas break. The 1/7.5 model was so precise that plans were drawn from it, which were then applied to the larger model. The T7 again took shape on a wooden buck, fitted with 356 axles to make the model movable. "If

20

you tried to lift a three-ton Plasticine model, it would immediately develop cracks," recalls Ernst Bolt.

To apply Plasticine, sticks of this brown material were heated in a pottery oven, which Heinrich Klie had brought with him from his previous job in ceramics (he was not only a pastry chef). Today, hot-air ovens are used to heat the putty. The material was heated to 50 or 60 °C (120 to 140 °F) and then pressed onto the buck with the heels of the hands and the thumbs. Ernst Bolt describes working with this hot material: "If you don't constantly work in Plasticine, the first thing that will happen is that you will develop some large blisters." Because new material had to be joined to existing layers, it had to be firmly rubbed onto the surface. For additional reinforcement, nails were pounded into the wooden buck; these were then covered with the putty.

The wooden buck was kept about 10 cm under the anticipated dimension. The thickness of Plasticine was constantly monitored by means of templates, and precisely located by means of a height gauge. The spacing of the templates was given by the drawings (see illustration). The model makers' job was first to apply enough Plasticine, then to work the model to the appropriate shape according to the drawing and in cooperation with the designer. (According to model maker Heinz Unger, "The interplay of designer and model maker is the most important part of automobile design.") Scraping and shaping is done with homemade tools. Butzi Porsche first shaped with coarse sawblades, "so that one doesn't get too close to the form while smoothing."

All four model department craftsmen worked on this full-scale version of the T7. Specialists Ernst Bolt, Hans Springmann and Heinz Unger were soon dubbed "The Three Musketeers," because of their remarkable teamwork. Heinz Unger joined Porsche on March 2, 1959, after training as a model maker at Berger und Mössner in Stuttgart-Feuerbach. For

Even before Butzi Porsche began his interpretation of a 356 successor in August 1959, he designed this Formula 2 racer.

The first Plasticine model of the Type 754 T7 was completed on October 9, 1959. This cast resin copy was pulled from the clay and given a fresh coat of blue paint.

years, this firm had been making 1/5 scale models and wooden steering wheels for Porsche. Hans Springmann came to Porsche in June, 1957; for years, his mother had worked as a housekeeper in the Porsche villa. A fourth model maker, Horst Handte, joined the model shop at about the same time, but in 1963 transferred to engineering.

The full-size Plasticine model was completed on December 28, 1959. The nose of the car was close to the final 901 shape, but the fuel filler lid was still missing from the left fender. The lower bodywork had the characteristic flowing fender contours which reminded all of the 356. Above all, the slightly raked headlights immediately said "Porsche." "For us, the headlights played a vital role in shaping the form, even then," recalls Butzi Porsche. The B-pillar, running along the rear edge of the door, was angled forward relatively steeply; the rake of the thin C-pillar

was even more pronounced. The large glass areas were untypical of Porsches up to that time; by comparison, the windows of the 356 T5 came across as peepholes or gun slits. The tail was strongly reminiscent of Pininfarina studies of the time, and was underscored by the huge backlight. Overall, the line of the rear bodywork flowed gently downward, but with a slight break. "We called it the step-down below the rear window," explains Butzi Porsche. Later, on the drivable prototype, the heads of rear-seat occupants brushed against the backlight. The rear seats were arranged as in the 356, that is, with two half-bucket seats, whose backrests could be folded down to make room for luggage. Butzi Porsche accepted the restricted headroom for rear seat passengers as part of the package; he wanted to avoid giving the T7 a hunchback, as the car was to have a decided fastback look. (A contemporary example would be the Bugatti EB 112, where the form created by Giorgetto Giugiaro's Italdesign follows function.) Today, the soft lines of the 911 are regarded as a masterpiece of postmodern automobile design.

As the T7 was originally conceived around a four-cylinder engine located under the floor, Butzi Porsche put slots in the rear flanks to admit cooling air. Later, it was determined that the openings were inadequate; but because air scoops were out of the question for a production car for styling reasons, the license plate was moved downward and a large opening was made at the rear, between the bumper guards.

Parallel to the construction of the full-size display model, the $1/7.5$ version was tested in Stuttgart University's wind tunnel. Heinrich Klie was always present for these tests, usually accompanied by one or two modelers, so that improvements could be carried out directly in the wind tunnel. Wool tufts were attached all over the body to pinpoint turbulence. The prepared model was tested at six different angles to the wind, and all aspects were photographed for reference. Porsche had available one of the best aerodynamicists to be found – Josef Mickl, who had already built the Auto Union racers for Professor Porsche. The rounded nose with its faired-in bumpers took shape in accordance with his expertise. In the wind tunnel, it quickly became apparent where flow separation occurred over the rear – much sooner on the steeply sloped fastback and with more turbulence, than would be the case with a flat roof and more rearward placement of the cutoff.

Finally, at the end of 1959, Ferry Porsche approved the design and development of a new Porsche model. The head of the firm further ordained that no feature of the 356 era should unconditionally be carried over to the new model.

First, it was decided to have a drivable prototype of the Type 754 made at the Reutter Body Works. The white experimental car (which may still be admired in the Porsche museum, now painted dark green) rolled out under its own power on November 1, 1960. At the wheel was Helmuth Bott, who soon pronounced a damning verdict: "We can forget about this!"

Bott was referring to the two-liter under-floor engine, which was exceptionally noisy because of its pushrods and twin cooling blowers. In contrast, the experimental team soon came to like the body shape.

A decisive step toward the 911 was Ferry Porsche's decree in favor of a more sporting, preferably smaller car. The wheelbase was to be 2.2 meters. Ferry Porsche wanted a fastback by all means, and his son Ferdinand Alexander showed that with the given wheelbase, an attractive four-seater could only be realized with a less steeply raked rear. Erwin Komenda was a champion of the fastback as well as the four-seat solution. Later, in a press release drafted by sales manager Wolfgang Raether, the new design direction was justified in the following terms: "All guesswork and speculation that Porsche intends to bring out a 4-seat model is unfounded; first of all because it contradicts the basic concept of Porsche and second because we are of the opinion that the present international automobile industry offers an adequate selection of 4-seat vehicle types."

The project was to be carried on under type designation 644 T8 by Butzi Porsche, as well as by Erwin Komenda under the designation 754 T9. Soon, two factions had formed. The chief of body develop-

Heinz Unger: "The interplay of designer and model maker is the most important part of automobile design."

23

Butzi Porsche with his crew, and a 912 predecessor. At left, Heinrich Klie.

Display model of the T7 with its large backlight, unusual for Porsche at that time.

Type 754 T7: The roofline sloped gently downward, with a slight break...

...the front aspect was virtually identical to the later 901 design.

25

The drivable T7 mockup, here repainted in dark green, retained the shift lever and steering wheel of the 356.

Today, the T7 in the Porsche Museum again carries a four-cam Carrera engine. In the early 1960s, tests were conducted with the six-cylinder Type 745.

For refueling, the trunklid had to be opened. The fuel filler lid on the left front fender would come later.

26

T7 wind tunnel tests in the model wind tunnel and at the University of Stuttgart.

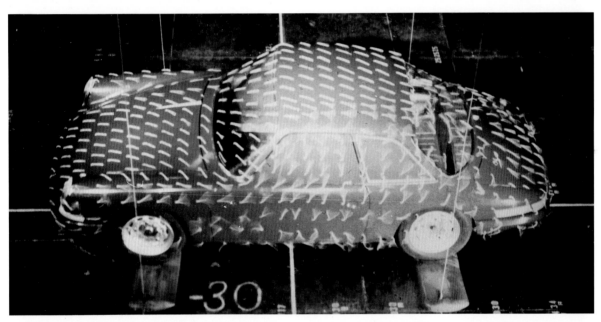

Small tufts are applied all over the $1/7.5$ model, to show turbulence.

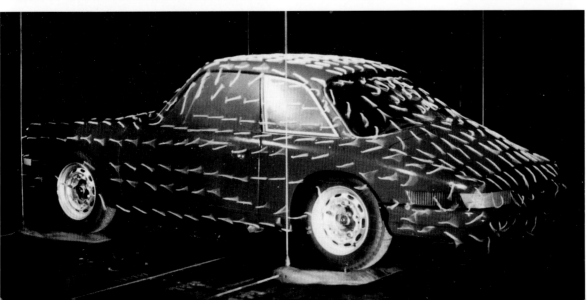

The prepared model was subjected to six different wind directions.

27

ment, who had worked for the firm since 1931, paid little heed to Ferry's instructions and held firm to his vision of a four-seat fastback. Today, Ferry Porsche declares "Besides which, he always changed my son's styling concepts in the direction represented by him and his team." By January 31, under Komenda's leadership, three full-scale viewing models of wood and metal had been built (designated as T 9/1, T 9/2, and T 9/3 in company memoranda). However, the bumpers appeared far too bulky (see photo on p. 29) and the turn signals seemed an afterthought. Above all, the Komenda designs were getting bigger and heavier. "The T9 had an inflated look to it," recalls Butzi Porsche. Ferry Porsche comments on the hostilities as follows: "I had to realize that a body designer was not necessarily a styling man, and vice versa." Ferry took an unusual step to ensure that the model developed by the styling team would not be altered by the body designers: "Now in the meantime we had taken over the Reutter company. So I went to Herr Walter Beierbach – at the time the chief executive officer of Reutter – and said to him, 'Herr Beierbach, here is my son's model. Could you have it drawn as you see it?' Herr Beierbach could do that, and translated the model into design drawings." The mockups were later used for detail development of the T8. For example, the rear license plate illumination was developed on them.

Erwin Komenda was thunderstruck by this move, but after several weeks he accepted the design direction and contributed to the effort. Ferry Porsche regrets that "Together with Walter Beierbach, they talked me out of the large opening rear window. This concept was later realized with the 928 and 944 models."

As of 1961, Ferdinand Alexander Porsche was named head of the model department, and Heinrich Klie slipped back to the second spot. At about the same time, engineers Theo Bauer and Werner Trenkler came to the model department to ensure that proposals were not only exhibited as renderings, but also translated into design drawings. Butzi's intent was to prevent the design and development team from shooting down a concept on the grounds that it "couldn't be done." If a styling idea was nevertheless discarded, Butzi would go to the floor above the model department and ask for an explanation. "Prob-

Ferry Porsche: "[Komenda] always changed my son's styling concepts."

ably because I was the son, possibly also because I had a feeling for the technology, more concessions were made to me than to my predecessor," he explains. The engineers had been referring to the model makers as "mudscrapers" and had not taken the department seriously. Because of Butzi's assertive stance, the model department's acceptance within the firm changed.

At this time, Butzi Porsche issued a memorandum ordering that "all departments involved in the development process should, in the event of any necessary modification of existing studio designs, first obtain the studio's approval or release." With that move, the chief of styling obtained continuous monitoring of all detail solutions to ensure a unified design.

Development work finally concentrated on a single design direction, designated Type 644 T8 , a two-seater on a 2100 mm wheelbase with rear-mounted fuel tank. The first Plasticine model in $1/7.5$ scale was completed in December 1961. In the meantime, the engineers had envisioned a very compact front suspension which permitted a better-protected fuel tank location. For that reason, the concept quickly deviated from the pure two-seater, and added another 100 mm wheelbase to result in a formally successful design for a 2+2 fastback, the eventual 911. Butzi Porsche: "I was completely convinced; this body would be super!"

This wood and metal display model of the Type 754 T9 was built in January 1962, under Komenda's direction.

Komenda's designs appeared clumsy and were getting bigger and heavier.

Parallel to the work of the model department, extensive negotiations with the management of Reutter were underway. A memorandum dated October 20, 1961, states that "The Reutter company has agreed to assume responsibility for the design of a T8 body on the present T6 chassis." The deadline was set: series production would begin in July 1963. Moreover, it was stated that the cost of the new body should under no circumstances exceed that of the T6 body (that is, the 356). To optimize cooperation between the body plant and Porsche, Erwin Komenda would assign a manager to Reutter. On November 13, 1961, he sent one of his best engineers, Gerhard Schröder, who had gained his early experience at the special body works of Ramseier & Cie in Worblaufen, Switzerland, the firm of Deutsch in Cologne (Ford 12 M Cabriolet) and Karmann. From there, he moved to Porsche in 1956 and at the beginning of the 1960s was primarily occupied with the 904. Cabriolet specialist Schröder was also the ideal choice because it was intended to involve his former employer Karmann in the design and production of the T8's exterior skin. (Karmann built 356 hardtop coupes (Karmann Hardtop model) until February 1962, and would soon take on part of the regular 356 coupe production to free up capacity at Reutter for the T8 design). The memorandum further notes that in the design of the exterior skin, "the vehicle also should be buildable as an open car."

In view of the tight schedule (20 months) Reutter immediately established a series of program stages, which was presented to Ferry Porsche and his team on November 2, 1961 (see box). In the explanation accompanying the plan, one may read that Reutter requested that the design drawings of the T7 car and, if possible, a $1/10$ scale model, be delivered without delay, as the T8 body would be based on the model. Reutter also asked that the body department of Master Gottlob Sturm be kept free of other projects while building the prototypes. From this we can see that Reutter considered this project most important, and delegated significant manpower to it. In the next six months, eight more Porsche employees were seconded to Reutter, including an additional designer to assist Werner Trenkler.

From the end of 1961, development work concentrated in a direction defined by the Type 644 T8. The first model, in $1/7.5$ scale, still envisioned a wheelbase shortened to 2100 mm.

30

This memo confirms that from this point onward, Butzi Porsche would bear sole responsibility for the body shape.
English translation page 388.

1962

Meanwhile, the T8 project was no longer merely a styling study; now all departments were under pressure. Porsche had decided on a completely new vehicle.

On January 11, 1961, Helmuth Bott drafted a T8 wish list for the road test department. Therein Bott expressed for the first time that a new suspension design could not be realized by July 1963. If, however, as he had heard, the body would be delayed until 1964, a new chassis with MacPherson struts and larger trunk space would be desirable.

The rough design of this suspension was laid out four days later during a T8 meeting by Leopold Schmid, design chief for engines and suspensions. Those present at the meeting were Porsche senior and junior, Hans Tomala, Karl Rabe (chief designer), Franz-Xaver Reimspiess, Richard Hetmann (chief of transmission testing), Erich Stotz (rear suspension designer) and Helmut Rombold (chief of testing). Schmid stressed that there was insufficient time for a completely new suspension and insisted on the 356 suspension with longer travel and ball joints, instead of kingpins. Ferry Porsche and Hans Tomala, who had overall responsibility for engineering, persisted in their demand for a modern suspension. They regarded this as the most significant improvement of the T8, beside the body and engine. In any event, Ferry Porsche wanted a vehicle concept that would remain viable for an extended time. According to the minutes of January 15, 1962, recorded by test driving chief Helmut Rombold, rack and pinion steering was discussed for the first time in a larger forum. It was recorded that a further advantage was that "the chassis is the same for left and right-hand-drive cars and, in the event of an impact, the articulated steering column could not be pushed into the car's interior." The test department, in cooperation with the design bureau, was to build a mock-up as quickly as possible to permit assessment of location and space requirements.

Description of the Type T8

On January 24, 1962, Hans Tomala summarized the type description of the T8:

1. The wheelbase was altered from 2100 to 2200 mm.

2. The concept is a 2+2, in which the fuel tank must again be located in the front of the car.

3. The openable rear window will be dispensed with. Access to the rear luggage space will be adequately improved by the enlarged doors.

4. According to Porsche's test department, the heating system must be improved.

5. Opening rear quarter windows for better ventilation are planned.

6. The Porsche design bureau is examining a new front suspension design, which should permit improved luggage space. Documents for this will be passed on to Reutter after the designs are complete. The space requirements for installation of this suspension will first be examined by the Porsche design bureau.

Thereafter, meetings between individual departments were called with ever-greater frequency. Between July 27, 1962 and December 18, 1964, a weekly technical meeting was initiated. In the minutes of the first regular meeting (1/62) the following explanation is found: "Purpose of the meeting was to bring forward all problems that fall into the technical area and to collectively initiate the required measures for their resolution. To this end, every Friday at 10:00 AM, the relevant points are to be discussed by representatives (department heads or their deputies) of the following departments:

– Work planning department

– Operations

– Inspection

– Design

– Patents

– Testing

Possibly, gentlemen from Purchasing and the Customer Service Department will be invited to these meetings. For control purposes, the individual points of discussion will be numbered consecutively." Present were *Herren* Hans Tomala, Ferdinand Alexander Porsche, Alfred Auwärter (Central Planning), Heinrich Gabrysch (director of quality control), Erich Herr (chief of engine testing), Erwin Komenda, Hans Mezger (engine design), Franz-Xaver Reimspiess, Emil Soukoup (patent department), and Eberhard Morr (assistant to Tomala in the design office). Naturally, in these meetings, the technically relevant points of all models were discussed. But at the second meeting, on August 3, 1962, the T8 was on the agenda, with problems regarding the checking of drawings.

Without regard to the formulation of technical problems, the model department was working at full speed. All decisions since January 1962 had been based on a 1:7.5 plasticine model. A full-scale viewing and seating model (illustrated on p. 33), made of wood and metal, with the new wheelbase (2200 mm) was finished on April 16, 1962. Items still to be resolved included the design of the air inlet in the engine lid. Due to the new turn of events, ten days later Hans Tomala and purchasing boss Wilhelm Albrecht travelled to Karmann in Osnabrück in order to set deadlines for further work. Herr Rutsch of Wilhelm Karmann GmbH emphasized that not a single day could be wasted if the T8 was to go into production immediately after the 1963 IAA (the Frankfurt International Automobile Show). To this end, he asked that Albrecht leave behind the not yet corrected line drawings (Tomala had scheduled the final line drawings for June 1962), so that he could carry out the preliminary work on the model. Plaster molds were to be made of the prototype models, and then plastic panels formed in the molds. These panels would be grafted together to form a master model of the exterior skin suitable for copying. In the same way, models for the interior skin and the new frame parts would be made. The complete set of masters

The metal and wood display model of the T8 was built in April 1962.

The air inlet below the backlight, here in a preliminary design stage, did not achieve its final shape until shortly before the September, 1963 Frankfurt IAA.

could be made within three months, at a price of 200,000 DM. Furthermore, the Karmann people felt it necessary to carry out the preliminary work for tooling (design and possibly manufacture of casting patterns) simultaneously with the work on the master models. In conclusion, it was proposed that the Reutter and Karmann body plants cooperate so that as many subcontracted parts as possible could be

The Reutter body works, in Stuttgart's Augustenstrasse, played a significant role in the development of the 901.

ordered from the same suppliers. This would reduce the high tooling costs and ensure interchangeability.

On May 10, 1962, Wilhelm Karmann and his co-workers Willi Rutsch and Helmuth Ukena travelled to Zuffenhausen to view the T8 model. Herr Walter Beierbach, chief executive of Reutter, also was present, as were Ferry and Butzi Porsche, Komenda, Schröder and Tomala. At the time, the bottleneck lay in the design of the frame and the front structure, which were being done under Komenda's direction. The chief of body engineering committed himself to having a line drawing ready on June 15, and to finish work on the floorpan by June 30. Based on those dates, Karmann agreed to have the "Kellerized model" of the exterior skin ready by September 30 ("Kellerizing," named for its inventor, is a process by which the lines, or strakes, of a vehicle are smoothed), and to have the Kellerized model of the inner skin finished by January 1, 1963. At this point, the costs were still not finalized. The tooling for the exterior skin was priced at 150,000 hours at 20 Marks/hour.

In the meantime, the new Porsche was named 901. This designation appears in writing for the first time on May 17, 1962. Initially, the T8 designation was still added in parentheses. The renaming did not mean that this car's design carried project number 901 in the sequence of all projects which the Porsche design bureau had taken on since its founding on April 25, 1931. The longest-serving Porsche employee, Karl Rabe, administrator of the project numbers, was far too unsystematic for that and the story is somewhat more complicated. At the beginning of the 1960s, a merging of the Porsche and Volkswagen organizations was envisioned. To that end, the computer in the spare parts department at Wolfsburg searched for unassigned numbers so that no complications would arise after the fusion. The computer spit out "901" as a suitable combination of numbers, so the new car received that designation. Even today, the designation of all new Porsche car models begins with a 9.

Also in the summer of 1962, during a meeting between Porsche and Reutter, Hans Tomala explained that the design of the front suspension and steering had at last been finalized, and that the design of the chassis in the area of the front suspension could get underway. As Erwin Komenda had given his assurance that the still-outstanding drawings for the chassis would be available in two weeks, Walter Beierbach, on behalf of Reutter, confirmed that the body for the first driving prototype would be ready on September 14, 1962. When the drawings were still not ready four weeks after this meeting, the tone of both parties became considerably sharper, as indicated by later correspondence. Time pressure became enormous; after all, a vehicle representing the later production cars was to be available for testing even before the tooling was finished and the cars were put into production. As the design of most Mechanical components had already been established, design engineer Hans Hönick could for the first time write a technical description of the 901 (in a report dated June 28, 1963 – see box on page 36, *English translation pages 388 - 389*) Drawings of individual components had hardly been finished before they were passed on to the company's patent department so that patent searches could be carried out in a timely manner. In this way, it was deter-

Right page: On July 4, 1963, Erwin Komenda wrote up the first short description of the body for the Porsche Type 901 coupe, in its left-hand drive version. English translation see pages 388 - 389.

Entwurf

Kurzbeschreibung

der Porsche-Karosserie Coupé 901.
Linkslenker-Ausführung.   Typ 901

1. Rohbau: Ganzstahlausführung mit festem Dach. Selbsttragender Verbundbau mit Bodenrahmen. Durchlaufende Einschalen-Außenhaut vom Windschutz bis zum Heckende. Vorderkotflügel abnehmbar.

2. Türen: Ganzstahlausführung, je eine Tür links und rechts, Scharnierseite vorn, Schloßseite hinten. Die Türaußengriffe mit Druckknopf-Betätigung und von außen mit gleichen Schlüssel abschließbar. Innensicherung durch Knopfbetätigung auf der Türschlüsselleiste. Das Türhauptschloß ist ein Kniehebelschloß mit Schließkeil und Türführung. Ein verdeckter Türhalter mit Bremse, Armlehne als Zuziehgriff und Innendrücker darunter sind eingebaut.

3. Deckel: Bug- und Heckdeckel sind mit innen liegenden Scharnieren ausgestattet und mit Gewichtsausgleich zum Offenhalten der Deckel. Die eingebauten Schlösser sind nur von Wageninnern aus durch Drahtzug zu öffnen. (Die Schloßsperrung des Bugdeckels öffnet sich wenn der Deckelzug reißt.) Der Bugdeckel ist gegen Aufspringen besonders gesichert. Der Heckdeckel trägt die Belüftungsgitter.

4. Fenster:
4.1 Die Windschutzscheibe ist eine einteilige, gebogene Rundsichtscheibe aus Schichtglas und in Gummiprofil mit Metallzierleiste gelagert.
4.2 Die Türscheiben bestehen aus gebogenem Hartglas und sind mittels Fensterkurbelapparat versenkbar. Sie sind in verchromten Messingrahmen mit Flüschprofil geführt.
4.3 Das Drehfenster in der Tür ist aus Hartglas mit verchromtem Rahmen. Es wird durch eine Bremse in jeder Stellung gehalten und in geschlossenem Zustand durch einen mit Sicherung versehenen Riegel verschlossen.
4.4 Die hinteren Seitenscheiben sind aus gebogenem Hartglas mit verchromten Rahmen
4.5 Die Rückwandscheibe ist sphärisch, aus Hartglas und in Gummiprofil mit Metallzierleiste gelagert.

-2-

- 2 -

5. Schalttafel:
Die Schalttafel ist mittragend verschweißt und enthält die Aufnahmeöffnungen für Instrumente und Betätigungen sowie einen Ablagekasten mit abschließbarem Klappdeckel. Abschluß der Schalttafel nach oben durch eine nicht spiegelnde Abdeckung mit gepolsterter Wulsthinterkante.
Eingebaut sind:
1 Drehzahlmesser mit Öltemperatur- und Öldruckanzeige, Kontrolleuchten für Batterieladung und Blinkleuchten.
1 Geschwindigkeitsmesser mit Wegstreckenzähler und Tageszähler, Kraftstoffanzeige mit Reservewarnleuchte, Fernlicht- und Handbremskontrolleuchten sowie Begrenzungslicht- und Nebellichtkontrolleuchten.
1 Lichtschalter mit Regler für Instrumentenbeleuchtung
1 elektr. Zigarettenanzünder
1 Handschuhkastenleuchte mit selbsttätigem Schaltkontakt
~~2 Türkontaktschalter für Innenleuchten~~ *gehört unter Punkt 5.*
1 Schalter für Frischluftklappenbetätigung
1 Aschenbecher
1 Haltegriff für Beifahrer neben dem Ablagekasten.
1 Radioblende (Einbau eines Radiogerätes auf Sonderwunsch).

6. Elektr. Einrichtung:
Der Kabelsatz wird mit Sicherungsdose, Relais usw. anschlußfertig verlegt. Angeschlossen sind die in der Schalttafel befindlichen Einrichtungen (siehe oben), sowie Anschlüsse zu Batterie und Anlasser, Radio, Nebelschlußleuchte und anderen elektrischen Geräten.
Sämtliche Leuchten und die Scheinwerfer sind mit Glühlampen montiert.
Asymmetrische "ES"-Scheinwerfer mit Fern- und Abblendlicht.
1 Paar Blink-Begrenzungsleuchten. Begrenzungsleuchte als Parkleuchte schaltbar.
1 Paar Heckleuchten, jede Leuchte enthält Brems-, Schluß- und Rückleuchte und Rückstrahler (Schlußleuchte als Parkleuchte schaltbar).
1 Anlasser-Batterie
Am Schaltblock des Lenkradlagers:
1 Einhebelschalter linksseitig für Blinker-, Abblend- u. Lichthupenbetätigung
1 Einhebelschalter rechtsseitig für Scheibenwischer- und Scheibenwascherbetätigung
1 Zündanlaß-Lenksperrschloß (mit Anlaßwiederholsperre), rechtsseitig.
1 Druckknopf für Signalhorn auf der Lenkrad-Nabe
2 Kennzeichenleuchten
1 Tandem-Scheibenwischeranlage, dreistufig schaltbar
1 Paar Starktonhörner (Zweiklang)
2 Innenleuchten am Dachrahmen links und rechts
1 Scheibenwaschanlage

-3-

- 3 -

1 Schaltkontakt zur Handbremskontrolle
1 Rückfahrleuchtenschalter am Getriebe
1 Kofferraumleuchte mit selbsttätigem Schaltkontakt

7. Heizung und Lüftung:
Für die Karosserie sind folgende Varianten von Heizung und Lüftung vorgesehen:
7.1 Motorheizung mit Temp.Regelung durch Frischluftzufuhr vom Motorgebläse
7.2 Frischluftzufuhr von vorn durch Luftschlitze im Windlauf.
Die Rohkarosserie ist grundsätzlich für den Einbau der Motorheizung vorgesehen.
Es sind alle Kanäle, Rohre, Anschlußlöcher usw. für den Einbau der Heizung und Lüftung vorhanden.

zu Punkt 7.1
Warmluftzuführung vom Motor durch Kanäle in den Längsträgern zum Wageninnern, zur Windschutzscheibe, Rückwandscheibe und Türscheiben. Die Betätigung für die Warmluftheizung befindet sich auf dem Mitteltunnel vor dem Schalthebel und kann beliebig ganz oder teilweise geöffnet werden.
Die Warmluftöffnungen zur Beheizung des Wageninnern können durch Schieber an den Längsträgern (vorn links und rechts) ganz oder teilweise geschlossen werden.

zu Punkt 7.2
Für die Frischluftzufuhr von vorn sind im Windlauf vor der Windschutzscheibe Lufteintrittsschlitze angebracht. Darunter ist ein Luftfangtrichter, der das mit der Luft eintretende Wasser im Wasserkasten abgeleitet. Das Wasser tritt aus einem Schlauch abgeleitet. Die Frischluft tritt nur aus einer in der Mitte des Windschutzscheibe angebrachten Düse in das Innere der Karosserie. Die Menge kann durch eine Regulierklappe im Wasserkasten eingestellt werden. Der Betätigungshebel befindet sich an der Schalttafel.

8. Sitze: Vorne 2 Sitze mit vorklapp- und verstellbarer Rückenlehne (Liegesitze). Zur Sicherung gegen Vorklappen, Rückenlehne mit Sicherung gegen Vorklappen. Sitze auf Federkästen gearbeitet, Rückenlehne mit Gummifederung. Im Fond ein 2-sitziger Notsitz mit geteilter Rückenlehne, diese vorklappbar als Gepäckauflage.

9. Gepäckräume:
Der Gepäckraum befindet sich unter dem vorderen Deckel, außerdem ist das Reserverad, die Batterie und das Werkzeug untergebracht.
Als weiterer Gepäckraum ist der Wagenfond vorgesehen. in dem bei vorgeklappter Notsitzrückenlehne eine breite, ebene Gepäckauflage entsteht.

-3-

- 4 -

10. Pufferstangen:
Die Pufferstangen sind an Bug und Heck lösbar aufgehängt und mit Leichtmetallzierleisten mit Plastikeinlage versehen.
Pufferhörner sind an der hinteren Pufferstange. Vorn können auf Wunsch Hörner angebracht werden.
Pufferstangen innen und außen in Wagenfarbe lackiert.

11. Beschläge: 11.1 Verkehrstechnische Beschläge:
1 Abblendbarer Innenrückspiegel
2 Sonnenblenden (vor dem Beifahrer mit Spiegel)
1 Außenrückblickspiegel (Inland serienmäßig, Ausland SW.)
11.2 Zierbeschläge, Oberflächen:
Zierleisten für Pufferstangen, Türeinstieg, Windschutzscheibe und Rückwandscheibe sowie Belüftungsgitter in Leichtmetall mit Hochglanz-Oberfläche.
Tür- und Seitenfensterrahmen, Aussteller, Fensterkurbel, Türaußengriff, vorderer Deckelgriff, Scheinwerferringe, Gehäuse für Schluß-Brems-Rückleuchten, Außen- und Innen-Rückblickspiegel nichtrostender Stahl (Halter verchromt).
Schriftzeichen "PORSCHE" vergoldet.
Scheibenwischerarme und -Blätter alu-lackiert.

12. Bodenbelag:
Gummimatten vor den Fahrersitzen, über dem Tunnel und im Fond Sperrholzauflagen auf der Pedalquerwand. Kofferraum vorn mit einer Matte ausgelegt.

13. Lackierung:
Alle Karosserieteile, die nach der Rohbaumontage miteinander Hohlräume bilden (Längs- und Querträger, Pfosten, Säulen, Verdeckholme und Abschlußbügel usw.), sind an den Zusammenpunkten an den Hohlräume bildenden Flächen mit Rostschutzfarbe zu versehen, desgleichen müssen sämtliche Punktschweißnaht rostgeschützt werden, ebenso die Tür- und Deckelfalznähte.
Nach dem Zusammenbau wird die Rohkarosserie sauber entfettet und entrostet. Alle mit Zinn ausgebesserten Stellen dürfen kein Abblättern der Grundierung zur Folge haben. Die Grundierung wird eingebrannt und danach gespachtelt, der Spachtel wird eingebrannt, geschliffen und der Vorlack gespritzt und gebrannt. Dieser wird ebenfalls geschliffen, danach der Decklack gespritzt und gebrannt. Alle Fugen, durch die Wasser in die Karosserie eindringen kann, müssen mit Karosserie-Abdichtzement vor dem Spritzen des Decklackes abgedichtet werden. Die Farbtöne sind auf den Farbkombinations-Blättern festgelegt.

-5-

- 5 -

14. Innenausstattung:
Der Seitenausschlag des Fonds, die Fondrückwand die Türen mit Taschen und Armlehne mit Zuziehgriff, die Türpfosten links und rechts, sind wie die Seitenbahn der Sitze und die Rückwände der Vordersitzlehnen mit Kunstleder ausgeführt.
Die Schalttafelabdeckung und die Fensterleisten sind mit Kunstleder bespannt. Der Himmel, die Tür- und Fensterjalusie, sowie die Sonnenblenden sind mit Kunstleder bespannt (Himmel perforiert).
Die Seiten des Fahrersitzraumes, Längsträger, Tunnel im Fond und Hinterseite der Notsitzrückenlehne werden mit Teppich verkleidet.
Die Farben und Qualität des Polsterstoffes, Kunstleders, Teppiche usw. sind auf den Farb-Kombinations-Blättern festgelegt.

15. Zubehör: 1 Schlüsseltäschchen mit:
2 Türschlüssel
2 Schlüssel für Zündanlaß-Sperrschloß
2 Schlüssel für Handschuhkastenschloß
1 Porsche-Lackstift in Wagenfarbe
1 Pflegeanweisung für die Karosserie.

16. Entdröhnung:

16.1 Spritzen:

16.11 **Außenteile**
Gesamter Boden und Rahmen von Bug bis Heck einschließlich der Hohlräume in der Vorder- und Hinterachse, alle Radkästen und Kotflügel, Bug- und Heckaußenhaut auf der Innenseite mit Entdröhnungsmittel.
Schwer zugängliche Stellen bei Bug und Heck nur mit Chassislack gespritzt oder gestrichen.
Besondere Verstärkung der Kotflügel gegen Steinschlag ist nicht vorgesehen.
Die ganze Karosserie-Unterseite wird, aber muß keinen Chassislack-Erstanstrich haben.

16.12 **Innenräume**
Bodenblech im Fahrgastraum einschließlich vorderer Querwand und Batteriekastenwand, hinteres Tunnelstück, hintere Radlaufkästen, Motorrückwand, Auflage des Notsitzkissens, Türschächte vor der Scharniersäule links und rechts einmal mit Entdröhnungsmittel (letzteres bei Bedarf in Wagenfarbe) überlackiert.
Innenseiten der Türen einmal mit Chassislack vorspritzen, einmal mit Entdröhnungsmittel. Vorderer Innenraum, Schloßquerwand, Radkasten, Tankraumboden, Querwand vorn, Kofferboden und Batterieraum einmal mit Entdröhnungsmittel.

- 6 -

16.13 **Motorraum**
Motorraum allseitig (Vorderwand, Seitenwände, Rückwand, Motorabschlußblech) zweimal mit Entdröhnungsmittel gespritzt.

16.2 **Weitere Entdröhnungsmaßnahmen, mit Dämpfungsmaterial ausgeklebt**

16.21 **Bugraum**
Kofferboden, Querwand.

16.22 **Fahrgastraum**
Pedalquerwand, Batteriekastenwand, Fußboden, Tunnel seitlich, Fersenblech, Notsitz und Kofferboden. Ferner Längsträger, hintere radlaufkästen, Fondrückwand und Dach.
Hohlraum zwischen Dach und Fondrückwand in vorgesehener Nut beim Rohbau mit Schaumstoff ausgefüllt.

16.23 **Motorraum**
Gesamter Motorraum einschließlich Motorraumabdeckblech.

16.24 **Außenteile**
Getriebeboden, Getriebemulde (Sitzmulde) und Türschacht vorn.

16.3 **Getriebedeckel am Tunnelende**
Deckel auf der Unterseite mit Dämpfungsmaterial beklebt, auf der Oberseite mit Teppich.
Angaben über die Dämpfungsmaterialien, Anzahl der eingeklebten Schichten usw. siehe Stückliste bzw. Zeichnung.

17. Besondere Ausstattung:
Ein Deckel im linken Vorderkotflügel verdeckt den Kraftstoffeinfüllstutzen. Der Deckel ist mit Drahtzug nur vom Wageninnern zu öffnen.

3.7.63   Dr.-Ing. h. c. F. Porsche K.-G. Stuttgart-Zuffenhausen   901.002.501.00

35

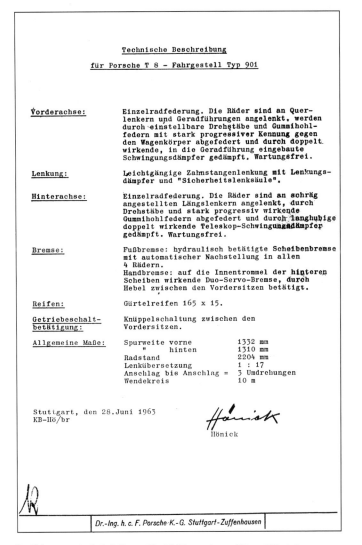

```
                    Technische Beschreibung
              für Porsche T 8 - Fahrgestell Typ 901


Vorderachse:        Einzelradfederung. Die Räder sind an Quer-
                    lenkern und Geradführungen angelenkt, werden
                    durch einstellbare Drehstäbe und Gummihohl-
                    federn mit stark progressiver Kennung gegen
                    den Wagenkörper abgefedert und durch doppelt
                    wirkende, in die Geradführung eingebaute
                    Schwingungsdämpfer gedämpft. Wartungsfrei.

Lenkung:            Leichtgängige Zahnstangenlenkung mit Lenkungs-
                    dämpfer und "Sicherheitslenksäule".

Hinterachse:        Einzelradfederung. Die Räder sind an schräg
                    angestellten Längslenkern angelenkt, durch
                    Drehstäbe und stark progressiv wirkende
                    Gummihohlfedern abgefedert und durch langhubige
                    doppelt wirkende Teleskop-Schwingungsdämpfer
                    gedämpft. Wartungsfrei.

Bremse:             Fußbremse: hydraulisch betätigte Scheibenbremse
                    mit automatischer Nachstellung in allen
                    4 Rädern.
                    Handbremse: auf die Innentrommel der hinteren
                    Scheiben wirkende Duo-Servo-Bremse, durch
                    Hebel zwischen den Vordersitzen betätigt.

Reifen:             Gürtelreifen 165 x 15.

Getriebeschalt-     Knüppelschaltung zwischen den
betätigung:         Vordersitzen.

Allgemeine Maße:    Spurweite vorne        1332 mm
                        "     hinten       1310 mm
                    Radstand               2204 mm
                    Lenkübersetzung        1 : 17
                    Anschlag bis Anschlag = 3 Umdrehungen
                    Wendekreis             10 m


Stuttgart, den 28.Juni 1963
KB-Hö/br                        Hönick
                                Hönick




                        Dr.-Ing. h. c. F. Porsche K.-G. Stuttgart-Zuffenhausen
```

In this report, dated June 28, 1963, engineer Hans Hönick provides a surprisingly accurate description of the 901 suspension. English translation see pages 389 - 390.

mined that the Porsche front suspension technically infringed on Sections 20 and 21 of the American patent 2 624 592, MacPherson/General Motors, dated March 21, 1947. But after reading a few additional sentences, the all-clear could be sounded: "However, the claims are anticipated by the German patent and Fiat, so that General Motors cannot make any valid claims." The design of the floorpan and the air vents above the rear window initially violated existing patent rights, but in the end they could be realized without changes.

Costs, too, were a pressing concern. For that reason, purchasing boss Wilhelm Albrecht also requested a bid from Karosseriewerke Weinsberg for the design of the production facilities. The small body maker was able to beat the Reutter offer by 40 percent and was issued a contract for part of the facilities. Now Porsche had to coordinate with three partners.

Body supplier Karmann (also not inexpensive, but with highly regarded quality), scheduled to switch production from the Type 356 C to the 901 in the fall of 1964, worked day and night shifts. On November 15, 1962, the first prototype models were viewed and signed off by a Porsche delegation consisting of Butzi Porsche (in early documents always referred to as Porsche Jr.), Tomala, Albrecht, designer Alfred Kühn, Schröder and Beierbach (now a Porsche employee, as Porsche had purchased Reutter). Porsche had asked the prototype models be painted black, polished, presented in a well-lit room and not on a pedestal. Although the Porsche men were well satisfied with the quality, some details still needed attention: the door handle depressions, the joints between the cowl and front fenders, the rear lid and the rear bumpers, the front bumper and the indentations for the windshield wipers in the cowl. To carry out the changes, two weeks were scheduled. Meanwhile, under drawing number 901.003.501.00, Porsche design engineer Robert Binder had completed the first relevant design drawing (illustrated on page 37). Drawings were always done in $1/10$ scale.

Technology was also making great strides. On Friday, November 9, 1962, Helmuth Bott undertook the first test drive in the 901 prototype. "The tension was enormous, even though I had already driven the rolling testbed on the T7 platform," recalls Bott, who had in the meantime become chief of the road test department. His impressions were recorded in his report dated November 12, 1962. Bott's second test drive came on Wednesday, November 14. The drives took place between 9 and 10 o'clock in the evening, so that the tests would be undisturbed by curious onlookers or other traffic. The test report attests to calm winds and an ambient air temperature of 6 °C (43 °F). The third test drive took place on Tuesday, November 27, in the company of Helmut

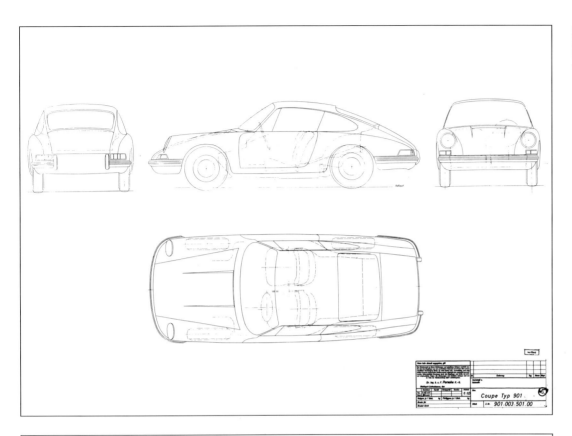

Porsche engineer
Robert Binder drew this
first definitive general
view in $\frac{1}{10}$ scale.

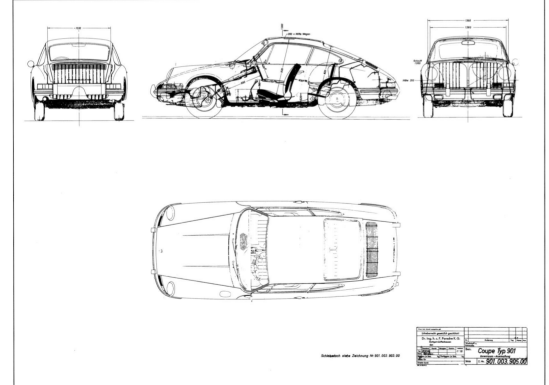

On this design drawing,
Porsche's characteristic
placement of the car's
key components and its
interior arrangement
are sketched in.

Verteiler:
Herrn Porsche
Herrn Porsche jr.
Herrn Tomala
Herrn Rombold
Herrn Reimspieß
Herrn Komenda
Herrn Linge
FV

Aktennotiz

Betr.: Erste Probefahrt mit Prototyp 901 am Freitag, 9.11.1962.

z.K. H.Kühn

A. Grundsätzliches

Sichtverhältnisse und Sitzposition sind gut.
Das Fahrzeug ist handlich und hat den Charakter des sportlichen
Wagens voll beibehalten. Die Fahreigenschaften entsprechen denen
unserer T 5 Vorläufer mit T 6 Karosse, d.h. das Fahrzeug übersteuert noch zu viel und spricht zu giftig an auf Lenkeinschläge,
in Wechselkurven noch nicht befriedigend. (Federabstimmung noch
nicht endgültig, fehlende neue Hinterachse).
Armaturen sind gut zu sehen, Sitze sind angenehm. Auf den Rück-
sitzen hat man nicht den Eindruck, besser untergebracht zu sein,
als im 356 B.
Stand- Brems- und Blinkleuchten sind gut sichtbar. Rückfahrschein-
werfer ergeben helles Licht und gute Streuung.

Vom Begleitfahrzeug aus wirkt das Fahrzeug von hinten fremd.
Man hat den Eindruck, als ob die Heckscheibe trapezförmig nach
hinten zusammenliefe. Das Fahrzeug wirkt zierlich und klein.

Gut ist auch die Abdeckung von Auspuff und Motor, wobei evtl. die
Begleiterscheinung, daß die Entdrunpappe am Motorblock schon
nach der ersten kurzen Fahrt sehr weich wurde, mit der schlechteren
Kühlung des Topfes durch den Fahrtwind zusammenhängen mag.

B. Karosseriebeanstandungen

Türen klappern.
Fenster klappern. (Behelfsanordnung).
Handschuhkastendeckel springt auf.
Fahrzeug ist insgesamt laut (nicht Antidröhn gespritzt)
Scheiben beschlagen sehr stark (reicht für Winterbetrieb Düsenquer-
schnitt aus?).
Motorraumbeleuchtung leuchtet durch Deckelkiemen (andere Anbringung
möglich?).
Warum kein symmetrischer Schlüssel für Tür- und Lenkschloß?

C. Fahrgestellbeanstandungen

Lenkung ist vor allem in Mittelstellung zäh und träge, trotzdem
bei Korrekturen giftig. hat in Mittelstellung etwas Spiel.
Fahrzeug übersteuert wie Wagen 109.
Heizung stinkt.
Getriebe heult.
Vorderachse falsch eingestellt, Fahrzeug hat zu wenig Bodenfreiheit.
Quertrennfugen kommen durch, als ob Gummipuffer anständen.
Vorderachse schlägt durch.
Lenkrad sitzt nicht in Mittelstellung.
Drehzahlmesser zeigt wahrscheinlich zu viel an.
Bremse hat starke Pedalwegänderungen. Nach einigen km Fahrt ohne
Bremsung ist man am Bodenbrett. Durch Pumpen kommt das Pedal wieder
zurück.

- 2 -

- 2 -

D. Sonstiges

Licht gut, Schaltung gut.
V_{max} Tunnel bei Behinderung 20,8 - 173 km/h. Anzeige Drehzahlmesser
6100 U/Min.

E. Montageprogramm für 12. und 13.10.62.

Lenkradstellung berichtigen.
Handschuhkastendeckel-Befestigung ändern.
Bodenbrett für Beifahrer anbringen.
Abstand Auspufftopf - Motorblock kontrollieren (Temperatur!).
Drehzahlmesser eichen.
Getriebe ausbauen und Tachometerantrieb einbauen.
Wenn Drehzahlmesser nicht korrigiert werden kann, zusätzlicher
Einbau Hartmann & Braun-Gerät.
Räderhebungen aufnehmen, Rahmenelastizität- und Lenkelastizität
messen.
Vorderachse richtigstellen.
Handbremse einbauen.
Bremse entlüften und untersuchen.

Stgt.-Zuffenhausen, 12.11.1962
FV/Bo-scho
(Bott)

Verteiler:
Herrn Porsche
Herrn Porsche jr.
Herrn Tomala
Herrn Rombold
Herrn Reimspieß/
Herrn Hönick
Herrn Komenda
Herrn Linge
FV

Aktennotiz

Betr.: Zweite Probefahrt mit Prototyp 901 am
Mittwoch, 14.11.1962.

Außentemperatur + 6° C, Straßen trocken.
Meßfahrten zwischen 21.00 und 22.00 Uhr, windstill.

Meßwerte:

Stehender km in 2 Richtungen gefahren: im Mittel = ~~35,3~~ 34,7
mittlere Geschwindigkeit 104 km/h. (Anfahrvorgang nicht ganz korrekt,
da Kupplung rupft).

Höchstgeschwindigkeit am Tunnel = 188 km/h bei Bremsleistung des
Motors 88,7 PS.

Bei Drehzahl 6100 abfallend auf 6000 nach Drehzahlmesser (Eichkurve
liegt im Augenblick noch nicht vor).
Tachoanzeige bei dieser Geschwindigkeit 197 km/h, Voreilung 5 %.
Tachoanzeige bei 60 km/h = 60 km/h
bei 120 km/h =120 km/h.
Abweichung also nur im oberen Bereich.

Lenkung:

Schon bei der Ausfahrt war die Lenkung nicht so lebendig wie unsere
Serienlenkung. Während der Fahrt wurde sie immer schwergängiger und
nach ca. 50 km mußte sie selbst bei engen Kurven in die 0-Lage zurück-
gezogen werden.

Bremsen:

Die eingebaute Girling-Bremse mit Girling-Hauptbremszylinder ist an-
genehm im Fußdruck, gut in der Bremswirkung und verzieht nicht aus hoher
Geschwindigkeit. Der Pedalweg wechselt immer noch stark.
Bei einer Vollbremsung aus 205 km/h war das Bremspedal am Bodenbrett.
Nach 5 Bremsungen aus 140 km/h bis nahezu Stillstand wurde ein starkes
Geräusch durch schleifende Bremsbacken an der Scheibe hörbar, das sich
im Verlauf von etwa 2 km wieder vollständig verlor. Außerdem qualmte
und stank die Bremse sehr stark bei den letzten beiden Bremsungen.

Drehzahlmesser:

Das Instrument funktionierte am Anfang sehr gut. Die Nadel stand ruhig
und eilte nicht merklich vor. Nach ca. 20 km Fahrt sprang die Nadel
plötzlich auf 0 zurück und setzte von Zeit zu Zeit stark zappelnd wieder
ein (Gerät nicht in Ordnung).

Motor:

Der eingebaute Motor hatte einen sehr schlechten Leerlauf (pendelnd von
800 auf 100 U/min). Starke Vibrationen wurden im Leerlauf auf den Wagen
übertragen.Im Gegensatz zu guten Serienmotoren fiel die Drehzahl bei
leichten Steigungen stark zurück. Die Probefahrt wurde unterbrochen, da die
Lenkung so stark klebte, daß das Fahrzeug nicht mehr betriebssicher war.

- 2 -

- 2 -

Weiteres Montageprogramm

1.) Motor ausbauen und an MV übergeben.

2.) Kupplung nachsehen (rupft stark).

3.) Motor-Getriebe-Aufhängung Shore-Härte prüfen
(Kupplungsrupfen, starke Geräuschübertragung).

4.) Bremsen überprüfen.
Bei Vollbremsung blockierten die beiden linken Räder.
Von den rechten Rädern zeichnet sich keine Bremsspur ab.
Bremspedal schlägt hart an beim Zurückschnellen.

5.) Drehzahlmesser Gerät ausbauen, überprüfen.
Eichkurve am Armaturenbrett ankleben.

6.) Spurstangen ausbauen, Reibung Lenkgetriebe und Lenkungsdämpfer
feststellen. Bei zu großer Reibung im Lenkgetriebe Lenkgetriebe
demontieren und Spezialfett einfüllen.

7.) Außenspiegel montieren nach Angaben der Abteilung Studie.

8.) Haltegriff für Beifahrer nach Anweisung Studio anbringen.

9.) Fahrzeug vermessen, Lenkradstellung korrigieren.

10.) Bedienung vom Scheibenwischer und -wascher angenehm, Lenk-
se los jedoch sehr schlecht zugänglich, unmöglich.

11.) Rahmenelastizitäts- und Lenkelastizitätsmessungen für Samstag
verbereiten.

Nächste Probefahrt voraussichtlich Montag, den 21.11.1962.

x) Handbremse in der Wirkung ausreichend nur bei sehr starkem Anziehen
des Handbremshebels (für eine Frau nicht mehr zumutbar).

Stgt.-Zuffenhausen, 15.11.1962
FV/Bo-scho
(Bott)

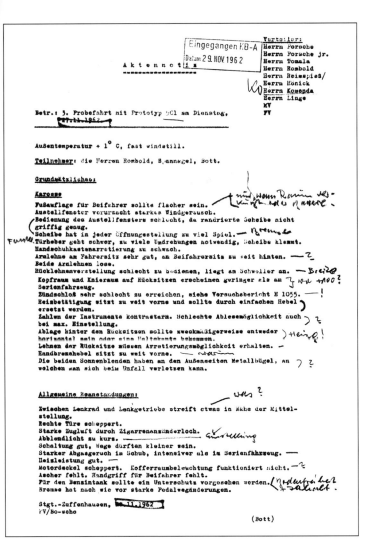

As early as November 1, 1960, the acting chief of the test driving department, Helmuth Bott, slid behind the wheel of a 911 predecessor. Bott drove the T7 with the two-liter engine mounted under the floor. His damning conclusion was "We can forget about this!" After the first three test drives with the 901, between November 9 and November 27, 1962, Bott was considerably more optimistic. Naturally, before the car was ready for production two years later, countless details had to be improved. The body had weak spots, especially in the door area; the windows bowed outward at high speed, creating objectionable wind noise. On the technical side, straight-line stability caused many an engineer's headache. Test drives took place between 9 and 10 PM, so that they might be undisturbed and unobserved. The second report mentions calm winds and an ambient temperature of six degrees (Celsius). English translation on pages 390 - 391.

Rombold and Hans Spannagel, members of the test driving staff primarily responsible for brakes and clutch. In the technical sector, too, there was no time to lose. On November 8, 1962, engine designer Hans Mezger, from the Swabian town of Besigheim, established a timetable for the Type 821 engine components, transmission, suspension, and road equipment (see pages 390 - 391 for English translation). In the meantime, it had become clear that the first production cars could not be built until the spring of 1964. The 901 would nevertheless be displayed at the Frankfurt Auto Show – the IAA – in September 1963, but not as a drivable car.

1963

Frankfurt was drawing ever closer. Like the parts of a puzzle, the many detail solutions slowly came together to form a whole. In March of 1963, it was decided that the fuel filler lid would be located on the left front fender. Two slightly different solutions were available, installed in the first and second prototypes. The fuel filler arrangement shown on the second prototype was rejected because of the risk of freezing shut.

The decorative grille for the air inlet under the windshield and the vent over the rear window still had to be finalized. The Reutter company developed some solutions for these.

Above all, the shape of the air inlet in the engine lid had to be developed, so that tooling could be made to stamp the required opening. Running prototype number II had a two-part solution like that of the 356, which had been advanced by the studio. (The model department had been renamed "Studio" in 1962). The Reutter design group also presented a solution, but only on paper. This proposal guaranteed the required area, determined by Egon Forstner of the calculating department, of 7 square decimeters (0.75 sq. ft.) and a good air flow path to the cooling blower. The disadvantage was that to realize this engine lid design, changes would have to be made to the decklid opening in the bodywork. Thereupon Butzi Porsche had six solutions made in the studio. "My idea was to have the grille located entirely out-

This first photo of the 901 prototype, nicknamed "Fledermaus" [Bat], moving under its own power, was taken on July 10, 1963 between Weilimdorf and Münchingen. For purposes of disguise, the car was fitted with additional parts and given a coating of olive drab German army wax.

side. As this would require reinforcing the lid below the grille, I could imagine that we could make the lid movable only below the grille." The Studio presented photos of all six solutions to Hans Tomala on August 16, 1963 – that is, three weeks before the opening of the IAA. Up to that point, nothing had been decided; but the delay to the last minute was not without reason. The effective air requirement for the engine was still to be determined by driving tests. How difficult this task would be had already been noted by the engineers on the first T7 running prototype and its under-floor motor. The definitive solution was completed only hours before the opening of the show.

Then there was the interior. The instrument panel was not yet formally completed. The construction team at Reutter developed several proposals. The type of vent window actuation was also not yet finalized. A decision on the different inner door actuation of the two prototypes was finally made on March 28,

1963. It would be a type of armrest pushbutton actuation. At the end of March, the construction of running prototype number III was begun.

Parallel to the technical meetings mentioned above, additional meetings, usually in Ferry Porsche's office, were called to discuss problems in the development of the T8. The new rack and pinion steering and the lack of adjustability of the front suspension were grounds for discussion. Under the leadership of Ferdinand Piëch, today chairman of the board of Volkswagen, the engine continued its development to production-ready status (see separate chapter). Hans Mezger added his racing engine design expertise. The transmission specialists, under their design chief Richard Hetmann, discussed four- or five-speed concepts.

From the beginning, the body of the 901 was designed to enable an open version to be built. Because of increasing time pressure, the other 901

Butzi Porsche created six proposals for the rear air inlet grille. The solution shown at left is that of the 356.

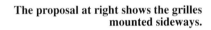

The proposal at right shows the grilles mounted sideways.

Butzi Porsche favored a solution with a transverse grille.

Design drawings of possible open versions: the removable steel roof could not be stowed.

Even a sunroof was not offered before June, 1965.

The Targa solution was developed from this design drawing.

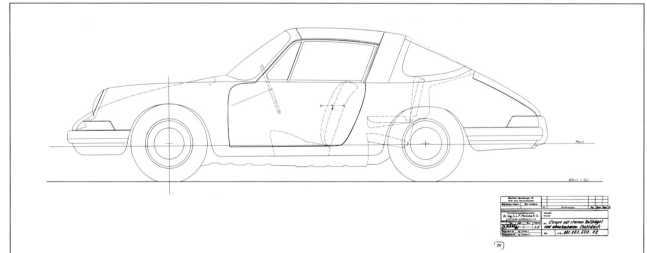

42

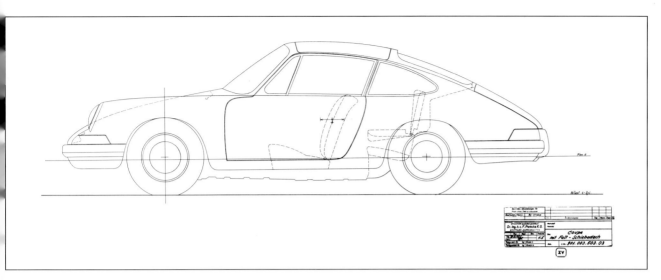

The folding sliding roof would hardly have been larger than the steel sunroof.

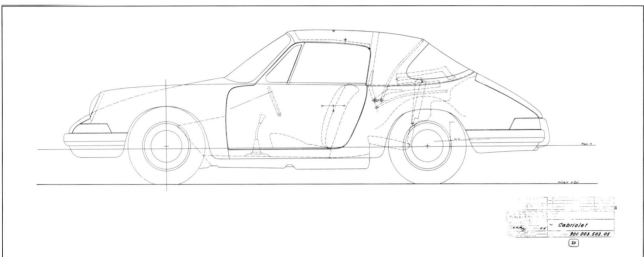

In the case of this Cabriolet top, there was no room left for the engine.

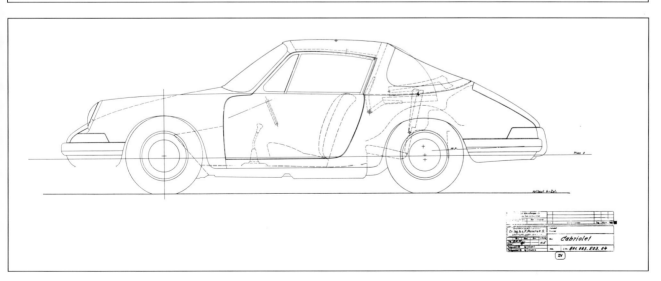

The Cabriolet with a larger rear window would only have been possible after extensive changes.

The cockpit of the first production cars, with a wood-rimmed steering wheel and wooden dash trim. The configuration of five round instruments has been retained to the present day.

variants were put on the back burner. Still, between June 26 and December 18, 1963, plans were drawn up for the widest variety of 901 versions: a coupe with steel sliding sunroof, a coupe with a removable steel roof, a coupe with a fixed roll bar, removable steel roof and folding rear window, a coupe with a folding sunroof and two cabriolet versions. Both cabrios sported a fixed roll bar, an accordion-like folding roof, and a folding rear window. The difference was to be found in the rear section, as Butzi had one version drawn with a slight break in the body contour. Today, he recalls this completely unknown version: "With that, I wanted to underscore the roadster feeling." A separate chapter, *The open 911,* describes development of the Cabriolet and Targa.

Meanwhile, sales, under the leadership of Wolfgang Raether, got involved in these discussions. The sales department is credited for the placement of the battery in the left front of the trunk, next to the spare tire, and not, as had been planned until May of 1963, in the passenger footwell or in the space then known as the "battery box" in the trunk to the right of the dashboard. The sales staff had a difficult position at the time; even as late as 1963, the 356 was still beloved. Ernst Bolt recalls the view in some quarters that "when this car comes out, we're sunk."

On July 4, 1963, Erwin Komenda signed a short description of the Porsche 901 coupe body, in the left-hand-drive version. (Box on p. 35). This was followed on August 1 by the written synopsis of the 901 technical specifications (Box on p. 45). These specifications also represent the status of the vehicle shown at the Frankfurt International Automobile Show beginning on September 12, 1963, to which a separate chapter is dedicated. At this point, the engines were still not equipped with a dry sump lubrication system or with heat exchangers. Experiments were underway to fit a heater, made by the Webasto company, into the battery box. Thereafter, the battery was finally moved to the left, next to the spare tire.

While the IAA car, number 5, travelled from show to show, work continued on the remaining six prototypes. Above all, the instrumentation was, according to a memorandum dated October 11, 1963, "newly defined for marketing and styling reasons." The two dominant instruments were replaced by five gauges: tachometer, speedometer, clock, oil pressure and temperature, and fuel level. Due to annoying reflections, the inclination of the instrument panel was increased by five degrees. To this day, the arrangement has remained almost

Technical Data of the Type 901 (effective August 1, 1963)

Engine Specifications 6 cylinders in boxer arrangement, bore 80 mm, stroke 66 mm, displacement 1991 cc, compression 9:1, 130 DIN hp at 6200 rpm, maximum torque 16.5 mkg (DIN) at 4600 rpm, specific output 66 DIN hp/liter/1000 rpm, octane requirement 96 Research Octane Number

Engine Design Air-cooled 6-cyl. boxer engine, 3 cylinders on each side, 8-bearing crankshaft, cylinders of cast gray iron, all other cast parts of light alloy, overhead valves in V arrangement, actuated by chain driven single overhead cams and rocker arms, dry sump lubrication (separate oil tank), with scavenge and pressure pump, oil cooler mounted on engine, disposable full-flow oil filter, 6 Solex carburetors, Micronic air filter, 12 V 360 W alternator, 45 Ah battery, electric fuel pump.

Power Transmission Single disc dry clutch with diaphragm spring, manual transmission with 4 or 5 forward gears, all forward gears with Porsche synchromesh. Final drive contained in same housing, ratio 4.43:1 (7/31). Limited slip differential available by special request. Shift actuation via conventional shift lever beside driver's seat.

Overall Gear Ratios

a) 4-speed transmission
- I. 13.69:1
- II. 8.12:1
- III. 5.39:1
- IV. 3.64:1

b) 5-speed transmission
- I. 13.69:1
- II. 8.37:1
- III. 5.84:1
- IV. 4.43:1
- V. 3.39:1

Theoretical speeds in gears

b: rpm for max. torque
c: rpm for max. power
d: approx. max. rpm

a) rpm	1st gear km/h	2nd gear km/h	3rd gear km/h	4th gear km/h
a: 1000	8	15	22	33
b: 4600	40	67	101	105
c: 6200	54	91	138	203
d: 6600	57	96	145	–

b) rpm	1st gear km/h	2nd gear km/h	3rd gear km/h	4th gear km/h	5th gear km/h
a: 1000	8	14	20	27	35
b: 4600	40	65	94	123	161
c: 6200	54	88	126	166	210
d: 6600	57	93	130	177	–

Suspension Front: independent suspension, transverse arms, trailing links, springing via adjustable torsion bars and hollow rubber bump stops, rear independent suspension with trailing arms, springing via torsion bars and hollow rubber bump stops, front and rear double-acting telescoping shock absorbers, hydraulic disc brakes on all four wheels, total brake swept area 185 cm^2, hand brake acting on rear wheels, rack and pinion steering with steering damper and safety steering column, fuel capacity 74 liters, radial tires 165 - 15.

Weights and dimensions Wheelbase 2204 mm, front track 1332 mm, rear track 1312 mm, ground clearance 118 mm (at maximum gross weight), turning circle 10 m, 2+2 coupe, length 4135 mm, width 1600 mm, height 1273 mm (at maximum gross weight), empty weight 998 kg.

Equipment Standard equipment: heater, windshield washers, individual seats, trip odometer, tachometer, oil temperature gauge.

Performance Fuel consumption 11 - 14 l/100 km, maximum speed approx. 211 km/h.

Specific performance (based on empty weight) Power to weight ratio 7.7 kg/hp, specific displacement 1.995 liter/ton, speed in 4th gear at 1000 rpm 35 km/h, blower volume in 5th gear 1710 liters/ton km.

This overview was created in the design office on July 19, 1963.

---

unchanged. Small details like the italic gold-anodized aluminum script were also finalized by the end of 1963.

The development costs of the 901 rose into the millions of Deutschmarks; by the time the new model was ready for production, they amounted to 15 million Marks, in addition to the takeover of the Reutter body plant. With this, Porsche's financial means were stretched so thin that the company had to abstain from several Grand Prix events. This emphasizes that Porsche could not afford to allow the new car to be a failure; its creators bore an enormous responsibility.

Wind tunnel tests with a full-size model were not carried out until March 1964. The tufts on the backlight indicate far less turbulence than had been noted in the T7 tests. Overall, the results were quite satisfactory.

1964

Throughout the year, during the so-called Thursday meetings, the individual problems of the seven prototypes were discussed. Present were all the specialists from the road test department including Hans Spannagel, Kurt Knoerzer, Peter Falk, Rolf Hannes, Herbert Linge, Helmuth Bott, and Helmut Rombold.

The meeting minutes indicate that the wind tunnel tests with full-scale models could not begin before March 1964, using Prototype Number 7. On the rear window, tests showed a limited separation of the streamlines with reverse flow and secondary flow, and thereby a much better result than with the T7 model. For the 901, Porsche used the wind tunnel of the Research Institute for Motor Vehicles and Automotive Engines (Forschungsinstitut für Kraftfahrwesen und Fahrzeugmotoren Stuttgart, FKFS), located in Untertürkheim.

On a less regular basis, discussions regarding assembly difficulties were held beginning in January

1964. In addition to the test engineers, those responsible for the body and several designers took part in these meetings.

After Porsche had refrained from demonstration drives during all of 1963 – and because the 901 shown at the IAA could not be driven by customers, as was the custom at the time – the sales department prepared a demonstration program for the domestic and European export markets. Salesmen Dieter Lenz and Hans Klink were to present the cars to dealers and provide an opportunity for prospective buyers to ride in it. It had been exceedingly difficult for the salesmen at the IAA to justify the increase in price of the 356 successor by 7000 Marks (to 23,900 Marks). By the time the first cars were delivered, sales chief Raether had been able to reduce the price by 1500 Marks. An internal memo dated December 9, 1963, indicates that three versions of the 901 were planned – first a 901 de Luxe, as shown in Frankfurt with full leather interior for 22,400 Marks; second, a standard version with a four-cylinder engine, leatherette interior and without chrome wheels or wooden steering wheel rim, for 17,500 Marks; and third, a

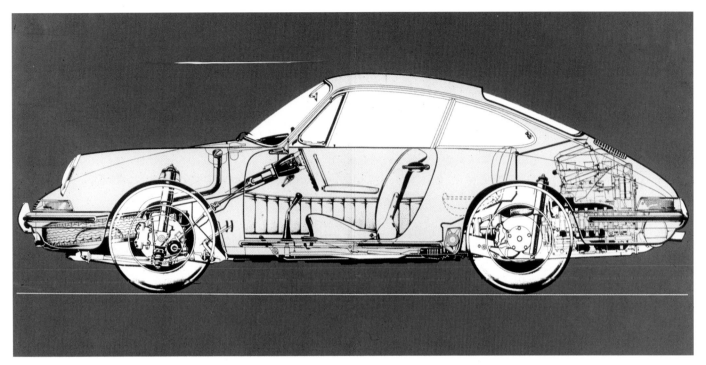

In terms of styling as well as function, the 911 was so thoroughly thought out that the basic concept has weathered thirty years. Even for occupant protection, the new Porsche more than met requirements by virtue of its angled steering column and a fuel tank protected by the front suspension.

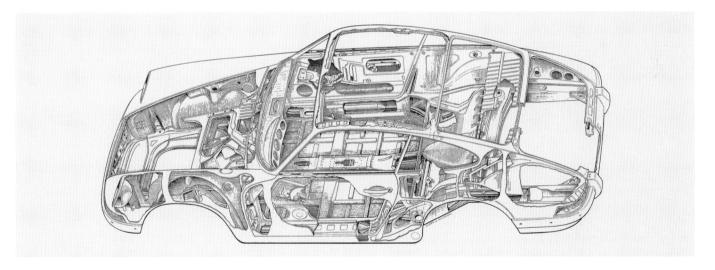

This phantom view of the Porsche 911 underscores the sturdy passenger cell, to protect its occupants, the short wheelbase of 2200 mm, and the relatively small front and rear overhang. The front fenders are bolted to the body.

901 "S" with a 150 horsepower engine, for 23,900 Marks. As only the first version could be delivered by the end of 1964, only this version was demonstrated on the sales tour. The program started on February 7, 1964, and developed into a unique adventure (see next two chapters); it became an endurance test which accelerated pre-production testing of the 901, as several suspension problems

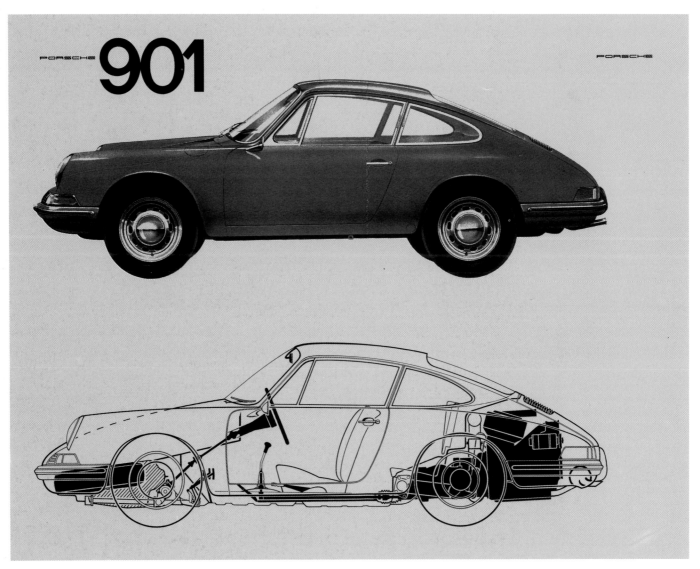

The stuff of dreams: a timeless, beautiful body with relatively short overhang, direct steering, five-speed transmission, six-cylinder boxer engine at the rear and thereby adequate weight on the drive wheels.

had not yet been resolved. Brake fading developed rapidly, and the pedal travel increased objectionably. In addition, the brake pads wore quickly, due to overheating brake discs. In test drives, which were mainly carried out in Wolfsburg, the body still showed some weak points. On all 901s made before March 25, 1964, the door windows were prone to flutter, and above a certain speed, were sucked outward. In addition, drafts were noted in several locations.

On August 25, 1964, Hans Tomala, speaking at a development meeting, declared that design work on the new Type 901 was, for all practical purposes, concluded. It was high time, as Porsche was behind schedule on the development contract for the Type 1764, for Volkswagen (This Beetle successor never went into production). But the file on the 901 could still not be closed as a more affordable version with a four-cylinder powerplant, a sunroof version and a competition car with lightweight body parts

48

Engine design:

1. Ruoff, Karl (chief of production engine design) 2. Hetmann, Richard (chief of transmission design) 3. Jäntschke, Leopold (engine designer) 4. Stotz, Erich (rear suspension designer) 5. Binder, Robert (production engine designer under Jäntschke) 6. Hofmann, Rudolf (front suspension designer) 7. Herzog, Hans (logistics, parts lists) 8. Hönick, Hans (Formula 1 engine designer) 9. Reimspiess, Franz Xaver (chief designer)

Body:

10. Kühn, Alfred (logistics within design department) 11. Bauer, Theo (body design within Reutter) 12. Klie, Heinrich (designer, model department) 13. Tengler, Edgar (parts procurement) 14. Beierbach, Walter (works manager at Reutter) 15. Komenda, Erwin (chief of body development) 16. Albrecht, Wilhelm (chief of purchasing) 17. Sturm, Gottlob (chief panelbeater) 18. Schröder, Gerhard (designer) 19. Mozelt, Karl (designer)

Experimental department:

20. Mezger, Hans ('experimental,' racing engine design) 21. Weyersberg, Ernst (planning) 22. Knoerzer, Kurt (road test department) 23. Metzger "senior", Karl (work planning, calculation in Werk II) 24. Martens, Hans (planning) 25. Bott, Helmuth (road test department) 26. Schneider, Adolf (leader of experimental shop) 27. Linge, Herbert (road test department and racing driver) 28. Schilling, Karl (leader of experimental purchasing department) 29. Storz, Eberhard (leader of all engine experimental work, production as well as racing engines) 30. Rombold, Helmut (leader of road test department) 31. Tomala, Hans (overall technical direction) 32. Piech, Ferdinand (engine testing department) 33. Porsche, F.A. (chief of model department) 34. Porsche, Dr. Ferry (chief).

49

remained on the agenda. The sliding roof had long been on the sales department's wish list, especially since no open version of the 901 could be offered to customers. Harald Wagner, at the time the domestic sales chief, recalls that 901 project leader Wolfgang Eyb had struck the sliding roof from the development program. The efforts of the sales department did get a steel sliding roof back into the program, but not until June 1965.

At the beginning of October, 1964, Porsche showed the 901 at the Paris automobile salon, and announced the imminent delivery of the first production examples. There, Peugeot's attention was suddenly drawn to the new sports car, more specifically to its model designation. As the French carmaker had given all its passenger cars since 1929 a three-digit model number with a zero in the middle, the French insisted on their copyright and asserted trademark protection claims. In a strictly legal sense, these demands were only enforceable in France. But to keep the same worldwide model designation for the new sports car – and as France was a vital export market – Porsche quickly changed the model designation to 911. Internally, on all drawings and in spare part numbers, the designation "901" was continued for quite a long time to avoid logical inconsistencies. In the same way, the not-yet-displayed four-cylinder model, the 912, was originally called the 902. The racing prototype 904, however, retained its designation. Racing director Huschke von Hanstein successfully argued that Porsche had had the 904 on the market for an entire year without any reaction from Peugeot. Later racing models also carried a zero as their central digit.

Now that the new sports car from Zuffenhausen finally had a name, from which incidentally much more attractive designations could be derived (at least in the German language, as "Neunelfer" or "Elfer"), the first production cars were delivered in Stuttgart on October 27, 1964, on the occasion of a sales conference. Naturally, the sports car still suffered some teething problems, which were addressed in so-called quality meetings. But the 911 was continuously improved and brought to the state of the technological art, a process which continues to the present day.

The 911 Prototypes

Rich in Experience

The occasion of a special anniversary is likely to result in the raiding of archives, extensive research and a host of new words. In the months preceding this book, there has been extensive speculation regarding the exact number of 911 prototypes, designated Type 901. Sellers of old Porsches took advantage of the upcoming festivities; in classified ads, they offered alleged 901s for sale. Further research clearly revealed that the cars in question were not 901s but rather early 911 models. Peugeot's veto of the 901 designation occurred immediately after the Paris Salon of October 1964; the first 911s were delivered to domestic and foreign distributors in Zuffenhausen on November 16 and 17 of that year. The first customers took delivery a few days later. All vehicles already carried the designation "911" and the first digit of the chassis number was "3." So, for example, a car with the chassis number 300 012 is the twelfth series-production 911.

Internally, a finer distinction was made. The first production chassis, serial number 300 007, left the assembly line on September 14, 1964. Interestingly, serial number 1 was not produced until September 17. As the production of these first cars occurred before Peugeot lodged its complaint, they were known internally as Type 901s. The switch to the 911 designation occurred on November 10, 1964,

with chassis number 300 049, that is, before delivery of the first vehicles. This is not to say that 49 cars carried the internal designation 901; as indicated by the first few cars and they were not produced with sequential serial numbers. So, for example, on November 5, 1964, cars numbered 74 and 79 were produced with the internal designation 901. All told, 82 vehicles carried the internal designation 901.

It is now possible to reconstruct the production sequence and production numbers for these early 911s. For the first time, we can say with certainty that exactly 232 vehicles were built in 1964. The last car of the year carried chassis number 233 and was assembled on December 23; the first car of the following year had its number, 235, assigned on January 4.

With regard to equipment, there was no difference between the cars designated internally as 901s and those introduced as of November 10, 1964 as 911s. Beginning with the very first chassis number, the cars were known as the so-called "Series 0," which remained in production until July 1967. This designation often leads to confusion, as the standard sequence adopted by the auto industry is as follows: the first cars are hand-built prototypes, followed by a pre-production series for development tests. Next

Externally, prototypes differed from early production cars in their lack of deco strips on the rocker panels.

come the "0 Series" or "Zero Series" cars, which incorporate production parts whenever possible. These cars, usually built in a series of fifty, are built using production tooling. In the case of the Porsche 911, however, "0 Series" does not refer to these, but rather the entire series prior to a later Series A (such as, for example, the 356, followed by the 356 A). Today, the identifiers within the car industry have been unified to avoid confusion.

Cars built within this first 911 series can be further subdivided. After the first year of production, which ended with the August 1965 plant holiday, the cars were fitted with a number of new details, which are chronicled at the back of this book. The last chassis number assigned to that first year of 911 production was 30 2104. This and 13 other cars were built on July 30, 1965. The first chassis number produced on August 16, 1965, after the plant reopened, was 30 2114.

In summary, it can be said that all cars built between September 14, 1964 and July 30, 1965 are cars of the first 911 generation. The true 901s are prototypes bearing chassis numbers of so-called replacement bodies, beginning with the number 13. The first 901 development car carries the chassis number 13 321. These forerunners were numbered chronologically only up to the tenth car. The eleventh car, numbered 13 352, fell out of sequence. The twelfth test car, numbered 300 001, bore the first production serial number.

Early company documents record how many prototypes were built and what they experienced. To clarify, once and for all, the history of these cars which bore witness to the early history of the 911, we present the data for each individual car. In compiling this information, the author has relied on the records of the development department. Naturally, there were more than the listed 13 prototypes, but these few cars defined the history of the 911 up to the delivery of the first production cars. Cars 12 and 13 are included, even though they already carried production numbers. The author has withheld one critical identifying characteristic for each car, in order to detect possible forgeries of these prototypes. In addition, for reasons of confidentiality, only subsequent owners who are or were Porsche employees are listed, although private owners are also known. In this way, the history of every single 901 may be reconstructed, to the point where it was scrapped. This information has only rarely been made available to the public. Car number 7 has survived, and was recently restored in the United States. This car is largely original; only the sunroof was added at some later date.

Various sources contributed to the following data. August Klie of the body department, responsible for the liaison between design, production and development, kept records of chassis number assignments for the prototypes. Chief of the road test department, Helmuth Bott, kept records of development tests. In a list dated July 29, 1963 (see illustration) the first

seven cars are mentioned. In addition, from January 1964 through 1965, Bott produced a monthly list of test vehicles, which was updated as required. From this, the mileage and application of individual cars could be determined. In 1965, Bott also kept independent records of fuel consumption. Other information could be garnered from the previously mentioned T 8 meeting minutes, Thursday meetings and technical meetings. Thanks to a report dated March 2, 1964, concerning the development status of the engines, it is possible to assign individual engine numbers to the prototypes. In this way, the facts for each prototype could be assembled; these agree with Helmuth Bott's personal records.

Illustrating the individual cars proved especially difficult, not least because there was a strict ban on photography in the individual departments. Here, too, an interesting collection could be assembled only through careful research and with the utilization of private photos, shot secretly by employees. Helmuth Bott provided previously unreleased motion picture film which had been shot in the early 1960s during test drives. By a costly process, stills were produced from these films, and matched to the prototypes. This process was made more difficult by the fact that the early cars were often fitted with temporary tags. To camouflage cars 2 and 3, Porsche even resorted to using American license plates.

One common feature of these 911 forerunners is the makeup of the chassis numbers. They all begin with 1332, and differ only in their end number. So the serial number of the very first car, as already mentioned, is 13 321. Until just before the start of production, there were seven pre-production cars (13 321 to 13 327). These were followed by two test cars for the 912 (originally called the 902) with numbers 13 328 and 13 329. Four additional prototypes (13 330 to 13 333) were built at the end of 1964.

In general, the prototypes could be differentiated from the later production cars by their lack of bumper guards, no deco strips on the rocker panels and no script on the engine lid. For some cars, however, components were added over the course of several years. The individual details follow:

Each vehicle has a log entry. They were not produced sequentially.

On July 24, 1964, Harald Wagner, at that time director of domestic sales, married his wife Christa. The wedding car was a prototype 901, already equipped with bumper guards.

Number 1 (901/1)(911/1)*

Chassis number: 13 321
Color: white
License plate: always without
Nickname: "Sturmvogel" (Storm Petrel)
Body built by: Reutter (1); chassis by Porsche
Year built: 1962
Application: Presentation and viewing; wind tunnel; later brake and carburetion tests
Front suspension: subframe

54

Rear suspension: 356 B (swing axles)
Brakes: Girling
Engine: S 90, later 901
Engine number: 08
Transmission number: 741/2A, No. 304 (4-speed);
gear ratios** 11/34, 17/30, 23/26, 27/22
Assembly: Body, to September 14, 1962; suspension
and drivetrain in boarded-up area of development
department; assembled by Albert Junginger and
Walter Bemsel (electrics)
Career highlights: In July 1963, vehicle could only
be rolled at low speed. Feb. 27, 1964: road tests with
light alloy wheel Early 1964, 5000 km on car, brake
tests with Dunlop light alloy brake (12.7 mm disk
thickness, 280 mm diameter, Ferodo DS 11 and DS
5 S pads) Wind tunnel tests on March 5, 1964. Wind
tests, October 1964 - February 1965, 25,200 km on
car, tests with rear swing axle, carburetor tests
Disposition: Scrapped in early 1965, after completion of carburetor tests

Number 2 (901/2)(911/2)

Chassis number: 13 322
Color: white, camouflaged with olive drab German
army wax
License plate: HEC 626 (USA, yellow); red (tempo-
rary) tags S-04324
Nickname: "Fledermaus" (Bat)
Body built by: Reutter (2); chassis by Reutter
Year built: 1963
Application: Body and engine tests, heating tests,
suspension tests, carburetor tests

Front suspension: subframe
Rear suspension: preliminary 901 (trailing arm)
Brakes: Girling, later Teves
Engine: 901 without dry sump lubrication; 821 valve
train; overflow carburetors
Engine number: 03*** (destroyed); later 12
Transmission number: 741/2A, No. 52 637 (4-
speed); gear ratios 11/34, 17/30, 23/26, 27/23
Equipment: Old outside rear view mirrors made by
Mall (644.731.111.06); Webasto and engine heat;
transversely mounted rear bucket seat on Nov. 19,
1963; first version of engine lid air inlets
Assembly: body, to October 12, 1963; suspension
and drivetrain in boarded up area of development
department; assembled by Albert Junginger and
Walter Bemsel (electrics)
Additional features: weight 1065 kg, fuel economy
14.5 liters/100 km (16.2 mpg)
Career highlights: first "planted" press photo,
between Weilimdorf and Münchingen; heating tests
with Webasto, Feb. 27, 1964; test drives between
June 10 and July 11, 1963 (pressure drop measure-
ments in interior and engine compartment);
Nürburgring tests from July 1 to July 5, 1963; early
1964, heating tests at 5900 km; wind tunnel tests on
Feb. 14, 1964; brake tests on June 10, 1964
Disposition: scrapped late 1964

---

*   as of November 1964
**   from first to fourth or fifth gear
***   900 003, to be exact

Number 3 (901/3)(911/3)

Chassis number: 13 323
Color: dark blue, sometimes camouflaged with olive drab German army wax; as of May 27, 1964, painted red
License plate: HEC 627 (USA, yellow); as of February 1964, S-SK 725; as of June 1965, none
Nickname: "Blaumeise" (Blue Titmouse)
Body built by: Porsche (1), built by Hans Fuchs; chassis Porsche
Year built: 1963
Application: Tests; suspension development; test car for Wolfsburg endurance tests and wind tunnel
Front suspension: 901 (subframe)
Rear suspension: 901
Brakes: Girling, later Teves
Engine: 901 with dry-sump lubrication, updated January 1964, engine damage on March 5, 1964; overflow carburetors with Knecht air filters; comparison with float-equipped Solex triple carburetors
Engine number: 05; later No. 4 with 142 hp at 6300 rpm
Transmission number: 901, No. 2 (5-speed); gear ratios 14/37, 19/32, 23/28, 26/25, 28/23
Equipment: sample mirror made by Mall with attachment to door frame; no heating
Assembly: to July 31, 1963
Career highlights: September 29, 1963 to October 5, 1963: VW test track in Wolfsburg; Nov. 8, 1963, performance tests; early 1964, endurance tests at 15,259 km; as of April 15, completely disassembled, paint stripped (at 45,000 km including 6500 at Weissach proving grounds, itself equivalent to 50,000

km); late 1964, installation of Type 1764 engine and Boge "Hydromat" shock absorbers; beginning March 1, 1965, carburetor tests; on May 27, 1964, taken to body shop for updating and repainting (red); June 1965, engine tests at 29,775 km (new speedometer/odometer); transferred to VW in September 1965.
Disposition: unknown

Number 4 (901/4)(911/4)

Chassis number: 13 324
Color: yellow
License plate: red (temporary) tags S-0436; S-SK 726 (beginning February 1964); no plates beginning June 1965; as of September 1965, registered and insured by Teves
Nickname: "Zitronenfalter" (Brimstone Butterfly)
Body built by: Porsche (2); chassis by Porsche; to the end of July 1963
Year built: 1963
Application: development; spare car for exhibits, originally intended as IAA show car; roadholding tests
Front suspension: 901 (new design, as of July 25, 1963)
Rear suspension: 901
Brakes: Girling, later Teves
Engine: 901 with dry sump lubrication (115.9 hp at 5500 rpm)
Engine number: 07; damaged on June 8, 1964; as of Nov. 2, 1965, 170 hp engine (at 6500 rpm) with 2195 cc displacement
Transmission number: 901, No. 4 (5-speed); gear

ratios 11/34, 18/33, 23/28, 26/25, 28/23
Equipment: Sample mirror from Fechenbacher, with Webasto gasoline heater, but without engine heat, front-mounted battery
Assembly: August 1963
Additional features: weight 1086 kg, fuel capacity 62 liters, fuel economy 21.8 liters (10.8 mpg)
Career highlights: initially for display, then development car; early 1963, suspension tests at 6916 km; March 19, 1964, conversion to new front suspension with short torsion bars and new subframe; late 1964, Teves brake tests; June 1965, transmission tests at 62,000 km; August 1965, brake tests at Teves (vehicle loaned to Teves)
Disposition: unknown

Number 5 (901/5)(911/5)

Chassis number: 13 325
Color: yellow
License plate: early 1964, none; then S-TC 1; as of September 1965, not registered for road use
Nickname: none
Body built by: Karmann (1); chassis by Porsche
Year built: 1963
Application: sales; first show car; demonstrator; development car (carburetion)
Front suspension: 901
Rear suspension: 901
Brakes: Girling
Engine: initially dummy engine, then 901 with dry sump lubrication
Engine number: 11 (overhauled at 31,900 km); later No. 15

Transmission number: 901, No. 3 (5-speed); gear ratios 11/34 (later 14/37), 18/33 (later 19/32), 23/28, 26/25, 28/23; ring and pinion 7/31
Equipment: steering wheel from 356; round instruments, Webasto gasoline heater; as of 1965, air conditioning system
Assembly: August 1963
Additional features: weight 1059 kg; oil consumption approx. 1.5 l/1000 km; fuel economy 14.3 l/100 km (16.4 mpg)
Career highlights: as of September 1963, Frankfurt IAA; 3-13 October, 1963, Paris auto show; 16-26 October, London auto show; Oct. 30 - Nov. 10, 1963, Turin auto show; early February 1964, noise tests; then on 50,000 km sales tour with Dieter Lenz; at 17,520 km Geneva auto show; first prototype tested by *auto motor und sport* (Vol. 8/1964); mid-September 1964, support vehicle for Tour de France (driven by von Hanstein and Barth); tire tests at Hockenheim, Sept. 29 to Oct. 1, 1964; then carburetor tests; automatic transmission tests from late 1964 to August 1965, to 76,100 km
Disposition: after accident during transmission testing, destroyed by drop testing on December 7, 1965

Number 6 (901/6)(911/6)

Chassis number: 13 326
Color: enamel blue 6403
License plate: LB-U 911
Nickname: "Quick Blue"
Body built by: Karmann (2); chassis by Porsche, to late August 1963
Application: sales, foreign auto shows

Today, this license plate can be found on an Austin Mini Clubman

Front suspension: 901
Rear suspension: 901
Brakes: Girling or Teves (depending on availability, according to memo dated July 25, 1963)
Engine: initially dummy engine, as of May 1964 Type 901 with dry sump lubrication
Engine number: 09; later 154
Transmission number: 901, No. 1 (5-speed); gear ratios 11/34, 18/33, 22/29, 26/26, 29/22
Equipment: new dashboard with five round instruments; Rosanil 705 leather; black seats with "Pepita" (houndstooth) center panels (7/127); leather door panels; carpets in black Besmer velour, IDEE 903
Assembly: September 1963
Career highlights: London auto show, 16-26 October 1963; Sweden, Berlin and Geneva; as of mid-1963, first car to be converted for demonstration purposes, finished January 1964; was to have been made drivable in March 1964; tire tests at Hockenheim, Sept. 29 - Oct. 1, 1964; bought privately by Ferdinand Piëch, Sept. 1965; sold to Hans Mezger on December 30, 1965; on December 12, 1967, had covered 63,381 km
Disposition: unknown

Number 7 (901/7)(911/7)

Chassis number: 13 327
Color: signal red
License plate: S-SX 564 (as of Feb. 1964)
Nickname: "Barbarossa"
Body built by: Porsche (3); chassis by Porsche; to November 1963
Year built: 1963

Application: development, wind tunnel, type certification (completed July 9, 1964)
Front suspension: 901
Rear suspension: 901
Brakes: Teves
Engine: engine installed on April 19, 1964; 901 with dry sump lubrication (126 hp at 6300 rpm); gray iron cylinders
Engine number: 14
Transmission number: 901 No. 6 (5-speed); gear ratios 11/34, 18/33, 23/28, 26/25, 28/23; transmission modified July 9, 1964
Equipment: two round instruments; steering wheel and horn ring like 356; old outside mirrors from Mall (901.731.111.00)
Assembly: September 1963
Additional features: turning circle, left, 10.16 m; right, 9.70 m; weight 1084 kg
Career highlights: February 1964, suspension tests at 1369 km; followed by wind tunnel tests; on March 19, 1963, converted to Flanbloc front suspension, which resulted in considerably better straight-line stability; on Nov. 5, 1964, conversion to production parts; as of December 1964, brake tests at 36,000 km; February 1965, suspension tests (front suspension) at 40,000 km; had covered a total of 43,927 km by October 15, 1965
Disposition: purchased in April 1965 by Richard von Frankenberg, who kept it until September 26, 1966; was restored in North America, 1993

Number 8 (911/8)

Chassis number: 13 328
Color: brown, with trunk lid highlighted in red
License plate: S-TV 112 (as of July 1964)
Nickname: none
Body built by: to December 1963, delivered July 1964
Year built: 1964
Application: development, type certification
Front suspension: 901
Rear suspension: 901
Brakes: Teves
Engine: 901 with dry sump lubrication; as of August 1965, four-cylinder engine Type 616/36
Engine number: 902 279
Transmission number: 901; as of August 1965, VW automatic transmission Type EA 080/3-IV (Porsche

Type 903/2)
Equipment: Longer window channels for test purposes; with Webasto gas heater and engine heat; front-mounted battery; new dashboard with five round instruments and wooden steering wheel
Assembly: unknown
Additional features: turning circle, left, 9.95 m; right, 11.08 m; weight 1066 kg; fuel economy 22.2 l/100 km (10.6 mpg); top speed 214 km/h (133 mph) measured on July 13, 1964
Career highlights: raw body shell completed April 10, 1964; suspension tests mid-1964; July, 1964, endurance testing at 3000 km; August, 1964, practice car for Tour de France; as of August 20, 1964, Alpine Trials (rally) with Herbert Linge; tire tests at Hockenheimring (Sept. 21 to Oct. 1, 1964); tests with Weber carburetors in December, 1964, at 40,000 km; brake tests as of January 1965 at 43,000 km; June 1 to 15, 1965, "intensive course" in Wolfsburg; June 1965, transmission development at 47,500 km
Disposition: sold on April 18, 1968

Number 9 (911/9)

Chassis number: 13 329
Color: unknown
License plate: S-UE 87
Nickname: none
Body built by: Reutter
Year built: 1964
Application: sales: demonstrator, type certification for Italy (November 1964); body development
Front suspension: 901
Rear suspension: 901
Brakes: Teves
Engine: 901 with dry-sump lubrication; later four-cylinder Type 616/36
Engine number: unknown
Equipment: electric sunroof (+10 kg), wind deflector across front of sunroof opening, attached via hinge; Webasto gas heater and engine heat; front-mounted battery
Assembly: unknown
Additional features: turning circle, left, 10.58 m; right, 10.30 m; empty weight 1034.4 kg with four-cylinder and 1086.5 kg with six-cylinder engine; top speed 212 km/h (132 mph) measured on July 13, 1964

Career highlights: March 1964, at Reutter, to prepare for series production; July 1964, pre-production tests; August 1964, on vacation with Ferry Porsche; September 25 - 28, 1964, cold chamber to -40° C (-40° F); January 1965, suspension tests at 15,200 km; January 1965, check of electrical system; February 8 - 12, 1965, Wolfsburg; thereafter body development between 16,700 and 30,886 km (August 1965); December 6 - 12, 1965, Bilstein; total km on December 28, 1965: 50,953
Disposition: unknown

Number 10 (902/10)(912/10)

Chassis number: 13 330
Color: unknown
License plate: S-UP 935 (as of December 1964)
Nickname: none
Body built by: Häusele
Year built: 1964
Application: Development
Front suspension: 901
Rear suspension: unknown
Brakes: Teves
Engine: four cylinder
Engine number: 830 001
Transmission: 4-speed
Equipment: rubber floor mats, no side pockets on doors, no dashboard covering; no bumper guards at front; Goodyear 695-15 HE tires; 6-volt electrical system
Assembly: unknown
Additional features: weight 989 kg
Career highlights: drivable as of Oct. 2, 1964; test drives in Monza, December 1964; early January 1965, conversion to 12 volts; Jan. 18 - 22, 1965, endurance testing at 1000 km; January 25 - 29, 1965, heating tests; Feb. 23, 1965, anti-roll bars installed; total km on Dec. 21, 1965: 20,100
Disposition: sold on Oct. 29, 1965

Number 11 (902/11)(912/12)

Chassis number: 13 352
Color: unknown
License plate: S-UP 934 (as of December 1964)
Nickname: none
Body built by: Karmann in Osnabrück; body delivered to Porsche on June 29, 1964

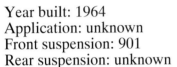

Year built: 1964
Application: unknown
Front suspension: 901
Rear suspension: unknown
Brakes: Teves
Engine: four-cylinder
Engine number: 813 422
Transmission: initially 4-speed with gear rations
similar to 356 SC; later, a 5-speed
Equipment: heat exchanger heating system; 12 volts;
3 instruments; Goodyear 695-15 HE tires; carpets
Assembly: unknown
Additional features: weight 1011 kg
Career highlights: Sept. 17, 1964: performance tests
with 4-speed; tire tests at Hockenheim, Sept. 29 to
Oct. 1, 1964; thereafter noise tests at 5500 km
(sound deadening); shock absorber tests; in Wolfs-
burg, April 26 - 30; noise tests in June, 1965, at
27,500 km; October 7 - 8, 1964, driven by Ferry Porsche to Wolfsburg; on Sept. 29, 1966, had covered
20,393 km
Disposition: sold on Sept. 17, 1965

Number 12 (911/12)

Chassis number: 300 001
Color: signal red 6407 B
License plate: S-UN 478 (as of November 1964)
Nickname: none
Body built by: Porsche; delivered Oct. 19, 1964
Year built: 1964
Application: development, endurance testing
Front suspension: 901

Rear suspension: 901
Brakes: Teves
Engine: 901 with dry sump lubrication; Feb. 15 - 19,
1965, converted to roller bearings
Engine number: 121
Transmission number: 100.018-901/0
Equipment: black leatherette; Dunlop 165-15
Assembly: unknown
Career highlights: November 1964, pre-production
tests at 4500 km; December 1964, suspension set-
tings tests at 7500 and 8300 km; Oct. 19 and 20,
1964, wind tests with various tires and toe-in combi-
nations at VW works; January 1965, installation of
Carrera engine; Feb. 8 - 12, 1965, test drives with
Carrera engine; thereafter straight-line stability at
9000 km; March 1 - 5, 1965, endurance tests in
Italy; April 26 - 30, 1965, Nürburgring; as of
December 6, 1965, Girling; December 20 - 30, 1965,
preparation for endurance testing; had covered
48,000 km on December 28, 1965
Disposition: unknown

Number 13 (911/13)

Chassis number: 300 002
Color: signal red 6407
License plate: S-UN 476 (as of November 1964)
Nickname: none
Body built by: unknown
Year built: 1964
Application: endurance testing
Front suspension: unknown
Rear suspension: unknown

Brakes: Teves
Engine: 901 with dry sump lubrication
Engine number: 103; later four-cylinder 832 060
Transmission number: 100 004
Equipment: black leatherette; Dunlop 165-15; standard production Solex carburetors
Assembly: unknown
Career highlights: June 1964, test drives on the Nürburgring and in Wolfsburg (approx. 13,000 km); November 1964, pre-production tests at 14,700 km; December 1964, tire tests in Monza (Michelin 155 HR 15, Goodyear HE, Dunlop 165 H 15 CB 57); thereafter endurance testing between 14,987 and 58,000 km; January 1965, practice for Monte Carlo rally; January 18 - 22, endurance testing for Monte Carlo; February 8 - 12, 1965, Wolfsburg; May 3 - 14, 1965, practice for Targa Florio; May 17 - 21, 1965, Nürburgring; July 19 - 27, practice for Sestrière rally; August 9 - 13, 1965, Wolfsburg; thereafter transmission development at 74,700 km
Disposition: sold on May 17, 1968

The interior of prototype number 7 (top) still contains a similar instrument cluster and the steering wheel of the Type 356. The signal red paint gave it the nickname "Barbarossa."

Naturally, there were other 911 prototypes in the course of the 32-year history of Porsche's six-cylinder sports car. The cars had to undergo a predefined test cycle before each model change. Further, alternative technology was often put to the test, but never reached the production line. For example, in 1975, Porsche coated several test cars with a vinyl skin, to make their external surfaces more resistant to rust and rock impacts. This rough skin covered regular production technology. They were powered by a 3.5 liter engine with roughly 225 hp, remarkable for its enormous torque output. Neither the surface treatment nor the engine went into production.

A Piece of Development History

Adventures in Car Building

More than three decades ago, the story of the 911 began in much the same way as the chronicle of a new car would begin today, if that car were to replace an extraordinarily successful model: with high expectations and tough requirements.

To formulate these requirements and then to meet them, step by step, is a special experience, then as now. The participants work closely, as a team. Top-level car designers develop general goals, designers generate drawings, model makers carve shapes, and engineers calculate. Project leaders discuss the earliest tests, discard some ideas and start the process all over again with their colleagues. Design studies and models take shape, as the requirements of the new automobile are laid down in a catalog of design targets. Design solutions are worked out to the last detail, then refined and improved to the point where one could at last venture to hand-build the first representative of the new automotive species.

These prototypes, the progenitors of the later production cars, will be tortured and mistreated, must undergo surgery and transplant operations, and, in their usually relatively short existence, undergo the most amazing mutations.

At the beginning, the Porsche 911 boasted seven

forefathers which underwent these difficult trials. Others were added in the course of development, until they totaled thirteen cars. Today, it is likely that only one has survived, Number 7, which is in private hands in North America. Every one of these cars represents a vital piece of the development story of the 911. As an example, we have reconstructed the fate of one of these early cars, Prototype Number 5, with chassis number 13 325. It was originally built for display purposes, and traveled to the greatest car shows of Europe in an enclosed trailer. Later, it was used for carburetor tests by the development department, and finally modified to meet the demands of the sales department. In the hands of Dieter Lenz, it visited all of the Porsche dealerships of Europe, covering 50,000 km (30,000 miles). In the story of the 911, there is no other car that has had so many co-drivers in the passenger seat. Among them was Reinhard Seiffert, the first member of the automotive press to describe this 356 successor, for *auto, motor und sport.* But first things first.

The body of Car Number 5 was hand-built in the summer of 1963 at the Wilhelm Karmann Karosseriewerk in Osnabrück. Porsche supplied the chassis. On July 27, 1963, an enclosed transporter delivered the finished assembly to the Reutter plant in Stuttgart; Project 901 was still top secret. At the time, the body manufacturer was located behind the old Werk I in Zuffenhausen. There, just before the annual plant vacation, Car Number 5 was painted yellow and fitted with sound deadening material. Assembly continued several streets away, in the Porsche experimental department. There, Number 5 was fitted with the complete 901 suspension. At the front, low-mounted transverse arms with longitudinal torsion bars provided the necessary space for the relatively large trunk. In place of conventional MacPherson struts, this system had only slim telescoping shock absorbers – a convincing solution which saved additional space.

The rear suspension design of the 901 also differed from Porsche tradition: semi-trailing arms and two-jointed driveshafts (Nadella joints) replaced the swing axles of the 356. Car number 5 was fitted with Girling brakes at all four corners, delivered precisely on schedule on August 5, 1963; there were some delivery problems with the brake backing plates. The yellow sheet metal initially covered a mockup of the planned six-cylinder boxer engine.

In the summer of 1963, the interior fittings were far from those which would eventually go into production. Car Number 5 was still fitted with three large round instruments, familiar from the Type 356. The driver faced a three-spoke steering wheel, likewise from the previous model.

Car Number 5 had two immediate relatives, another yellow car and a blue car. All three were given an especially smooth finish, as they were earmarked as exhibition cars. Car Number 5 had to be completed especially quickly, as it was to sound out potential customers at the Frankfurt International Automobile Show (IAA) on September 12, 1963. It would be the first 901 seen by the public. Immediately after Frankfurt, Number 5 undertook its first foreign journey; from October 3 to 13, 1963, it charmed visitors at the Paris Auto Salon. From there, it was carefully packed up for a longer journey and sent to London, where it was on display from October 16 to 26 at the Earls Court Motor Show. There was only enough time to wipe off the finger prints of its admirers before Car Number 5 was loaded up and sent to Turin, where it cheered the hearts of Italian sports car fans from October 30 to November 10.

In mid-November, Prototype 5 was being eagerly awaited in Stuttgart. Chief engineer Hans Tomala had earmarked the car to be prepared as a demonstrator. As individual components had undergone steady development in the previous months, Car 5 would first be completely disassembled. New parts provided by the development department would be installed in the assembly shop, under Willi Kahnau. This work was covered by experimental work order E 1085, HA.E 47. At the same time, Number 5 was finally fitted with an engine, Number 11, with dry-sump lubrication. But the six-cylinder powerplant was still far from production-ready. The cast iron cylinders, developed with the Mahle company, were still far from optimized, and the heat range of the spark plugs had not yet been determined. Furthermore, at the time, the following components were still untested: oil pump, hydraulic chain tensioners, cylinder head studs, flywheel, exhaust valves, valve springs, rocker shafts and oil cooler. In other words, burnt pistons were almost guaranteed, and only a matter of time; but more on that later. In any case, under today's conditions it would be inconceivable to install such an early development engine in a demonstrator. At this point, the development history of three decades ago deviates sharply from modern practice. What was once developed with ingenuity, improvisation and hard work, is today calculated by powerful computers before any actual prototyping begins.

In 1964, the engineers experienced adventures in car building with, among other things, fuel delivery. At the time of assembly, the first prototypes of the Solex overflow carburetors planned for production had not been tested; in fact, they were not even available. But the development engineers of thirty years ago were blessed with an amazing talent for improvisation, and made the six-cylinder run with carburetors borrowed from the Lancia V6 models (also made by Solex). For this reason, Car Number 5 went into service a bit down on power, with about 120 hp (production cars would have 130 hp).

In February 1964, the life of the yellow test car took on a new dimension. From now on, it would travel under its own power; Car Number 5 was ready for the road. In the meantime, the 901 had been shown to the public all across Europe, and the proto-

Prototype Number 5, painted yellow with chassis number 13 325, was initially built for display purposes. Beginning in early 1964, it went on a sales tour with salesman Dieter Lenz, responsible for the domestic market.

types could go out into traffic without camouflage. One young engineer who was closely involved with chassis development would one day become chief of the research and development center in Weissach: Helmuth Bott. He documented the last of Herr Tomala's handling complaints regarding Car 5. On February 5, 1964, Tomala drove to Wolfsburg, arriving without incident. Only the idle speed of the six-cylinder was too high, and the spark plugs fouled on long downgrades. On the other hand, noise from the fuel pump was a constant irritant to Tomala. He ordered the pump relocated to the engine compart-

ment. After taking care of these small complaints, the development department handed the car over to the sales department on February 7, 1964. Number 5 had only 3500 km on the odometer; a spare tire and tool kit were delivered with the car.

Under its new masters, the car would very soon run up many more kilometers. The Porsche sales department had a daring plan: two prototypes, including Number 5, would be demonstrated to all European dealers nearly a year before delivery of the first production cars, in order to give potential customers an opportunity to ride in the new car.

What led to such an extraordinary sales promotion – especially considering the early prototype condition of the car, still far removed from production? The story begins at the Frankfurt IAA, in September 1963. Although the 901 was a great attraction, the announced price of 23,900 Marks shocked a large part of the traditional Porsche clientele. Porsche personnel at the IAA display had a difficult job justifying the fact that the 356 successor would cost 7000 Marks more (the 356 SC cost about 17,000 Marks). The sports cars from Zuffenhausen would enter a price class that some customers simply could no longer afford. But quality has its price. And a 130 hp six-cylinder simply costs more than a 95 hp four-cylinder powerplant. That may sound good in theory, but one wanted to convince the customers by example. And that could only be accomplished by a test ride, at the earliest opportunity.

Porsche's domestic sales manager, Harald Wagner, called a meeting with his two salesmen and discussed the mammoth plan. Dieter Lenz, at the time only 28 years old but well qualified thanks to his technical apprenticeship at Porsche and many years as a career salesman, would start the sales tour with Number 5. His territory in Germany included the Frankfurt area, with all dealers north and west of that city, and Bavaria. Outside Germany, his range included Scandinavia, Holland, Belgium and Luxembourg. A few months later, his colleague Hans Klink would visit the rest of Germany, France, Italy, England and Switzerland.

As there was no time to lose, and Number 5 was ready to go, Dieter Lenz planned his route in minute detail. Appointments followed in rapid succession. Lenz would visit a dealer, who would have customers waiting at half-hour intervals. The plan would have worked, except for one detail: the car. The yellow 901 was a pure prototype, for which there were no spare parts available, anywhere.

But young Lenz knew nothing of this delicate situation as he picked up Number 5 from test driver Kurt Knoerzer. Innocently, Lenz asked his colleague Knoerzer for an introductory drive, so that he might learn the car's characteristics. Instead of explana-

tions, the young salesman got an earful of depressing news: this isn't right yet, that doesn't work too well, and that over there definitely needs improvement. But Lenz wasn't easily discouraged, as Number 5 gave him a great deal of driving pleasure. In particular, after only moments in the car, he was impressed by the free-revving six-cylinder engine and the car's impressive performance.

Even Mrs. Lenz put the brakes to the salesman's euphoria. Lenz proudly picked up his wife at their home in Leinfelden, near Stuttgart. After only a few yards, Lenz' better half told him to turn around. Otherwise, she would immediately get out of this "horrible thing." But Lenz didn't give up. Holding firm to the belief that he was driving a predecessor of the production cars, he took his assignment seriously and kept minute records of all positive and negative details noticed in his early days with Number 5.

Number 5 had been issued license plate S-TC 1, and was ready to go. But before starting his first sales tour, Lenz had a few improvements carried out in the development department. As Number 5 still did not have heat exchangers, the prototype was fitted with a Webasto gas heater. This was simply mounted transversely in the luggage compartment. It was not until the car went into production that it would be moved to a space at the right of the lug-

Dieter Lenz: "The customer in the passenger seat took it well."

65

gage compartment, under the brake fluid reservoir, where the battery was installed in the prototype. Lenz had to protest loudly before the heater was at least fitted with an aluminum shield. Otherwise, he would have had to reach even further into his bag of salesman's explanations to counter customer criticism.

On February 16, Number 5 was loaded with some luggage and, by February 28, had covered more than 5000 km in the Ruhr Valley. Lenz recorded that test drives were conducted only with customers selected by the dealerships, resulting in about 15 demonstration drives per day. "I really put a lot of effort into it," recalls the 901 pioneer today. Every test drive followed a logical sequence, and popularly rumored problem areas, such as poor straight-line stability, were discussed from the outset in terms of theory and practice. To demonstrate stability, Lenz would jerk the steering wheel at various speeds, to demonstrate that the 901 would resume its course without further input. "You only need to give the steering wheel enough freedom," explains the Porsche man. And his demonstrations had repeated success. After the first few days, Lenz had five firm orders.

A memo dated March 2, 1964, records several points criticized by the sales prospects. The most prominent was price. This was followed by unacceptable rolling noise over transverse grooves, cobblestones and potholes. The instrument panel, many control details and the side panels left a negative impression with potential customers. High marks were given to the shape, comfortable entry, outward visibility, trunk (in spite of the auxiliary heater), acceleration and flexibility of the engine, the pleasant engine note audible inside the car, suspension comfort and handling.

Lenz and Number 5 brought home a similar good news/bad news report from the Geneva Auto Salon. At that time, it was still customary to allow visitors to drive the vehicles on display, and manufacturers were expected to have prototypes available. So Dieter Lenz, with Number 5, and Hans Klink with Number 6 drove to Switzerland in early March, to be available for prospective customers. By tradition, a closed road along Lake Geneva, heading toward France, became the scene of duels between manufac-

turers – with customers in the passenger seat. In the past, the 356 set the pace for these contests, and could humiliate the considerably more powerful Ferraris, Maseratis or Aston Martins. Thanks to their lower weight, the Porsches always had the advantage in braking for hairpins. With Number 5, Lenz even established a new record time. An American car, powered by an imposing 300 hp 7-liter engine, was able to stay close up to the mountain section, but at a crest just before the turnaround point, the American competition went airborne and landed in the weeds. Number 5 returned safely, ready for the next lap. Today, Lenz describes these private races as "unimaginable by today's standards."

Above all, the oft-repeated praise for Number 5's good handling baffled the responsible parties in Zuffenhausen, who knew better. In fact, Lenz was able to suppress this early 901 shortcoming by virtue of his driving skill. Lenz, although trained as a salesman, found that the addition of about 50 kg (110 lbs.) to the trunk made a remarkable difference in handling. The fuel tank was also kept well filled.

"But not too well filled," says Dieter Lenz, recalling a sudden spin on an Autobahn off-ramp near Munich at the end of March. As he had often done, Lenz was demonstrating the car's handling by drifting through the turn, when the 901 suddenly spun. "The customer on the passenger seat took it well," recalls Lenz. But since he had always mastered this car, he looked for a different cause. He smelled gasoline, and Number 5 had painted the road with a broad stream of fuel. Conclusion: fuel had dripped onto the road from the fuel tank vent line, and the left rear tire was running through this fuel trail. Under such conditions, even the best driver could not avoid spinning. Lenz considered it his duty to immediately inform the development department in Zuffenhausen. But instead of technical assistance, Lenz received ridicule. He was told "We've known about that problem for ages. Just don't fill the tank all the way."

In other respects, too, the sales tour from March 23 through May 13, in the regions of Munich, Stuttgart, Dortmund and Hagen taxed the driver's nerves and endurance. At 19,700 km, power suddenly dropped, smoke poured from the exhaust, and the oil

Dieter Lenz (sitting in trunk) at a Porsche dealer, presenting the new 901. This car is prototype Number 3, which had been repainted red just before this photo was taken.

temperature skyrocketed. Lenz drove a few more customers around, but 500 km later had to break off the program because of excessive smoke. Instead of standing around in confusion, which one would expect of a present-day salesman, Lenz analyzed the problem: a hole had been burned through the number two piston. At times like these, the highly-regarded salesman gladly recalled his apprenticeship at Porsche, which he had begun in 1956. The sports car manufacturer made it quite clear to its new charges: if you want to become a salesman at Porsche, you have to know the product. He was first assigned to the repair shop, to perform routine inspections and later entire engine overhauls. After such experience, every Porsche employee was expected to have complete familiarity with the product.

Now, however, he had to bring Number 5 back to

Stuttgart as quickly as possible. That was feasible, even with the holed piston. Thanks to its dry sump lubrication system, the six-cylinder lost relatively little oil. Still, Lenz bought a few spare liters of oil and proceeded on the Munich-Stuttgart Autobahn with no more than 3000 rpm. Every 30 kilometers, he stopped to check the oil level and to top off if necessary. On the downgrade from the Swabian Alb, S-TC 1 covered the Autobahn with a smoke screen. Cars behind switched on their lights, suspecting bad weather ahead, but they broke into sunlight the instant they passed Number 5.

The technicians in the development department switched engines overnight, and, according to Dieter Lenz' records, performed other repair jobs. At five in the morning, the intrepid salesman was back at the shop, inquiring about the condition of Number 5.

At eight o'clock, the first prospect would be waiting at a dealership. But this passenger was not especially happy with his seating position; after only a few kilometers, the seat recliner broke at its pivot point. And that wasn't all; on the drive back to the nearest Porsche dealership, at 21,826 km, the upper attachment of the left rear Boge shock absorber failed. The dealers again postponed demonstrations, and Number 5 headed back to Stuttgart minus its left rear shock absorber.

Number 5 and Dieter Lenz could find no peace. Only two days later (the pair was in Cologne, after the shock mounts had been strengthened by welding in sheet metal reinforcements the night before) the front left torsion bar broke, shortly thereafter the speedometer shaft gave up the ghost, and the door panels came loose. Now the car was well and truly jinxed. During a later demonstration drive, with two prospects instead of the usual one passenger, Lenz suddenly noticed that he could no longer see the person in the rear seat. The headliner had come loose and was hanging down. Ever the clever salesman, Lenz opened the window, and the air pressure forced the headliner back up. The remaining drives were carried out with open windows. Not surprisingly, Lenz came home with not only a chronically ailing S-TC 1, but also a severe cold for himself. It finally dawned on Dieter Lenz that Number 5 was no pre-production car, but rather one of the first 901 prototypes. Only nobody had bothered to tell him.

This knowledge was little comfort to the dynamic duo. Both had to get well, as quickly as possible. Ferry Porsche himself had decreed that the editor-in-chief of *Auto, Motor und Sport* (later style: *auto motor und sport*), Heinz Ulrich Wieselmann, should be allowed to examine the yellow prototype over the Easter holidays. After a test drive, Reinhard Seiffert would write the first test drive report on the 901. Lenz picked up Seiffert in Leonberg and demonstrated the car's Porsche-untypical, unproblematical straight-line stability to the critic. He jerked the wheel at 50 km/h, then at 100 km/h and finally at 180 km/h. Seiffert was highly impressed, but commented that the top speed claim was probably a bit exaggerated. So Lenz floored the throttle through the Leonberg tunnel. The speedometer needle ran up to nearly 220 km/h, and at the Ditzingen exit, where the

road rises slightly, dropped back to 210 km/h – and all this in wet conditions. The speed indicated at this point on the road is fairly close to the actual top speed of any given car. Porsche engineers had determined this in the late 1950s, and it was a well-known fact in the automotive scene. Seiffert was convinced and, in Volume 8, dated April 18, he wrote a glowing review of the new Porsche.

But Lenz had no time to lose. Thanks to the published review, he was no longer under such pressure to prove the car, yet prospective buyers did not want to forego their scheduled test drives. Until May 13, 1964, Lenz demonstrated the car to potential clients, a new prospect every half hour – until another forced retirement. At 30,000 km, Number 5 again exhibited a loss of power, and at 31,420 km another piston had been holed.

As the engines had become more durable by mid-year, Lenz' attention during demonstration drives from May 19 to June 16 in northern Germany was directed at the brakes and steering. One complaint was excessive fading when braking from high speed, with extremely high pedal pressure. In addition, many customers demanded a dual-circuit brake system. The angled safety steering column introduced in the Porsche Formula II racer aroused displeasure due to its transmission of jolts from uneven road surfaces.

On July 3, 1964, Dieter Lenz returned Number 5, license plate S-TC 1, to the development department, with 46,987 km on the odometer. The yellow prototype had been continuously improved by may repairs, but Lenz had aged by years. He had spent days and nights behind the wheel of this car, and achieved incredible feats. He returned the car with reluctance.

For the benefit of all departments, Dieter Lenz summarized his demonstration drives on August 14, 1964. He asked that the points criticized not be dismissed out of hand, as in his opinion they would be decisive for sales of the 901. These points were the unsatisfactory brakes, hopping over cobblestones, wind noise from poor window seals and the transmission of road irregularities through the steering wheel.

In September, Number 5 got a whiff of rally atmosphere. It was delegated as a support vehicle for the Tour de France, with racing director Huschke von Hanstein at the wheel. As of September 2, Number 5 appeared regularly in the development department's inventory of cars. It was available for suspension tests. After November 4, 1964, Number 5 disappeared from these lists, after having covered a distance of 66,000 km. And no wonder – the yellow prototype had suffered a severe accident while being used for transmission development. On November 29, 1965, Helmuth Bott pronounced the death sentence: Number 5 would be scrapped two days later.

Meanwhile, Project 901 was several years old, the first production cars had already been delivered, the engines were reliable, the brakes offered the good performance expected of a Porsche, and the handling had been improved. The yellow prototype with license plate S-TC 1 had lived for just a little over two years, but it had had an intensive life. In those few months, it had experienced countless adventures with a multitude of people. Number 5, with chassis number 13 325, is a piece of Porsche 911 history.

The Frankfurt Auto Show, 1963
Then as now

E ven in 1963, a festival atmosphere reigned at the IAA (International Automobile Show), and Frankfurt was a major convention town. Thirty years ago, every last hotel room, even the guest rooms of private homes, was occupied by visitors to the International Automobile Show. It might have been possible to get a room in Mainz, miles away. Every parking space and every taxi had been spoken for.

These inadequacies came as no surprise to those who had attended the show in previous years. Still, in 1963, 850,000 visitors streamed into the exhibit halls, in addition to the several hundred employed at the stands and in service jobs.

Back then, a visit to the show implied dealing with the same onerous conditions as today. One approached the fairgrounds as part of a traffic jam; three decades ago, one could figure on three and a half hours for the short distance from Bruchsal to Frankfurt. Until they reached the fairgrounds, the ladies and gentlemen of the press might still have felt themselves privileged; a fat, green letter P (for press parking) decorated their windshields. But they soon discovered that this free pass, obtained by pulling every string they could think of, was no benefit at all. Once they had fought their way through to the press parking lot, they were turned away. The

stressed-out journalists were simply told that the lot was full. Guards chased them away with exhortations to "Move along, move along." But press people don't give up that easily. They continued on, in a traffic jam of course, to the regular visitor's parking lot.

An eternity or two later, one finally climbed into an ancient and completely overloaded bus (after a fruitless search for a taxi), paid 40 Pfennigs to be carted to the main entrance. Visitors were allowed into the halls in batches; the waiting period could be used for choral griping practice. Fritz B. Busch summed up the intolerable conditions of the time for *Auto, Motor und Sport:* "A town that is so crowded, and then insists on hosting trade shows, should be penalized for bodily injury, loss of personal freedom, pandering, usury, harassment, negligence and violation of Section 1 of the Motor Vehicle Code."

At the manufacturer's stands, one might even glimpse some sheet metal, if one could see past the sweat-soaked backs and dandruff-covered shoulders of one's fellows. That is, if there were not at least ten Japanese lying, kneeling or possibly even standing to photograph every possible detail. But perhaps seeing cars wasn't even the point. The honorable automobile salons had become vacation spots and

The new Porsche caused a sensation at the IAA. Even though the 901 could nòt yet be test driven, and was quite expensive at 23,900 Marks, several sales contracts were signed at the Frankfurt show.

the destination of pilgrims. Thousands of visitors were regularly attracted by an undefinable atmosphere. In short, the halls were entirely overfilled, the air was rank and the temperature decidedly too high. That was the case thirty years ago and it remains so to this day.

Once they had reached the halls, the invited ladies and gentlemen of the press could attend briefings from 7 PM on Tuesday, September 10 through 8:30 PM on Friday, September 13. All told, there were 21 meetings, presented as special occasions behind velvet partitions. Rumor has it that there were even a few journalists who examined the cars with their

own eyes, without benefit of orchestrated press presentations. The best time to do this was September 12, the day before the official show opening. The displays of most carmakers were already in their full glory. Among the accessory dealers, however, one had to climb over steel frames or carpet remnants. Men in coveralls were still swinging hammers and wielding paint brushes; even though deadlines had been set more than a year earlier, car shows, then as now, are not ready until the very last moment. But this did not seem to bother the organizers, nor the actors.

The Porsche stand, too, glittered under neon lights

well before the official opening. For the first time, the 901, successor to the 356, was shown to the public. Its comfort, safety and remarkable engine output were intended to place the 901 in the international luxury class. Indeed, the yellow sports car attracted the public like a magnet. In carmakers' suites, behind their stands, confidential meetings took place and quickly took on the form of cocktail parties. Porsche, on the other hand, held its internal meetings externally, as it were. The sales department met its distributors at the private home of the largest Porsche dealership in the Frankfurt area, Glöckler. Meanwhile, probably by pure coincidence, the highest-ranking Mercedes delegation visited the Porsche stand. The 901 was inspected critically; after all, the men from Untertürkheim had brought a new car of their own, the competing 230 SL sports car, to Frankfurt. They withdrew, deep in thought. A rear-engined sports car with such a spacious luggage compartment had been regarded as technically impossible.

The car on display was the fifth prototype, chassis number 13 325. The body, built by Karmann of Osnabrück, had been painted yellow. At the front,

the show car had the new 901 suspension, which had already undergone tests in other prototypes. This consisted of a transverse arm, controlled by MacPherson struts. These, however, were reduced to slim shock absorbers with reinforced piston rods; instead of the coaxial coil spring of a conventional MacPherson strut and springing was by longitudinal torsion bars. At the rear, too, Number 5 was fitted with a new suspension design, which had already undergone endurance testing. The swing axles of the Porsche 356 had been replaced by semi-trailing arms and two-joint halfshafts. This suspension resulted in considerably smaller camber and toe changes, and the possibility of tuning the suspension for comfort or performance. The brakes were by Girling.

For the IAA of 1963, Number 5 was fitted with a mockup of the six-cylinder engine. Because Porsche recognized the show's importance for the trade magazines, the technology of the new boxer engine was released to the press shortly before the IAA. Reinhard Seiffert, writing in the large auto show edition of *Auto, Motor und Sport* (No. 19, 1963), was able to provide a highly detailed report on the new engine and compare it with the 2000 GS Carrera power-

Hall 1a, stand number 27, 211 square meters: the Porsche display just before the onslaught of visitors.

plant. A photo, an angled view from above, was also released. It showed the two Solex three-barrel carburetors, which at that time had not even been tested yet. The flat air filter with its low-mounted intake snorkel was completely reworked before the car went into production. And the muffler still had two outlets. At the end of 1963, this mockup was replaced by a drivable version. Nevertheless, at that point, the state of engine development was still far from satisfactory, especially in view of the impending start of production. (See previous chapter, "Adventures in Car Building.")

But back to the 1963 IAA. Because of the dual exhausts, the rear valance had matching cutouts. The angled, gold-plated 911 script, introduced with the 0-series, did not yet decorate the engine lid. The missing bumper guards and lack of deco strips on the rocker panels immediately distinguish the IAA prototype from the first production cars.

Porsche made no secret of the fact that several months would pass before the 901 was ready for production. Insiders even suspected that the company would have to pay a penalty to the show organizers, the VDA (Association of German Auto Manufacturers). This would be imposed if a displayed car did not go into production within nine months of the show. Whether this fine was actually paid can no longer be determined. One thing is certain: Porsche was not able to put the 901 into production within the allotted nine months.

This came as no surprise to those in charge at Porsche, even though it had been hoped to deliver the first cars in early summer of 1964. But domestic sales boss Harald Wagner had spent nine years with the sports car maker and had lived through several new car introductions. Because there had always been delays, he gave his salesmen strict instructions not to promise the 901 for the summer of 1964. He feared that customers would be disappointed and angry if they ordered the car based on this timetable, possibly with thoughts of taking the much roomier 356 successor on their summer vacation.

Because long delivery times were not customary and the imposing price of 23,900 Marks had already been announced (including leather upholstery, which

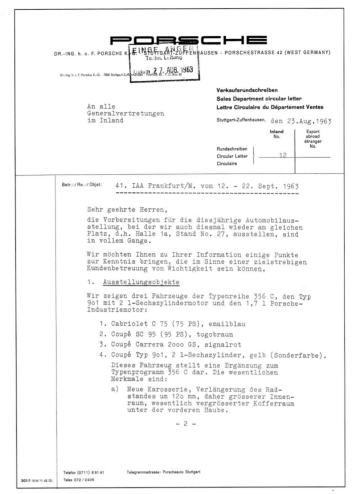

This memo records that three 356 C models were displayed alongside the 901. English translation on page 391.

however was not even available as an option when production started), the crew representing Porsche at the IAA display found itself on the defensive against continuous criticism. But they had several positive responses. Compared to its predecessor, the 901 had not only a larger luggage compartment thanks to its space-saving front suspension design, but the wheelbase increase from 2100 to 2200 mm also provided a larger interior. The articulated steering column attached to the rack-and-pinion steering had two advantages: it saved space and, above all, was an important contribution to occupant protection in accidents. The bolted-on front fenders simplified body repair.

Then there was the engine. Porsche customers got a free-revving six-cylinder powerplant with every bit of 130 horsepower. Porsche developed a fully-synchronized five-speed transmission especially for this new engine generation. Naturally, a 12 Volt electrical system was standard.

The handling characteristics were still anybody's guess. Normally, at car shows, it was customary to have demonstrators available for test drives. In this way, the customer would be able to actually test the car rather than buy a pig in a poke, as it were. This combination of showroom glamour and hard-edged practicality had proven itself in prior years. In this way, in spite of the novelty of the 901, more than 400 potential 356 customers were identified during the ten days of the IAA, and about 280 took advantage of the opportunity for a test drive. But sales contracts were also drawn up for the 901, without test drives, without delivery dates, and despite a price starting about 7000 Marks higher than that of the 356. This reaffirmed Porsche's rear engine philosophy and encouraged those responsible in Zuffenhausen to forge ahead with the 901 project. For in 1963, there was yet another handicap which confronted all auto manufacturers: the auto industry was in a state of change, as it has always been, and as it remains today.

Traffic jams formed, new roads were built and were immediately clogged – naturally on a different scale than today, but no less annoying for the drivers of that time. Then the market began to be saturated, international competitors gained market share (other European car makers could produce at lower cost), and finally the German auto industry came under strong criticism, even more so after the 1963 IAA. The public and the industry had expected a display of progress, but genuine progress for the average car buyer went begging. If anything was undertaken at all, it was only partial improvement of existing products. In this, Porsche was certainly the exception, but then Porsche was in the highest priced market segment. There was a genuine desire for advances for the average consumer, such as automatic transmissions for cars with 1. 5 liter engines, bumpers worthy of the name, height-adjustable headlights, smaller turning circles or new models with smaller external dimensions without loss of interior space. The automotive press of 1963 found only two significant new developments at the IAA: first, the normally conservative English firm, Rover, displayed a turbine-powered car. And second, NSU of Neckarsulm showed the first car with a rotary piston engine. Both concepts were revolutionary, but were never successful. The 901, on the other hand, became a long-running hit, and has remained so for 30 years.

Engine Development
Clearly defined expectations

At the end of the 1950s, engines displacing two liters were considered quite large by the standards of German car makers. This seemingly magical threshold was exceeded only by large sedans like the Mercedes 220; Mercedes vehicles with three liters were almost exclusively reserved for government use.

Porsche had just developed a two-liter, four-cam engine, which celebrated its debut in the Carrera 2 at the 1961 Paris auto salon. In the customer version, it developed an impressive 130 horsepower; a prototype even managed 135 hp. "One of my most memorable experiences was a drive with the very first two-liter prototype, Ernest Fuhrmann's company car," recalls Helmuth Bott, at that time still working in the road test department. Bott continues: "He had designed the engine, and I did the suspension. Both systems were so well matched that for the first time, we were able to take all the curves on the Autobahn between Stuttgart and Heilbronn at more than 200 km/h [124 mph]." Porsche, and indeed the entire sports car world, had a new benchmark.

But the Carrera 2 engine was a thoroughbred racing powerplant, much too complicated and expensive for use in larger numbers. "Exactly eight mechanics worldwide were qualified to set up the camshaft drive," recalls Hans Mezger, who was already active in the racing engine department in the late 1950s. One of these specialists came from Porsche's own ranks, the foreman of the engine test department, Eberhard Storz.

At the same time, Ferry Porsche approved the design and development of a new Porsche model. Body designs were already on hand, but which powerplant would be appropriate for this new car? "I pointed out the excellent acceleration performance of the Carrera to my people and told them that this is how it should go, except it should also be quiet, it should not be as noisy as a race car," explains Ferry Porsche.

The message from the boss was unambiguous, and the engine designers had a new challenge.

By this time Porsche was no longer firmly wedded to the principle of air cooling nor to rear-mounted engines. In this regard, Ferry Porsche himself often pointed to the Porsche-Cisitalia, which was water cooled. On the other hand, there were strong incentives to retain the traditional concepts. Sports cars with racing potential (Ferry Porsche never saw a compelling difference between a touring sports car and a competition vehicle) carried a high percentage of their weight on the drive wheels; a

fore he again chose an air-cooled, rear-mounted boxer engine solution.

However, the desired combination of power and low noise could not be achieved with a four-cylinder engine. The only other engine projects at Porsche at the start of the 1960s were the eight-cylinder Types 753 and 771 (for the Type 804 Formula 1 racers), which had just been designed for the 1962 racing season. But these, too, would have been impossible to build in large quantities. To keep development costs at an acceptable level, Porsche split the difference and chose a six-cylinder concept. To achieve the desired power output of 130 horsepower, a displacement of two liters was calculated. "That was a big decision for that time," explains Helmuth Bott. "Each new design requires certain built-in reserves, at least for motor sports," adds Hans Mezger, looking ahead to future developments. In the early 1960s, no one would ever have guessed that the six-cylinder, two-liter engine would grow to 3.6 liters (even 3.8 liters for the Carrera RS).

Type 745

Under the direction of chief development engineer Klaus von Rücker, who had previously been closely involved in a Porsche development project for the American car maker Studebaker, work on the new engine began under the type designation 745. In Leopold Jäntschke, the development chief had a designer who specialized in boxer engines. Jäntschke came to Porsche from the Czech car maker Tatra, based in Nesseldorf, Moravia (Koprivnice). The Tatra 603, introduced in 1955, was powered by a V8 engine weighing only 175 kg [385 lbs.], with two axial cooling blowers and tubular oil coolers. These engines, with a displacement of 2545 cc, put out 95 horsepower in street trim, and as much as 175 hp in racing form. Together with his deputy, Robert Binder, Jäntschke designed a robust pushrod engine. The valves formed a 59-degree V and were actuated by rocker arms. As with air-cooled aircraft engines, each rocker operated in its own chamber, with its own cover (partly covered with cooling fins), held down by two bolts. Experience with the Carrera four-cylinder engines resulted in short pushrods, driven by two camshafts, located above (for the inlet

mid-engine concept would excessively restrict interior space, and in the case of front-wheel drive, it was feared that the front wheels would spin under full throttle acceleration with the anticipated power. In the early 1960s, the predominant opinion was still that manufacturers of front-engined cars needed to build mid-engine cars for racing purposes if they expected to be competitive. Ferry Porsche wanted to avoid such redundancy if at all possible, and there-

A Porsche eight-cylinder engine, here the Type 771, would have been far too expensive for mass production.

valves) and below (for the exhausts) the crankshaft. This complicated solution was derived from the eight-cylinder engines. The camshafts, each with six lobes, ran in four bearings. Again borrowing from the Grand Prix engines, both camshafts were driven at half engine speed by timing gears at the front of the crankshaft.

The crankshaft ran in only four bearings. Air cooling was accomplished by a pair of axial blowers, comparable to those of the Tatra engines, located at the rear of the engine and driven by v-belts from the end of the crankshaft. These permitted a relatively low engine and had the added advantage that each bank of cylinders could be cooled individually. The low installed height of the Type 745 resulted in a so-called "under-floor engine." This meant that the engine was hardly any taller than the transmission and therefore, when installed, rose only slightly higher than the floorpan of the car. This term is used primarily in truck design.

Fuel delivery was by individual Solex downdraft carburetors, which were later modified for the first production cars.

The first dynamometer tests quickly showed that the conventional valve train, despite its short push-rods, did not allow high rpm. The result for this complex design was a modest 120 horsepower at 6500 rpm and a peak torque of 123 ft.-lbs. Nevertheless, this engine was installed in the prototype 754 T 7.

In this form, on November 1, 1960, the 356 successor, fitted with an engine of a new design, moved under its own power for the first time. The Type 754 T 7 may still be seen in the Porsche Museum, in Zuffenhausen. With Helmuth Bott at the wheel, the first test drive was even more sobering than the dynamometer results. Bott recalls that "Because it was as loud as a threshing machine, that immediately became its nickname." Somebody in the development department even adapted a poem by Rilke to the hapless design and its builders. Yet they didn't give up.

The cylinder bore was increased to 84 mm; this gave a displacement of 2195 cc and achieved the desired 130 hp at the same rpm. However, because

The six-cylinder Type 745 still actuated its valves by means of pushrods.

Porsche production engines are expected to show potential for racing applications, which the Type 745 could only achieve by means of yet another displacement increase but not through higher rpm, the project came to a standstill. Added to that, Klaus von Rücker was replaced by Hans Tomala in the spring of 1962; Tomala's area of responsibility had expanded from design and manufacturing to include development. Finally, Ferry Porsche, who had driven the T 7 prototype with the 745 engine for several months, banned the design of other new pushrod engines once and for all. It would be necessary to design a six-cylinder with overhead cams.

Type 821

For this assignment, an experienced engineer, Hans Mezger, was borrowed from the racing engine department. Mezger had gone directly to Porsche after graduating from the University of Stuttgart. His first job was in the calculating department, under Egon Forstner, where he soon became a valve train specialist. From there, he went to the racing engine design department under Hans Hönick, where he gained valuable experience, including new discoveries regarding combustion chamber shape and oil circulation. Beginning in 1962, Mezger integrated these findings into the 821 engine design, after Porsche had terminated its Formula 1 activities for cost

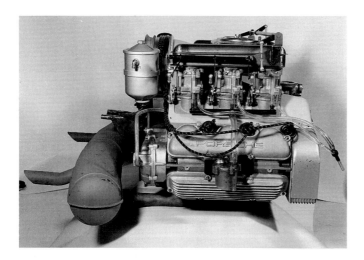

The engine shown here, with two single overhead cams, was built in 1963 and served in a 901 prototype. For production, the air filters and the muffler were changed.

Technische Daten - Motor Typ 821/1

Bauart	Boxer
Zylinderzahl	6
Kühlung	Luft
Bohrung	80 mm
Hub	66 mm
Hub-Bohrungsverhältnis	0,825
Hubvolumen	1990,7 cm^3
Leistung Ne	130 PS
bei Motordrehzahl n	6500 U/min
entsprechend einem pme	9 kg/cm^2
max. Drehmoment	16,5 mkg
bei Motordrehzahl n	4600 U/min
entsprechend einem pme	10,4 kg/cm^2
Hubraumleistung	65 PS/l
Verdichungsverhältnis ε	9:1
Pleuelstangenverhältnis	0,262
spez. Kolbenbelastung	0,434 PS/cm^2
mittl. Kolbengeschwindigkeit bei 6500 U/min	14,3 m/sec.
Kurbelwelle	7fach gelagert
Nockenwelle	obenliegend, durch Kette gesteuert
Elektrische Anlage	12 V

KB-Bi/si 11.7.1962	Dr.-Ing. h. c. F. Porsche K.-G. Stuttgart-Zuffenhausen	821.002.101.00

This memo dated July 1962 already indicates that the camshafts were to be chain-driven. English translation on page 391.

reasons. "At the time, engine development was not organized very rigidly, so that I was continually put to work on production engines, even though I was officially working in the racing engine department," explains Mezger. The successful engineer underscores his dual relationship with racing and mass-produced engines: "I always wanted to be involved with production engines, and not be limited to racing engine design, and that remains so today."

Mezger agreed with Ferry Porsche's decision to avoid pushrods: "If we are already installing two camshafts, we might as well move them to the top of the cylinder head." This naturally led to the question of how to drive the single overhead cam per cylinder head. To answer this elementary question, four alternative solutions were presented to Hans Tomala. Shaft-driven cams were no longer considered because of difficult assembly, high manufacturing costs and tremendous noise levels. Similar considerations ruled out gear-driven cams, such as those used successfully by motorcycles like the MV Agusta. The Glas company had pioneered the use of rubber timing belts; their advantages were low noise and sufficient elasticity to take up the thermal expansion of the engine without resorting to a tensioner. Nevertheless, this was a new concept, and one had too little confidence in rubber belts for high-performance engines. The former chief of the development department, Paul Hensler, emphasizes that "The timing belt was considered unpredictable." For these reasons, the engine was given a cam drive consisting of high-grade IWIS timing chains and an oil-hydraulic chain tensioner, developed by Hans Mezger and the present chief of all research and develop-

ment, Horst Marchart.

In Ferdinand Piëch, the engine design department had a second man with an impressive understanding of modern engine design. Piëch, who had studied at the Swiss Technical Institute in Zürich, could hardly wait to begin work on this fascinating project. For this reason, he spent his school vacations in the design department, and as of April 1963, was entirely at Porsche's disposal. His former colleague, Hans Mezger, recalls the then 26-year-old engineer: "Ferdinand Piëch always paid close attention to quality." To this day, Piëch is still regarded as a hard-core engineer. Because Piëch was a member of the Porsche family, he was always able to insist on the highest quality materials (quality is always expensive), overcoming the objections of the purchasing department. This consequently contributed greatly to the durability of the new engines.

Based on experience with the eight-cylinder 754, the engineers knew that the crankshaft should have a bearing on either side of each connecting rod, to

As early as 1963, Ferdinand Piëch (left) had an excellent feel for engine design. To his right are his brother Michael and Ferdinand Alexander Porsche.

79

prevent distortion of the crankshaft at high rpm (6500 rpm had been targeted). This naturally results in seven main bearings and an additional eighth bearing at the nose of the crank to admit lubricating oil. The 745 had run in only four bearings. In June of 1963, mechanics Himmelseher and Herrmann were assigned the task of installing an eighth bearing in Type 901/1 engine number 4. The first three engines had only seven bearings.

In addition, after countless test drives and races, it was known that under hard cornering, oil would be forced to the outer cylinder bank of boxer engines. This physical problem could only be solved by a deep oil pan. This provided enough oil for lubrication, but increased engine height.

For cooling, a centrally mounted fan dominated the engine. While the pushrod engines were equipped with radial impellers (purchased from Volkswagen), the 821 engine employed an axial cooling blower. The axial arrangement improved the blower efficiency to such an extent that a light-alloy fan of only 245 mm diameter was required. The number of fan blades was also decreased, from the initial 17 (for the first test cars) to only 11. The cooling air was distributed to the cylinders and cylinder heads by a plastic shroud. According to Hans Mezger, Porsche's air cooling system absorbed less engine power than the cooling fans and water pumps of comparable water-cooled engines.

Type 901/01

On January 9, 1963, the designation "901" for the new six-cylinder first appears in documents. It took several weeks before the new type designation was applied universally. On October 30, 1963, development chief Helmut Rombold received a memo from the development department, which recorded the following: "This shall establish that for the foreseeable future, the Type 901 engine, intended for production, will be numbered sequentially beginning with the number 900 001. It should be noted that the numbers 900 001 to 900 100 are reserved for experimental engines. Consequently, actual production numbers begin with 900 101."

At this stage, designers Piëch and Mezger began their fine-tuning of the engine design. The Type 821 had defined their approach. The basic difference between the two engines lay in one feature, their lubrication systems. In spite of its high cost, Ferry Porsche, at the urging of the designers, approved the dry-sump lubrication system. This was the only way to ensure satisfactory lubrication of the entire engine in every situation, and permitted a lower engine. This required an additional shaft to drive the necessary oil pumps. This shaft was mounted centrally, directly under the crankshaft, and gear-driven at half crankshaft speed. This in turn drove two gear pumps, one pressure pump and one scavenge pump. Oil was drawn from a separate tank and fed to the lubrication points by the pressure pump. Afterwards the oil was captured in the sump and fed back through a cooler to the oil tank by the scavenge pump.

The combustion chamber was again reworked and made more compact. In the production version, the valves formed an included angle of 59 degrees. The inlet valves were set 27 degrees, and the exhaust valves 32 degrees from vertical. Hans Mezger had done a lot of fine tuning to this arrangement, and explains that "There is no other two-valve engine in which the valves can be arranged in such an ideal fashion. On the other hand, we recognized early on that air-cooled four-valve engines would not be possible."

Taking a cue from the eight-cylinder Formula 1 engines, the 901 powerplant also used individual cylinders and cylinder heads. The cylinder heads in particular had a large potential for continuous displacement increases. Before production got underway, the cast iron cylinder liners were surrounded by pressure-cast alloy jackets with cooling fins (so-called Biral cylinders). Undercuts in the rough surface of the liner resulted in a very solid mechanical connection between light alloy and gray iron. This process was developed by the piston specialists at Mahle in Stuttgart. Its advantage was that the pistons ran on the relatively durable cast gray iron surfaces, while the pressure-cast aluminum cooling fins resulted in optimum heat transfer. The first Biral cylinders were made available to Porsche in May of 1963, and were immediately installed in six test engines.

Engine cutaway. Two banks of Solex carburetors provided the air-fuel mixture.

The five-speed transmission, here shown as a cutaway model, had a tall first gear.

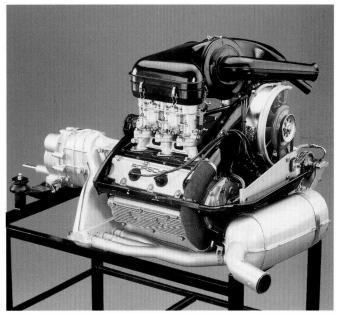

The two-liter boxer engine, with 130 horsepower, had great potential.

In the early stages, a large number of detail experiments were conducted. As in the racing engine department, mechanics took individual responsibility for the powerplants which they assembled. English translation on page 392.

English translation on page 392.

Dr.-Ing. h.c. F. Porsche K.-G. Stuttgart-Zuffenhausen

Mot. Nr.	Gehäuse	K-Welle	Kolben Zyl.	Köpfe	Steuerg.	N-Welle	Vergaser	Versuchs-zweck	Monteur	Typ
1	Silumin alte Ausführg. Ölkanäle 901	901	Ferral	821	1007 starr	821 normal 2	40 PICB	Temperaturmessungen	Dellin, 1 Brems.	821/1
2	Elektron-Gehäuse 821	821	Ferral	821	1007 starr	821 normal 2	40 schwimmerlos	Fahrzeug T 8	Rapp, (Kolb)	821/1
3	Silumin alte Ausführg. Ölkanäle 901	901	Ferral	821	1007 starr	821 normal 2	36 schwimmerlos	Saugrohrversuche Vergaser	Munding, Hahn	821/1
4	Silumin-Gehäuse Ausführg. 821/901	901	Ferral	901	1008 starr	901 normal 2 verstellbar		Nockenversuche	Herrmann, Himmelseher	901/1
5								Ölversuche	Klißer Boilel.	901/2
6								Kettenversuche	Enz, Binder, Ost	901/2
7								Nockenaggregat	1 Monteur	901/1 u. 901/2

MV-Wi/kü, 21.3.1963

The new oil-hydraulic chain tensioners were developed by Horst Marchart, today chief of all Porsche research and development activities, and Hans Mezger.

In the 1970s, aluminum cylinders containing 17 percent silicon were used. A special process exposed silicon crystals above the aluminum matrix of the cylinder surface, and the nickel or iron plated pistons slid on these crystals. This technology, pioneered on the 911, is still used in Porsche's water-cooled four- and eight-cylinder engines. The Biral process was replaced by this new aluminum-silicon alloy (SAE 390), which also permitted a larger cylinder bore and therefore larger displacement. The test reports also tell us that much experimental effort went into the arrangement of cooling fins. For Biral cylinders, a fin spacing of less than 5 mm was not possible. A spacing of 5.5 mm was established, as tooling was already available.

Most recently, Porsche's successful cylinder coating technology was replaced by an even better method. Instead of the SAE 390 alloy, an 0.06 to 0.10 mm (.0024 to .0040 in.) layer of nickel embedded with hard silicon carbide particles is galvanically deposited. The process, called Nikasil, was also developed by the piston manufacturer Mahle.

Nikasil cylinder walls result in quick break-in and rapid seating of the piston rings. Combined with Nikasil's low friction losses, further advantages are gained in terms of engine output, piston ring blow-by, oil consumption and cylinder wear.

The engine of the 911 has undergone constant development for thirty years. The individual development stages are outlined in the following contribution by Heinz Dorsch, Hans-Joachim Esch and Paul Hensler, Porsche engine specialists working in the Weissach research and development center.

The two-liter engine, mounted on an assembly stand, is dominated by the large, centrally mounted eleven-blade fan and the three intake runners per side.

Sonderdruck aus MTZ Motortechnische Zeitschrift, Jahrgang 26, Heft 1, Januar 1965, Seite 13–17
Franckh'sche Verlagshandlung Stuttgart

Der neue Porsche-Motor Typ 911

Dipl.-Ing. Egon Forstner, Stuttgart-Zuffenhausen

Dipl.-Ing. Egon Forstner, Stuttgart-Zuffenhausen

Der neue Porsche-Motor Typ 911

Porsche hat auf der Internationalen Automobilausstellung 1963 in Frankfurt einen neuen schnellen Reisewagen — den Typ 911 — gezeigt. Die Serie lief im September 1964 an und den Interessenten für besonders leistungsfähige Wagen steht damit neben dem bekannten Typ 356 C ein noch schnelleres Porsche-Fahrzeug, das mit dem hier beschriebenen Motor ausgestattet ist, zur Verfügung.[*]

Der Motor ist im Heck angeordnet, wie beim jetzigen Serienwagen und den verschiedenen sportlichen und rennsportlichen Fahrzeugen, die von Porsche in den letzten Jahren gebaut und eingesetzt worden sind. Der Motor, ein Sechszylinder in Boxerausführung mit 21 Hubvolumen ist wieder luftgekühlt. Hohe Leistung und ausgeglichene Laufruhe kennzeichnen die neue Konstruktion. Gegenüber dem Serienmotor des 356 C ist das Hubvolumen um 25 % und die Leistung um 40 % gesteigert. Das gewählte Konzept läßt aber noch viel Raum für wesentliche Entwicklungsschritte zu höheren Leistungen. Es ist das Ziel weiterer Entwicklungsarbeiten, den neuen Motor in forcierter Ausführung auch für den Rennsport reif zu machen und so die Serie und den Sport zum wechselseitigen Nutzen eng zu verknüpfen.

Das Bild 1 zeigt die Leistungslinien des neuen Motors Typ 911. Zum Vergleich sind vier weitere Porschemotoren des laufenden Serienprogramms und der Stoßstangen. Die Typen 1600 C und 1600 SC sind zwei unterschiedlichen Leistungen der Typ 587/3 ist vom Vier-Nockenwellen-Rennmotor abgeleitet, der vom Spyder, vom Carrera, dem Formel II- und dem Formel I-Wagen her bekannt ist.

Aus der Zahlentafel können die Hauptdaten der oben genannten Motoren und — um einen Überblick zu geben — auch die Daten der zugehörigen Fahrzeuge und ihre wichtigsten Fahrleistungswerte abgelesen werden. Der Gran-Turismo GTS 904 wird seit Frühjahr 1964 in internationalen Sport eingesetzt.

Im Bild 2 ist der neue Sechszylinder-Motor mit angebautem Schalt- und Ausgleichgetriebe gezeigt. Hinzuweisen ist auf das axiale Kühlgebläse, die drei Vergaser (je Motorseite (hier nicht in der endgültigen Ausführung), das großvolumige Ansaugluftfilter, den Vorauspufftopf und den hinten

[*] Über den zugehörigen Wagen (früher 901 genannt) siehe: H. Tomala u. E. Forstner, Der neue Porsche-Wagen Typ 901 und GTS 904 ATZ 66 (1964) H. 5, S. 139/139 und H. 6, S. 169/175

Zahlentafel. Motor-, Fahrzeug- und Fahrleistungsdaten

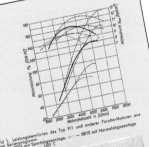

Bild 2, Motor 911 mit angebautem Schalt- und Ausgleichgetriebe. Triebwerk, Kühlanlage, Heizung und Abgasanlage sind eine geschlossene unabhängige Montageeinheit.

liegenden Abgasschalldämpfer. Die Auspuffrohre unter dem Motor ummantelt und dienen als Wärmeaustauscher für die motorabhängige Wagenheizung. Die Heizluft wird durch die beiden Schlauchleitungen vom Gebläse zu den Wärmeaustauschern rechts und links geführt.

Motor	Zylinder Zahl Z	Steuerung NW — Nockenwelle	Bohrung Hub	Hubraum V_H cm³	Verdichtung ε	N_e DIN PS	Fahrzeug Typ und Verwendung	η_r Luftwiderstandsfläche m²	c_w Luftwiderstandsbeiwert	Leergewicht kg	Leistungsgewicht mit Fahrer (75 kg) kg/PS	Höchstgeschw. v_{max} km/h	Zeit für um stehenden sec
911	6	1 NW pro Seite	66/60	1991	9,0	131	911 Reisewagen	1,66	0,36	1080	8,8	210	29,9
							911 Reisewagen			935	13,5	175	34,4
		Stoßstange	74/82,5	1582	8,5	75	356 C Reisewagen	1,61	0,398	935	10,6	185	32,6
1600 C	4	Stoßstange	74/82,5	1582	9,3	95	356 C Reisewagen	1,61	0,398	935	8,8	250	25,7
1600 SC	4	2 NW pro Seite	74/92	1966	9,8	155	904 GTS Gran Tourismo Sport	1,32	0,33	740	5,3	265	24,6
587/3 Serien abgas-A.	4	2 NW pro Seite	74/92	1966	9,8	180	904 GTS Gran Tourismo Sport	1,32	0,33		4,5		

Bild 1. Leistungskennlinien des Typ 911 aus dem Serienprogramm der Sportabgasanlage, ---- 587/3 mit Normalabgasanlage. ---- 1600 SC ---- 1600 C

Luft- und wassergekühlte Motoren sind nach Jahrzehnten der Entwicklung in der Leistung völlig gleichwertig, wie im Bild 3 zu sehen ist. Hier sind die Literleistungen verschiedener Viertakt-Ottomotoren über der Drehzahl aufgezeichnet. Es sind wenige Punkte eingetragen, um die Übersichtlichkeit zu wahren. Ein Vergleich der ganzen Vielzahl aufgeführter Personenwagen-Motoren zeigt noch deutlicher, daß die Leistungen der luftgekühlten Motoren an der oberen Grenze des Feldes liegen. Der jetzige Standort des Typs 911/1 läßt erkennen, beim Vergleich mit den anderen Porsche-Konstruktionen, daß im zunehmender Drehzahl die Leistung noch sehr wesentlich gesteigert werden kann.

Die eingezeichnete mittlere Kurve folgt einer starken Progression mit steigender Drehzahl, die besonders deutlich durch die Mitteldrucklinien hervorgehoben wird. Dieser Effekt kann zum geringen Teil auf die höhere Verdichtung forcierter Motoren, die im Diagramm weiter rechts liegen, zurückgeführt werden. Einen wesentlich stärkeren Einfluß haben zweifellos verbesserte Gaswechselvorgänge, die bei den hohen Drehzahlen besonders gute Zylinderfüllungen ergeben. Voraussetzung dafür sind allerdings widerstandsarme, sorgfältig ausgebildete und abgestimmte Ansaug- und Auspuffsysteme. Wichtig ist auch, daß die mechanischen Verluste im Triebwerk, wie Kolben-, Lagerreibung und Olpantscharbeit klein gehalten werden.

Der Motorlängsschnitt nach Bild 4 zeigt bemerkenswerte Details. Die Kurbelwelle ist vollgelagert. Zwei Olpumpen sorgen für den Schmierölumlauf. Die eine saugt das Ol aus dem Trockensumpf ab, die andere fördert es zu den Lagerstellen. Es ist ein Axialgebläserad verwendet, das auf der Welle der WechselstromLichtmaschine sitzt und durch einen Keilriemen angetrieben wird. Die sechs Vergaser sind an ein Trockenluftfilter angeschlossen. Rechts unten im Nockenwellenraum sind zwei Kettenräder zu erkennen, die je eine Kurbelwelle pro Motorseite antreiben. Die verwirklichten konstruktiven Lösungen und der nur 333 cm³ große Zylinderhubraum sind Grundlagen für spätere wesentliche Drehzahl- und Leistungssteigerungen.

Kurbelwelle

Die Vollagerung der Kurbelwelle ist bei Boxermotoren dieser Größe ungewöhnlich, gibt aber Sicherheit gegen zu hohe Biegebeanspruchung selbst bei extremen Drehzahlen. Im Laufe der Zeit sind die Triebwerksbelastungen ganz allgemein stark gewachsen. Mit der Verdichtung zum Beispiel wurden die Zünddrücke wesentlich höher, wie im Bild 5 zu erkennen läßt. Verstärkt wird ihre Wirkung durch die größeren Bohrungen zusätzlich größere Lagerabstände und Biegelängen zur Folge haben. Mit der Drehzahl sind in ähnlicher Weise auch die Massenkräfte größer geworden. Die Vollagerung im Dieselmotor allgemein verwendet — war ein Mittel dem zu begegnen. Gleichzeitig sind übrigens auch auf dem Werkstoffsektor und besonders durch entsprechende Wärmebehandlung wie z. B. das Teniffer-Verfahren viel erreicht worden[**].

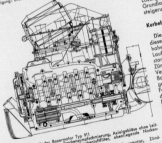

Bild 4. Sechszylinder Boxermotor Typ 911. Vollagerte Kurbelwelle, Trockensumpfschmierung, Axialgebläse ohne Leitrad, Wechselstromlichtmaschine, Trockenluftfilter, obenliegende Nockenwelle

Luftgekühlter Boxermotor,	Zündfolge 1-6-2-4-3-5
Bohrung	66 mm
Hub	60 mm
Zylinderzahl	6
Hubraum	1991 cm³
Verdichtung	131 PS
DIN Leistung	6100 U/min
bei Drehzahl	17,8 kpm
max. Drehmoment	4300 U/min
bei Drehzahl	65 PS/l
spezif. DIN-Leistung	96 ROZ
Oktanzahlbedarf	

8fach gelagerte Kurbelwelle
Ventile in V-Form hängend, Kipphebel mit obenliegender Nockenwelle durch Kette angetrieben.

Trockensumpfschmierung mit Saug-
und Druckpumpe, Ölfilter mit
Papierpatrone
Ölkühler am Motor.

Solex-Vergaser
Micronic-Luftfilter
12-Volt-Lichtmaschine 490 Watt.

Bild 5. Maximaler Zünddruck, abhängig vom Verdichtungsverhältnis.
a. Theoretisch, vollständige Gleichraumverbrennung.
b. Praktisch, gemischte Verbrennung.
$\eta_1 = 0,95$

[**] Über das Teniffer-Verfahren, das die Festigkeitserhöhung und Dauerfestigkeitserhöhung nitrierter Teile von Verbrennungskraftmaschinen, MTZ 25 (1964) H. 6 S. 245/247

Bild 3. Hubraumleistung luft- und wassergekühlter Viertakt-Vergaser-Ottomotoren. Typ 901/1 heißt jetzt Typ 911
[*] Berichtigung: Diese Zeile muß lauten: Nr. 23 Porsche 587/3/4Z/1966 Sp. A.

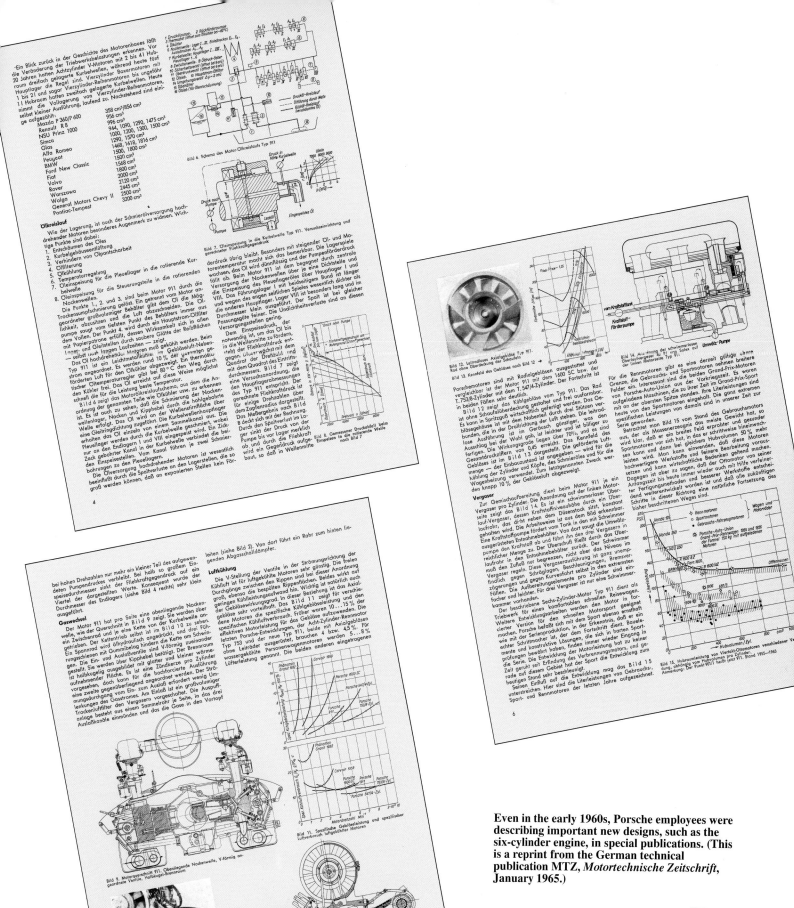

Even in the early 1960s, Porsche employees were describing important new designs, such as the six-cylinder engine, in special publications. (This is a reprint from the German technical publication MTZ, *Motortechnische Zeitschrift*, January 1965.)

Three Solex overflow carburetors, Type 40 PI, shared a common float bowl. They were difficult to synchronize.

For the 1969 model year, the 170 hp two-liter "S" engines were the first to be fitted with Bosch mechanical fuel injection.

Digital Motor Electronics

1. Fuel pump
2. Fuel filter
3. Pressure damper
3a. Pressure regulator
4. Fuel injection lines
5. Idle stabilizer
6. Air flow meter
7. Throttle switch
8. Induction air temperature sensor
9. Engine temperature sensor
10. TDC sensor
11. Reference mark sensor
12. Control unit
13. Fuel injectors
14. Ignition coil
15. Ignition distributor
16. Dual fuel pump/control unit relay
17. Idle switch
18. Fusebox

At the end of the 1960s, the era of carburetors at Porsche was nearly past. Injected engines formed the basis for future power increases.

Blue = fuel supply

Yellow = vacuum controls

Red = transistorized ignition

Kraftstoffversorgung

Unterdrucksteuerung

Transistorzündung

86

Great Potential

1. Introduction

The past thirty years of automotive engine development have been characterized by formidable environmental standards, high customer demands in terms of performance, reliability, economy and ease of maintenance, as well as the necessity for cost effective and dependable manufacturing methods. In this time period, no engine in the abundant worldwide palette of automotive powerplants outlines the history of engine evolution more convincingly, without changing its basic concept and without sacrificing its sporting character, than the air-cooled six-cylinder boxer engine of the Porsche Type 911.

This is ample justification to examine this extremely interesting thirty-year period of Otto-cycle engine development from the point of view of the 911 engine's history.

2. Design development

2.1 Engine layout

The fact that the 911 engine was capable of continuous development over the course of thirty years

can be attributed to the farsightedness of its original designers. In particular, the already mentioned modular construction of the engine played a significant role in this capability. Despite a multitude of detail changes, the basic design of the engine has not changed during its entire development life.

Engine cross sections from three decades of 911 engine development (see Figs. 2, 3 and 4) clearly show the basic engine layout. The development of engine displacement, power output and basic engine specifications of the various evolutionary stages are summarized in Table 1. The significant features of the engine and their development history will be briefly outlined in the following.

2.2 Crankcase

The pressure die-cast crankcase is split vertically.

Up through the 1969 model year, the crankcase was made of magnesium. For strength reasons, aluminum alloys have been used as of the 1970 model year.

2.3 Crankshaft

From the very beginning until the present day, the crankshaft has run in eight bearings. To ensure reliable oil supply to the connecting rod bearings at high engine speeds, oil is supplied to the crankshaft through bearings 1 and 8.

The Porsche 911 has always employed a forged crankshaft. To reduce bearing loads, the number of counterweights has been changed in the course of development. The crankshafts of the first engine variants had no counterweights at all.

When piston stroke was increased from 66 mm to 70.4 mm, one counterweight per cylinder was introduced. Later, all crankshafts had two counterweights per cylinder.

2.4 Camshaft drive and oil pump

The two overhead cams are driven by an intermediate shaft and double chains. The intermediate shaft is located under the crankshaft and is driven by a

Fig. 2
How it all started: cross section of the two-liter engine.

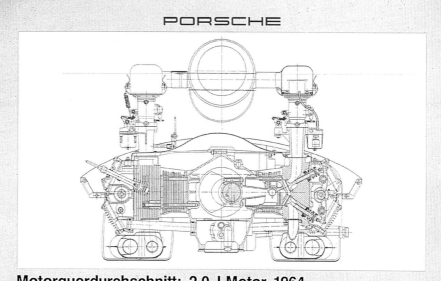

PORSCHE
Motorquerdurchschnitt: 2,0 l-Motor 1964

Fig. 3
Trimmed for fuel economy: three-liter engine.

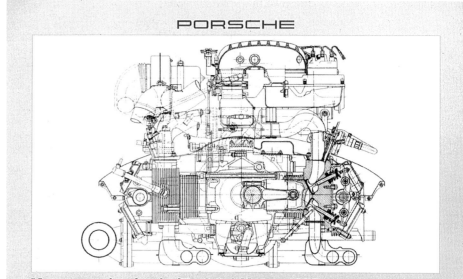

PORSCHE
Motorquerdurchschnitt: 3,0 l-Motor 1975

Fig. 4
The latest evolutionary stage: 3.6 liters.

PORSCHE
Motorquerdurchschnitt: 3,6 l-Motor 1994

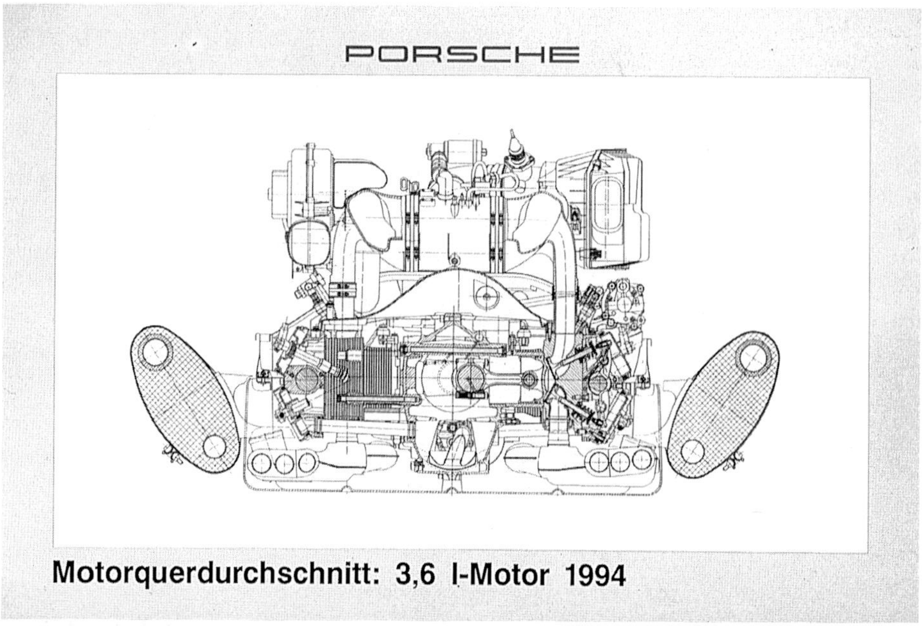

PORSCHE

| | Modelljahr | Hubraum (dm^3) | Bohrg. x Hub (mm) | Verdichtung | Kurbelwelle | | | Pleuelstangen-Verhältnis | Leistung (kW) | Drehmoment (Nm) | Kraftstoff ul=bleifrei (ROZ) | Gemischaufbereitung |
					Hauptlager (mm)	Pleuellager (mm)	Gegengewichte					
Saugmotoren	1964-1966	2,0	80 x 66,0	9,0	57	57	0	0,25	96	175	98	Verg.
	1967-1969	2,0	80 x 66,0	9,9	57	57	0	0,25	125	178	98	Verg.
	1970-1971	2,2	84 x 66,0	9,8	57	57	0	0,25	132	200	98	m.E.
	1972	2,4	84 x 70,4	8,5	57	52	1	0,28	140	215	92	m.E.
	1973-1975	2,7	90 x 70,4	8,5	57	52	1	0,28	154	255	92	m.E.
	1975	2,7	90 x 70,4	8,5	57	52	1	0,28	128	235	92	K-Jet
	1976-1977	3,0	95 x 70,4	8,5	57	52	1	0,28	147	255	92	K-Jet
	1978-1979	3,0	95 x 70,4	8,5	60	53	2	0,28	132	245	92	K-Jet
	1980	3,0	95 x 70,4	8,5	60	53	2	0,28	138	265	92	K-Jet
	1981-1983	3,0	95 x 70,4	9,5	60	53	2	0,27	150	265	98	DME
	1984-1988	3,2	95 x 74,4	10,0	60	55	2	0,29	170	285	98	DME
	1987-1988	3,2	95 x 74,4	10,0	60	55	2	0,29	160	285	95ul	DME
	1989-1993	3,6	100 x 76,4	11,3	60	55	2	0,30	184	310	95ul	DME
	1994	3,6	100 x 76,4	11,3	60	55	2	0,30	200	335	98ul	DME
Turbomotoren	1975-1977	3,0	95 x 70,4	6,5	57	52	1	0,28	191	343	98	K-Jet
	1978-1989	3,3	97 x 74,4	7,0	60	55	2	0,29	221	430	98	K-Jet
	1991-1992	3,3	97 x 74,4	7,0	60	55	2	0,29	235	450	95ul	K-Jet
	1993-1994	3,6	100 x 76,4	7,5	60	55	2	0,30	265	530	95ul	K-Jet

Hauptabmessungen und Leistungsdaten der 911-Motoren

Table 1
Overview of principal dimensions, output and torque for 911 production engines; it all started with 130 horsepower (96 kW).
Left column
    Saugmotoren = normally aspirated engines
    Turbomotoren = Turbo engines
Top row
    Model year
    displacement
    bore x stroke
    compression ratio
    Kurbelwelle = crankshaft
    main bearing diameter
    connecting rod bearing diameter
    connecting rod ratio
    power output, kW
    torque, Nm
    fuel, ul = unleaded
    fuel supply system

pair of gears from the crankshaft. In addition to the valve train, the intermediate shaft also drives the oil pressure and scavenge pumps, located in a separate housing.

In the course of development, due to increasing camshaft drive loads, the gears and hydraulic chain tensioner were redesigned several times.

The capacities of the pressure and scavenge pumps were also repeatedly increased.

2.5 Connecting rods

From the beginning until the present day, forged steel connecting rods have been used exclusively in the 911. In order to realize the evolution of engine displacement from the original 2.0 liters to the present 3.6 liters, it was necessary to change the connecting rod bearing diameter and connecting rod length several times.

When the stroke was increased from 66 to 70.4 mm, the connecting rod bearing diameter was reduced from 57 to 52 mm to allow clearance between the connecting rods and oil pump.

Later, when stroke was increased again, it was necessary to increase the bearing diameter to 55 mm due to crankshaft strength considerations and connecting rod bearing loads.

Connecting rod clearance was achieved by accompanying changes to the crankcase, connecting rods and oil pump.

The significant progress in the load-driven design of components by means of modern development methods may be seen in Fig. 5, which compares connecting rods from the 1964 and 1994 model years.

Despite considerably higher loads, the mass of the current connecting rod is 15 percent lower than that of the 1964 connecting rod.

2.6 Cylinders

The 911 engine employs individual cylinders, which are fitted to bores in the crankcase.

In particular, the development of cylinder technology permitted a bore increase from 80 to 100 mm without increased cylinder spacing. For special motor sports applications, the bore has even been increased to 102 mm.

At the beginning of its development history, the engine was fitted with cast iron and aluminum composite cylinders (Biral process). Engines with both 80 and 84 mm cylinder bore were fitted with such cylinders (Fig. 6). Later, a special engine variant with reduced power output was fitted with cast iron cylinders.

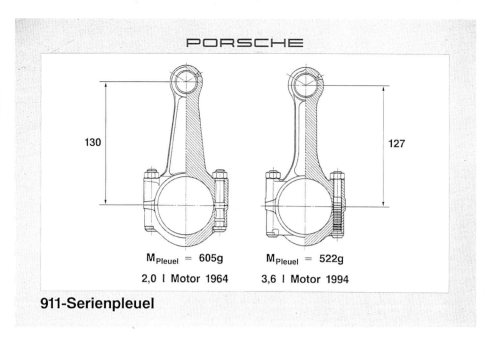

Fig. 5
Comparison of 1964 and 1994 connecting rods.

911-Serienpleuel

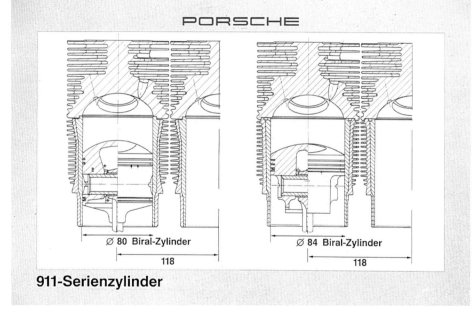

Fig. 6
Comparison of 80 and 84 mm cylinders.

911-Serienzylinder

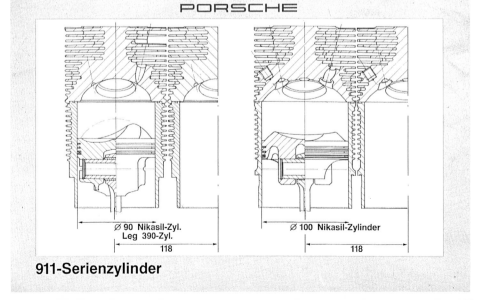

Fig. 7.
Comparison of 90 and 100 mm cylinders.

90

911-Serienzylinder

The development of monometallic aluminum cylinders was the decisive step which permitted larger cylinder bores.

One unique problem of the air-cooled engine is that with constant cylinder spacing, an increased bore reduces the cooling fin length and therefore decreases heat transfer.

The development of monometallic aluminum cylinders made increased displacement possible because this particular technology enables the necessary cooling air flow required for increased heat transfer.

In 1973, monometallic aluminum cylinders with a nickel dispersion coating (Nikasil process) were introduced on the 2.7 liter engine, which had a 90 mm cylinder bore.

A year later, an alternative process was introduced in production, employing cylinders of SAE 390 hypereutectoid aluminum-silicon alloy.

Over the years, the Nikasil cylinders have proven themselves to be the best solution in terms of wear, oil consumption and friction losses, and remain in production today with a bore of 100 mm.

Fig. 7 compares the 90 mm and 100 mm cylinders. The illustration emphasizes the problem of ensuring adequate cooling fin length with increasing bore.

2.7 Cylinder heads

Analogous to the cylinders, the 911 engine employs individual cylinder heads. The heads of each cylinder bank are bolted to the camshaft housing, and this subassembly is then installed as a single unit.

In the course of development, many detail improvements were made to the cylinder heads. In particular, the cooling fin arrangement underwent continuous refinement.

Among other measures, oversized Plexiglas scale models were built and tested in a water tank.

Because of the high thermal load on the cylinder heads, only high-grade aluminum alloys are used. All turbocharged engines use the alloy GK AlCu5Ni1.5CoSbZr (RR 350). In the past, the heads for normally aspirated engines were cast of GK AlCu4Ni2Mg (so-called Y alloy). Primarily for casting considerations, the 1994 model year witnessed a switch to the RR 350 alloy for non-turbo engines as well.

The most important step in cylinder head development was the introduction of ceramic port liners for the exhaust passages in 1988. This resulted in a significant decrease in the thermal load on the cylinder heads, and improved catalytic converter response.

3. Maintenance reduction

The history of the 911 engine, which now spans thirty years, provides an impressive illustration of the extraordinary progress in reducing the engine's maintenance requirements.

At the beginning of its development history, the 911 engine required numerous maintenance procedures at short intervals. In the course of many years, improvements in engine management, lubricating oil quality, spark plug life and V-belt durability reduced its maintenance requirements. An additional measure to reduce service requirements is the introduction of hydraulic valve lash adjustment.

Figure 8 shows that the number of recommended service visits between vehicle delivery and 40,000 km [25,000 miles] has been reduced from the original six to the present two visits. In the same period, the number of service items has been reduced from 43 to seven. With its recommended oil change interval of 20,000 km, introduced in the 1983 model year, the 911 retains a unique position among automobile powerplants.

4. Power output, fuel economy, exhaust and noise emissions

The chief characteristics of a sports car are its vehicle dynamics and performance, both determined to a large extent by engine output. Even if other conditions have changed in many different ways, 911

Fig. 8.
Maintenance intervals
for the 911 engine have
become progressively
longer over the years.

M = change engine oil
and filter
F = change air filter
K = change spark
plugs
C = check
compression
U = check breaker
points
Z = check and adjust
ignition
R = check and adjust
belts
L = check and adjust
idle speed
V = check and adjust
valve lash

PORSCHE

bis 3.000 km	MRLV	MUZRV	MRV	
bei 5.000 km	UZR			
bei 10.000 km	MFKCUZRLV	M		
bei 20.000 km	MFKCUZRLV	MFKUZRLV	MFZRLV	MFR
bei 30.000 km	MFKCUZRLV	M		
bei 40.000 km	MFKCUZRLV	MFKUZRLV	MFKZRLV	MFKR
	MJ 64 – MJ 72	MJ 73 – MJ 82	MJ 83 – MJ 93	MJ 94
Service / Positionen	6 / 43	5 / 23	3 / 16	2 / 7

M Motoröl u. Motorölfilter wechseln   C Kompression messen   R Riemen prüfen und einstellen
F Luftfilter wechseln   U Unterbrecherkontakte prüfen   L Leerlauf prüfen und einstellen
K Zündkerzen wechseln   Z Zündung prüfen und einstellen   V Ventilspiel prüfen und einstellen

Wartungsintervalle und Wartungsaufwand für die 911-Serienmotoren

customers have always had high expectations for power output. In the continuous evolution of the 911, power output (Figs. 9, 10 and Table 1), environmental compatibility, comfort, and reliability have been regarded as interrelated development goals, and have undergone a constant, steady improvement for thirty years.

Examination of the development of power, fuel economy and emissions indicates that the evolution of the 911 engine may be divided into four decades, with different emphasis in each decade.

4.1 The first decade

The first ten years (1964 - 1973) were characterized by engines with high specific output. Individual carburetors or separate intake runners permitted peak values of 82 horsepower per liter (60 kW/l) at high rpm. The earliest displacement increases, from 2.0 to 2.2 and later to 2.4 liters, were carried out entirely for higher power and torque. While the 2-liter engines were fitted with individual carburetors, mechanical fuel injection by means of a two-row mechanical injection pump was introduced on the 2.2 liter engines. Porsche had successfully applied this system to racing engines. As early as 1966, Porsche conducted its first exhaust emissions tests. The goal was to meet California exhaust emissions standards at a time when Germany was still debating the merits of a 4.5 percent idle CO limit. At the end of the first decade, an exhaust system concept including a catalytic converter for the U.S. market was discussed. For this, unleaded fuel would be required, which at that time was only available with a Research Octane Number of 91.

To reduce the number of 911 engine variants, even non-U.S. market engines were designed to operate on regular grade gasoline. Despite this, a displacement increase to 2.4 liters resulted in increased power.

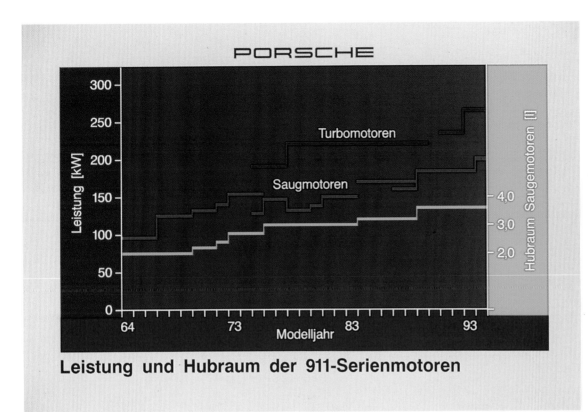

Leistung und Hubraum der 911-Serienmotoren

Fig. 9
Power output and displacement of 911 production engines in the course of 30 years.

Red bar, power output (kW)

green bar, displacement (normally aspirated engines) (liters)

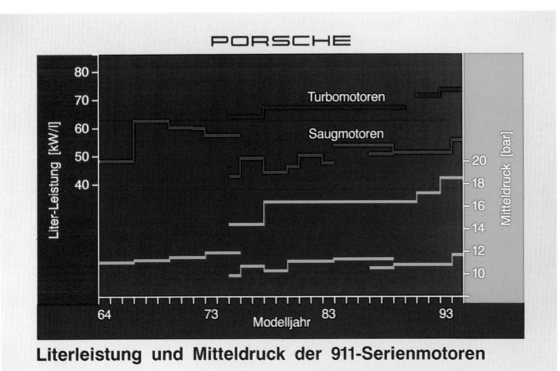

Literleistung und Mitteldruck der 911-Serienmotoren

Fig. 10
Specific output and brake mean effective pressure of 911 production engines between 1964 and 1993.

red bar, specific output (kW/liter)

green bar, brake mean effective pressure (bar)

93

4.2 The second decade

The second decade (1974 - 1983) was characterized by worldwide oil and economic crises. Reduction of the lead content in German fuel from 0.5 grams/liter to less than 0.15 g/l led to further uncertainty regarding fuel availability and quality. In developing the "non-U.S." engines, these additional requirements had to be taken into consideration.

A significant step toward reducing fuel consumption and to increased environmental compatibility was achieved with the K-Jetronic. This fuel injection system was developed by Bosch, in close cooperation with Porsche, and first installed on a 911 engine in mid-1973. Reduced fuel octane and the intake system typical of the K-Jetronic permitted specific output of only 68 hp (50 kW) per liter. With a displacement of three liters, the K-Jetronic engines achieved a maximum of 204 hp (150 kW).

For customers who demanded more power, development of a production turbocharged engine was begun in 1972, despite market uncertainty; Porsche had been highly successful with turbocharged racing engines. In 1974, Porsche's new flagship model, the 911 Turbo, was introduced, powered by a three-liter engine with an exhaust-driven turbocharger and exhaust-side boost control. The 911 Turbo represents the first production application of this boost control method. The advantage over all previous turbocharged road vehicles was apparent in improved response even at low rpm, and higher reliability even when driven in normal traffic. Despite critical

The engine of the three-liter 911 Turbo was based on the normally-aspirated engine of the Carrera 3.0.

The 300 horsepower 3.3 liter engine is recognizable by its large intercooler.

comments in the automotive world, this model was so successful that after the originally planned 400 examples had been built, a new, more powerful engine was developed. A 3.3 liter engine, improved by the addition of intercooling, represented the most powerful 911 model from 1977 to 1989.

The originally planned 400 examples were only the beginning. Since then, more than 25,000 turbocharged 911s have been delivered to customers.

4.3 The third decade

In the third decade (1983 - 1993) was characterized by accumulating engineering demands. 911 customers expected more performance. Environmental concerns and fuel economy were important factors in purchasing decisions. As of 1983, Porsche met these demands with a new 231 horsepower (170 kW) engine with a displacement of 3.2 liters, a high compression ratio of 10.0:1 and electronic engine management. For the U.S and Canada, oxygen sensors and three-way catalysts were standard equipment, while internal engine measures were sufficient to meet all European requirements. As of 1986, Porsche successfully offered its European customers this modern exhaust emissions technology, with an output of 160 kW.

The 1989 model year saw the introduction of 3.6 liter engines with 250 horsepower (184 kW). Selective knock control and dual ignition permitted an extremely high compression ratio of 11.3:1. This engine fulfilled customer expectations and regulatory requirements worldwide, and represents a genuine Porsche "world engine."

The Turbo engines were also matched to the new regulations. Even though a catalytic converter was required, in 1990 it was possible to increase power output of the 3.3 liter engine to 320 hp (235 kW), and in 1992, a displacement increase to 3.6 liters yielded 360 hp (265 kW). These powerplants are also genuine "world engines."

4.4 The fourth decade

The 911's fourth decade begins with the high point of an engine history which extends from 1964 to the present day. A 3.6 liter normally-aspirated engine with 272 horsepower (200 kW), which meets all worldwide exhaust and noise standards, is at the heart of the new 911 Carrera.

4.5 Power development

The steady increase in power output of 911 production engines over the past 30 years (see Table 1, page 89) is primarily due to the progressive increase in displacement from 2.0 to 3.6 liters. Secondary contributions are attributable to progress in intake system design. Fig. 11 schematically shows the concept of the resonance pipe intake system (1964 - 1983), the single-stage resonant induction system (1984 - 1988), and the two-stage resonant induction system (since 1989).

Despite increasing restrictions on valve timing and on the design of exhaust systems, development of these intake systems permitted increases in engine volumetric efficiency. Porsche 911 engines have always achieved volumetric efficiency greater than 100 percent, even though these air-cooled engines have only one intake and one exhaust valve per cylinder.

4.6 The development of exhaust and noise emissions

When California introduced exhaust emissions standards in 1966, internal engine modifications were sufficient, as they were for European standards before 1988. Later U.S. standards required more extensive measures for exhaust gas treatment, such as secondary air injection for thermal reactors and later for oxidation catalysts. As of 1980, 911 engines have been fitted with oxygen sensors combined with three-way catalysts. Since 1989, metal substrate catalysts have been fitted. Porsche is the first manufacturer anywhere in the world to install a metal substrate main catalyst. Today, Porsche 911 production engines meet all U.S. standards; in Europe, they meet Stage II requirements, which are mandatory as of 1996.

Fig. 13 shows the development of California exhaust standards. Because of the importance of the California market to Porsche, the 911 has always

Fig. 11
911 production engine
intake systems.

Title:
Development of intake
systems

Upper right:
Schematic of
individual resonance
stacks

Upper left:
Schematic of
single-stage resonance
induction system

Lower:
Schematic of two-stage
resonance induction
system

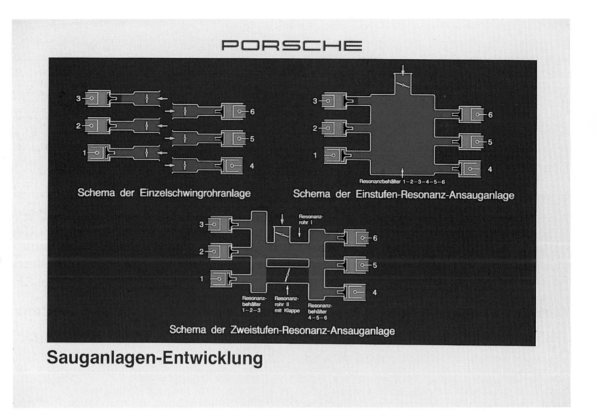

Sauganlagen-Entwicklung

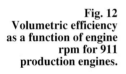

Fig. 12
Volumetric efficiency
as a function of engine
rpm for 911
production engines.

Title:
911 induction systems

green = dual resonance
system
yellow = plenum
system
red = individual
resonance stacks

Luftaufwand =
volumetric efficiency

Drehzahl = rpm

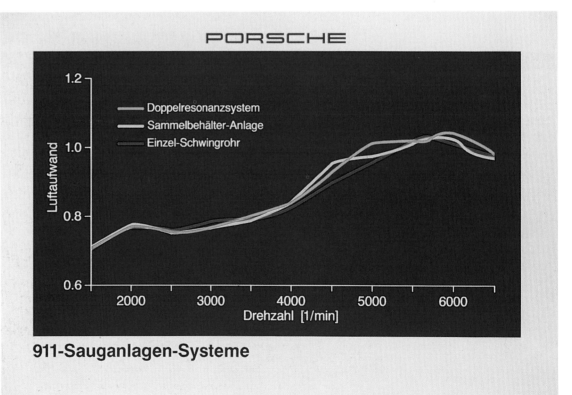

911-Sauganlagen-Systeme

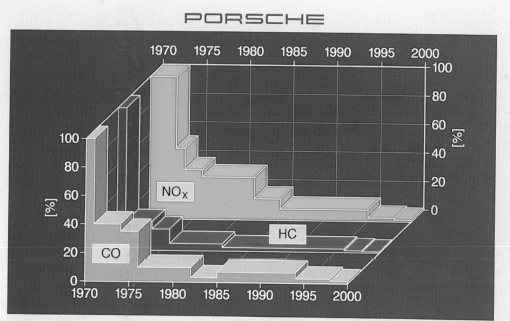

Entwicklung der Abgasgrenzwerte Kalifornien

Fig. 13
Harbingers of the future: California emissions limits

Maßnahme						
Gemisch-Aufbereitung	V.	Mech. einspritzg.	K-Jetronik		L.mengen-messung	L.massen-messung
Zündung		Fliehkraft + Unterdruckverstellung			DME Einzel-zündung	DME Doppel-zündung
Abgastechnik Motor Intern	SLE		SLE + AGR			
Abgastechnik Motor Extern		Thermo-reaktor	OK	3 Wege Katalysator mit λ Sonde		

1968　1972　1976　1980　1984　1988　92　94　93

MJ

DME: Digitale Motor Elektronik　　V:　Vergaser
SLE: Sekundär-Luft-Einblasung　　L:　Luftmassenmessung
AGR: Abgas-Rückführung　　　　　OK: Oxydations-Katalysator

Abgastechnologie zur Erfüllung der kalifornischen Abgasvorschriften

Fig. 14
Exhaust system technology required to meet California exhaust standards over the years.

Vertical labels on left:
Gemischaufbereitung = fuel supply
Zündung = ignition
Abgastechnik Motor intern = internal engine emissions reduction measures
Abgastechnik Motor extern = external engine emissions reduction measures

DME: Digital Motor Electronics
SLE: secondary air injection
AGR: exhaust gas recirculation
V: carburetor
L: mass air flow metering
OK: oxidation catalyst

in diagram:
Mech. Einspritzung = mechanical fuel injection
L.mengenmessung = volume air flow metering
L.massenmessung = mass air flow metering
Fliehkraft + Unterdruckverstellung = centrifugal & vacuum advance
DME Einzelzündung = DME single ignition
DME Doppelzündung = DME dual ignition
Thermoreaktor = thermal reactor
3 Wege Katalysator mit (Greek letter lambda) Sonde = 3-way catalyst with oxygen sensor (Lambda sonde)

Fig. 15
European Common
Market noise limits
and Porsche 911 noise
levels.

green line: Maximum
permissible

red line: Porsche 911
Schalldruckpegel in
dB(A) = sound pres-
sure level in dB(A)

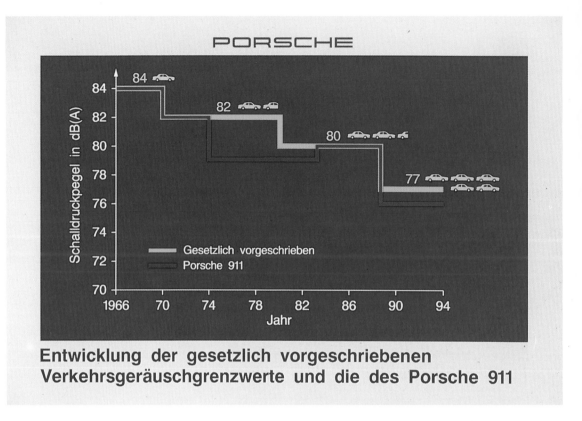

PORSCHE

Entwicklung der gesetzlich vorgeschriebenen
Verkehrsgeräuschgrenzwerte und die des Porsche 911

met these standards, the strictest in the world. The technology developed to meet these standards is shown in Fig. 14.

With regard to noise emissions, the 911 has a special handicap. Both main noise sources, engine and exhaust pipe, are located at the rear. While power output and acceleration performance have increased, noise levels have been reduced from 84 to the present 76 dB(A) (Fig. 15).

The main feature of this modern exhaust sound-proofing is the application of reflection and absorption systems. In the latest engine model, additional interference phenomena are utilized to reduce exhaust system noise.

Transmission development
Geared for performance

**Porsche synchromesh from 1952
to the end of the 1988 model year**

The history of the house of Porsche is closely tied to its patented synchromesh system. As in the case of engines, the first sports cars to carry the Porsche name (1950-1952) relied on a transmission developed using items from Volkswagen parts bins. This modified VW transmission was unsynchronized, and was known internally by the English epithet "crash box." At the time, the synchromesh systems employed within the auto industry were hardly worthy of the name. For this reason, Porsche decided to forge ahead with its own ideas. A small team working under Dr. Ernst Fuhrmann, consisting of Leopold F. Schmid and Richard Hetmann, developed a system based on "a slotted synchro ring with spring type action" and shift collars whose teeth also serve as friction surfaces during the synchronization process.

Extensive durability tests in cars and on synchronizer test benches, which in some tests simulated a 3 - 2 downshift up to 200,000 times, underscored the reliability of the Porsche synchromesh.

By 1960, more than seventy international patents protected the Porsche synchromesh system from unauthorized reproduction.

The Porsche system was licensed to many of the world's foremost automotive manufacturers. Alfa Romeo, Simca, Ferrari and Fiat, to name just a few, used the system. Transmission manufacturer Getrag delivered units with Porsche synchromesh to Audi, BMW, and Glas in Germany. In the truck sector, Berliet, Unic, OM and Hanomag, among others, used a Porsche system designed for their higher loads. British Motors Corporation (BMC) was also interested in Porsche synchromesh, but at the time, British manufacturing equipment was unable to produce the molybdenum-coated synchro rings of the required quality.

Although Porsche synchromesh is superior to other systems for fast shifts, and is also unaffected by transmission oils with higher than normal additive content, one basic disadvantage cannot be denied. To shift out of a selected gear, or to select a gear from standstill, the friction between the teeth of the shift collar and the rough molybdenum-coated surface of the synchro ring must be overcome. Depending on conditions, this could result in hanging up or blocking of the shift linkage. For this reason, Porsche switched to a modern development of the cone synchronization system in 1989.

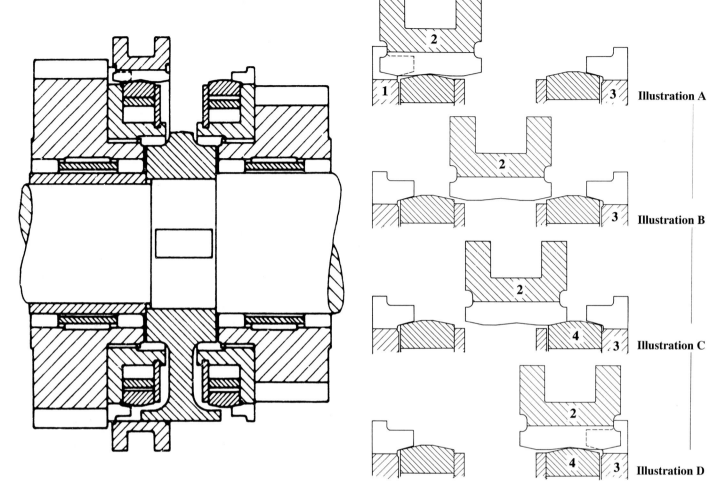

Illustration A

Illustration B

Illustration C

Illustration D

Operation of the Porsche synchromesh
Shifting gears:

The synchromesh uses friction to match speeds between the shaft and gear, and simultaneously prevents the shift collar from touching the clutch body for the selected gear before speeds are matched.

During the shift process, the clutch connecting engine and transmission must be disengaged.

The above illustrations demonstrate events during a gear shift.

Illustration A represents an engaged gear; the clutch body of the left gear (1) is rigidly connected to the shaft by means of the shift collar (2).

A gear change occurs when the shift collar is moved from this position, through its neutral position (Illustration B) and all the way to the right into its synchronizing position (Illustration C), so that the clutch body of the right gear (3) is rigidly connected to the shaft by the shift collar (Illustration D).

The actual matching of speeds occurs in the synchronizing position (Illustration C). The speed difference between the shaft and gear is eliminated by friction between the shift collar (2) and the synchronizer ring (4). Blocking elements located between the synchro ring and the clutch body can be used to increase the effectiveness of the synchronizing system over a wide speed range.

The Type 901 transmission, from 1965 to the end of 1971

The 901 transmission family is based on a three-piece transmission case. These initially consisted of die casting light alloy parts and later pressure-cast housings.

The large transmission housing also contains the clutch, clutch release mechanism and the final drive.

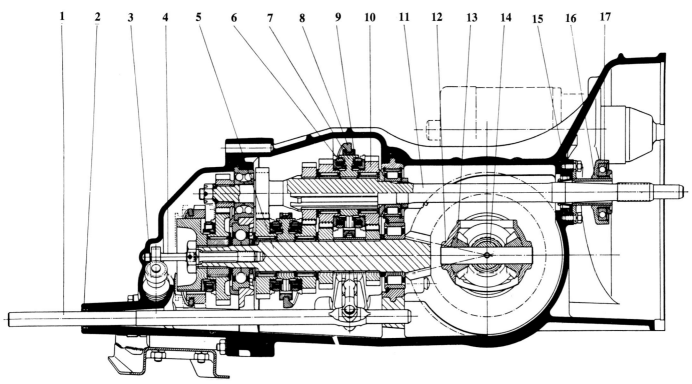

1 Shift rod	7 Guide sleeve	13 Differential pinion
2 Seal ring	8 Shift fork	14 Side gear shaft
3 Speedometer cable connection	9 Shift collar	15 Seal ring
4 Gear shaft for speedometer drive	10 Gear 1 (free) for 1st gear	16/17 Throwout bearing
5 Output shaft	11 Input shaft	
6 Synchronizer ring	12 Differential housing	

All forward gears are equipped with Porsche's own synchromesh system, which offered distinct advantages over competitors' systems (ZF, Borg-Warner, etc.) until well into the 1980s. Even during very quick shifts, the synchros are unbeatable. Shift forces, especially in the case of a quick, sporty driving style, are considerably lower. Given correct clutch actuation, their service life is comparable to that of the entire vehicle. This was not the case for other manufacturers of the time.

Within the large housing, the transmission input and output shafts are carried only by roller bearings. The intermediate plate is attached to the large transmission housing. The transmission shafts are precisely located in the intermediate plate by four-point ball bearings. The front transmission housing mates to the intermediate plate. The 901 transmissions were built as four-speeds as well as five-speed units; most customers opted for five forward gears.

In the five-speed transmission, first gear, reverse, and the mechanical speedometer drive are located in the front housing. In the four-speed, all forward gears are located in the large transmission housing.

The differential is placed transversely in the main transmission housing and located by two tapered roller bearings. Installation of the differential and ring gear is accomplished through a round opening in the side of the transmission housing, which is closed off by side plates after assembly.

The output shaft and ring gear are matched, and during assembly these must be fitted together very carefully. This is done at the differential by means of shims, which set the preload of the two tapered roller bearings at the differential, and, when selectively installed on the left and right side, locate the ring gear accordingly and set the backlash between the ring and pinion.

The output shaft is marked by the manufacturer (Hurth in Munich or Getrag in Ludwigsburg) to permit approximate setup during assembly. Precise measurement of the installed dimension between the face of the output shaft and the axis of the ring gear determines the final adjustment. This is achieved by installing paper shims between the transmission housing and intermediate plate, to an installed tolerance of +/- 0.05 mm (0.002 in.).

All forward gears are equipped with Porsche's own synchromesh system, which offered distinct advantages over competitors' systems (ZF, Borg-Warner, etc.) until well into the 1980s. Even during very quick shifts, the synchros are unbeatable. Shift forces, especially in the case of a quick, sporty driving style, are considerably lower. Given correct clutch actuation, their service life is comparable to that of the entire vehicle. This was not the case for other manufacturers of the time.

Porsche never deviated from the floor-mounted shift lever. The shift train runs from the driver-actuated shift lever, through a shift linkage, back to the transmission. The shift rod extends through the front transmission housing. The shift linkage is connected to the rod by a coupling in the central tunnel, which reduces vibration and noise transmission

through the shift mechanism. The shift rod incorporates a linkage which distributes shift action to three shift selectors:

Five-speed transmission
- shift selector for reverse and 1st gear
- shift selector for 2nd and 3rd gear
- shift selector for 4th and 5th gear
This results in the following shift pattern: reverse is left forward, 1st is left and back. Second and 4th are forward, 3rd and 5th are back.

Four-speed transmission
- shift selector for reverse only
- shift selector for 1st and 2nd gear
- shift selector for 3rd and 4th gear
Reverse is left forward, first is in the middle and forward. Third and fourth gear are in the rightmost gate (conventional H-pattern).

The shift pattern
for the five-speed has two advantages:
- for rocking (for traction, as in snow), first and reverse gears are located in the same plane
- the common shift from 4th to 5th or 5th to 4th takes place in only one shift plane
Disadvantages: shifting between 1st and 2nd involves a jog; if the shift is not performed cleanly, reverse gear may be touched briefly.

The four-speed shift pattern is a conventional H pattern, in which reverse lies at the left and forward, and 1st gear is forward, in the central plane.

The Type 915 transmission, from 1972 to the end of the 1986 model year

The 915 family of transmissions represents a further development of the Type 901 transmission. The high torque of the 2.4 liter engines required reinforcement of the entire transmission. The chief differences compared to earlier transmissions are:

- larger spacing between the input and output shafts
- reinforced gears for all speeds
- reinforced and improved Porsche synchromesh
- greatly improved bearings for transmission shafts

- no intermediate plate; instead, output shaft axial bearings and output shaft adjustment directly behind pinion gear
- new clutch operation, with pull-actuated clutch release bearing
- different shift pattern: 5th and reverse gear in same plane
- possibility of installation of transmission oil pump to supply oil to highly-stressed components

The Type 915 transmission was well suited to power increases up to 1986. The new generation of radial and axial bearings for both transmission shafts is especially noteworthy.

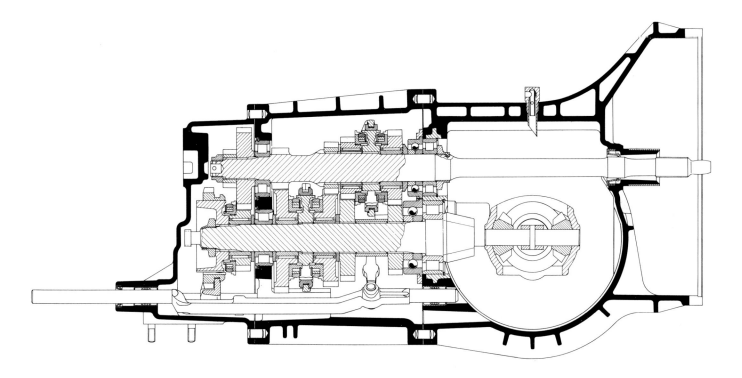

The combination of roller bearings and four-point ball bearings at the transmission housing parting line permits a much more precise adjustment of the ring and pinion gear, using thin steel shims, and ensures that the transmission will operate under all temperature conditions without affecting the ring and pinion wear pattern due to thermal expansion.

The shift pattern was changed at the request of many Porsche drivers. As in the 901 transmission, the shift rod includes an internal linkage, which distributes shift action to three shift selectors.

This results in the following shift pattern:

Five-speed transmission
- shift selector for 1st and 2nd gear
- shift selector for 3rd and 4th gear
- shift selector for 5th and reverse gear
The first four gears are in a normal H pattern, 5th

103

 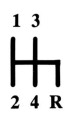

gear is right forward, reverse is right and back.

Four-speed transmission
- shift selector for 1st and 2nd gear
- shift selector for 3rd and 4th gear
- shift selector for reverse gear only
The four forward gears are in a conventional H pattern, while reverse is in an unconventional location, right and back.

The shift pattern of the five-speed transmission has one advantage:
- the 1 - 2 and 2 -1 shifts, often encountered in city traffic and motor sports, are in a single plane.
Disadvantages: shifts between 4th and 5th involve a jog. This is a burden on inexperienced drivers, as these shifts take place at high speeds.

When rocking (for traction), going from 1st to reverse involves traversing the entire shift pattern.

A mechanical lockout prevents accidentally going from 4th or 5th to reverse.

The four-speed shift pattern consists of a conventional H pattern, in which reverse gear is in an unconventional location.

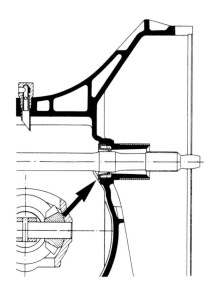

Important changes during production:

At the beginning of production, the seal ring for the input shaft was installed from the inside of the transmission (arrow). As of 1973, it is mounted directly in the throwout bearing guide sleeve and can be removed from outside, without special tools.

As of the 1976 model year, the guide sleeve is removable, making seal replacement even easier.

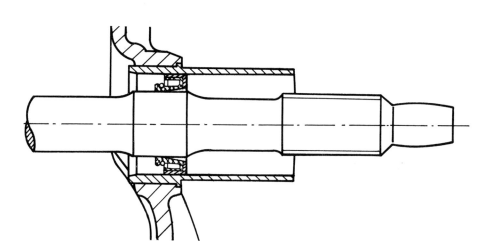

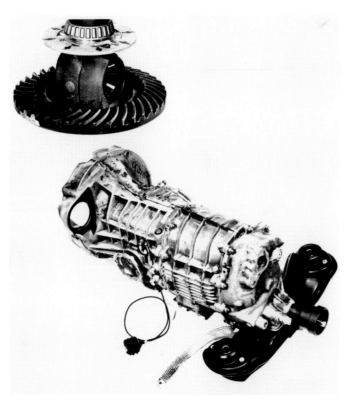

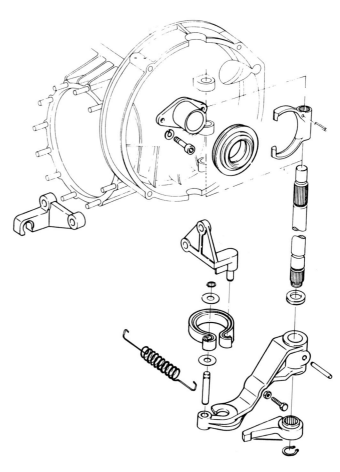

Electronic speedometers were installed beginning with the 1976 model year. This eliminates the mechanical drive from the output shaft through intermediate gears to a speedometer cable in the center tunnel. Instead, a light alloy disc containing eight tiny magnets is attached to the differential carrier. A reed switch mounted to the outside of the transmission housing is activated by the rotating magnets. This gives eight square-wave pulses per rotation of the differential.

As of the 1977 model year, clutch release mechanisms incorporating assist springs were installed, to reduce clutch pedal effort.

For the 1984 model year, coinciding with the introduction of the 3.2 liter Carrera engines, the Type 915 transmissions were fitted with a road speed dependent transmission oil pump and a finned tubular oil cooler mounted next to the transmission. This cooling system reduces the temperature of transmission internal parts by about 20° C. (36° F.)

105

The G 50 transmission family, as of the 1987 model year

The five-speed G 50 transmission represents a completely new design. It shares almost no features with the long-serving Type 915 transmission. Important new features include:
- altered shift pattern. Reverse is now left forward (four-plane shift pattern)
- new, reinforced housing components
- larger spacing between input and output shafts
- reinforced hypoid final drive, with 16 mm offset
- reinforced shafts and roller bearings
- reinforced gear sets, gear ratios altered
- shift rods mounted in roller bearings instead of sliding bearings

- full-cone synchromesh (parts shared with 928)
- synchromesh for reverse gear
- new sensor system for electronic speedometer
- shift gate inside transmission
- switch to multi-grade SAE 75 W 90 GL5 transmission oil

Shift actuation of the G 50 transmission
The shift lever, shift linkage and shift actuation inside the transmission are completely new.

The shift pattern and internal shift rod attachment "five-speed" were taken from that of the Porsche 959 (initially without its sixth gear). A shift gate inside the transmission ensures precise shifts and facilitates finding the gears.

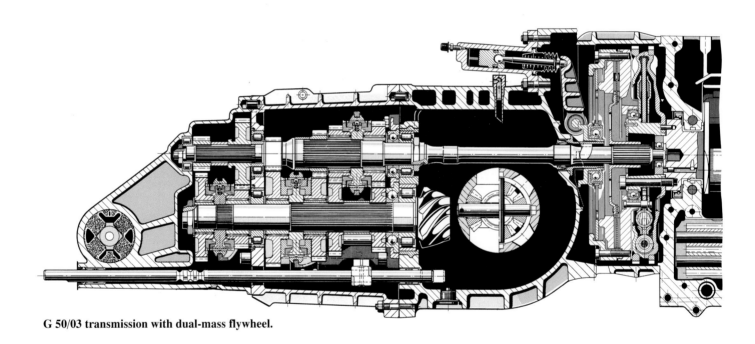

G 50/03 transmission with dual-mass flywheel.

Reverse gear is now located "left forward" in its own shift plane; the first four gears are in an H pattern, and 5th gear is also in its own plane, "right forward."

The six-speed G 50/21 transmission for the new Carrera generation (Type 993) as of the 1994 model year

A thin-wall pressure-cast light-alloy transmission housing and lightweight design of the transmission components result in the same overall weight as the previous five-speed transmission.

The bell housing incorporates new ventilation ducts to cool the pressure plate, which is fitted with an impeller for cooling air flow.

The transmission has six forward gears, which are matched to the vehicle's improved performance. Dual-cone synchronizers for 1st and 2nd gear result in noticeably lower shift effort.

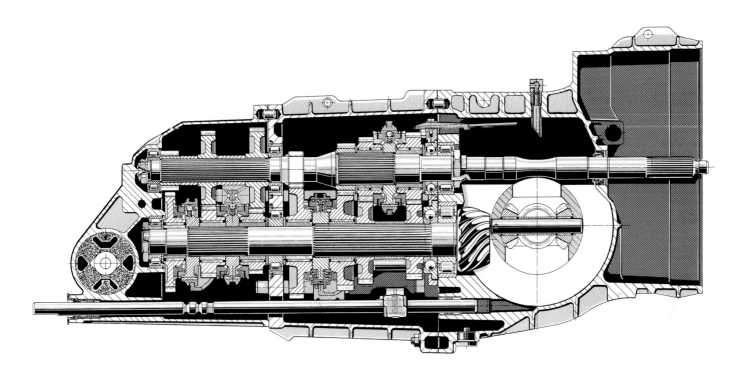

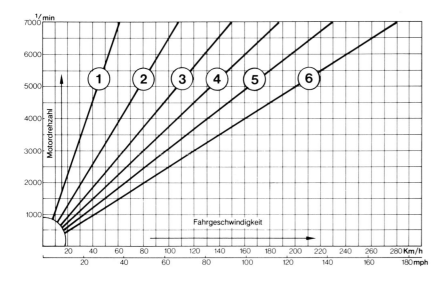

The transmission has six forward speeds, matched to the improved vehicle performance.

The shift pattern was adopted from the Porsche 959. Sixth gear is located at the right rear, in the same plane as 5th gear.

The G 64 transmission family, for all-wheel-drive models as of 1989

Overview:

The transmission system of the 911 Carrera 4 consists of a fully synchronized five-speed transmission (1) with integral rear differential (2) as well as transfer case (3) for its full-time all-wheel drive system.

The connection to the front differential (4) is accomplished by a proven transaxle system consisting of a rigid torque tube (5) containing the driveshaft (6).

The external shift mechanism (7) with its coupling rod (7a) is attached to the torque tube (5).

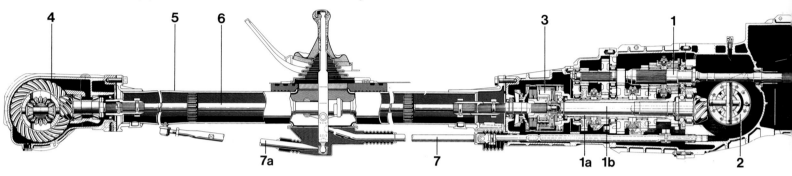

1 Five-speed manual transmission Input shaft	2 Rear differential
1b Pinion shaft	3 Transfer case
	4 Front differential

5 Central tube (torque tube)	7 External shift mechanism
6 Driveshaft	7a Coupling rod

Power flow

The G 50 and G 50/50 transmissions represent a new transmission family for the six-cylinder 911 model line. Provisionally, the G 64 unit of the Carrera 4 represents the ultimate development of the model line.

This new transmission family enables largely identical parts to be used for all six-cylinder models.

The extension to all-wheel drive is accomplished by means of a transfer case (3) in the front transmission housing. Instead of a normally solid output shaft, drive to front wheels is facilitated by a hollow

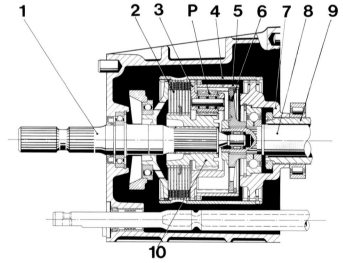

The heart of the all-wheel drive system: the transfer case. Its main task is to distribute the engine torque between the front and rear axles, with a nominal 31/69 torque split. This 31/69 ratio is achieved by the planetary gearset (P), whose gear diameters (planetary gear 31, sun gear 69) are selected accordingly.

In the event of wheelspin at the front or rear axle, this mechanical relationship can be varied continuously, without discrete steps, in a fraction of a second from 0/100 to 100/0, by locking the center clutch (2).

1 Drive shaft to front axle
2 Center clutch plates
3 Planetary gear carrier
4 Coupling sleeve
5 Planetary ring gear set
6 Drive plate
7 Bearing carrier
8 Pinion shaft to rear axle
9 Five-speed transmission output shaft
10 Sun gear
P Planetary gears

108

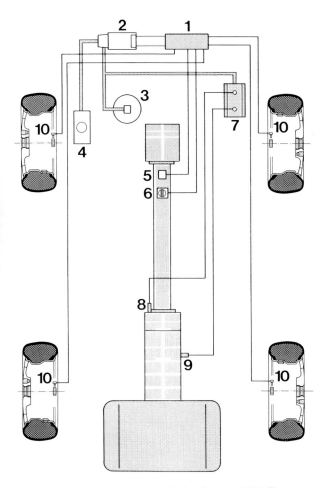

Porsche Dynamic All-Wheel Drive System (PDAS)

1 ABS and locking differential control unit
2 Pressure pump with pressure switch
3 Pressure reservoir
4 Supply tank
5 Lateral acceleration sensor
6 Differential switch
7 Valve body
8 Center differential slave cylinder
9 Rear differential slave cylinder
10 Wheel rpm sensor

shaft (1a) containing bearings and a coaxial pinion shaft (1b). The transfer case is driven by the hollow shaft. The transfer case (3) distributes drive torque to the pinion shaft (1b) driving the rear axle (2) and to the central driveshaft (6) driving the front differential (4).

The mechanical design of the transfer case results in the Carrera 4's basic 31 percent front/69 percent rear torque split. This torque distribution, determined after extensive driving tests, ensures that the Carrera 4 retains the handling characteristics of a rear-drive car, making it very similar to the rear-wheel-drive 911.

The transfer case has a limited slip function which alters the distribution of drive torque between the front and rear axles. At the rear, an electronically controlled limited slip differential ensures maximum traction for both rear wheels. Both limited slip differentials are managed by an electronic control system which obtains traction information for all four wheels via the anti-lock brake system (ABS) rpm sensors. Additional inputs are provided by a lateral acceleration sensor and a driver-controlled lockup switch which locks both differentials below about 30 km/h (20 mph) for better startup traction under difficult conditions.

Under normal driving conditions, both differentials are open, resulting in the nominal 31/69 front/rear torque split. The rear differential is applied in stages to improve vehicle dynamics during weight transfer in cornering. The limited slip center differential stabilizes the vehicle while accelerating out of corners.

The anti-lock braking system remains fully operational in all driving situations.

The 930 transmission family from 1975 to the end of the 1988 model year

To cope with the increased performance of the 911 Turbo, a new transmission had to be developed. Because of the shorter space between the transverse chassis tube and the rear axle drive flanges, the transmission had to be shortened, which was only possible by deleting fifth gear. In all other respects, the transmission was identical to that of the normally aspirated engines.

Following are the important changes and new features compared to the Type 915 transmission:

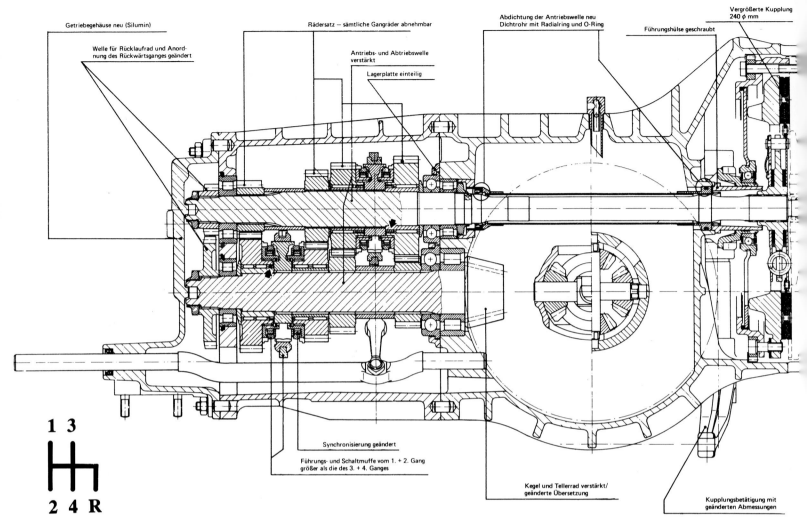

Getriebegehäuse neu (Silumin)

Welle für Rücklaufrad und Anordnung des Rückwärtsganges geändert

Rädersatz – sämtliche Gangräder abnehmbar

Antriebs- und Abtriebswelle verstärkt

Lagerplatte einteilig

Abdichtung der Antriebswelle neu Dichtrohr mit Radialring und O-Ring

Führungshülse geschraubt

Vergrößerte Kupplung 240 ⌀ mm

Synchronisierung geändert

Führungs- und Schaltmuffe vom 1. + 2. Gang größer als die des 3. + 4. Ganges

Kegel und Tellerrad verstärkt/geänderte Übersetzung

Kupplungsbetätigung mit geänderten Abmessungen

1 3
2 4 R

The gears are reinforced. All gears are a slide fit on their shafts, and special gear rations can be quickly installed for motor sports applications.

For this transmission, the Porsche synchromesh has been redesigned. Particular attention was given to reducing rpm sensitivity, so that smooth shifts could be carried out even with high input rpm.

The sealing of the input shaft is of interest. The seal is located in a long sleeve, and seals the input shaft near its main bearing. Input shaft vibrations, which could occur under high loads, can no longer result in leakage past the seal.

A clutch-type limited slip differential, made by ZF, is available as an option. Its slip factor is preset at about 40 percent. For motor sports applications, other factors can be achieved by changing the clutch packs.

Important changes during production:
Gear ratios were changed for the 1978 model year (911 Turbo 3.3)

A modified clutch was installed, with a rubber hub in the clutch disc developed by Porsche. This system permits up to 30 degrees of twist under load or engine braking.

Due to this torsional vibration damper, the transmission housing had to be extended by 40 mm.

The engine was moved back by the same amount.

The G 50/50 series transmission from 1989 to the end of the 1994 model year

Beginning with the 1989 model year, the 911 Turbo was also given a stronger five-speed transmission with synchromesh on reverse gear.

The installation of the five-speed transmission was made possible by extensive changes to the floorpan. The transverse tube is split in the area occupied by the nose of the transmission.

The G 50/50 transmission is functionally identical to the G 50 transmission, which had been installed in the normally-aspirated 911 Carrera since 1987.

To accommodate the higher performance of the 911 Turbo, several components had to be reinforced:
- light alloy transmission housing, with integral cast iron girdle in the area of the roller bearings
- hypoid final drive (Klingenberg type), ring gear diameter 215 mm
- larger, stronger side plates
- reinforced bearing carrier plate
- needle bearings for differential pinion gears

The shifter and shift pattern are identical to those of the G 50 transmission.

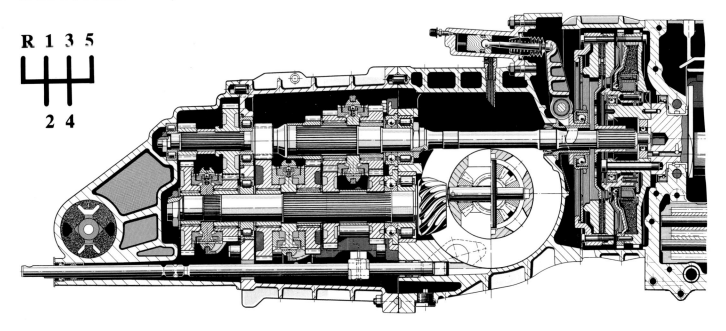

R 1 3 5

2 4

Clutch and torsion damper

Until the introduction of the dual-mass flywheel in the Carrera 2 and 4, clutches were supplied solely by Fichtel & Sachs of Schweinfurt. The clutch diameter was initially 215 mm, later 225 mm (as of the 1971 model year) and, beginning with the production of the 911 Turbo as a 1975 model, 240 mm.

The clutch discs supplied to Porsche were always special versions, particularly in their use of dampers to reduce annoying transmission noises at low rpm.

In addition to the steel spring torsion dampers used initially, rubber dampers were soon put in service.

An appreciable reduction of driveline noise was not achieved until 1990, with the introduction of the dual-mass flywheel developed in cooperation with Freudenberg. This reduces the critical resonant speed of the transmission input shaft below 500 rpm, a speed which is never encountered in service.

Angular displacement of as much as 30 degrees in either direction between the primary mass (rigidly

Cutaway of dual-mass flywheel
 1 Primary flywheel
 2 Ring gear for timing marks
 3 Starter ring gear
 4 Cover plate
 5 Rubber damper
 6 Damper segments
 7 Secondary flywheel
 8 Clutch disc
 9 Ball bearing (sealed, permanently lubricated)
10 Retaining ring
11 Plug
12 Bolt
13 Pressure plate housing
14 Pressure plate
15 Clutch slave cylinder
16 Throwout fork
17 Throwout bearing
18 Transmission input shaft
19 Crankshaft

● The primary flywheel (1) and the cover plate (4) are rigidly connected to the crankshaft.

○ The rigid clutch disc (8) is splined to the transmission input shaft (18).

● The secondary flywheel consists of the pressure plate housing (13), the pressure plate (14) and the secondary flywheel (7).

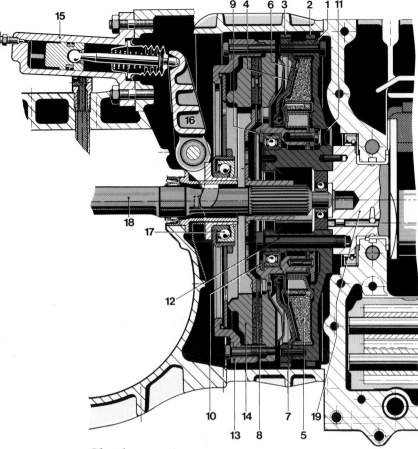

bolted to the flywheel) and the secondary mass are possible. The vibration damper consists of a ring-shaped rubber damper, assisted by a silicone-filled damper.

The secondary mass, which is locked to the input shaft (18) by the clutch disc (8) when the clutch is engaged, shifts the resonant frequency of the driveline to very low rpm and thereby ensures a quiet transmission, especially at low operating rpm.

As of the 1991 model year, the 911 Turbo is also fitted with a dual-mass flywheel developed in cooperation with the firm LUK. The LUK system differs from the Freudenberg system in its use of steel springs instead of rubber torsion dampers.

The Sportomatic Types 905 and 925 transmission families, from 1968 to the end of the 1990 model year

Clutch actuation

For the 901 and 915 transmission families, the clutch is actuated mechanically by means of a cable. For the Type 901 transmission, a conventional throwout bearing was used, which presses against the clutch spring diaphragm when the clutch is disengaged.

For the Type 915 and 930 transmissions, as well as the following G 50 generation, the throwout bearings are pull-actuated and constantly rotating. This design requires less space.

Beginning with the G 50 (1987 model year) the clutch is actuated hydraulically via master and slave cylinders.

At Porsche, the idea of producing a sports car with an automatic or at least a semi-automatic transmission had already reached maturity in the late

1950s. During the production run of the 356 B (1961 - 1962) several experimental vehicles were fitted with an interesting semi-automatic gearbox. In cooperation with the Swabian turbine and transmission manufacturer J.M. Voith, based in Heidenheim, a transmission suitable for sports car use was developed, based on a successful mass-transit bus transmission known as the "Diwabus." (Diwa was derived from 'Differential-Drehmomentwandler,' differential torque converter). The Diwabus had two conventional forward gears with synchromesh and one reverse gear.

Added power flow variations were provided by adding a planetary gear set behind the torque converter to give four forward gear ratios. After reaching the top of second gear, the high speed range (giving 3rd and 4th gears) had to be engaged manually. The technical complexity of this system did not justify putting it into production.

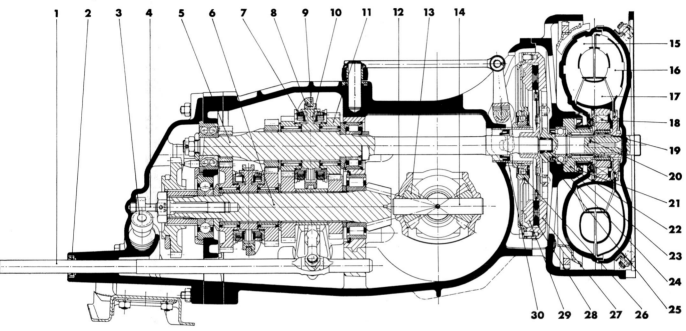

1 Shift rod
2 Seal ring
3 Speedometer cable connection
4 Gear shaft for speedometer drive
5 Input shaft
6 Output shaft
7 Porsche synchro ring
8 Shift collar
9 Shift fork
10 Guide sleeve
11 Gear 1 (free) for 4th gear
12 Differential housing
13 Differential pinion
14 Differential gear shaft
15 Torque converter impeller
16 Torque converter turbine
17 Torque converter reactor
18 Free wheeling mechanism for reactor
19 Turbine shaft sleeve
20 Nozzle in turbine shaft
21 Seal ring
22 Free wheel support
23 Needle bearing for input shaft
24 Seal ring
25 Seal ring
26 Clutch throwout bearing
27 Clutch carrier
28 Clutch disc
29 Pressure plate
30 Seal ring

Sportomatic

The second road to a semi-automatic transmission led to Fichtel & Sachs in Schweinfurt. F&S had developed a drive system consisting of a mass-produced torque converter and an additional friction clutch (WSK-type); the F&S system was nearly production-ready. With the simple addition of a four-speed synchromesh transmission, the semi-automatic Sportomatic was born.

In truth, it wasn't that simple; initially, the torque converter and mechanical clutch took up too much of the limited space at the back of the 911. The problem was solved by the addition of a pull-type throwout bearing. This space-saving design, first used on the Sportomatic, would be used for all later Porsche manual transmissions.

Providing working fluid to the hydraulic torque converter was easy: one of the camshafts is coupled to a small ZF-Eaton supply pump, which feeds oil from the engine oil tank to the torque converter and back. To eliminate the possibility of engine damage due to lack of oil caused by a leak in the torque converter oil circuit, the suction side for the torque converter oil supply was located at a certain level in the oil tank. If the oil level dropped too low, the torque converter would no longer be supplied with oil and the car would stop, but without incurring engine damage.

The manual clutch, necessary to disconnect the transmission from the crankshaft during shifts, is actuated by a vacuum servo. The required vacuum is provided by engine manifold vacuum and a vacuum reservoir.

When the driver moves the shift lever, an electrical contact activates a vacuum switch which connects the vacuum servo to manifold vacuum. A lever system engages the throwout bearing, and in a fraction of a second the clutch is disengaged.

If the shift lever is released at idle rpm, the clutch engages gradually, with a specific time delay. If, however, the shifter is released and the throttle opened immediately, the clutch engages as quickly as possible. Under acceleration, shift times of less than half a second are achievable.

The four-speed transmission is similar to the Type 901. Synchromesh parts, shift collars and shaft bearings are identical.

The first generation Sportomatic transmission (Type 905) was used until the introduction of the higher-torque 2.7 liter engines. This stronger version of the Sportomatic, the Type 925, was matched to the more powerful engines and higher vehicle performance and introduced in 1973.

New, tougher drive-by noise standards for several European countries and the U.S. made it necessary to "amputate" one forward gear beginning with the 1975 model year. The resulting decrease in acceleration performance allowed the car to pass its certification tests.

Gear selection and shifting to "Park" is accomplished by means of the floor-mounted shifter. This lever activates the vacuum servo for the mechanical clutch through a solenoid valve.

Shift patterns for the four-speed and three-speed Sportomatics:

P Park	**D** Drive
L Low	**D3** Drive 3
R Reverse	**D4** Drive 4

The Sportomatic was offered until the end of the 1980 model year. It was stricken from the lineup, without replacement, until the fully automatic Tiptronic of the 911 Carrera 2 was introduced in 1990.

From the Porsche Dual Clutch (PDK) transmission to the Tiptronic A 50

The PDK Porsche Dual Clutch transmission

In the early 1970s, Porsche pursued a line of investigation to find a way to shift gears automatically, that is without interruption of the engine power flow, but without the unavoidable inefficiencies of a hydraulic torque converter. After initial feasibility tests using two mechanical dry-plate clutches and a conventional synchromesh gearbox, a prototype transmission for racing applications was ready for installation. After driving off normally, this is capable of shifting through the gears without interruption of the power flow. This is possible by means of two coaxial transmission input shafts, each connected to the engine by means of its own clutch.

One input shaft is responsible for gears 1, 3 and 5;

the other for 2, 4 and 6. The gears are preselected automatically. For example, when accelerating in first gear, the second gear is already selected but not engaged to the engine. At the shift point, the first clutch disengages, while the second engages, completing the 1-2 shift. These shifts can occur automatically or by means of a driver-actuated pushbutton. Because the interruption of power during acceleration has been eliminated (each shift can take about one half second in a conventional transmission), such a six-speed automatic transmission can result in an advantage of as much as three seconds in accelerating from a standstill to top speed.

The PDK transmission was installed in several Porsche Type 962 Group C race cars and entered in German national motorsports events as well as world sports car championship races. Hans Joachim Stuck achieved notable successes with the PDK, particularly with its final variation, which had two buttons on the steering wheel to initiate up- and downshifts.

Due to its limited numbers, manufacturing costs of the PDK system for Porsche production sports cars would have been prohibitive.

The Tiptronic system

Cost considerations forced Porsche to seek an automatic transmission which would be suitable for the special circumstances of a rear-engined sports car, specifically the 911. Such a device was found at the Zahnradfabrik Friedrichshafen (ZF). The ZF 4HP22HL is the result of close cooperation between both companies, and is manufactured at ZF's Saarbrücken plant.

The Tiptronic consists of a conventional four-speed automatic transmission with two sets of planetary gears and a lockup torque converter. In contrast to all other cars with automatic transmissions, the Carrera 2 Tiptronic has two shift lever planes. The left plane selects conventional automatic up- and downshifts, according to the shift lever position in P, R, N, D, 3, 2, and 1, exactly like a fully-automatic transmission.

If the shift lever is moved rightward from the D position into the second shift plane, tipping the lever forward or back results in lightning-quick shifts; tipping forward to shift up, back to shift down.

1 **ATF pump (Automatic Transmission Fluid)**
2 **Lockup clutch**
3 **Torque converter reactor**
4 **Torque converter turbine**
5 **Torque converter impeller**
6 **Torque converter housing**
7 **Ring gear, lapped gear faces**
8 **Right drive flange**
9 **Differential**
10 **Output shaft**
11 **Tapered roller bearing unit**
12 **Plastic protective sleeve**
13 **Side shaft**
14 **Tapered roller bearing unit**
15 **Helical drive gear**
16 **Helical idler gear**
17 **Helical driven gear**
18 **Parking pawl wheel**
19 **Road speed sensor**
20 **Disc clutch brake F**
21 **Clutch pack E**
22 **Planetary gear set**
23 **Simpson planetary gear set**
24 **Disc clutch brake D**
25 **Disc clutch brake C1**
26 **Disc clutch brake C2**
27 **Clutch pack B**
28 **Clutch pack A**
29 **Left drive flange**

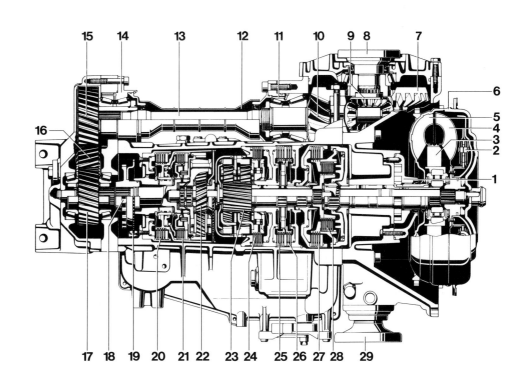

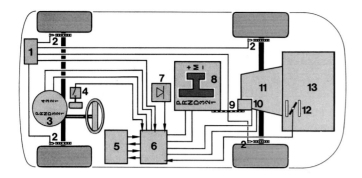

1 ABS control unit
2 ABS wheel sensors
3 Speedometer
4 Kickdown switch
5 DME control unit
6 Tiptronic control unit
7 Lateral acceleration sensor
8 Gear selector system, two shift planes
9 Actuating cable
10 Position switch
11 A 50 automatic transmission
12 Throttle butterfly with potentiometer
13 Engine M 64

The Porsche Tiptronic automatic shift strategy

The Tiptronic electronic control unit (6) serves as the command and information center for the entire system. Control of the transmission, in the form of commands to shift or hold in gear, result from evaluation of a multitude of sensory inputs which are compared to several performance profiles and their respective shift maps.

Information processing in the Tiptronic control unit

- Potentiometer resistance (throttle position)
- Rate of resistance change in potentiometer (speed of throttle actuation)
- Frequency signal from DME (engine rpm)
- Pulse frequency from transmission output shaft inductive sensor (road speed)
- Lateral acceleration signal (sensor in car's center console)
- Rate of inductive sensor pulse frequency change (vehicle acceleration or braking)

These parameters are read several times per second and processed by the control unit.

Comparison of these parameters with values stored in memory determines which of five shift maps will be used by the system.

Short-term driver influences: In addition to the five shift maps which can be selected by the Tiptronic control system according to driving style, the driver may exert a short-term influence on the system:

- Suppression of upshifts under engine braking prior to a corner
- Locking in gear through corners
- Actively shifting to the highest-performance shift map (SK5)
- Upshifts during engine braking on slippery (icy) surfaces
- Kick-down function without full throttle by means of rapid throttle pedal movement

Limp-home mode: In the event of an electrical or electronic fault, the control system deactivates itself and switches to a mechanical-hydraulic limp-home program. The car may be driven without difficulty in this mode (third gear). A red warning light in the clock indicates that the limp-home mode is active.

Tiptronic S

For the 1995 model year, Porsche introduced the Tiptronic S variation of the Tiptronic transmission. Taking a cue from current Formula One practice, which in turn had been inspired by Porsche's own PDK system, the Tiptronic S incorporates two rocker switches in the steering wheel for quick shifts in a manual mode. When the Tiptronic is in its manual mode (lever in right shift gate), activating the rocker switches has the same effect as tipping the shift lever. The Tiptronic S allows the driver to keep both hands on the wheel and his eyes on the road and instruments.

Suspension development
Genius in the details

The first developments which would eventually lead to the 911 suspension were undertaken to improve the handling of the 356. "With the 356, we were restricted by the welded-in front suspension and the VW-derived rear suspension," recalls Helmuth Bott, who served as acting chief of the road test department in the 1950s. "From today's perspective, these designs offered few development opportunities. That makes our achievements with this concept all the more remarkable," adds the Swabian engineer, speaking from retirement in Buttenhausen, near Münsingen. Indeed, the suspension of the 356 was greatly improved during its sixteen year production run. In particular, the last version used in the Type 356 C, with front stabilizer bar and rear compensating spring, was still considered a modern design in the early 1960s, and its concept was validated by its many motor sports successes.

In the 1950s, Porsche test cars still had names. Back then, suspension tests were first carried out on "Ferdinand." This early 356, internally labeled as Test Car Number 1, was the first Porsche to carry a stabilizer bar, over forty years ago. In 1954, this car, named for the firm's founder, Professor Ferdinand Porsche, was also the first to have a bolted-in front suspension. Initially, this permitted setting various caster angles; later, with ball joints instead of king-pins, camber and cornering angle differential (the angular difference between the front wheels when the steering wheel is turned) could be set. For camber, values between -2 to +4 degrees could be set. Stabilizer bars in particular resulted in a noticeable improvement in vehicle dynamics. "I did my journeyman work on the 356 A. Thanks to numerous changes to suspension, steering, wheels and tires, it had substantially better handling characteristics than its predecessors," recalls Bott.

Meanwhile, development chief Helmut Rombold had acquired more vehicles for his motor pool, including Test Car Number 35, known as "Gottlieb." Based on a crashed 356, it was fitted with a Mercedes-Benz front subframe and suspension from the Mercedes 180, with parallel transverse arms. Even the subframe and self-centering recirculating ball steering were taken from an Untertürkheim product. Helmuth Bott remembers this important test bed: "Gottlieb looked like a really cobbled up job, it wasn't even painted." Later, it was fitted with a modified rear suspension.

The actual predecessor to the 911 suspension was born on the drawing board of Wolfgang Eyb, who would later serve as project leader for the 928. In this front suspension, each wheel was located by a

Personal photo dated May, 1963: Ekkehard Keifer, Heinz Bäuerle, Theo Häuser, Martin Kopp, Kurt Knoerzer, and Günther Steckkönig (left to right).

trailing link and sprung by a transverse torsion bar. A large-capacity telescoping shock absorber on each side completed the suspension. As in the case of "Gottlieb," the front suspension of this car was fitted with ball joints, which permitted greater turning lock. Because the test car with this suspension had a higher front ride height than the production car, it was nicknamed "The Stork."

"Combined with the rear swing axles, the Stork was not an especially good driver. Still, it had longer suspension travel and therefore was quite comfortable. But with an empty tank and empty trunk, it had too much front end lift and poor straight-line stability," says Helmuth Bott, recalling the first long-distance test drive to Le Mans with customer service director Hans Klauser. However, the development engineers felt that the front suspension showed great promise. In their extensive test drives, Bott and race driver Richard von Frankenberg found that fitting a stabilizer bar improved the car's handling.

Another prototype had a so-called Watt axle, with both upper and lower links, "fitted so that one pickup point was ahead of, and the other behind the axle," explains Bott. The advantage of the Watt linkage is that the toe-in does not change during suspension travel.

The combination of different front and rear sus-

pensions, and careful detail engineering, resulted in valuable lessons and ideas for new 356 suspension systems. Bott emphasizes that "Without years of testing in 356 models, we would never have been able to realize our expectations for the 911 in such a short time. At the time, these valuable lessons could best be learned by experiment," concludes Bott, who joined Porsche in 1952.

It was not until the company's chief executive, Ferry Porsche, officially gave the go-ahead to design a new Porsche model in 1959 that the team under the direction of Leopold Schmid, chief designer for engines and suspensions, and test director Helmut Rombold, began development of completely new suspensions in earnest. Rombold's second in command, Bott, front suspension and steering specialist Rudolf Hofmann, and rear suspension specialist Erich Stotz formed a capable team. Yet in a memo dated January 11, 1961, Bott records that a new design could not be realized before July 1963. On the other hand, a new suspension with McPherson struts, giving a larger trunk, was desired by all concerned. As it had also been realized that the first six-cylinder engines would arrive no earlier than mid-1964, Ferry Porsche and Hans Tomala, responsible for all engineering, insisted on a modern suspension. Besides the new body and engine, they regarded this as the most important innovation incorporated in the T 8.

118

The new Porsche was to be designed as a Grand Touring car, and have greater ride comfort than its predecessor. For this reason, the relatively direct connection between the chassis and suspension found on the 356 (front suspension with trailing arms and transverse torsion bars) was out of the question. This design had no adjustment capability and took up too much space at the front of the car, space which could be used for a larger trunk. A planned subframe for the new suspension provided better noise isolation, but was rejected because of its added weight and space requirements. Finally, a McPherson suspension was designed, but with torsion bars replacing the usual space-robbing coil springs of the classic McPherson design. The wheels were connected to the chassis by a lower transverse link and the shock absorber strut, which was braced against the wheel well. The longitudinal torsion bars were carried in a subframe connected to the chassis by four elastic mounts.

Tests drove home the realization that the space-saving McPherson design would do quite nicely without a separate subframe. Drawings for a front suspension design without the benefit of a subframe were prepared in time for a T 8 meeting on January 9, 1963. The solution seemed so plausible that the necessary components were ordered immediately. To assist in springing, each double-acting hydraulic strut was fitted with a progressive rubber stop. Cornering behavior was improved by a transverse stabilizer bar connecting the front wheels, actuated by crank arms and links. The front suspension was maintenance-free, with permanently lubricated joints.

But it would be a long road before this design reached maturity. First, suitable suppliers would have to be found. To this end, Helmuth Bott and his colleagues conducted their test drives with struts from Koni and Boge. Boge could call upon four years of McPherson strut experience, thanks to cooperation with Ford and BMW.

The rear suspension provided headaches of its own. Prototype Number 1 ran up its test miles with a 356 B rear suspension, i.e., swing axles with transverse torsion bars and camber compensator spring. At some point, the complex suspension of the Type

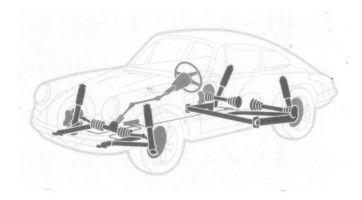

Phantom drawing of the 911 suspension, showing the safety steering column.

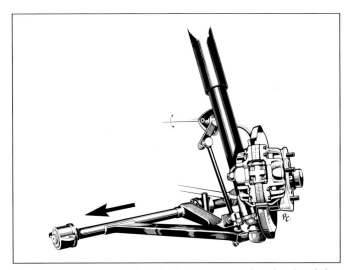

McPherson suspension: the wheels are connected to the chassis by lower transverse arms and shock absorber struts.

718 Spyder of 1959 was considered (independent suspension and coil springs). But as with the front suspension, Ferry Porsche elected to go with a new design, albeit relatively late in the 911 development process.

In a memo dated August 10, 1962, addressed to design chief Franz-Xaver Reimspiess, a patent evaluation conducted by Emil Soukup describes the design as follows: "As may be seen from the accompanying sketch X 229, the rear wheels of the vehicle are driven by double-jointed driveshafts with a sliding joint, and are located by A-arms, which, in conjunction with a flat spring blade standing on edge,

119

forms a crank arm carrying the wheel bearing. The A-arm is connected to a torsion bar. The diagonal member of the A-arm rotates in a rubber bushing and is connected to a torsional stabilizer bar."

So the rear wheels were suspended and located by trailing arms as on the 356, supported by transverse torsion bars. With a diameter of 23 mm, these had the same diameter as those of the 356 Carrera and ensured that the desired camber of slightly more than one degree did not vary greatly over the entire range of suspension movement, thereby increasing the available tire cornering force. The 911 was given independent suspension at the rear as well, with one added advantage: because the telescoping shock absorbers were mounted in this way behind the wheel, they had a long travel. Tests with the new rear suspension were universally positive. In a test report dated December 13, 1963, test driver Kurt Knoerzer recorded that "With the current state of suspension development, no rear stabilizer bar is required for the Type 901. No further tests of rear stabilizers are planned before production of the T 8 begins."

By contrast, the front suspension still posed problems for the development engineers. The primary reason was technical director Hans Tomala's opinion that while the prototypes were adjustable, the bolted-in suspension of the production cars would not require any adjustability. At the time, he remarked to his co-workers that "The production tolerances of the body are very tight, and if the holes for mounting the upper ends of the struts are drilled after the body has been welded together, they can be located in such a manner that the suspension settings are exactly right." By March of 1963, Tomala had designer Hans Hönick calculate the allowable assembly tolerances. In addition, it was believed that if the body assembly tolerances should be larger than expected, the desired camber of 0° 15' could be achieved by adjusting the ball joint at the transverse arm. On November 8, 1963, the test department asked that the caster be increased from 7° to 8° 30' and the camber from 0° to -30'. To achieve this, the upper mounting points for the struts had to be moved 4 mm back and 5 mm inward.

Despite these careful preparations, theory was not

borne out in practice. In October 1964, test driver Rolf Hannes conducted a series of examinations on the first twelve production cars and reached a devastating conclusion: the mean deviation of the left front camber was +8', with extreme values of 20' positive and negative. This required a transverse correction of about 3 mm at the upper mounting point.

The mean camber deviation on the right side was even more extreme: +34.5'. Extreme values were an astounding 50' positive and 15' negative. The upper mounting point would have to be moved 8.3 mm.

On the left side, caster angle was an average of 51' too small, on the right the mean was 49'. This required mounting point corrections of 12.5 and 17.5 mm.

After his first cross-country trip, Ferry Porsche, who drove one of the first pre-production 911s as his company car, criticized its unsatisfactory straight-line stability. He complained to the first suspension engineer he could find, who happened to be Helmuth Bott. He promised his boss that he would return a perfectly stable car within two days. Bott immediately installed adjustable suspension pickup points as had been used on prototypes. After another long test drive, Ferry Porsche was satisfied. "That's how we'll do it," he ordered. Meanwhile, thanks to their poor straight-line stability, the first 911s had already

Rolf Hannes: "The tolerances at the front suspension were too large."

The first 911s, without stabilizer bars, showed excessive lean in corners. At the limit of adhesion, the unloaded front tire provided no steering forces.

Test drives with the Type 912: Heinz Bäuerle, Hans Hermann, Rolf Hannes and Kurt Brose (left to right).

121

Due to their rearward weight distribution, the first 911s had a basic oversteering tendency, poor straight-line stability and high crosswind sensitivity.

earned the nickname "Blindschleiche" (slow worm or blind worm, actually a legless lizard).

Unfortunately production of the first examples of the so-called zero series, built between November 1964 and July 1967, had already begun. The front suspension settings of the first model year, until July 1965, were not adjustable. Because Porsche, from the beginning of the 1960s, was the first car maker to check suspension settings of every car at the end of the production line, the chassis mounting spar could be adjusted in the event of excessively large deviations from the target settings. Still, many customers were extremely unhappy with the handling characteristics of their cars. This was not due to the basic character of any rear-engined design, already familiar from the 356. Due to the larger proportion of vehicle weight over the rear axle, this principle pro-

vides a basic oversteering tendency, poor straight-line stability and high sensitivity to crosswinds, as the vehicle's center of pressure is far ahead of the center of gravity giving aerodynamic forces a longer lever arm.

The first item was relatively easy to solve. To make the first 911s controllable at the limit, they were deliberately set up with ample understeer. Installation of narrow 4 1/2" wheels and modest 165 HR-15 tires, taken directly from the 356, emphasized this understeering tendency. The narrow Dunlops naturally ran at high slip angles.

Because of the large manufacturing tolerances, straight-line stability remained unsatisfactory despite costly corrective measures. The first comprehensive test report, by Reinhard Seiffert in *auto motor und*

sport, 2/1965, twisted the knife in the wound. Among other problems, Seiffert listed the following:
- unsatisfactory directional stability in crosswinds and on uneven road surfaces;
- steering sensitive to road surface, and requires high steering effort;
- excessive engine noise;
- several body details still not satisfactory

Seiffert's article caused considerable consternation at Porsche. On January 20, 1965, P. Gockenbach of the sales support department sent a memo to several large distributors: "The 911 test report dated January 23, 1965 is unfavorable. This is not only our impression, but also that of our sales organization, as evidenced by numerous telephone conversations... We cannot allow the burden of a negative image of the Type 911 to be imposed upon our sales team... Please give us your support in this matter."

Only five days later, Helmuth Bott had prepared a report which addressed and explained each of the criticized points. It didn't end there; the chief test driver was assigned the task of doing something, anything to improve the behavior of the 911, and doing it quickly. As the root of the problem lay in the car's weight distribution, Bott first conducted skid pad tests in Weissach with sand bags in the trunk. Bott recalls that "There was a marginal improvement in handling." Then he installed cast lead weights in the ends of the bumpers, to place ballast farther forward. Suddenly, the car was a joy to drive again. When he removed the bumper weights and placed them in the trunk, the car's handling immediately deteriorated, indeed, it was worse than with the heavy sandbags.

Further important discoveries resulted from tests with a steering wheel marked to measure the wheel's angular deflection as a function of speed. Fitting the "lead horns," which have erroneously entered some history books as production items, resulted in an appreciably higher self-centering moment for the wood-rimmed wheel. When Bott mounted both weights at the center of the bumper, to move the weight still farther forward, handling characteristics once again deteriorated. The inescapable conclusion was that the handling problem was not only caused by the weight distribution, but was also sensitive to the car's polar moment of inertia. Helmuth Bott draws an analogy: "These laws of physics are even used by ice skaters, when they spread their arms to slow their rotation, or pull them in to turn faster."

Filling the bumpers with lead would have been very costly and would have resulted in unpleasant surprises in the event of disassembly. Furthermore, the weights were still not mounted at the extreme perimeter of the car. Bott had one of his mechanics, Theodor Heuser, bend tubes in the shape of the front bumper tips, fitted with two mounting brackets. Mechanic Wolfgang Kubach melted lead sticks with a welding torch to fill the tubes. Driving tests were convincing; the solution now established had to be optimized for the expected small production run. Chief test driver Bott took a front bumper to the Bodenmüller foundry, located across the street from Porsche, and had sand molds of the bumper tips made. These molds provided iron castings weighing 11 kilograms (24 lbs.), which were cemented into the bumpers with a particularly tough adhesive and also clamped by the bumper mounts (see illustration.) This design had the advantages of not being visible when installed and of reducing the amount of work required to repair minor frontal accidents.

Helmuth Bott recalls that "We didn't want to publicize this solution with its reinforced bumpers, but we were happy to have found a bolt-on remedy."

Wolfgang Kubach (left) and Albert Junginger: "We filled tubes shaped like the front bumper ends with lead."

Indeed, even today, when picking up one of these cast iron bumper tip inserts, one is surprised by their weight. The crucial point, however, is the genuinely improved handling. Because steering effort was higher, self-centering action was improved, equivalent to increasing caster angle, and the steering was smoother.

The cast iron parts, officially listed as bumper reinforcements and given a replacement part number, were installed as standard equipment for several months, and were retrofitted in the event of customer complaints – usually without telling the customers exactly what had been done to improve their cars. Naturally, further tests were conducted to find a more elegant solution that did not add weight. However, this was not introduced until the 1969 model year. The 45 Ampere-hour battery was replaced by two 36 Ah batteries located in the front fenders, below the headlights. This did move weight to the outside front of the 911 Series B through F, but had the drawback of difficult battery access. Also, this

was a very expensive solution, as the body and therefore the body tooling had to be altered. As of August 1973, with the introduction of the G Model, this solution was abandoned, as the new bumpers did not allow sufficient space for two batteries. Instead, a 66 Ah battery was mounted at the far left of the trunk, its weight compensated by the space saver spare tire on the opposite side.

By this time, the car's handling characteristics were no longer as strongly dependent on weight distribution and polar moment of inertia. As of the 1966 model year, the top strut mounts of all 911 suspensions were adjustable, and camber could be modified by small amounts. With the introduction of the 1968 911 S model, 5 $\frac{1}{2}$" wide Fuchs alloy wheels, 185/70 VR 15 tires, a stiffer front stabilizer bar and a rear stabilizer bar became available. According to the factory test numbers, these improvements increased the lateral acceleration measured to 0.78 g, compared to 0.65 to 0.70 g for the earliest standard models.

These cast iron bumper reinforcements were installed in production cars beginning with serial number 301340.

For improved weight distribution, batteries were located in the left and right front fenders.

The decisive difference in achieving optimum weight distribution was the lengthened wheelbase introduced with the 1969 models, achieved without relocating the engine. "That was only possible after we had developed an angled driveshaft for the semi-automatic 'Sportomatic' transmission," recalls Helmuth Bott. The Sportomatic had the same axle location as the manual transmission. Because the addition of a torque converter meant that the differential was moved forward, angled driveshafts were required. Wear of the Rzeppa constant-velocity joints fitted to the driveshafts is dependent on their operating angle. For example, this angle was the root cause of problems with early front-drive cars; the halfshafts had to be replaced at relatively low mileage. The Sportomatic shafts, however, had endured more than 100,000 test kilometers. Moreover, three factory cars fitted with the Sportomatic transmission had survived the 84 hours of the "Marathon de la Route" on the Nürburgring, indeed had finished first and second. Those responsible confidently approved the change.

To stretch the wheelbase, the rear suspension arms had to be lengthened by 57 mm and the wheel wells altered appropriately, resulting in different fenders and different front and rear bumpers for this 911 evolution. Another change for improved weight distribution was the relocation of the nine-liter oil tank from behind the rear axle to a location ahead of the right rear axle, introduced with the 1972 model year E series. This modification is immediately recognizable by the outside oil filler lid on the right rear fender. When several customers confused the oil filler with the fuel filler, this change was once again abandoned.

Meanwhile, racing experience had shown how aerodynamic improvements could affect driving characteristics. This knowledge was first applied to the E-series of 1972. The 911 S model was given a front air dam, to deflect air to the sides and thereby reduce front end lift. A rear spoiler was first introduced on the Carrera RS, which celebrated its debut at the Paris salon in October 1972. The combination of front and rear spoilers dramatically improved the car's behavior. With this model, Porsche was the first manufacturer to fit different tire sizes front and rear (185/70 VR 15 on 6-inch wheels at the front, 215/60 VR 15 on 7-inch wheels at the rear), which resulted in an excellent lateral acceleration value of 0.9 g.

In the following years, the handling of the 911 was steadily improved. However, an entirely new dimension was created in 1988 with the introduction of the new Carrera 2/4 generation (Type 964). The all-wheel-drive Carrera 4 represented the highest development stage of the production 911. The classic shape hides a completely new car. Eighty-five percent of all components differ from their predecessors. The advanced engineering of this model is most clearly demonstrated by the all-wheel drive system. A central differential attached to the rear-mounted engine/transmission unit normally sends 39 percent of the drive torque to the front, where it is divided by another differential and then transmitted to the individual tires. Hydraulically activated, electronically controlled locking differentials modify the torque distribution according to wheel slip. Wheel slip is detected by sensors shared by the ABS system, also introduced at this time.

Beginning with the 1972 model year, the S models were fitted with a front air dam to reduce lift.

The combination of front and rear spoilers greatly improved the behavior of the Carrera RS 2.7.

126

Thanks to myriad detail improvements and countless tests, today's 911s achieve incredible lateral acceleration values. Tires always play a decisive role in reaching higher handling limits.

A new era for rear-drive Porsches dawned with the introduction of the new 911 generation, the Type 993, at the 1993 Frankfurt IAA.

The outstanding driving characteristics of the Type 993, combined with large safety reserves, were achieved by two changes. The front suspension of the preceding model, a McPherson strut system, was completely redesigned. It was given a different suspension geometry with negative steering offset. At the same time, the previous rear suspension system, with semi-trailing arms and struts, was replaced by a completely new multi-link suspension, incorporating Porsche's LSA (lightweight-stable-agile) system. Matching the entire vehicle to the suspension, steering and various tire combinations is of course part of the development engineer's task. The new all-wheel-drive 911, introduced in September 1994, indicates the ultimate direction of 911 development.

Other basic chassis components, such as steering and brakes, are examined in the following chapter.

Erich Stotz, 27 years a designer: "To design a new rear suspension, we needed new driveshafts. The shaft introduced by the Nadella company was a remarkable invention."

Kurt Knoerzer former member of the Porsche road test department: "The main emphasis of my work was testing 901 components, mostly on the 356 C chassis."

Porsche's saftey consciousness
Always a step ahead

Thirty years of 911 production represent thirty years of safety development for Porsche customers. But the origins of Porsche's safety engineering lie even farther back.

Unlike a new transmission or larger engine, safety cannot be built into a car overnight. Rather, safety technology emerges as the result of a prolonged process. In the 1950s, manufacturers as well as customers first had to comprehend the need for safety before individual features would be taken seriously. It was considered a matter of course that in the event of a severe frontal impact, the driver would be impaled on the car's steering column; that's just the way it was. But at Porsche, a handful of people began to think about changing this situation.

The first safety feature incorporated in a Type 356 was, of all things, the coat hook. In the early 1950s, a child riding in the rear seat of a 356 received severe head injuries as a result of striking the chrome-plated coat hook during an accident. Helmut Rombold, known for his meticulous attention to every detail, called a meeting of his colleagues in the development department to discuss the causes of this accident. It was immediately resolved to replace the chrome plated coat hooks with hooks consisting of a rubber-covered metal strip. As it was the custom of

that time to wear heavy coats, many coat hooks succumbed to their heavy loads and dropped their burdens to the floor. This resulted in a reinforced version, which still satisfied safety requirements.

Sensitized by examining wrecked customer cars, most of which arrived at Porsche's own repair department, and by conversations with customers who had been in accidents, Porsche gradually eliminated all sharp corners of the 356 interior. A major contribution toward occupant protection was the addition of a padded dashboard top, introduced in 1955.

Another safety pioneer was chief body designer Erwin Komenda. His colleague Helmuth Bott, second in command of the road test department, recalls the growing safety consciousness of the time: "We spent eight, ten, or twelve hours of every day sitting in cars; this gave us plenty of time to think."

The Stuttgart team was dealt a particular blow when Wilfried Krüger, who had played the leading role in the German motion picture "0-8-15," was killed in his 356 while driving home from the film's premiere. His car had left the road and struck a tree. Cause of death: speared by the steering column. Shortly thereafter, a scientist, well known to television viewers, died under similar circumstances when he lost control of his car as a result of hydroplaning, and struck an unprotected steel girder of an autobahn bridge over the Lech River near Augsburg. Helmuth Bott investigated many accidents of that era; race driver and journalist Richard von Frankenberg often recommended Bott to third parties as an accident investigator. This brought the man who would eventually become Porsche's research and development chief into early and profound contact with safety problems.

Bott recalls that a close relationship with the race drivers of the 1950s resulted in a heightened sense of responsibility among the engineers. If a technical fault caused a race driver to suffer an accident, the

Chief designer Leopold Schmid used sand bags to simulate impact with a steering wheel.

development engineers not only blamed themselves, but also began immediate work on the appropriate improvements. Helmuth Bott emphasizes that "Everybody knew everybody else."

Almost from its very beginnings as a car company, Porsche began to explore new safety ideas. Steering wheel impact tests were conducted as early as 1952. Active as well as passive safety features were investigated. In 1954, production vehicles incorporated the results of this research in the form of a new steering system, new tires, the addition of stabilizer bars and completely different suspension tuning. A few years later, Daimler-Benz promulgated the deliberate deformability of the front of the car (crush zone) and the impact-absorbing steering wheel pad. At the same time, Porsche settled on the deep-dish steering wheel. In the early 1960s, the articulated steering column of the 911 drew considerable attention. Experience gained with the similar steering column design of the Type 719 RSK racer of 1959 played a decisive role in this development. Helmuth Bott recalls that "This steering system was a child of necessity. We wanted to use the left-mounted steering box of the 356 for a center-seat race car. This was made possible by an angled steering column."

Shortly before, *Quattroruote,* the leading Italian automotive magazine, had written "... the most life threatening of the thousands of individual parts that make up a car is and remains the steering column." In 1957, Cornell University had published a study of more than 1000 accidents. Of the 1678 persons injured in these accidents, 29.4 percent, or nearly one-third, had received injuries from the steering wheel and steering column. The study clearly demonstrated the need to find a remedy. Still, many carmakers continued to install long steering columns connected directly to the steering box, as if the results of accident investigations by Cornell and others did not even exist.

The reasons are easy to see. Consumers did not demand this contribution to their own safety. Cars were selected by other criteria, such as styling, powertrain and price. The buyer did not exert pressure on the industry, which in turn had no reason to invest additional funds on the development of safety

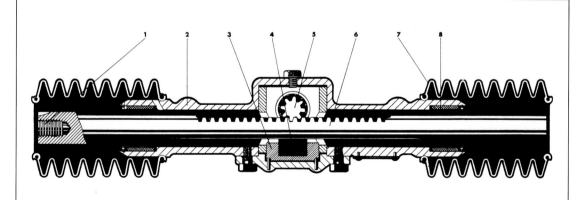

Safe and compact: the
911 front suspension,
with its safety steering
system.

1. Thread for tie rod joint
2. Housing
3. Adjusting nut
4. Pressure block

5. Steering pinion
6. Steering rack
7. Rubber boot
8. Bushing

The rack and pinion
steering box in
detail.

131

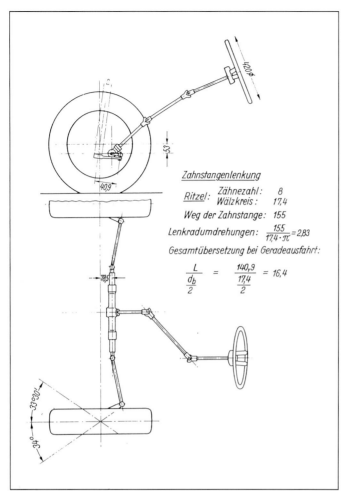

Zahnstangenlenkung

Ritzel: Zähnezahl: 8
Wälzkreis: 17,4

Weg der Zahnstange: 155

Lenkradumdrehungen: $\frac{155}{17,4 \cdot \pi} = 2,83$

Gesamtübersetzung bei Geradeausfahrt:

$$\frac{L}{\frac{d_b}{2}} = \frac{140,9}{\frac{17,4}{2}} = 16,4$$

This top view reveals how the intermediate steering shaft is deflected in the event of an accident.

features. Porsche, on the other hand, despite its position as a maker of limited-production specialty cars and anything but financially well endowed, forged ahead voluntarily. Even in the 1950s, thanks to their creativity and dedication, the people working for the young car company in Zuffenhausen could compete with the huge engineering apparatus of the major car makers. With the introduction of the 901 at the 1963 Frankfurt auto show, the combination of exciting styling, potent powerplant, above-average quality and maximum safety represented by this car became the embodiment of Porsche's company philosophy. The six-cylinder was the first sports car with an

effective safety steering system. Years before, Porsche had developed a telescoping steering column. But the 911 solution was much simpler; Porsche achieved its safety goals by placing the ZF (Zahnradfabrik Friedrichshafen) rack and pinion steering box very low and on the car's centerline. ZF had also designed the steering box for the Type 804 Grand Prix car.

This location enabled the installation of an articulated steering column, consisting of three very short segments connected by universal joints. In the event of a frontal impact, the intermediate shaft, which is not restrained by bearings, is displaced to one side and prevents intrusion of the steering column into the cabin. Combined with the three-point harness offered since 1962 (lap belts since 1956, shoulder belts since 1961) and locking seat backs, Porsche offered optimum crash protection. This may all sound simple and logical, but its design was very complicated and correspondingly expensive. The development of the steering column alone consumed 250,000 Marks before it was deemed ready for production, a great deal of money for the time. This upfront investment for development was not the only cost involved; the more complex steering column incurred additional production costs of two million Marks per year. But the investment proved worthwhile. Porsche customers appreciated that the sports cars from Zuffenhausen provided not only the highest levels of quality, but also met the most rigorous safety demands.

Even the company's cost accountants could be appeased; part of the cost of the new steering system was recovered because the centrally located rack and pinion steering box could be used without modification for right-hand-drive vehicles. Peter Falk, at the time employed in the road test department and later chief of the racing department, recalls that "Actually, this was the main reason for the design of an articulated steering column. The safety factor was a welcome side benefit."

At its introduction, the steering system was not fully developed. The small splines joining its individual components were found to lack durability. Larger splines were introduced for the 1966 model year, and retrofitted to older vehicles.

The centrally located rack and pinion steering unit could be used for right-hand-drive cars without modification.

Despite the clear safety benefits offered by the 911, advertising did not stress this aspect to the degree which is customary today. In the 1960s, customers reacted primarily to sporty styling and powerful engines. Furthermore, safety was not strictly equated with passive occupant protection; active safety dominated the issue. In 1965, Porsche's house magazine, *Christophorus,* wrote: "It has always been the main concern of Porsche designers to build a vehicle with substantial accident safety, that is, a vehicle whose technical prerequisites, including outstanding roadholding, rapid acceleration, first-class brakes and tires, prevent an accident from happening in the first place. Because human errors imply that accidents can never be entirely eliminated, the cars from Zuffenhausen are well equipped for this eventuality. To this end, the most important safety component of all is the articulated steering column."

Peter Falk: "The safety factor was a welcome side benefit."

133

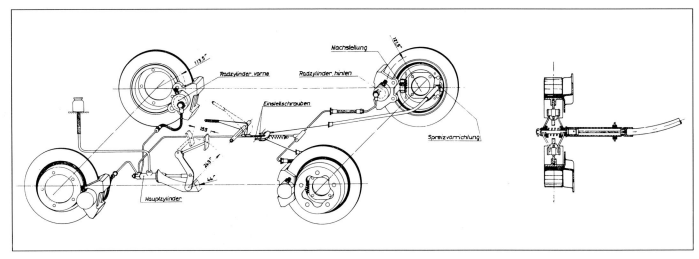

Porsche has always been known for its excellent brake systems. From the very beginning, the 911 employed four disc brakes. The single-circuit brake system shown here was replaced by a safer dual-circuit system for the 1968 model year.

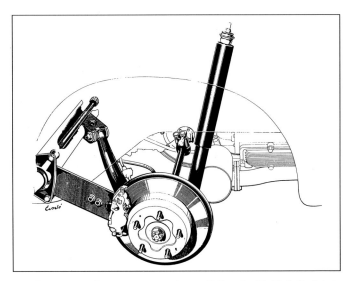

The first generation rear suspension, still fitted with Nadella joints and without ventilated brake rotors.

Two safety aspects are given lesser emphasis in this article. Dunlop, not Porsche, invented disc brakes, but Porsche developed its own system for the 356 Carrera 2, shown at the end of 1961. This unusual system grew out of a standard drum brake system. Helmuth Bott recalls the first disc brake experiments: "We cut segments out of an aluminum brake drum, mounted the disc and caliper inside. This had the advantage of permitting a larger disc diameter."

Brake specialist Alfred Teves, now owned by an American firm and known as Ate, bought the Porsche patents and produced its own disc brake system (licensed from Dunlop) for Porsche. The first Porsche to be fitted with disc brakes as standard equipment was the 356 C. These were carried over, almost without modification, to the first generation 911. Only the front disc diameter was increased by 5 mm to 285 mm. Ventilated discs were introduced on the 1967 911 S.

Tires are also extremely critical for active safety. With the 911, Porsche was the first German car maker to mount radial tires. This need was already apparent in the 356 era; the Carrera 1600 GS with its two-liter four-cam engine achieved a top speed of 210 km/h (130 mph), a speed which the conventional tires of the day could not withstand for very long.

In the mid-1960s, highway safety organizations expressing their safety recommendations advised buyers to select conspicuous colors for better visibility. The "camouflage colors" popular at the time, such as a delicate blue or light gray, were easily overlooked in conditions of low light and twilight. Porsche product planners had already recognized this; the color palette included bright colors such as Bahama yellow and Irish green.

Porsche worked steadily on safety issues. In

Early 911s had to make do with 165-15 tires. Primary suppliers were Dunlop and Michelin. In the spring of 1993, Porsche and German tire manufacturer Pneumant developed a modern tire in the 165 VR 15 dimension for vintage 911s.

During the 356 era, Porsche literally drove the tread off of their test tires.

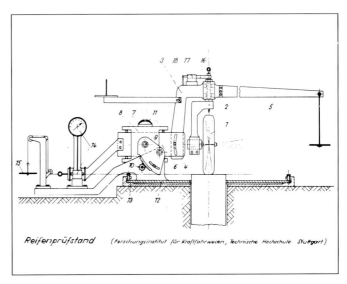

Until Porsche had its own tire test rig, a facility at the Stuttgart Technical University was used.

In the mid-1960s, safety experts advised car buyers to select conspicuous colors. Porsche's program has always offered "safety colors" which complemented its products.

March of 1966, drop tests were begun in Zuffenhausen. These were predecessors of today's crash tests. Vehicles were hoisted exactly ten meters (32.8 ft.) by a crane, and released like a sailplane. The glide ratio, however, was not comparable. The frontal impact simulated a 50 km/h (31 mph) crash. Even rare, limited-production racing prototypes, such as the Porsche 904, were tested in this manner. These tests examined how the vehicle structure behaved in a crash; in other words, whether the passenger cell could be expected to act as a survival capsule. These were completely new considerations; in the mid-1960s, the body and structural members were

designed to be as rigid as possible to achieve optimum driving characteristics, and not to absorb the maximum amount of energy in a crash to protect the occupants. Between 1966 and 1971, a total of 71 drop tests were carried out. For special purposes, the impact speed was increased to 80 km/h (50 mph). Weissach's first crash facility was operational in 1973; a much more modern indoor facility was built in 1986.

Crane drop tests provided valuable information about the impact and fire resistance of fuel tanks. The location of the 911 tank, between the front axle

136

The entire model line was crash tested, including this 904.

Danger: the wood-rimmed steering wheels which were standard equipment in the first model year could splinter as a result of an accident.

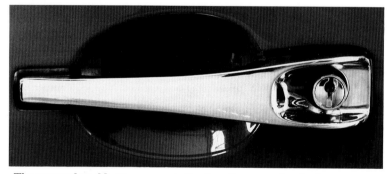

The recessed pushbutton prevents the door from opening during a rollover accident.

and the cabin, continued to occupy the attention of Porsche designers, especially since the 901 design specifications had always called for a large tank (the first models had a 62 liter, or 16.4 gallon, fuel tank) to provide adequate range at high cruising speeds. As fuel tanks for race cars were to have even greater capacity, tests with plastic tanks were begun in the mid-1960s. These tanks are lighter and more corrosion resistant than steel tanks and can be shaped to fit the available space. Sheet metal, on the other hand, can only be bent to specific radii. Porsche's first use of a plastic fuel tank was in the 911 R race car of 1967. In 1973, plastic tanks were first used for

a special application, the U.S. model 911. Initial manufacturing difficulties prevented the plastic tanks from sweeping aside steel fuel tanks in all applications; it was not until the 928 was introduced in 1977 that they were deemed completely production-ready.

The world's first safety convertible, the 911 Targa with its rigid roll bar and removable rear window, represented more than a mere detail solution. Targa deliveries commenced in 1967. In the early 1960s, designers feared that American safety standards would soon lead to the extinction of the open

At Weissach, Porsche doesn't skimp on crash tests. After evaluation, the wrecks are scrapped.

A 50 km/h (30 mph) front barrier crash test.

138

Passive Safety at Porsche

Chronology of Porsche passive safety innovations

1952	Porsche 356: single-piece V-shaped laminated safety glass windshield
1955	Porsche 356 Speedster: first German production car with curved safety glass windshield
1956	Porsche 356 A: lap belts offered
1959	Porsche 718 RSK: articulated safety steering column
1961	Porsche 356 B: shoulder belt offered
1962	Porsche 356 B: three-point belts offered, seat backs locked during braking
1964	Porsche 911: safety steering system
1966	Porsche 911 Targa: safety convertible
1967	Porsche 911 R: safety fuel tank
1969	Porsche 914: integral head rests
1971	Galvanized floor pan
1972	Automatic three-point harnesses for U.S. market
1973	Porsche 911: plastic fuel tank, fire-resistant interior materials, introduction of door beams (U.S. market)
1974	Porsche 911: safety steering wheel with additional deformable element
1975	–
1976	Introduction of hot dip galvanized body
1980	–
1982	–
1984	–
1985	Door reinforcement for all models, worldwide
1986	–
1987	Porsche 944 Turbo: first car from a European manufacturer with driver and front passenger airbags (standard for U.S. market cars)
1989	Driver and front passenger airbags standard for all models (U.S. market)
1991	Porsche provides standard driver and front passenger airbags for German market
1993	Numerous detail improvements in 993. Introduction of a further optimized airbag in the new 911 Carrera.

Pioneering Porsche developments for passive safety

Steering wheel impact tests and experiments with safety steering systems

–

–

–

–

–

Drop tests begun in Zuffenhausen
Fuel tank tests
Air bag experiments begin
Weissach acceleration test sled, airbag sled tests (911 and 914)
Rollover tests with 911, side impact tests
First crash test facility in Weissach

–

Tests with corroded cars
Fuel tank fire tests, crash tests of repaired cars
Development of deformable barrier for CCMC, airbag development begins
Pole impact tests (front and side)
Crash tests with 50% offset
Investigation to improve race track safety
Second crash test facility at Weissach

–

–

–

Presentation of side airbag study
Achievement of new European Common Market frontal and side crash standards, provisionally effective October 1, 1995

convertible. Porsche did not want to be caught out by such a possible change in regulations, and began looking for an alternative. A report by the body manufacturer Wilhelm Karmann, dated October 18, 1962, presented Porsche body planners with three variants: first, a conventional cabriolet with a padded folding top, second, a type of roadster with a removable top, and third, a version in which the main top bow was replaced by a rigid roll bar. It was this proposal which formed the basis of the Targa concept, which would provide open-air motoring without depriving its occupants of rollover protection.

Individual safety features have undergone continuous improvement to the present day (see overview). A further vital advance in occupant protection was the introduction of the airbag system. Porsche's airbag experiments began as early as 1969. Two years

Beginning with
the 1976 model
year, Porsche
pioneered the use
of the
fully-galvanized
body. Earlier
Targa models
were particularly
prone to rust.

140

later, the first airbag test sled was available. Actual airbag development began in 1980. In 1987, the 944 Turbo was the first European-built car to be equipped with standard driver and front passenger airbags as standard equipment. Since 1991, all German-market Porsches have been equipped with these life-saving devices for both front occupants.

Although styling sacrifices were made to the early airbag systems, with their plump steering wheel hubs, with the 993 Porsche stylists showed how pleasantly an airbag can be integrated in a steering wheel. The latest four-spoke safety steering wheel is well integrated in the overall interior design; its ergonomics and operating comfort are most satisfying. What is not immediately apparent is the advanced technology hidden under its leather skin. The internal structure consists of a die-cast skeleton. The driver airbag module is attached via four special rubber-metal elements, and simultaneously serves as horn button.

The improved airbag is not the only component contributing to increased safety in the 993. Every detail was rethought and reexamined. Changes include the air inlets in the front bumper, which provide better heat transfer from the front brakes. As on the earlier 964, an asymmetric hump on the outer bead of the optional 17-inch wheels prevents the tire from slipping off the wheel in the event of a complete loss of air pressure. More sensitive steering response optimizes road feel. Elastic tie rod ends greatly reduce transmission of road impacts through the steering column. The new suspension makes weight transfer reactions in corners even easier to master, eliminates instability during sudden lane changes, allows higher lateral acceleration, minimizes movements in roll and pitch, and improves stability under braking. Body reinforcements and integral door sills provide increased chassis stiffness.

The list goes on, and clearly shows that today, safety is built into every single detail. Safety has become an extremely complex subject, which makes the highest demands of man and machine. Yet Porsche's designers have a great advantage in mastering this subject; they can call on more than four decades of experience.

Production and development
Made by hand

During the 1960s, craftsmanship and the enthusiasm to go with it were still in high demand. Note the optional "ram protection" bar between the bumper overriders.

Heinz Fuchs:
"We made it work
because we had
to."

Werner Zahs:
"Anyone who
served an
apprenticeship at
Porsche knew his
trade."

Carburetor banks were carefully checked before installation.

Name des Lehrlings: **Harald Keller**

Geburtsdatum: **18.2.1949** Geburtsort: **Stuttgart**

Lehrberuf: **Feinblechner**

Wohnung: **S-Feuerbach Stuttgarter Str. 171**

Beginn der Lehrzeit: **1.4.1966** Ende der Lehrzeit: **31.3.1969**

Lehrvertrag abgeschlossen am: **1.4.1966** und eingetragen in die Lehrlingsrolle

der Industrie- und Handelskammer am:

Lehrbetrieb: **Dr. Jng. hc F. Porsche KG**

Name des Lehrbeauftragten: **Herr Wagner Herr Ocker**

Ausbildungsgang

(Für die Regelmäßigkeit dieser Eintragungen ist der Lehrbeauftragte verantwortlich).

Lehr- oder Betriebsabteilung	Dauer von	Dauer bis	Wochen	Unterschrift des Ausbilders
Rohmontage: Fondseiten-teil, Seitenteile, St.III Punkt-schweißen, St.I Boden u.	3.4.	19.5.	7	Dr. Ing. h. c. F. Porsche KG. Stuttgart-Zuffenhausen Porsche-Str. Fernruf 891 41 Lehrlingsabteilung
Heizleitung, Türen an-schlagen, Vorferl. Motor-raumdeckel, Konstr. Büro,	22.5.	23.6.	5	Dr. Ing. h. c. F. Porsche KG. Stuttgart-Zuffenhausen Porsche-Str. Fernruf 891 41 Lehrlingsabteilung
Kofferraumdeckel anschl, Motorraumdeckel anschl, Vorfertigung Türen,	26.6.	1.9.	10	Dr. Ing. h. c. F. Porsche KG. Stuttg. Porsche-Str.
Lötverputzen, Ausrichten u. Endverp., Polizeiwagen, Auslöten, Konstr. Büro,	4.9.	1.12.	13	Dr. Ing. h. c. F. Porsche KG. Stuttgart-Zuffenhausen Porsche-Str. Fernruf 891 41 Lehrlingsabteilung
Auslöten, Fertigmontage;	4.12.	29.12.	4	Dr. Ing. h. c. F. Porsche KG. Stuttgart-Zuffenhausen Porsche-Str. Lehrlingsabteilung
Kunststoffabteilung;	2.1.	26.1.	4	Dr. Ing. h. c. F. Porsche KG. Stuttgart-Zuffenhausen Porsche-Str. Lehrlingsabteilung
Flaschnerei - Versuch;	29.1.	29.3.	9	Dr. Ing. h. c. F. Porsche KG. Stuttgart-Zuffenhausen Porsche-Str. Fernruf 891 41 Lehrlingsabteilung

Harald Keller, today a paint specialist in Göppingen near Stuttgart, was honored for his well-kept apprentice notebook.

143

Porsche has had a test track at Weissach since 1969. The 911 shown here is driving through a salt water bath, part of an endurance test.

At Porsche, the name Fuchs often leads to confusion. It appears twice in Porsche's history. Each time, it stands for exceptional quality. The Otto Fuchs Metallwerke of Meinerzhagen, in the Sauerland district of North Rhine-Westphalia, has given us the legendary Fuchs alloy wheel, while Heinz Fuchs from the Swabian town of Rutesheim, halfway between Zuffenhausen and Weissach, built VW-based Formula Vee and Super Vee monoposto racers for amateur motorsports. In the 1950s and 60s, before his career as race car designer, he had spent two years at the Reutter body plant and six years at Porsche in Zuffenhausen. The sheet metal specialist worked as a mechanic on the first 901 prototypes. In addition, he trained apprentices in the craft of metal finishing. One of his protégés was Werner Zahs of Stammheim, who to this day earns his living as an

auto body craftsman. In the mid-1960s, it was primarily Zahs who welded three stainless steel 911s together for display at the 1967 Frankfurt auto show. Porsche wanted to demonstrate that it was possible to build absolutely rust-free cars. But Zahs recalls that the costs were prohibitive: "The roof consisted of two halves and had to be joined by a thin stainless steel strip." One of these cars is still on display in the Deutsches Museum in Munich. Zahs was an accomplished welder, but was less meticulous with the notebook which all apprentices had to keep. The Swabian craftsman recalls that "Once, Fuchs even picked me up at home, so I wouldn't forget my notebook again." By contrast, his fellow apprentice Harald Keller of Stuttgart-Feuerbach took theory to heart. He was honored by his employer for his minutely detailed notebook.

Porsche 912

Little brother

Development of the 911 was already well advanced before Porsche began to consider a more economical version. It was not until the end of 1962 that company management issued a work order to have a stock 1.6 liter Type 616/7 engine, as used in the 356 SC, installed in a 901 prototype. Paul Hensler, who had come to Porsche directly from college, recalls "My first assignment in the development department was to install the four-cylinder 616 engine in the 901 body." In the process, the engineers encountered problems. A new flywheel was required. As a result, on June 22, 1963, engine designer Leopold Jäntschke recorded his department's recommendation that the stronger Fichtel & Sachs clutch be used for the smaller engine. Moreover, because of the rear engine mounts, a new transom was required for the engine bay. "The assignment was more difficult than we had expected, as on top of it all, the engine was to be matched to a five-speed transmission," adds Hensler, who would later become director of Porsche development activities.

The first test drives were satisfactory; this combination of two existing components resulted in a thoroughly acceptable Porsche. The goal of the "small Porsche" was to match the performance of the 1600 SC, but offer the advantages of the 911 body and chassis.

The decisive factor in continuing development of this 901 sibling was the Frankfurt International Automobile Show in September, 1963. In particular, the anticipated price of the 901 had drawn criticism. The sum of 23,900 Marks seemed much too high, even if leather had been included. This made the 901 about 7000 Marks more expensive than the last 356. Of course, the car that would later be sold as the 911 offered much more in the way of comfort, features and performance than the 356, but at that time, price regions above 20,000 Marks were the domain of only very special customers.

Because four-cylinder engines were appreciably less expensive than six-cylinder powerplants, company management decided to offer the 901 with the smaller engine. During a technical meeting on June 15, 1962, the type designation 902 was assigned to this project.

The body of Prototype Number 10 (see "The 911 Prototypes," pages 51 and 54) was completed at about the time this decision was made. The car, with chassis number 13 330, was drivable on October 2, 1964. Installed in the rear was a forerunner of the new Type 616/36 four-cylinder engine, with the same 1582 cc displacement as the 356 powerplant. The entire valve train, including the valves and cam-

shaft, was slightly modifed to allow continuous full-throttle operation at 5800 rpm with a 9.3:1 compression ratio. Experiments had even been carried out with hydraulic valve lifters. Porsche engineers reduced induction noise by mounting large air filters, made by Mann und Hummel, on the Solex 40 PII-4 two-barrel downdraft carburetors. The muffler resembled that of the 911, and likewise exhaled through an exhaust pipe at the lower left. These modifications cost the engine 5 horsepower compared to its 356 counterpart, but it soon proved to be considerably more robust. It developed 90 horsepower at 5800 rpm and accelerated the 902 to 100 km/h (62.1 mph) in 12.8 seconds. During the course of 1964, all technical details were discussed in so-called "Type 616 Engine Meetings," usually documented by Paul Hensler.

Tooling for the 902 (later renamed 912) was made by the Wilhelm Karmann body works in Osnabrück.

This entailed modifications and additions to tooling for the Type 901. The major changes were to the rear engine mounts and a dashboard for three instead of five round gauges. The original production schedule called for Karmann to build only 912s; the sales department anticipated brisk sales for the economy model. Coordination of the two firms was handled by Herr Schlosser of Karmann and Porsche's purchasing chief, Wilhelm Albrecht.

The major characteristic differences between the 911 and 912 were established during a special meeting of Porsche management on December 1, 1964. The dashboard would not have a wooden fascia, the door panels would have a storage pocket, a 12-volt electrical system would be installed, and the Webasto gasoline heater would not be available, even as an option. Furthermore, it was decided that vehicles with sunroofs would be built only after production had been well established. Porsche strove to approach the price of the 356 C coupe. There were minor changes to standard equipment. There was no oil pressure gauge, a simple horn button replaced the expensive 911 horn ring, the steering wheel rim itself was made of plastic instead of wood, and the road wheels were painted instead of chrome plated. Standard equipment included a four-speed transmission, while the five-speed option added 340 Marks to the price.

Early in 1965, in the middle of the model year, Porsche introduced the 912 to the public. It was presented as a so-called "Euro type," but because of certain regulatory hurdles, it could only be sent to continental European distributors and could not be sent overseas or to Great Britain.

When the 912 was announced, traditional customers breathed a sigh of relief; its price of 16,250 Marks was close to that of the 356.

The motoring press was quick to test Porsche's latest baby. *auto, motor und sport* labelled it an "everyday Porsche," that is, suitable for ordinary daily use. In the United States, *Car and Driver* saw it as a car which any enthusiast could afford. This may have been a bit of an exaggeration; at its presentation, the 912 cost exactly 16,250 Marks, making it 5650 Marks less expensive than the lowest-priced 911. Naturally, this four-cylinder offshoot of the 911 had lower maintenance costs. The "little" Porsche used 12 to 13 liters per 100 km [18.0 to 19.6 mpg], or 3 to 4 l/100 km less than the 911 (which got about 15 mpg). This was in part due to the lower weight of the 912, which weighed 100 kg [220 lbs.] less than the 911. The weight difference resulted from the lighter powerplant and the lack of a separate oil tank, required for the 911's dry sump lubrication system. Naturally, this altered the weight distribution to 44 percent front/56 percent rear, compared to the 41/59 distribution of the 911. This imbued the 912 with more balanced handling characteristics, and made it more docile in corners, exhibiting pronounced understeer. *Car and Driver* reported that the only way to bring the tail out was to suddenly brake in the middle of a turn.

The 912 became an instant sales hit. It was especially attractive to customers who liked the lines of the 911, but did not need the performance of the six-cylinder Porsche. It sold well in the United States because American customers were even more price-conscious than the Europeans, and in a land of permanent speed limits, the performance of the 912 was more than adequate. By the end of 1965, Porsche counted 6401 customers for the 912, twice as many as for the 911. During the 912's production run, Porsche built a total of 27,738 912 coupes and 2562 Targas.

At the 1965 Frankfurt International Automobile Show, the 912, like the 911, was displayed as a Targa with a rigidly mounted roll bar. The first Targas were not delivered until early 1967. After the 1968 plant vacation, the 912 underwent its most important alteration. As on the 911, the wheelbase was stretched by 57 mm to 2268 mm. In addition, the fenders were widened slightly to accommodate 5 1/2" wheels, and the interior trim was upgraded.

At the end of 1967 (1968 model year), Porsche introduced a new economy model, the 911 T. This entry level 911, with its 110 hp two-liter six-cylinder engine, would eventually replace the 912, which was ptoduced through the 1969 model year. The four-cylinder experienced a brief renaissance in the 1976 model year, when Porsche offered the 911 body powered by the engine of the 914/4. This 912 E was sold only in the United States. The 1971 cc power-plant developed 90 hp at 4900 rpm and accelerated to a top speed of 180 km/h (112 mph). The economi-cal engine met the strict American exhaust emissions standards. Trim and equipment were identical to Porsche's 911 export models, recognizable by their upright sealed beam headlights. Only a year later, the 911's little brother disappeared for the second and last time, after 2099 had been built. The 924 would take over the role of entry level Porsche.

Porsche's 1967 model lineup. The 912, at the left front, had painted rims and a less fully equipped interior.

148

The open 911
Hats off

The history of open Porsches is as old as that of the company itself. In 1948, the first car to carry the Porsche name was fitted with only a rudimentary top. Porsche Number One was also designated as the Type 356 Roadster in Porsche's sequential project numbering system. Ever since that first car, open Porsches would continue to enjoy strong demand. During the 356 C era, at a time when 901 development was at an advanced stage, open cars made up 16.5 percent of Porsche's sales volume. It was only logical that there should also be an open version of the new Porsche. To that end, a memorandum dated October 20, 1961 recorded that an agreement between Porsche and Reutter had been reached, to the effect that "The body shall be patterned after the prototype T7 built by Reutter, taking into consideration that the vehicle should also be buildable in an open version." As we shall see later, this intent was not in fact translated into hardware.

At the time, the 356 program had not yet been abandoned. On October 23, 1961, Porsche requested in a letter that Reutter's chief executive, Walter Beierbach, "study options for delivering a simplified and lower-cost cabriolet, which can fill the market niche of the discontinued Roadster." Despite a detailed 25-point program outlining such a stripped model, the project never materialized. The firm's

resources were fully occupied with development of the 901. Even the design of an open 901 was moved to the back burner, as the timetable for bringing the coupe to market was already very tight.

Yet the subject of a 901 cabriolet remained a topic of discussion. In the fall of 1962, three proposals were presented as $1/10$ scale drawings and a $1/7.5$ scale model, sent to the Wilhelm Karmann Company. The Osnabrück-based body manufacturer was asked to evaluate these designs for manufacturing feasibility. A letter from Porsche, dated October 18, 1962, reiterates the design variations.
a) Normal cabriolet with full folding padded top and full boot, Polyglas [clear flexible plastic] rear window, removable via zipper as necessary. When stowed, the top is to present as low a silhouette as possible.
b) Collapsible version with partial top bows, but stowable after folding in a completely recessed position by means of a top boot. (When stowed, top mechanism may be protected by cover held in place by snap fasteners.) In this case, the top fabric would be removed completely.
c) The main top bow would be formed by a protective sheath (roll bar), rigidly mounted or collapsible, possibly painted, with removable rear section and forward roof panel.

At this time, it was not yet foreseeable that this last version would be the one ultimately chosen. A memo from Porsche draftsman Fritz Blaschka, dated May 28, 1963, records further concepts. The possibility of a "simple roll-up roof, similar to that of the Opel cabriolet sedans of 1933-1935" was discussed. The idea was suggested by technical director Hans Tomala, because it would retain the luggage and passenger spaces, including the rear jump seats.

A concept by Ferdinand Alexander ("Butzi") Porsche envisioned a "rigid steel roof, easily removed by hand, between the windshield and the rigidly mounted roll bar." Chief criticism for the design was its awkward operation, which would force the driver to stop and get out of the car. A conventional sliding roof would not suffer from this restriction, but one would have to be content with a much smaller roof opening. Also, there was as yet no way to store the roof once removed.

A third possibility raised by the Blaschka memo was a "normal folding-top cabriolet with components that could mostly be stowed below the body line." Of course, the disadvantage of this design was that the jump seats could only be used with the top erected.

Chief designer Butzi Porsche had a completely different concept of the open 901: "It was my opinion that the open car should have a distinct break in the roof line, to underscore the Roadster feeling." A design drawing for this cabriolet shape is dated December 2, 1963 (see illustration below). Compared to the coupe, its greatest disadvantage was its reduced interior space. What finally killed this design was cost. Stamping the new rear sheet metal would have required new tooling, which, in view of the enormous development cost of the 901 coupe, Porsche could not and would not incur.

The folding top cabriolet would also have been very expensive. Blaschka's memo goes on: "As no consideration for a cabriolet version was given during design of the coupe, modification or rework of doors, side windows, and rear lid would be necessary to make the roll bar fully collapsible." Nevertheless, design drawings for complete cabriolets were made. Contemplating a drawing dated December 18, 1963, designer and top specialist Gerhard Schröder points out that no engine was sketched in. Now living in Weissach, craftsman Schröder emphasizes that "With this top, there would have been no space left over for an engine." It was not until two decades later that he was assigned a full cabriolet Porsche project. Schröder adds, "With the engine in place, the folded top would have stood above the body, like a VW Beetle cabriolet, and that would not have been acceptable for a sports car of Porsche's stature."

Between June 26 and December 18, 1963, six design concepts were created, reflecting the more important considerations on the subject of the "open

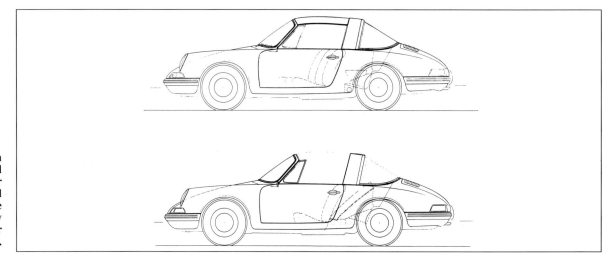

For the open car, Ferdinand Alexander Porsche wanted a break in the body line below the rear window.

901." These are illustrated in the first chapter of this book, "Beginnings." The term cabriolet is applied to vehicles with rigid bows, removable roof and folding rear window. The following were considered:

- a coupe with steel sliding roof;
- a coupe with removable steel roof;
- a coupe with a rigid roll bar and removable steel roof;
- a cabriolet with a break in the rear roof line; and
- a cabriolet.

After the successful presentation of the 901 coupe at the 1963 Frankfurt IAA, and visitors to the Porsche display repeatedly asked for a cabriolet, the model and design departments intensified their work on an open 901. A movie made at the end of 1963 records a preliminary model viewing by Ferry Porsche and his son Ferdinand Alexander. The studio contains three white Plasticine models in $1/_{7.5}$ scale, behind them two Studebaker studies in black lacquer. Among the Porsches we see a cabriolet version with a removable black roof, a roll bar painted in body color and still steeply raked aft, and a rear folding top section. A second model also has a removable roof, a silver-colored roll bar and the roof line break favored by Butzi Porsche. The monochrome third version explores different orientations for the roll bar.

At this preliminary viewing, it was decided that Porsche would not forego the built-in roll bar. For one, it represented a unique design element, and for another Porsche feared that U.S. regulations would someday eliminate open vehicles without rollover protection. Because American as well as all other European car manufacturers were still happily producing full convertibles, this could not have been the

Butzi Porsche and his creation, in scale. The open car, with its silver-colored roll bar and foldable rear window, was initially called the 901 cabriolet.

sole, decisive factor in favor of the Porsche roll bar. Moreover, as was often reiterated, the roll bar was originally intended to be collapsible with the top down. The only problem was that this could not be realized due to space constraints. It was also decided that the rear window would extend to the roll bar, and attach to it by means of a zipper. The cloth part of the zipper on the roll bar side would be attached to the inner wall of the roll bar.

Porsche's first internal presentation of the "open 901" mockup to a larger audience took place on June 12, 1964, in a separate building of the body plant. Present were Ferry Porsche, his son Ferdinand Alexander, Hans Tomala, Walter Beierbach, domestic sales chief Harald Wagner, chief body engineer Erwin Komenda, and Fritz Blaschka, who took notes. Harald Wagner once again pleaded for a full cabriolet without roll bar. Eventually he realized that too many expensive changes, such as a lower windshield and altered rear shape, would be necessary. On this day, Porsche management agreed upon the design variation based on the rigid roll bar. Ferry Porsche requested a few changes. The forward roof receiver, at the top of the windshield, was to be kept as small as possible for easier entry and closer similarity to a true cabriolet. Further, the rear edge of the roll bar was to be altered, and the originally planned folding top bows were to be dropped to increase rear seat headroom. The basic door assemblies, including vent windows, were to remain unchanged, but the A-pillars were to have heavily reinforced bases. Ferry Porsche also suggested that the rigid removable top be stowed ahead of the jump seats. Roof stowage, however, was one aspect which still needed work. All other changes were to be carried out on the existing mockup, which consisted of aluminum sheet metal on a wooden buck. Komenda immediately drew up a timetable, divided into the following Targa-specific segments:

 – Body,
 – Rigid, non-removable roll bar,
 – Doors and windows,
 – Plastic forward roof section,
 – Fittings,
 – Polyglas rear section, and
 – Seals

Emil Soukup, chief of the patent department, immediately began a search for prior claims to similar designs. He found the Triumph TR 4 and several Daimler-Benz patents, which in some ways resembled the Porsche solution, but whose overall concept differed from it. The only danger was from a patent filed on June 1, 1964, by the Braun company, for a top with roll bar. Nevertheless, in a memo to Porsche management dated February 5, 1965, Soukup concluded that "It does not appear to me that a design change for the cabriolet, as already represented by two vehicles, is necessary."

At the end of January, 1965, the first test drives with the cabriolet prototype took place. Helmuth Bott paid particular attention to wind noise, fluttering of the rear window and lack of body stiffness. On January 28, 1965, Bott reports that "The cabriolet gives a good overall impression... driving over cobblestones (bridges) at high speed, one notices the familiar lack of stiffness common to cabriolets, but it is no more pronounced in this car than in the 356 C cabriolet... Tests with the roof installed could not be carried out, as the rigid panel is still not available."

Indeed, the roof panel was not yet finished when the test crew travelled to Wolfsburg for their test session. Porsche employee Knoll was to arrive a day later with the completed panel. Knoll arrived in Wolfsburg the following evening, but minus roof, which he had forgotten. His punishment was simple: that same night, he had to spend seven hours driving back to Stuttgart to get the missing part. During a second test drive, Helmut Bott was able to close the roof and determine that "Even at 55 km/h [34 mph] strong wind noise is audible, which increases with speed to the point where one can converse only by shouting. The main source of noise is the gap between top and windshield frame." The chief of the road test department had a complaint regarding safety aspects: "The (temporary) top catches installed on Cabriolet 1 are not acceptable in their present form, as they present many possibilities for injury in the event of an accident." However, Bott's overall conclusion was positive: "In summary, it may be said that, after the listed faults have been corrected, the cabriolet is usable under all driving conditions, without major design changes."

152

Shortly thereafter, Bott presented his findings to the individual departments at a large internal meeting. On display was the first cabriolet test car, with prototype chassis number 13 360, built by Karmann in Osnabrück and delivered to Porsche on September 10, 1964. It was decided to cover the removable panel with grained black vinyl, as was done on the Opel Diplomat, to reduce the width of the roll bar, and to mount two Porsche crests, like those on the wheel covers but in gold. These crests did appear on the dark green Targa of the first sales brochure, but never went into production.

On June 9, 1965, Rolf Hannes of the road test department drove the second experimental cabriolet, chassis number 13 396. Hannes found a new problem: "With the roof panel removed and the rear window closed, there is an intense draft in the area of the driver's head, which blows the hair forward. But worse, there is a strong forward draft under the seats, which picks up dirt from the floor and slings it into the faces of driver and passenger. For these reasons, it is almost impossible to drive without wearing a cap and glasses." Fortunately, this could be solved relatively easily.

The roof panel did not work entirely as planned. During the design phase, Butzi Porsche believed that one could drive this new type of convertible in its closed form at high speed without having the top inflate like a balloon. In practice, this was only possible under certain conditions. Despite stiff side frames and front and rear transverse ribs, the collapsible, rubber-coated cloth design bowed upward at high speeds.

On August 11, 1965, Porsche registered its top design with the patent office, under the number 1455743. The invention was not officially disclosed until May 22, 1969, and, after the relatively long appeal period had expired, became legally binding by means of an announcement on October 14, 1976. Hans Tomala, who as chief engineer had overall responsibility for the project, and designers Gerhard Schröder and Werner Trenkler were named as the inventors.

In view of the planned design solution, it no longer made sense to call the open car a cabriolet. During a brainstorming session in Zuffenhausen, Walter Schmidt (nicknamed the "General"), chief of purchasing and responsible for central planning, export sales boss Erich Hirsch, domestic sales director Harald Wagner and customer service chief Hans Klauser listed all the race tracks of the world and considered their names for possible use. Mercedes had a model named the Nürburg, Opel had a Monza. The name of the long-distance event run in the hills of Sicily, the Targa Florio, had not yet been claimed. As "Florio" didn't have the right ring and would not have been understandable in every foreign language, Harald Wagner simply proposed the designation "Targa." The proposal was approved by those present. What was not realized at the time, but which turned out to be a happy coincidence, was that the Italian word "Targa" translates as "shield," and indeed the safety hoop does serve as a sort of shield for the car's occupants.

Harald Wagner, who remained a Porsche employee until very recently, was expected to supply estimates of expected Targa sales as a portion of total 911 sales. Wagner, who had the lack of an open version pointed out to him on a daily basis by customers, estimated that Targas would represent an incredible 40 percent of 911 sales. This, despite the fact that he had only seen the mockup, with its much wider roll bar. "A gigantic thing," he recalls today. Wagner's belief in the open 911, thenceforth called the Targa, was confirmed at the 1965 Frankfurt International Automobile Show.

Porsche's newest model was described in a press release dated September 1, 1965: "The Targa is neither a cabriolet nor a coupe, not a hardtop nor a sedan, but rather something completely new."

"With this model, we not only present a new car, but also a new idea: the application of a safety hoop in a production car and thereby the world's first safety cabriolet... It is Porsche's privilege to be the first auto manufacturer in the world to offer a roll bar on a production car..."

Targa Spyder. Without roof panel and with folded rear window, Targas offered virtually all the pleasures of a full convertible.

154

Targa Bel Air. "Topless," with a huge sunroof.

Targa Hardtop. As well sealed as a coupe, but with wind noise included at no additional charge.

Targa Voyage. Folding top and the rear window can be removed by means of a single zipper.

155

The press release also emphasizes the Targa's possible variations:

1. Targa Spyder
"The completely open version, i.e. without roof panel and with folded rear section..."

2. Targa Hardtop
"With a rigid roof panel, made of heavy, extremely durable plastic, the Targa turns into a hardtop..."

3. Targa Voyage
"In place of the rigid roof panel, a folding panel is available for touring..."

4. Targa Bel Air
"In this case, one can leave the rear section in place and drive without the top, i.e. 'topless,' as with a giant sunroof, to enjoy fresh air and sunlight from above, or leave the roof in place and release the rear section by opening a single zipper..."

At the Frankfurt show, the price had not yet been announced, but the sales staff gave an approximate added cost of about 1500 Marks above the price of the coupe. The car was to be delivered in the spring of 1966 and would be available with the four and

six-cylinder engines.

Porsche had a winner on its hands. The Targa was the hit of the Frankfurt show. The newest Porsche graced every magazine cover, and even the president of the Federal Republic of Germany expressed intense interest as Ferry Porsche explained the thinking behind the roll bar.

Before the car was ready for delivery, there remained a great deal of detail work. On September 27, 1965, Helmuth Bott commenced an endurance test on the torture track section of the Wolfsburg proving grounds. Although the car was a pre-production example, its serial number, 500 002, was consistent with later production cars. In early November, the car was disassembled for inspection. The results were less than satisfactory. For prototype number 4, reinforcements were welded into the rear door sills, and the heater tube was altered. On January 6, 1966, this car was ready for testing at Wolfsburg, survived the torture track and, after examination, finally met Porsche's quality standards. To minimize resonance effects in the body, all Targas were equipped with radial tires and Boge shock absorbers.

As the Targa had already garnered worldwide praise as a safety convertible, on November 10, 1965, Targa test car number 28 was subjected to a drop test. The car was lifted to a height of two meters (6 ft. 8 in.) and dropped upside down. Porsche's engineers were not satisfied by the results, and designer Werner Trenkler was assigned the task of reworking the roll bar. The hammerforms and the final components of the top design could also not be completed before early January 1966, pushing delivery of production Targas back from spring of 1966 to January 23, 1967. When it finally arrived, three variations were available: the 911 and 911 S with chassis numbers beginning with 500 001 and the Type 912 with numbers starting at 550 001.

Meanwhile, Ferry Porsche had decided that the Targa, which still appeared in most reports and memos as "Cabriolet" or "Cabriolet Targa," would not be equipped with an air conditioning system. The company's chief executive based this decision on a memo dated October 27, 1965, from Egon

Harald Wagner: "By happy coincidence, the Italian word 'Targa' translates as 'shield'."

At the 1965 Frankfurt show, Porsche presented the world's first safety convertible.

The full convertible shown here is allegedly a prototype, built in 1964.

Roland Wolf: "The Porsche began to fill with water."

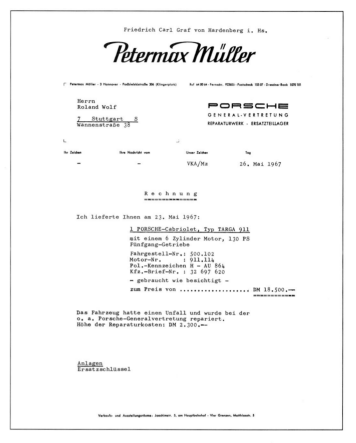

Forstner, chief of the calculating department. Forstner reported that "it would not be possible to install a compressor, as the bulkhead between the cabin and the engine compartment has a different shape from that in the coupe."

In contrast, Porsche tried to ease the burden on its customers who chose to drive in the winter. A ski

Today, prices like these can only be found in dreams. Roland Wolf bought the 102nd Targa ever made for 18,500 DM (about $4625).

For races organized by the Academic Motor Sports Club of Stuttgart University, car numbers were applied by hand.

Grunt work. Installation of the rigid rear window requires a great deal of experience. Many a Targa backlight has been broken in the process.

holder was developed especially for the cabriolet "Targa," available as of June 1965 as part no. 901.801.013.40.

For most Targa customers, winter was the last thing on their minds as they took delivery of their cars in the spring of 1967. Independent businessman Roland Wolf of Stuttgart was one of the first to drive a Targa. The enterprising Swabian had obtained his open 911 by means of a slight detour. In early May, Wolf flew up to the Hannover trade fair, but on that fine day had no great desire to march through its stuffy exhibit halls. The words of a press release about the new open Porsche kept running through his head, and he had already sold his 1963 356 C cabriolet. Wolf also knew that even in these first months of production, demand already exceeded supply, even though the car was not even being exported yet. He

speculated that the supply in Hanover might be somewhat better. As soon as he arrived at the airport, he reached for a telephone directory and found Petermax Müller's Porsche dealership. There, he and salesman Friedrich Carl, Count von Hardenberg, closed the deal. Roland Wolf was the first owner of a red Targa, chassis number 500 102, of which he took delivery in Stuttgart after a minor body repair. Today, Roland Wolf wistfully recalls that "Back then, we almost always drove at the limit." Old race results from the Academic Motor Sports Club of Stuttgart University document that Wolf and his Targa competed successfully against the likes of BMW 2002, 1800 TI, and Alfa Romeo 2600.

But the Targa had its dark side, too. Wolf recalls a drive to Lake Constance, on back roads. Suddenly, the outside air temperature plummeted and hail

159

began to fall. He tried to close the unzipped rear section, in vain, and soon the second-generation bathtub Porsche began to fill with water. The temperature drop had shrunk the plastic, and it could no longer be closed. For this reason, Porsche service shops recommended that customers not open the rear section if the temperature dropped below 15 °C (about 60 °F). No wonder then that a huge 60 mm (nearly 2½ inch) outside thermometer, part no. 644.741.601.06, was one of the most popular Targa accessories, at a price of 75 Marks.

Of course, Porsche continued to improve the Targa. As of chassis no. 500 464 (911) and 550 341 (912), Porsche installed an improved latch for the folding top. As of the 1968 model year, an optional rigid rear window was available; the glass rear window was made standard during the 1969 model year. This move was forced by American safety standards; as of January 1969, U.S. market Targas with plastic rear windows had to be registered as two-seaters. Instead of the rear jump seats, these cars had two small locking compartments. When fitted with a permanently mounted glass backlight, however, the Targa could be registered as a 2+2. The solid glass window had other advantages: rear visibility was greatly improved. Thanks to embedded heating elements, this was also true in bad weather. Because wind noise was reduced, and the Targa more closely resembled the coupe, the solid rear window model became increasingly popular. Its devoted following included a large proportion of women. In early 1970, the Targa exceeded the 40 percent share of 911 production predicted by Harald Wagner.

The 911 Cabriolet

Popular as the Targa was, some would always regard it as a half-hearted stopgap measure. What they really wanted was an uncompromising open Porsche. Ernst Fuhrmann, company president between 1972 and 1980, wouldn't even consider an open 911. Quite the contrary, after he had introduced the Turbo in 1974, despite the oil crisis, Fuhrmann's attitude had undergone a transformation. He wanted the 911 to die quietly, and regarded the 928 as its rightful successor. But long before that, Helmuth

Gerhard Schröder: "We didn't have much time to design the top."

Bott had recorded his prognostications for the future of the 911. He and his team continued to believe in the success of the 911 and could well imagine a 911 cabriolet. To be safe, at the 1981 Frankfurt Auto Show, Porsche tested the attitude of press and customers with a cabriolet prototype. (Gerhard Schröder's drawings for this show car still labeled it a "Speedster.") The car had one additional remarkable feature: it was equipped with all-wheel drive. Although the new drivetrain technology was made visible by means of mirrors, interest for the AWD system remained lukewarm; it was the uncompromising 911 convertible concept that drew the attention of show goers. After a long dry spell without a true cabriolet, Porsche fans heaved a sigh of relief.

To save time, Bott did not go through the usual channels. Instead of issuing a work order to the design department for a new cabriolet, he engaged convertible top specialist Gerhard Schröder directly. On Maundy Thursday (the last working day before the Easter holidays), Schröder arrived at Bott's home in Buttenhausen at the wheel of a dark blue prototype, to have his handiwork appraised by Porsche's chief engineer. Bott recalls that "My designers and I were enthusiastic about the top design." Schröder says "To some extent, I was able to use the reference materials I had gathered during my time at the specialist coachworks manufacturer Ramseier & Cie. in Worblaufen, Switzerland." From these,

160

specialist Schröder developed a new top bow design for the 911, in which about half of the roof consisted of stamped steel panels. Yet the entire top could be lowered completely into the bodywork. This ingenious new design ensured that it would retain its shape even at high speeds, up to the top speed of 245 km/h (152 mph), and also provided good rollover protection. Today, Helmuth Bott declares that "What Gerhard Schröder achieved in record time was a masterpiece."

Schröder never got rich from the patents registered with his name as inventor. German patent law specifies that Porsche must pay the inventor 33 Pfennigs per car produced. With 41,436 cabriolets produced to May 1993, that works out to 13,673.88 Marks. Not a fortune, but not at all bad either.

New benchmarks. About half of the 911 top consists of stamped steel panels.

Opening or closing the manual top is accomplished in seconds.

Of course, removal of the Targa bar exacted a toll in terms of chassis stiffness. Extensive stiffening of the floorpan compensated for this loss. This, of course, again required a multitude of tests.

At first, the top was still manually operated. A zipper permitted opening the flexible plastic rear window. However, from the very beginning, Ferry Porsche had desired an electrically operated top. One of the design targets was officially stated as follows: "A system is to be devised which will perform the transformation from closed to open top, and vice versa,

without manual intervention. Furthermore, it is desired that the top opening and closing process be possible from within the car, without opening doors or windows." This catalog of requirements seemed realizable, but would have required too much development time; the plan was to offer the cabriolet as of 1983. The solution was to first offer a manual top, followed as soon as possible by the automatic top.

Again, it was Schröder who was given a direct assignment to build the prototype. The manually operated roof was an ideal starting point for the desired automatic. The roof latches were modified for electrical operation, and space had to be found for the electric drive components. Both motors disappeared under a cover behind the rear seat backs. Power was transmitted by two flexible shafts to gear-driven arms located under the rear side upholstery. The windshield frame provided adequate room for the top latches; the top was located by two pins. The top mechanism was activated by a pushbutton which was only active when the car was parked.

This may all sound quite simple, but in fact the drive motors activate 13 moving bows as well as the top frame and linkage arms, with 22 pivots in the top and on the body. The sequence of operations is monitored by a microprocessor control unit. After a top closing operation, an indicator light in the dashboard notifies the driver that the top has been properly latched. The entire operation takes 20 seconds. Automatic operation provided the 911 with the best convertible top on the market. In addition, wind tunnel tests showed that the convertible had a better C_d than the coupe, because the soft top could conform to the air flow. The high-grade mechanism had its price; electrical operation added about 4000 Marks to the cost of a new car.

And what of the Targa? It remained a sales success. The cabriolet brought a new group of customers to the Porsche fold. Targa fans remained loyal, with few changing over to the completely open model. After all, the Targa also provides open-air motoring; if desired, rolling up the side windows makes its interior virtually draft free. The customer is able to control the flow of fresh air and, in bad weather, gives up nothing to the coupe. On the other hand, the cabriolet could be brought up to the standard of an

162

The drive motors for the electric top must actuate 13 movable bows, as well as the roof frame and linkage levers, with 22 pivots.

all-season vehicle by the installation of a particularly attractive hardtop. Porsche's engineers were able to install the rear quarter windows and the backlight of the coupe in a galvanized roof. A cabriolet fitted with the hardtop was almost indistinguishable from a 911 coupe, even at short range. The stiff price of 6585 Marks (unpainted) was attributable to the limited, hand-made nature of the top. It was advisable to order the hardtop along with the car, so that it could be precisely fitted to the body. Thereafter, for winter driving, the hardtop could be attached by two people. At the windshield frame and the B-pillars, the hard-

top uses the same attachment points as the fabric top. At the rear, six bolts and pre-existing fittings attach the top to the bodywork.

For the 1985 model year, the Targa and cabriolet were even offered in the wide-body "Turbo Look," but without the Turbo rear wing. In the following model year, and continuing to the 1989 model year, both body styles were even available as bonafide 3.3 liter Turbos. Also in the 1989 model year, an additional open Porsche joined the family: the two-seat Speedster. This return to a tradition from the 356 era

163

The hardtop should be ordered with the new car, so that it may be custom-fitted to the bodywork.

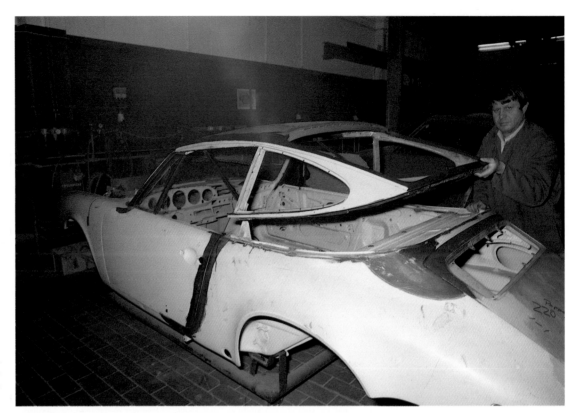

As of the spring of 1987, the Targa and cabriolet were available as genuine Turbos.

The Speedster revival began with the 1989 model year.

The Clubsport variation of the Speedster could only be seen as a styling study at the 1987 Frankfurt auto show.

165

The new Speedster, with its 964 bodywork, presents a much more integrated appearance than its predecessor.

In its Turbo Look version, the cabriolet continued in production until December 1993.

Even before the new wore off, the 1989 Speedster was a classic. The manually operated roof disappeared under the twin fairings of the composite rear deck cover.

(the Porsche 356 Speedster was born in 1954) fulfilled a dream for many Porsche drivers. This most open of all 911s was based on the 911 Carrera Turbo Look, but could also be ordered with the narrow body. The windshield was lower, and the manually operated rudimentary top disappeared under the twin fairings of the composite body-colored turtledeck.

At the 1987 Frankfurt auto show, Porsche showed a Speedster Clubsport, completely devoid of any sort of windshield and with only one seat backed by a small roll bar. This version never went into production. The roadgoing Speedster went out of production after the 1989 model year. The planned 2100 examples were quickly sold, despite styling which may have required some getting used to, as it was based on the new 964 bodywork. Nevertheless, prices escalated well over the original selling price, and did not stabilize until two years later.

As of the 1990 model year, the Targa and cabriolet were available with the new 964 bodywork. However, demand for the Targa was declining. Both versions were available with Carrera 4 drivetrains, and the Turbo Look was optional for rear-wheel as well as all-wheel drive models. It was not until the Paris salon of October 1992 that the Speedster experienced a revival, in its new form. It was to be offered only with the standard narrow-body Carrera cabriolet bodywork. It didn't take long for customers to

protest this limitation, and the Turbo Look Speedster was made available in the summer of 1993.

The new Speedster generation did not incorporate the characteristic features of its predecessor within its newer bodywork. Components such as the top mechanism had to be re-engineered, for which Lutz Podewski bore responsibility. Podewski emphasizes that "In keeping with the good old Speedster tradition, the top is opened and closed manually. This chore has gotten easier, though." Indeed, compared to the 1989 version, the latch mechanism was extensively reworked. After a short introduction and observing the prescribed sequence of operations, the fabric top is easily managed. Sealing was also optimized; Podewski explains that "If a Speedster passes our sealing test using artificial rain, it is perfectly suitable for everyday use." The rigidly attached windshield and improved rubber seals, including those on the side windows, improved matters considerably. Moreover, the latching of the composite cover, which completely hides the lowered top, was improved.

The Carrera RS seat shells, painted in body color, and leather upholstery specifically designed for the Speedster provide visual accents. Other conspicuous features include body-colored instrument panel accents, shift lever and parking brake handle. Porsche returned to the Speedster philosophy of the 1950s; at its German market introduction in the spring of 1993, this minimalist car with maximized qualities was priced at 131,500 Marks, 8457 Marks less than the comparable Carrera 2 cabriolet. And this despite inclusion of conveniences such as electric windows and air conditioning. Initially, the low windshield did not provide adequate support for an inflating airbag; minor modifications later allowed airbags to be available on the Speedster.

This does not in any way diminish the pleasure of driving a Speedster. The low windshield lets the driver experience the pure joy of driving. The two-seater blasts to 100 km/h (62 mph) in 5.7 seconds. Like the other Carrera models, top speed is listed as 260 km/h. Theoretically, it should be higher, as the Speedster has a smaller frontal area.

The new Speedster, which had a production run of

With the cabriolet, Porsche offers a solution for those seeking an open sports car with everyday utility.

Exciting from every aspect: the 911 Carrera cabriolet, available as of March, 1994.

The shape of the new cabriolet top complements the integrated lines of the new Carrera generation.

exactly 930 cars, continued in production to the end of 1993. Even though the new Carrera generation (internally designated the 993) had already been revealed at the 1993 Frankfurt auto show, the Speedster continued to sell, often with optional Turbo bodywork.

The Porsche 911 Carrera cabriolet, introduced in March 1994, is based on the Carrera coupe which celebrated its debut in September 1993. Compared to its predecessor, numerous cabriolet-specific components were optimized and integrated into the latest iteration of the classic sports car. Thanks to a new restraint system for rear seat passengers, housed in a seat belt dome, the cabriolet can once again be sold as a full-fledged 2+2 in the United States. A new wind blocker, which raises automatically when the roof is lowered, offers a completely new, user-friendly solution to unwelcome turbulence in the Carrera cabriolet.

The roof raises or lowers in only 13 seconds. Compared to its predecessor, top operation has been altered. In the new cabriolet, top operation is possible while the engine is running, but for safety reasons the vehicle must not be moving. To ensure that this condition is met, the top functions only when the parking brake is applied. The ignition key must be in the "run" position.

The interior of the new 911 cabriolet is more attractive than ever. The entire top mechanism and the attachments for the top fabric are now covered by a headliner, which results in a neat, smooth environment. The new headliner is made of a material which acts as an excellent sound deadener and also folds very easily.

Due to insufficient demand, the Targa will not be offered, at least for the time being. Nevertheless, open cars will always be part of the Porsche legend.

The Carrera RS 2.7 and its successors

Highly addictive

If forced to choose the one definitive 911 model from a 30-year history of superlative six-cylinder sports cars, one very special model immediately comes to mind: the Carrera RS 2.7, introduced at the Paris salon in October, 1972. When production ended in the fall of 1973, 1580 examples had been built. Why this car, above all other 911 models? There are several good reasons. For one, this particular model is visually very attractive. The RS is an especially well balanced compromise between visual appeal and engineering necessity. The Carrera RS wears a steel suit cut in the original 911 style, and carries it well despite the addition of very necessary aerodynamic aids. The front air dam and rear "ducktail" spoiler add an aggressive dash to the car's outfit, without becoming obtrusive. Second, it was the first 911 to carry wider rims at the rear (7 inch) than at the front (6 inch), and its fenders were flared accordingly. These fender flares were restrained enough to allow the 2.7 RS to go down in Porsche history as the epitome of the pure, slim-bodied 911.

The RS hardware is fascinating, but not sensational. The 2.7 liter powerplant is the logical outgrowth of the production 2.4 liter engine. Not surprisingly, the 190 horsepower of the 2.4 grew to 210 hp in the 2.7. The RS was developed at a time when considerations of unleaded fuel and noise standards took a back seat to pure performance, and loud, relatively thirsty cars were not yet stigmatized. However, by the time the RS came to market, the first oil crisis had changed all that. From that point on, engine designers would have to meet environmental standards in their search for more power. For this reason, the effortless power and acoustic presence of the potent 2.7 liter powerplant would make it the ultimate 911 engine from the days when sporting ability went unchecked by environmental concerns.

Then there was its lightweight design philosophy, which actually was not a philosophy at all but rather an honest assessment of reality: the decisive factor in sports car design has always been the car's power to weight ratio. Lightweight construction is the most efficient method of improving performance. Braking distances are shorter, and the car accelerates more quickly. Aside from the 911 R of 1967 and the 911 ST of 1970, both rare, uncompromising production-based derivatives, the RS was Porsche's first effort to offer a race-capable machine to a wider circle of enthusiasts. Later, as customer demands for comfort increased, this would become increasingly difficult.

But the success secret of the 1973 RS is its overall balance. Everything fits together: the body, the engine and the suspension harmonize with one

Uncompromisingly sporting: the 911 R of 1967 was the first lightweight 911.

The 911 ST of 1970, a hybrid of the "S" and "T" models.

Forerunner: this Carrera 2.7 RS prototype is not fitted with the later spoiler package.

Sobering: without the ducktail spoiler, rear lift is drastically increased.

Endurance test: the Carrera RS was also tested for rally applications. For the East African Safari, Porsche installed 210 hp production engines, but modified the suspension.

another. Purists maintain that it's all the car anyone would ever need – or want. The 911 RS is now over 20 years old, by any ordinary definition a vintage car. Yet this bit of reality is forgotten the instant one drives the car. The 2.7 RS was so advanced for its day that its performance is impressive even in a modern context. When the throttle is floored, its 210 horses mobilize its lightweight structure with a vehemence matched only by much more powerful modern sports cars. Full application of this sports car's power yields a clearly perceived, distinctive sound lacking in more modern vehicles. Even today, The 2.7 RS provides pure, unadulterated driving pleasure. The realization that its performance was sensational for its day naturally adds to the enjoyment.

In contemplating the 2.7 RS, we must not lose sight of one thing. Porsche would long since have ceased to exist if the sports car smiths of Zuffenhausen had only built the RS or only the 2.7 RS. This

pure sports car appeals to a very limited group of hard-core fans. So we come to an alternative answer to our original question, the question of the definitive 911. Only 1580 examples of the RS were built, including 55 iterations of the racing Carrera RSR. This naturally increases its exclusivity. And hardly two examples are alike. There is a deep-rooted fallacy that all RSs were delivered in Grand Prix White, as the original plan to make the car available only in a single exclusive color was not adhered to. The RS was available in every regular and special order color, as well as colors to sample, but not in metallic paint. Admittedly, the first RSs were delivered in white. However, they were distinguished by the Carrera script on the doors and their painted wheels, which could be ordered in blue (205 cars), green (60 cars) or red (185 cars). Light yellow was the color chosen for 296 Carreras. The Carrera script on doors and engine lid also leads to confusion. The original sales brochure shows them as "positive" script, but

174

Even parked, the Carrera RS of 1973 makes a dynamic impression, without becoming obtrusive. The model shown here is an RS Sport (option code M 471).

A splendor of colors: most RS Carreras were delivered in white, but differed in the color of their Carrera script and wheel centers. Bright colors were also available.

175

in fact "negative" script was applied to production cars. The three colored scripts (red, blue, or green) could only be applied to white cars. All other colors came with black script. For the RSR, any script color could be ordered.

Further RS paint details will not be mentioned in this volume. Readers interested in more detailed information are referred to a magnificent work, unique among automotive books, by Austrian enthusiasts Thomas Gruber and Georg Konradsheim. Their meticulous three-year research project is the last word in Carrera RS history.

Naturally, each RS is a lightweight 911, but there are differences. The lightest version was the RSH, intended strictly for homologation. For weight reasons, it was not even fitted with stabilizer bars and carried tiny 165 tires at the front. Only 17 were built.

The RS Sport (option code M 471) was intended for club racing and amateur motorsports activities, yet fully capable of everyday service. Porsche reduced the weight of the touring version from 1075 kg (2370 lbs.) to the RS Sport weight of 975 kg (2150 lbs.) by painstaking detail work. For example, the bumper deco strips were deleted, as were the engine lid latch and the rear rubber bumper guards. Decals replaced Porsche crests, and the rear quarter windows could not be opened. The interior lacked a clock, comfortable carpeting, passenger sun visor, arm rests, door storage pockets and rear seats. The door latch was actuated by a pull strap. Only one battery was fitted, on the left side, and only one low-frequency horn. The spare tire was a collapsible "space saver" supplied with an inflator bottle.

The Sport was built during the entire RS production run. This should also lay to rest the second erroneous legend, that the first 500 were built as lightweights. How then could the fourth from last car (of the 1580 built) have been a Sport? A total of 200 RS Sport editions were built.

Customers ordered the RS Touring (M 472) a total of 1308 times. Equipment was virtually identical to that of the 911 S. On this model, in particular, equipment and accessories could be combined freely. The standard equipment fitted to each car may be found

in Gruber and Konradsheim's RS book.

The 55 examples of the RSR racing version (M 491) deviated much more from the production models. Their main differences were fender flares resembling those of the later Turbo model, a roll bar, a 2.8 liter engine and the braking system of the 917 race car.

The technology of the 2.7 liter Carrera is described in the year-by-year model descriptions, while detailed facts and figures may be found in the technical specifications, both at the back of this book. The story of the RS' breakthrough in motorsports is presented in a separate chapter.

The 2.7 liter Carrera does not by any means represent the end of the lightweight Porsche story. In 1974, it was followed by yet another high point in sports car history, the 230 horsepower Carrera RS 3.0. It was half a second faster to 100 km/h [62 mph], but *auto motor und sport* observed a top speed of "only" 238.4 km/h [148 mph], where the 2.7 RS had gone 240 km/h. This was attributable to its wider bodywork, based on that of the newer G-model. However, the three-liter RS used thinner sheet metal. The muscular fenders permitted fitting 8-inch wheels at the front and 9-inchers at the rear. Behind the wheels, Porsche installed the brake system of the 917 Turbo to provide stopping performance matching the acceleration potential of the 3.0 RS, especially important in the 330 hp racing version. A newly developed rear spoiler, with a conspicuous rubber surround, provided directional stability and downforce.

To meet the homologation requirements for FIA Group 4 (Special GT), 100 units had to be sold. Porsche built exactly 111 of these cars, of which six were right-hand drive; five went to Britain and one to Japan. The exact breakdown of subtypes is as follows: 54 roadgoing cars (Group 3), 42 RSRs (Group 4), and 15 IROC cars. These last were ordered by Roger Penske for the "International Race of Champions." Visually, the cars appeared to be standard production vehicles, but their bodywork covered RSR mechanicals. In view of the hefty price tag of 64,900 Marks, there was some initial concern about sales; due to the ongoing energy crisis, German

Rarity: the
Carrera RS shown
here, chassis
number
9114609018, is one
of only five
right-hand-drive
examples exported
to Britain. A sixth
went to Japan.

Club racer:
the 911 Carrera
SC RS was
equipped with a
three-liter engine.

autobahns were speed limited to 100 km/h. The Carreras sold quickly after the German government declared the crisis over.

Because of its limited numbers, the three-liter Carrera cannot be regarded as a successor to the 2.7 RS. The same applies to the three-liter 911 SC RS, sold in 1984 as a customer car for amateur motorsports. Only twenty left the plant, conceived for the race track. With 935 cylinder heads, more radical cams and other race-tested modifications, the car developed 255 hp and achieved a top speed of 255 km/h [158 mph]. In fighting trim for Group B racing, the SC RS weighed in at only 960 kg [2115 lbs.], thanks to its aluminum front fenders, front lid and doors, plastic bumpers and front air dam, and thinner glass all around. The brake system was that of the 911 Turbo. Cigarette manufacturer Rothmans entered several 911 SC RS in the European Rally Championship, with Finnish rally ace Henri Toivonen contracted as lead driver.

The next limited-production racer also represented the absolute pinnacle of 911 evolution to date. In 1986, Porsche surprised the automotive world with its technology demonstrator, the 959, which is covered in a separate chapter (pages 191 - 200).

For the 1987 model year, Porsche built 340 examples of the 911 Carrera Club Sport (option code M 637) with a 231 hp 3.2 liter powerplant, exhausting through an environmentally correct catalytic converter. The rev limit was raised to 6840 rpm. This 82,275 Mark piece of sporting equipment was available for three model years. Eighty-one were built in 1987, 21 in 1988 for the U.S. market and 148 for the rest of the world. In 1989, seven examples went to the U.S. and 83 to the remaining markets. The two-seater had no sound deadening material, no rust-proofing sprayed into its body cavities and no undercoating; the increased interior sound level provided drivers with a constant reminder of their investment. Interestingly, Porsche did not offer Club Sport customers their customary long-term anti-corrosion warranty; instead, the warranty against rust perforation was limited to only two years.

Externally, this athletically inclined 911 was recognizable by the "Club Sport" script on the left front fender. Right hand drive versions for Britain carried "Carrera CS" script on the doors and on the rear lid, similar to the Carrera 2.7 RS. The interior atmosphere was best described as Spartan. Many items not deemed absolutely necessary were simply left out, yet the electrically adjustable and heatable outside mirrors were retained.

Model differences: For the British market, the 911 Carrera Club Sport, available as of the 1987 model year, had bold "Carrera CS" script on the doors. The German and U.S. versions had only a discreet decal on the left front fender.

Worthy successor: The Carrera legend was reborn on September 18, 1990, at the Birmingham Motor Show. 260 horsepower gave a top speed of 260 km/h [162 mph].

In 1990, Porsche announced its Carrera Cup racing series. Customers with sporting ambitions could buy one of the identically-prepared racers for the relatively reasonable price of 123,000 Marks. In addition, they had to pay a security deposit of 75,000 Marks, which was returned only if the driver regularly took part in races. This was Porsche's strategy to prevent speculators from buying the Carrera Cup cars solely to turn them over for a quick profit.

When customers clamored for a new Carrera RS for the street, Porsche reacted quickly. The new Carrera RS celebrated its world premiere on September 18, 1990, at the Birmingham motor show. The legendary Carrera 2.7 was reborn. And again, reduced weight was a primary feature. By leaving out creature comforts, curb weight was reduced about ten percent to 1240 kg [2731 lbs.] Compared to the Carrera 2, detail work raised power output by 10 hp to 260 hp, which enabled a top speed of 260 km/h [162 mph]. As on the SC RS, the brake system was borrowed from the Turbo.

One thousand examples would be required for homologation in FIA Group N/GT, but Porsche raised production to 2164 units (not including the RS America). Of these, a total of 2051 were built as the standard street version and the more expensive sport version. The remaining 113 cars were built as race cars equipped with the M 003 option package. As it turned out, Porsche built too many Carrera RSs; on the used car market, virtually new examples dropped to rock-bottom prices, and Porsche was barely able to sell its stock of new cars.

But Porsche's RS philosophy was right on target. Customers wanted a sports version, but they also demanded exclusivity. Concurrently with the RS, the customer racing department in Weissach built a lightweight version of the Carrera 4 for the race track, without a catalytic converter. Twenty copies of this hand-built lightweight were made, at a price of over 300,000 Marks. This, presumably, was exclusive enough.

The 1992 Carrera Cup version of the RS cost 148,000 Marks, put out 275 hp and had a modified suspension mounting 18-inch wheels. No street version was ever built.

In 1992, Porsche revealed yet another confection: the 911 Turbo S. With a base price of 295,000 Marks, it was conceived for club racing, but its limited production ensured that collectors would also be interested. Extensive fine tuning raised the 3.3 liter engine's power output to 381 hp. A weight reduction of 180 kg [396 lbs.] provided an incredible power to weight ratio of 3.4 kg/hp [7.5 lbs./hp]. For comparison, the 959 had a power to weight ratio of 3.2 kg/hp [7.2 lbs./hp].

For 1993, Porsche developed a particularly attractive model lineup for production-based racing (see motorsports chapter). Weissach developed the "911 Turbo S Le Mans," with its twin-turbo engine developing about 475 hp, specifically to meet the Le Mans GT regulations. The modified 911 Turbo 3.6 was available for the IMSA Supercar Championship, and the Carrera RSR 3.8 competed for the ADAC [German Auto Club] GT Cup. This especially attractive evolution of the Type 964 Carrera weighs only 1120 kg [2467 lbs.] and is propelled by a powerplant developing 325 hp at 6900 rpm and 360 Nm [265 ft.-lbs.] of torque at 5500 rpm. Ready to race, with numerous aluminum and composite components, the ADAC GT Cup cars were initially priced at 270,000 Marks.

For the 1994 season, the German Porsche Carrera Cup racing series, already a classic, was run with brand new cars, based on the new Type 993 Carrera. Again, a street version was available.

A completely new Carrera RS, based on the radically redesigned 911 Carrera (Type 993), was introduced in February 1995. The engine displacement was raised to 3.8 liters by increasing cylinder bores to 102 mm. The 1995 Carrera RS included a completely new induction system, known as "Varioram," which provides variable intake tract length dependent on engine rpm. As a result, power increased to 300 hp (221 kW) from the stock 272 hp (200 kW), yet torque at low rpm was also increased. At low engine speeds, the intake tracts of the Carrera RS were nearly twice as long as those of the stock Carrera. As revs increase, vacuum-actuated slides, one per cylinder bank, shorten the intake runner length. This makes the RS especially tractable even in city traffic.

This new Carrera RS weighed only 1270 kg (2797 lbs.), 100 kg less than the standard Carrera. This weight reduction was achieved by deleting comfort items including rear seats, electric windows, electric mirrors, central locking, headlight washers and stereo speakers. The windshield washer system holds only 1.2 liters (instead of 6.5l). The extensive interior illumination of the 911 Carrera has been replaced by the smaller interior light of the Speedster. Airbags were available as an option.

A special version of the Carrera RS, the Clubsport, was available for racing activities. Like the RS, it was available in most markets as a street-legal car. The anticipated production run of 100 units, in left or right hand drive, qualifies the car for the FIA GT2 racing class. In the German market, the 1995 Clubsport was priced at 164,700 Marks. That price includes a welded-in roll cage, shock tower brace, special racing seats for driver and passenger, six-point harnesses, battery kill switch and fire extinguisher. The modified front spoiler and adjustable but non-retractable rear spoiler provide added downforce. The rear spoiler angle of attack can be adjusted between zero and 12 degrees to match it to different race tracks. The rear spoiler also includes engine combustion and and cooling air inlets.

The Clubsport has even more Spartan equipment than the RS. The interior sheet metal is painted in body color, without sound deadener, carpeting or upholstery. The dual-mass flywheel was deleted, and an airbag is available as an option only on the driver's side. The engine and suspension are identical to those of the Carrera RS.

Porsche 911 Turbo
New dimensions

In the early 1970s, Otto-cycle [gasoline] engines with exhaust-driven turbochargers were almost exclusively found on racing engines. To achieve the highest possible power output from a given displacement, the amount of air drawn in naturally on each cylinder's intake stroke was and still is simply inadequate. However, normally wasted energy in the exhaust gas stream may be used to drive a turbine, which in turn drives a compressor mounted on the same shaft. The compressor draws air, compresses it, and forces it into the cylinders. When combined with a correspondingly higher fuel injection rate, it is possible for such turbo-supercharged engines to achieve more than double the specific output [horsepower per liter, or horsepower per cubic inch] of normally-aspirated engines.

As far back as the 1920s and 1930s, racing engine designers put this priciple to good use, albeit with mechanically-driven compressors. The Auto Union series of Grand Prix cars, developed by Porsche, is only one of many examples from this golden age of auto racing. But exhaust-driven turbocharging was not invented by the men from Untertürkheim [Mercedes], Zwickau [Auto Union] or Zuffenhausen [Porsche]. The principle was patented by a Swiss engineer, Alfred Büchi, in 1905. Initially, it was diesel engines which benefited from exhaust turbocharging.

Paul Hensler, director of Porsche engine research and development, explains that "Lack of compressed air was never a problem. But in the late 1960s, matching the supply of high-pressure air to driving conditions was regarded as an insoluble problem." On the race track, this was merely a secondary concern, especially in the American Can-Am racing series; Porsche's turbocharged Type 917 Can-Am racers, with twelve-cylinder turbocharged engines developing up to 1200 horsepower, could be driven at full throttle for most of each lap.

For road use, however, other criteria become important. What was lacking was some arrangement which could regulate the amount of power produced. Even the inventive Swiss engine specialist Michael May could not solve the problem. In the late 1960s, he installed a small turbocharger, capable of supplying useful boost even at low rpm, on a Ford Capri V6 engine. "Development chief Ferdinand Piëch assigned Julius Weber and myself to drive over to the Schwabengarage in Stuttgart, to test drive the May Turbo," recalls turbo specialist Heinz Dorsch, at the time a development engineer at Porsche. "That wasn't the right answer either."

BMW also played a decisive role in the development of turbocharging. In 1969, the Bavarians won

Not just for dreamers. The 911 Turbo exudes power from every perspective

182

the European Touring Car Championship using turbocharged engines. At the 1973 Frankfurt Auto Show, BMW presented the 2002 turbo, a sport sedan which quickly disappeared from the scene thanks to poor engine durability and the oil crisis.

"Still, we were highly motivated by our racing success (we had convincingly won the American Can-Am championship on our first try) to make turbo technology socially acceptable," says Paul Hensler. Porsche engineers visited the leading turbocharger suppliers of the time, including Garrett in the U.S., Bosch in Stuttgart and Eberspächer in Esslingen. Ultimately, though, in 1971, a cooperative deal was struck with the lesser known firm of Kühnle, Kopp & Kausch (KKK for short) in Frankenthal.

The main objective of the cooperative effort was to find a suitable means of boost regulation. The response of any supercharged engine, whether turbocharged or equipped with a mechanical blower, is dependent on boost pressure. When the throttle is opened, boost pressure must be available quickly; conversely, when the throttle is closed, it must be reduced. Therefore, full boost should not be provided at all times, as had been the prior state of the art. Instead, boost pressure has to be modulated. Porsche's engine development engineers saw the answer in exhaust-side boost regulation. If too much boost pressure was available, exhaust gases were not directed to the turbine, but rather diverted by a wastegate. If more power was desired, the wastegate was closed. "Although this sounds like a simple solution, at the time it was completely new, but turbocharger technology had its own unique problems," recalls Heinz Dorsch. Oil supply to the turbocharger presented difficulties; because the low turbocharger location mandated by a boxer engine, unpressurized oil could not return to the main lubrication circuit. If the oil were left in the turbocharger, it would seep into the turbine section and would have produced blue exhaust smoke as it was burned. The answer was an additional scavenge pump to draw oil from the turbocharger housing and feed it back to the oil tank.

"Then we had thermal problems," recalls Dorsch. The turbine inlet temperature was as high as 900 °C [1650 °F]; turbochargers on diesel engines saw only

Heinz Dorsch: "Turbocharger technology had its own unique problems."

600 °C [1100 °F]. Because both the turbine and the turbine housing were subject to hot exhaust gases, new materials and welding techniques had to be applied to withstand these temperatures. Then there were problems with seals and bearings. All in all, it was a difficult job to add turbocharger technology to the cramped engine compartment of the 911, even though the first Porsche Turbos were not yet fitted with the boxy intercooler.

Heinz Dorsch recalls that "Internally, at this stage, the turbocharger was still regarded as a tuning trick." But initial trials were so successful that soon the question of building a turbocharged production car was raised. The market environment for such a high-performance sports car was anything but favorable. Porsche was feeling financial pains and Heinz Dorsch recalls that "Prophets inside the company prognosticated that in ten years, there would be no more gasoline." Still, Porsche swam against the tide and built a production turbocharged car. The decisive event which led to this decision was experienced by Porsche's manager, Ernst Fuhrmann, during a 1972 race at Hockenheim. Wolfgang Berger, at the time working with Norbert Singer in the racing department, clearly recalls that "We watched a race in which a Ford Capri was running well in the lead, followed by a BMW. The fastest Porsche, from the Kremer team, had already been lapped. At that point,

First series: The Turbo was available with a three-liter powerplant beginning in 1975. Its 12 psi of boost provided 260 horsepower, at the time a stunning power output.

Professor Fuhrmann asked me why the competition was running away from [our product]." Berger's reply led to Porsche's decision to reenter production-based racing. The Carrera RS 2.7 was quickly developed. The rules for the so-called Group 4 (special GTs) required 500 units. But soon, Porsche's powerful normally-aspirated engine was made uncompetitive by a new racing regulation, known as Appendix J. Porsche decided to concentrate on Group 5 racing, with the Type 935, but also wanted a car for homologation in Group 4. In November 1973, company management decided to build the required 400 cars. This marks the birth of the 911 Turbo, which would be developed under the type designation Porsche 930.

The fact that it was the only car in the product line to require leaded premium fuel made the decision to go ahead with a street turbo all the more remarkable. All intake system parts were made in Weissach, as it would not have been cost effective to have outside suppliers tool up for such limited production runs. Similarly, the fender flares were welded on by hand, as new tooling would have been too costly.

Working with Bosch, Porsche also sought out the most cost-efficient solution for the fuel injection system. Optimum results would be provided by air metering at constant pressure upstream of the compressor, and fuel injection above the intake valve. The state of the art for such a system was the Bosch K-Jetronic, which, however, did not have a suitable air metering unit to meet the airflow demand of the six-cylinder Turbo. Instead, an available eight-cylinder unit was used, having an air metering capacity sufficient for 400 hp. Heinz Dorsch explains that "we simply closed off two outlets." This method was still used in 1994, after just under 30,000 911 Turbos had been built. Within the Porsche model line, the Turbo was always the one model which could be offered for the longest time without changes, and therefore was developed accordingly. Dorsch emphasizes that "The Turbo always had the lowest warranty claim rate."

The three-liter Turbo bowed at the Paris salon in the fall of 1974; a year earlier, a turbocharged racing version of the Carrera RSR had been shown. The Turbo was a success for two reasons. First, 1975 saw an economic upturn, and not a moment too soon. Second, according to Paul Hensler, "The Turbo conveyed something that even we had not anticipated. Its tremendous acceleration, the feeling of being pressed back into the seat, still excites Turbo customers to this day. And we must continue to nurture this unique fascination." Naturally, in the mid-1970s, the Turbo's wide-bodied stance and its huge rear spoiler contributed to its sales success as well as its image. Soon the Porsche 911 Turbo was simply called "Turbo" – a word to command the respect of competitors.

The very first Turbo was a unique example fitted with a 250 hp 2.7 liter powerplant, tested in daily use by Louise Piëch, Ferry Porsche's sister and chief executive of Porsche Austria. A three-liter version priced at 65,000 Marks was available beginning in March of 1975. A boost pressure of 0.8 atmosphere [12 psi] provided 260 hp, an impressive torque of 343 Nm [253 ft.-lbs.] at 4000 rpm, and acceleration from zero to 100 km/h [62 mph] in 5.5 seconds. In 1974, the editor of *auto motor und sport*, Clauspeter Becker, described his first encounter with Porsche's flagship: "With the turbocharger, Porsche has achieved that which all of the previous displacement increases never quite managed: abundant power at moderate rpm."

The Turbo 3.3

Naturally, development of the Turbo continued, if for no other reason than the fact that turbocharging presented one way of making enormous power output possible, yet was also capable of meeting more stringent emissions requirements. Laboratory tests showed that without changing compression ratio or fuel octane rating, charge air cooling would permit

appreciably higher boost and therefore higher power output. In the real world, engine intake air temperatures just upstream of the intake valve ranged between 140 and 150 °C [284 and 302 °F]. This, of course, increased the thermal load on the engine, which meant that the intake air pressure had to be reduced. If this was to be achieved without a loss of power, a greater air volume would have to be supplied, which in turn required more power for the turbocharger to feed air to the combustion chambers. The intercooler lowered air temperatures by 50 to 60 °C [90 to 108 °F], allowing higher boost pressures. As this required smaller air volumes, smaller turbochargers could be used. The lower thermal load on the engine also led to a lower tendency toward pre-ignition, reducing the likelihood of engine knock. Heinz Dorsch emphasizes the benefits of intercooling: "With increased cooling, the same engine power can be achieved with lower compressor pressure ratios. But the temperature should not be decreased beyond a certain point. An optimum value has to be found, otherwise there would be too much flow restriction from the intercooler. This in turn would require more power to drive the turbocharger and therefore higher exhaust back pressure in the turbine. We have to find the best compromise between increasing the back pressure and reducing the air temperature."

Although this knowledge was incorporated in the second generation Turbo, introduced as a 1978 model, it was kept secret for several years to maintain Porsche's competitive advantage. The intercooler was placed above the six-cylinder engine, under a rear spoiler designed specifically to provide space for the large boxlike structure.

Zuffenhausen's new weapon, code named 930/60, developed 300 hp from a displacement of 3.3 liters.

In 1986, the Turbo line was expanded by the addition of Targa and Cabriolet versions. At the time, there was much discussion about the reasoning, or lack thereof, behind a 300 horsepower Cabriolet. And the factory Turbo "slant nose" conversions were not a matter of opinion, rather a matter of taste. The special order department led by Rolf Sprenger and Elmar Willrett kept an open ear (and mind) to power hungry customers. Turbo engines could be

modified to put out 330 hp, and even 350 hp in the case of the 964 Turbo.

Porsche was still struggling with one technical problem. Lead contained in gasoline formed deposits on the turbine blades. After about 35,000 km [22,000 miles], deposits would be so heavy that a portion could peel off and cause turbine imbalance. At typical turbine operating speeds of 100,000 to 120,000 rpm, such an imbalance would shake the turbine to pieces. Later examination showed that the lead deposits occurred only if the temperature reached 600 °C [1100 °F], making the interval between such occurrences dependent on driving style. In Germany, this problem was minimized as the lead content of fuel was reduced. In the United States, where the lead content was even higher, unleaded fuel was required even though the Turbo was not equipped with a catalyst.

And it was believed that catalysts would determine the fate of the Turbo. "We saw no possibility of fitting the Turbo with a catalyst," says Paul Hensler. With the technology then available, it would have been theoretically possible, but with too much power loss. Heinz Dorsch sums up the problem: "Of the original 300 hp, only 240 would have remained." For this reason, the Turbo disappeared from the U.S. lineup in 1985, and in 1990 even in Germany. This resulted in incredible prices for used Porsche Turbos, especially those with the five-speed transmission. Even some older models were selling for more than their original sticker prices.

Meanwhile, development work on a successor, code named 965, was proceeding at full steam. This car was to have many components taken from Porsche's rolling technology showcase, the 959, including a twin turbo system. Two turbochargers, one on each side, would have permitted much better heat management, and the thermal energy of the exhaust gases would have been available on even shorter notice. The 965 was also fitted with a modern Motronic engine management system (long standard on Porsche's four-cylinder turbocharged models), which would have made it more fuel efficient. All-

Can't touch this: fascination for the turbocharged 911 continues unabated. The imposing rear spoiler provides downforce and houses the intercooler.

wheel drive would have made the 965's 360 hp more usable. From the fall of 1988 to the spring of 1989, the biturbo 965, bearing a strong resemblance to the 959, was tested on the roads of southern France (see illustration). At the last minute, the new director of research and development, Ulrich Bez, shifted the project goals to building a "more civilized version." In charge of Weissach since the fall of 1988, Bez' primary concern was the car's high price. Customers for the 965 would have been expected to ante up about 200,000 Marks. Still, in view of its technical complexity, production costs for the 965 would have been quite reasonable, as a large part of its development cost had already been written off on the Carrera 4.

Instead, the 911 Turbo, after a hiatus of nearly a year and a half, celebrated a less than successful comeback. For one, its price of 178,500 Marks was more than 40,000 Marks higher than that of its predecessor. It carried 964 bodywork, and was again fitted with the customary rear spoiler, which was 20 mm lower for aerodynamic reasons. Its styling included a dynamic new shape for the rear view mirrors, and the design of its 17-inch aluminum wheels was strongly reminiscent of those on the 959.

With a maximum output of 320 hp, its performance was no longer significantly better than that of its lesser brethren, the Carrera 2 and 4; success eluded the new Turbo. But this Turbo had strengths of its own, particularly its suspension and new brakes. In terms of environmental responsibility, it even set new standards for turbocharged cars. With its oxygen-sensor equipped three-way metal monolith catalyst and increased muffler volume, the new exhaust system provided lower back pressure and thereby reduced catalyst-induced power losses. Even the separate exhaust from the wastegate was provided with an unregulated metal substrate catalyst.

The chief complaint concerning this second-generation Turbo voiced by experienced turbo tamers was that it didn't have enough power. No wonder then that in March of 1992, Porsche's display of a lightweight Turbo study at the Geneva auto show was greeted with enthusiasm. As a result, the sports car maker laid on a small production run of this super sports car, intended primarily for motor

Top secret. Project 965 was cancelled at the last minute.

Turbo S 3.3: The script on the rocker panels reading "Supercar Champion IMSA" commemorates Porsche's victory in the American production car racing series.

188

sports activities. For 295,000 Marks, customers got a car that was 180 kg [396 lbs.] lighter, propelled by 381 hp at 6000 rpm and riding on an uncompromisingly racing-oriented suspension. The catalyst for this development was the overwhelming triumph of the 911 Turbo in IMSA's Supercar Championship, a series for production-based sports cars.

The Turbo 3.6

Meanwhile, Porsche engineers continued development of the production Turbo to once again raise its power output. The next Turbo model, available as of November 9, 1992, boasted the following vital statistics: 360 hp at 5500 rpm, maximum torque 520 Nm [383 ft.-lbs.] at 4200 rpm, top speed 280 km/h [174 mph], braking from 200 km/h [124 mph] to a standstill in 131 meters [430 ft.], all for a price of 204,000 Marks. These figures demonstrate that the prime objective of the development team was not merely to increase power, but also to provide more torque and improved fuel economy. They were able to achieve a remarkable balance between these criteria. Even when off boost, the engine pulls so willingly that the Turbo-typical kick at about 4000 rpm seems far less abrupt than before. Still, the effect of the turbo is unmistakable. That exciting feeling of being forced back into the seat is still there. "We have to keep that as part of the Turbo," says Paul Hensler.

A further Turbo highlight is its brake system, long recognized by the motoring press as the world's finest. A 20 percent increase in front pad area makes the third generation Turbo brakes even more capable. This was made possible by 18-inch wheels derived from the Carrera Cup cars; keen observers can glimpse the red four-piston aluminum brake calipers through their generous openings. This impressive brake system is not merely a visual delight for technology fans; braking from 100 km/h [62 mph] to a standstill consumes only 38.6 meters [127 ft.] with cold brakes, while warm pads and rotors will stop in 117 ft. This braking performance is repeatable, stop after stop, without the slightest trace of fading.

The suspension was matched to these new levels of performance. The ride height was lowered by 20 mm, the springs are 12 percent stiffer, with degressive shock absorber calibration. As this reduces body lean, driving the Turbo requires a delicate touch. When driven hard, its stiff suspension tuning behaves virtually as precisely and with nearly the sensitivity of a racing suspension, and demands gentle steering wheel movements. Yet detail development has kept the Turbo a comfortable car. Hensler underscores that "In terms of comfort, the Turbo is the top model in the 911 lineup, even for those who drive frequently or for long distances."

The overall harmony of the Turbo is all the more remarkable when one considers how quickly Porsche can develop such a car, in this case in less than one year. The engineering team under project leader Friedrich Bezner received their orders on October 7, 1991. Their target was to increase the power output of the 3.3 liter Turbo by at least 10 percent, while reducing fuel consumption. On October 22, the engineers presented two proposals to management. One of these was selected on October 28, 1991; the project's development plans were approved on November 18. In the following weeks, the engineering goals were catalogued, and then were confirmed on February 18, 1992. A decision on visual changes from the previous model was not made until May 20. Nevertheless, production of the 3.6 liter Turbo started on schedule, at the beginning of October, 1992.

At its presentation in southern France, the reaction of the automotive press was overwhelming. Turbo fans were again enthusiastic about their flagship. Even the high price of admission no longer seemed a handicap. It was the right product, and in 1993, even in the typically slow selling summer months, the Turbo was a hot item. Since the begin of production on October 5, 1992, daily production numbers of the Turbo have spiraled upward. In October 1992, two Turbos per day left the assembly line; in December, this rose to six cars per day. By January, a daily total of ten Turbos rolled out of Werk II.

Despite this success, the third Turbo generation had a short life span. The last examples left the line at the end of December, 1993. After that, all 911 production capacity was dedicated to the new Type 993 Carrera.

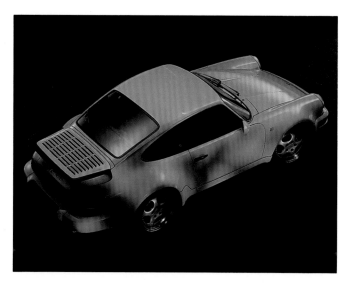 

The march of time: visually, the Turbo 3.6 was adapted from the new generation (Type 964) Carrera. The wide fenders are an unmistakable element of the Turbo look.

The twin-turbo that was first seen at the 1995 Geneva Auto Show introduced the popular "turbo" model to the new 993 generation. Note the 18" cast alloy wheels.

In developing the 3.6 liter, Porsche established tough benchmarks for its successor. This was code-named the UST, and its development began in early 1993. The new twin-turbo was introduced at the 1995 Geneva Auto Show in March of 1995, and went on sale in the following month.

The engine employs two small turbochargers to force engine power past the 400 horsepower mark – 408 hp (300 kW) to be exact. Power is transmitted to all four wheels by a new six-speed manual transmission designed to cope with the Turbo's prodigious power and torque output. All Turbos, worldwide, are fitted with four oxygen sensors and a new "On Board Diagnosis II" system which is required for all vehicles sold in the U.S. The 18-inch aluminum alloy wheels (8 inches wide at the front, 10 inches at the rear) are made using a new hollow-spoke casting

method, reducing each wheel weight by at least 20 percent. The Turbo's brake system is virtually race ready, with larger 322 mm rear brake discs. Acceleration to 100 km/h (62 mph) takes only 4.5 seconds, while braking from the same speed takes place in only 2.61 seconds.

The front aspect is virtually identical to that of the new Carrera 993, but the rear is heavily modified and fitted with an attractive spoiler. Performance fulfills any buyer's wildest dreams.

Even in the Turboless time before the newest model became available, the 911 Turbo remained the ideal and embodiment of a unique automobile. While the 911 is a long-established 30-year legend, for twenty of those years, the Turbo has been a legend in its own right.

All-wheel-drive
The ultimate 911

With its Type 959, Porsche demonstrated what is possible when money is no object; there was never any question of showing a profit for the 284-car production run of this 450,000 Mark exotic sports car. As turbo specialist Heinz Dorsch recalls, "No limits were ever imposed on us." For practical purposes, the 959 served as a technology showcase providing dramatic proof of Porsche's engineering expertise.

Manfred Bantle, leader of the 959 project, adds that "The Porsche 959 was conceived as a development testbed for future Porsche products. It explores new frontiers which had previously been the exclusive province of race car development." For the first time, Weissach engineers were able to apply lessons learned from racing, without the concessions typical of regular production vehicles. In the engine depart-

The distinctive air inlets and vents were added during development.

Composite construction resulted in reduced vehicle weight.

Doors and front lid were of aluminum.

ment this included water-cooled four-valve cylinder heads mounted on air-cooled cylinders (this so-called "mixed cooling" was taken from the 956/962 racing engine), polished titanium connecting rods, a forged chrome-moly crankshaft, hydraulic valve lash adjustment and two turbochargers which were activated progressively with increasing load. Porsche calls this advanced turbocharger concept "Registeraufladung" – sequential turbocharging. At low rpm, the engine is fed by only one relatively small turbocharger, capable of reacting quickly to throttle changes. When this small turbocharger is no longer capable of providing the desired boost, at about 4300 rpm, a valve opens to admit boost from the second, larger turbocharger, located on the right side of the engine. To bring this turbo up to speed even before its output is directed to the engine, a portion of the exhaust gas stream has already been directed through it. Sequential turbocharging may be compared to a relay race; one runner for initial, low-rpm operation, the second for high-load, high-rpm duty.

The center bearings of both turbochargers are water cooled, like those of the four-cylinder 944 Turbo. The rapid response of the first turbocharger and the immediate availability of boost from the second turbocharger prevent the notorious "turbo lag" experienced with older designs. The 959 provides its turbocharged acceleration, cherished by those who master it and feared by those forced to compete against it, with a vehemence that slams passengers back into their bucket seats, especially in the three lower gears. The turbocharged 2.85 liter powerplant develops 450

horsepower, without the encumbrance of a catalytic converter. With 158 horsepower per liter, the 959 has the highest specific output ever realized in a production car, yet theoretically it remains perfectly suitable for everyday use.

The 959's unusual engine displacement is the result of Group B racing rules. Porsche planned to compete in the four-liter class, which permits normally aspirated four-liter engines. The displacement of 2.85 liters results because turbocharged engines are assessed a displacement handicap factor of 1.4.

The 959 fuel injection system was not even remotely related to production technology. Bosch developed an electronic system known as MP-Jetronic (M for Motronic, P for pressure regulated) especially for the 959. The required fuel injection quantity is determined by pressure measurement between the throttle butterfly and the intake valves. The principle is similar to that of the Bosch D-Jetronic, first used in a much more restricted form in the late 1960s. The MP-Jetronic's central processing unit is also responsible for boost regulation.

Power is managed by a six-speed transmission and directed to all four wheels. The six gear ratios divide the 959's top speed of 315 km/h [196 mph] into more manageable portions; first gear alone is good for more than 100 km/h [62 mph]. The transmission is connected to the front differential by means of a so-called "transaxle tube." Located in the tube is Porsche's PSK variable center differential,

Walter Röhrl: "A fascinating car."

which determines how torque is divided between the front and rear axle. The same component is installed in the rear axle to act as a variable limited-slip differential. These two components enabled Porsche to design a very versatile all-wheel drive system which allowed the driver to select one of four basic traction programs: 'traction,' 'ice and snow,' 'wet,' and 'dry.' Fine tuning of the torque distribution is then managed by the electronic control system. Rally champion and 959 fan Walter Röhrl is particularly impressed by "the ability to directly compare such markedly different configurations."

Helmuth Bott, Porsche's former chief engineer and effectively the 'father' of the 959, explains that "The more evenly you divide lateral and longitudinal

forces among all four wheels, the better the handling. The purpose of the 959 was to explore the possibilities of such a system." But Porsche was no newcomer to all-wheel drive. "In the 1960s, we bought a Jensen FF and carried out numerous driving tests with it." Lessons learned on the test track were incorporated in the rear-engined, 911-based all-wheel-drive concept car shown at the 1981 Frankfurt auto show. But it would not remain a mere show car. An interoffice memo to Peter W. Schutz confirms that in 1983, Helmuth Bott proposed, among other things, a 'super Porsche' (911/930) with added features providing exceptional versatility: all-wheel drive, ride height adjustment and turbocharging.

Meanwhile, Helmuth Bott had been collecting all-wheel drive experiences of his own; he drove a four-wheel-drive 911 as his personal vehicle. The first version, which he had ordered built in the early 1980s, was still fitted with an Audi transmission.

The project began to gain momentum, and soon the 959 project would occupy the full attention of Porsche's engineers. In 1984, an all-wheel-drive 911 Carrera fitted with a normally aspirated engine won the 'Paris-Dakar,' the most difficult rally in the world. The following year, Porsche again entered the race across the desert. Porsche's entry was fitted with what would later become the 959 suspension, but a second victory was prevented by minor mishaps. In the 1986 running of the Paris-Dakar rally, Porsche entered purebred 959 Group B coupes, with electronically-controlled power distribution as well as speed-dependent ride height adjustment; 959s finished first and second. For Porsche, this was an important victory and underscored a long-standing company tradition: new systems must first be proven on the race track before they are installed in production cars. Still, Helmuth Bott emphasizes that "The basic concept of the 959 is not that of a rally or off-road vehicle." Rather, while planning the 959, Porsche had hoped that cars meeting Group B regulations would one day compete on the race track. Indeed, Group B rules determined the basic parameters of the 959, including the aforementioned engine displacement, the production run of at least 200 units, and the use of lightweight materials to achieve the 1100 kg [2423 lbs.] minimum weight established for the 959's displacement class. Like the production

The cockpit of Porsche's technology showcase, the 959, recalls that of the 911. Two knobs on the center console control ride height and shock absorber damping.

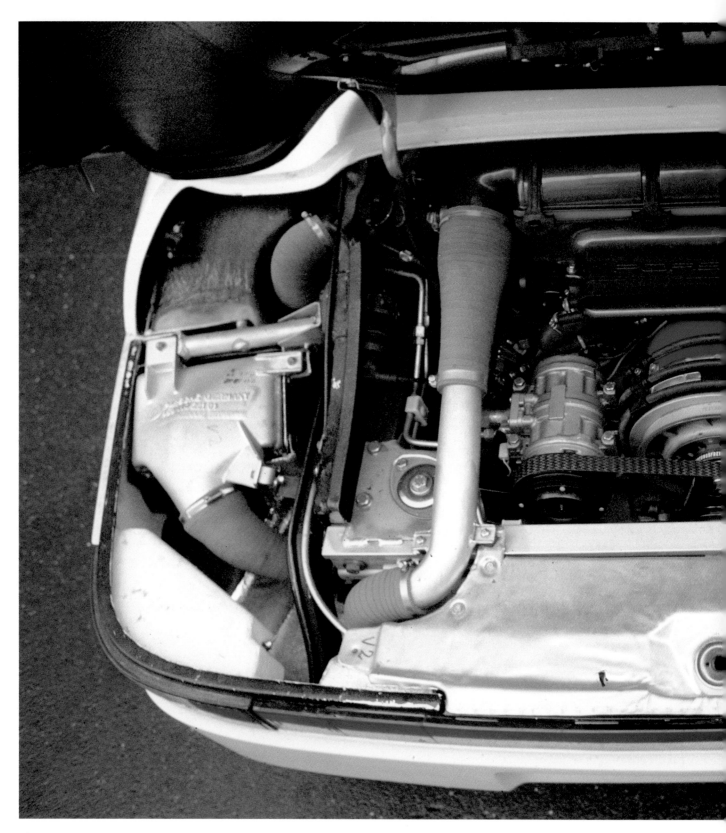

The most exciting
powerplant ever
installed in a
roadgoing Porsche.
It squeezes 450
horsepower out of
only 2.85 liters.

911, its core consists of hot dip galvanized steel. The rear of the car, the rocker panels, the roof and fenders were made of an aramid and fiberglass reinforced composite material. The doors and front lid were of deep-drawn aluminum panels, while the front fascia was of fiberglass reinforced plastic. To this day, the multi-media construction of the 959 remains unique among Porsche products. The 959 chassis is not only lightweight and torsionally rigid, but also an aerodynamic masterpiece, with a drag coefficient of only 0.31. Even at 300 km/h [186 mph] the body does not generate lift.

Although the 959 was not equipped with an anti-wheelspin system, as this was not deemed appropriate for a Porsche, the technology demonstrator is fitted with an ABS (anti-lock braking) system. This, combined with a brake system developed in cooperation with Wabco-Westinghouse, operates at an unusually high pulse rate, which enables the system to react rapidly to even minimal changes in wheel rpm. Processing of anti-lock information is carried out by two computers. The 959's deceleration capability is even greater than its outstanding acceleration performance, thanks to the larger brakes made possible by 17-inch wheels. Even the 959's tire pressure is electronically monitored. Two sensors per wheel and a rigidly mounted induction pickup report to a processing unit, which activates a dash-mounted display in the event of a deflating tire.

In view of all of the advanced technology packed into the 959, it is obvious that at 450,000 Marks, the selling price of this automotive superlative cannot possibly cover its development and production costs. Yet in many respects the 959 has fulfilled its mission, even though no Group B sports car races ever took place. First and foremost, it served as a calling card for Porsche and the entire German automotive industry, and generated unprecedented media response. Second, it served as a technology demonstrator. At the unveiling of the 959, Helmuth Bott predicted that "In the future, many discoveries resulting from the 959 project will be incorporated in our other models, above all the next 911 generation." This, of course, includes visual highlights of future 911s.

On the 959, the typical 911 headlights were installed at a lower angle; this treatment is also used for the new Carrera, the Type 993. As the chief engineer ultimately responsible for Porsche's supercar project, Helmuth Bott explains his position on headlights: "For me, integrated headlights represent an optimal solution, and I have always pleaded for them." The long cooling air inlets in the lower part of the front valance are also echoed by the new generation Carrera.

Porsche introduced a new era in spoiler design with the 959 rear spoiler, which sprouted directly from the rear fenders. Japanese manufacturers in particular have demonstrated their approval by copying the design. At Porsche, though, this spoiler variation has remained a one-off; the cancelled Type 965, originally planned to replace the Turbo, would have had a modified 959 rear end treatment. The new Turbo generation introduced in 1995, again resembles the legendary 959, at least in appearance. The design of the 959 rear view mirrors was slightly modified and adopted for the Type 964 (Carrera 4) in 1988.

Of course, with a production run of only 200 units, every 959 is an exclusive sports car, but apparently not exclusive enough for one German collector, who used a wrecked 959 formerly owned by German race driver Jürgen Lässig to build his own 959 Cabriolet. Recently, the men at Zuffenhausen built three additional 959s for customers, using excess spare parts.

Porsche AG offered customers two versions of its ultimate sports car: the 959 and 959 Sport. Because the 959 was fitted with comfort and convenience items such as electric windows, air conditioning and rear seats, it tipped the scales at 1450 kg [3194 lbs.] despite its lightweight design. The rare, lightweight Sport version was intended for club racing.

As prices for used examples rose to a value considerably higher than the original selling price, the 959 became an object of speculation. However, its uniqueness is based not on price, but rather on the fact that with the 959, Porsche created a design study on wheels capable of achieving in practice what had only been possible in theory. The 959 went down in history as the "Wonder of Weissach."

The Carrera 4

A direct line of development leads from the 959 to the Carrera 4. Helmuth Bott explains that "This is at least in part traceable to personnel. Manfred Bantle, for example, had done his part in suspension development and tuning of the 908/03 and 928 with great dedication, and was named project leader of the 959 effort. He also contributed to the suspension tuning of the Type 964 all-wheel-drive 911. An entire series of systems, particularly all-wheel drive technology, locking differential control, anti-lock braking systems and aerodynamics profited from knowledge gained in 959 development. In its first version, the transaxle tube carrying drive to the front wheels was routed above the central tunnel and hidden by a plastic cover. Not least because of a suggestion by Professor Porsche, we then decided to design the driveline so that it could be installed as a unit from below. This would require a complete redesign of the floor pan and front end of the car, which we were only able to realize when the new production facilities in Zuffenhausen became available."

Engineering changes incorporated in the Carrera 4 are covered in detail in the description of the 1989 model year lineup. Power management of the G 64 transmission used in the all-wheel drive system is described in the transmission chapter, while driving impressions are collected in the chapter entitled "Experiencing the 911 Story" (page 209). It should

be pointed out at this time in the company's history, the oft-posed question of whether Porsche's rear-engined concept is still viable can be answered in the affirmative. The introduction of the Carrera 2 for the 1990 model year, visually differentiated from the Carrera 4 only by the script on the engine lid, made purchasing choices even more difficult. The detectable difference between the Carrera 2 and Carrera 4 was quite minimal, much less so than during the previous Carrera generation. Those satisfied with rear-wheel drive saved 13,100 Marks and 100 kg [220 lbs.] of vehicle weight, yet this did not provide any significant performance benefits. In a comparison test, the German magazine *auto motor und sport* measured the Carrera 2's top speed at 264 km/h [164 mph], 4 km/h [2.5 mph] higher than that of its all-wheel-drive sibling. On the Hockenheim race track, the lighter Carrera 2, driven by an experienced 911 pilot, was always able to stay ahead, but the Carrera 4 driver no longer needed to guard against escape attempts by the rear end. The all-wheel drive car exhibited consistent understeer and mastered weight transfer without drama. With the Carrera 4, Porsche has attained new dimensions in active safety.

The Carrera 4 quickly achieved market acceptance within the Porsche model line. At the end of its career, 30 percent of all 911 buyers ordered the all-wheel-drive 911. Nevertheless, in formulating the design specifications for the new Carrera 4 generation, customer-oriented priorities were redefined. The vehicle's dynamic behavior was to retain more

Three of a kind: at left the rally version, in the center the civilian version priced at 450,000 Marks, and at right the somewhat bulky-appearing 961, developed to meet Group B racing rules.

rear-drive character. Moreover, the weight of the all-wheel-drive components was to be reduced to the point where no loss of performance compared to the rear-drive Carrera could be detected.

These criteria were met in the design of the new Carrera 4. Porsche's latest all-wheel-drive 911 combines the agility and driving pleasure of the 911 Carrera with the advantages of an all-wheel drive system. Its performance virtually matches that of the Carrera, and the weight increase due to its all-wheel-drive components is only half that of its predecessor.

The critical components of the new Porsche all-wheel drive system are:

- all-wheel drive via central tube containing a drive-shaft (transaxle) and a viscous clutch connecting the front and rear axle
- a dynamic limited slip differential for the rear axle
- the automatic brake differential (ABD)

The viscous clutch is located at the transmission output side, forward of the rear axle. This clutch automatically distributes the output torque between the front and rear axles, dependent on wheel slip. The viscous clutch is connected to the compact, weight-optimized front differential by means of a hollow driveshaft. The maintenance-free viscous clutch operation is based on the interaction between clutch packs running in silicone oil; operation is dependent on rpm, transmitted power, and temperature. In addition, the viscous clutch provides the required speed differentiation between the front and rear axles while cornering.

To counteract any tendency of the rear wheels to spin, the viscous clutch reacts in a fraction of a second to divert torque to the front wheels. Thanks to operating characteristics specifically tailored to the Carrera 4, the viscous clutch always provides the ideal torque split to the front axle, and provides stable vehicle dynamics under all conditions.

The dynamic rear limited slip differential has asymmetric locking characteristics, i.e. the lockup factor is 25 percent while accelerating and 40 percent while braking or coasting. As a result, to promote understeer under engine braking, the vehicle's

yaw moment is nearly doubled compared to when the vehicle is accelerating. This provides a stabilizing effect during abrupt throttle changes (backing off the throttle) in turns, which keeps the vehicle on the desired line. However, in accordance with the development goals and as the result of careful tuning, under throttle the new Porsche 911 Carrera 4 exhibits the high cornering capability and agile handling which have always been a decisive, highly esteemed factor in the 911's appeal.

The automatic brake differential (ABD), which is standard equipment on the 911 Carrera 4 and an option on the rear-drive 911 Carrera, is the ideal complement to the function and effect of an all-wheel-drive system based on a viscous center clutch and limited slip rear differential. The ABD uses the anti-lock braking system (ABS) sensors to detect individual rear wheelspin; the control system applies the appropriate braking force to the individual wheel to restore optimum traction.

In the case of split-coefficient road surfaces, such as right wheels on pavement and left wheels on ice, the rear limited slip differential engages smoothly to divert drive torque to the wheel with the greatest traction. If this is not sufficient and slip continues at one rear wheel, the ABD system applies the brake to the spinning wheel. This braking moment is transferred as drive torque to the opposite wheel. This function is effective up to a speed of 70 km/h (43 mph) and is especially helpful in overcoming weather-related starting traction difficulties. The complete system, with all-wheel drive via viscous clutch, limited slip rear differential, and ABD, automatically provides maximum traction under all road conditions.

The all-wheel drive system of the Porsche 911 Carrera 4 is ideally suited to the demands of this high-performance sports car; for this reason, its design and performance have been dynamically optimized. The character of the rear-drive 911 Carrera was retained, deliberately and undiluted. The continuously variable, traction-dependent torque distribution provides even greater vehicle stability under all conditions, without any driver intervention. In addition, the Carrera 4 offers maximum traction in wet and wintry conditions.

Strictly limited editions

While it seems that great automobile marques have no difficulty finding cause for celebration in the form of anniversaries and other milestones, it is most unusual for an auto maker to successfully produce a single sports car model for a period of thirty years, and be able to celebrate the highlights of a career spanning three decades. For Porsche, the 911's success story is a welcome excuse to carry on a tradition which has existed since the firm was founded: offer

Porsche aficionados a limited special anniversary model. In the case of the special "30th Anniversary Edition," this takes the form of a Carrera 4 in the body of a 911 Turbo. The Turbo's trademark rear spoiler was deleted, giving the anniversary model an especially well integrated look. The wide front and rear fenders over 17-inch diameter "Cup Design" wheels, emphasize the lines of this special edition. To Friedrich Bezner, Weissach's six-cylinder project

In 1981, the 928, 911 and 924 models shown here were available to commemorate "50 Years of Porsche."

Turbo fender flares and 17-inch wheels add appeal to the special "30th Anniversary" model 911.

leader, this car represents the culmination of the thirty-year history of the 911.

A special color, violet metallic, was developed for this special series, built in the 1993 model year. The exterior color harmonizes with the full-leather interior in another special color, Rubicon Gray. Embroidered into each carpeted fold-down rear seatback is a subtle "911" script. The shift lever is topped by a silver-colored metal plate, engraved with the shift pattern. Another silver-colored metal plate on the rear package shelf carries the sequential number of the car within a limited production run totaling 911 units. Finally, these cars are identified by a silver

semi-matte rear model designation bearing the subscript "30 Jahre" [30 Years].

Porsche had cause for celebration during the 1988 model year as well; by June 3, 1987, a quarter million units of the classic Porsche had been sold. Porsche produced a total of 875 special editions for all markets, painted in Diamond Blue Metallic (color code F5F5) with body-colored wheels and silver-blue gathered leather upholstery. The headrests featured the stitched signature of the firm's chief, Ferry Porsche. Even the carpets were dyed an elegant shade of silver gray. German customers took 250 examples of the special edition in coupe and Targa

Porsche sold the 250,000th 911 in 1988. To celebrate, it produced this special model in Blue Diamond Metallic.

A total of 250 anniversary model Coupes and Targas were delivered in Germany, 300 in America and 325 elsewhere. This is a German specification car.

form; American buyers accounted for 300 units (120 coupes, 80 Targas and 100 Cabriolets). The rest of the world took the remaining 325 cars. Of these, 50 right-hand-drive cars went to Britain: 30 coupes, ten Targas and ten Cabriolets.

Porsche offered special models of the 924, 911 SC coupe and Targa and 928 S in time for Porsche's 50th Anniversary celebration on the Nürburgring, in August 1981.

The 200 911s of this series, painted Meteor Metallic, had an especially luxurious interior featuring a combination of burgundy leather and fabric. The center section of the front and rear seats, the door panels, rear side panels and rear panel were of red and silver striped fabric. The three-spoke steering wheel and headliner were burgundy in color, and the

head rests were decorated by an embroidered "F. Porsche" signature. Customers who parted with 57,500 Marks for the coupe or 60,500 Marks for the Targa also received a rear wiper, motorized antenna, two speakers in the rear package shelf, tinted glass, and 7- and 8-inch alloy wheels with black centers carrying 185/70 VR 15 tires at the front and 215/60 VR 15 at the rear.

For the 1980 model year, Porsche produced a run of 400 "Weissach" special models (option code M 439) strictly for the American market. Half of the cars were painted Black Metallic, the other 200 were Platinum Metallic. The Doric Gray interior was off-set by burgundy beading on the seat edges. The price of this car, completely unknown in Germany, was $30,000.

204

For 1975, The 25th anniversary of Porsche car production in Stuttgart was marked by a special model, available as a 911, 911 S and Carrera. A special identifying feature of all 400 examples was a plaque on the glovebox, engraved with Ferry Porsche's signature, the number of the car within the series, and the customer's name.

Further, each car in this anniversary edition was painted Silver Metallic, normally an optional color, and equipped with a wide range of otherwise optional items. For the 911 and 911 S, this included a two-stage heated rear window, headlight washer system, 6-inch ATS pressure cast alloy wheels painted Diamond Blue-Gray, stabilizer bars front and rear, matte black anodized exterior trim, and a five-speed transmission. The Carrera received the tinted rear window, headlight washers and five-speed transmission, as the other components were already standard on this model. The roll bar of Targa models was painted flat black.

The interior was in blue-black leatherette, with "Tweed" seat center sections. A 38 cm [15 inch]

A special edition 911 was available for the firm's 25th anniversary in 1975.

Several body designers accepted the challenge to build a four-seat 911. This is Pininfarina's version.

The Boxster styling study, shown in 1993, points the way to Porsche's future.

sport steering wheel and a Blaupunkt "Bamberg Stereo" radio were also part of the package. Door panels, rear side panels, rear panel, rear seat cushions and rear backrests were in blue-black tweed. Deep-pile blue-black carpeting added the finishing touch to the interior. Prices ranged from 33,350 Marks for the 911 Coupe and 45,350 Marks for the Carrera Targa. The advertising slogan "25 years of driving in its finest form" was coined for this model.

Truly unique among rare 911s are the four-seat prototypes. Four-seat cars have been a recurring topic for Porsche and its body makers. In the late 1960s, Porsche commissioned famed automotive couturier Pininfarina to build a one-off two-door coupe offering true seating space for four. Wheelbase grew to 2460 mm, and the turning circle to 11.7 meters [38.4 ft.] Known internally as Prototype B 17, it retained the serial number of the 911 on which it was based – 320 020. Handling worsened considerably, as the weight distribution of the 1135 kg [2500 lb.] car shifted rearward, to 39 percent front/ 61 percent rear. Rear passengers were comfortably ensconced in luxurious leather seats, and were given considerably more legroom than in the production coupe. In 1975, the one-off prototype, originally

Porsche's Panamericana study was the surprise sensation of the 1989 Frankfurt auto show.

painted a dark color, was repainted and fitted with a front air dam, fender flares and a 210 hp Carrera engine. In June of 1993, Swedish owner Nisse Nilsson arrived in Stuttgart for the "30 Years of Porsche 911" rally, with what was allegedly the original Pininfarina styling study. It had been freshly restored and repainted acid green.

By June 6, 1970, Porsche had also built its own four-seat 911. The approximately 300 mm [12 inches] longer car, internally known as 911/C 20, bore chassis number 911 030 0004 and is presently stored in the Porsche museum warehouse. Like the Pininfarina study, the drivable prototype was powered by a 2.2 liter six-cylinder developing 180 horsepower and driving through a stock five-speed transmission. The rear suspension had to be modified and its arms lengthened by 50 mm [20 inches]. Wheelbase was stretched to 2615 mm, increasing the turning circle to 12 meters [39.4 feet]. Except for the visibly longer rear fenders, the 911 silhouette was retained.

In the early 1990s, Porsche made its last attempt at a four-seater, under the 989 type designation. The project, intended for production, was finally put on ice when management and owners began to doubt the marketability of a 150,000 Mark sport sedan. Thereafter, Porsche would concentrate only on two-seaters with rear jump seats. Indeed, the "Boxster" sports car study is a pure two-seater.

Time machines

The opportunity to experience three generations of 911 on one extended journey is a rare one indeed. In this way, the driver can immerse himself in a different epoch, almost feel the ethereal presence of the *Zeitgeist,* simply by switching cars. This is especially true in the early 911, in this case a car first registered on May 6, 1965; the driver feels as if he has been transported to an earlier age, as if by a time machine.

The wooden dashboard trim, today again regarded as chic and available at a substantial added cost, was standard equipment of the day. Even the thin-rimmed, large-diameter steering wheel is made of fine wood. To this day, the instrument layout has not changed significantly; the large tachometer takes center stage, with its red range beginning at 6800 rpm. To its right is the somewhat smaller speedometer, calibrated to 250 km/h [155 mph]. In 1965, this speed instilled awe in children and adults alike.

A twist of the ignition key, and the loud whirring of the electric fuel pump is heard. Its hum reminds the driver to pause for a moment while it tops off the float bowls of the Solex three-barrel carburetors. Once that has been done, the 96 kW (130 hp) short-stroke engine takes up its task willingly. The mechanical symphony so beloved of Porsche pilots,

more readily heard in this earliest of 911s than in other models, conveys the engine's willingness to explore the upper regions of its rev range. We might as well get underway, leaving behind us the mechanical noises of idle rpm.

In the later sport transmissions, first gear is located left and back. First gear is too tall to allow easy creeping along; there must have been far fewer traffic jams in 1965. Slow, steady motion is possible only by continuous, skilled slipping of the clutch. Enough of this; let's engage second gear, good for 110 km/h [68 mph], and leave the city limits in our wake. Finally, on country roads, the nine liters of engine oil reach their operating temperature of 90 °C [194 °F] and the 911 is in its element. It cries for more rpm; its maximum output of 96 kW (130 hp) is not reached until revs have climbed to 6100 rpm. This earliest of 911s doesn't get serious until engine speed climbs above 4000 rpm. Third gear in particular, which covers the range from 30 to 155 km/h [19 to 96 mph], underscores the uncommon agility of this 1080 kg [2379 lb.] sports car. The broad speed ranges covered by third and fourth gear ensure that the full range of the engine's output is readily available to the driver.

The brake system is designed for rapid progress,

Three generations of 911. From left to right: the original 911 of 1965, a 1974 Carrera and a Carrera 2/4 of 1993. At the far right, the "30 Years of 911" anniversary model.

as well. It grabs firmly and steadily, but requires firm pedal pressure. Drivers with an enthusiastic throttle foot may feel somewhat inhibited when they recall that this is a single-circuit brake system. And if that doesn't instill some circumspection, then the first set of corners taken at speed will result in a rude awakening. The original 911 may have breathtaking engine characteristics, but by today's standards it permits only average cornering speeds, if only because of its skinny 165 HR 15 Dunlop SP tires on 4 1/2" chrome rims taken from the 356 C. The narrow tires express their pleasure in taking corners at the limit by squealing in delight, while those driving ahead anxiously check their mirrors in unwarranted concern. The terminal oversteer so feared by inexperienced Porsche drivers is not yet a consideration; with this car, on dry pavement, oversteer can only be achieved by deliberate provocation, by cranking in more steering in fast corners while lifting off the gas.

When the rear of this basically well-behaved 911 finally does break away, it comes around instantly

and without warning. Then the driver has to counter with the steering wheel if he is to have any hope of catching the car; the typical panic reaction of getting off the gas will only make matters worse.

Finally, let's see how this veteran behaves on the autobahn. On ordinary highways, we are able to drive casually, one hand on the wheel and the other resting on the window sill. But on the autobahn, all that changes. The original 911 quickly tells its driver that both hands belong on the wheel. Straight-line stability is this 911's weak point; the culprit is poor aerodynamics. In the mid-1960s, engineers still did not know of any means to combat front-end lift. With increasing speeds, the 911 gets progressively lighter. Every bump or road irregularity results in a change of direction, which must be corrected by the driver, who by this time has developed a case of sweaty palms. At speeds in excess of 150 km/h [93 mph] and in the presence of gusty crosswinds, one instinctively tends to stay in the middle of the road, to maintain some runoff space to either side. This condition is unimaginable by today's standards, and would not be acceptable even in the lowliest economy car. For safety reasons, we won't try to verify the impressive top speed claim of 210 km/h [130 mph] recorded in the car's registration papers, especially since at higher speeds, the driver of this sports car feels downright naked without modern head rests and safety belts (lap belts were an option in 1965).

Today's driver of an early 911 has two possibilities. High-speed travel on the autobahn is possible under absolutely calm wind conditions; otherwise, he must conduct his 911 in a manner befitting a classic car – somewhat slower, but with style.

The driver of a 1974 Carrera is not limited by such

restrictions. Porsche's 911 entered its tenth year of production with the so-called G Series. In the intervening decade, the men of Zuffenhausen had learned a thing or two.

The most important change, the addition of aerodynamic aids, is immediately apparent. Porsche did not apply the hard-won lessons of racing until 1972. From that point, however, it became obvious that even production cars needed a deep front air dam to prevent front-end lift, and a rear spoiler for increased downforce.

Yet the huge rubber-edged rear spoiler, characteristic of the first generation Turbo of the following model year, was earmarked only for certain markets.

While the basic shape remains, details of the early 911 at the far left seem overly fussy in comparison.

As of 1989, the Carrera is not only faster, but also cleaner. Its catalyst-equipped engine develops 250 horsepower.

But this spoiler is an attractive addition to our test vehicle, which was supplied by a private collector. And it's an absolute necessity: by 1974, the engine output of 155 kW [210 hp], achieved despite increasingly tight emissions regulations, had to be safely transferred to the road.

Porsche first used the Carrera name for a 911 model at the 1972 Paris automobile salon, where the sports car makers of Zuffenhausen premiered Germany's fastest sports car, the Carrera RS. While the legendary Carrera, with its trademark "duck tail" spoiler, represented an uncompromising design for ultimate performance, its successor, the G-model Carrera, contains a hint of luxury. Rear jump seats, a clock, and electric windows are but a few of the many convenience features of the later Carrera. The

result: 1180 kg [2600 lbs.] in fighting trim, while its predecessor, the RS, tipped the scales at 1010 kg [2225 lbs.] with a full tank of fuel.

In those turbulent times, even makers of pure sports cars, Porsche included, had to adapt to changing conditions. Cars which, like the Carrera RS, were conceived as thoroughbred high-performance vehicles would have been unmarketable in 1974. Thanks to the oil crisis, customer attention had shifted from performance numbers to fuel economy figures; to compensate for lost driving thrills, more luxury was added. Adding insult to injury, Germany instituted not only carless Sundays but also speed limits on the autobahn (100 km/h or 62 mph) and on secondary roads (80 km/h, 50 mph). Yet Porsche maintained its emphasis on performance and kept the sporting Carrera in the model line. A mechanical manifold injection system provided fuel for the 2.7 liter powerplant and moves this luxury-oriented Carrera in a manner which is simply captivating. Second gear will see the car past 100 km/h [62 mph], and fourth gear will just reach 200 km/h [124 mph]. At that point, the tach reads 7200 rpm and urgently reminds the driver to shift. The upward climb continues to 240 km/h [149 mph].

Even today, this Porsche can be driven at speeds well above average. Like its predecessors, the Carrera is still a car which demands a firm hand at the wheel. Its straight-line stability (or lack thereof) still requires some familiarity, and the wide tires result in high steering forces in corners. The Carrera's trademark rear fender flares cover 8-inch wheels wrapped with Dunlop SP Sport tires, size 225/50 R 15. At the front, the Carrera is fitted with 205/50 R 15 rubber. Combined with its stiffer suspension tuning and larger stabilizer bars, these tires permit enormous cornering speeds. However, when all available power is called up, the rear has a tendency to break away, as if there is some invisible demon just waiting to strike. When that happens, the Carrera 2.7, like its predecessors, demands quick corrective measures.

The only thing that gives this Carrera away as a product of the past is its garish green paint. A female pedestrian, who apparently did not recognize this as an older car, was particularly indignant. "How can anyone paint a Porsche in that horrible color?" was her unsolicited comment to the driver. But in 1974, things which today would be surprising or shocking were definitely "in:" shoulder-length hair, bellbottoms, and bright colors like yellow, orange or this brilliant acid green. The spirit of the times also inspired the Carrera script at the lower edge of the doors, which many customers ordered as a 95 Mark option.

With the 1974 Carrera 2.7, Porsche substantiated

Interim solution: The potent 210 horsepower 2.7 liter engine was available in the G-model only in 1974.

In 1965, 130 horses qualified as high output. The original 911 reached a top speed of 210 km/h [130 mph]. Today, it is best driven as a revered vintage car.

that safety and emissions regulations need not dilute the concept which gave life to the 911. The Porsche Carrera 4 created a third dimension of 911 performance. While it continues the distinctive lines of earlier 911 generations, it is in fact virtually a completely new car, which sets new standards in active safety. Sweaty palms on the steering wheel are once and for all banished to the past. The appeal of the Carrera 4 is not its unpredictability, but rather its effective exploitation of the available power.

And the new model has no shortage of power. With 184 kW [250 hp] on tap, Porsche equipped the 1989 Carrera with the most powerful normally aspirated engine ever fitted in the rear of the 911 at that time. The torquey 3.6 liter engine employs a digital electronic engine management system and dual ignition. As a result, it provides ample push at all engine speeds, yet whirs away quietly at idle. The new Carrera engine is eminently suited for the traffic situations of our time and transforms the 911 into a multifaceted car with everyday utility and enormous reserves. But once traffic has been left behind, the all-wheel-drive Carrera shows its stuff. Thanks in part to the retractable rear spoiler, even the Turbo-bodied anniversary edition is a wolf in sheep's clothing. The boxer-powered sports car weighs in at 1410 kg [3106 lbs.] yet catapults from a standstill to 100 km/h [62 mph] in only 5.1 seconds. Engine speeds between 4000 and 6900 rpm show it at the peak of performance.

On the autobahn, in contrast to its forebears, the new 911 is a genuine pleasure to drive. In the earliest 911s, one might as well turn off the radio at speeds above 150 km/h [93 mph] as the tremendous wind and engine noises would not tolerate any other aural entertainment; the Carrera 4 permits undiminished musical enjoyment even at speeds on the far side of 200 km/h [124 mph]. Nevertheless, dedicated sports car enthusiasts might prefer to turn off the radio in order to delight in the muffled bark of the boxer engine, which enters the cabin in a restrained manner without unpleasant additional noises.

Even in the rarefied regions of top speed, the Carrera 4 remains glued to the road. Crosswinds are of no consequence to the C4; even the floor pan offers virtually no grip for the wind, which would result in unwelcome turbulence. The servo-assisted steering and ABS brakes compensate for its appreciably greater weight compared to its progenitors, and contribute to its stress-free driving characteristics.

On the one hand, the perfect balance of the vehicle is pleasant, but this refined manner, without flaws or idiosyncrasies, does diminish the impression of riding in a sports car. Precarious drifts at the limit of the laws of physics do not necessarily reflect the type of sporting performance which inspired the Carrera 4 engineering team. But the concept of the sports car can be interpreted in many ways: as a high-energy physical workout or as a pleasant diversion, as a merciless duel for every last inch of road or as a refreshing release from everyday tension. With that, Porsche is again ahead of its time. From the moment of its introduction in the fall of 1994, this 911 embodies the *Zeitgeist* of tomorrow.

Racing the six-cylinder Porsches
Back to Basics

It takes no more than a quick glance at Porsche's corporate history to realize that Porsche has always offered limited production runs of race-ready cars for customers with sporting ambitions. As early as 1955, privateers stormed the race tracks of Europe with a lightened and more powerful version of the Type 356, a secret weapon which answered to the now legendary name "Carrera." Porsche did not choose this designation at random; the Spanish word "la carrera" translates as "race" or "competition." The victory of the Franco-German team of Strähle and Buchet in the 1959 Liège-Rome-Liège endurance run, and a second place by the semi-works team of Walter and Nathan in the arduous Acropolis Rally of the same year, are highlights of Porsche's early rally history.

In these early years, Porsche was accused of concentrating on campaigning its purpose-built race cars, even though the firm's products seemed predestined to dominate production-based rallying. (At the time, no one could have foreseen that the 356's successor would have an unprecedented rally career.) Still, Porsche took these accusations seriously and, in the early 1960s, decided to offer competition machinery not only to privateers but also to take part in rallies as a factory team. To this end, former racer Herbert Linge and the man who would one day head

Porsche's research and development facilities, Helmuth Bott, sketched out the first proposals for a lightweight, motorsports-oriented 911, in November 1964, before the 911 had even been introduced to the market. Chief body engineer Erwin Komenda compiled their suggestions in a report dated November 26, 1964. Concurrently, the director of engine R&D, Ferdinand Piëch, and engine specialist Hans Mezger tinkered with methods to increase power output of the stock 130 hp six-cylinder boxer engine. Time was of the essence; the racing 911 had to be homologated as quickly as possible. The target date was the occasion of the 34th Monte Carlo Rally, in January of 1965.

Thanks to the efforts of all concerned, a rally-prepared 911 awaited the starter's signal on the ramp at Chambéry, France, in a driving snowstorm. Herbert Linge, at the time foreman of the development department's mechanics, sat behind the wheel. Beside him sat Peter Falk, at the time an engineer in the road testing department. They would tackle the 4600 kilometers [2860 miles] of Monte Carlo in their green 911, chassis number 55, propelled by a 160 horsepower engine. At the end of the brutal event, they found themselves in fifth place overall, a sensational result. Their colleagues Böhringer and Wütherich, in a 904, took second overall and first

elegante sportiva
sportiva *elegante*

PORSCHE

Race on Sunday, sell on Monday. This advertising poster emphasizes Porsche's racing philosophy.

How it all started. Falk and Linge at the Monte Carlo Rally.

Huschke von Hanstein: "Racing was an adventure."

217

Powered by four- and six-cylinder engines, the lightweight 904 raced to victory after victory.

Racing historic 911s is a popular hobby of the 1990s.

A profusion of power: the Porsche 917.

place in the under-two-liter GT class. Porsche had cause to celebrate; the first works effort in the demanding Monte Carlo Rally could not have been more successful.

To everyone's amazement, Porsche's rally activities in the following years were quite restrained. The reasons are simple: first, the research department's "racing wizards," including road test chief Helmuth Bott, suspension specialist Peter Falk and R&D boss Ferdinand Piëch, were fully occupied with the design and deployment of the 906, 910, 907, 908 and 909 sports prototype racers (some fitted with six-cylinder engines). Furthermore, Ferdinand Piëch wanted to field a new, different prototype for each racing season, and complained that Porsche was only achieving class victories; the company should be chalking up overall wins. In 1968, this new emphasis on beating all comers marked the beginning of the 917 era, which lasted until the end of 1971 (and until the end of the 1973 season in the North American Can-Am racing series). On the other hand, the sports car wizards of Stuttgart wanted to play it safe in rallys. A

factory entry would be fielded when victory was not merely possible, but probable. Meanwhile, private entrants demonstrated the potential of the 911 with impressive success.

It was not until 1968 that Porsche again sent an official works team to the Monte Carlo Rally. The effort was headed by Reiner Engels, who in that year succeeded Helmuth Bott as chief of the road testing department. Bott, in turn, advanced to chief of research and development. Piëch's orders to Engels were to concentrate on production cars, but Engels also formed a small department dedicated to customer racing development. In addition, this department supported factory efforts which fielded production-based cars. The new team enjoyed instant success. Vic Elford and Pauli Toivonen crewed a pair of bright orange 911s, in which they had trained for six weeks and almost 12,000 miles. The professionalism of the Porsche team paid off: Porsche's pilots brought home a decisive double victory. Waldegaard and Helmer gave Porsche a Monte Carlo hat trick with their back-to-back victories in 1969 and 1970.

Short reign. The 914/6 was intended to be even more successful on the race track than the 911.

Hausmitteilung

An

Abteilung: __Presse__   z. Hd. von: __Herrn von Hanstein__
                                    __über Herrn Piëch__
                                    Verteiler:

ausgestellt von	27. 6. 67
	VF/Bo-kf
	Datum und Diktatzeichen

Betreff:

__Marathon de la Route__
__Ihre Hausmitteilung vom 21. 6. 67__

Wie ich Sie mündlich bereits unterrichtet habe, wollen wir
für diese Veranstaltung ein Fahrzeug präparieren:

Karosse 911 R,
Sport-o-matic-Getriebe mit erhöhter Wandler-Festbrems-
drehzahl,
Motor 911 S mit Sportkit.

Als Besetzung für dieses Fahrzeug schlage ich die Fahrer
Elford, Herrmann, Neerpasch vor, die alle drei auf der Fahrt
nach Sizilien und beim Vortraining das Sport-o-matic-Getriebe
kennengelernt haben.
Während des Rennens gibt der Fahrversuch eine Betreuung
von 2 Mechanikern und 1 Ingenieur (Sachbearbeiter Sport-
o-matic). Diese Leute können selbstverständlich auch das
zweite serienmäßige Sport-o-matic-Fahrzeug mitbetreuen.
Sollte eine Zeitnahmemannschaft von Ihnen erwünscht sein, so
bitte ich Sie, mich dies wissen zu lassen.

__Alpenfahrt__
__Ihre Hausmitteilung vom 21. 6. 67__

Die Teilnahme eines "R" an der Alpenfahrt hängt davon ab,
ob wir unser Mugello-Auto ohne Schaden wieder nach Hause
bringen.

Bott

PORSCHE

| Erledigt - Ablage | Zur weiteren Bearbeitung an: | Zur Kenntnis genommen: |

20 P

Inter-office memo:
racing as a means of
product testing.
Translation page 392

Present at the creation: Günther Steckkönig (left) and Peter Falk.

Heavyweight: 911 prepared for the London to Sydney Rally.

Riverside, 1973: the Porsche 917/30 Can-Am racer, series champion Mark Donohue at the wheel.

Group 5: the Porsche 935, powered by a turbocharged six-cylinder boxer engine.

The long string of 911 victories had begun, but would soon be put on hold by a massive works effort based on the new 914/6. Porsche management believed that the image of the new model could be enhanced by racing. This philosophy had already been applied to the base version of the 911, the 911 T; most rally cars carried a "T" nameplate, even though the sportier "S" model was better suited for racing. It was expected that the mid-engine "VW-Porsche," with its standard 110 horsepower engine taken from the 911 T, would enjoy better sales as a result of racing, but excepting a class win at the 1970 "Marathon de la Route," Porsche had only limited success with this model. The 911 remained impressive in its role as a multitalented racer, equally at home on rally special stages or race tracks, even if rally efforts occurred only sporadically.

In 1967, to replace the classic over-the-road Liège-Rome-Liège rally, which could no longer be run for organizational reasons, the Royal Motor Union of Liège instituted an 84 hour (later 86 hour) endurance test, the Marathon de la Route, held on the Nürburgring. Porsche immediately seized on this venue as a testing ground for new developments. The first year saw the debut of the newly developed Sportomatic transmission, transplanted into an uncompromisingly lightened 911. Driving this 170 hp racer, Hans Herrmann and Jochen Neerpasch won the first running of this enduro.

With its extensive use of lightweight materials, this two-liter 911 R tipped the scales at only 830 kg [1828 lbs.], making it the lightest of the 911 family. Composite lids, aluminum doors, lightweight seats and thin glass all served to reduce weight. Still, rally cars tended to gain weight because of skidplates and other equipment. Little was done to the suspension; stiffer torsion bars, shock absorbers and stabilizer bars, and more negative camber for the rear suspen-

Flying on the ground. "Moby Dick" reached speeds of 227 mph on the long straight at Le Mans.

Le Mans, 1979: both factory 936s dropped out.

sion were all that was necessary to make it raceworthy. Limited slip differentials, even locked differentials for some racing applications, served to improve the rear-engined car's already excellent ability to transfer power to the road.

Porsche developed increasingly powerful versions of the 911. The 2-liter 911 S "Rally," with its 170 horsepower, was replaced by the 180 hp 911 S-2.2 "Rallye." Displacement grew in stages to 2.8 liters, and power output increased to 330 hp (see table). These racers chalked up a long string of race and rally victories, including the highly competitive "Tour de France."

All the while, Porsche prices remained reasonable. In 1972, a 911 S 2.5 could be bought for 49,000 Marks; in 1974, a Carrera RS 3.0 cost 65,000 Marks. Attractive pricing encouraged private teams to compete in motorsports. One of the most active privateers was Polish driver Sobieslav Zasada. It was his ambition to win the East African Safari Rally at the wheel of a 911, the only great rally which did not appear on the list of Porsche victories despite the extensive efforts of works and private teams. Test driver Günter Steckkönig remarks appreciatively that "It was fascinating to see how this man, usually accompanied by his wife as co-driver, repeatedly achieved good finishes on race tracks all over the world. That's why we were happy to support Zasada." Peter Falk, Porsche's long-serving racing director, recalls a rally in the Balkans: "As usual, Zasada arrived at Weissach on the evening before the rally. He was looking for a shock absorber that would withstand even the most severe impacts over long distances. Because there was no such shock, we worked a night shift to limit the shock travel with steel cables. The results were enormously successful. One by one, competing works teams dropped out. It was not until Mercedes engineers inspected Zasada's car during an ocean passage, and discovered this simple but effective solution, that they were able to beat his private effort."

Zasada is still active today. He intends to take part in the revived "London to Sydney" classic rally in the spring of 1994, at the wheel of a 1966 911 S.

Compatriots who did their racing on road courses can point to their own proud victories. Günter Steckkönig recalls that "With the development of the so-called 'duck tail' rear spoiler and widened rear fenders, the Porsche gradually evolved away from the original shape laid down by Butzi Porsche. The wide fenders were necessary to accommodate rear tires which were wider than those at the front, a first in production car history." This spoiler did not enjoy universal appeal, but Porsche engineers did accede to the realization that a spoiler would only be effective if the trailing edge was mounted a certain distance from the bodywork. Peter Falk adds that "Even Helmuth Bott was not easily convinced that it was necessary to add fender flares. As a tire and suspension specialist, he felt that all four wheels must be interchangeable." Meanwhile, the 911 continued its winning ways. Aside from various class wins, Peter Gregg and Hurley Haywood won at Daytona and Sebring in 1973, Müller and Van Lennep won the Targa Florio, Gregg and Haywood repeated their Daytona success in 1975, and in 1976 Holbert and Keyser again won the American 24-hour event in a Carrera RSR.

Porsche had shifted its factory efforts to the big sports prototypes, powered not only by the 911's six-cylinder but also by eight-cylinder and later even twelve-cylinder engines. This was also the first application of turbocharging to increase power output; the 917/30, with more than 1000 horsepower, still stands as one of the most potent race cars of all time. Nevertheless, the six-cylinder boxer engine was by no means ignored; instead, it embarked on a new career in the form of the Turbo. This began in 1973 with the Carrera RSR-derived Turbo RSR, the first turbocharged racing version of the 911. This was followed by the racing version of the 911 Turbo, which carried the production type designation 930.

The Group 4 version was designated the 934, while the Group 5 car was called the 935. In addition, the 936 Spyder, also powered by a turbocharged six-cylinder, joined the lineup to take part in Group 6 competition, which had no requirement for "silhouette" bodywork. These vehicles displayed the 911's talents to even better effect. World-beating race cars were developed on the basis of the production 911.

The most memorable success of this era. Porsche's brand-new 956 finished first, second and third at Le Mans.

The Types 934 and 935, developed in Weissach, were built in Zuffenhausen under the direction of Elmar Willrett. From the outset, the 934 was intended as a customer race car. The fact that the factory itself entered both the 934 and 935 models in competition is due to a change in the rules, which were influenced by various international interests. Porsche adapted to the changes, prepared only one works 935 for the 1976 season, and won the world championship for the fourth time, repeating its 1969, 1970 and 1971 success but this time with a production-based car instead of a sports prototype.

In 1977, it was the privateers' turn. The Cologne-based Kremer brothers had already prepared their own 935 in 1976. Rolf Stommelen, driving the Loos Porsche, was German racing champion in 1977. In the same year, Peter Gregg, driving a 934, won the American IMSA Camel GT series. The following year, 1978, brought even more success to privately-entered Porsches; from then until the mid-1980s, the 935 was one of the most attractive and spectacular phenomena to grace the world's race tracks.

The 935 era was not only a period of spectacular successes, but also a time of explosive technical change. In 1977, a very limited production run of the 935 was built for the small-displacement division of the German Racing Championship series; this was done to counter press accusations that Porsche was only capable of building ever-larger engines. The car, which the Weissach engineers and soon the rest of the world dubbed "Baby," provided impressive proof of Porsche's potential at all levels of motorsport. In less than four months, the team built the lightest Porsche 911 ever. It was pared down to the minimum permissible weight of 735 kg [1619 lbs.], and was powered by a 1.4 liter, 370 horsepower turbocharged engine. After only two races, with Jacky Ickx at the wheel, "Baby" was rolled into the museum. The same fate awaited the fastest and most powerful 911 ever built. The rolling powerhouse of the 1978 season had a nickname of its own – "Moby Dick." Its tube frame chassis, first used on the 935 "Baby," underwent additional development. In addition, this supreme 911 had 6 cm of its floor pan trimmed away. This was the only possible means of lowering the car, as the rules stipulated that the roofline had to remain unaltered. "Moby Dick" was not

only the most powerful of its breed, but also the fastest. In Le Mans, it was clocked at 366 km/h [227 mph] down the Hunaudières straight.

As Group 5 cars got faster, they gradually lost their resemblance to production cars. Only the silhouette remained, but even that was buried under spoilers. The 935's carefully tailored racing bodywork covered impressive technological achievements; it had evolved into a thoroughbred racing car, with water-cooled four-valve heads, intercooling, and more than 750 hp. In 1979, at Le Mans, Klaus Ludwig achieved the third-fastest qualifying time, behind the two works 936s. During the race, the 936s dropped out, leaving Ludwig and his co-drivers, the Whittington brothers, to win the dramatic event.

After the factory had frozen development of the 935, customers carried the torch themselves. Peter Falk tells us that this was not at all easy. "Only a few top teams could manage this car." Among these were Reinhold Joest, who built his own "Moby Dick". The Kremer brothers even had a small production run, with their own 935 K3 and K4 models.

Two years later, despite this lack of continued factory development, a works car was again able to win at Le Mans. Tests at Paul Ricard demonstrated that the 944 Turbo earmarked for Le Mans was not capable of overall victory. An alternative was sought and finally found in the 936 stored in the factory museum. The engine was no longer competitive, but Porsche mechanics transplanted the turbocharged six-cylinder powerplant developed for Indianapolis, capable of well over 600 hp when fueled with methanol. In record time Bosch developed a fuel injection system designed to operate on Euro Super gasoline, allowing the car to complete a 30-hour Le Mans simulation on the dyno. Lap after lap, this test program cycles the car through every gear shift and every speed encountered during the gruelling race. Research and development chief Helmuth Bott received project approval from Porsche's new chairman of the board, Peter W. Schutz, but the only sponsor who could be found on such short notice was Christian Dior, manufacturer of the men's cologne "Jules", who was not as financially well endowed as Porsche might have wished. Schutz repeatedly distinguished himself by his optimistic attitude, and was always happy to entertain new ideas. Porsche's courageous efforts were rewarded when the 936 brought home the 1981 Le Mans laurels.

The 935 and 936 epoch finally came to an end in 1981, when FISA's rules changed to move the sport away from the concept of production-based race cars. There followed the era of the "Group C" racers, which Porsche again contested with turbocharged six-cylinder cars. "This is the most unbelievable story in the history of auto racing," recalls project leader Norbert Singer. For more than a decade, Porsche's Group C cars dominated various racing series all over the world. The results speak for themselves: five manufacturer's and team championships with 43 decisive victories, including six Le Mans wins, five driver's world championships. Added to these are four IMSA titles and 53 victories including nine wins at the Daytona and Sebring enduros. Between 1983 and 1991, the cars won numerous successive

national championships in Europe and Japan. Singer adds that "No other sports prototype was built in such numbers." A total of 150 examples of the 956 and 962 sports racers was produced. This was made possible by the efforts of many Porsche people; outstanding among these were racing chief Peter Falk, project leader Norbert Singer, designer Horst Reitter, body specialist Eugen Kolb and engine designers Valentin Schäffer and Hans Mezger. The most memorable success of this era, which lasted until Porsche's withdrawal from sports car racing in 1988, was the finish of the 1982 Le Mans race, without doubt the most difficult race in the world. With a brand-new car, developed in record time, Porsche's works entries, numbered 1, 2, and 3, took first, second, and third place respectively.

In 1984, while the Group C cars were at the peak of their dominance, another new development achieved its first milestone. After presentation of the 911 all-wheel-drive study at the 1981 Frankfurt auto show, Porsche continued development of this new

Just before Porsche's racing withdrawal in 1988: Wolfgang Porsche (left), 956 and 962 project leader Norbert Singer and Susanne Porsche.

Important 911 racing victories

1965

| Monte Carlo Rallye | Linge/Falk (5th overall) | **911** |

1967

| Marathon de la Route | Herrmann/Neerpasch/Elford | **911 R** |
| 24 Hours of Spa | Gaban/"Pedro" | **911** |

1968

| Monte Carlo Rallye | Elford/Stone | **911 T** |
| Swedish Rallye | Waldegaard/Helmer | **911** |

1969

Monte Carlo Rallye	Waldegaard/Helmer	**911 S**
Austrian Alpine Trial	Waldegaard/Helmer	**911 S**
Swedish Rallye	Waldegaard/Helmer	**911 S**
Tour de Corse	Larrousse/Gelin	**911 R**
Tour de France	Larrousse/Gelin	**911 R**

1970

| Monte Carlo Rallye | Waldegaard/Helmer | **911 S** |

1971

| Swedish Rallye | Waldegaard/Helmer | **911 S** |

1972

| 24 Hours of Daytona | Gregg/Haywood | **911 S** |

1973

24 Hours of Daytona	Gregg/Haywood	**Carrera RSR**
12 Hours of Sebring	Gregg/Haywood/Helmick	**Carrera RSR**
Targa Florio	Müller/van Lennep	**Carrera RSR**

1975

| 24 Hours of Daytona | Gregg/Haywood | **Carrera RSR** |

1976

6 Hours of Dijon	Ickx/Mass	**935**
6 Hours of Mugello	Ickx/Mass	**935**
12 Hours of Sebring	Holbert/Keyser	**Carrera RSR**
6 Hours of Watkins Glen	Stommelen/Schurti	**935**

1977

6 Hours of Brands Hatch	Ickx/Mass	**935**
24 Hours of Daytona	Gregg/Haywood/Helmick	**935**
German Racing Championship, Hockenheim	Ickx	**935 1.4 liter Turbo**
2 x 3 Hours, Hockenheim	Wollek/Fitzpatrick	**935**
6 Hours of Mosport	Heimrath/Müller	**934**
6 Hours of Mugello	Stommelen/Schurti	**935**
Nürburging 1000 km	Stommelen/Hezemans/Schenken	**935**

1977

6 Hours of Silverstone	Ickx/Mass	**935**
6 Hours of Vallelunga	"Dino"/Morchi	**935**
6 Hours of Watkins Glen	Ickx/Mass	**935**

1978

24 Hours of Daytona	Stommelen/Hezemans/Gregg	**935 3.0 T**
Dijon 1000 km	Wollek/Pescarolo	**935 3.0 T**
6 Hours of Misano	Wollek/Pescarolo	**935 3.0 T**
6 Hours of Mugello	Hezemans/Heyer/Fitzpatrick	**935 3.0 T**
Nürburging 1000 km	Ludwig/Heyer/Hezemans	**935 3.0 T**
Monte Carlo Rallye	Nicolas/Laverne	**Carrera RS**
6 Hours of Silverstone	Ickx/Mass	**935**
6 Hours of Vallelunga	Wollek/Pescarolo	**935 3.0 T**
6 Hours of Watkins Glen	Gregg/Hezemans/Fitzpatrick	**935 3.0 T**

1979

24 Hours of Daytona	Ongais/Haywood/Field	**935**
24 Hours of Le Mans	Ludwig/Whittington/Whittington	**935**
6 Hours of Mugello	Schurti/Fitzpatrick/Wollek	**935**
Nürburging 1000 km	Schurti/Fitzpatrick/Wollek	**935**
6 Hours of Silverstone	Wollek/Heyer/Schurti/Fitzpatrick	**935**
6 Hours of Vallelunga	Calderrari/Spattetti/Martz	**Carrera RSR**
6 Hours of Watkins Glen	Ludwig/Whittington	**935**

1980

24 Hours of Daytona	Stommelen/Joest/Merl	**935**
Dijon 1000 km	Pescarolo/Barth	**935 3.0 T**
6 Hours of Watkins Glen	Gregg/Hezemans/Fitzpatrick	**935 3.0 T**

1981

24 Hours of Daytona	Garretson/Rahal/Redman	**935**
Monza 1000 km	Dören/Lässig	**935**
Silverstone 1000 km	Schornstein/Grohs/Röhrl	**935**

1982

| 24 Hours of Daytona | Stommelen/Paul/Paul | **935** |

1984

| Quatar Rallye | Al Hajri/Spiller | **935** |
| Paris-Dakar Rallye | Metge/Lemoyne | **911 AWD** |

1985

| Pharaohs Rallye | Al Hajri/Spiller | **959** |

1986

| Paris-Dakar Rallye | Metge/Lemoyne | **959** |

drivetrain concept under racing conditions. In 1984, a normally aspirated all-wheel-drive 911 Carrera, with alterations almost entirely confined to the front axle, won the most difficult rally in the world – the Paris-Dakar. Peter Falk underscores the importance of this accomplishment: "This victory, in new territory and on the first try, is one of the greatest achievements in Porsche racing history." With these words, the man who served as Porsche's racing boss for so many years reveals that he always felt a special affinity for rallying. With this predecessor of the 959, Porsche had reentered the rally arena. The production-based SC/RS emerged as a winning machine in national as well as the European championships.

In the following year, the Carrera was fitted with the suspension of the later 959 and underwent bodywork modifications, yet victory eluded its grasp. Soon, however, rally victories achieved by normally-aspirated engines were eclipsed by the 400 horse-power 959 Group B with its sequentially turbo-charged and intercooled powerplant. In 1986, this version took the first two finishing positions in the Paris-Dakar – a major success not only for Porsche but also for Jacky Ickx, who had dedicated himself to the project and finished second behind the more experienced rallyist René Metge.

Due to changes in the Group B rally regulations, the 959 was never entered in the very events for which it was originally conceived. However, its close cousin, the 961, generated valuable all-wheel-drive data during two Le Mans efforts and one entry in the Daytona 6 Hours. For awhile, Porsche had not offered cars for club racing, and forced privateers to compete with cars that were more than a decade old. Though these comparatively antiquated cars were not always doomed to defeat, customers demanded an affordable, competitive race car, which could be campaigned without extensive modifications.

Success eluded Porsche and its 959 prototype in the 1985 Paris-Dakar rally...

...but 1986 saw Porsche take home a double victory in the Paris-Dakar. In desert trim, the 959 developed 400 horsepower.

Porsche fulfilled this desire in 1985, when it created the Porsche 944 Turbo Cup. Once again, the sports car maker came up with an attractively priced alternative to professional racing. The Turbo Cup quickly became the favorite single-marque championship among drivers as well as spectators. From an engineering standpoint, the Turbo Cup, as it was soon known, was also a harbinger of future trends. Porsche was the first carmaker to go racing with catalytic converters and ABS anti-lock brakes.

In 1990, the Cup series was expanded with the introduction of the Carrera Cup. Porsche's gamble paid off; after only one season, interest in the single-marque championship was so great that a "minor league," the Carrera Trophy, had to be introduced to make affordable racing available to even more customers.

This success is attributable to three decisive fac-

tors. First, company management was united in its support of the single-marque racing series. Second, the Cup racing concept, with its virtually identical cars, provided spectacular competition. And third, the unique flair of this legendary sports car spurred the series to success; the Porsche 911 represents the epitome of the sports car concept for the public road, as well as the race track. Thanks to the continued development of this definitive sports car, the Porsche 911 has always remained competitive within the industry. And with the Carrera Cup, Porsche offers a brilliant example of the state of the art in automotive engineering. The high degree of reliability built into every mechanical component virtually guarantees affordable racing. Generally, engines can serve for an entire racing season with only routine maintenance and without overhaul. And lap times are at a level that only a few years ago would have ensured a mid-field position in the German Touring Car Championship.

This is indicative of highly developed racing technology, as well as the degree of experience achieved by today's drivers. Naturally, this benchmark makes it increasingly difficult to find qualified drivers for the "celebrity cars" entered for every race. Many a candidate is wary of embarrassing him or herself.

The popularity of the Carrera Cup is documented by the multitude of race reports found in newspapers and the motoring press. The collected press clippings for the 1992 season fill two 500-page scrapbooks.

For Porsche, this press approbation represents a welcome opportunity to advance the company's image, but on the other hand implies a great responsibility to the fans. The Porsche Carrera Cup organization is aware of this obligation, and is even now setting the course of its own future. Cup manager Jost Capito underscores that "We must look ahead at least three to five years. The cornerstones of our successes in 1996 must be laid today." To this end, the 1993 season reflected a step-by-step evolution of the Cup rules. Carrera Cup races were conducted at tracks all across Europe, which increased the series' stature by yet another step. Immediately below the Carrera Cup in order of importance was the national

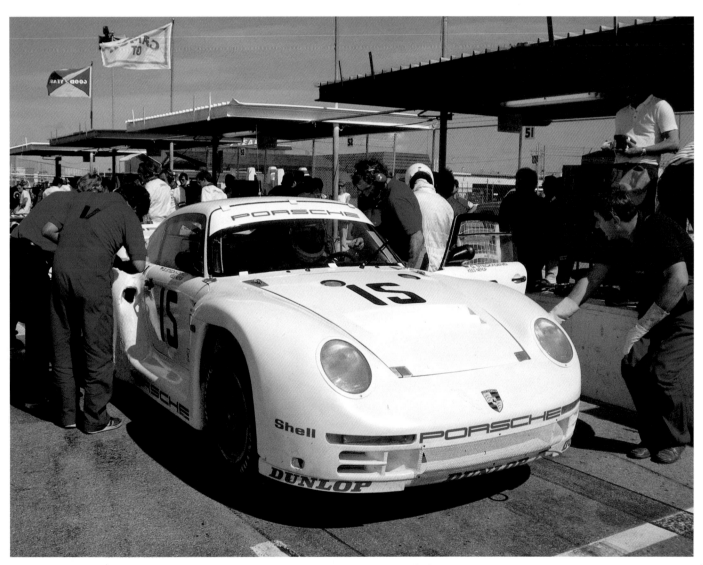

A 959 derivative for the race track, the 961 served as a racing all-wheel-drive testbed.

Good to go: Racer and author Jürgen Barth.

cup series, which Jost Capito regards as an intermediate level between the erstwhile national Carrera Cup and the Carrera Trophy.

As of 1993, a distinction was made between the international "Porsche Supercup" and the individual national "Carrera Cup" series of Germany, France and Japan. Six of the eight Porsche Supercup races were held in conjunction with Formula One race weekends; the year before, the Carrera Cup had already been invited to share the bill with four events in the world's premier auto racing series. Evidently, by 1992, the Carrera Cup teams had achieved a stature which allowed the series to complement Formula 1 events. Nevertheless, each team had to enter two cars for the 1993 season.

The German Touring Car Championship race at the Norisring, with its huge spectator turnout, provided yet another excellent forum for the Supercup. During the season's eight events, the Supercup teams were able to provide fans with spectacular entertainment. Their sponsors were rewarded with excellent marketing exposure, thanks to the international aspect of the Cup series which drew the attention of television, especially the DSF sports channel.

Carrera Cup 1992: the Strähle 911 on the Norisring.

Opening act for Formula 1: Supercup race in Monte Carlo, 1993.

The 911 Carrera RSR 3.8, built for the ADAC GT Cup.

To underscore the multinational flavor of the series, Jost Capito introduced a national points championship, in which the two top-placed drivers of each country garnered points for their nation's points fund. In this way, individual drivers or teams not only competed against each other, but also against other nations.

The Cup cars entered the new season with only minor modifications. The most significant change was the addition of built-in jacks. This had been long overdue, and enabled teams to make more effective use of the 30-minute practice sessions.

This technical stability fulfilled the wishes of many a team which could not or would not buy new cars every season. The fact that several cars from the 1990 season were still front runners in 1992 is proof of the Carrera's durability and reliability. For the 1993 season, it was again the task of the mechanics to apply their skills in preparing cars for each racing venue while staying within the rigid rules – their efforts are limited to optimizing engines within production tolerances, any suspension settings excluding ride height, and tire pressure. Pole position was often decided by fractions of a second. Porsche's strict controls virtually eliminated any unfair advantage or unsportsmanlike conduct in car preparation.

A new chapter began in 1994. In January, only three months after the market introduction of the new Carrera (Type 993), Porsche offered a new Cup racer. Porsche's intent is to once again demonstrate the near-production status of these race cars. Of course, this technology has its price, but the teams accept this, even if the new Carrera Cup cars cost in excess of 200,000 Marks. Even with its higher price of admission, a Porsche still represents a cost-effective way to go racing.

There are plenty of alternatives for those who don't want to ante up for a new Cup racer. The playing field for the approximately 200 Cup cars built to date provides a variety of racing opportunities. If the Porsche Supercup is too professional, the Carrera Cup too ordinary and the Alpine Cup, sanctioned by Swiss and Italian clubs, too one-sided, one could compete in the Veedol Endurance Trophy series, the Ferrari-Porsche Challenge or various club racing events.

Porsche's current racing efforts are not restricted to its single-marque series. Thirty years after that

first Monte Carlo Rally effort, after three decades in which Porsche had earned for itself the image of a winner, the racing department faced a new challenge. Beginning in 1993, the ADAC [German Auto Club] and FISA, the worldwide governing body of motor sports, had instituted a GT racing series, with the express purpose of popularizing racing with production cars. Nineteen ninety-three was still an interim year, but in 1994 a GT World Championship was created. Even though there was no minimum number of cars required for homologation, only a requirement that each car be licensable for road use, Porsche laid on a small production run of about 50 cars for sale to customers. In these recessionary times, when most car manufacturers have withdrawn from the top echelons of motorsports competition, Porsche's decision was especially noteworthy. And it again demonstrates that Porsche and racing are and always have been inseparable. Of all the world's car makers, the Zuffenhausen sports car builder is the only manufacturer to offer race-ready competition cars directly for sale to customers. The racing department in Weissach even provides customers with two attractive alternatives for competition in

Designed for Le Mans: the 911 Turbo S Le Mans GT, driven by Walter Röhrl, Hans-Joachim Stuck and Hurley Haywood.

For the 1994 Supercup series, the new Cup Carrera engine is enlarged to 3.8 liters, giving 300 horsepower.

An exciting start to the 1994 season, at Interlagos, Brazil. Christian and Wilson Fittipaldi won in their Carrera RSR 3.8.

the GT Cup. One choice is the nimble four-cylinder 968 Turbo S; the other is a modified Carrera Cup car with a 3.8 liter engine, known as the 911 Carrera RSR 3.8. Naturally, the production Carrera 2, Carrera 4, 911 Turbo and 928 GTS are also suitable for racing, with minor modifications.

To take advantage of the special GT rules structure which were in effect for Le Mans, a special twin-turbo 911 was developed, carrying the official designation 911 Turbo S Le Mans GT. Porsche team drivers Walter Röhrl, Hans-Joachim Stuck and Hurley Haywood took a class win at the Sebring 12 Hours with this 475 horsepower, 1000 kg [2200 lb.] Porsche GT.

With its unshakeable dedication to motor sports,

in 1993 as in other years, Porsche affirms what has become the company creed for more than a quarter century: Porsche is the quintessential sports car, and the people of Zuffenhausen have one goal in motor sports – to promote a broad base of popular racing activities, and to make racing more accessible by providing a unified system of competition rules.

The success story of the racing 911s would easily fill volumes. Ulrich Upietz, who has contributed significantly to this chapter, has written a book whose 380 pages and 600 color illustrations encompass the Group C era. Beyond this work, his Gruppe C Motorsport-Verlag [Group C Motorsport Publishing] will issue a comprehensive yearbook chronicling Porsche racing activities, so that all may enjoy this fascinating continuing story.

The activities of the Porsche fraternity
Good fellowship

The ties that bind the members of this family are not those of blood, but rather constitute a special form of association by choice. It is an association based on a shared personal passion and by a common active lifestyle. These traits characterize the countless Porsche drivers who congregate to enjoy exclusive sporting, social, and special events spanning a wide range of activities. For example, by invitation from the Porsche Centers and Porsche AG, customers may take part in golf or tennis tournaments throughout Germany. More passive tennis fans meet annually at the Womens' Tennis Grand Prix in Filderstadt, near Stuttgart. Porsche driver training events promote customer confidence in their own and their cars' abilities. Drivers can demonstrate their driving talent at numerous club sport events. And in the winter months as well as throughout the year, the bimonthly magazine *Christophorus* expresses the spirit of Porsche in words and pictures.

Of course, not all of these activities are financed or organized by Porsche AG. The Zuffenhausen-based car maker works closely with its partners, the Porsche Centers. In addition to continuous advice and support, the dealerships receive an annual catalog of marketing incentives. At the back of this catalog is a collection of ideas outlining possible activities which may be offered to customers. Dealers

draw inspiration from these ideas, indeed they are almost required to do so; by the terms of the franchise contract, a fixed proportion of their wholesale discount must be applied to advertising and marketing activities. Marketing chief Georg A. Ledert places a high value on such activities, and encourages dealers to organize special customer events unique to their regions. As an example, in 1994, the Porsche Center Pforzheim organized a exhibition of environmental technology, with support from Porsche AG, at the annual Baden-Württemberg State Garden Show. Porsche Center customers were invited to the opening of the show.

Another example: on the occasion of German reunification in 1990, the Porsche Center Berlin reacted quickly. Only weeks after the opening of the Wall, customers were invited to a driving tour of the Mark Brandenburg. Participants explored their newly accessible suburbs with great interest.

By contrast, the Hamburg Porsche Center offers an annual event typical of its own region: a polo tournament. And as Porsche drivers are often also active in diverse sporting disciplines, Porsche owners in Hamburg recently formed their own polo team. The Porsche Center Baden-Baden in Sinzheim also has a special equestrian event taking place virtu-

Early 911s in rank and file. From July 23 to July 25, 1993, Fred Hampton, board member of the Porsche Club Great Britain, organized an anniversary display at the Silverstone "Historic Festival."

ally next door: Horse Racing Week. Porsche AG itself is also interested in exclusive horsepower of yet another kind: every June, customers are invited to join the company at a special display of Arabian stallions, also in Baden-Baden.

The Munich branch has an annual convocation in a beer tent at Oktoberfest, and Viennese Porsche drivers meet at the yearly Opera Ball.

The possibilities are endless. Ledert sums up the marketing challenges of the last few years: "It's worthwhile to discuss every idea, no matter how crazy it may sound." So, for example, Mardi Gras princes in Heilbronn and Kaiserslautern have been chauffeured in Porsche Cabriolets. Afterwards, Porsche drivers celebrated Carnival among the other costumed revelers.

Even in the absence of a special social occasion, Porsche customers can find activities tailored around their sports car interest. Examples include a rally

ending at an automotive museum or a vision test at a local Porsche Center. In the latter case, the connection to the sports cars from Zuffenhausen is the Carrera line of eyewear, created by Butzi Porsche's firm, Porsche Design. Fashion shows, on the other hand, are often presented without spotlighting any Porsche products.

Including the entire family is gaining increasing importance at customer events which address not only Porsche drivers, but also their spouses and children. The woman of the house is often a key decision maker in the purchase of a car. Sales professional Ledert identifies three typical cases. In the first, a successful female entrepreneur buys the car for herself; second, the woman is a joint user of the car; and third, the spouse is forced to accept the purchase decision made by her husband. The last of these points has presented Porsche with a perennial problem, resulting in a new form of customer relations. The new motto is "Women experience Porsche." To realize this, the ladies are invited to Ludwigsburg to experience the Porsche fraternal spirit. An interesting daylong agenda emphasizes placing them behind the wheel of Porsche products. Past events have yielded convincing results, with attendees expressing greater interest in Porsche. In some cases, they wished to drive a sports car from Zuffenhausen of their own. Of nearly equal importance to Porsche AG, other attendees began to understand their husbands' fascination for driving a Porsche. This would hopefully make the next Porsche purchase a joint decision by both partners.

In contrast to the specific rationale of such marketing activities, mens' and womens' golf tournaments have been organized since 1988. Taking place throughout the year, Porsche presented 19 tournaments. Individual Porsche Centers sanctioned 16 qualification rounds; Porsche AG underwrote two additional rounds and the final round in the fall, at Konstanz, where the best Porsche-driving golfers in Germany met to decide a champion. In 1993, the series had an added international flair as Japanese and Canadians accepted Porsche AG's invitation to play for national points in the guest class. Georg Ledert underscores the desire of most participants to measure themselves against international competition in the Golf Cup finale.

Driving a Porsche and driving a golf ball has become inseparable for many customers, and interest in this combination increases yearly. Sometimes, these sportsmen exhibit an almost irrepressible competitive spirit. Andrea Schwegler, who works as Golf Cup liaison in the sales development department, recalls one man who bought a Porsche for his wife so that she could take part in the finale; the rules stipulate that participants in the last championship round must also be Porsche owners.

For those who don't want the challenge of stowing golf clubs in a 911, transporting tennis rackets to one of the qualifying rounds of the Tennis Cup, supported by the Porsche Centers, presents much less of a problem. Porsche's association with tennis has nearly two decades of history behind it, but golf seems to be edging ahead. Claudia Schäffner, who has been working in Porsche's sales development department for more than fifteen years, attributes the decrease in Porsche-sanctioned tennis activities to the limited

On September 12, 1992, a gigantic fireworks display highlighted the Porsche Parade in Cortina d'Ampezzo.

resources of the Porsche Centers. The large variety of possibilities forces dealers to establish priorities and select criteria, and at the moment golf is more popular.

Still, the tennis championship has its own finale, to which Porsche AG invites approximately 60 winners of qualification rounds. In 1993, the final round took place in Salzburg, Austria.

In roughly the same time frame, the world's top women tennis players meet to decide the winner of the Porsche Tennis Grand Prix. As main sponsor, Porsche presents a Porsche sports car as a prize for the champion, an incentive that has repeatedly attracted the elite among women tennis professionals for more than 16 years. Their male counterparts only had one opportunity to take part in a Porsche Tennis Grand Prix, in its first year – 1977.

For this annual tennis spectacle, Porsche Centers are offered ticket blocks for their customers. Porsche's hospitality tent has developed into an annual meeting place for friends and like-minded fans from all over Germany.

In the same way, Porsche distributes tickets for the hospitality tents at Carrera Cup events and the Nürburgring Oldtimer Grand Prix, held in mid-August. At Carrera Cup races, Porsche relies on its many years of experience in providing trackside hospitality. Between 1986 and 1989, Porsche provided culinary service for more than 9000 guests at sixteen events in the 944 Turbo Cup series. During the Carrera Cup era, between 1990 and 1992, nearly the same number, 8500 visitors, visited the Porsche tent at eleven events. An even larger swarm of fans was expected for the 1993 Super Cup series. Porsche's hospitality services expanded in 1993; the tent was open for business on Saturday, not only on Sundays as in years past. The ticket packet given to Porsche customers included reserved space in an exclusive Porsche parking area, admission to a covered grandstand and passes to the hospitality tent on Saturday and Sunday.

Porsche offers a high performance driving school which provides more than mere drivers' education. On the evening before the event, participants gather for an evening of Porsche camaraderie; many an enduring friendship has ensued. And no wonder: in the last fourteen years, the driver training program (which has been in existence for nineteen years) has improved the skills of more than 12,000 drivers. Of these, nearly 95 percent drove Porsche products of every description, the remaining five percent drove other marques. Zuffenhausen's six-cylinder products dominate the mix, making up about 80 percent of the turnout at nearly every event.

Training takes place on closed courses. Claudia Schäffner, responsible for organizing and processing applications for participation in Porsche's driving schools, explains that "This is a basic requirement, to provide the maximum level of safety. Participants should experience driving at the limit and repeat the correct reactions as often as possible, so that they will react properly in the event of an actual emergency." Schäffner, an experienced Porsche employee, adds that "We want customers to get to know their own cars." However, this requirement is becoming an increasing problem for the sports car maker. In Germany, race tracks are few and far between, and a veritable flood of events (nowadays, race tracks even host rock concerts) has left only limited openings for the auto industry. For this reason, Porsche has added the Salzburgring in Austria, the race track in Rijeka, and on occasion race tracks at Zolder, Zandvoort or Imola to its driving school calendar. Unfortunately, this means that travel time to the event becomes more time-consuming than the program itself, which occupies a day and a half.

The number of participants is determined by the length and character of the available race course. On the Hockenheimring, the location of choice for Porsche's "basic training," up to 120 cars can take part. By contrast, winter training on the small Seefeld course is limited to 42 cars.

Clearly, demand exceeds supply. Courses are booked solid only weeks after mailers announcing the courses are sent out. In addition, applicants from the United States, Japan or New Zealand have expressed interest in taking part in Porsche driver training. In 1992, Claudia Schäffner had to send out more than 300 letters of regret; she estimates that the future number will be even greater.

Concours d'élégance at the first Porsche Parade Europe, Cortina d'Ampezzo, Italy.

Students at a Porsche driver training event fling this Tiptronic-equipped buggy through a tight slalom course.

241

The only alternative to factory-sponsored training among like-minded Porsche fans are those training programs offered by a very few Porsche Centers on their own initiative. Whenever possible, the factory supports these efforts by loaning instructors – enthusiastic Porsche employees from all branches, who provide special expertise and sacrifice their weekends to the cause.

These would-be schoolmasters are prepared for their important tasks during instructor seminars. These training sessions for the trainers themselves repeatedly stress that the driver training program is intended to improve driver skills and techniques, and not achieve maximum top speeds.

To gauge customer satisfaction, Claudia Schäffner conducts a survey of school participants at irregular intervals. The latest survey indicated that at the end of their training program, 95 percent of the students agreed that they were now better able to control their vehicle in extreme situations, and that they have learned how their car reacts at the limit. Many expressed the feeling that they now suddenly owned "more car." This is convincing proof of the effectiveness of Porsche's sport driver training program.

Those who would like to improve their newly found driver skills by taking part in motorsports within the Porsche fraternity are well advised to join a Porsche club. The clubs regard themselves as ambassadors in matters of motorsport. To put this ideal into practice, Porsche clubs organize countless slaloms and time trials on race tracks. Besides the shared pleasure of high-performance driving, social events are an equally vital part of club life. Many different activities take place within this circle of friends with shared interests: photo rallyes, ski trips and river rafting excursions, to name only a few. In recent years, these club gatherings have extended far beyond the borders of the home country; the Porsche Parade Europe takes place every other year. This international convocation was first held at the English channel resort of Brighton in 1990; in 1992, fans of the sports cars from Zuffenhausen met in the Italian ski resort of Cortina d'Ampezzo, scene of the 1956 Winter Olympics and championship skiing events. In 1994, Porsche AG hosted the parade on its home turf in Stuttgart.

Celebrations marking the thirtieth anniversary of Porsche's 911 resulted in a shift in this regular schedule. To mark the occasion, between June 10 and 13, 1994, Porsche fans from all over the world journeyed to the home of their favorite sports cars. For this special event, Porsche's organizers had to be highly selective. Worldwide, more than 300 Porsche clubs encompass over 120,000 members. No other marque club in the world even comes close. Another unusual aspect of this circle of ardent Porsche fans is that since 1976, the company has had its own department responsible for providing support to all of the Porsche clubs. This area is headed by Ilse Nädele, a dedicated employee and ardent Porsche fan.

To speak with Ilse Nädele about Porsche clubs is an enlightening experience. Frau Nädele bubbles over with enthusiasm for the high-performance machines from Zuffenhausen, indeed her passion for Porsche has not diminished in more than seventeen years at her post. She does not hesitate to take responsibility for hundreds of Porsche owners at a time, and thanks to her efforts, all participants in a Porsche Parade can be assured of meticulously organized activities. Frau Nädele explains the enormous turnout at Porsche meets with the following: "Because participants don't need to worry about anything once they reach the Parade, they get the greatest possible enjoyment from the event, and even the longest possible journeys to reach a Parade site seem well worth the effort." Frau Nädele adds that "Porsche drivers, who are usually under great stress occupationally, experience a kind of inner regeneration just through their travel to the event." The lady who makes these events happen is also optimistic about the future. Her eyes light up as she says that "Every year, there's something new."

For 1993, this "something new" was represented by the newly created Anniversary Parade. But she also regards smaller gatherings with happy anticipation, such as when a Porsche club spends a day or two in Stuttgart. On these occasions, she is wholly committed to arranging an enjoyable factory visit for the "friends of the House." This may include a "live" factory tour with Herr Karger as well as a visit to the factory museum under the direction of Rolf Koch; both of these men are carved from the same Porsche stock as Ilse Nädele. Schedule and organiza-

On June 11, 1993, to celebrate the 911's thirtieth anniversary, 320 Porsche 911s lined up to for inspection in the courtyard of the Ludwigsburg palace.

tional details permitting, visitors may also have the opportunity to experience a few laps of the Weissach test track before gathering over cocktails and dinner to reflect on the day's events.

By creating a special department responsible for club support, Porsche recognizes that Porsche clubs and their presidents are the most effective ambassadors of the marque. It was decided to invite all of the world's club presidents to a biennial Porsche Club Presidents' Meeting, falling in the years between Porsche Parades. The year 1993, with its Parade celebrating the 30th anniversary of the 911, represented an exception to the rule, as the Presidents' Meeting took place later in the same year, October 1 to 3.

Professor Dr. Ferry Porsche also cherishes the great value of Porsche clubs, and their presidents, to the family business; he has been personally present at all seven events to date. Perhaps this is one reason

that overseas participants gladly submit to more than 20 hours of air travel to attend. And to listen as Professor Porsche recounts, as he did in Karlsruhe in 1989, how his late wife, on seeing a Porsche in the 1950s and 1960s, would say to her husband "Look, there goes one of your children." Upon which Ferry Porsche bid the club presidents to "Take good care of my children."

Of course, such a sentimental side of the honorary chairman of the board may not be glimpsed at every Porsche gathering, but there are other highlights as well. As diverse as these activities may be, they have one common goal: they are intended to intensify and cultivate the relationship between the manufacturer, the dealerships and the customers. It has long been clear to Porsche that the salesman is usually not the most significant opinion maker in closing the sale; rather, it is another Porsche driver, another member of the large and unique Porsche family.

The development of the Fuchs alloy wheel
Trendsetter

Wheels appear to offer automotive stylists with unlimited opportunities to demonstrate their creative skill. Their main criterion is that they have to be round. Beyond that, material and dimensions are a given, and therein lies the challenge. The visual design of this seemingly simple element plays an important role in shaping the image of a car; after all, what would a car be without its own unique wheels?

This consideration may have contributed to Porsche's decision to ask the specialist wheel manufacturer Fuchs whether light alloy wheels could be realized for a production car. Both parties had worked together before: Fuchs had delivered forged wheels for armored military vehicles. Porsche's contact at Fuchs was technical consultant Herr Kretsch, who travelled southern Germany on behalf of the Meinerzhagen-based Otto Fuchs Metallwerke, offering Fuchs products and specialized know-how to German car makers. What Kretsch offered Porsche must have come as a complete surprise, in view of the state of the art at the time; the Fuchs representative outlined the possibility of mass producing a high-quality forged alloy wheel. Nothing on this scale had yet been attempted in Germany. Cast alloy wheels were still unknown at the time, because no alloys were available which would have the required

mechanical properties. The auto industry expressed a desire to install light alloy wheels because they had hoped to match the positive experience of the aircraft industry in using high quality, lightweight aluminum components. Porsche became a pioneer in the field of alloy wheel development when it and Mercedes-Benz (who, also in cooperation with Fuchs, brought out a forged alloy wheel for their midrange models almost at the same time as Porsche) were the first German car makers to offer aluminum wheels.

Once the decision to go ahead with this new type of wheel had been made, Heinrich Klie of the Porsche model department (later known as the styling studio) was given the assignment to style a light alloy wheel for the 911. He became the "father" of the Fuchs wheel.

Klie was born in 1914 and changed careers after the Second World War. He underwent training in creative arts and opened his own ceramics studio. One day, Porsche placed an order for ceramic models of the Type 356 as promotional gifts. This opened the door, and after a short stint in the Volkswagen model department, Klie founded the Zuffenhausen sports car maker's model department in 1953.

With astonishing confidence in his own style, Klie modeled many a detail of the 911, such as the complete dashboard. But the Fuchs wheel would be his masterpiece. Porsche had obtained an aluminum wheel from the American firm Alcoa, but this did not meet the sports car maker's quality requirements and seemed far too pudgy to serve as an inspiration.

Klie and his colleagues received no precise instructions for the development of the light, corrosion-resistant new wheel. Klie recounts that "Whenever we got an assignment to do this or that, to develop a detail part of a new car or whatever, we didn't waste much time talking about it. We just got to work and made something. And that's the way it was with this wheel."

Klie gathered ideas for his wheel creation at auto shows or by observing details in the traffic around him. He did not proceed systematically, but rather had faith in his instincts and in what developed during the modeling process. Klie replaced the center section of a conventional steel wheel with a wooden disk, which served as a base for Plasticine modeling clay. After he had applied the Plasticine, he began sculpting the wheel center by forming the clay with his hands or various scrapers and blades. Klie says that "Drawings made little sense at the time, if one wanted to develop something like that, because one was working in three dimensions. Modeling something [in clay] resulted in completely different proportions from what one would get in a drawing. If I had followed a drawing, this would have resulted in a completely distorted, lame impression. Working in Plasticine, I can add material, remove it, and change things at will. On top of that, this is the shortest and clearest path: the viewer can see instantly whether or not the result meets his expectations."

Many styling assignments were characterized by weeks of trial and error, changes, reshaping. Not so the alloy wheel. According to Klie, the design was successful "with a wave of the hand," as Klie puts it. His model was quickly approved by Ferry Porsche and went to the suspension design department, where engineer Rudolf Hoffmann was responsible for drawing the wheel and calculating its physical properties.

Leaders of Porsche management and the styling department rapidly reached a consensus during one of the few Fuchs wheel working meetings.

Fifty-eight manufacturing steps were required to make a single Fuchs wheel. The process begins with the pressed blank at the right.

Fuchs chief engineer Karl-Heinz Ochel was responsible for the wheel on the manufacturing side. For its production, Fuchs developed a completely new process, using rolling machines supplied by the Kieserling company of Esslingen, near Stuttgart. The manufacturing process was extremely complicated: 58 steps were required to make a single "Fuchs" wheel. Karl-Heinz Ochel explains that "It had to be preformed, a blank had to be forged, the center had to be mechanically rolled, the holes had to be drilled, and many other steps had to be carried out. Because of its propeller-like appearance, Fuchs employees soon dubbed it the 'Flügelrad' – the fan wheel."

To be precise, the Fuchs wheel was formed by the following steps. A pressed piece of stock was forged to make a forging blank. Next, drop forging the blank produced the ventilation holes and deburred the flange. A further drop forging step resulted in a split flange, before the workpiece was widened by rolling. And here is the secret advantage of this complex manufacturing process: the Fuchs wheel stayed in production for so many years because it could be rolled to any width desired. The forming process resulted in a wheel with a completely finished inner side. The outer, visible side of the wheel was turned on special lathes, which resulted in the smallest possible wheel imbalance. A carefully developed surface finish – polishing, anodizing, and painting – permitted different design variations over the years and assured high corrosion resistance.

Prototype wheels were tested directly on the car. Test drivers drove in circles at high speed, continuously subjecting the samples to the highest possible side forces. Afterwards, they were checked for cracks and deformation. After minor dimensional modifications, the "Fuchs wheel" was approved and

Heinrich Klie: "Drawings made little sense at the time."

went into production in time to appear on the 1967 models.

In 1967, the sales brochure for the newly introduced 911 S highlighted the Fuchs wheel, even though its appearance had resulted in some internal controversy at Porsche. Its design was intended to express sportiness, strength and power, and to make the new model even more desirable. The marketing strategists who prevailed in their support of the Fuchs wheel already suspected what the following 20 years would prove beyond doubt: the wheel would become a runaway success, an enduring favorite, indeed almost a trademark for the 911. Today, Heinrich Klie downplays his greatest achievement. "When I designed this wheel, I had no idea that it would remain current for so long. Back then, we did this job more or less on the side."

Automotive photography

Nothing by chance

Surely it is the dream of every photographer to work unmolested by his environment. In 1986 René Staud fulfilled this dream by creating a partitionable 6500 square foot photo studio in Leonberg, just a few Autobahn minutes south of Zuffenhausen. Driven by a quest for perfection, the inventive Swabian developed his own lighting system, dubbed "Magic-flash," to provide illumination comparable to natural daylight. Magicflash has a decided advantage over natural light: it doesn't change. This large-area flash unit with its 250,000 Watt output is driven by fifty generators. Eighty individual and effect lights, with a total area of 80 square meters (860 square feet) can, for example, simulate a cloudy sky or dusk conditions. Staud's studio adds one superlative to another.

Perfect auto photography requires more than just gargantuan gadgetry. The decisive element is appreciation for the automotive subject. Photographer Staud underscores the need to fully understand the object in his viewfinder: "For this, contact with the car's designers, even in the early stages of development, is imperative. To photograph the new Carrera generation, the Type 993, I repeatedly met with chief designer Harm M. Lagaay. Only when the concept of the individual car has been fully grasped can the design's vital shapes be emphasized by sophisticated lighting techniques." With Staud, every exposure is a

synthesis of hard work, professionalism and inspiration. This last ingredient comes easily; cars are his abiding passion.

Inspection of the Swabian's work shows that not even the smallest light reflection is by chance. Staud allows that "It takes three times as long to set up lighting for a 911 as for any other car. This is due to its different shapes, that is, a soft line from the roof to the tail, a characteristic front with steeply angled headlights, and the recessed hood and rounded tail." Every viewing angle results in a different lighting condition. For a side view of the 911, Staud positions the camera a little above wheel height. This way, the hood line and the cowl can still be seen. On the other hand, the camera must not be raised so high that the rear fenders stick out like an unrelated object. "That just looks impossible," reflects Staud. For a tail shot, the camera should look down slightly, and from the front, care must be taken with the view through the greenhouse. Staud criticizes the cluttered underbody of some vehicles, particularly older models. "For me, a car ends at the bottom of the bumper; everything below that is only a means to an end."

Staud's first Porsche experiences were gathered with the legendary 959 (see also illustrations in the

René Staud and a Turbo 3.6: "The photographer needs to understand the automobile."

chapter "The Ultimate 911," pages 191-200). "In producing these photos, I learned the importance of cooperation with the designers. They create lines which cannot be realized in production, and they would like to recreate these shapes in photos. On the other hand, highlights must not be forced to the point where they create a new shape. In photo production, the various views expressed by designers and salesmen must also be considered. The designer naturally wants every photo to show the details which he has so lovingly worked out, while the salesman simply wants photos which will entice consumers to buy. For each photo, I have to stay within these two extremes."

Naturally, there are basic rules that apply to every perfect photo, rules which the master photographer has absorbed after years of practical experience. Staud can list a thousand details for each photo; a brief selection should give us some idea of what is involved.

- Before shooting, each car is thoroughly cleaned
- appropriate polishing compounds provide the desired effect

- chrome can be brought to a high luster with a diamond compound
- matte spray minimizes unwanted reflections
- black dulling spray emphasizes the cloth character of cabriolet tops
- after cleaning, lint can be removed from interior upholstery with adhesive tape
- glass can be cleaned with denatured alcohol
- before shooting, tire pressure is increased to about 100 psi, so that the tires will appear perfectly round
- tires can be "lightened" by a light application of baby powder
- cockpit spray brings out a shine on tires
- the car's stance is corrected by adding sandbags to the trunk or engine compartment
- interior shots require stabilizing the car with jacks,
- spinning wheels can be simulated by evenly jacking the car until the tires have one or two mm of clearance. Just before the exposure, they are spun.

This list can be continued at much greater length, but the few points mentioned give us a sense of the work behind every photograph. René Staud has opened new dimensions in automotive photography.

Paint jobs
Artistic freedom

Graphic designer Rainer E. Taxis works out all details to the same degree of precision. In the process, shadows and reflections which automatically result in natural-light photographs are faithfully reproduced.

For each subject, automotive designer Georg F. Simonis decides what is most important. His illustration of the anniversary model (top) makes a powerful impression. Taxis, on the other hand, interprets the same subject using a photorealistic style.

Georg F. Simonis underscores the car's dynamics with visual cues, including dust clouds and visible exhaust gases.

Drawing the 911 is a similar proposition to photography. An artist who creates an illustration of an automobile can faithfully draw upon shapes and shadings present in photographs or in nature or deliberately alter these to serve his artistic purpose. This spectrum of choices is vividly demonstrated by two illustrators, each of whom has given his interpretation of two identical subjects. An early 911, as delivered in November 1964, was one subject, chosen in honor of the model's 30th anniversary; the other subject is the Turbo Look anniversary model.

For illustrations created in response to specific customer requests, Rainer E. Taxis is a proponent of a form of photorealism. The graphic designer, based in Plochingen near Stuttgart, carefully outlines an existing subject. Reflections are added, with almost pedantic accuracy, particularly noticeable in the drawing of the anniversary model. When photographed under natural light, such reflections result almost automatically. Taxis works out all details with the same attention to detail, even coincidental items.

Georg F. Simonis espouses a different philosophy. Like Taxis, he also draws cars to order. A professional automotive designer, Simonis employs a greater degree of artistic license and decides what he regards as important or superfluous for each subject.

The Pforzheim-based artist regards his work idealistically, as he does not illustrate an existing situation, but rather creates a new one. For him, an oblique view is characteristic for an early 911, especially when the car is able to express its dynamism in a turn. For the anniversary model, he even chose an unconventional low perspective to emphasize the powerful lines exhibited by the car even at a standstill. Reflections in the vividly colored bodywork run more evenly than they ever could under natural conditions. It is interesting to compare the perfect lines of Simonis' illustrations with the deliberate trick lighting of René Staud's photography.

Simonis emphasizes "that it is very difficult to draw the 911. The car has very sensitive lines, and even slight deviations can drastically alter the car's proportions." Yet most artists credit the 911 with a particularly pleasing shape, if for no other reason than the fact that the car's overall shape can be drawn with a single stroke.

Among artists, the right tool contributes to perfection. To aid draftsmen and artists, so-called "Porsche curves" are available, consisting of a set of curve templates from 30 to 150 cm (1 to 5 ft.) long, similar in function to "French curves." Exclusivity has its price: this drafting aid demands an investment of 10,000 Marks.

Styling
Form follows function

Engineers define a car's design specifications and determine basic conditions which a design must fulfill. Yet in spite of these engineering constraints, a car's styling takes shape in an atmosphere of artistic freedom.

Ferdinand Alexander ("Butzi") Porsche interprets this as a freedom "which is never absolute, but rather always relative." In the 30-year history of the 911, design constraints have gained increasing importance: knowledge of aerodynamics, technical imperatives, modern manufacturing methods and regulatory requirements have become increasingly important in defining the work of a designer. A stylist must therefore have a broad technical background, and today, engineers work side by side with designers in the styling studio. For the new skin of the 993, a further critical factor restricted the design team's freedom of expression: cost.

Anthony R. (Tony) Hatter, the English project leader responsible for the 993's styling, makes it clear that "costs dictated our limits." Without monetary constraints, the new Carrera generation would have undergone even further visual development. But conditions laid down at the very beginning of the project required that the roof and greenhouse, the doors and the trunk lid were to be retained almost without alteration. The development of a new roof would have cost several million Marks. However, the constraints do provide an inherent benefit: the silhouette of the 911 remains essentially unchanged, and the vehicle is immediately identifiable as a Porsche 911.

Regarded solely from a styling standpoint, the 993 does not represent an entirely new vehicle, but rather a major facelift, a visual development, an evolution. Because the basics were retained, this naturally simplified many aspects. The clay modelers were able to build upon the original styling model used for the previous Carrera generation.

For years, the Porsche studio has used the same technique to build both wind tunnel and display models. On the basis of preliminary drawings, a full-scale basic model, divided down its centerline, is built on a surface plate. This gives two separate car halves, which may be connected to provide literally a back-to-back comparison. To give an overall view of the car, a mirror cut to match the car outline is attached to the parting line. Using modern materials, this first model consists of a rigid foam core covered by brown Plasticine modeling clay. In the past, in the era of the 356, wood was used to support the clay. This model only serves to realize design

The final stage of Project 993, undergoing wind tunnel testing. Headlights and wheels do not represent production pieces.

Extensive experiments were carried out on the rear quarter windows to minimize wind noise.

The rear of the car appears wider and lower than that of its predecessor.

Air vents ahead of the front tires are part of "the visual language of the car."

255

concepts; it possesses neither an adequate suspension nor even a chassis. For this reason, a similar $1/5$ scale wind tunnel model is made, for which every underbody detail is recreated in Plasticine. Running changes must be added to both models.

Once the design's aerodynamic development has reached a more advanced stage, details such as the size of air openings or the shape of spoilers are finalized and precise coordinates are taken from the full-size Plasticine model. The data gained from the model is fed to a CAD (computer-aided design) program, in this case a software package known as "Catina," which generates optimized coordinates for the body shape. These values serve as a basis for design drawings. Using the computer-generated data, the engineering department mills the actual master model using a hard material known as "Ureol," comparable to laminated wood, which reproduces the final form of the new car. This is taken by truck to the styling studio, where wide strips of chrome adhesive tape are stuck to the surface and the body lines are checked once again. Equally spaced lines of black tape are applied to a board which is mirrored by the chrome-covered body. The true body shapes can be recognized in the reflections of the black tape lines. Tony Hatter says that "This examination of the master model requires a trained eye; we're dealing with tenths of a millimeter." Necessary corrections are applied directly to the master model by adding hard filler or grinding away excess material.

Parallel to creation of this master model, an additional 993, as realistic as possible, was built for studio work. It was based on a Type 964 chassis, without fenders, door sills, engine or trunk lids. To make these parts, molds were taken from the Plasticine model to form the missing parts in plastic.

This plastic and metal model employed detachable fenders. Various diameter wheels and tires could be mounted, and different track dimensions simulated. It served as a basis for all detail design work, such as interior modifications and the creation of a new wheel design. Using this model as a baseline, Harm M. Lagaay's styling department worked simultaneously on this 964-based mockup and on individual Plasticine models. Designers expressed their ideas, which model makers translated into reality on the

model. Model makers and designers work as a team; from the very beginning of the project, model makers' ideas contributed to the shape of the new Porsche.

This process is repeated many times before the final shape is realized. The model makers' depth of experience proved to be of great assistance to the 993's designers. More than thirty years earlier, Ernst Bolt and Heinz Unger (since retired) had already worked with Ferdinand Alexander Porsche on models of the 901. Project leader Hatter: "For me, it was an honor to work with these craftsmen." Designers, model makers and engineers are equally excited when Professor Ferry Porsche conducts one of his periodic visits to the Weissach studio to examine new projects. Usually, hc nods approval and heads back to his office in Zuffenhausen; Porsche goes in to work nearly every day. This gesture is without doubt a valuable contribution to the collegial atmosphere among the nearly 40 employees in Porsche's styling studio.

In addition to the 993 project, part of the styling department also works on outside projects. Harm Lagaay assigns individual employees in his department to various projects and agrees on timetables with other Porsche departments. Drawing on his creative skills, Porsche's styling chief solves not only styling problems, but also coordination and management challenges.

Normally, a facelift should not take more than three years. The 993 project took longer. In 1989, as Dr. Ulrich Bez, chief of research and development, and chief stylist Harm Lagaay directed the course of future of Porsche development, the evolution of the Carrera was redefined, and work had to start afresh. Two designers, one studio engineer, several model makers and project leader Tony Hatter pursued their new assignment by first determining which Carrera features would be carried over to maintain the unique identity of the classic Porsche.

The roof plays a central role in this process, particularly in side view. The roofline drops in a gentle line from its peak just behind the windshield, ending in the steeper downward slope of the car's tail. Also from a lateral perspective, the side glass helps to

Chief designer Harm M. Lagaay points out to the author which styling elements were inspired by the 959 technology demonstrator.

define the 911's visual character. The trunk lid and strongly defined fenders, with their soft curves and round headlights, dominate the front view. Overall, the concept of the fully integrated vehicle shape, which Porsche has cultivated for more than thirty years, is still appealing.

The current Carrera generation lives up to this styling demand for evolution rather than revolution. This next stage in the evolution of the 911 provided a particular challenge for Porsche's designers, and imposed on them a considerable responsibility. The design team did an admirable job in meeting these goals. Despite the 993's diverse design requirements, Porsche designers have once again drawn a thoroughly modern car which is nevertheless recognizable as a traditional Porsche from every angle.

Seen in silhouette, the 993 conveys a unified design impression even more strongly than its predecessor. Front and rear bumpers blend into the overall shape more smoothly. "Today, all international requirements must be considered from the very outset of a design," explains Hatter. For this reason, designers sought a visually acceptable solution for the black rubber bumperettes required for the American market; U.S. standards specify a minimum distance between the bodywork and the outer edge of the bumpers. As on the Porsche 968, the bumperettes are attached separately, but as on the 928, they are not particularly obtrusive.

The rocker panel area also underwent considerable restyling. As on much earlier 911 models, the outer rocker panels incorporate additional reinforcements and are an integral part of the body, and no

Numerous renderings are made before the first model is begun. Opposite, top, shows styling project leader Tony Hatter flanked by veteran Porsche modelers Heinz Unger (left) and Ernst Bolt.

259

longer a bolted-on valence panel as on more recent 911s. Window seals were altered to bring the rear window flush with the bodywork. Body-colored exterior door handles are more appealing than previous black handles. Even the electrically actuated rear spoiler is shaped to match the curves of the engine lid, with no unnecessary edges and corners to spoil the overall harmony of the design. As a result of these styling elements, the compact, uncluttered shape of the 993 conveys an impression of tremendous dynamism, even when standing still.

In front view, the 993 remains a typical 911. Completely new ellipsoid headlights are installed for the first time. To maintain the 911's characteristic "face," they were designed as large, round units. Thanks to the softer, flatter lines of the front fenders, the headlights are mounted at a lower angle to the wind than before, which results in appreciable aerodynamic advantages. Also, their lower angle of incidence reduces the risk of stone impact damage.

Chief designer Lagaay places particular emphasis on integrating headlights into the lines of the bodywork, rather than having them as individual styling elements. Dutch-born Lagaay explains that "Every detail is important. Even the ridges in the headlight cover glass are an intentional styling element."

For the first time, the windshield wiper arms are located closer to the car's centerline (Lagaay: "They have character") to give the windshield a clearer, more structured appearance, and also serve to improve wiping action. Turn signals and auxiliary lights are clustered in compact units. In addition, the headlight units offer added practicality. A lever inside the trunk releases the entire unit for servicing; integral connectors eliminate the need to connect plugs or wires.

Likewise, the air vents ahead of the front tires are not only functional elements to improve aerodynamics. They were deliberately styled as readily visible "gills," and are part of "the visual language of the car," to quote design chief Lagaay. He adds that "Without such elements, a car would resemble a rubber raft."

According to designer Hatter, the car's rear shapes were especially difficult to sculpt, but the results are convincing; the car appears wider and lower than its predecessor. This is mainly attributable to the black-painted air inlet grille and the full-width light strip, which will emerge as a particularly characteristic feature of the new generation. The exhaust pipes on either side were a specific engineering requirement listed in the design specifications, a requirement gladly embraced by the designers because it conveys an impression of power.

Today, because of their size, wheels contribute to the appearance of the 911 to an even greater degree than in the past. Early 0-series 911s of 1964 still rolled out of the plant on 15-inch rims; for a short time, some models even had 14-inch wheels. By contrast, the 993 is fitted with standard 16-inch and optional 17-inch light alloy wheels. For a stylist, designing a new wheel is an especially attractive assignment. The only precondition was that they should be attractive and simple. To this end, several designs were created, of which one variation was especially pleasing, as it echoed the soft lines of the overall vehicle concept. The gentle shapes of the five spokes had an additional advantage: the wheel is easy to clean.

The interior of the Carrera, of particular importance to the emotional response of the driver, underwent few visual changes, although essential elements such as safety, functionality and ergonomics were improved. "Drivers of the 911 love the dramatics of five instruments; we didn't want to change any of that," explains Harm Lagaay. The most apparent change is the airbag-equipped steering wheel, whose appealing simplicity harmonizes with the elegant lines of the dashboard. The steering column stalks are more practical, and the once almost impossible to find switches for auxiliary functions such as sunroof and rear window defrost are now clearly arrayed in a console ahead of the shift lever. The so-called "knee bar," which blends smoothly into the inner door panels, increases crash safety in the footwell area. Switches on the inner door panels are now easier to operate, and the panels are fitted with roomy storage pockets and flush-mounted stereo speakers. The seats have a new stitching pattern and no longer use traditional, sometimes visually unappealing welting.

The first model consists of a rigid foam core covered by brown Plasticine modeling clay. The suspension is borrowed from the older Carrera generation, known internally as the 964.

For a time, stylists considered accenting the rocker panels as well as the front and rear valances in black.

A small strip mounted above the rear window provided a particular challenge for the 993's designers. Visually, this mini-spoiler was intended to make the roof appear longer, a particular advantage for export versions fitted with the additional black rubber bumperettes. The spoiler also had a technical rationale: first, it resulted in a slight improvement in drag coefficient, and second, for the U.S. market and countries with similar regulations, it serves as a housing for the center high mounted stop light. In this way, no additional lights had to be added to the rear deck or stuck against the inside of the rear window, design solutions that had always seemed an afterthought on previous generations. After this problem had been satisfactorily solved, work continued on the not yet production-ready open versions, the Targa and Cabriolet. Their market introduction would be delayed for several months after delivery of the coupes had begun.

In talking to the designers responsible for the 993, one is repeatedly struck by their desire to create a compact, unified design, in which all individual components were integrated into the overall shape and all elements were mounted flush with the surrounding bodywork. In view of this, one would expect a low drag coefficient, but the wind tunnel results were not as good as expected. Numerous costly wind tunnel studies lowered the C_d by only .04, to 0.31, but this was achieved despite the new car's wider rear fenders. Such a purely theoretical comparison also does not consider the aerodynamic advances previously realized in the second Carrera generation, with its rounded, integrated front and rear bumpers and race-proven flat underbody tray.

Significant improvement in the drag coefficient could only have been achieved by reducing the car's overall frontal area. However, due to the wide tires required by the 993's power output, this is not possible without compromising the stability and handling of this high-performance sports car. If only for technical considerations, aerodynamics will always represent a compromise.

Biased reviewers might denounce the 993 styling from a purely formal aspect. They might overlook the loving attention to design detail and dismiss the exterior with a blunt characterization of "968 front,

Panamericana tail." On closer examination, these do not represent negatives; on the contrary, the 968 and Panamericana were drawn almost simultaneously (the 968 barely preceding the show car) under Harm Lagaay's direction. Naturally, in directing work on these projects, Porsche's chief stylist was applying a single unifying Porsche philosophy.

When introduced to the market in 1991 (rhd models in 1992), the 968 incorporated more 911 styling elements than had been given to its predecessor, the 944, to give it a Porsche family look. Also, work on the 993 was begun before the first renderings for the 968 had been made. Similarity to the 993 is neither coincidental nor unintentional; both cars represent

In viewing yard behind the Weissach studio, full-scale models were repeatedly contemplated under natural lighting conditions. The development stage shown here does not yet have fully developed fender contours.

Eberhard Brose, shown working on a 993, has been modeling the 911 for more than 20 years.

Porsche design philosophy and were drawn nearly in parallel. Examined more closely, thanks to its characteristic fenders, the 993 has a more clearly defined "face," resembling that of the earlier 959 technology carrier.

Consequently, similarities with the rear aspect of the Panamericana study, particularly the light strip, may be regarded as positive attributes. Styling studies such as the Panamericana and the Boxster, shown in early 1993, demonstrate Porsche's styling potential. It is quite reasonable to expect styling elements from Porsche concept cars to find their way to the production line in the future.

Impressive though they might be, styling studies alone do not show Porsche's future direction, as the new Carrera generation amply demonstrates. Its designers made it plain that even today, cars must have character. The 993's 39-year-old project leader draws an international styling comparison: "The Japanese go too far." Indeed, sports cars, full-size sedans and even small cars built in the Orient display increasingly smooth, almost featureless shapes. Hatter adds reflectively that "Cars should not look like eggs." For him, the 911, with its controlled round shapes, still represents an ideal design for today, a styling composition offering a multitude of perspectives for the future.

Biographical Sketch: Tony Hatter

Anthony R. (Tony) Hatter (born December 13, 1954), after studying industrial design in England, attended the Royal College of Art in London to specialize in automotive design. Even then, he considered that someday he might work at Porsche.

Hatter's first practical experiences were gained at Opel, where he contributed to the styling of the Opel Omega. After five years in Rüsselsheim, he moved to Porsche. He was named project leader responsible for styling the 993. By his own admission, Hatter is a complete auto fan. For him, the 911 represents the ideal design.

Road testing the 993 prototype

Eyes on the prize

At their Weissach proving grounds, Porsche engineers have created a very special torture track. To evaluate long-term durability and life expectancy of vehicles and individual components, patched pavement, hunchbacked curves, Belgian blocks, rough railroad crossings and a launching ramp compress years of driving into only a few days. At Porsche, a car design travels a long, tortuous path before it is deemed ready for production.

Every morning, at about 5:30, long before the tiny village of Weissach awakens, the first commuters of the workday make the turn between the church and the Gasthaus Löwen [the Lion Inn], traveling the small road that connects this town of 6000 inhabitants with the outside world. Every morning, a handful of Porsche employees enter the grounds of the research and development center well ahead of the rest of its 2000 employees. The gate swings up, and these early risers go to work. A few minutes later, one hears six-cylinder boxer engines being fired up, and one by one, the 993 prototypes roll toward the nearly three kilometer long test track, each with a new, remarkable rasp in its exhaust note. On their way to the track, one more barrier blocks their path. It opens only after the driver's company ID tag is inserted and read, registering the driver. At Porsche, nothing is left to chance.

Two drivers per car make up the morning shift. They trade places every hour. "In the long run, that's all that the men will take," explains Peter Sharpf, one of the individual team leaders on the 993 project. And after 20 years at Weissach, he should know; for years, engineer Scharpf served as his own test driver. Today, Scharpf primarily works on organizational problems, yet work draws him onto the test track again and again. Each time, this veteran engineer is again fascinated by the extraordinary standard of quality exhibited by sports cars from Zuffenhausen. Prototypes are abused on the test track until the design is released for production. "Under the same treatment, competing cars just fall apart," says Scharpf, clearly proud of his own company's product.

Today, durability testing on the Weissach test track covers a distance of 6000 km [3600 miles]. Twenty years ago, the distance was twice as great, and for a time dropped to 8000 km. But tighter development deadlines, and the increased cost and complexity of development to meet modern demands, required some way of packing more driving into a shorter time. The torture course was made so difficult that today, prototypes undergo the same cumulative punishment as in the past, despite the shorter overall distance.

September, 1991: wet handling tests at the Contidrom. This Type 964 Carrera, with the narrow front and wide rear track of the Turbo-look package, is powered by an early version of the 993 powerplant.

On European roads, these 6000 test kilometers must be multiplied by 27 to reach an equivalent distance. This works out to the equivalent 162,000 km – 100,000 miles – which, on the Weissach track, can be compressed into only two or three working weeks. The resulting collective wear and tear applies to all components which are considered to be "load-carrying structure." This includes the crankcase, transmission case, steering, suspension, body shell, and mountings for auxiliary components. For the cabriolet, it also includes the mechanical parts of the top. "Open cars cover half of the total distance, that is, 3000 km, with the top open, even in winter," adds Scharpf, unable to hide a grin. Today, it's easy for him to find this amusing; the white Carrera 2 (993), only slightly camouflaged, is reeling off today's

mileage with its top raised. And a good thing, too; the outside temperature is 1° C [34 °F].

The engine lets out an unmuffled roar; under our feet, bare, unpainted metal is visible. We're on our way. Just after we enter the test track, the Carrera bounces over clearly marked obstacles; half of the nearly three kilometers of the course consist of so-called "condition sections," segments which simulate the most wretched road conditions imaginable. The prototypes catch their breath only briefly before the shaking and pounding begins all over again. After potholes equaled only by those found on the roads of Baja California comes the washboard road, and then the pancake section. This last looks as though a herd of cattle was driven along it, leaving

266

January 1992, on the Turracher Höhe in Austria. The Turbo bodywork covers a complete 993 suspension package and a prototype of the more powerful engine.

behind road muffins which have petrified to asphalt. The bouncing steering wheel speaks of the enormous impacts which the suspension has to absorb on this section.

On the test track, different rules of behavior apply. In everyday driving, one usually slows down for potholes and rough roads. Instead, Scharpf accelerates, explaining, "We have to cover this section at 80 km/h [50 mph]." He adds a friendly comment: "Don't panic, but we're coming up on a launching ramp." I have just enough time to grab the door handle before the Carrera goes airborne, only to slam onto its bump stops a moment later. The boxer engine is sluggish in answering the throttle pedal; test equipment records misfiring. The jump, followed by acceleration in

sixth gear, is too much even for the highly refined six cylinder engine. The driver explains this odd behavior: "It wasn't designed for this, but I wanted to see if sixth gear pops out." There is no rest for the car; we're coming up on the hunchback curve. The 993 prototype shakes and squirms toward the outside of the turn, but only reluctantly; wheel bearings and axles are subjected to extraordinary loads. The speedometer indicates nearly 90 km/h [55 mph]. Then a quick left hander on smooth asphalt, squealing tires, and hard braking before entering "Road Condition Section I." There, the Carrera deals with torsion humps, which twist the body to simulate a 4.9 meter long stretch of the nearby country road to Wiernsheim; then several meters of "Pforzheim pavement," followed by a brief rest.

June, 1992, at the Contidrom. The new skin of the 993 is hidden by the so-called "heavy camouflage" kit.

Endurance testing at the Nürburgring, June 1992.

268

Even rest periods for the car – or perhaps they are intended for the driver – are carefully planned into the schedule. After just one lap of the test track, it becomes obvious that the mileage multiplier of 27 was not reached arbitrarily. "If anything, it is a bit conservative," confirms Peter Scharpf, as he discusses work in the testing department. It is apparent that discipline and attention to detail are primary concerns. After about 1000 km [600 miles] the suspension geometry is checked. In addition, technicians check the tightening torques of all safety-related fasteners. All parts of the car undergo a visual check. Engineers keep careful notes to record all observations. In the event of a defect, no matter how small, the appropriate department is immediately notified. As an example, Scharpf cites that "If a hydraulic lifter clatters repeatedly in the same corner, we have to schedule a lubrication endurance test."

Even if a specific part has no detectable flaws, test engineers are still not satisfied. Three samples of every part, all representing the same development level, must survive the torture test without damage. Only then can the part be approved for production.

Meanwhile, the specified rest time has passed. The six-cylinder engine roars again, and it's off to the next lap. In the "Road Condition Section II," the car encounters a 77.8 meter section of Belgian blocks, followed by 315.7 meters of transversely grooved pavement, transversely wavy pavement for the same distance, and then 20.3 meters of a 2.5 percent salt water solution. To deliberately hasten corrosion effects, many prototypes do not have undercoating.

Suddenly, Peter Scharpf slams on the brakes. The 993 prototype comes to an abrupt stop. Scharpf explains that "Naturally, on these road condition sections, no significant demands are placed on the brakes. Still, I need to know from time to time what the ABS system is doing after a given test distance."

269

Tire tests at the Contidrom, September 1992, with a 993 prototype.

The test engineers are given a certain degree of freedom, and can act spontaneously within the parameters of the endurance test program.

An hour later, the white prototype, with its taped-on camouflage, again pulls up to the barrier. Again the employee ID card is fed into the slot and is recorded by a computer. The car, known internally as "R 34," heads straight for its parking space behind workshop doors. Project 993 is still top secret. A large sticker on the driver's door serves as a constant reminder: "Achtung! Do not drive without camou-flage! Check attachment of 'light camouflage' before every drive! Loose areas are to be retaped or must be replaced by ETW 45 [author's note: the department responsible for camouflage]. Camou-flage will reduce headlight range."

In keeping with Porsche's testing philosophy, this intensive endurance test is only the first hurdle in a prototype's complete testing program. Early in the development process, vehicles must prove their mettle in a real-world endurance test. At 2 PM of every work day, the integrated vehicle road test department's second shift goes to work. Department chief Wetschky sends his drivers out on a predetermined course on country roads around the Weissach R&D center. Here, a more customer-oriented driving style is simulated. The course offers a balanced mix of different road surfaces. By way of Hochdorf, the road leads to Öschelbronn, to Tiefenbronn and Rutesheim and back to Weissach. The loop takes about one hour, depending on weather and traffic. At this stage of development, only 993 prototypes fitted with "heavy camouflage" are allowed out on public roads. These Porsches look like something from the wildest days of show tuning. Camouflage panels are often only riveted in place; for this reason, the registration book of every road-registered prototype carries an annotation certifying it as a test vehicle. Once aware of this, the police look the other way. Even the guardians of public decency realize that real-world tests are necessary.

Porsche has spent billions to provide its Weissach development staff with a wealth of test equipment. An unmatched collection of climate chambers, wind tunnels, engine and chassis dynamometers, noise chambers and vibration test stands are only a small part of the extensive repertoire. Yet regardless of how perfect the test results may be, they cannot replace that most unique test instrument, the human being. This person, the customer of tomorrow, will drive the car. He will steer and operate all of the technical marvels designed by people using the finest tools and computers. But ultimately it is the driver who must control the wondrous devices so carefully engineered into the car. The human being is the one incalculable factor in the high technology of the car. For Porsche, now and in the future, real-world tests are without a doubt unavoidable.

November 1992, at the Weissach proving grounds. Even in the depths of winter, Cabriolets must cover 3000 km, half of the test distance, with the top down.

Only part of a car's durability testing takes place on public roads, within the rules and regulations required by traffic. Other tests are conducted on special courses such as the north circuit of the Nürburgring. Such demanding race courses place especially high loads on suspension and brakes. Full-load engine durability is tested on the high-speed test track at Nardo, in southern Italy. In general, three different test combinations are presently available. Most common is the 80,000 km [50,000 mile] mixed endurance test. This simulates Porsche's assessment of the usual stress placed on a vehicle within its

expected service life at the hands of European customers. In 18 to 20 weeks, the test covers the following test segments: 6000 km of the Nürburgring north course; 22,000 km country roads around Weissach; 27,000 km Autobahn. These tests generally are conducted in the third shift, which goes on duty at 10 PM. Road and traffic conditions permitting, autobahn mileage is accumulated on the stretch from Baden-Baden to Basel. This is followed by 10,000 km in city traffic, if possible under stop-and-go conditions. Finally, 15,000 km are covered at the high speed test track in Nardo.

January 1993: ice tests on a frozen pond in St. Martin.

January 1993, winter tests on the Turracher Höhe.

March 1993, Michelin proving grounds in Ladoux, France.

Photographed in front of the backdrop of "La Grand Motte" on the French Riviera, this white prototype is fitted with only the taped-on "light camouflage" kit.

In order to obtain data on component durability as quickly as possible early in the development process, an intensified 40,000 km endurance test is available. This can be finished in eight to ten calendar weeks.

To ensure real-world durability, an additional 160,000 km [100,000 mile] endurance test is available. This simulates customer-specific situations, without the added strain of acceleration factors. This will consume 27 to 29 calendar weeks, in other words, nearly seven months. Despite the time-consuming nature of this test, it will soon be part of the general test program. American emissions regulations require that all vehicle components related to exhaust emissions must be able to withstand 100,000 miles of use.

The third type of testing at Porsche may be summarized under the concept of "function tests." Pre-production cars are put through a strenuous road test regimen across a wide spectrum of climatic and road conditions. Engineers make a distinction between summer, winter and mountain testing. In the Rocky Mountains of North America, individual vehicle components are subject to high operating temperatures in low humidity. In the snowy wastes of Alaska, the mercury may drop to -30 °C [-22 °F]. The air-cooled engines of the Carrera will not tolerate still lower temperatures, but water-cooled vehicles can at least be pre-heated. In tests on Alpine passes, engines experience a large difference in air density. Testing and evaluation of prototypes for a new model add up to millions of kilometers. Years before the

This prototype, photographed in March 1993 in Arjeplog, Lapland (northern Finland), has only the taped-on "light camouflage" package. The front fenders and headlights of the production version can be recognized.

car goes into production, highly qualified Porsche technicians reel off the miles that make up these rigidly defined test programs. In the beginning, testing is disguised by the unassuming bodywork of the current production model. Later, camouflaged versions of modified bodies are placed in service.

In this age of sophisticated electronics, the complexity of a car which will be driven by human beings, who bring to the driving experience their own subjective perception, presents its development engineers with a multitude of problems and design targets, problems which must appear overwhelming to the layman. Porsche's Weissach employees (Porsche Engineering Services) have specialized in the solution of such problems. At Weissach, develop-

ment of each vehicle, system, and component is carefully planned and, in keeping with a strict development timetable, results in a new automobile.

Every test driver had his eye on the most important deadline of the project: the latest master stroke from Porsche, the new Carrera, known internally as the Type 993, which was revealed to the public at the 1993 Frankfurt auto show. Meanwhile, the Weissach road test team was already working on the next project. The legendary Turbo was to be replaced by a successor, propelled by a twin-turbo powerplant, internally carrying a mysterious designation, "UST."

The company ID card is inserted, the barrier swings up, and we're off on another lap.

Development of the 993
Greater than the sum of its parts

Modern automobile manufacturing is far from the individualistic undertaking it once was. The car of today is far too complex a creation to permit such expressions of personal genius. Each new car represents so many design goals and challenges that the burden must be shared by many individuals. In this way, the 993 Carrera project was divided among specialists responsible for engine, transmission, suspension, bodywork, body ancillaries, systems and electrical/electronics; seven project subgroups, each with one or two project leaders responsible for the 993 alone. The various 911 models in turn are served by their own project teams, which expands the company organization chart by a multitude of individual groups.

Despite the absence of any one individual's design imprint on the modern car, names may still be associated with the development of a new design. Engineers Friedrich Bezner and Bernd Kahnau are the team leaders responsible for every 911 variant. The exceptions to this rule are exclusive limited-production models such as the Turbo S or the Carrera Cup cars, which are conceived and built directly by the racing department. For these models, the 911 project leaders serve only in an advisory role.

At Porsche, Friedrich Bezner is one of three project leaders who has held this post since its inception in 1979. At that time, distinction was still made among four, six, and eight-cylinder projects. Because Porsche's chairman of that era, Ernst Fuhrmann, intended to phase out production of the 911 by 1981 (Fuhrmann regarded the 928 as a worthy successor), the six-cylinder project leader's position appeared to be a thankless job of only limited duration. This didn't deter Bezner, a dedicated fan of the 911; today, his eyes still hold a gleam as he recounts how he applied for the position and was accepted. Bezner had been assistant to Helmuth Bott, chief of research and development. Bezner comments on the five years of his career with Bott: "That gave me valuable insights into the company's operation." In his new position, he continued to work closely with the R&D chairman. Helmuth Bott expected his project leaders to maintain a steady stream of suggestions for the future model lineup. Bezner recalls these early years: "With our never-ending suggestions, we were a real pain to the responsible departments." Despite the very limited development budget for the six-cylinder line, project leader Bezner and his team wanted to give their engine more horsepower. This could only be achieved if the engines were once again tuned for premium fuel. Bezner received approval for this step, even though Fuhrmann originally resisted investing in the soon to be

The new Carrera represents a logical development of the original 911's unique features.

Despite its lower front fenders, the 911 has given up none of its classic profile.

Overall, smoother body transitions are apparent, especially between the front hood and bumper.

Pure driving
pleasure: the new
911 responds to
the throttle as
willingly as its
ancestor, the
Carrera RS 2.7.

Driving for
enjoyment: the
new 911 makes a
wonderful sound.

Details: the interior (top) is only slightly changed from that of the predecessor; 40 percent of the engine components are newly developed.

phased out 911. Thanks to Bezner's team, the 911 SC put out 204 horsepower as of the 1981 model year, which resulted in an immediate increase in its popularity among buyers. While only 9475 911s were sold in 1980, sales in 1982 rose to 11,627 units, and 13,320 in 1983. By 1982, Peter W. Schutz had replaced Fuhrmann as chairman of the board. Friedrich Bezner had achieved his goal; the future of the 911 was secure.

According to Bezner, who started his Porsche career on April 20, 1954 as an apprentice, the pinnacle of 911 evolution has already been reached: the 30th anniversary model. Regarding the Turbobodied Carrera 4, painted a special shade of violet metallic, this Porsche veteran enthuses that "For me, this is the most beautiful 911." He is particularly intrigued by the wide body with its spoiler retracted at rest. Bezner describes the handling of this special model, limited to only 911 numbered examples: "On top of that, the car corners as if on rails."

Bezner's enthusiasm for the 911 remains unbroken, even after 14 years of team leadership and 30 years of 911 production, mainly due to the evolutionary history of the model. For some time now, the six-cylinder engine has been Porsche's mainstay; it is responsible for two-thirds of sales. It is readily apparent that the success of the 993 Carrera generation is vital to Porsche. This fact was not lost on Bezner or his team when they undertook the 993 project. With undiminished zeal, they created, with the 993, one of the most important evolutionary stages in the development history of the six-cylinder engine. Bezner's department still exemplifies the Porsche team spirit which some assert, often erroneously, has been lost from many departments in Porsche's recent difficult times.

The division of responsibility among the project teams has changed slightly. Since the inception of the stillborn four-seat Project 989, which was to have an eight-cylinder powerplant, Bezner's team is no longer referred to as the "six-cylinder project group," but rather the "911 model line project group."

Then as now, the most important task for a project leader is coordinating the efforts of various specialized project groups involved in a development project. Added to this is cooperation with other departments such as production, customer service, sales, marketing or company management. Each of these departments has its own expectations of the project, and each department's suggestions must be taken into consideration whenever possible. This is a difficult assignment for a project leader, especially since he is expected to develop cost-reducing measures rather than costly improvements.

Horst Marchart, board member for research and development, makes no secret of the fact that the 911 is still his one and only automotive love.

The rough outlines of Project 993 were first defined at a management board product meeting in early 1989. At that time, Weissach was under the leadership of Dr. Ulrich Bez, chief of Porsche research, development, and motorsports activities from October 1, 1988 to September 30, 1991. These first discussions leading toward a decision to go ahead with Type 993 development took place at a time when Porsche was still building 16,460 examples of the 911 annually; a year later production

would even climb to 20,855 units, exceeding the magic 20,000 unit threshold. No wonder then that the first ideas for an even better 911 were greeted with high enthusiasm. Bezner recalls the beginnings of Project 993: "Originally, we had planned to build a completely new car." But the automobile industry was soon plunged into crisis; enormous financial pressures dictated plans and decisions. Bezner summarizes the situation: "The 993 was put on a diet." In addition, the order of the day was that the immediate successor to the then-current 911, the 964, should achieve higher performance but without increased costs.

One of the highlights of the 993 was to have been the engine. After the four-door Project 989 was shelved once and for all, thought was given to installing the water-cooled eight-cylinder rear-mounted engine, developing 300 horsepower, in the 993. By mid-1989, though, it was realized that the required design effort would have been too great and costs would have skyrocketed; the six-cylinder was back in the picture. The output of the six-cylinder boxer would be raised from 250 to 270 horsepower; it would be based on the engine of the 964. A year later, it was thought that cylinder head cooling would raise output to 285 hp, but in January 1991 this far too complicated variation was also rejected

Bernd Kahnau, 993 project leader from 1989 to 1994: "Overall, the new 911 Carrera is a more agile car."

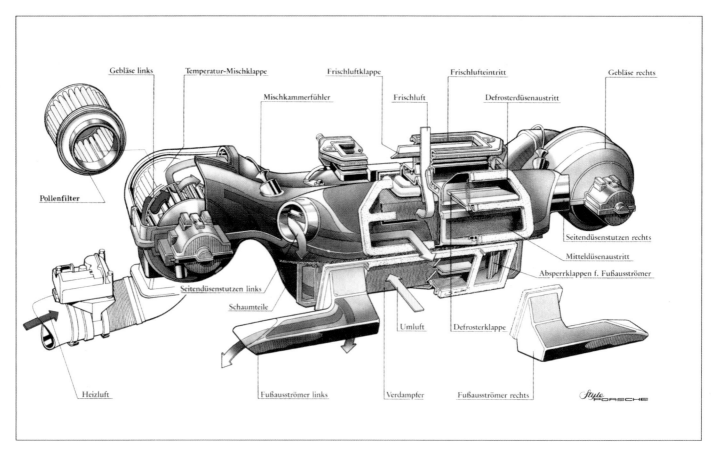

Gebläse links
Temperatur-Mischklappe
Frischluftklappe
Frischlufteintritt
Gebläse rechts
Mischkammerfühler
Frischluft
Defrosterdüsenaustritt
Pollenfilter
Seitendüsenstutzen rechts
Mitteldüsenaustritt
Absperrklappen f. Fußausströmer
Seitendüsenstutzen links
Schaumteile
Umluft
Defrosterklappe
Heizluft
Fußausströmer links
Verdampfer
Fußausströmer rechts
style PORSCHE

The new heating system assures rapid warming of the cabin.

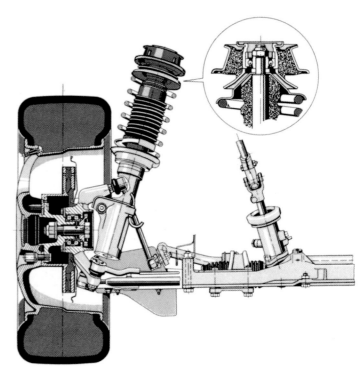

To reduce front suspension weight, aluminum components replace steel.

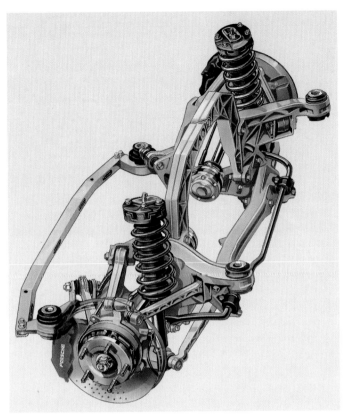

The multi-link rear suspension improves ride comfort.

and it was agreed to raise power by 15 hp, to 265 horsepower. The most difficult engine change was a new exhaust system, which meets the new, stricter noise standards [as of 1995, reduction of maximum noise level from 77 dB(A) to 75 dB(A)] by increasing muffler volume. As always, the exhaust tip is the dominant source of noise. Still, it was possible to design the exhaust system so that the already developed multi-link rear suspension, with its wide front crossmember, could be accommodated with only minor modifications. This was achieved by directing exhaust gas to a central catalytic converter, but then again splitting the exhaust into two separate streams. Dual exhaust not only had engineering advantages, but was also welcomed by the styling department.

Other noise sources were optimized. Hydraulic valve lash adjustment reduced valve train noise, an altered air filter system reduced intake noise, and improved engine encapsulation reduced overall engine noise. This made the 993 so quiet that Porsche's acoustic engineers could "play" with the engine sound spectrum. Bezner voices his opinion about the sound of the 993: "A sports car does not have to be loud, but should have a pleasant sound. On long stretches, loud cars are annoying."

This phantom view shows the modified drivetrain and the new exhaust system.

283

The transmission was also brought in line with Porsche's new philosophy for an economical sports car. In December, 1990, its six speeds were to be geared for maximum speed; only two months later, a more fuel-efficient layout was chosen.

The suspension provided the greatest headaches for all concerned. Originally, the 993 was to have the sophisticated suspension of the never-realized Turbo successor, the 965. In August 1989, it was decided to use the conventional semi-trailing arm suspension. Bernd Kahnau says that "This decision was not very satisfactory." He summarizes concerns about the old suspension design: "After all, we wanted to reduce the thumping noises from the rear suspension." Indeed, the decision would be reversed. In early 1990, after the engine designers had indicated the feasibility of the new exhaust system, the better isolated, steerable rear suspension was back in the picture. The project was rushed through development, and exactly one year later the project leaders decided in favor of the much more comfortable suspension with upper and lower A-arms as standard equipment, but in a non-steerable version.

Naturally, these decisions also had a direct effect on the stylists. The voluminous exhaust system and elaborate rear suspension required space under the rear fenders. To meet this requirement, in early 1989 it was still intended to use the outer skin of the cancelled Turbo successor, the 965, with its rigid rear spoiler. Shortly thereafter, the designers and engineers came up with an electrically retractable rear spoiler for the 965. In June of 1989, it was decided instead to design a new, narrower body. By October, the Porsche styling department was ready with its own version, which was approved and underwent only minor detail changes before the begin of production.

Additional details were originally planned, but time was growing short. Shelved plans included slightly relocated seats, a new steering wheel with reach adjustment, new inner door panels and use of the seats conceived for the [four-seat] 989. "We haggled about every single little button or knob," says Bezner, describing the detail change discussions. In view of these considerations, the speed with which Project 993 was realized is especially impressive. In October 1992, the first cars of the pre-production run (PV 1) were built in Zuffenhausen. To these were added four all-wheel-drive prototypes. All of these were extensively hand-built cars. PV 2 followed in December 1992 and January 1993, with a total of 21 cars, and in March the first 0-series, with 25 cars, came off the assembly line. Next were 26 press fleet cars, seven right-hand-drive cars and several Cabriolet prototypes. Compared to 30 years ago, many more cars are needed today for type certification and model introduction activities such as advertising and brochure photography, dealer introductions, multimedia shows, service manuals and owner's handbooks. Preparations were made for press and dealer introductions. Once past the Frankfurt auto show, in September, and press and dealer introductions, in October, the development process continued unabated. Variations on the 993 theme are already in the pipeline, to be introduced at planned intervals over the coming months and years.

When asked how perfect the 993 is, Bezner quickly replies that "In car design, total perfection is impossible." He regards the 993 Carrera as the most important 911 evolutionary stage since the 964, especially since many of the "lovable idiosyncrasies" have finally been eliminated: a new rear suspension, an optimized heating system with integral pollen filter as standard equipment, a new wiper design and a more user-friendly shift console. Yet the Carrera has retained the character, indeed even that charm which make it so unique. Regarding the future, Bezner allows that "It might even become a little more perfect." As always, the 911 and its variations hold enormous development potential.

Evolution of the 911
Chronology of model development

The following pages document the most important changes to Porsche production vehicles of the types 911, 912 and 911 Turbo. The section headings from 1 through 10 reflect similar divisions within the factory repair manuals, parts catalogs and flat rate manuals, and in Porsche technical bulletins. In addition to factory documents, information from individual Porsche specialists was taken into consideration. For this work, retired Porsche engineer and customer service instructor Jörg Austen generously gave his valuable time and assistance. Herr Austen retired after many years of responsibility for technical literature and, in particular, for technical training.

Each model year begins on August 1 of the previous year. This does not necessarily mean that all changes take effect at the beginning of the new model year. Moreover, some changes were introduced within the course of a model year, in keeping with Porsche model policy. These changes were also applied to various export countries at various times. For this reason, modifications for the German market take precedence in this chronology. These are supplemented by information regarding foreign models, particularly when these are indicative of future changes for all models worldwide. The following 911-specific criteria are of particular interest:

• development of the air-cooled boxer engine
• emissions reduction for all engines, worldwide
• transmission development from the manual transmission through the Sportomatic to Tiptronic
• wheels and tires
• corrosion protection and the resulting long-term anti-corrosion warranty
• passive safety features
• development stages for heating and air conditioning systems
• evolution of the electrical system from DC generators to on-board computers
• individual visual modifications

The upper half of the text gives a brief summary of changes. Following text in italics explains these changes and puts them into perspective. "RoW" designates "Rest of World."

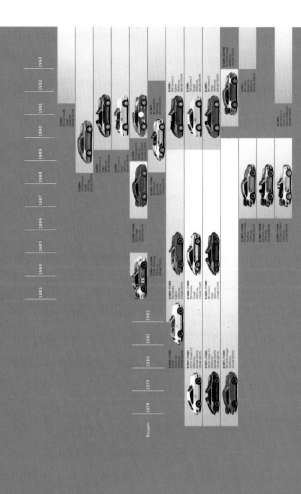
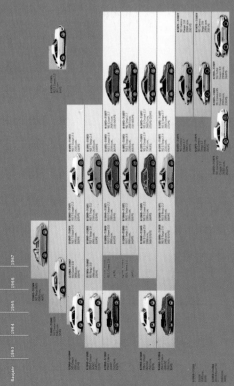

PORSCHE

1963–1993

911 prototypes, 1963/1964

Type designation: Porsche 901

Description
Before the 911 went into production in November 1964, a total of thirteen 911 prototypes were built, with chassis numbers 13 321 to 13 333. Numbers 13 330 and 13 331 were predecessors of the four-cylinder 912. No two examples were alike. They were used for display purposes as well as testing, underwent continuous modification and differed from later production cars in many details. The Frankfurt International Automobile Show (IAA) in September, 1963 marked the official birth of the 911.

1. Engine
The six-cylinder boxer engine was developed in early 1960, under type designation 745. This version still employed pushrods, four main bearings and two axial blowers driven by fan belts from the crankshaft. The next development stage was designated Type 821 and closely resembled the later production engine. The main difference was that this type did not employ dry sump lubrication.

After extensive test drives with the T7, a predecessor to the 911, fitted with a Type 745 engine, Ferry Porsche resolved to discontinue pushrod engines.

2. Fuel and ignition systems
Even the early Type 745 engine relied on downdraft Solex carburetors for its supply of air-fuel mixture. Before the production 40 PI carburetors were ready, Porsche conducted its tests with a Solex application used for Lancias, the Type 40 PBIC.

The Solex overflow carburetors required costly development; simultaneously, Porsche conducted experiments with Weber carburetors.

3. Powertrain
Tests were conducted with four- and five-speed manual transmissions. To achieve the desired comfort, the five-speed gearbox was selected. In order to provide a shift pattern which would also be suitable for racing, first gear was located to the left and back, reverse gear left and forward. Development of the new transmission was relatively free of problems; as inventor of the blocking synchromesh system, Porsche had access to enormous technical expertise.

4. Suspension
Porsche had already experimented with a new suspension design on the 356. Both 901 prototypes were still fitted with front subframes and 356 rear suspensions. At the last moment, it was decided to use a new suspension system at the rear. Fuel tank volume was maximized at 62 liters [16.4 gallons] to emphasize the car's Grand Touring character.

Without numerous tests on 356 models beginning in the mid-1950s, it would not have been possible to develop a completely new suspension for the 911.

5. Bodywork
The first renderings, carrying the designation Type 695, were done in 1957, largely by Graf Goertz. Ferdinand Alexander Porsche created the Type 754 T 7 in 1959, with a slight break in the roofline between the backlight and engine lid. A rather overloaded design, Type 754 T 9, was drawn by Porsche's chief of body engineering, Erwin Komenda. The 901 was eventually developed from F.A. Porsche's design for the 644 T8, which was still the subject of experimentation to find an acceptable wheelbase. The prototypes had no bumper guards, no side deco strips and dual exhaust outlets.

It was hard to imagine any Porsche other than the 356. As a result, the new styling was received with great skepticism.

6. Equipment
The new Porsche had large glass areas – a genuine 2+2, with fold-down rear seat backs like its predecessor.

In the beginning, two large round instruments were employed; the combination of five round instruments with green faces was not completed until 1964. The interior of the prototype shown at the 1963 IAA differed greatly from the later production version.

7. Seats and trim
Porsche intended to offer the new model with a full leather interior as standard equipment, but in fact leatherette was combined with fabric. Seat height was the object of extensive experimentation.

Porsche placed great emphasis on a comfortable seat position for its sporty Grand Touring car.

8. Heating system
Because the heating system was engine speed and load dependent, tests were also conducted with an auxiliary heater. This was later available as an option, mounted in a well in the right side of the trunk ahead of the dashboard. Originally, the battery was to be mounted in this well.

Initially, the prototypes did not have a heating system, as heat exchangers were not ready until much later. For this reason, some versions had only an auxiliary heater mounted in the trunk.

9. Electrical system
Early in the development of the 901/911, Porsche decided to install a high output 12 Volt system. Prototypes still used 360 Watt generators.

The location of the windshield wiper arms was the subject of extensive discussions. Early versions had their wipers parked on the right to provide a larger field of view.

Model year 1965

Type designation: Porsche 911

Changes
After fourteen years of building the Porsche 356, its successor goes into production, using the same basic concepts: air-cooled boxer engine combined with clutch, transmission and final drive to form a compact powertrain unit. Engine and drivetrain mounted at the rear of the vehicle. Fully synchromesh manual transmission employing Porsche's patented synchromesh system. Torsion bar suspension. Trunk at front of car.

1. Engine
Six-cylinder boxer engine, Type 901/01, with displacement of 1991 cc. Air cooled via cooling fan, mounted coaxially with the alternator. Dry sump lubrication system with separate oil tank. Engine output 130 hp [96 kW] at 6100 rpm. Cylinder bore 80 mm, piston stroke 66 mm, compression ratio 9.0:1. Pressure die cast alloy crankcase, Biral aluminum cylinders with iron liners. Alloy pistons. Eight main bearings. One camshaft per cylinder bank. Camshaft drive via two timing chains.

From the very beginning, the six-cylinder boxer engine was designed for future power increases. The cooling fan, belt driven from the crankshaft, not only supplied engine cooling air, but also cooled the engine oil by means of a separately mounted oil cooler. The overhead cams permitted high engine rpm which would be essential for later sport and racing engines. Also noteworthy was the futuristic dry sump lubrication system, which completely eliminated crankshaft splashing losses at high rpm.

2. Fuel and ignition systems

6 Solex PI overflow carburetors with one float bowl serving three carburetors. Firing order 1-6-2-4-3-5. Ignition distributor Marelli S112 AX.

The two banks of Solex carburetors were a short-lived solution, as they were difficult to synchronize. Ignition was by conventional coil ignition with breaker points in the distributor.

3. Powertrain

Standard five-speed manual transmission, Type 901, with final drive in same housing. Shift pattern: first gear left and back, reverse left and forward, spring loaded lockout for 1-2 shift. All forward gears equipped with Porsche synchromesh. Final drive via spiral-cut bevel gears. Bevel gear differential, ZF limited slip differential available as option. Drive to rear wheels by means of Nadella joints. The outer universal joint was of conventional configuration, while the inner "Nadella" joint employed a hinged connection to permit driveshaft length variations.

For the 901/911, Porsche employed a further improvement of the Porsche synchronizing system. Porsche synchromesh was patented worldwide and was licensed for installation in all Alfa Romeo, Simca and AUDI models, and in some Fiat, Ferrari, Maserati and Lamborghini models. For trucks, Porsche blocking synchromesh was used by Fiat-OM, Unic, Berliet and in some diesel-powered forklifts.

4. Suspension

Welded steel box frame, welded directly to body. Front suspension: independent suspension with struts and lateral arms. Rear suspension: independent suspension on trailing arms. Rear drive by means of jointed halfshafts. Front springing by means of separate longitudinal torsion bar for each wheel. At the rear, one transverse round torsion bar per wheel. Shock absorbers: front double acting MacPherson struts, rear double acting telescoping shock absorbers. Toe-in and track not adjustable in first model year. Articulated multi-link safety steering column

as standard equipment. ZF rack and pinion steering, still employing fine pitch gearing. Steering ratio 16.5:1. Wheels: slotted disc steel wheels, optionally available with chrome plating, 4 $^1/_2$ J x 15 deep-bed rims with 165 HR 15 tires. Brakes: single-circuit hydraulic brake system. Front disc diameter 282 mm, rear 285 mm. Mechanical drum parking brake acting on both rear wheels.

Porsche had chosen a self-supporting floorpan for its design of the VW Beetle. Even for the 356, the box frame was rigid enough to permit test drives without bodywork.

The ZF rack and pinion steering was new for the 901/911. In this, Porsche broke ground for the entire auto industry, which still employed worm and nut or cam and peg steering systems. The new suspension system retained torsion bars for its springing, a system which Porsche had developed. The longitudinal orientation of the front torsion bars was completely new. The four disc brake system of the 901/911 was virtually a luxury in the 1960s, but Porsche did not use its own development of the inside-acting calipers (used in the 356 Carrera 2 and Porsche Formula 1 race car), but instead used conventional outside calipers. The brake system was still single-circuit type.

5. Bodywork

Coupe body style only, all-steel construction. A sunroof is not yet available. Seat and shoulder belts can be fitted. Comprehensive instrumentation, including for the first time an oil level indicator which reads while the engine is running. Considerably more trunk and interior space compared to the 356. The wiper blades are parked on the right side of the windshield.

The classic Porsche line was retained in styling the new 901/911: angled headlights in the front fenders, air inlets in the rear lid and at the front next to the front turn signal units. External identifying characteristics of this so-called "Series Zero" model line are the gold-plated 911 script on the rear lid, chrome plated bumper guards without rubber inserts, and optional rocker panel deco strips.

6. Equipment

Safety glass windshield, round outside mirror.

Curved safety glass was largely unknown in 1963/1964. Porsche used this safety feature from the very beginning of 911 production.

7. Seats and trim
Completely new interior trim and seats. Luxurious appointments; interior trim and seats in partial leatherette. Wood steering wheel and wood veneer dashboard, silver script on right of dash. Entry area of door sills covered by rubber mat.

8. Heating system
Standard heating system uses engine waste heat. The engine cooling fan blows fresh air through the engine heat exchangers and forces the warmed air to

the cabin. In addition, a Webasto gasoline heater (Type P1018) is available as an option, but it is not remembered for its reliability.

The heating system, considerably improved from that of the 356, satisfies the customer demands and regulatory requirements of the 1960s. Air conditioning is not yet available as production begins.

9. Electrical system
12 Volt electrical system as standard equipment. Asymmetric low beam pattern. Three wiper speeds. Electric windshield washer system.

Advanced electrical equipment made the 901/911 one of the most modern cars of its day.

10. Miscellaneous
Originally, a luxury version of the 911 had been planned, but this was postponed. In the beginning, few options were available.

Model Year 1966

Type designation: Porsche 911, Porsche 912

Changes
The Porsche 912 is new in the model lineup. It uses the four-cylinder engine of the 356 SC, with output reduced to 90 hp [66 kW] as installed in the 912.

The 912 was conceived as the entry-level Porsche. The economical and affordable 912 found ready acceptance, particularly in the United States, where strict speed limits were already commonplace in 1965.

1. Engine
The Type 901/01 and 901/05 engines were used for the six-cylinder. The 616/36 was used in the 912.

2. Fuel and ignition systems
Modification of Solex carburetor emulsion tubes: now open at the bottom. The 901/05 engine is equipped with Weber 40 IDA 3L & 3C1 carburetors.

Porsche switches mid-year 1966 to Weber carburetors, which are considerably easier to adjust.

3. Powertrain
Five-speed manual transmission, Type 901/02, standard for the 911. Five-speed Type 902/01 available as an option for the 912.

Porsche recognized that vehicles with a top speed above 200 km/h [120 mph] require a five-speed manual transmission. With only four speeds, gear ratios cannot be optimized. For this reason, a five-speed gearbox was also available as an option for the 912.

4. Suspension
Altered brake calipers.

5. Bodywork
Angled bright anodized rear script on 912.

6. Equipment
Wooden steering wheel or black plastic wheel on 912 models. Wood veneer on instrument panel of 911 painted or brushed aluminum on 912. Soft plush carpeting for 911; square weave wool on 912s.

7. Seats and trim
No changes.

8. Heating and air conditioning system
No changes.

9. Electrical system
490 Watt alternator.

Model year 1967

Type designation: Porsche 911 Coupe and Targa, Porsche 911 S Coupe and Targa
Porsche 912 Coupe and Targa

Changes
The first power increase: 911 S. The Types 911 and 912 continue as before. A new body variation, the Targa, a safety convertible with built-in roll bar, is introduced.

A frequently expressed customer wish is granted in 1967: increased power (to 160 hp). Suspension and brakes are upgraded in keeping with the power increase. In the tradition of Porsche's successful 356 Cabriolet, Roadster and Spyder models, the Porsche 911 Targa once again offers open-air motoring. The name "Targa," Italian for "shield," becomes an identifying model feature all over the world, in the form of its removable roof (shield). Porsche's trademarked name is also intended to recall racing successes in Sicily, in the "Targa Florio" road race.

1. Engine
In addition to the Type 901/06 for the 911, with altered camshafts and improved heat exchangers, Porsche offers increased power with the same displacement with the 901/02 installed in the 911 S. The power increase is achieved by
- compression ratio increase to 9.8:1
- Biral cylinders, aluminum with cast iron liners
- soft nitrided forged steel connecting rods
- forged light alloy pistons
- altered camshafts
- 42 mm intake valves, 38 mm exhaust valves
- two springs per valve
Engine performance data:
Maximum output 160 hp [118 kW] at 6600 rpm.
Specific output 80 hp/liter. Maximum rpm 7200.

The 911 S engine was developed from the basic engine without incurring any reduction in service life. In view of the fuel available at the time, the high compression of 9.8:1 is noteworthy. Interesting cylinder design: as before, the pistons run inside a cast iron bore, but an aluminum cooling fin jacket is shrunk onto this liner for improved heat transfer.

2. Fuel and ignition systems
Two Weber three-barrel carburetors, Type IDA (S) or 40 IDS 3C and 3C1, are used for the "Super" (911S) engine. A Bosch ignition distributor, no. 0 231 159 002, with a yellow label, is used. Spark plugs have a heat range of 260. Premium fuel (98 Research Octane Number) is required.

All six-cylinder engines are now equipped with Weber carburetors. The ignition system is now made by Bosch; distributor, coil and spark plugs are all production items made by Porsche's neighbors in nearby Stuttgart-Feuerbach.

3. Powertrain
The five-speed 901/02 transmission is standard equipment for the 911 S. Optionally, the 901/51 (sportier gear ratios), 901/52 (for hillclimbs), 901/53 (airport gears), 901/54 (for high-speed races), and 902/0 (Nürburgring gears) are available.

In addition to the standard transmission, which differs from the original transmission only in minor details, customers with racing ambitions may select from special gear ratios for competition use.

4. Suspension
New for the 911 S:
- transverse anti-roll bars front and rear
- Koni shock absorbers front and rear
- Fuchs forged alloy deep-bed 4 1/2 x 15 wheels
- ventilated brake rotors front and rear

For the first time, Porsche offers alloy wheels. To this day, the forged (or better said pressed) five-spoke wheel enjoys unprecedented recognition and the favor of Porsche fans. This is often described as the "Fuchs wheel." The wheel was designed by Studio Porsche and was manufactured, to Porsche drawings and specifications, by the alloy metalsmiths of the Fuchs company in Meinerzhagen.

5. Bodywork
The Targa, a "safety cabriolet," is new to the Porsche model line. The B pillar is designed to act as a sturdy roll bar. The removable roof, between the windshield header and the roll bar, can be folded like an accordion and stowed in the front luggage compartment without significant loss of space. The rear window of Targa models (between the Targa bar and bodywork) is flexible and unzips to fold down or can be removed completely.

While little regard was paid to accident safety in most car designs of the time, Porsche soon recognized the importance of occupant protection. With its flexible rear window design, Porsche attempted

to retain the feeling of driving an open car. Three open-air configurations are possible:

- *roof installed, rear window open*
- *roof and rear window open*
- *roof open, rear window closed*

6. Equipment
Leather-covered steering wheel standard for 911 S. Engine oil pressure and oil level analog gauge standard on 911 S only.

7. Seats and trim
No changes

8. Heating system, air conditioning system
A gasoline-electric auxiliary heater is an option.

9. Electrical system
Addition of analog oil pressure and level gauge for 911 S.

Model year 1968 (A-Series)

Type designation: Porsche 911 T, L, S, Coupe or Targa, Porsche 912 Coupe or Targa

Changes

Introduction of the "Sportomatic" semi-automatic transmission for the 911 and 912. First cars equipped with exhaust emission controls for the U.S. market. Also new: the Type 911 T, a six-cylinder car with reduced power output (110 hp), also available with Sportomatic. The 911 L models are powered by the 901/06 carbureted engine carried over from 1967 (130 hp) or when ordered with the Sportomatic, the 901/07 engine.

Major changes for the 1968 model year: a semi-automatic transmission, the Sportomatic, is available for all models. The 911 T, a reduced-output six-cylinder car, with a market position similar to that of the 356 "Dame" [Lady, the 356 Normal], is intended as an entry level car which is also attractive to female buyers.

1. Engine

For the first time, U.S. market cars have emission-controlled engines (Types 901/14 for manual transmissions and 901/17 for Sportomatics). Six-cylinder engines with reduced output are built for the 911 T models: 901/03 for manual transmissions and 901/13 for Sportomatics. The compression ratio of these 110 hp [81 kW] engines is reduced to 8.6:1, and maximum power is reached at only 5800 rpm. These engines employ cast iron cylinders.

The first emission-controlled cars are delivered to the United States. Due to the fact that 50 percent of its production is allocated to the American market, Porsche has done ground breaking work in emissions control from the very beginning, and met even the strict California emissions standards without loss of power and with nearly no effect on driving comfort. Porsche's products, although still equipped with carburetors, exhibit reduced emissions thanks to exhaust gas recirculation.

2. Fuel and ignition systems

The 911 T engine is fitted with two Weber three-barrel carburetors and a Marelli S 112 AX ignition distributor. Spark plug heat range 230.

3. Powertrain

No changes to the manual transmissions. The semi-automatic four-speed Sportomatic transmission is available for all models: Type 905/00 for the four-cylinder 912 models and Type 905/01 for the 911 T, L and S. The difference between the two transmissions is their top gear ratio, which is matched to the performance potential of each engine. The Sporto-matic drive system incorporates a hydraulic torque converter rigidly attached to the engine flywheel, a manifold vacuum actuated clutch, a four-speed Porsche synchromesh transmission and a 7:27 final drive ratio. Sportomatic cars do not have a clutch pedal. If a gear is to be selected, it is only necessary to touch the shift lever; in a fraction of a second, a vacuum servo disengages the clutch, interrupting the power flow to the transmission, and the next gear can be selected by manually moving the shift lever. After shifting, releasing the shift lever reengages the clutch.

Market research has shown that especially in the United States, a new generation of customers who have never learned how to operate a clutch pedal is entering the marketplace. In addition, stop-and-go traffic in large cities is becoming so common that even a sports car might be more enjoyable with a torque converter. The Sportomatic drive system is equipped with a Fichtel & Sachs torque converter and a conventional clutch. Because the rear-engine design of the 911 severely limits the space available for installation of the Sportomatic, Porsche developed a pull-type clutch release system. This type of clutch actuation, in which the throw out bearing spins at engine rpm, requires less space and eventually found worldwide application on manual transmissions. Oil supply to the hydraulic torque converter is taken from the engine oil tank. A ZF-Eaton pump, driven by one camshaft, supplies a stream of oil to the torque converter and assures filling and cooling during operation. Engine damage due to oil loss from the torque converter or its oil supply and return lines is not possible; the suction lines to the torque converter supply pump are located high in the oil tank to insure that there is always an adequate oil supply to the engine.

4. Suspension

Boge shock absorbers are standard equipment for the 912, 911 T and L, as well as all Targa models. Koni shocks are used on the 911 S. Front anti-roll bar diameter is 11 mm for the 911 L, 15 mm on the 911 S. Rear anti-roll bar is 15 mm on 911 S. Wider 5 $\frac{1}{2}$ J x 15 wheels. Dual-circuit brake system for all six-cylinder models.

Porsche tests have shown that wider wheels, combined with modified chassis tuning, result in better performance.

5. Bodywork

Black wiper arms and blades. Rubber strip on front and rear bumper guards are standard equipment on all models.

Porsche is the first car maker to recognize that chrome plated wiper arms may be visually attractive, but can also dazzle the driver in bright sunlight.

6. Equipment

No changes.

7. Seats and trim

No changes.

8. Heating system, air conditioning system

No changes.

9. Electrical system

No changes.

Model year 1969 (B-Series)

Type designation: 911 T, E, S Coupe and Targa 912 Coupe and Targa

Changes

Extensive body changes take effect with the B series: longer wheelbase, altered fenders, redesigned lighting system. New fuel injected engines for the 911 E and S; power output of 911 S increased to 170 hp [125 kW].

Documentation of Porsche models often refers to internal model year designations: A for 1968, B for 1969, etc. Major body and engine changes are introduced for the 1969 model year. The longer wheelbase will make future suspension geometry changes easier.

1. Engine

The 911 E (for Einspritzung – fuel injection) as well as the 911 S are equipped with Bosch mechanical fuel injection. The Type 901/09 engine (901/11 for Sportomatic) develops 140 hp [103 kW] at 6500 rpm from a 9.1:1 compression ratio. The 911 S is fitted with an oil cooler in the right front fender, in addition to the normal engine-mounted cooler. The exhaust valves of all six-cylinder models are sodium filled and have hardened seating surfaces.

The injected 911 E and S engines are the basis for future power increases and reduced exhaust emissions. Sodium-filled exhaust valves are normally only used in racing engines, to transfer heat from the valve face to the valve stem and out through the valve guides to the cylinder head. Although sodium filling and hardening the seating surfaces increases manufacturing costs, all six-cylinder Porsche engines are fitted with sodium-filled valves to ensure full-load engine durability.

2. Fuel and ignition systems

Two Weber 40 IDT3 C three-barrel downdraft carburetors for the 911 T. Bosch twin-row injection pumps for the 911 E and S. Capacitive discharge ignition for all six-cylinder engines.

At Porsche, the era of carburetors is nearing its end. Only the touring model, the 911 T, is still equipped with carburetors.

3. Powertrain

Reinforced M 215 KL clutch with increased pressure (530 - 590 kp, 1168 - 1300 lbs.) for the 911 S. No significant transmission changes. The 911 T is also equipped with the five-speed manual transmission as standard equipment.

4. Suspension

Longer wheelbase (2268 mm). Only the 911 E uses hydropneumatic struts; for this model, the front torsion bars are deleted. The front calipers of the 911 E and 911 S are made of aluminum alloy. The 911 E and S are fitted with 6 J x 15 alloy wheels and 185/

70 VR 15 tires as standard equipment. The 911 T and 911 E may also be fitted with 5 1/2 J x 14 wheels and 185/HR14 tires.

Hydropneumatic struts are a new development. These struts, jointly development by Boge and Porsche, are self-leveling.

5. Bodywork

Targa models have ventilation slots in the stainless steel safety bar, and the optional rear window is rigidly mounted (heatable safety glass). These had been occasionally fitted the prior year. Wheel wells of all 911 models are slightly flared. Larger front turn signal lenses, smaller horn grilles.

Porsche replaces the flexible rear window of Targa models with rigid glass incorporating heating elements. This greatly improves rearward visibility.

6. Equipment

Analog oil pressure gauge for the 911 E.

7. Seats and trim

Day-night inside rear view mirrors glued to windshield. Smaller steering wheel with padded horn button. Flip-out ashtray on bottom edge of dashboard. Door panels with larger storage pockets. Inside door release is a pull handle integrated in the armrest. Improved seat back locking.

8. Heating system, air conditioning system

Three-stage heating and ventilation system.

9. Electrical system

Wiring harness changes. Fuse box in front trunk. Two batteries (each 35 Ah) for all models in the front fenders. 770 Watt alternator for all 911 models. Dual-reflector H1 halogen headlights. Altered taillights. Emergency flashers as standard equipment. Illuminated glove compartment.

Replacing the single 45 Ah battery with a pair of 35 Ah units, one in each front fender, not only improves the electrical system but also benefits the car's handling; the two masses provide a marked improvement in straight-line stability.

Model year 1970 (C-Series)

Type designation: 911 T, E, S Coupe and Targa

Changes

Production of the 912 ends. All 911 models have 2.2 liter engines.

The affordable entry level Porsche, the 912, is no longer built. In its place, VW-Porsche, a marketing organization founded by both companies, offers the Porsche 914, powered by the 2-liter six-cylinder Porsche engine of the 911 T.

1. Engine

Enlarging the cylinder bore to 84 mm results in a displacement of 2195 cc. Performance specifications of the three engine variants increase as follows:

Engine designation		911T-C	911E-C	911S-C
Manual trans. engine		911/03	911/01	911/02
Sportomatic engine		911/06	911/04	----
Compression ratio		8.6:1	9.1:1	9.8:1
Fuel requirement	(RON)	98	98	98
Power output	(hp/kW)	125/92	155/114	180/132
at	(rpm)	5800	6200	6500
Torque	(Nm)	177	192	200
at	(rpm)	4200	4500	5200

The crankcase is a pressure-cast magnesium die casting. The crankshafts are forged steel, and are tenifer treated for the 911 S. Light alloy die cast pistons, except for the 911 S which uses forged alloy pistons. Biral cylinders for the 911 E and S. All engines have improved cylinder heads with larger valves: inlet valves 46 mm, outlet valves 40 mm.

With the displacement increase to 2.2 liters, Porsche once again satisfies customer demands for more power and torque. Use of magnesium for the crankcase and other weight reduction measures reduce the DIN empty weight from the 1080 kg [2379 lbs.] of the 1969 911 E to 1020 kg [2247 lbs.] The 911 S also weighs only 1020 kg. This is clearly the mark of Porsche's new chief engineer, Ferdinand Piëch.

2. Fuel and ignition systems

911 T: two three-barrel Zenith or Weber downdraft carburetors. 911 E and S: Bosch two-row mechanical injection pump. Ignition system for all engines: Bosch BHKZ (high performance capacitive discharge battery ignition, with breaker points).

3. Powertrain

All 911 models are equipped with a larger 225 mm F&S clutch system. The pressure plate (MFZ 225 KL) pressure is increased to 600 - 670 N [135 - 150 lbs.] The 911 T is equipped with the Type 911/00 four-speed manual transmission as standard equipment, while the 911 E and S have the 911/01 five-speed. The 911 T and 911 E are also available with the 905/20 Sportomatic transmission.

The clutch is completely redesigned for positive power transmission. The working diameter of the clutch disc is 225 mm. This change will permit years of power increases without problems.

4. Suspension

Ventilated disc brakes now for the 911 T.

5. Bodywork
No changes.

6. Equipment
911 E equipment identical to that of the 911 S. Use of "Skai" leatherette.

7. Seats and trim
No changes.

8. Heating system, air conditioning system
Gasoline-electric auxiliary heater standard for 911 S.

9. Electrical system
Additional fuses for electrical components. Additional fusebox in engine compartment. Rear window wiper available as an option.

Model year 1971 (D-Series)

Type designation: 911 T, E, S Coupe and Targa

Changes
Nearly no changes to the 911 model line for the 1971 model year.

1. Engine
No mechanical changes.

2. Fuel and ignition systems
Due to stricter emissions standards in various export markets, the fuel injection systems have been modified. The pressure sensor, ignition distributor, throttle body and ignition control unit have been reworked. The fuel supply pump is relocated between the torsion bar tube and the rear semi-trailing arms.

3. Powertrain
No changes to clutch or transmissions.

4. Suspension
No changes

5. Bodywork
all models fitted with rubber strips on the front and rear bumper guards.

6. Equipment
No changes.

7. Seats and trim
No changes.

8. Heating system, air conditioning system
911 S changed to engine heat (instead of gasoline heater).

9. Electrical system
Three wiper speeds instead of two speeds plus an intermittent setting.

Model year 1972 (E-Series)

Type designation: 911 T, E, S Coupe and Targa

Changes
In addition to a displacement increase to 2.4 liters and corresponding power increases, body changes are introduced. An engine oil filler lid is added to the right rear fender. All Porsches may be operated with regular gasoline. New transmission design with different shift pattern.

Progressively tighter emissions regulations, particularly in the United States, require a complete rethink of the engine design. High-octane fuel, with high concentrations of tetraethyl lead, is no longer available in several export markets. As a result, Porsche redesigned the engines to operate on regular-grade fuel.

1. Engine

The engine family has undergone a redesign; altering the crankshafts to give a 70.4 mm stroke results in a displacement increase to 2341 cc. The compression ratio is reduced to a point where all Porsche models may be operated on regular grade (91 Research Octane Number) fuel. The engine oil tank, necessary for the dry sump lubrication system, has been moved ahead of the right rear wheel. Oil is added through a separate oil filler lid below the right rear quarter window. An aluminum oil cooler is installed in the right front wheel well. Engine and power specifications:

Engine designation		911TV-E	911E-E	911S-E
Manual trans. engine		911/57	911/52	911/53
Sportomatic engine		911/67	911/62	911/63
Compression ratio		7.5:1	8.0:1	8.5:1
Fuel requirement (RON)		91	91	91
Power output	(hp/kW)	130/96	165/121	190/140
at	(rpm)	5600	6200	6500
Torque	(Nm)	196	206	216
at	(rpm)	4000	4500	5200

Despite reduced compression ratios, the displacement increase to 2.4 liters results in higher power output for all models. Torque increases of approximately ten percent are particularly noteworthy. As a result, the engines perform better; the 911 can accelerate smoothly from low engine rpm.

2. Fuel and ignition systems

The fuel injection systems have been modified to comply with stricter emissions regulations in several export markets.

3. Powertrain

Single disc dry plate clutch, MFZ 225, pulled release bearing. New Type·915 transmission family. Characteristics: reinforced transmission housing, gears, and final drive. Better bearings for transmission shafts, improved heat transfer and lubrication by means of auxiliary pump. Porsche patent blocking synchromesh with less sensitivity to transmission lubricant grade. Limited slip differential with adjustable lockup values available as an option. Altered shift pattern: first gear left and forward, reverse gear right and back, fifth gear right forward. Engine power increases also affect the semi-automatic Sportomatic (Type 925) transmissions: altered torque converter with improved mounting, larger vacuum servo. Modifications to the Porsche patent blocking synchromesh on the four forward gears.

The new Type 915 transmission family will be able to cope with engine power increases planned for the coming years. The new design takes advantage of experience gained with the racing Type 908 transmission: the output shaft is located by two tapered roller bearings directly behind the ring gear, a cylindrical roller bearing takes up radial loads, and a large four-point ball bearing takes axial loads. Thermal expansion of the alloy transmission case no longer affects the preset mesh of the ring and pinion gears. Because these highly stressed components place high demands on the transmission lubricant as a result of gear tooth loads, friction between the pinion gear teeth, and high operating temperature, Porsche approves a blended transmission oil with API (American Petroleum Institute) service grade GL5 (MIL-L 2105B). This is made possible because the Porsche synchromesh system is easily adapted to reduced friction coefficients.

The altered shift pattern fulfills the wishes of rally drivers, who prefer first and second gear in the same shift plane. In tight corners, it is often necessary to shift from second to first and back up again.

4. Suspension
No changes

5. Bodywork
Moving oil tank ahead of the right rear wheel necessitates body changes. A body-colored lid near the right side B pillar covers the oil filler neck. All models are equipped with rubber pads on the front and rear bumper guards. Rectangular outside mirrors. "2.4" script on the engine air inlet grille. The 911 S has a steel front spoiler.

Moving the oil tank forward is intended to improve the front to rear weight distribution.

6. Equipment
Door panels and instrument panel center section in interior color.

7. Seats and trim
No changes.

8. Heating system, air conditioning system
No changes.

9. Electrical system
No changes.

Model year 1973 (F-Series)

Type designation: 911 T, E, S Coupe and Targa, 911 Carrera RS only as Coupe

Changes
All 911 models can be equipped with front spoilers. The 911 E and S are fitted with 85 liter [22.5 gallon] fuel tanks. Oil tank moved back to original location, behind right rear wheel. Some U.S. models [911 T beginning with January 1973 production] are delivered with the new K-Jetronic fuel injection system. A new six-cylinder model is introduced, the 911 SC (Carrera RS) available in sport and touring versions and powered by a 2.7 liter engine. In standard trim, its DIN empty weight 1075 kg [2368 lbs.], while the "Lightweight Carrera" racing version with a 2.8 liter engine weighs only 900 kg [1982 lbs.]

Inspired by wind tunnel studies of the 908 and 917 race cars, aerodynamic improvements are applied to the 911 model line. A steel front air dam reduces front end lift at high speeds, resulting in improved straight-line stability and better control. The "duck tail" rear spoiler of the new Carrera RS provides improved flow separation in the rear body area and results in a higher top speed. Ferdinand Piëch, chief of research and development, emphasizes lightweight design, resulting in the racing version of the Carrera RS, which weighs in at only 900 kg and is available to the general public.

1. Engine
No changes for 2.4 liter engines. The Carrera RS is powered by a new engine, displacing 2687 cc. Like the 2.4, this engine can also operate on regular-grade gasoline (RON 91). The displacement increase is the result of larger 90 mm pistons. The Carrera RS is the first model to use aluminum alloy cylinders with Nikasil bores.

Engine designation		911 SC-F
Manual trans. engine		911/83
Compression ratio		8.5:1
Fuel requirement	(RON)	91
Power output	(hp/kW)	210/154
at	(rpm)	6300
Torque	(Nm)	255
at	(rpm)	5100

The cylinders of the Type 911/83 engine are made entirely of aluminum alloy. Because nearly all aluminum alloys exhibit poor sliding qualities when mated with other aluminum alloys, they are normally not suitable for use as both pistons and cylinders. However, by coating the aluminum cylinder walls with a layer of nickel, Porsche achieved optimum sliding properties while taking advantage of aluminum's improved heat transfer properties through the cylinder walls and to the cooling fins.

2. Fuel and ignition systems

The 911 T continues to use a three-barrel Zenith Type 40 TIN downdraft carburetor. The 911 E, S, and Carrera RS are fitted with Bosch twin-row fuel injection pumps. For the first time, the exhaust systems are made of stainless steel. The first K-Jetronic equipped engines are delivered for sale in the United States. These 2.4 liter engines develop 140 hp [103 kW] when equipped with the K-Jetronic. Their exhaust gas CO level of 1.5 - 2.0% is surprisingly good.

Porsche is aware of the damage which may result to body and exhaust system components as a result of the growing worldwide use of corrosive road salt to melt snow and ice. Porsche's first step to combat this is the installation of exhaust systems made of rust-resistant steel. In its quest to build the pollution-free car, Porsche is the first auto manufacturer to install the Bosch K-Jetronic fuel injection system. The K-Jetronic, a continuous fuel injection system, is the first to use a flat plate to measure air flow to the engine and distribute fuel to the injector valves accordingly.

3. Powertrain

No changes for the transmissions fitted to 2.4 liter engines. The Type 915/08 transmission is developed for the Carrera RS, incorporating ground gear sets, and a transmission oil pump for improved cooling and lubrication on factory-entered race cars. Third, fourth and fifth gear ratios are modified in keeping with the higher engine power. The shifter and shift lever are redesigned, and shift quality improved. A true reverse gear lockout prevents accidental selection of reverse gear.

It is the task of the Type 915/08 transmission oil pump to cool and lubricate critical areas within the transmission. For racing purposes, the oil may also be circulated through an external oil cooler.

4. Suspension

The wheelbase is increased yet again, to 2271 mm. Hydropneumatic front struts, formerly standard on the 911 E (as of the 1969 model year) are now available as options for the T, E and S; all 911 models return to front torsion bars as standard equipment. The 911 E is fitted with 6 J x 15 cast alloy wheels

(made by ATS), shod with 185/70 VR 15 tires. The 911 S continues to use 6 J x 15 forged alloy wheels. The Carrera RS uses forged alloys, 6 J x 15 at the front, with 185/70 VR 15 tires, and 7 J x 15 with 215/60 VR 15 tires at the rear. The 911 E, S and Carrera RS are equipped with a space-saver spare tire on a 5 1/2 J x 15 rim.

While the standard hydropneumatic struts of the 911 E improved ride comfort, this feature was not appreciated by sports car fans. Nevertheless, the system remains available as an option on all 911 models (with the exception of the Carrera RS) for customers desiring a higher degree of comfort.

5. Bodywork

The engine oil tank moves back to its original location behind the right rear wheel. Oil is added through a filler neck on the inside right wall of the engine compartment. An 85 liter (22.5 gallon) plastic fuel tank is installed in the 911 E, S and Carrera RS. The rear fenders of the Carrera RS are flared. Various body parts, including the front lid, are made of thinner gauge metal, while a fiberglass "duck tail" spoiler is added to the engine lid.

The oil tank ahead of the right rear wheel, used in 1972 in an effort to achieve better handling, was an unsatisfactory solution; gas station attendants often confused the oil filler lid with the fuel filler, and added gasoline to the oil tank. Also, it radiated more heat to right rear seat passengers. It was quickly decided to move the tank back behind the rear wheel.

The "duck tail" rear spoiler was a sensation. Factory documents record every conceivable response, from enthusiastic acceptance by customers to total rejection by various national regulatory authorities.

6. Equipment
Front horn grilles made of black plastic.

7. Seats and trim
No changes.

8. Heating system, air conditioning system
No changes.

9. Electrical system
For weight reasons, the Carrera RSR is fitted with only one 36 Ah battery (while the RS Touring has two 36 Ah batteries). Conversion of main headlights to dual-filament H4 bulbs. U.S. market vehicles continue to be fitted with sealed beam headlights.

Model Year 1974 (G-Series)

Type designation: 911, 911 S, 911 Carrera Coupe and Targa

Changes
Main features for 1974 are extensive body changes and increased occupant protection. Larger engine displacement again results in power increase. Model designation changed. For drivers with sporting aspirations, the Carrera RS is available, powered by a three-liter engine. Only 111 examples of this car were built for Group 3 homologation.

U.S. bumper regulations require that cars withstand 5 km/h impacts without incurring repair costs. Porsche has modified its models for all markets worldwide with light alloy bumpers. U.S. vehicles additionally mount the bumpers to the frame via shock absorbers. Displacement of all engines is increased to 2.7 liters.

1. Engine
All models fitted with 2687 cc engine. 911 S and Carrera have added oil cooling by means of trombone in right front wheel well. All engines equipped with Nikasil cylinders.

Engine designation		911	911 S	911 SC-F
Manual trans. engine		911/92	911/93	911/83
Compression ratio		8.0:1	8.5:1	8.5:1
Fuel requirement	(RON)	91	91	91
Power output	(hp/kW)	150/110	175/129	210/154
at	(rpm)	5700	5800	6300
Torque	(Nm)	235	235	255
at	(rpm)	3800	4000	5100

Displacement and power output of all engines is increased by enlarging the cylinder bore. All engines are fitted with light alloy cylinders and Nikasil coated cylinder walls. Again, all engines can be operated with regular-grade gasoline, RON 91; Porsche again demonstrates that even sports cars can be environmentally friendly.

2. Fuel and ignition systems
911 and 911 S are fitted with Bosch K-Jetronic fuel injection system. The Carrera retains the mechanical twin-row injection pump.

3. Powertrain
Longer pedal shafts. The clutch pedal is fitted with an assist spring for reduced effort. Choice of manual transmissions: 915/16 (four-speed) or 915/06 (five-speed). Gear ratios are matched to engine power output. Sportomatic transmission (Type 925/02) is only available for 911 and 911 S. The top gear ratio (28:23) reflects increased engine output.

The pedal cluster has also been reworked. The pedals are longer and more user-friendly. An assist spring is located at the clutch actuating lever on the transmission housing. Its over-center layout significantly reduces the high pressure required to disengage the clutch. Clutch actuation can now be carried out without difficulty by even less athletically inclined drivers.

4. Suspension

The load-leveling hydropneumatic suspension formerly available as an option is no longer available. Cast light alloy rear semi-trailing arms. Front anti-roll bars for all vehicles (911 and 911 S, 16 mm; Carrera, 20 mm). The 911 S is fitted with pressure cast alloy 6 J x 15 wheels. All vehicles are fitted with a 165 x 15 collapsible spare tire.

The standard 80-liter fuel tank leaves little trunk space for a spare tire. Porsche used experience gained in sports car racing, where rules require cars to carry spare tires. Even the 917 carried a lightweight, compact collapsible spare tire, stowed above the transmission during races.

5. Bodywork

Extensive, readily visible changes are introduced for the 1974 model year. Front and rear bumpers are made of light alloy and attached to the frame via easily replaced collapsible tubes (U.S. cars: shock absorbing mounts). Bumpers are painted in body color and are fitted with wraparound rubber trim strips. Front turn signals are integrated into the bumpers. Black flexible accordion sections are fitted between the bumpers and the bodywork. Rectangular outside mirrors are painted in body color. All vehicles are fitted with 80 liter [21.2 gallon] plastic fuel tanks. For the Carrera, the headlight trim rings, previously chrome plated, are painted in body color. The space between the taillights is taken up by a dark red (but non-reflecting) strip with black PORSCHE script.

Porsche's design solution for energy-absorbing bumpers clearly demonstrates a visually attractive alternative to other carmakers' designs. Mounted without visible gaps to the bodywork, the bumpers can compress on resilient mounts (as on U.S. market Porsches) or collapse by as much as 50 mm in the case of the simpler crush tubes. These cost-effective tubes are easily replaced after a minor impact. The resilient bumper U.S. mounts are available as options worldwide.

6. Equipment

Foam plastic steering wheel rims for 911 and 911 S, leather covered sport steering wheel for the Carrera. Energy-absorbing steering column section immediately below steering wheel for increased occupant protection. Standard three-point safety belts for driver and front passenger.

For years, safety steering wheels had incorporated large impact pads. Porsche introduced an additional safety element, an energy absorbing section between the steering wheel and steering column. In the event of an accident and the driver's impact with the wheel, this section collapses, enabling the wheel to move away from the driver and minimize injuries.

7. Seats and trim

New door panels and trim. New seat design with integrated, fixed head rest.

8. Heating and air conditioning system

Defroster vents for side windows.

9. Electrical system

911 and 911 S are fitted with higher output (980 Watt) alternators. For weight reasons, the Carrera retains the previous 770 Watt alternator as standard equipment. The previous installation of two batteries, each with 36 Ah, in the front fenders is abandoned. Instead, all models are fitted with a 66 Ah battery in the trunk. A headlight washer system is available as an option.

10. Miscellaneous

911 Carrera RS 3.0: for homologation purposes, a special series of 100 street-legal examples is built. The car includes fender flares similar to the later Turbo, and is fitted with a three-liter 230 hp [169 kW] engine. This power increase is achieved by fitting 90 mm cylinders. Compression ratio is 9.8:1. Minimum fuel octane requirement is 96 RON.

Model year 1975 (H-Series)

Type designation: 911, 911 S, 911 Carrera Coupe and Targa, 911 Turbo Coupe, 912 E Coupe

Changes

No significant alterations are made to the types 911, 911 S and Carrera introduced a year earlier. However, a new model, the 911 Turbo, is the world's first turbocharged production sports car. Its three-liter engine develops 260 hp [191 kW]. The Turbo is exclusively a coupe with a top speed in excess of 250 km/h [155 mph]. Internally, the 911 Turbo is known as the "930 Turbo;" engine as well as transmission design carry 930 type numbers.

With the introduction of the 911 Turbo, Porsche transferred its successful experience with turbocharged race cars to production street-legal cars. Initially, only a small production run was planned, but worldwide demand for the Turbo was so great that Porsche's flagship would become an object of desire for all sports car enthusiasts.

1. Engine

No mechanical changes for normally aspirated engines, but improved heat exchangers are installed. The engine of the 911 Turbo is based on the normally aspirated engine of the 911 Carrera RS 3.0. An exhaust-driven turbocharger is fitted for increased power output. For durability reasons, the crankcase is made of an aluminum-silicon alloy. Forged aluminum pistons. Auxiliary tubular oil cooler located in right front fender.

Engine designation		Turbo
Engine type		930/50
Displacement	(cc)	2994
Compression ratio		6.5:1
Fuel requirement	(RON)	96
Power output	(hp/kW)	260/191
at	(rpm)	5500
Torque	(Nm)	343
at	(rpm)	4000

Porsche pulled out all the stops to make its most powerful production engine. Experience gained in the merciless arena of endurance racing proved valuable in the first turbocharged production sports car engine.

2. Fuel and ignition systems

Two series-mounted electric roller cell pumps supply fuel for the 911 Turbo. Fuel metering: Bosch K-Jetronic. Ignition: breakerless high output coil ignition (BHKZ)

Because of the Turbo engine's high fuel demand at full load, Porsche conservatively placed two fuel pumps in series. This principle had already proven itself in the 917 race car.

3. Powertrain

No transmission changes for normally aspirated cars. Exception: U.S. market cars are fitted with taller gears and final drive ratios to reduce fuel consumption and thereby exhaust emissions. The 911 and 911 S are also available with the Sportomatic transmission. The powertrain was completely redesigned for the 911 Turbo: a 240 mm pull-type single dry plate clutch.

A completely new four-speed manual transmission (Type 930/30) is designed for the 911 Turbo. Compared to the similar Type 915 transmission design, its shafts, bearings, gear sets and final drive have undergone extensive reinforcement. A new variation of the Porsche blocking synchromesh permits shifting with transmission internal speeds as high as 10,000 rpm. The four-speed Type 930/30 transmission represents a new design appropriate for the limited space and high power and torque demands of the Turbo. The necessarily wider gear sets and increased ring gear diameter dictated a four-speed transmission. Because future racing applications of this transmission would require very high transmission rpm, a newly developed, less speed-sensitive Porsche synchromesh system was installed. Porsche had already gathered valuable racing experience with similar designs; in 1973, Porsche had developed a racing transmission for the French firm, Matra, easily capable of withstanding up to 12,000 rpm produced by the Matra twelve-cylinder engines. With this transmission, Matra defeated Porsche at the 1973 and 1974 Le Mans races.

4. Chassis and suspension

Compared to the non-Turbo models, the suspension of the 911 Turbo has been completely reworked. Front transverse arms with light alloy support members, and light alloy semi-trailing arms at the rear, were developed for the 911 Turbo. Bilstein shock absorbers, 18 mm front and rear anti-roll bars. Lever arm links for the anti-roll bars. Dual-circuit brake system with failure warning light. Front and rear ventilated brake rotors. Light alloy front brake calipers, cast iron rear calipers. Forged alloy wheels, front 7 J x 15 with 185/70 VR 15 tubeless tires; rear 8 J x 15, with 215/60 VR 15 tubeless tires.

Initially, Turbos, with their horizontal rear spoiler (known as a "wing" to regulatory agencies) had to be presented for individual inspection to the German TÜV before a road license was issued, as "there is a danger that bicyclists hitting the car from the rear,

especially children, might be injured."

5. Bodywork

Body with fender flares, polyurethane front spoiler, horizontal rear spoiler with polyurethane edging. Fiberglass engine lid. Outside mirrors and headlight rings painted body color.

6. Equipment

Three-spoke leather-covered steering wheel for 911 Turbo. Electrically adjustable and heated outside mirrors. Electric windows, also for 911 Carrera. For the Turbo, first use of production electronic speedometer and odometer. Inertia reel safety belts for front occupants. The 911 Carrera Targa is fitted with a matte black Targa bar.

Porsche is probably the first carmaker to fit a production car with a speedometer that uses electronic impulses for speed and distance measurement. This, too, is a spinoff from racing technology: Ferry Porsche was to receive a Porsche 914 fitted with a fixed roof and three-liter, eight-cylinder racing engine as a birthday present. For use on public roads, a speedometer was required. After some thought, Porsche engineers developed a distance sensor consisting of a tiny bar magnet attached to the transmission output shaft, and a 15 mm long reed switch, which senses the magnetic field of the rotating magnet through the transmission housing. Each output shaft rotation results in two pulses, which are converted to speed and distance signals by separate electronic components.

7. Seats and trim

Full leather or leather combined with plaid fabric.

8. Heating and air conditioning system

Automatically controlled heating system, controls located on center tunnel.

For air-cooled cars, continuous readjustment of heat output is unavoidable, as a great deal of heat is generated at full load, and virtually no heat is produced at idle or while coasting. A temperature sensor in the cockpit is first installed on the Turbo, to report cabin temperatures to an electronic control system. This unit compares the actual temperature with the desired temperature, which has been set by

the driver by means of a rotary potentiometer. Depending on engine load, the heater flaps are adjusted to admit more or less hot air to the cabin.

9. Electrical system
Battery 66 Ah, alternator 980 W

Stereo radio with two additional speakers in the rear shelf, electrically retractable antenna.

10. Miscellaneous
912 E: Once again, a four-cylinder engine is offered in the 911 body, exclusively for overseas markets, particularly for the U.S. The two-liter engine is derived from the VW-Porsche 914/4, develops 90 horsepower [66 kW] and is fitted with airflow-sensing electronic fuel injection (L-Jetronic). As the compression ratio is only 7.6:1, the 912 E is content to operate with regular gasoline. Exhaust emission control is by means of thermal reactors. A type 923/02 five-speed manual transmission is fitted as standard equipment. Optionally, a ZF limited slip differential with 40 percent lockup factor is available.

The fact that Porsche once again offers a four-cylinder model is attributable to undiminished American demand for an economical and affordable sports car in the wake of the first energy crisis of 1973 and 1974. Even though the new, fuel-efficient Porsche 924 was introduced in 1975, Porsche produced 2092 examples of the 912 E, most sold in the United States.

Model year 1976 (J-Series)

Type designation: 911, 911 Carrera 3.0 Coupe and Targa, 911 Turbo Coupe

Changes
Reducing model proliferation at Porsche: there are only two normally aspirated models, the 911 and 911 Carrera, and the turbocharged 911 Turbo. The 911 Carrera is fitted with a three-liter engine and K-Jetronic fuel injection system. The semi-automatic transmission, available only for the non-turbocharged models, is fitted with three forward gears. Structural parts of all bodies are made of hot dip galvanized steel. Six-year warranty against rust perforation of floorpan.

Because an entry-level Porsche is now available in the form of the 125 hp [92 kW] Porsche 924, the range of six-cylinder models is reduced. The 911 with its 2.7 liter engine remains, the 911 Carrera 3.0 uses a three-liter normally aspirated engine, and the 911 Turbo continues with the turbocharged engine developed from the Carrera powerplant. Fruits of Porsche's extensive research in reducing corrosion reach the production line: hot dip galvanized steel sheet is used for structural body members. This results in a milestone in automotive construction: a long term (six year) warranty against rust perforation. Previously, Porsche had conducted extensive experiments with stainless steel bodies. Three prototypes were built at great expense, one of which may be seen in the Deutsches Museum in Munich. Drawing and welding the steel sheets provided the greatest difficulties.

1. Engine
Changes to the Carrera 3.0 engine: in addition to a displacement increase to 2994 cc and larger valves, fuel is metered by a K-Jetronic continuous injection system. The engine of the 911 also gets a power increase by means of higher compression. Both nor-

mally aspirated engines are fitted with five-blade cooling fans. The blower ratio is changed: alternator and fan spin faster.

Engine designation		911	Carrera
Engine type		911/81	930/50
Displacement	(cc)	2687	2994
Compression ratio		8.5:1	8.5:1
Fuel requirement	(RON)	91	91
Power output	(hp/kW)	165/121	200/147
at	(rpm)	5800	6000
Torque	(Nm)	235	255
at	(rpm)	4000	4200

Higher rpm for the cooling fan and alternator are necessary because the electrical demand of cars idling in city traffic is often greater than the available supply from the alternator.

2. Fuel and ignition systems
The Turbo engine is fitted with an auxiliary air valve, auxiliary air injection to reduce exhaust emissions, a fuel pressure accumulator between the fuel pumps and an improved fuel distributor. With the changeover of the Carrera to K-Jetronic fuel injection, all Porsche models, including the 924, are fitted with the same fuel injection system for the first time. The fuel pump for the 911 and 911 Carrera is moved to the tank and and steering box area.

The Turbo fuel system incorporates several components to improve comfort or hot and cold starting.

3. Powertrain
Both Sportomatic transmissions, Type 925/09 for the 911 and 925/13 for the 911 Carrera 3.0 are fitted with only three forward gears. Manual transmissions for the normally aspirated engines are fitted with gears matched to the engine output. Due to the newly available wider tires, the 911 Turbo is available with two transmissions which differ only in their final drive ratio: Type 930/30, final drive 9:38, normal tires, and Type 930/32, final drive 9:36, for 50-series tires.

The fact that the Sportomatic is only available with three forward gears is attributable to tougher noise standards in several vital export markets. When accelerating through the test section, cars with

four-speed Sportomatics reach their rev limit, for example 6800 rpm, in second gear. The resulting exhaust and mechanical noise exceed the new regulatory limits.

4. Suspension
No change for normally aspirated vehicles. For the Turbo, two tire choices are available: as before, front 185/70 VR 15, rear 215/60 VR 15, or a new choice, front 205/50 VR 15, rear 225/50 VR 15.

For the first time, Porsche offers 50-series tires, i.e. tires whose sidewall height is 50% of their tread width. Customer demand for 50-series tires is so great that a production bottleneck at the tire manufacturers results, particularly for replacement tires.

5. Bodywork
Introduction of hot dip galvanized sheet steel for structural members of the body, for all cars. Improvement of surface and cavity treatment in the manufacturing process and in painting. The Carrera and Turbo are also fitted with headlight rings painted in body color. Headlight washers are standard for 911 Carrera and Turbo.

Porsche is the first car maker to manufacture cars using hot dip galvanized deep-drawing steel sheet metal. After attempting to make stainless steel bodies, Porsche in Zuffenhausen and Audi in Neckarsulm (contract manufacturer of the Porsche 924) adopted galvanized sheetmetal. Despite costly prepaint preparation, the familiar high standard of Porsche paintwork is achieved even on galvanized bodywork.

6. Equipment
The 911 Carrera and 911 Turbo have pleated door panels, and carpeting extended upward from the floorboards. Illuminated door and ignition key.

7. Seats and trim
No changes.

8. Heating and air conditioning system
No changes.

9. Electrical system
All vehicles fitted with electrically adjustable and

heated outside mirrors. 911 and 911 Carrera 3.0: electronic speedometer. Two speakers in doors. The 911 Turbo has two speakers in the doors and two in the rear shelf. Automatic speed control is available for all six-cylinder models.

10. Miscellaneous
For production reasons, 123 examples of the 911 Carrera are fitted with the more powerful 210 hp [155 kW] engine.

Model Year 1977 (K-Series)

Type designation: 911, 911 Carrera 3.0 Coupe and Targa, 911 Turbo Coupe

Changes
Not much new for 1977: altered heating and ventilation controls for normally aspirated engines. The Carrera 3.0 and 911 Turbo are fitted with power-assisted brakes. The 911 Turbo gets 16-inch wheels.

1. Engine
Engines for U.S.-specification cars have air injection downstream of the exhaust valves, exhaust gas recirculation (EGR) and thermal reactors. Japanese models are additionally fitted with a visual exhaust gas temperature indicator; if normal exhaust gas temperatures are exceeded (for example, 750 °C in the case of the Turbo) the driver is warned of possible exhaust system overheating. Turbo engines are fitted with a sensor for the exhaust temperature indicator.

The United States, Canada and Japan have increasingly tighter exhaust emissions regulations. These regulations can only be met, and cars can only be sold in these countries, by installing air injection for exhaust gas oxidation, recirculating part of the exhaust gas to the intake system, and installing thermal reactors in the exhaust system.

2. Fuel and ignition systems
A new fuel supply pump design makes its first appearance: the Bosch EKP IV. These pumps are quieter and have higher output volume. Henceforth the Turbo is fitted with two EKP IV pumps in series.

3. Powertrain
Improved clutch assist for the 911 Carrera and 911 Turbo; declutching is even more comfortable. The 915/60 transmission (911) and 916/61 (911 Carrera 3.0) have improved shift components for first gear. Selecting first gear from a standstill is improved.

Introduction of asymmetrically pointed dogs on the first gear clutch body and its associated operating sleeve make it easier to engage first gear.

4. Suspension
Vacuum brake power assist is installed on the 911 Carrera 3.0, 911 Turbo and Sportomatic-equipped 911 models. The brake system is modified accordingly. Further changes for 911 Turbo: Front anti-roll bar 20.0 mm, rear 18.0 mm. All Turbos are fitted with 16-inch wheels and tires. Front wheels 7 J x 16, rear 8 J x 16. Front tires 205/55 VR 16, rear 225/50 VR 16.

Cars get heavier from year to year, top speeds increase, and even the 911 can't continue without power assisted brakes. To keep pedal pressures acceptably low, Teves vacuum assist brake boosters are installed.

5. Bodywork
No changes

6. Equipment
Tamper-resistant door locks with rotating locking knob. The locking pin disappears completely when the door is locked, and can no longer be pulled up manually. To increase security of Targa vehicles, the front vent windows are replaced by non-opening windows. 911 Turbos are equipped with a boost

pressure gauge. The boost gauge, which reads to 1.5 bar, is located within the centrally mounted tachometer.

Auto theft is becoming a worldwide problem. As had long been done on the coupe, Porsche installs fixed triangular side windows on the Targa model to eliminate this potential break-in path, and makes the door lock pins flush with the door sill when locked. Manual locking and unlocking from inside the vehicle is accomplished by a twist knob.

7. Seats and trim
Front and rear seats available with pinstripe fabric.

8. Heating and air conditioning system
Dual ventilation levers (right and left sides of cabin), illuminated at night. For better interior ventilation, all cars are fitted with twin central vents in the dashboard. The 911 Carrera 3.0 is equipped with automatic heating controls like the 911 Turbo.

9. Electrical system
Seat belt warning light for all models.

Model Year 1978 (L-Series)

Type designation: 911 SC Coupe and Targa, 911 Turbo 3.3 Coupe

Changes

Only two six-cylinder models are offered, the 911 SC and the 911 Turbo 3.3, with its engine enlarged to 3.3 liters. The 911 SC combines the body features of the 911 S with the three-liter Carrera engine. The 911 Turbo is fitted with a larger 3.3 liter engine and a charge air intercooler.

Because the Porsche model range has been expanded by the addition of the 924 and 928, the number of 911 models has been reduced to only two models with different performance potential. These are the 911 SC, whose letters are a combination of the previous year's S, with its "Super" equipment, and the C representing the more powerful Carrera engine. The increased power of the 911 Turbo 3.3 maintains its performance edge over the new 928. Nevertheless, in this model year it becomes apparent that the 911 will be allowed to die and be replaced by the 928.

1. Engine
Due to differing exhaust requirements for various export markets, six different normally aspirated engines are installed in the 911 SC alone.

Desig-nation	Type	Displace-ment (cc)	Compression ratio	Octane (RON)	Power (hp/kW)	Torque (Nm)	Remarks
911 SC	930/03	2994	8.5:1	91	180/132	265	RoW manual trans.
911 SC	930/13	2994	8.5:1	91	180/132	265	RoW Sportomatic
911 SC	930/04	2994	8.5:1	91*	180/132	265	USA manual trans.
911 SC	930/05	2994	8.5:1	91*	180/132	265	Japan manual trans.
911 SC	930/15	2994	8.5:1	91*	180/132	265	Japan Sportomatic
911 SC	930/06	2994	8.5:1	91*	180/132	265	California

*: Unleaded fuel required.
RoW: Rest of World, not including USA, Canada or Japan.

Exhaust gas treatment for these individual engine types is accomplished as follows:

Engine	Country	Secondary air injection	Exhaust Catalyst	Exhaust gas recirc.	Heat shield
930/03	RoW manual trans.	yes	---	---	---
930/13	RoW Sportomatic	yes	---	---	---
930/04	USA + CDN	yes	yes	---	---
930/05	Japan manual trans.	yes	yes	yes	yes
930/15	Japan Sportomatic	yes	yes	yes	yes
930/06	California	yes	yes	yes	---

Further changes for normally aspirated engines: reinforced crankshaft, main bearings enlarged to 80 mm. The connecting rods are modified to match the new crankshaft.

The Turbo's displacement increase to 3.3 liters is accomplished by a larger 97 mm cylinder bore and a new crankshaft providing a 74.4 mm stroke. Here, too, the connecting rods are matched to the new crankshaft. Comparison of these engines underscores how much power is lost to environmental demands.

Desig-nation	Type	Displace-ment (cc)	Compression ratio	Octane (RON)	Power (hp/kW)	Torque (Nm)	Remarks
911 Turbo	930/60	3299	7.0:1	98	300/221	412	for RoW
911 Turbo	930/61	3299	7.0:1	96+	265/195	395	for USA + CDN
911 Turbo	930/62	3299	7.0:1	96+	265/195	395	for Japan
911 Turbo	930/63	3299	7.0:1	96+	265/195	395	for California

+: Unleaded fuel required.
RoW : Rest of World, not including USA, Canada or Japan.

Exhaust gas treatment:
930/60 (RoW):   Secondary air injection
930/61 (USA + CDN): Secondary air injection + thermal reactors + exhaust gas recirculation
930/62 (Japan):   Secondary air injection + thermal reactors + exhaust gas recirculation + heat shield
930/63 (California):   Secondary air injection + thermal reactors + exhaust gas recirculation + ignition advance

Porsche eliminates break-in requirements for its engines. Thanks to modern manufacturing methods and materials, it is now only necessary to stay below 5000 rpm for the first 1000 km [600 miles].

2. Fuel and ignition systems

Fuel metering for all engines is achieved via Bosch K-Jetronic. The 911 Turbo 3.3 has a charge air intercooler mounted downstream of the turbocharger. All engines are fitted with a Bosch breakerless HKZ 12 V ignition system. Upon reaching the rev limit, for example 6800 rpm in the case of the 911 SC, the rev limiter for U.S., California and Japan engines does not interrupt the spark but rather cuts out the fuel pump(s).

Emission-controlled engines fitted with thermal reactors cannot be allowed to have the ignition cut out while fuel flow continues, as the unburnt fuel would then burn in the exhaust system, resulting in overheating and destruction of the thermal reactors.

3. Powertrain

The 911 SC clutch disc is fitted with a torsional vibration damper developed by Porsche. When starting from rest and at low rpm, it permits up to 28 degrees of angular deflection. The clutch disc of the Turbo 3.3 is also fitted with a new vibration damper which permits up to 34 degrees of twist. The manual transmission (Type 930/34) is fitted with a "taller" fourth gear in keeping with improved performance potential. Larger angular deflection of the clutch discs permits better damping of engine irregularities at low rpm. Engine torsional vibrations, even at idle, excite resonance in the drivetrain, particularly when starting off at low rpm. The new torsional damper fitted to all six-cylinder cars helps to damp these vibrations and virtually eliminate annoying transmission rattle at very low rpm.

4. Suspension

The 911 SC is fitted with 20 mm front and 18 mm rear anti-roll bars. Its braking system includes power assist. Cast alloy wheels are 6 J x 15 at the front, 7 J x 15 rear. Tires are 185/70 VR 15 at the front, 215/60 VR 15 at the rear. The SC is available with optional 16-inch wheels and tires. A completely new brake system is introduced for the 911 Turbo: wide, ventilated and cross-drilled rotors front and rear. Front and rear brake calipers were developed by Porsche and adapted from those of the 917 race car. These feature four-piston light alloy fixed calipers. The power booster is modified for the new brake layout. Forged 9 J x 16 rear wheels are permissible.

For the new brake system, Porsche once again benefits from its racing experience. The Turbo 3.3, now reaching speeds of 260 km/h [162 mph] and weighing in at 1680 kg [3700 lbs.], is fitted with a brake system which has proven itself in long distance races including Le Mans and the Nürburgring: ventilated brake rotors with perforated ("cross drilled") surfaces. Sturdy four-piston calipers and excellent heat rejection (light alloy). The brake calipers bear the name of their developer: Porsche.

5. Bodywork

Bonded-in rear quarter windows for all models. The Turbo 3.3's front and rear spoilers have been reshaped. The engine lid is steel, the rear spoiler is part plastic.

6. Equipment

Altered instruments for all vehicles: the combination instrument has different ranges. The tachometer range ends at 7000 rpm. Turbo only: 300 km/h speedometer and improved boost pressure gauge.

7. Seats and trim

No changes.

8. Heating and air conditioning system

No changes.

9. Electrical system
No changes.

10. Miscellaneous
The Porsche 928 is introduced for this model year.

Model year 1979 (M-Series)

Type designation: 911 SC Coupe and Targa, 911 Turbo 3.3 Coupe

Changes
No significant changes to the six-cylinder models for 1979.

1. Engine
No changes.

2. Fuel and ignition systems
No changes.

3. Powertrain
No changes.

4. Suspension
Fixed caliper brake system for the 911 SC.

5. Bodywork
Tinted glass for the Turbo 3.3.

6. Equipment
Floor covering: short pile carpeting.

7. Seats and trim
No changes.

8. Heating system, air conditioning system
Automatic warm air regulation

9. Electrical system
No changes.

Model year 1980 (A Program)

Type designation 911 SC Coupe and Targa, 911 Turbo 3.3 Coupe

Changes
Power increase for the 911 SC to 188 hp [138 kW]. First application of an oxygen sensor ("Lambda sonde") for U.S. engines. Dual exhaust tips standard for Turbo 3.3.

1. Engine

Changes to SC engine: larger cooling fan from Turbo engine, improved oil scavenging from crankcase. Changes to SC and Turbo engine: stiffening ribs on lower valve cover, improved valve cover gaskets. New front oil cooler. Different 911 SC engines for various markets:

Desig-nation	Type	Displace-ment (cc)	Compression ratio	Octane (RON)	Power (hp/kW)	Torque (Nm)	Remarks
911 SC	930/07	2994	9.3:1	91+	180/132	245	for USA+CDN
911 SC	930/08	2994	9.3:1	91+	180/132	245	for Japan
911 SC	930/09	2994	8.6:1	91	188/138	265	for RoW

+: unleaded fuel required
RoW : Rest of world, not including USA, Canada and Japan.

Exhaust gas treatment:

Engine	Country	Type
930/07	(USA + CDN):	Secondary air injection + Exhaust gas catalyst + oxygen sensor
930/08	(Japan):	Secondary air injection + Exhaust gas catalyst + oxygen sensor
930/09	(RoW):	Secondary air injection

All normally aspirated engines are fitted with the higher volume cooling fan of the 911 Turbo 3.3.

2. Fuel and ignition systems

The 930/07 and 930/08 are fitted with oxygen sensors (Lambda sonde) for the first time. To take advantage of the oxygen sensors, the following fuel system components have been added: solenoid valve in fuel distributor, throttle butterfly switch, engine temperature sensor, control unit. The 911 Turbo 3.3 is fitted with a dual outlet exhaust system.

Porsche builds its first engines equipped with three-way catalysts. The Lambda sonde, developed by Bosch, is used to measure oxygen content of the exhaust stream. Signals from the Lambda sonde are processed by a control unit, which sends pulses to a fuel valve which reduces the instantaneous fuel injection quantity at the fuel distributor (leaner mixture) or increases the injected quantity (richer mixture.)

3. Powertrain
No changes.

4. Suspension
No changes.

5. Bodywork
No changes.

6. Equipment
Three-spoke leather-covered steering wheel for SC, center console for all vehicles.

7. Seats and trim
No changes.

8. Heating system, air conditioning system
No changes.

9. Electrical system
An alarm system is available as an option. It must be armed before locking the driver's door. All models: engine compartment illumination.

Model year 1981 (B Program)

Type designation: 911 SC Coupe and Targa, 911 Turbo 3.3 Coupe

Changes
No significant changes to Turbo 3.3. Again, a power increase for the 911 SC, to 204 hp [150 kW]. Anti-rust warranty period extended to 7 years and expanded to cover entire body.

1. Engine
Normally-aspirated engines for countries without unleaded fuel have been reworked again. By increasing compression ratio, altering valve timing and using 98 RON premium fuel, maximum output of 204 hp is available. Engines for USA, Canada and Japan are given new type designations (930/16 and /17) but retain the same technical and performance specifications.

Following are specifications of the 204 hp RoW engine:

Engine designation		911 SC
Engine type		930/10
Displacement	(cc)	2994
Compression ratio		9.8:1
Fuel requirement	(RON)	98
Power output	(hp/kW)	204/150
at	(rpm)	5900
Torque	(Nm)	267
at	(rpm)	4300

As 98 octane fuel is available in nearly all foreign markets as well as the Federal Republic of Germany, Porsche uses every opportunity to increase output of its engines. Raising the compression ratio and changing ignition timing results in a secondary benefit: reduction in brake specific fuel consumption.

2. Fuel and ignition systems
The increased power of the 930/10 engine is made possible by an increase in compression ratio to 9.8:1, more performance oriented valve timing and altered ignition timing.

3. Powertrain
911 SC uses a clutch disc with steel spring vibration dampers. The 911 Turbo 3.3 retains the rubber-damped clutch with its greater angular deflection capability. The Sportomatic transmission is no longer available. No changes to manual transmissions.

Manufacturing problems encountered with the 911 SC rubber-centered clutch disc force a return to steel-spring clutches for the normally aspirated engine.

4. Suspension
No changes.

5. Bodywork
Extension of long-term rust perforation warranty to 7 years, covering the entire body. Side turn signal lights for all vehicles.

By this time the entire body is made of two-sided hot dip galvanized steel. Porsche is the first car manufacturer in the world to provide a seven year warranty against rust perforation of the entire body. Also noteworthy: 80 percent of all Porsches ever built are still operational.

6. Equipment
Illuminated switches.

7. Seats and trim
New optional sport seats, also available are seats entirely covered with cloth.

8. Heating system, air conditioning system
No changes.

9. Electrical system
No changes.

Model year 1982 (C Program)

Type designation: 911 SC Coupe and Targa, 911 Turbo 3.3 Coupe

Changes
Only minor changes from the previous model year.

1. Engine
No changes.

2. Fuel and ignition systems
No changes.

3. Powertrain
The 911 SC differential is reinforced.

4. Suspension
Cast alloy wheels with black painted centers and polished rims are standard on the 911 SC.

5. Bodywork
The 911 SC is available with the rear wing of the 911 Turbo 3.0 as an option.

6. Equipment
The oil temperature gauge is recalibrated. The white band begins at about 20 °C [68 °F] and ends at 60 °C [140 °F]. Two marks indicate 90 °C [194 °F] and 120 °C [248 °F].

7. Seats and trim
Special child seats are available for the rear seats.

8. Heating system, air conditioning system
The side vents are connected to the hot air ducts. Warm air is now available for the side windows.

9. Electrical system
Installation of a 1050 Watt alternator (A 14 N11) for all six-cylinder engines.

10. Miscellaneous
Special edition "Ferry Porsche" 911 is offered, based on the 911 SC. This includes comfortable interior appointments and Ferry Porsche's signature embroidered in the seat backrests. A 911 Turbo 3.3 with increased power (65 additional horsepower, 47 more kW) is built and sold for Group B racing. An optionally available roof rack system permits loads of up to 75 kg [165 lbs].

Model year 1983 (D Program)

Type designation 911 SC Coupe, Targa and Cabriolet, 911 Turbo 3.3 Coupe

Changes

No significant changes to engine or drivetrain components. New regulations necessitate an improved muffler. A Porsche cabriolet is once again available.

Legal requirements to reduce automobile-induced noise are becoming increasingly stringent. Switzerland in particular makes type certification more difficult. After almost a two-decade hiatus, Porsche again offers a cabriolet. For years, regulatory agencies in the United States had been preparing safety laws which would have made it impossible to certify new convertibles for road use. These pending laws were finally scrapped. Porsche's 911 Cabriolet motivated nearly all car makers to once again build open cars.

1. Engine

No changes to engine mechanics.

2. Fuel and ignition systems

New exhaust resonator for 911 SC. Special muffler for Switzerland. Altered main muffler for 911 Turbo. The wastegate exhaust no longer enters the main muffler but rather escapes through a pipe under the main exhaust outlets. This pipe is fitted with its own muffler. Detail engineering on the 911 Turbo's K-Jetronic and ignition system.

3. Powertrain

The 930/34 transmission (Swiss market 911 Turbo) is given a taller second gear (24:30) to meet drive-by noise regulations.

Even the transmission had to be changed to reduce engine rpm and enable the Turbo to meet Swiss drive-by noise limits.

4. Suspension

For the 911 SC, front 6 J x 17 and rear 7 J x 16 wheels are approved.

5. Bodywork

The 911 SC is also available as a Cabriolet. The cabriolet top employs a new mechanism in which 50 percent of the roof consists of stamped steel panels. This new development ensures a stable shape even at high speeds and offers added accident protection.

The top is manually operated. The flexible rear window can be opened by means of a zipper. Cabriolets have two electrically adjustable and heated outside mirrors.

Several factors had to be considered during development of the Cabriolet. The loss of the Targa bar reduced body stiffness, which had to be regained by extensive stiffening of the floorpan. Safety aspects also influenced the design of the top. Extensive research resulted in a top design employing metal panels which form a cage over the cabin when the top is raised.

6. Equipment

No changes.

7. Seats and trim

Mechanical safety belts for rear seat passengers. All Cabriolets are fitted with leather-covered seats as standard equipment.

8. Heating system, air conditioning system

Two additional electric heating blowers provide more warmth for occupants of the 911 Turbo, particularly during the engine's warm-up phase. The 911 SC is fitted with automatic warm air control. The 911 SC Cabriolet retains manual heat controls because driving with the top open would result in incorrect heat control by the automatic system.

9. Electrical system
New Blaupunkt radio generation, SQR 22 Köln with ARI (automatic traffic information system) for Germany, Atlanta without ARI for Rest of World, and Monterey for USA.

SQR 22 means:

S Search
Q Quartz Tuning (with station memory)
R Reverse (cassette autoreverse)
2 20 Watt output
2 Sold beginning in 1982.

Model year 1984 (E Program)

Type designation   **911 Carrera Coupe, Targa and Cabriolet**
911 Carrera Coupe Turbo Look
911 Turbo 3.3 Coupe

Changes
New 3.2 liter engine family. Digital Motor Electronics. Improved brake system. 911 Carrera Coupe available in Turbo Look. The Turbo continues to be available for Canadian customers.

The normally-aspirated engines are designed to meet new exhaust emissions standards. Even though many European countries do not yet have unleaded fuel, the engines are already designed to use it when it becomes available. The 911 Turbo is still not available in the United States because its engine has not yet been developed to work with a catalytic converter.

1. Engine
The normally aspirated 911 Carrera engine has been extensively reworked. In addition to a displacement increase to 3.2 liters, the crankcase has been stiffened, the chain tensioners improved and connected to the engine oil supply. The crankshaft, with its stroke of 74.4 mm, is nearly identical to that of the 911 Turbo.
Carrera engine specifications:

Application		Rest of World	USA+Japan
Engine designation		911 Carrera	911 Carrera
Engine type		930/20	930/21
Displacement	(cc)	3164	3164
Compression ratio		10.3:1	9.5:1
Fuel octane	(RON)	98	91 unleaded
Power output	(hp/kW)	231/170	207/152
at	(rpm)	5900	5900
Torque	(Nm)	284	260
at	(rpm)	4800	4800

No mechanical changes for Turbo engine.

Major changes have been made to the normally aspirated engines. The crankshaft is new, and functionally identical to that of the Turbo engine. The two tensioners for the camshaft timing chains have been redesigned for increased operating reliability.

2. Fuel and ignition systems
Digital Motor Electronics (DME) is employed for the Carrera engine's fuel injection and map ignition. The DME includes fuel cutoff while coasting and an oxygen sensor (Lambda control) for the U.S., Californian, Canadian, and Japanese markets. All Lambda sensors are electrically heated. No changes to the ignition system or the fuel management system of the Turbo engine.

Digital Motor Electronics (DME) is now also available for the Carrera engine. The timed, electronically controlled fuel injection and spark timing via an ignition map stored in electronic memory are controlled by a single digital microprocessor. The fuel injection is based on the familiar Bosch L-Jetronic system. When the DME recognizes that the vehicle is coasting, it cuts out the fuel injection. Depending on the car's destination country, an oxygen sensor can be installed in the exhaust system to provide additional information to the control system and modify the fuel injection quantity accordingly.

3. Powertrain

The Type 915/67 manual transmission (Carrera RoW) and 915/69 manual transmission (Turbo Look RoW) differ only in their drive flanges. Both transmissions incorporate a road speed dependent transmission oil pump and a finned oil cooler attached to the outside of the transmission case. Gearing in fourth and fifth gears has been changed in keeping with the increase in engine output.

The transmission oil cooling system lowers oil temperatures by approximately 25 °C [45 °F]. In addition to improved cooling, the viscosity of the transmission oil is higher (under identical operating conditions) and therefore mechanical noise is reduced.

4. Suspension

The 911 Carrera is fitted with a more powerful brake system including a brake pressure limiting valve, venturi-type vacuum amplifier and a larger brake power booster. Turbo Look vehicles are fitted with front hubs, rear torsion bar tube, suspension arms

and brake system taken from the Turbo, plus forged alloy wheels, 7 J x 16 with 205/55 VR 16 tires at the front and 8 J x 16 with 225/50 VR 16 at the rear. All six-cylinder cars are equipped with brake pad wear indicators and lug nut locks to prevent wheel theft.

The brake pad wear indicator is an added safety feature for customers. Scheduled service intervals have been extended to 20,000 km [12,000 miles].

5. Bodywork

Foglamps of all models are integrated into the front spoiler. Option M 491 allows customers to order the 911 Coupe with the Turbo Look package. Front and rear fenders, rear fender flares, front and rear spoilers are identical to those of the 911 Turbo.

6. Equipment

Black "Carrera" script on the engine lid. Tinted rear window, two-stage rear defroster for Coupe and Targa. The Targa top and its seals have been redesigned. Lockable trunk release handle now provided on coupe. Cabriolet top now also available in brown and blue.

Apparently, the Women's Liberation movement finally reaches the 911. That, or men feel a need for mirrors in the driver's sun visor.

7. Seats and trim

New two-tone fabrics with Porsche script. Inside door handles matched to interior color.

8. Heating system, air conditioning system

Two auxiliary blowers in heater ducts added to Carrera models for improved heating. Conversion of air conditioning system to ten-cylinder swashplate compressor.

9. Electrical system

New 92 A alternator, with 1288 Watt output.

10. Miscellaneous

A limited production run (20 examples) of a special model, the 911 SC RS, is built for Group B racing purposes. Its 3.0 liter engine develops 250 hp [184 kW] at 7000 rpm. A 280 hp [206 kW] engine is also available for racing and rallys.

Model year 1985 (F Program)

Type designation **911 Carrera Coupe, Targa and Cabriolet**
911 Carrera Turbo Look Coupe, Targa and Cabriolet
911 Turbo Coupe

Changes

The Turbo Look 911 Carrera is also available with Targa and Cabriolet bodywork. A first for the German market: catalytic converter and Lambda sonde (oxygen sensor). A new seat design is available for all models.

Within the European Common Market, Porsche is a leader in implementing unleaded fuel. Although the number of gasoline stations capable of dispensing unleaded fuel is still far from satisfactory, Porsche is the first to offer a regulated catalytic converter to European customers.

1. Engine

All six-cylinder models are fitted with a finned oil cooler in the right front fender, ahead of the wheel. Air enters under front bumper, above the foglight.

Improved engine oil cooling by means of the cooler's large surface area.

2. Fuel and ignition systems

In addition to the M 930/20 and M 930/21 engines of 1984, option M 298 for Germany (mandatory for Austria, Australia, and Switzerland) equips the M 930/21 engine with a catalytic converter and Lambda sonde (oxygen sensor). Because unleaded premium fuel is not yet available, this engine has a compression ratio of only 9.5:1, resulting in power reduction to 207 hp [152 kW].

Unleaded fuel available in Europe ("Eurosuper unleaded") has a Research Octane Number of only 95. Note: fuel refined from mineral oil always contains some naturally occurring Pb (lead). To increase knock resistance of the fuel, it had been customary to mix additives to the fuel at the refinery. These additives had a high lead content, and therefore posed a health hazard. For these reasons, it is more appropriate to refer to the new generation of fuels as "unleaded" rather than "lead free."

3. Powertrain

The transmissions available for the Carrera, the 915/72 with transmission oil pump and oil cooler for all non-catalyst engines, and 915/73* without oil cooling for all catalyst-equipped engines, now incorporate a reinforced transmission housing. The Porsche patent synchromesh is reworked: shifting forces, particularly for engaging first gear, are further reduced. The shift lever ratio is changed, resulting in noticeably shorter and therefore "sportier" shift throws.
* Transmission 915/73 : Gear ratios for 2nd, 4th and 5th are shorter to match the reduced engine output.

Without a change in gear ratios, cars equipped with the less powerful engine would not be able to reach top speed.

4. Suspension

Boge dual-tube gas-pressure shocks, type "GZ," are installed in all six-cylinder models. The suspension of the 911 Turbo has been retuned and equipped with stiffer anti-roll bars, 22 mm at the front, 20 mm at the rear. The brake power booster ratio for all Turbo Look models has been changed, resulting in appreciably lower brake pedal effort.

5. Bodywork

The Targa and Cabriolet body variations are also available with the Turbo Look option, but without the Turbo rear wing. Changing to heavier-gauge sheet metal and added chassis reinforcement make the open bodies capable of withstanding the demands of the Turbo suspension.

6. Equipment

Four-spoke steering wheel for all six-cylinder models. Electric central locking can be activated by a switch on the center console. Electrically heated windshield washer nozzles. Sekuriflex windshield available as an option.

The Sekuriflex windshield has a perfectly clear plastic film on its inner surface which protects occupants from sharp glass fragments in the event of severe stone impact or head contact in an accident.

7. Seats and trim
New seat generation for all Porsche models: basic seat, also with partial power features, fully electric comfort seat, and partial-power sport seat.

8. Heating system, air conditioning system
No changes.

9. Electrical system
Rear window now with only single-stage defrost. Active windshield antenna embedded in the passenger side of the windshield. Antenna amplifier in trunk.

Porsche's windshield antenna is based on experience gained with systems proven in service on supersonic aircraft.

Model year 1986 (G Program)

Type designation: **911 Carrera Coupe, Targa and Cabriolet**
911 Carrera Turbo Look Coupe, Targa and Cabriolet
911 Turbo 3.3 Coupe, Targa and Cabriolet

Changes
No major changes for the 911 Carrera and RoW (Rest of World) Turbo. New Turbo engine for U.S. market, with feedback catalytic converter. Extension of long-term warranty against rust perforation to ten years. Three year paint warranty, two-year unlimited mileage warranty on remainder of vehicle. Twelve month warranty on Porsche replacement parts purchased at franchised Porsche dealerships. 911 Turbo offered with Targa and Cabriolet bodywork for the first time.

1. Engine
The U.S. market Turbo engine differs from the more powerful RoW engine by its fuel system and ignition. Comparison of Turbo engines:

Engine application	USA	Rest of World
Engine designation	911 Turbo	911 Turbo
Engine type	930/68	930/66

Displacement	(cc)	3299	3299
Compression ratio		7.0:1	7.0:1
Fuel required	(RON)	96	98
Power output	(hp/kW)	282/210	300/221
at	(rpm)	5500	5500
Torque	(Nm)	390	430
at	(rpm)	4000	4000

* unleaded fuel required

2. Fuel and ignition systems

No changes to RoW engines. The Turbo USA is equipped with a Lambda sonde (oxygen sensor) and three-way catalytic converter. Exhaust gas treatment: with cold engine, auxiliary air is injected downstream of the exhaust valves; once the engine warms up, air is injected directly into the catalytic converter. The ignition system is modified to meet strict U.S. emissions regulations.

The Turbo equipped with a feedback-controlled catalytic converter was developed especially for the U.S. market. American exhaust emissions standards can only be met with expensive modifications to the K-Jetronic fuel injection system, which includes a solenoid valve to modify the air-fuel ratio.

3. Powertrain

No changes to RoW powertrains. The Turbo USA is equipped with the four-speed 930/36 manual transmission, which had been installed in RoW vehicles during the previous model year.

4. Suspension

Altered suspension tuning for the Carrera. The 20 mm front anti-roll bar is replaced by a 22 mm bar; the rear 24 mm torsion bars are replaced by 25 mm torsion bars. The rear anti-roll bar diameter is also increased, from 18 to 21 mm. The 911 Turbo and Turbo Look have larger rear forged alloy wheels, 9 J x 16 H2, with 15 mm offset*, carrying 245/45 VR 16 tires.
* offset: distance between center of wheel and mounting surface of wheel.

5. Bodywork

Electrically operated Cabriolet top option available.

6. Equipment

U.S. market vehicles are fitted with a third, high-mounted brake light (CHMSL: Center High Mounted Stop Light). New anti-theft protection for lug nuts. All vehicles equipped with intensive windshield washer system. Vanity mirrors in sun visors are equipped with sliding covers. Larger air vents.

7. Seats and trim

Front seats 20 mm lower. Trunk lining matches interior carpeting.

8. Heating system, air conditioning system

New cabin temperature sensor.

9. Electrical system

Changes to antenna amplifier. New radio family, Bremen SQR/Toronto SQR.

Model year 1987 (H Program)

Type designation: 911 Carrera Coupe, Targa and Cabriolet
911 Carrera Turbo Look Coupe, Targa and Cabriolet
911 Turbo Coupe, Targa and Cabriolet

Changes
No major changes for the 911 Turbo, except addition of Turbo Targa and Turbo Cabriolet variants. Due to the increasing worldwide availability of unleaded fuel, 1987 sees a wide variety of normally aspirated 911 engines. New for all Carreras: G 50 transmission and clutch.

Worldwide as well as within the Common Market, unleaded fuel becomes more readily available. However, there is no shortage of confusion, as many countries, even within the EC, do not offer premium grade fuel. Manufacturers are forced to design cars specifically for individual countries.

1. Engine
Comparison of normally aspirated 911 engines:

Engine application		RoW + D, no cat. Japan	USA + D+A+CH+ Japan	Australia	Sweden
Engine designation		All engines:		911 Carrera	
Engine type		930/20	930/25	930/25	930/26
Displacement	(cc)	3164	3164	3164	3164
Compression ratio		10.3:1	9.5:1	9.5:1	9.5:1
Fuel requirement	(RON)	98 +/-	95 *	91 *	98 +/-
Power	(hp/kW)	231/170	217/160	207/152	231/170
at		5900	5900	5900	5900
Torque		284	265	260	265
at		4800	4800	4800	4800
Comments		without cat.	with cat. (M 298)	with cat. (DME)	without cat. (aux. air inj.)

+/- = unleaded or leaded, observe octane requirement
* = unleaded fuel
(M 298) = engine available with feedback catalytic converter as option
(DME) = change to Digital Motor Electronics: later ignition timing
(aux. air) = auxiliary air injected downstream of exhaust valves
Normally aspirated and Turbo vehicles with catalytic converter are equipped with an electric cooling fan for the engine oil cooler in the right front fender. When retrofitted with catalytic converters, 231 hp engine output drops to 207 hp, not the 217 hp of powerplants originally fitted with converters.

2. Fuel and ignition systems
Six different DME control units are used for Carrera engines:
911.618.111.12   for high compression engines, worldwide
911.618.111.13   for countries with low octane fuel (i.e. Belgium, France, Greece)
911.618.111.14   for USA, California, Japan, Canada, Austria, Switzerland and Europe/RoW with catalytic converter
911.618.111.15*   for high compression engines with "sports package I"
911.618.111.16*   for low-octane fuel and "sports package I"
911.618.111.17*   for USA etc. with "sports package I"
* = higher rev limit of 6840 rpm (standard: 6520 rpm)

3. Powertrain
Carrera models are equipped with a hydraulic clutch (F&S MFZ 240) and a rubber-damped clutch disc (F&S 240 GUD). The five-speed G 50 transmission is a completely new transmission design. Shafts, gears, roller bearings and pinion gears are considerably reinforced. New housing design, hydraulic clutch actuation. New synchromesh system, reverse gear also fully synchromesh. Longitudinal support of shift rails by means of low-friction ball bushings. New four-plane shift pattern: reverse at left forward, fifth gear right forward.

After a fifteen year production run for the Type 915 transmission, a new transmission family is introduced: the G 50. The new manual transmission is in many respects identical or similar to that of the Porsche 959. Experience gained in developing the 959 is introduced here: easier shifting thanks to reduced shift linkage friction, relocation of main bearings, clutch actuation, etc. Also new is the fully synchromesh reverse gear, making it possible to engage reverse while still rolling forward. The four-plane shift pattern simplifies later development of a six-speed transmission.

5. Bodywork
No changes.

6. Equipment
All models with leather-covered shifter and leather shift boot.

7. Seats and trim
Turbos equipped with full power seats.

8. Heating system, air conditioning system
No changes.

9. Electrical system
Two rear fog lights for all models.

10. Miscellaneous
The 911 Carrera is available in a Club Sport version (Sport Package, M 637). This provides a higher engine rev limit, sport shocks, 7 and 8 J x 16 wheels, and stiffer engine mounts. Elimination of many interior and equipment items reduces empty weight to 1160 kg [2555 lbs.]; for comparison, empty weight of RoW 911 Carrera is 1210 kg [2665 lbs.]

4. Suspension
The new G 50 transmission necessitates a new torsion bar tube. Rear torsion bars have SAE fine-pitch splines.

Model year 1988 (J Program)

Type designation: **911 Carrera Coupe, Targa and Cabriolet**
911 Carrera Turbo Look Coupe, Targa and Cabriolet
911 Turbo Coupe, Targa and Cabriolet

Changes
No major changes to 911 Carrera or 911 Turbo. Clutch linings for all markets now asbestos free. Brake pads for Scandinavian markets now asbestos free.

As of January 1, 1988, Scandinavian countries outlaw the use of materials containing asbestos.

1. Engine
No significant engine changes.

2. Fuel and ignition systems
No changes.

3. Powertrain
Asbestos-free clutch linings (Porter Thermoid).

4. Suspension
Asbestos-free brake pads for Scandinavian countries. The Carrera is now fitted with Fuchs five-spoke forged alloy wheels, 7 J x 15 at the front, 8 J x 15 at the rear.

Back to basics: forged five-spoke light alloy wheels similar to those first used in 1967.

322

5. Bodywork
Improved gas pressure struts for engine & trunk lid.

6. Equipment
New on-board air compressor in tool kit. The steering wheel hub pad, which also serves as the horn button, includes a horn symbol.

U.S. law requires that the button or lever used to activate the horn must be marked for visual identification.

7. Seats and trim
Carrera has electric seat height adjustment standard.

8. Heating system, air conditioning system
No changes.

9. Electrical system
Temperature control system now with more sensitive electric adjustment (replacing vacuum servos). Electric motors for central locking system, with safety switch on center console. 911 Turbo with 8-speaker "sound package" as standard equipment.

10. Miscellaneous
The 911 Turbo is also offered in a "slant nose" version:
- front bodywork with flat fenders, retractable lights
- vents atop front fenders
- rocker panel fairings
- air inlets with strakes in rear fenders
- oil cooler with fan in rear air inlet
- more powerful 330 hp [243 kW] engine in Europe
- standard tires: Bridgestone RE 71 N0.

The shape of the front bodywork and fender vents are adapted from that of the successful Porsche 935 race car. In contrast to the plastic components offered by Porsche "tuners," the factory slant nose consists of two-side hot-dip galvanized steel panels. Corrosion prevention measures and painting of the bodywork are carried out on the Zuffenhausen production line, enabling Porsche to provide the same long-term warranty extended to regular production models. The slant nose found favor among customers for only a short time before becoming unfashionable.

Model year 1989 (K Program)

Type designation: 911 Carrera Coupe, Targa and Cabriolet and Speedster
911 Carrera Turbo Look Coupe, Targa, Cabriolet and Speedster
911 Carrera 4 Coupe
911 Turbo Coupe, Targa and Cabriolet

Changes
The 911 Carrera continues for 1989 with only minor changes. The 911 Turbo is fitted with the long-awaited five-speed transmission. A further body variant of the 911 Carrera is the Speedster. See Section 10 (Miscellaneous) for details. Beginning in January 1989, the body assembly line begins production of the all-wheel-drive 911 Carrera 4. Bodies for the 911 Carrera and Turbo, which are completely different from the new body of the Carrera 4, continue in production until the end of the model year (July 1989), at which point the "old" body plant is temporarily closed.

Assembly of the old body enters its last days in the old body plant. Porsche's new, modern body plant, on the other side of Federal Highway 10, is already producing the new 911 Carrera 4. The last cars to use the old basic body shell are 911 Speedsters.

After a short conversion period, the old Zuffenhausen body plant begins contract production of approximately 20 unfinished Mercedes-Benz 500 E bodies per day. In the so-called "Rösslebau," where the 959 had been built, the bodies, after painting and fitting at the Mercedes-Benz plant, are again returned to Porsche for installation of drivetrains and suspensions, and completed for delivery.

1. Engine

Engine types 930/20 and 930/25 for the 911 Carrera, as well as the 930/66 and 930/68 for the 911 Turbo, continue in production without any significant changes. The engine of the Carrera 4, Type M64/01, is based on the familiar Porsche six-cylinder powerplant. It displaces 3.6 liters and delivers 250 hp [184 kW] with or without catalytic converter.

Technical specifications for the Carrera 4 engine:

Application		Worldwide
Engine type		M64/01
Bore	(mm)	100
Stroke	(mm)	76.4
Displacement	(cc)	3600
Compression ratio		11.3:1
Fuel requirement	(RON)	95 +/- (Eurosuper)
Power output	(hp/kW)	250/184
at	(rpm)	6100
Torque	(Nm)	310
at	(rpm)	4800

+/- = unleaded. For markets where unleaded fuel is not yet available, vehicles are delivered without a catalytic converter and without a Lambda sonde (option M 150). Additional engine features:
- two spark plugs per cylinder (twin plug ignition)
- knock sensors
- exhaust passages in cylinder heads formed by ceramic port liners
- camshaft drive by means of duplex roller chains
- hydraulic chain tensioners
- separate drives for engine cooling fan & alternator
- oil cooler with two-stage fan in right front fender
- two-stage resonance induction system

The proven aluminum-silicon alloy crankcase remains largely unchanged, but the crankshaft has been completely redesigned. The new engine was developed expressly to take advantage of exhaust emissions controls and regulated catalyst technology. With a cylinder bore of 100 mm, twin plug ignition reaps benefits: two ignition sources in each combustion chamber result in more consistent combustion and lower pollutants in the exhaust stream even before it reaches the catalytic converter.

2. Fuel and ignition systems

Improved Digital Motor Electronics:
- sequential fuel injection
- knock sensors, one sensor per cylinder bank
- adaptive Lambda control
- new metal substrate catalyst
- electronically controlled fuel tank ventilation
- twin-plug ignition distributor with Hall effect triggering
- exhaust system made entirely of stainless steel

Knock sensors are now available for the air-cooled engines, as well. Since universal availability of unleaded 95 RON fuel is not yet guaranteed, knock sensors provide added protection against engine damage.

The 911 Carrera 4 is the first passenger car to be fitted with a metal substrate catalytic converter as standard equipment. Porsche conducted basic research and development on metal substrate catalysts. Advantages:
- *especially low flow restriction*
- *0.04 mm (0.0016 in.) thick stainless steel sheets provide 14% greater surface area*
- *faster "light off" after cold start*
- *improved high temperature behavior.*

3. Powertrain

911 Carrera: no changes to powertrain.
911 Turbo: new hydraulic clutch actuation, like 911 Carrera. New five-speed transmission G50/50, basically identical to G50/00 but reinforced in several areas.

911 Carrera 4: hydraulically actuated single dry plate clutch (F&S GMFZ 240), rubber-damped clutch disc (F&S GUD 240). New G64/00 drive system. The drive system of the 911 Carrera 4 consists of a fully synchromesh five-speed manual transmission with integral rear differential, as well as an integral transfer case for full-time all-wheel drive. Connection to the front differential is accomplished by a proven transaxle design, with a rigid torque tube carrying a central drive shaft. The five-speed manual transmission is assembled from existing G50 components, with additional parts for the transfer case and permanent all-wheel drive. The transfer case splits the engine torque, 31 percent going to the front axle, 69 percent to the rear. In the event of tire spin, this torque split can be altered in a fraction of a second by the central clutch. The range of front/rear torque split is 0:100% to 100:0%. Rear axle drive is integrated in the transmission housing, and includes a slip-sensitive Porsche clutch-type limited slip differential. This transverse limited slip differential provides a stabilizing yaw moment in cornering situations. If the ABS wheel sensors detect rear wheel spin, the limited slip differential can develop up to 1000 Nm of blocking torque in a fraction of a second.

The new five-speed transmission of the 911 Turbo results in improved acceleration performance, as the engine and therefore the turbocharger spins at higher rpm after each shift due to closer gear ratios.

The Porsche Dynamic All-Wheel Drive System (PDAS) includes a planetary gearbox to split torque between the front and rear axle. Under normal conditions, torque is distributed in such a way as to give the driver the impression of driving a rear-wheel-drive sports car. If the ABS sensors detect wheelspin at either the front or rear wheels, the central differential may be partially or fully locked. The PDAS system is based on the interaction between the transverse and longitudinal limited slip differentials.

4. Suspension

The 911 Carrera 4 rides on a completely new suspension:
- front suspension via MacPherson strut independent suspension with light alloy transverse arms
- rear suspension via light alloy semi-trailing arms
- power assisted rack and pinion steering
- front and rear coil springs
- dual-circuit brake system with hydraulic brake booster
- ventilated front and rear disc brakes
- anti-lock brake system (ABS)
- cast alloy wheels front 6 J x 16 H2, ET 52.3*
  rear   8 J x 16 H2, ET 52.3*
- tires front 205/55 ZR 16 N1
  rear   225/50 ZR 16 N1

* ET = offset

The Turbo suspension also undergoes changes. The center of the rear torsion bar tube is modified to make room for the five-speed transmission. Rear torsion bars machined with SAE splines. Torsion bar diameter increased to 27 mm (from 26 mm). The anti-roll bar diameter is reduced from 20 to 18 mm to reduce oversteer. Bilstein gas pressure shock absorbers front and rear with degressive damping characteristics (improved comfort). Asbestos-free brake pads for all Porsche vehicles.

Except for the 959, the Carrera 4 is the first Porsche 911 which does not employ torsion bars. Power steering and ABS brakes are standard on the Carrera 4.

5. Bodywork
While the body of the Carrera 4 resembles that of the previous 911 Carrera, it has been completely redesigned. Front and rear bumpers have been integrated into the body shape, the rear spoiler extends automatically, and the car is fitted with a smooth undertray. The body structure and the floorpan are modified for the all-wheel drive system.

Special attention has been paid to overall vehicle aerodynamics. The absolute drag coefficient, C_d, of 0.32 is not the deciding factor; C_d multiplied by the frontal area of the car, A_f, in this case 1.79 m², results in the actual drag value, 0.57. The fact that aerodynamic lift, C_l, is nearly zero at all speeds is a further source of pride for Porsche's aerodynamicists. The smooth body lines did not immediately appeal, but soon gained market acceptance.

6. Equipment
The shaft of the Carrera 4 rear windshield wiper passes directly through the rear window.

7. Seats and trim
The interior trim of the Carrera 4 has been completely redesigned. The seats are similar to those of Porsche's other production models.

8. Heating system, air conditioning system
The Carrera 4 is available with two different systems. Option M 573 provides an automatic heating and air conditioning system. Seat heating is adjustable by means of thumbwheels. The seat side bolsters are also heated.

9. Electrical system
The electrical system of the 911 Carrera 4 is completely different from that of earlier Carrera models:
- central electronics are located in the trunk
- all instruments newly designed, with backlighting
- central warning light and acoustic signal for warning lights
- electrothermal fuel level gauge
- completely new wiring harness
- the alarm system of the 928 is adapted for the Carrera 4: arming is accomplished by locking the door. Light emitting diodes (LEDs) in the door lock buttons flash to indicate that the system is armed.

10. Miscellaneous
Expansion of the six-cylinder model range with the addition of the 911 Speedster:
- based on the 911 Carrera Turbo Look, but also available in a "narrow body" version
- shorter windshield
- manually operated top
- composite cover completely conceals stowed top
- powerplant is the 3.2 liter Carrera engine, available with or without catalytic converter

The dream of many Porsche drivers becomes reality: fans of open-air motoring may opt for the 911 Speedster, designed primarily for good-weather driving conditions. In contrast to the 911 Cabriolet, which is perfectly usable in winter conditions thanks to its all-weather top, the 911 Speedster is fitted with only a rudimentary top.

Model Year 1990 (L Program)

Type designation: 911 Carrera 2 Coupe, Targa and Cabriolet
911 Carrera 4 Coupe, Targa and Cabriolet

Changes
Model reduction at Porsche: the rear-drive Carrera 2 is built alongside the all-wheel-drive 911 Carrera 4. With the exception of all-wheel-drive technology, the Carrera 2 shares major components with the Carrera 4. Turbo, Turbo Look and Speedster models are not available during the 1990 model year. The Carrera 2 is available with the Tiptronic transmission, an intelligent drive system with load-dependent shift points.

The 911 Carrera 2 is new for the 1990 model year and represents a logical expansion of the six-cylinder program: a vehicle without all-wheel drive. The 911 Carrera 2 is also available with a new drive system which permits up- and downshifts without interruption of power flow to the wheels.

1. Engine
No significant changes to the Type M64/01 engine. For the German market, only vehicles with three-way catalytic converters and Lambda control are offered.

"Eurosuper unleaded" is finally available everywhere in Germany.

2. Fuel and ignition systems
No changes to the DME, with the exception of the Carrera 2, where the DME and Tiptronic control unit work together.

3. Powertrain
The 911 Carrera 2 may be equipped with the Tiptronic drivetrain as of January 1990. Like a conventional automatic transmission, the four-speed Tiptronic transmission permits automatic up- and downshifts without interrupting the power flow to the drive wheels. If, however, the shift lever is moved from the D position to the rightmost shift plane, rocking the lever in either direction easily and quickly selects the next desired gear. Rocking the lever back results in a downshift, while momentarily moving it forward immediately shifts up a gear. The 911 Carrera 2 may alternately be equipped with a five-speed manual transmission (G50/03). The 911 Carrera 4 is only available with a five-speed manual transmission, Type G64/00. All models of the 911 Carrera 4 and 911 Carrera 2 equipped with manual transmissions are fitted with a dual-mass flywheel to reduce annoying transmission noises at low engine rpm. The system employs a rubber-damped flywheel developed in cooperation with the Carl Freudenberg company.

Porsche's development of the Tiptronic drive system is based on racing experience. Over the course of several years, a drive system known as "PDK," for Porsche Doppel-Kupplung (Porsche Dual Clutch) was tested in Type 962 race cars. PDK was the predecessor to an entire generation of automatic racing transmissions, which have the advantage of shifting up or down without interrupting the power flow to the drive wheels, i.e. without lifting from the throttle pedal. On the 962 race car, shifts were initiated by means of electrical switches on the steering wheel. The Tiptronic shifts when the shift lever is moved.

An engine's power strokes and firing order result in rpm variations which excite torsional vibrations in the drivetrain. At low rpm, these vibrations result in driveline clatter and rattling noises. To avoid this, before they are introduced into the transmission, vibrations must be reduced to the point where they are no longer objectionable. This is achieved by the dual-mass flywheel.

4. Suspension
The suspension of the 911 Carrera 2 is basically identical to that of the 911 Carrera 4. The rear brakes of the 911 Carrera 2 are equipped with dual-piston calipers; the 911 Carrera 4 has four-piston rear calipers. Wheels are identical for both models: cast light alloy "Design 90" wheels. The wheel width in inches and offset in mm (for example, 8 and 52 respectively) are cast into the wheel, immediately left and right of the tire valve. Forged alloy wheels (Disc Wheel Design) are available as option M 395.

On the 911 Carrera 4, the brake power assist is achieved by means of a high pressure hydraulic system. By contrast, the power booster of the 911 Carrera 2 employs engine manifold vacuum.

5. Bodywork
The long awaited and complex all-electric top mechanism is standard equipment for all Cabriolets. U.S. and Canadian cars are equipped with driver and front passenger airbags.

Excellent experience with airbags in the U.S.-market 944 Turbo prompt the decision to equip all 1990 U.S. specification Porsches with airbags. Porsche is of the opinion that the driver as well as the passenger must be protected by airbags.

327

a remotely mounted 1.7 kW starter is installed. All six-cylinder cars are fitted with a switch on the center console to extend or retract the rear spoiler.

Remote headlight aiming becomes mandatory in Germany. The trip computer provides the following information:

- distance to empty
- trip odometer
- average fuel consumption
- digital speed readout
- average speed
- outside air temperature

6. Equipment
With the exception of the Cabriolet, three-way automatic safety belts for rear-seat occupants are standard equipment.

7. Seats and trim
No changes.

8. Heating and air conditioning system
No changes for the Carrera 4; systems identical to those of the Carrera 2.

9. Electrical system
All vehicles equipped with remote headlight adjustment. Tiptronic-equipped vehicles are fitted with a trip computer as standard equipment. The electronic speedometer is no longer driven by impulses from the transmission, but rather by wheel impulses from the ABS sensors. Because of the dual-mass flywheel,

10. Miscellaneous
In addition to the production Carrera 2, Porsche builds "Carrera Cup" cars for racing purposes, based on the standard production 911 Carrera 2.

- engines are selected at the plant for identical power output
- no air filter
- no dual-mass flywheel
- engine control units are tested for identical performance and sealed
- brake system includes large ventilated rotors and the four-piston aluminum calipers of the 911 Turbo. Hydraulic brake booster and ABS.
- alloy wheels with asymmetric safety hump to prevent separation of tire from rim in the event of air loss
- welded-in steel roll bar (made by Matter).

Model Year 1991 (M Program)

Type designation: 911 Carrera 2 Coupe, Targa and Cabriolet
911 Carrera 4 Coupe, Targa and Cabriolet
911 Turbo Coupe

Changes
The 911 Carrera 2 and 4 carry over to the 1991 model year with only minor changes. The 911 Turbo returns, with a three-way catalytic converter, Lambda sensor and 320 hp [235 kW]. With the re-introduction of the Turbo, the 911 model line is again highlighted by the rich tradition of its flagship model. Despite similarities in major body structure to the normally aspirated models, the Turbo-typical appearance and widened fenders have been retained. The large rear wing houses an enlarged intercooler.

1. Engine

New pistons are installed in the Carrera's Type M64/01 engine. Cylinder head sealing has also been modified. Spark plug change intervals have been doubled to 40,000 km [24,000 miles]. All models of 911 Turbo, worldwide, use a new engine, Type M30/69. Following are the most important engine specifications:

Application		worldwide
Engine type		M30/69
Bore	(mm)	97
Stroke	(mm)	74.4
Displacement	(cc)	3299
Compression ratio		7.0:1
Fuel requirement	(RON)	95 unleaded
Power	(hp/kW)	320/235
at	(rpm)	5750
Torque	(Nm)	450
at	(rpm)	4500

Further improvements to the Turbo engine:
- new thermally optimized cylinders
- stainless steel cylinder head gasket
- oil filter in main oil stream
- separate alternator (115 A) and cooling fan belt drives

Common Market regulations now necessitate a three-way catalytic converter and lambda control for the Turbo.

2. Fuel and ignition systems

The new Turbo engine is fitted with the familiar, proven K-Jetronic system with Lambda control used on the Turbo USA. Electronic map ignition, metal substrate catalytic converter and a larger intercooler permit increased power while reducing exhaust emissions.

As all 911 models now use unleaded fuel, which results in considerably reduced combustion chamber deposits and reduced spark plug electrode erosion, the permissible service life of spark plugs is doubled.

3. Powertrain

No changes to the drive trains of the Carrera model line. Dual-mass flywheel for the 911 Turbo. However, its design differs considerably from that of the system used in the Carrera models: instead of an elastic rubber vibration damper, the 911 employs steel springs and mechanical friction dampers. The system is manufactured by LUK. Also new is a five-speed manual transmission, Type G50/52, with a ZF mechanical limited slip differential as standard equipment. The new transmission is based on the G50/50 unit of the earlier Turbo model, and is functionally identical to the 911 Carrera 2 transmission. In contrast to previous systems, which achieved identical lockup factors of about 40 percent under acceleration as well as braking, the new unit has different lockup factors when under load or braking:
- lockup under load: 20%
- lockup under braking: 100%

Reducing the lockup factor under load to 20 percent appreciably improves cornering behavior and increases traction compared to a conventional differential without limited slip. Increasing the lockup factor under braking to 100 percent reduces trailing throttle yaw moments in corners (oversteer effect) and has a stabilizing effect on the car.

4. Suspension

At the rear, the 911 Carrera models are fitted with a thicker (20 mm) anti-roll bar. Although the suspension of the new 911 Turbo is based on that of the 911 Carrera series, it has undergone further development in view of the 911 Turbo's higher performance potential:
- MacPherson independent front suspension with light alloy transverse arms
- rear wheels independently suspended by track correcting light alloy semi-trailing arms
- power assisted rack and pinion steering
- front and rear coil springs
- dual circuit brake system with hydraulic power booster
- anti-lock brake system (ABS)

Front anti-roll bar 21 mm, rear 22 mm. New "Cup Design" pressure cast light alloy wheels.
front 7 J x 17 H2 ET 55,* 205/55 ZR 17 tires
rear 9 J x 17 H2 ET 55,* 255/40 ZR 17 tires
* ET = offset

For the first time, Porsche approves a 17-inch wheel for production car use. The aspect ratio of 40 for the Turbo's rear tires is also new territory for production cars.

329

5. Bodywork

As of February 1, 1991, all left-hand-drive Porsche vehicles are fitted with driver and front passenger airbags as standard equipment. Structure of the Turbo raw body shell is identical to that of the 911 Carrera models. Front and rear fenders and attached body parts have been modified in keeping with the Turbo's wider exterior skin.

- drag coefficient C_d 0.32
- frontal area A 1.89 m²
- actual aerodynamic drag C_d x A 0.68
- lift coefficient C_l nearly zero

The Turbo is fitted with a new outside mirror design: oval in shape, improved appearance, reduced drag, lower wind noise, lighter weight.

The management decision to fit all left-hand-drive cars with dual airbags is based on the principle that "At Porsche safety is not an option; it is standard equipment."

6. Equipment
No changes.

7. Seats and trim
Unlocking of the rear seat backs is by means of a push button release. The dashboard of the 911 Turbo is covered in leather to match the upholstery color.

8. Heating and air conditioning system
The 911 Turbo has two rear heating blowers in its rear fenders. From the heat exchangers onward, the warm air system is identical to that of the 911 Carrera models. The air conditioning system is nearly identical to the Carrera's.

9. Electrical system
Modified anti-theft alarm control units for all models. The 911 Turbo is fitted with a trip computer as standard equipment, which also provides a digital readout of turbo boost pressure.

Model year 1992 (N Program)

Type designation: **911 Carrera 2 Coupe, Targa, Cabriolet and Cabriolet Turbo Look**
911 Carrera RS and 911 RS America Coupe
911 Carrera 4 Coupe, Targa and Cabriolet
911 Turbo Coupe

Changes

For the 1992 model year, changes to the 911 Carrera 2, 911 Carrera 4 and 911 Turbo are limited to minor modifications made in the interest of technological progress and improved quality. All models: elimination of engine oil and filter change, valve lash adjustment and transmission oil level check at first scheduled service (3000 - 4000 km). The 911 Carrera 2 Cabriolet Turbo Look is a new model for 1992, with suspension, brakes, 17-inch wheels and fender flares identical to those of the 911 Turbo. Engine, clutch and transmission are the same as those of the 911 Carrera 2. Also new in the lineup is the 911 Carrera RS, a coupe with improved performance capability conceived for racing applications in Group N or Group GT. As the 911 Carrera RS is not certified for the U.S. market, a special model, the 911 RS America, is built exclusively for American customers. This is equipped with the drivetrain technology of the 911 Carrera 2, but has more sporting suspension tuning, 17-inch wheels and a fixed rear spoiler.

Extensive testing and precision manufacturing methods enable Porsche to eliminate the first scheduled oil change, valve adjustment, and other service procedures. This results in lower maintenance costs for the customer, and helps to preserve the environment by eliminating one more batch of waste oil and used oil filter cartridge. After the successful 911 Cup racing series of the previous year, Porsche makes the 911 Carrera RS available as a "civilian" model. With this model, Porsche travels a new road: away from comfort and convenience, and toward the pure driving machine. Everything that is not absolutely essential is deleted. For the basic version, the 7.5 liter windshield washer reservoir is reduced to only 1 liter.

1. Engine

911 Carrera 2 and 4: no significant changes
911 Turbo: no significant changes
911 Carrera RS: higher output M64/03 engine
- matched pistons and cylinders
- sport flywheel for base model
- alternator and cooling fan driven by common belt
- firmer rubber mounts replace hydrolastic engine mounts

Major engine specifications:

Application		worldwide, except U.S.A.
Engine type		M64/03
Displacement	(cc)	3600
Compression ratio		11.3:1
Fuel requirement	(RON)	98 unleaded
Power output	(hp/kW)	260/191
at	(rpm)	6100
Torque	(Nm)	325
at	(rpm)	4800

2. Fuel and ignition systems

911 Carrera 2 and 4: No changes.
911 Turbo: changes to Lambda control unit, warmup regulator, new Bosch WR6 DPO spark plugs. 911 Carrera RS: DME control unit altered in comparison to 911 Carrera 2 and 4; more ignition advance, 98 octane fuel required. If 95 RON fuel is used, the knock sensor modifies the ignition advance accordingly (and reduces power output).

Although the engine of the RS resembles a racing powerplant, it should not be forgotten that it is equipped with a Lambda sensor and three-way catalytic converter. Improvements to the Tiptronic include
- *improved reaction of shift components during coasting kickdowns*
- *kickdowns to first gear are possible below 55 km/h (34 mph) for engine braking effect*

- *special warmup program: first acceleration after cold start always in first gear*

Keylock: removal of ignition key is only possible with the transmission in Park. Insurance against inadvertently letting the vehicle roll away. Shiftlock: once the ignition has been activated, the gear selector can only be moved out of Park while the service brakes are applied.

3. Powertrain

911 Carrera 2 and 4: clutch pressure increased to 10,600 - 11,500 N [2400 - 2600 lbs.]

The 911 Turbo pedal cluster, which includes an assist spring to reduce clutch pedal effort, is now also used for normally aspirated models. The G64/00 transmission of the Carrera 4 incorporates improved friction discs for its transverse limited slip differential. Tiptronic A50/02 drivetrain:
- transmission mount in front transmission cover identical to 911 Carrera 2 manual transmission mount
- controlled-friction limited slip clutch discs, improved shifting comfort
- U.S. vehicles equipped with different final drive ratio, 9:32, and unique A50/03 Tiptronic drivetrain
- Tiptronic control unit modified for improved comfort and sporting driving style
- indication of selected gear in speedometer
- keylock and shiftlock safety systems for U.S. and Canadian vehicles; added security with shift lever/ignition lock and shift lever lock, respectively

The 911 Carrera RS, developed for racing purposes, is built in three different variations: (1) The basic version, road licensing possible, with minimal comfort. (2) The touring version, road licensing possible, with added comfort. (3) The racing version (NGT), road use not possible, intended solely for competition use. The base version is fitted with a lightweight flywheel, and its clutch disc contains steel spring vibration dampers instead of the dual-mass flywheel. The "touring version" is equipped with the dual-mass flywheel of the Carrera 2. The "sport version" has a rigid sintered clutch disc and lightened flywheel. All three versions are fitted with the five-speed G50/10 transmission, which differs from the G50/03 (Carrera 2) transmission by taller first and second gear ratios. Additional transmission differences:

- harder rubber center mount (60 Shore hardness) in the front transmission cover
- limited slip differential as standard equipment (lockup factor under braking up to 100 percent, 20 percent under power, like 911 Turbo)
- steel synchronizer rings, altered shift sleeves
- 3.4:1 shifter ratio replaces 4.0:1 for sportier feel

All German-market vehicles are the "base version." To keep weight and rotating masses as low as possible, some transmission noise at low rpm was considered an acceptable tradeoff. Positive experience gained with the 911 Turbo is applied to other models: like the Turbo, the RS is fitted with a limited slip differential whose lockup factors under load and braking are different.

4. Suspension
Altered ZF power steering for the 911 Carrera 2 and 4, with steering stops to accommodate 17-inch wheels. Identical rear coil springs (33 N/mm) for both Carrera models. The U.S. market Carrera 2 is fitted with alloy four-piston brake calipers like those of the Carrera 4 and a 55/5 brake pressure reduction valve (switching pressure 55 bar). Cup Design 16-inch cast alloy wheels are standard equipment, optional 17-inch wheels as follows:
front wheels 7 J x 17 AH* ET 55, with 205/50 ZR 17 tires; rear wheels 8 J x 17 AH* ET 52, with 255/40 ZR 17 tires

* AH = asymmetric hump in outer half of rim prevents tire from slipping into the deep bed of the wheel in the event of pressure loss. A high degree of steerability, directional stability and braking ability are retained. ET = offset.

911 Carrera RS: suspension completely reworked, 40 mm lower ride height. Springs, shock absorbers and anti-roll bars are stiffer and result in uncompromisingly sporty ride and handling. Non-assisted rack and pinion steering. Front brake system taken from the 911 Turbo, rear brakes from the Carrera Cup cars. Hydraulic brake power assist. Cast magnesium wheels; front wheels 7 1/2 J x 17 AH, ET 55, with 205/50 ZR 17 tires; rear wheels 9 J x 17 AH, ET 55, with 255/40 ZR 17 tires

The expensive and complex manufacture of magnesium wheels for the Carrera RS (specific gravity 1.74) results in a weight reduction of 10.6 kg per car. Comparison of empty weights (to DIN 70020):
911 Carrera 2 coupe   1350 kg [2974 lbs.]
911 Carrera RS   1220 kg [2687 lbs.]

5. Bodywork
911 Carrera 2 and 4: No changes.
911 Turbo: No changes.
911 Carrera 2 Cabriolet Turbo Look: fenders, front and rear valances taken from 911 Turbo, with extending rear spoiler of 911 Carrera 2 & 4.

6. Equipment

Full leather interior for 911 Carrera 2 Turbo Look Cabriolet. Oval outside mirrors. 911 Carrera RS: base model without undercoating, only three year warranty against rust perforation. Touring version like Carrera 2, with undercoating and long-term warranty. No airbag system available for 911 Carrera RS. Light alloy trunk lid. Oval outside mirrors.

Six-point harnesses and mandatory helmet use in racing events compensates for lack of airbags.

7. Seats and trim

911 Carrera RS: base model, racing seats for driver and front passenger, prepared for six-point safety harness. Touring version with sport seats and electric seat height adjustment.

8. Heating system, air conditioning system

All six-cylinder cars fitted with a new heating and air conditioning control unit. 911 Carrera 2 Cabriolet Turbo Look has an air conditioning system as standard equipment.

9. Electrical system

New radio generation: "Symphony RDS" (RDS = Radio Data System).

Model year 1993 (P Program)

Type designation: 911 Carrera 2 Coupe, Targa, Cabriolet and Cabriolet Turbo Look
911 Carrera 4 Coupe, Targa, Cabriolet and Coupe Turbo Look
911 RS America Coupe
911 Turbo 3.6 Coupe

Changes

911 Carrera 2 and 4 carry over into the 1993 model year with minor changes. After a small production run of the 911 Turbo "S," with 381 hp [280 kW], the 911 Turbo 3.6 begins production in January 1993. The Turbo 3.6 has identical cylinder bore and stroke dimensions as the concurrent normally aspirated models. Power output 360 hp [265 kW]. For the first time, the Turbo is fitted with 18-inch wheels.

The 911 Turbo S is built by the "Exclusive Department" (Special Order Department) in Zuffenhausen. It is based on modifications made to an already completed production 911 Turbo which is differentiated by higher boost pressure, altered ignition map and body and wheel changes.

1. Engine

As of 1993, all Porsche engines are factory filled with Shell TMO Synthetic, a fully synthetic engine oil, SAE 5W-40. No significant engine changes for 911 Carrera 2 & 4. 911 Turbo 3.6: major components of the Turbo's 3.6 liter engine, including the crank train, cylinders and other components, are identical to those of the concurrently produced Carrera engines. Pistons, camshafts and the further optimized K-Jetronic injection system are matched to the particular circumstances of the turbocharged engine.

Major engine specifications:

Application		worldwide
Engine type		M64/50
Stroke	(mm)	76.4
Bore	(mm)	100
Displacement	(cc)	3600
Compression ratio		7.5:1
Fuel requirement	(RON)	95 unleaded
Power output	(hp/kW)	360/265
at	(rpm)	5500
Torque	(Nm)	520
at	(rpm)	4200

Additional Turbo engine features:
- oil filter in main oil stream
- crankshaft torsion damper
- stainless steel cylinder head ring seals
- chain drive and chain housings identical to normally aspirated Carrera
- new camshaft and cam timing
- altered wastegate

Fully synthetic engine oil has the advantage of a very wide viscosity range; compared to conventional (mineral) oils, it flows more easily in winter service,

333

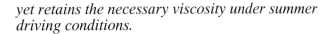

yet retains the necessary viscosity under summer driving conditions.

For the Turbo engine, increased power output via larger engine displacement, also results in massive torque: 520 Nm [383 ft.-lbs.], a value unmatched even by the 928 GTS with its 5.4 liter engine.

2. Fuel and ignition systems

All six-cylinder models: a 92-liter fuel tank is available as option M 545. 911 Turbo 3.6: in keeping with the larger displacement and higher power output, the K-Jetronic fuel injection system and the ignition system were modified in several areas. The engine is fitted with auxiliary air injection; auxiliary air is diverted via a selector valve to the exhaust ports or to the catalytic converter, depending on conditions.

The 92 liter fuel tank is a customer request with particular relevance to those who drive their 911

Turbos at high speeds over long distances, reducing the annoying frequency of fuel stops.

3. Powertrain

911 Carrera 2 only: application of the LUK dual-mass flywheel of the 911 Turbo, which uses steel coil springs to eliminate engine low-rpm variations. All Tiptronic models are now fitted with the keylock and shiftlock security systems introduced a year earlier on U.S. models. 911 Carrera 4 only: change of clutch pack discs for longitudinal and transverse limited slip differentials to more comfortable Valeo clutch discs. 911 Turbo 3.6: the G50/52 five-speed manual transmission of the Turbo 3.3 is carried over without modifications.

The coil-spring dual mass flywheel provides more reliable power transmission but cannot yet be applied to the equally powerful Carrera 4 because its all-wheel drive system results in different torsion-

al vibrations which can result in transmission noise in certain rpm ranges.

4. Suspension
All Porsche vehicles factory filled with DOT 4 - 200 brake fluid. Advantages: increase in recommended brake fluid change intervals to three years, higher boiling point, very low moisture absorption.
911 Carrera 2 only: installation of four-piston brake calipers for rear wheels is now worldwide.
911 Turbo 3.6: suspension similar to Turbo 3.3, but with 20 mm lower ride height and very sporting suspension tuning. The vehicle is fitted with a front shock tower brace. Front suspension: newly optimized MacPherson struts with dual tube gas pressure shocks. Rear suspension: light alloy semi-trailing arms, spring and suspension struts modified in keeping with higher performance potential. Wheels and tires: the 911 Turbo 3.6 is equipped with three-piece Cup Design 18-inch light alloy wheels. Front: 8 J x 18 H2 ET 52 wheels with 225/40 ZR 18 tires; rear 10 J x 18 H2 ET 61 wheels with 265/35 ZR 18 tires.

For years, DOT 4 - 200 was used in works Type 962 racing efforts, as well as all 911 Carrera Cup vehicles. Racing experience was applied directly to production models.

Similarly, for the suspension of the 911 Turbo 3.6, lessons learned in racing were carried over to production. The Carrera Cup suspension tuning was directly applied to the Turbo.

At Porsche, the 18-inch wheel has now made its way from racing to production. The three-piece wheels and the tire aspect ratio of 35 represent new territory for Porsche production vehicles.

5. Bodywork
All right-hand drive vehicles are fitted with a driver side airbag, worldwide. The entire Vehicle Identification Number (VIN) is also visible from outside the vehicle, mounted on the A-pillar and visible through the windshield.

For years, placing the VIN number in a location where it is easily visible to police has been standard practice for all cars sold in the U.S. With this step, Porsche increases anti-theft security for all other markets as well.

6. Equipment
No changes.

7. Seats and trim
No changes.

8. Heating system, air conditioning system
All Porsche air conditioning systems use a CFC-free refrigerant, R 134a. This necessitates modification of all air conditioning components. Porsche is probably the first car maker to make the switch to CFC-free refrigerant for all of its production models, as early as July/August 1992.

9. Electrical system
New radio model "London RDM 42" with CD Tuner and Key Card to reduce risk of theft.

Model year 1994 (R Program)

Type designation: 911 Carrera 2 Cabriolet and Speedster
911 Carrera 4 Turbo Look special edition
911 RS America Coupe
911 Turbo 3.6 Coupe
911 Carrera (993) Coupe and Cabriolet

Changes
The basic 911 has been redesigned: new front and rear sections, higher output engine, six-speed manual transmission, completely new rear suspension, new interior. Initially, the "new Carrera" is available with rear wheel drive only. As of the end of 1993, due to production considerations, the previous Coupe, Targa, Cabriolet, Speedster and Turbo body variants can no longer be produced concurrently with the new design.

The first major changes to the 911 Carrera models, with the internal type designation 993: clearly visible body changes in the front and rear sections result in a "corporate identity" in common with the other Porsche models, the 968 and 928.

1. Engine

Power output of the M64/05 engine for the "new Carrera" is raised to 272 hp (200 kW). This is achieved by the following modifications:

- torsionally stiffer crankshaft
- improved and lightened connecting rods
- lighter, improved pistons, reduced oil consumption
- pressure cast aluminum cylinders with nickel-silicon bore surfaces
- larger valves and passages in cylinder heads
- hydraulic valve lash adjustment on rocker arms
- cam shafts matched to new engine, with altered valve timing
- additional main flow oil filter (micro filter, 20 microns, = 0.0008 in.)

The power increase was achieved without changing displacement or compression ratio. Previously, the M64/01 engine types provided well over 250 hp, and in some cases more than 260 hp as installed at the factory.

2. Fuel and ignition systems

The sequential fuel injection and the ignition system of the previous engine were carried over. The Digital Motor Electronics (DME) were improved (now version M 2.10.1). This results in lower fuel consumption, reduced exhaust emissions and smoother operation. Intake air metering is accomplished by means of a hot film air mass sensor. Increased power output is made possible by a completely new exhaust system with considerably reduced back pressure:

- improved exhaust manifold, part of heat exchanger
- mixing chamber with Lambda sensor downstream of manifolds combines exhaust gas streams from left and right cylinder banks
- separate entry of exhaust gas streams into two (left and right side) metal substrate catalytic converters
- post-catalyst exhaust gas directed to two mufflers located left and right of engine

The modified exhaust system is a case of having one's cake and eating it too:

- *lower exhaust back pressure results in appreciable increase in engine power*
- *the large volume mufflers, to either side of the engine, reduce drive-by noise levels below 75 dB (A), which, as of October 1995, is the European Common Market noise limit.*

3. Powertrain

Intensive ventilation of the bell housing by means of radial vanes in the pressure plate and vents in the area of the diaphragm spring retaining ring. Hot/cold air exchange by means of openings in transmission housing. G50/20 six-speed manual transmission matched to engine characteristics. Dual-cone synchros on first and second gears result in appreciable reduction in shift effort. Pinion shaft and ring gear are ground and matched after hardening for lower operating noise. Thinwall pressure-cast light alloy housings result in same overall weight as the previous five-speed transmission. Tiptronic A50/04 automatic transmission: improved shift strategies within the individual shift maps. Software in the control unit has been modified for increased comfort as well as more spirited performance. In the manual mode, downshifts can be accomplished while braking. An Automatic Brake Differential (ABD) is optional for both transmission systems. This traction aid applies the service brake to a spinning drive wheel at speeds below 70 km/h [43 mph].

Reducing the operating temperature of clutch components, particularly the clutch disc, results in a higher coefficient of friction between the clutch lining and the flywheel and pressure plate. This improves clutch reliability.

The 270 km/h [168 mph] top speed of the car resulted in such a tall top gear that the steps between the individual gears of a five-speed transmission would have been too great; an upshift would have placed engine revs too low in the succeeding gear for satisfactory acceleration. More gears mean better matching of the selected gear to the driving situation.

ABD can be quite helpful in starting up on slick surfaces; generally, if a wheel spins, traction also breaks down on the opposite wheel. As the Tiptronic drivetrain is not available with a conventional limited slip differential, ABD offers a useful traction aid.

4. Suspension
Redesigned Carrera 2 front suspension, with light alloy suspension bearings. Negative steering radius of -11.5 mm (previously 0). Modified power steering system results in better straight line stability and more sensitive steering. Subframe-mounted multi-link rear suspension enables higher lateral acceleration values. Appreciably lower road noise within the cabin. Wider wheels all around and 20 mm wider tires at the rear:
front tires 205/55 ZR 16 on 7J x 16 ET 55 wheels
rear tires 245/45 ZR 16 on 9J x 16 ET 70 wheels.
Reinforced and improved brake system, cross-drilled brake discs. New ABS 5 anti-lock braking system:
- shorter braking distances, especially on uneven surfaces
- better deceleration characteristics for the duration of the braking event

The ABS 5 system is fitted with a sensor which continuously monitors road roughness during a braking event. Appreciably shorter braking distances on rough roads are possible by varying ABS action during braking.

5. Bodywork
New front and rear bodywork. Lower inclination for special headlights in front fenders, lower, wider appearance to rear section of car. Rear quarter windows mounted flush with bodywork. Simplified top actuation for Cabriolet: the electric top mechanism is operable when the car is stopped and the parking brake applied.

Previously, the engine had to be turned off and, with the vehicle at a standstill, the ignition switch had to be returned to the "run" position before the top could be opened or closed.

6. Equipment
Modified airbag steering wheel. Altered steering column stalks. User-friendly heating controls. Doors openable from inside even when locked.

A contribution to safety: often, the car was locked by its occupants using the electric locking switch. In the event of an emergency, opening the doors could

only be accomplished after again pressing the locking switch on the center console.

7. Seats and trim
Only minor changes to seats. Completely new door panels with different stereo speaker locations.

8. Heating system, air conditioning system
User-friendly heating and air conditioning system. Push button for maximum cooling of vehicle interior. Heater flaps close when in reverse gear. Rear window defrost switches to an energy-saving setting after 12 minutes.

The "Max cool" button delivers the full cooling capability of the air conditioning system to the cabin, via center and side air outlets, regardless of the position of the conventional climate control knobs.

9. Electrical system
Combined central locking and alarm system. New radio model, Blaupunkt Bremen RCM 43. Completely redesigned windshield wiper system:

- wiper arm pivots relocated toward center of windshield
- considerably larger wiped area
- excellent wiping action ensured at high speeds

Modular wiring harness: a basic harness, plus additional vehicle-specific harnesses. Headlights take advantage of new lighting technology and improved light output; an ellipsoid H1 headlight for low beam and a variable focus reflector system for high beam are incorporated in a single housing. Front and rear light units are integrated into the new body shape.

The development goal for the new headlights was to exceed the excellent light output of the 928, which has an inherent advantage in having higher-mounted headlights.

10. Miscellaneous
Production startup of the "new Carrera Cabriolet" began in January 1994, along with new Cup cars for racing activities.

338

Production Numbers of Porsche Six-Cylinder Models

Year	901	911/964* Coupe	911/993 Coupe	911/964 Targa	911/964 Cabriolet Speedster	911/993 Cabriolet	912/912E Coupe Targa	930/964 Turbo Coupe	930/964 Turbo Targa	930/964 Turbo Cabriolet	906	914/6**	959
1963	13												
1964		230											
1965		3154					6401						
1966		3724		10			9325				54		
1967		3222		2323			5429						
1968		6039		3089			5501						
1969		9107		3493			2579					20	
1970		9280		4749								72	
1971		5817		4789								34	
1972		8688		5566								236	
1973		9560		5855									
1974		6148		3761				7					
1975		4643		3270			873	284	1				
1976		6015		4768			1216	1174					
1977		6642		5050				1422					
1978		4719		3564				1257					
1979		5333		3607				2052					
1980		5010		3603				840					
1981		5458		3592				761					
1982		6199		4124	337			1027					
1983		5077		2267	5000			1080					
1984		5604		3123	2303			881					
1985		6756		3900	3354			1028					
1986		6733		3663	4654			2773	1	3			1
1987		6904		3583	4019			2481	114	528			60
1988		5362		2094	3252			2128	127	782			223
1989		10232		1105	4851			2204	56	330			
1990		10705		2744	7217								
1991		8232		1109	4476			3298					
1992		6243		457	3053			618					
1993		2878	2368	238	2149	22		1350					
Total	**13**	**183714**	**2368**	**89496**	**44665**	**22**	**31324**	**26665**	**299**	**1643**	**54**	**3352**	**284**

* Of these, beginning with the 1990 model year, a total of 10047 examples with Tiptronic transmission and 17767 Carrera 4.
** Not including 11 examples of Type 916.
Note: 912 and 912E models have four-cylinder engines.

Porsche 911 by the numbers
Technical specifications

Technical specifications for all Porsche 911 models, beginning with the first production cars of 1964 up to and including the 1994 model year (including the Type 993 Carrera) have been collected from numerous factory documents, such as, annual service information, specification books, and owner's manuals.

Due to rapidly changing exhaust gas regulations and fuel octane changes in smaller markets (i.e. Sweden or Australia), engines for these markets underwent engine, fuel system and gear ratio modifications to permit certification in those countries. For space reasons, not all variations can be covered in this book. Therefore, as in the case of the model chronology, vehicles for the German and American market take precedence.

Special attention was given to the capacities and specifications of engine and transmission oil for older models, as today these must often be replaced by more modern products. In general, it can safely be said that modern multigrade engine oils with their broad viscosity range are suitable for older cars. Naturally, the single-viscosity oils approved when the cars were new are also usable – insofar as they are still available. Care should be exercised when filling an older car, which has been operated with an unknown oil, with a modern oil. Modern oils contain detergents which loosen and suspend engine oil and dirt deposits. This can cause an older car to suffer blocked arteries after an oil change, with plugged oil passages and increased wear of moving parts due to abrasive deposits carried in the oil, and possibly result in engine damage. In such cases, several oil and filter changes should be carried out in the first 1000 km [600 miles].

In the case of transmission oils, a somewhat different but equally critical situation results when modern transmission oils are used in older vehicles. In the Porsche 911, the manual transmission, synchronizers, and final drive with its highly stressed ring and pinion gears are all contained within a single housing. As of approximately 1970, the oil industry began to make available a highly blended transmission oil capable of withstanding higher contact pressures at the most critical points (on the faces of gear teeth). Oil additives greatly reduce friction, resulting in appreciably longer life for highly stressed gears. However, lower friction results in a chemical smoothing action on the friction surfaces of the synchro rings, and failure of their synchronizing action, without any trace of measurable wear.

Porsche reacted quickly and modified the synchronizers to work at lower friction levels. As of 1972, transmissions have been filled with the new, blended GL5 (MIL-L 2105 B) transmission oils. Both oil specifications are permitted until the end of the 1973 model year, and as of 1974 only the blended oils are approved. Older vehicles should always use the most modern brake fluid; recent years have seen great advances in high temperature properties and resistance to aging.

Model years 1964/1965

Model designation		911

1. Engine

Engine type, manual trans.		901/01
No. of cylinders		6
Bore	(mm)	80
Stroke	(mm)	66
Displacement	(cc)	1991
Compression ratio		9.0:1
Power output	(kW/hp)	96/130
at rpm	(rpm)	6100
Torque	(Nm)	174
at rpm	(rpm)	4200
Specific output	(kW/l)	48.6 (65hp/l)
Maximum rpm	(rpm)	6500
Engine weight	(kg)	184

2. Fuel system, Ignition, Settings

Fuel supply		Solex overflow downdraft carburetor, Type 40PI
Fuel, Research Octane No.		96
Ignition system		conventional battery ignition
Firing order, all 911 eng.		1 - 6 - 2 - 4 - 3 - 5
Ignition distributor		Marelli S 112 AX
Spark plugs, Bosch		W225T7 W200T35
Beru		P 225/14
Spark plug gap	(mm)	0.6...0.7
Idle rpm	(rpm)	850...950

3. Powertrain

Clutch, pressure plate		M 215K
Clutch disc		215
Manual transmission type		901/02
Gear ratios		
1st Gear		3.091
2nd Gear		1.888
3rd Gear		1.318
4th Gear		1.000
5th Gear		0.758
Synchromesh syst. Gears 1-5		POSY
Final drive ratio		4.4285
Limited slip differential		M
Lockup factor Load/Coast, %		40/40

Abbreviations:
M Optional equipment
S Standard equipment
POSY Porsche Blocking synchromesh system, molybdenum-coated synchro rings

4. Steering, Suspension, Wheels, Brakes

Front suspension		
Stabilizer bar dia.	(mm)	...
Steering ratio		17.87
Turning circle dia.	(m)	10.7
Rear suspension		
Stabilizer bar, dia. man. trans.	(mm)	...
Brake system		Single-circuit brake system
Master cylinder dia.	(mm)	19.05
Brake caliper piston dia.		
front	(mm)	48
rear	(mm)	35
Brake disc diameter		
front	(mm)	282
rear	(mm)	285
Brake disc thickness		
front	(mm)	12.7 U
rear	(mm)	10.0 U
Total eff. pad area	(cm²)	185
Parking brake		Mechanical, acting on both rear wheels
Brake drum diameter	(mm)	180

Model designation		911

Total pad area	(cm²)	170
Wheels and tires		
Standard tires front		165-15 radial
on wheel size		4 ¹/₂J x 15
Standard tires rear		165-15 radial
on wheel size		4 ¹/₂J x 15
Tire pressure, front	(bar)	2.0
rear	(bar)	2.4

Abbreviations:
12.7 U = unventilated, solid brake disc, 12.7 mm thick

5. Body, interior equipment (Dimensions at empty weight)

Length	(mm)	4163
Width	(mm)	1610
Height	(mm)	1320
Wheelbase	(mm)	2211
Track, front	(mm)	1367
rear	(mm)	1335
Ground clearance at legal maximum weight	(mm)	150

9. Electrical system

Generator output	(W/A)	490/30
Battery	(V/Ah)	12/45

Weights according to DIN 70020

Empty weight	(kg)	1080
Maximum permissible total weight	(kg)	1400

Performance

Maximum speed		
Manual trans.	(km/h)	210
Acceleration 0...100 km/h		
Manual trans.	(s)	9.1
Standing start kilometer	(s)	29.9

Capacities

Engine oil capacity 1*	(l)	9
Oil change qty. 1*	(l)	8...9
Manual trans. 2*	(l)	2.5
Fuel tank capacity	(l)	62
Brake reservoir 6*	(l)	0.20

* Notes
1* Approved motor oils: API SE/SF when combined with API SE/CC - SF/CC -SF/CD - SE/CD
Multigrade oils approved by factory, (SAE 10 W/50 or 15 W/40 or 20 W/50). Single grade oils (brand name HD oils) are also approved. Summer SAE 30. Winter SAE 20.
2* Single-grade transmission oil SAE 90 to MIL-L 2105 or GL 4.
Not approved: transmission oil SAE 90 MIL-L 2105 B or API classification GL 5.
6* Use only brake fluid meeting SAE J 1703 or DOT 3 or 4.

Model year 1966

Model designation		911

1. Engine

Engine type, manual trans.		901/01 and 901/05
No. of cylinders		6
Bore	(mm)	80
Stroke	(mm)	66
Displacement	(cc)	1991
Compression ratio		9.0:1
Power output	(kW/hp)	96/130
at rpm	(rpm)	6100
Torque	(Nm)	174
at rpm	(rpm)	4200
Specific output	(kW/l)	48.6 (65 hp/l)
Maximum rpm	(rpm)	6500
Engine weight	(kg)	184

2. Fuel system, Ignition, Settings

Fuel supply Type 901/01		Solex overflow downdraft carburetor 40PI
Type 901/05		Weber carburetor 40IDA 3L and 3C1
Fuel, Research Octane No.		96
Ignition system		conventional battery ignition
Firing order of all 911 engines		1 - 6 - 2 - 4 - 3 - 5
Ignition distributor		Marelli S 112 AX
Spark plugs, Bosch		W225T7 W200T35
Beru		P 225/14
Spark plug gap	(mm)	0.6...0.7
Idle rpm	(rpm)	850...950

3. Powertrain

Clutch, pressure plate		M 215K
Clutch disc		215
Manual transmission type		901/02
Gear ratios		
1st Gear		3.091
2nd Gear		1.888
3rd Gear		1.318
4th Gear		1.000
5th Gear		0.758
Synchromesh syst. Gears 1-5		POSY
Final drive ratio		4.4285
Limited slip differential		M
Lockup factor Load/Coast, %		40/40

Abbreviations:
M Optional equipment
S Standard equipment
POSY Porsche Blocking synchromesh system, molybdenum-coated synchro rings

4. Steering, Suspension, Wheels, Brakes

Front suspension		
Stabilizer bar dia.	(mm)	...
Steering ratio		17.87
Turning circle dia.	(m)	10.7
Rear suspension		
Stabilizer bar, man. trans.	(mm)	...
Brake system		Single-circuit brake system
Master cylinder dia.	(mm)	19.05
Brake caliper piston dia.		
front	(mm)	48
rear	(mm)	35
Brake disc diameter		
front	(mm)	282
rear	(mm)	285
Brake disc thickness		
front	(mm)	12.7 U
rear	(mm)	10.0 U
Total eff. pad area	(cm²)	185
Parking brake		Mechanical, acting on both rear wheels
Brake drum diameter	(mm)	180
Total pad area	(cm²)	170
Wheels and tires		
Standard tires front		165-15 radial
on wheel size		4 ½J x 15
Standard tires rear		165-15 radial
on wheel size		4 ½J x 15
Tire pressure, front	(bar)	2.0
rear	(bar)	2.4

Abbreviations:
12.7 U = nonventilated, solid brake disc, 12.7 mm thick

5. Body, interior equipment (Dimensions at empty weight)

Length	(mm)	4163
Width	(mm)	1610
Height	(mm)	1320

Wheelbase	(mm)	2211
Track, front	(mm)	1367
rear	(mm)	1335
Ground clearance at legal maximum weight	(mm)	150

9. Electrical system

Generator output	(W/A)	490/30
Battery	(V/Ah)	12/45

Weights according to DIN 70020

Empty weight	(kg)	1080
Maximum permissible total weight	(kg)	1400

Performance

Maximum speed		
Manual trans.	(km/h)	210
Acceleration 0...100 km/h		
Manual trans.	(s)	9.1
Standing start kilometer		
Manual trans.	(s)	29.9

Capacities

Engine oil capacity 1*	(l)	9
Oil change qty. 1*	(l)	8...9
Manual trans. 2*	(l)	2.5
Fuel tank capacity	(l)	62
Brake reservoir 6*	(l)	0.20

* Notes:
1* Approved motor oils: API SE/SF when combined with API SE/CC - SF/CC - SF/CD - SE/CD
Multigrade oils as approved by factory, (SAE 10 W/50 or 15 W/40 or 20 W/50).
Single grade oils (brand name HD oils) are also approved. Summer SAE 30. Winter SAE 20.
2* Single-grade transmission oil SAE 90 to MIL-L 2105 or GL 4.
Not approved: transmission oil SAE 90 MIL-L 2105 B or API classification GL 5.
6* Use only brake fluid meeting SAE J 1703 or DOT 3 or 4.

Model year 1967

Model designation		*911*	*911S*
1. Engine			
Engine type, manual trans.		901/06	901/02
No. of cylinders		6	=
Bore	(mm)	80	=
Stroke	(mm)	66	=
Displacement	(cc)	1991	=
Compression ratio		9.0:1	9.8:1
Power output	(kW/hp)	96/130	118/160
at rpm	(rpm)	6100	6600
Torque	(Nm)	174	179
at rpm	(rpm)	4200	5200
Specific output	(kW/l)	48.6	59.2
Maximum rpm	(rpm)	6500	7200
Engine weight	(kg)	184	184

2. Fuel system, Ignition, Settings			
Fuel supply		WV 40IDA	WV 40IDS
Fuel, Research Octane No.		96	96
Ignition system		conventional battery ignition	
Firing order of all 911 engines		1 - 6 - 2 - 4 - 3 - 5	
Ignition distributor		Bosch	Bosch
Spark plugs, Bosch		W230T30	W250P21
Beru		P 225/14	...
Spark plug gap	(mm)	0.6...0.7	0.35

Model designation		911	911S
Idle rpm	(rpm)	850...950	=
Abbreviations:			
WV = Weber carburetor 40 IDT P			

3. Powertrain

		911	911S
Clutch, pressure plate		M 215K	=
Clutch disc		215	=
Manual transmission type		901/02	901/03
Gear ratios			
1st Gear		3.091	=
2nd Gear		1.888	=
3rd Gear		1.318	=
4th Gear		1.000	=
5th Gear		0.758	=
Synchromesh syst. Gears 1-5		POSY	=
Final drive ratio		4.4285	=
Limited slip differential		M	M
Lockup factor Load/Coast, %		40/40	=

Abbreviations:
M Optional equipment
S Standard equipment
POSY Porsche Blocking synchro system, molybdenum-coated synchro rings

4. Steering, Suspension, Wheels, Brakes

		911	911S
Front suspension			
Stabilizer bar dia.	(mm)	M	14
Steering ratio		17.87	=
Turning circle dia.	(m)	10.7	=
Rear suspension			
Stabilizer bar, man. trans.	(mm)	M	14
Brake system		Dual-circuit braking system	
Master cylinder dia.	(mm)	19.05	=
Brake caliper piston dia.			
front	(mm)	48	=
rear	(mm)	35	38
Brake disc diameter			
front	(mm)	282	=
rear	(mm)	285	=
Brake disc thickness			
front	(mm)	12.7 U	20, ventilated
rear	(mm)	10.0 U	20, ventilated
Total eff. pad area	(cm²)	185	=
Parking brake		Mechanical, acting on both rear wheels	
Brake drum diameter	(mm)	180	=
Total pad area	(cm²)	170	=
Wheels and tires			
Standard tires front		165-15 radial	=
on wheel size		4 1/2J x 15	=
Standard tires rear		165-15 radial	=
on wheel size		4 1/2J x 15	=
Tire pressure, front	(bar)	2.0	=
rear	(bar)	2.4	=

Abbreviations:
12.7 U = nonventilated, solid brake disc, 12.7 mm thick

5. Body, interior equipment (Dimensions at empty weight)

		911	911S
Length	(mm)	4163	=
Width	(mm)	1610	=
Height	(mm)	1320	=
Wheelbase	(mm)	2211	=
Track, front	(mm)	1367	=
rear	(mm)	1335	1339
Ground clearance at legal maximum weight	(mm)	150	=

9. Electrical system

		911	911S
Generator output	(W/A)	490/30	=
Battery	(V/Ah)	12/45	=

Model designation		911	911S
Weights according to DIN 70020			
Empty weight	(kg)	1080	1030
Maximum permissible total weight	(kg)	1400	=

Performance

		911	911S
Maximum speed			
Manual trans.	(km/h)	200	225
Acceleration 0...100 km/h			
Manual trans.	(s)	9.1	7.6
Standing start kilometer			
Manual trans.	(s)	32.1	27.55

Capacities

		911	911S
Engine oil capacity 1*	(l)	9	=
Oil change qty. 1*	(l)	8...9	=
Manual trans. 2*	(l)	2.5	=
Fuel tank capacity	(l)	68	=
Brake reservoir 6*	(l)	0.20	=

* Notes:
1* Approved motor oils: API SE/SF when combined with API SE/CC - SF/CC - SF/CD - SE/CD
Multigrade oils approved by factory, (SAE 10 W/50 or 15 W/40 or 20 W/50).
Single grade oils (brand name IID oils) are also approved. Summer SAE 30. Winter SAE 20.
2* Single-grade transmission oil SAE 90 to MIL-L 2105 or GL 4.
Not approved: transmission oil SAE 90 MIL-L 2105 B or API classification GL 5.
6* Use only brake fluid meeting SAE J 1703 or DOT 3 or 4.

Model year 1968

Model designation		911T	911 L	911S
1. Engine				
Engine type, manual trans.		901/03	901/06	901/02
No. of cylinders		6	=	=
Bore	(mm)	80	=	=
Stroke	(mm)	66	=	=
Displacement	(cc)	1991	=	=
Compression ratio		8.6:1	9.0:1	9.8:1
Power output	(kW/hp)	81/110	96/130	118/160
at rpm	(rpm)	5800	6100	6600
Torque	(Nm)	157	174	179
at rpm	(rpm)	4200	4200	5200
Specific output	(kW/l)	40.7	48.2	59.2
Maximum rpm	(rpm)	6500	6500	7200
Engine weight	(kg)	184	184	184

2. Fuel system, Ignition, Settings

		911T	911 L	911S
Fuel supply		WV 40IDT P	WV 40IDA	WV 40IDA
Fuel, Research Octane No.		96	98	98
Ignition system		conventional battery ignition		
Firing order of all 911 engines		1 - 6 - 2 - 4 - 3 - 5		
Ignition distributor		Marelli	Bosch	Bosch
Spark plugs, Bosch		W230T30	W250P21	W265P21
Beru		P 225/14	...	...
Spark plug gap	(mm)	0.6...0.7	0.35	0.35
Idle rpm	(rpm)	850...950	=	=
Abbreviations:				
WV = Weber carburetor				

3. Powertrain

		911T	911 L	911S
Clutch, pressure plate		M 215K	=	=
Clutch disc		215	=	=
Manual transmission type		901/03	901/50	901/50
Gear ratios				
1st Gear		3.091	=	=
2nd Gear		1.888	=	=
3rd Gear		1.318	=	=
4th Gear		1.000	=	=
5th Gear		0.758	=	=

Model designation		911T	911 L	911S
Synchromesh syst. Gears 1-5		POSY	=	=
Final drive ratio		4.4285	=	=
Limited slip differential		M	M	M
Lockup factor Load/Coast, %		40/40	=	=
Sportomatic transmission		905/00	=	...
Torque converter dia.	(mm)	F&S 190	=	
Converter stall rpm		2500...2700	=	
Gear ratios				
1st Gear		2.400	=	
2nd Gear		1.631	=	
3rd Gear		1.217	=	
4th Gear		0.926	=	
Synchromesh on fwd gears		POSY	=	
Final drive ratio		3.857	=	

Abbreviations:
M Optional equipment
S Standard equipment
F&S Manufacturer Fichtel & Sachs
POSY Porsche Blocking synchromesh system, molybdenum-coated synchro rings

4. Steering, Suspension, Wheels, Brakes

		911T	911L	911S
Front suspension				
Stabilizer bar dia.	(mm)	M	14	14
Steering ratio		17.87	=	=
Turning circle dia.	(m)	10.7	=	=
Rear suspension				
Stabilizer bar, man. trs.	(mm)	M	14	14
Brake system		Dual-circuit braking system	=	
Master cylinder dia.	(mm)	19.05	=	=
Brake caliper piston dia.				
front	(mm)	48	=	=
rear	(mm)	35	38	38
Brake disc diameter				
front	(mm)	282	=	=
rear	(mm)	285	=	=
Brake disc thickness				
front	(mm)	12.7 U	20, ventilated	
rear	(mm)	10.0 U	20, ventilated	
Total eff. pad area	(cm²)	185	=	=
Parking brake		Mechanical, acting on both rear wheels		
Brake drum diameter	(mm)	180	=	
Total pad area	(cm²)	170	=	
Wheels and tires				
Standard tires front		165HR15	165VR15	=
on wheel size		4 ¹/₂J x 15	5 ¹/₂J x 15	5 ¹/₂J x 15 LM
Standard tires rear		165HR15	165VR15	=
on wheel size		4 ¹/₂J x 15	5 ¹/₂J x 15	5 ¹/₂J x 15 LM
Tire pressure, front	(bar)	2.2	=	2.2
rear	(bar)	2.4	=	2.2

Abbreviations:
12.7 U = nonventilated. solid brake disc, 12.7 mm thick
LM = forged alloy wheels, manufacturer Fuchs

5. Body, interior equipment (Dimensions at empty weight)

		911T	911L	911S
Length	(mm)	4163	=	=
Width	(mm)	1610	=	=
Height	(mm)	1320	=	=
Wheelbase	(mm)	2211	=	=
Track, front	(mm)	1367	=	=
rear	(mm)	1335	=	=
Ground clearance at legal maximum weight	(mm)	150	=	=

9. Electrical system

		911T	911L	911S
Generator output	(W/A)	490/30	=	=
Battery	(V/Ah)	12/45	=	=

Model designation		911T	911 L	911S
Weights according to DIN 70020				
Empty weight	(kg)	1080	=	1030
Maximum permissible total weight	(kg)	1400	=	=
Permissible towing load				
unbraked	(kg)	480	=	=
braked	(kg)	600	=	=
Performance				
Maximum speed				
Manual trans.	(km/h)	200	215	225
Acceleration 0...100 km/h				
Manual trans.	(s)	10.0	9.0	8.0
Standing start kilometer				
Manual trans.	(s)	32.1	29.8	28.8
Capacities				
Engine oil capacity 1*	(l)	9	=	10
Eng. Oil qty. w. SPM	(l)	+ 2	=	...
Oil change qty. 1*	(l)	8...9	=	=
Manual trans. 2*	(l)	2.5	=	=
Sportomatic 2*	(l)	2.5	=	=
Fuel tank capacity	(l)	62	=	=
Brake reservoir 6*	(l)	0.20	=	=

* Notes:
1* Approved motor oils: API SE/SF when combined with API SE/CC - SF/CC - SF/CD - SE/CD
Multigrade oils as approved by factory, (SAE 10 W/50 or 15 W/40 or 20 W/50).
Single grade oils (brand name HD oils) are also approved. Summer SAE 30. Winter SAE 20.
2* Single-grade transmission oil SAE 90 to MIL-L 2105 or GL 4.
Not approved: transmission oil SAE 90 MIL-L 2105 B or API classification GL 5.
6* Use only brake fluid meeting SAE J 1703 or DOT 3 or 4.
Abbreviations:
SPM Sportomatic

Model year 1969

Model designation		911T	911 E	911S
1. Engine				
Engine type, manual trans.		901/03	901/09	901/10
Bore	(mm)	80	=	=
Stroke	(mm)	66	=	=
Displacement	(cc)	1991	=	=
Compression ratio		8.6:1	9.1:1	9.9:1
Power output	(kW/hp)	81/110	103/140	125/170
at rpm	(rpm)	5800	6500	6800
Torque	(Nm)	157	175	182
at rpm	(rpm)	4200	4500	5500
Specific output	(kW/l)	40.7	54.5	62.5
Maximum rpm	(rpm)	6500	6800	7200
Engine weight	(kg)	176	182	182

2. Fuel system, Ignition, Settings

		911T	911 E	911S
Fuel supply		WV 40IDTHPMSE	MSE	
Fuel, Research Octane No.		96	98	
Ignition system		conventional BZ BHKZ	=	
Ignition distributor		Marelli	Bosch	=
Spark plugs, Bosch		W230T30	W265P21	=
Beru		240/14/3P	265/14/3P	=
Spark plug gap	(mm)	0.6	=	=
Idle rpm	(rpm)	850...950	=	=

Abbreviations:
BZ = battery ignition
BHKZ = Battery high voltage condenser ignition
WV = Weber carburetor 40 IDT3C
MSE = Bosch mechanical port injection
by means of 6-plunger two-row injection pump

Model designation		911T	911 E	911S
3. Powertrain				
Clutch, pressure plate		G MFZ 215KL	=	=
Clutch disc		215	=	=
Manual transmission type		911/01	=	=
Gear ratios				
1st Gear		3.091	=	=
2nd Gear		1.777	=	=
3rd Gear		1.217	=	=
4th Gear		0.926	=	=
5th Gear		0.758	=	=
Synchromesh syst. Gears 1-5		POSY	=	=
Final drive ratio		4.4285	=	=
Limited slip differential		M	M	M
Lockup factor Load/Coast, %		40/40	=	=
Sportomatic transmission		905/20	=	=
Torque converter dia. (mm)		F&S 190	=	=
Converter stall rpm		2600	=	=
Gear ratios				
1st Gear		2.400	=	=
2nd Gear		1.555	=	=
3rd Gear		1.125	=	=
4th Gear		0.857	=	=
Reverse Gear		2.533	=	=
Synchromesh on fwd gears		POSY	=	=
Final drive ratio		3.857	=	=

Abbreviations:
M Optional equipment
S Standard equipment
F&S Manufacturer Fichtel & Sachs
POSY Porsche Blocking synchromesh system, molybdenum-coated synchro rings

4. Steering, Suspension, Wheels, Brakes				
Front suspension				
Stabilizer bar dia.	(mm)	M	M	15
Steering ratio		17.87	=	=
Turning circle dia.	(m)	10.7	=	=
Rear suspension				
Stabilizer bar, man. trs.	(mm)	M	M	15
Shock absorbers		Boge	HPF*	Koni
Brake system		Dual-circuit braking system	=	
Master cylinder dia.	(mm)	19.05	=	=
Brake caliper piston dia.				
front	(mm)	48	=	=
rear	(mm)	35	38	38
Brake disc diameter				
front	(mm)	282	=	=
rear	(mm)	285	=	=
Brake disc thickness				
front	(mm)	20, ventilated		=
rear	(mm)	20, ventilated		=
Total eff. pad area	(cm²)	185	=	=
Parking brake		Mechanical, acting on both rear wheels		
Brake drum diameter	(mm)	180	=	
Total pad area	(cm²)	170	=	
Wheels and tires				
Standard tires front		165HR15	185/70VR15	=
on wheel size		5 ½J x 15	6J x 15	6J x 15 light alloy
Standard tires rear		165HR15	185/70VR15	=
on wheel size		5 ½J x 15	6J x 15	6J x 15 light alloy
Tire pressure, front	(bar)	2.2	=	=
rear	(bar)	2.4	=	=

Abbreviations:
HPF* = self-regulating hydropneumatic struts

5. Body, interior equipment (Dimensions at empty weight)				
Length	(mm)	4163	=	=
Width	(mm)	1610	=	=

Model designation		911T	911 E	911S
Height	(mm)	1320	=	=
Wheelbase	(mm)	2268	=	=
Track, front	(mm)	1362	1374	=
rear	(mm)	1343	1355	=
Ground clearance at legal maximum weight	(mm)	150	=	=
9. Electrical system				
Generator output	(W/A)	770/55	=	=
Battery	(V/Ah)	2 x12/36	=	=
Weights according to DIN 70020				
Empty weight	(kg)	1020	=	=
Maximum permissible total weight	(kg)	1400	=	=
Permissible towing load				
unbraked	(kg)	480	=	=
braked	(kg)	600	=	=
Performance				
Maximum speed				
Manual trans.	(km/h)	200	215	225
Acceleration 0...100 km/h				
Manual trans.	(s)	10.0	9.0	8.0
Standing-start kilometer				
Manual trans.	(s)	30.35	28.5	27.5
Capacities				
Engine oil capacity 1*	(l)	9	=	10
Eng. Oil qty. w. SPM	(l)	+ 2	=	...
Oil change qty. 1*	(l)	8...9	=	=
Manual trans. 2*	(l)	2.5	=	=
Sportomatic 2*	(l)	2.5	=	=
Fuel tank capacity	(l)	62	=	=
Brake reservoir 6*	(l)	0.20	=	=

* Notes:
1* Approved motor oils: API SE/SF when combined with API SE/CC - SF/CC - SF/CD - SE/CD
Multigrade oils as approved by factory, (SAE 10 W/50 or 15 W/40 or 20 W/50).
Single grade oils are also approved. Summer SAE 30. Winter SAE 20.
2* Single-grade transmission oil SAE 90 to MIL-L 2105 or GL 4.
Not approved: transmission oil SAE 90 MIL-L 2105 B or API classification GL 5.
6* Use only brake fluid meeting SAE J 1703 or DOT 3 or 4.
Abbreviations:
SPM Sportomatic

Model year 1970

Model designation		911T	911 E	911S
1. Engine				
Engine type, manual trans		911/03	911/01	911/02
Bore	(mm)	84	=	=
Stroke	(mm)	66	=	=
Displacement	(cc)	2195	=	=
Compression ratio		8.6:1	9.1:1	9.8:1
Power output	(kW/hp)	92/125	114/155	132/180
at rpm	(rpm)	5800	6200	6500
Torque	(Nm)	176	191	199
at rpm	(rpm)	4200	4500	5200
Specific output	(kW/l)	41.9	51.9	60.1
Maximum rpm	(rpm)	6500	6700	7200
Engine weight	(kg)	176	182	182
2. Fuel system, Ignition, Settings				
Fuel supply		WV 40IDT3C	MSE	MSE
Fuel, Research Octane No		98	=	=
Ignition system		BHKZ	=	=
Ignition distributor		Bosch	=	=

Model designation		911T	911 E	911S
Spark plugs, Bosch		W230T30	W265P21	=
Beru		240/14/3P	265/14/3P	=
Spark plug gap	(mm)	0.6	=	=
Idle rpm	(rpm)	850...950	=	=
Fuel consumption	(l/100 km)			
		9.0	9.5	10.2

Abbreviations:
BHKZ = Battery high voltage condenser ignition
WV = Weber carburetor 40 IDT3C
MSE = Bosch mechanical port injection
by means of 6-plunger two-row injection pump

3. Powertrain

		911T	911 E	911S
Clutch, pressure plate		G MFZ 215KL		=
Clutch disc		215	=	=
Manual transmission type		911/01	=	=
Gear ratios				
1st Gear		3.091	=	=
2nd Gear		1.777	=	=
3rd Gear		1.217	=	=
4th Gear		0.926	=	=
5th Gear		0.758	=	=
Synchromesh syst. Gears 1-5		POSY	=	=
Final drive ratio		4.4285	=	=
Limited slip differential		M	M	M
Lockup factor Load/Coast, %		40/40	=	=
Sportomatic transmission		905/20	=	=
Torque converter dia.	(mm)	F&S 190	=	=
Converter stall rpm		2600	=	=
Gear rati				
1st Gear		2.400	=	=
2nd Gear		1.555	=	=
3rd Gear		1.125	=	=
4th Gear		0.857	=	=
Reverse Gear		2.533	=	=
Synchromesh on fwd gears		POSY	=	=
Final drive ratio		3.857	=	=

Abbreviations:
M Optional equipment
S Standard equipment
F&S Manufacturer Fichtel & Sachs
POSY Porsche Blocking synchromesh system. molybdenum-coated synchro rings

4. Steering, Suspension, Wheels, Brakes

		911T	911 E	911S
Front suspension				
Stabilizer bar dia.	(mm)	M	M	15
Steering ratio		17.87	=	=
Turning circle dia.	(m)	10.7	=	=
Rear suspension				
Stabilizer bar, man. trs.	(mm)	M	M	15
Shock absorbers		Boge	HPF*	Koni
Brake system		Dual-circuit braking system =		
Master cylinder dia.	(mm)	19.05	=	=
Brake caliper piston dia.				
front	(mm)	48	=	=
rear	(mm)	35	38	38
Brake disc diameter				
front	(mm)	282	=	=
rear	(mm)	285	=	=
Brake disc thickness				
front	(mm)	20, ventilated =		=
rear	(mm)	20, ventilated =		=
Total eff. pad area	(cm²)	185	=	=
Parking brake		Mechanical, acting on both rear wheels		
Brake drum diameter	(mm)	180	=	
Total pad area	(cm²)	170	=	

Model designation		911T	911 E	911S
Wheels and tires				
Standard tires front		165HR15	185/70VR15	=
on wheel size		5 ¹/₂J x 15	6J x 15	6J x 15 light alloy
Standard tires rear		165HR15	185/70VR15	=
on wheel size		5 ¹/₂J x 15	6J x 15	6J x 15 light alloy
Tire pressure, front	(bar)	2.2	=	=
rear	(bar)	2.4	=	=

Abbreviations:
HPF* = self-regulating hydropneumatic struts

5. Body, interior equipment (Dimensions at empty weight)

		911T	911 E	911S
Length	(mm)	4163	=	=
Width	(mm)	1610	=	=
Height	(mm)	1320	=	=
Wheelbase	(mm)	2268	=	=
Track, front	(mm)	1362	1374	=
rear	(mm)	1343	1355	=
Ground clearance at legal maximum weight	(mm)	150	=	=

9. Electrical system

		911T	911 E	911S
Generator output	(W/A)	770/55	=	=
Battery	(V/Ah)	2 x12/36	=	=

Weights according to DIN 70020

		911T	911 E	911S
Empty weight	(kg)	1020	=	=
Maximum permissible total weight	(kg)	1400	=	=
Permissible towing load				
unbraked	(kg)	480	=	=
braked	(kg)	600	=	=

Performance

		911T	911 E	911S
Maximum speed				
Manual trans.	(km/h)	200	215	225
Acceleration 0...100 km/h				
Manual trans.	(s)	9.5	9.0	7.0
Standing-start kilometer				
Manual trans.	(s)	30.35	28.5	27.5

Capacities

		911T	911 E	911S
Engine oil capacity 1*	(l)	9	=	10
Eng. Oil qty. w. SPM	(l)	+ 2	=	...
Oil change qty. 1*	(l)	8...9	=	=
Manual trans. 2*	(l)	2.5	=	=
Sportomatic 2*	(l)	2.5	=	=
Fuel tank capacity	(l)	62	=	=
Brake reservoir 6*	(l)	0.20	=	=

* Notes:
1* Approved motor oils: API SE/SF when combined with API SE/CC - SF/CC - SF/CD - SE/CD
Multigrade oils as approved by factory, (SAE 10 W/50 or 15 W/40 or 20 W/50).
Single grade oils are also approved. Summer SAE 30. Winter SAE 20.
2* Single-grade transmission oil SAE 90 to MIL-L 2105 or GL 4.
Not approved: transmission oil SAE 90 MIL-L 2105 B or API classification GL 5.
6* Use only brake fluid meeting SAE J 1703 or DOT 3 or 4.
Abbreviations:
SPM Sportomatic

Model year 1971

Model designation		911T	911 E	911S
1. Engine				
Engine type, manual trans.		911/03	911/01	911/02
Bore	(mm)	84	=	=
Stroke	(mm)	66	=	=

Model designation		911T	911 E	911S
Displacement	(cc)	2195	=	=
Compression ratio		8.6:1	9.1:1	9.8:1
Power output	(kW/hp)	92/125	114/155	132/180
at rpm	(rpm)	5800	6200	6500
Torque	(Nm)	176	191	199
at rpm	(rpm)	4200	4500	5200
Specific output	(kW/l)	41.9	51.9	60.1
Maximum rpm	(rpm)	6500	6700	7200
Engine weight	(kg)	176	182	182

2. Fuel system, Ignition, Settings

		911T	911 E	911S
Fuel supply		SZV	MSE	MSE
Fuel, Research Octane No.		98	=	=
Ignition system		BHKZ	=	=
Ignition distributor		Bosch	=	=
Spark plugs, Bosch		W230T30	W265P21	=
Beru		250/14/3P	265/14/3P	=
Spark plug gap	(mm)	0.6	=	=
Idle rpm	(rpm)	850...950	=	=
CO level	(%)	2.5...3.5	=	=
Fuel consumption, l/100 km		9.0	9.5	10.2

Abbreviations:
BHKZ = Battery high voltage condenser ignition
SZV = Solex-Zenith carburetor 40TIN
MSE = Bosch mechanical port injection

3. Powertrain

		911T	911 E	911S
Clutch, pressure plate		G MFZ 225	=	=
Clutch disc		225	=	=
Manual transmission type		911/01	=	=
Gear ratios				
1st Gear		3.091	=	=
2nd Gear		1.777	=	=
3rd Gear		1.217	=	=
4th Gear		0.926	=	=
5th Gear		0.7586	=	=
Reverse Gear		3.325	=	=
Synchromesh syst. Gears 1-5		POSY	=	=
Final drive ratio		4.4285	=	=
Limited slip differential		M	M	M
Lockup factor Load/Coast, %		40/40	=	=
Sportomatic transmission		905/20	=	=
Torque converter dia. (mm)		F&S 190	=	=
Converter stall rpm		2600	=	=
Gear ratios				
1st Gear		2.400	=	=
2nd Gear		1.555	=	=
3rd Gear		1.125	=	=
4th Gear		0.857	=	=
Reverse Gear		2.533	=	=
Synchromesh on fwd gears		POSY	=	=
Final drive ratio		3.857	=	=

Abbreviations:
M Optional equipment
S Standard equipment
F&S Manufacturer Fichtel & Sachs
POSY Porsche Blocking synchro system, molybdenum-coated synchro rings

4. Steering, Suspension, Wheels, Brakes

		911T	911 E	911S
Front suspension				
Stabilizer bar dia.	(mm)	M	M	15
Steering ratio		17.87	=	=
Turning circle dia.	(m)	10.7	=	=
Rear suspension				
Stabilizer bar, man. trs.	(mm)	M	M	15
Shock absorbers		Boge	HPF*	Koni
Master cylinder dia.	(mm)	19.05	=	=
Brake caliper piston dia.				
front	(mm)	48	=	=
rear	(mm)	38	=	=
Brake disc diameter				
front	(mm)	282.5	=	=
rear	(mm)	290	=	=

		911T	911 E	911S
Brake disc thickness				
front	(mm)	20, ventilated =		=
rear	(mm)	20, ventilated =		=
Total eff. pad area	(cm²)	210	=	257
Parking brake		Mechanical, acting on both rear wheels		
Brake drum diameter	(mm)	180	=	=
Total pad area	(cm²)	170	=	
Wheels and tires				
Standard tires front		165HR15	185/70VR15	=
on wheel size		5 1/2J x 15	6J x 15	=
Standard tires rear		165HR15	185/70VR15	=
on wheel size		5 1/2J x 15	6J x 15	=
Spare wheel		Space saver, 5 1/2 J x 15		
Tire pressure, front	(bar)	2.0	=	=
rear	(bar)	2.4	=	=
Space saver spare	(bar)	2.0	=	=

5. Body, interior equipment (Dimensions at empty weight)

		911T	911 E	911S
Length	(mm)	4163	=	=
Width	(mm)	1610	=	=
Height	(mm)	1320	=	=
Wheelbase	(mm)	2268	—	=
Track, front	(mm)	1362	1374	=
rear	(mm)	1355	=	=
Ground clearance at legal				
maximum weight	(mm)	150	=	=

9. Electrical system

		911T	911 E	911S
Generator output	(W/A)	770/55	=	=
Battery	(V/Ah)	2 x12/36	=	=

Weights according to DIN 70020

		911T	911 E	911S
Empty weight	(kg)	1020	=	=
Maximum permissible				
total weight	(kg)	1400	=	=
Permissible towing load				
unbraked	(kg)	480	=	=
braked	(kg)	600	=	=

Performance

		911T	911 E	911S
Maximum speed				
Manual trans.	(km/h)	200	215	225
Acceleration 0...100 km/h				
Manual trans.	(s)	9.5	9.0	7.0
Standing-start kilometer				
Manual trans.	(s)	30.35	28.5	27.5

Capacities

		911T	911 E	911S
Engine oil capacity 1*	(l)	9	=	10
Eng. Oil qty. w. SPM	(l)	+ 2	=	...
Oil change qty. 1*	(l)	8...9	=	=
Manual trans. 2*	(l)	2.5	=	=
Sportomatic 2*	(l)	2.5	=	=
Fuel tank capacity	(l)	62	=	=
Brake reservoir 6*	(l)	0.20	=	=

* Notes:
1* Approved motor oils: API SE/SF when combined with API SE/CC - SF/CC - SF/CD - SE/CD
Multigrade oils as approved by factory, (SAE 10 W/50 or 15 W/40 or 20 W/50).
Single grade oils are also approved. Summer SAE 30. Winter SAE 20.
2* Single-grade transmission oil SAE 90 to MIL-L 2105 or GL 4.
Not approved: transmission oil SAE 90 MIL-L 2105 B or API classification GL 5.
6* Use only brake fluid meeting SAE J 1703 or DOT 3 or 4.
Abbreviations:
SPM Sportomatic

Model year 1972

Model designation		911T	911 E	911S
1. Engine				
Engine type, manual trans.		911/57	911/52	911/53
Bore	(mm)	84	=	=
Stroke	(mm)	70.4	=	=
Displacement	(cc)	2341	=	=
Compression ratio		7.5:1	8.0:1	8.5:1
Power output	(kW/hp)	96/130	121/165	140/190
at rpm	(rpm)	5600	6200	6500
Torque	(Nm)	196	206	216
at rpm	(rpm)	4000	4500	5200
Specific output	(kW/l)	41	52	60
Maximum rpm	(rpm)	6500	7000	7300
Engine weight	(kg)	176	183	182

2. Fuel system, Ignition, Settings				
Fuel supply		SZV	MSE	MSE
Fuel, Research Octane No.		91	=	=
Ignition system		BHKZ	=	=
Spark plugs, Bosch		W230T1	W265P21	=
Beru		225/14/3	235/14/3P	
Spark plug gap	(mm)	0.7	0.5...0.6	=
Idle rpm	(rpm)	850...950	=	=
CO level	(%)	2.5...3.5	=	=

Abbreviations:
BHKZ = Battery high voltage condenser ignition
SZV = Solex-Zenith carburetor 40TIN
MSE = Bosch mechanical port injection

3. Powertrain				
Clutch, pressure plate		G MFZ 225	=	=
Clutch disc		GUD 225	=	=
Manual transmission type		915/03	=	=
Gear ratios				
1st Gear		3.181	=	=
2nd Gear		1.833	=	=
3rd Gear		1.261	=	=
4th Gear		0.9615	=	=
5th Gear		0.7586	=	=
Reverse Gear		3.325	=	=
Synchromesh syst. Gears 1-5		POSY	=	=
Final drive ratio		4.4285	=	=
Limited slip differential		M	M	M
Lockup factor Load/Coast, %		40/40	=	=
Sportomatic transmission		905/21	925/00	925/01
Torque converter dia. (mm)		F&S 190	=	=
Converter stall rpm		2600	2600	3000
Gear ratios				
1st Gear		2.400	=	=
2nd Gear		1.555	=	=
3rd Gear		1.125	=	=
4th Gear		0.857	=	=
Reverse Gear		2.533	=	=
Synchromesh on fwd gears		POSY	=	=
Final drive ratio		3.857	=	=

Abbreviations:
M Optional equipment
S Standard equipment
F&S Manufacturer Fichtel & Sachs
POSY Porsche Blocking synchromesh system, molybdenum-coated synchro rings

4. Steering, Suspension, Wheels, Brakes				
Front suspension				
Stabilizer bar dia.	(mm)	M	M	20
Steering ratio		17.87	=	=
Turning circle dia.	(m)	10.80	=	=
Rear suspension				
Stabilizer bar, manual trans.	(mm)	M	M	15
Master cylinder dia.	(mm)	19.05	=	=

Model designation		911T	911 E	911S
Brake caliper piston dia.				
front	(mm)	48	=	=
rear	(mm)	38	=	=
Brake disc diameter				
front	(mm)	282.5	=	=
rear	(mm)	290	=	=
Brake disc thickness				
front	(mm)	20	=	=
rear	(mm)	20	=	=
Total eff. pad area	(cm²)	210	=	257
Parking brake		Mechanical, acting on both rear wheels		
Brake drum diameter	(mm)	180	=	
Total pad area	(cm²)	170	=	
Wheels and tires				
Standard tires front		165HR15	185/70VR15	=
on wheel size		5 ¹/₂J x 15	6J x 15	=
Standard tires rear		165HR15	185/70VR15	=
on wheel size		5 ¹/₂J x 15	6J x 15	=
Space saver spare wheel		5 ¹/₂ J x 15		
Tire pressure, front	(bar)	2.0	=	=
rear	(bar)	2.4	=	=
Space saver spare	(bar)	2.0	=	=

5. Body, interior equipment (Dimensions at empty weight)				
Length	(mm)	4227	=	4147
Width	(mm)	1610	=	=
Height	(mm)	1320	=	=
Wheelbase	(mm)	2271	=	=
Track, front	(mm)	1360	1372	=
rear	(mm)	1342	1354	1354
Ground clearance at legal maximum weight	(mm)	150	=	=

9. Electrical system				
Generator output	(W/A)	770/55	=	=
Battery	(V/Ah)	12/66	=	=

Weights according to DIN 70020				
Empty weight	(kg)	1050	1075	=
Maximum permissible total weight	(kg)	1400	=	=
Permissible towing load				
unbraked	(kg)	480	=	=
braked	(kg)	600	=	=

Performance				
Maximum speed				
Manual trans.	(km/h)	205	220	230
Acceleration 0...100 km/h				
Manual trans.	(s)	9.5	7.9	7.0
Standing-start kilometer				
Manual trans.	(s)	30.35	28.5	27.5

Capacities				
Engine oil capacity 1*	(l)	11	13	=
Eng. Oil qty. w. SPM	(l)	+ 2	=	=
Oil change qty. 1*	(l)	10	=	=
Manual trans. 2*	(l)	3.0	=	=
Sportomatic 2*	(l)	2.5	=	=
Fuel tank capacity	(l)	62	=	=
Brake reservoir 6*	(l)	0.20	=	=

* Notes:
1* Approved motor oils: API SE/SF when combined with API SE/CC - SF/CC - SF/CD - SE/CD
Multigrade oils approved by factory, (SAE 10 W/50 or 15 W/40 or 20 W/50). Single grade oils are also approved. Summer SAE 30. Winter SAE 20.
2* Single-grade transmission oil SAE 90 to MIL-L 2105 B or API classification GL 5.
Also permissible: transmission oil SAE 90 MIL-L 2105 or API classification GL 4.
6* Use only brake fluid meeting SAE J 1703 or DOT 3 or 4.
Abbreviations:
SPM Sportomatic

Model year 1973

Model designation		911T	911E	911S	911 RS 2.7

1. Engine

		911T	911E	911S	911 RS 2.7
Engine type, manual trans.		911/57	911/52	911/53	911/83
Bore	(mm)	84	=	=	90
Stroke	(mm)	70.4	=	=	=
Displacement	(cc)	2341	=	=	2687
Compression ratio		7.5:1	8.0:1	8.5:1	8.5:1
Power output	(kW/hp)	96/130	121/165	140/190	154/210
at rpm	(rpm)	5600	6200	6500	6300
Torque	(Nm)	196	206	216	255
at rpm	(rpm)	4000	4500	5200	5100
Specific output	(kW/l)	41	52	60	57
Maximum rpm	(rpm)	6500	7000	7300	7300
Engine weight	(kg)	176	183	182	182

2. Fuel system, Ignition, Settings

		911T	911E	911S	911 RS 2.7
Fuel supply		SZV	MSE	MSE	MSE
Fuel, Research Octane No.		91	=	=	=
Ignition system		BHKZ			
Spark plugs, Bosch		W230T1	W265P21	=	W260P21
Beru		225/14/3	235/14/3P	265/14/3P	265P21
Spark plug gap	(mm)	0.7	0.5...0.6	=	=
Idle rpm	(rpm)	850...950	=	=	=
CO level	(%)	2.5...3.5	=	=	2.0...3.0

Abbreviations:
BHKZ = Battery high voltage condenser ignition
SZV = Solex-Zenith carburetor 40 TIN
MSE = Bosch mechanical port injection

3. Powertrain

		911T	911E	911S	911 RS 2.7
Clutch, pressure plate		G MFZ 225	=	=	=
Clutch disc		GUD 225	=	=	=
Manual transmission type		915/03	=	=	915/08
Gear ratios					
1st Gear		3.181	=	=	=
2nd Gear		1.833	=	=	=
3rd Gear		1.261	=	=	=
4th Gear		0.9615	=	=	0.925
5th Gear		0.7586	=	=	0.724
Reverse Gear		3.325	=	=	=
Synchromesh syst. Gears 1-5	POSY		=	=	=
Final drive ratio		4.4285	=	=	=
Limited slip differential		M	M	M	M
Lockup factor Load/Coast, %		40/40	=	=	=
Sportomatic transmission		905/21	925/00	925/01	...
Torque converter dia. (mm)		F&S 190	=	=	...
Converter stall rpm		2600	2600	3000	...
Gear ratios					
1st Gear		2.400	=	=	
2nd Gear		1.555	=	=	
3rd Gear		1.125	=	=	
4th Gear		0.857	=	=	
Reverse Gear		2.533	=	=	
Synchromesh on fwd gears		POSY	=	=	
Final drive ratio		3.857	=	=	

Abbreviations:
M Optional equipment
S Standard equipment
F&S Manufacturer Fichtel & Sachs
POSY Porsche Blocking synchromesh system, molybdenum-coated synchro rings

4. Steering, Suspension, Wheels, Brakes

		911T	911E	911S	911 RS 2.7
Front suspension					
Stabilizer bar dia.	(mm)	M	M	20	15
Steering ratio		17.87	=	=	=
Turning circle dia.	(m)	10.80	=	=	=
Rear suspension					
Stabilizer bar, man. trans.	(mm)	M	M	15	=
Master cylinder dia.	(mm)	19.05	=	=	=

Model designation		911T	911E	911S	911 RS 2.7
Brake caliper piston dia.					
front	(mm)	48	=	=	=
rear	(mm)	38	=	=	=
Brake disc diameter					
front	(mm)	282.5	=	=	=
rear	(mm)	290	=	=	=
Brake disc thickness					
front	(mm)	20	=	=	=
rear	(mm)	20	=	=	=
Total eff. pad area	(cm²)	210	=	257	=
Parking brake		Mechanical, acting on both rear wheels			
Brake drum diameter	(mm)	180	=	=	=
Total pad area	(cm²)	170	=	=	=
Wheels and tires					
Standard tires front		165HR15	185/70VR15	=	=
on wheel size		5 1/2J x 15	6J x 15	=	=
Standard tires rear		165HR15	185/70VR15	=	215/60VR15
on wheel size		5 1/2J x 15	6J x 15	=	7J x 15
Space saver spare wheel		5 1/2 J x 15			
Tire pressure, front	(bar)	2.0	=	=	=
rear	(bar)	2.4	=	=	=
Space saver spare	(bar)	2.0	=	=	=

5. Body, interior equipment (Dimensions at empty weight)

		911T	911E	911S	911 RS 2.7
Length	(mm)	4227	=	4147	=
Width	(mm)	1610	=	=	1652
Height	(mm)	1320	=	=	=
Wheelbase	(mm)	2271	=	=	=
Track, front	(mm)	1360	1372	=	=
rear	(mm)	1342	1354	1354	1394
Ground clearance at legal maximum weight	(mm)	150	=	=	=

9. Electrical system

		911T	911E	911S	911 RS 2.7
Generator output	(W/A)	770/70	=	=	=
Battery	(V/Ah)	12/66	=	=	=

Weights according to DIN 70020

		911T	911E	911S	911 RS 2.7
Empty weight	(kg)	1050	1075	=	=
Maximum permissible total weight	(kg)	1400	=	=	=
Permissible towing load					
unbraked	(kg)	480	=	=	=
braked	(kg)	600	=	=	=

Performance

		911T	911E	911S	911 RS 2.7
Maximum speed					
Manual trans.	(km/h)	205	220	230	240
Acceleration 0...100 km/h					
Manual trans.	(s)	9.5	7.9	7.0	6.3
Standing-start kilometer					
Manual trans.	(s)	30.35	28.5	27.5	26.5

Capacities

		911T	911E	911S	911 RS 2.7
Engine oil capacity 1*	(l)	11	13	=	=
Eng. Oil qty. w. SPM	(l)	+ 2	=	=	...
Oil change qty. 1*	(l)	10	=	=	=
Manual trans. 2*	(l)	3.0	=	=	=
Sportomatic 2*	(l)	2.5	=	=	...
Fuel tank capacity	(l)	62	62	85	85
Brake reservoir 6*	(l)	0.20	=	=	=

* Notes:
1* Approved motor oils: API SE/SF when combined with API SE/CC - SF/CC - SF/CD - SE/CD
Multigrade oils as approved by factory, (SAE 10 W/50 or 15 W/40 or 20 W/50).
Single grade oils are also approved. Summer SAE 30. Winter SAE 20.
2* Single-grade transmission oil SAE 90 to MIL-L 2105 B or API classification GL 5.
Also permissible: transmission oil SAE 90 MIL-L 2105 or API classification GL 4.
6* Use only brake fluid meeting SAE J 1703 or DOT 3 or 4.
Abbreviations:
SPM Sportomatic

Model year 1974

Model designation		911	911 S	911 Carrera
1. Engine				
Engine type, manual trans.		911/92	911/93	911/83
Bore	(mm)	90	=	=
Stroke	(mm)	70.4	=	=
Displacement	(cc)	2687	2687	2687
Compression ratio		8.0:1	8.5:1	8.5:1
Power output	(kW/hp)	110/150	129/175	154/210
at rpm	(rpm)	5700	5800	6300
Torque	(Nm)	235	235	255
at rpm	(rpm)	3800	4000	5100
Specific output	(kW/l)	41	48	57
Maximum rpm	(rpm)	6400	6400	7200
Engine weight	(kg)	182	182	182

2. Fuel system, Ignition, Settings

		911	911 S	911 Carrera
Fuel supply		K-Jetronic	K-Jetronic	MSE
Fuel, Research Octane No.		91	91	91
Ignition system		BHKZ	BHKZ	BHKZ
Spark plugs, Bosch		W215T30	W225T30	W260T2
Beru		215/14/3	225/14/3A	260/14/3
Spark plug gap	(mm)	0.7	=	=
Idle rpm	(rpm)	850...950	=	=
CO level	(%)	2.5	=	=
Fuel consumption, city-highway average	(l/100 km)	12...14	13...15	15...18

Abbreviations:
BHKZ = Battery high voltage condenser ignition
SLE = Secondary air injection. ZLP = Air pump
MSE = Bosch mechanical port injection

3. Powertrain

		911	911 S	911 Carrera
Clutch, pressure plate		G MFZ 225	=	=
Clutch disc		GUD 225	=	=
Manual transmission type		915/06	915/40	915/06
Gear ratios				
1st Gear		3.181	=	=
2nd Gear		1.833	=	=
3rd Gear		1.261	=	=
4th Gear		0.9259	=	=
5th Gear		0.7241	=	=
Reverse Gear		3.325	=	=
Synchromesh syst. Gears 1-5		POSY	=	=
Final drive ratio		4.4285	=	=
Limited slip differential		M	M	M
Lockup factor Load/Coast,%		40/40	=	=
Sportomatic transmission		925/02	=	...
Torque converter dia. (mm)		F&S 190	=	...
Converter stall rpm		2000	=	
Gear ratios				
1st Gear		2.400	=	
2nd Gear		1.555	=	
3rd Gear		1.125	=	
4th Gear		0.821	=	
Reverse Gear		2.533	=	
Synchromesh on fwd gears		POSY	=	
Final drive ratio		3.857	=	

Abbreviations:
M Optional equipment
S Standard equipment
F&S Manufacturer Fichtel & Sachs
POSY Porsche Blocking synchromesh system, molybdenum-coated synchro rings

4. Steering, Suspension, Wheels, Brakes

		911	911 S	911 Carrera
Front suspension				
Stabilizer bar dia.	(mm)	16	16	20
Steering ratio		17.87	=	=
Turning circle dia.	(m)	10.80	=	=
Rear suspension				
Stabilizer bar, man. trs.	(mm)	M	M	18

Model designation		911	911 S	911 Carrera
Master cylinder dia.	(mm)	19.05	=	=
Brake caliper piston dia.				
front	(mm)	48	=	=
rear	(mm)	38	=	=
Brake disc diameter				
front	(mm)	282.5	=	=
rear	(mm)	290	=	=
Brake disc thickness				
front	(mm)	20	=	=
rear	(mm)	20	=	=
Total eff. pad area	(cm²)	210		257
Parking brake		Mechanical, acting on both rear wheels		
Brake drum diameter	(mm)	180		
Total pad area	(cm²)	170	=	
Wheels and tires				
Standard tires front		165HR15	185/70VR15	=
on wheel size		5 ½J x 15	6J x 15	=
Standard tires rear		165HR15	185/70VR15	215/60VR15
on wheel size		5 ½J x 15	6J x 15	7J x 15
Space saver spare wheel		5 ½ J x 15		
Tire pressure, front	(bar)	2.0	=	=
rear	(bar)	2.4	=	=
Space saver spare	(bar)	2.0	=	=

5. Body, interior equipment (Dimensions at empty weight)

		911	911 S	911 Carrera
Length	(mm)	4291	=	=
Width	(mm)	1610	1610	1652
Height	(mm)	1320	=	=
Wheelbase	(mm)	2271	=	=
Track, front	(mm)	1360	1372	=
rear	(mm)	1342	1354	1380
Ground clearance at legal maximum weight	(mm)	150	=	=

9. Electrical system

		911	911 S	911 Carrera
Generator output	(W/A)	770/70	=	=
Battery	(V/Ah)	12/66	=	=

Weights according to DIN 70020

		911	911 S	911 Carrera
Empty weight	(kg)	1075	=	=
Maximum permissible total weight	(kg)	1440	=	1400
Permissible towing load				
unbraked	(kg)	480	=	=
braked	(kg)	800	=	=

Performance

		911	911 S	911 Carrera
Maximum speed				
Manual trans.	(km/h)	210	225	240
Acceleration 0...100 km/h				
Manual trans.	(s)	8.5	7.6	6.3
Standing-start kilometer				
Manual trans.	(s)	29.0	28.0	26.5

Capacities

		911	911 S	911 Carrera
Engine oil capacity 1*	(l)	11	13	=
Eng. Oil qty. w. SPM	(l)	+ 2	=	...
Oil change qty. 1*	(l)	10	=	=
Manual trans. 2*	(l)	3.0	=	=
Sportomatic 2*	(l)	2.5	=	...
Fuel tank capacity	(l)	80	=	=
Brake reservoir 6*	(l)	0.20	=	=

* Notes:
1* Approved motor oils: API SE/SF when combined with API SE/CC - SF/CC - SF/CD - SE/CD
Multigrade oils as approved by factory, (SAE 10 W/50 or 15 W/40 or 20 W/50).
Single grade oils are also approved. Summer SAE 30. Winter SAE 20.
2* Single-grade transmission oil SAE 90 to MIL-L 2105 B or API classification GL 5
6* Use only brake fluid meeting SAE J 1703 or DOT 3 or 4.
Abbreviations:
SPM Sportomatic

...el year 1975

...esignation		911	911S	911 Carrera	911 Turbo
...ne					
...type, manual trans.		911/41	911/42	911/83	930/52
	(mm)	90	90	90	95
	(mm)	70.4	=	=	=
...ement	(cc)	2687	2687	2687	2994
...ssion ratio		8.0:1	8.5:1	8.5:1	6.5:1
...output	(kW/hp)	110/150	129/175	154/210	191/260
	(rpm)	5700	5800	6300	5500
	(Nm)	235	235	255	343
	(rpm)	3800	4000	5100	4000
...e output	(kW/l)	41	48	57	64
...m rpm	(rpm)	6500	6500	7300	7000
...weight	(kg)	195	200	200	207

...system, Ignition, Settings

...pply		K-Jetronic	K-Jetronic	MSE	K-Jetronic
...esearch Octane No.		91	91	91	96
...n system		BHKZ	BHKZ	BHKZ	BHKZ breakerless
...lugs, Bosch		W215T30	W225T30	W260T2	W280P21
Beru		215/14/3	225/14/3A	260/14/3	...
...lug gap	(mm)	0.7	=	=	=
...n	(rpm)	850...950	=	=	900...950
...t emission control		...	...	...	...
...el	(%)	2.5	=	=	=
...nsumption, city-highway					
...e	(l/100 km)	12...14	13...15	15...18	14...18

...viations:
= Battery high voltage condenser ignition
Secondary air injection. ZLP = Air pump
Bosch mechanical port injection

...ertrain

...pressure plate		G MFZ 225	=	=	G MFZ 240
...disc		GUD 225	=	=	GUD 240
...l transmission type		915/43	915/40	915/06	930/30
...tios					
...ar		3.181	=	=	2.250
...ar		1.833	=	=	1.304
...ar		1.261	=	=	0.893
...ar		0.9615	1.000	0.9259	0.656
...ar		0.7241	0.8214	0.7241	
...se Gear		3.325	=	=	2.437
...romesh syst. Gears 1-5		POSY	=	=	POSY
...drive ratio		4.4285	=	=	4.222
...d slip differential		M	M	M	M
...o factor Load/Coast, %		40/40	=	=	=
...matic transmission		925/02	925/13	...	...
...e converter dia. (mm)		F&S 190	=	...	...
...rter stall rpm		2000			
...tios					
...ar		2.400	=		
...ear		1.555	=		
...ear		1.125	=		
...ear		0.821	=		
...se Gear		2.533	=		
...romesh on fwd gears		POSY	=		
...drive ratio		3.857	=		

...viations:
...tional equipment
...ndard equipment
...Manufacturer Fichtel & Sachs
Porsche Blocking synchromesh system, molybdenum-coated synchro rings

...ering, Suspension, Wheels, Brakes

...suspension					
...izer bar dia.	(mm)	16	16	20	20
...ing ratio		17.87	=	=	=
...ng circle dia.	(m)	10.80	=	=	=
...suspension					
...izer bar, man. trans.	(mm)	...	...	18	18

Model designation		911	911S	911 Carrera	911 Turbo
Brake system					
Master cylinder dia.	(mm)	19.05	=	=	=
Brake caliper piston dia.					
front	(mm)	48	=	=	=
rear	(mm)	38	=	=	=
Brake disc diameter					
front	(mm)	282.5	=	=	=
rear	(mm)	290	=	=	=
Brake disc thickness					
front	(mm)	20	=	=	=
rear	(mm)	20	=	=	=
Total eff. pad area	(cm^2)	210	=	257	257
Parking brake		Mechanical, acting on both rear wheels			
Brake drum diameter	(mm)	180	=		
Total pad area	(cm^2)	170	=		
Wheels and tires					
Standard tires front		185/70VR15 =		=	205/50VR15*
on wheel size		6J x 15	=	=	7J x 15
Standard tires rear		185/70VR15		=	215/60VR15 NNNNNNNI
on wheel size		6J x 15	=	7J x 15	8J x 15
Space saver spare wheel		5 1/2 J x 15			
Tire pressure, front	(bar)	2.0	–	=	=
rear	(bar)	2.4	=	=	=
Space saver spare	(bar)	2.0	=	=	=

* Optional: 185/70VR15 front. 215/60VR15 rear

5. Body, interior equipment (Dimensions at empty weight)

Length	(mm)	4291	=	=	=
Width	(mm)	1610	1610	1652	1775
Height	(mm)	1320	=	=	=
Wheelbase	(mm)	2271	=	=	2272
Track, front	(mm)	1372	=	=	1438
rear	(mm)	1354	=	1380	1511
Ground clearance at legal maximum weight	(mm)	120	=	=	=

9. Electrical system

Generator output	(W/A)	980/70	=	=	=
Battery	(V/Ah)	12/66	=	=	=

Weights according to DIN 70020

Empty weight	(kg)	1075	=	=	1140
Maximum total weight	(kg)	1440	=	1400	1470
Permissible towing load					
unbraked	(kg)	480	=	=	none
braked	(kg)	800	=	=	none

Performance

Maximum speed					
Manual trans.	(km/h)	>210	>225	>240	>250
Acceleration 0...100 km/h					
Manual trans.	(s)	8.5	7.6	6.3	5.5
Standing-start kilometer					
Manual trans.	(s)	29.0	28.0	26.5	24

Abbreviations: > = greater than, < = less than

Capacities

Engine oil capacity 1*	(l)	11	13	=	=
Eng. Oil qty. w. SPM	(l)	+ 2	=	...	...
Oil change qty.1*	(l)	10	=	=	=
Manual trans. 2*	(l)	3.0	=	=	3.7
Sportomatic 2*	(l)	2.5	=	...	...
Fuel tank capacity	(l)	80	=	=	=
Brake reservoir 6*	(l)	0.20	=	=	=

* Notes:
1* Approved motor oils: API SE/SF when combined with API SE/CC - SF/CC - SF/CD - SE/CD
Multigrade oils as approved by factory, (SAE 10 W/50 or 15 W/40 or 20 W/50).
Single grade oils are also approved. Summer SAE 30. Winter SAE 20.
2* Single-grade transmission oil SAE 90 to MIL-L 2105 B or API classification GL 5
6* Use only brake fluid meeting SAE J 1703 or DOT 3 or 4.
Abbreviations:
SPM Sportomatic

Model year 1976

Model designation		911	911 Carrera	911 Turbo
1. Engine				
Engine type, manual trans.		911/81	930/02	930/52
Bore	(mm)	90	95	95
Stroke	(mm)	70.4	70.4	70.4
Displacement	(cc)	2687	2994	2994
Compression ratio		8.5:1	8.5:1	6.5:1
Power output	(kW/hp)	121/165	147/200	191/260
at rpm	(rpm)	5800	6000	5500
Torque	(Nm)	235	255	343
at rpm	(rpm)	4000	4200	4000
Specific output	(kW/l)	45	50	64
Maximum rpm	(rpm)	6700	7000	7000
Engine weight	(kg)	195	200	207
2. Fuel system, Ignition, Settings				
Fuel supply		K-Jetronic	K-Jetronic	K-Jetronic
Fuel, Research Octane No.		91	91	96
Ignition system		BHKZ	BHKZ	BHKZ breakerless
Spark plugs, Bosch		W225T30	W260T2	W280P1
Beru		225/14/3	260/14/3	225/14/3A
Spark plug gap	(mm)	0.7	=	0.7
Idle rpm	(rpm)	850...950	=	900...950
Exhaust emission control		...	...	SLE+ZLP
CO level	(%)	2.5	2.5	2.5

Abbreviations:
BHKZ = Battery high voltage condenser ignition
SLE = Secondary air injection
ZLP = Air pump

		911	911 Carrera	911 Turbo
Fuel consumption, city-highway average	(l/100km)	13...15	14...16	14...18
3. Powertrain				
Clutch, pressure plate		G MFZ 225	=	G MFZ 240
Clutch disc		GUD 225	=	GUD 240
Manual transmission type		915/44	915/44	930/33
Gear ratios				
1st Gear		3.181	=	2.250
2nd Gear		1.833	=	1.304
3rd Gear		1.261	=	0.893
4th Gear		1.000	=	0.656
5th Gear		0.821	=	...
Reverse Gear		3.325	=	2.437
Synchromesh syst. Gears 1-5		POSY	=	POSY
Final drive ratio		3.875	=	4.222 and 4.000
Limited slip differential		M	M	M
Lockup factor Load/Coast, %		40/40	=	=
Sportomatic transmission		925/09	925/13	...
Torque converter dia. (mm)		F&S 190	=	...
Converter stall rpm		1900	=	
Gear ratios				
1st Gear		2.400	=	
2nd Gear		1.428	=	
3rd Gear		0.926	=	
4th Gear		...	...	
Reverse Gear		2.533	=	
Synchromesh on fwd gears		POSY	=	
Final drive ratio		3.375	=	

Abbreviations:
M Optional equipment
S Standard equipment
F&S Manufacturer Fichtel & Sachs
POSY Porsche Blocking synchromesh system, molybdenum-coated synchro rings

4. Steering, Suspension, Wheels, Brakes		911	911 Carrera	911 Turbo
Front suspension				
Stabilizer bar dia.	(mm)	16	20	18

Model designation		911	911 Carrera	911 Turbo
Steering ratio		17.87	=	=
Turning circle dia.	(m)	10.80	=	=
Rear suspension				
Stabilizer bar, manual trans.	(mm)	...	18	18
Brake system				
Brake booster dia.	(in.)	...	7	7
Master cylinder dia.	(mm)	20.64	=	23.81
Brake caliper piston dia.				
front	(mm)	48	=	=
rear	(mm)	38	=	=
Brake disc diameter				
front	(mm)	282.5	=	=
rear	(mm)	290	=	=
Brake disc thickness				
front	(mm)	20	=	=
rear	(mm)	20	=	=
Total eff. pad area	(cm²)	257	=	=
Parking brake		Mechanical, acting on both rear wheels		
Brake drum diameter	(mm)	180	=	=
Total pad area	(cm²)	170	=	=
Wheels and tires				
Standard tires front		185/70VR15	=	185/70VR15*
on wheel size		6J x 15	6J x 15	7J x 15
Standard tires rear		185/70VR15	215/60VR15	215/60VR15*
on wheel size		6J x 15	7J x 15	8J x 15
Space saver spare wheel		165-15 89P		
Tire pressure, front	(bar)	2.0	=	2.0
rear	(bar)	2.4	=	3.0
Space saver spare	(bar)	2.2	=	2.2

* Optional: 205/50VR15 front, 225/50VR15 rear

5. Body, interior equipment (Dimensions at empty weight)				
Length	(mm)	4291	=	=
Width	(mm)	1610	1652	1775
Height	(mm)	1320	=	=
Wheelbase	(mm)	2272	=	=
Track, front	(mm)	1369	=	1438
rear	(mm)	1354	1380	1511
Ground clearance at legal maximum weight	(mm)	120	=	=

9. Electrical system		911	911 Carrera	911 Turbo
Generator output	(W/A)	980/70	=	=
Battery	(V/Ah)	12/66	=	=

Weights according to DIN 70020				
Empty weight	(kg)	1120	=	1195
Maximum permissible total weight	(kg)	1500	1440	1525
Permissible towing load				
unbraked	(kg)	480	=	none
braked	(kg)	800	=	none

Performance				
Maximum speed				
Manual trans.	(km/h)	>210	>230	>250
Acceleration 0...100 km/h				
Manual trans.	(s)	7.8	6.5	5.5
Standing-start kilometer				
Manual trans.	(s)	29.0	27.0	24.0

Abbreviations: > = greater than, < = less than

Capacities				
Engine oil capacity 1*	(l)	13	=	=
Eng. Oil qty. w. SPM	(l)	+ 2	=	...
...				
Oil change qty. 1*	(l)	10	=	=
Manual trans. 2*	(l)	3.0	=	3.7
Sportomatic 2*	(l)	2.5	=	...
Fuel tank capacity	(l)	80	=	=
Brake reservoir 6*	(l)	0.20	=	=

* Notes:
1* Approved motor oils: API SE/SF when combined with API SE/CC -
SF/CC - SF/CD - SE/CD
Multigrade oils as approved by factory, (SAE 10 W/50 or 15 W/40 or 20
W/50).
Single grade oils are also approved. Summer SAE 30. Winter SAE 20.
2* Single-grade transmission oil SAE 90 to MIL-L 2105 B or API
classification GL 5
6* Use only brake fluid meeting SAE J 1703 or DOT 3 or 4.
Abbreviations:
SPM Sportomatic

Model year 1977

Model designation		*911*	*911 Carrera*	*911 Turbo*
1. Engine				
Engine type, manual trans.		911/81	930/02	930/52
Bore	(mm)	90	95	95
Stroke	(mm)	70.4	70.4	70.4
Displacement	(cc)	2687	2994	2994
Compression ratio		8.5:1	8.5:1	6.5:1
Power output	(kW/hp)	121/165	147/200	191/260
at rpm	(rpm)	5800	6000	5500
Torque	(Nm)	235	255	343
at rpm	(rpm)	4000	4200	4000
Specific output	(kW/l)	45	50	64
Maximum rpm	(rpm)	6700	7000	7000
Engine weight	(kg)	195	200	207

2. Fuel system, Ignition, Settings				
Fuel supply		K-Jetronic	K-Jetronic	K-Jetronic
Fuel, Research Octane No.		91	91	96
Ignition system		BHKZ	BHKZ	BHKZ breakerless
Spark plugs, Bosch		W225T30	=	W280P21
Beru		225/14/3		225/14/3A
Spark plug gap	(mm)	0.7	=	0.6
Idle rpm	(rpm)	850...950		900...950
Exhaust emission control		ZLP+TR +EGR*	=	SLE+ZLP
CO level	(%)	2.0...2.4	2.0...4.0	

Abbreviations:
BHKZ = Battery high voltage condenser ignition
SLE = Secondary air injection. ZLP = Air pump
TR   = Thermal reactors. EGR = Exhaust gas recirculation. * = USA only

Fuel consumption, city-highway				
average	(l/100km)	13...15	14...16	14...18

3. Powertrain				
Clutch, pressure plate		G MFZ 225	=	G MFZ 240
Clutch disc		GUD 225		GUD 240
Manual transmission type		915/60	915/60	930/33
Gear ratios				
1st Gear		3.181	=	2.250
2nd Gear		1.833	=	1.304
3rd Gear		1.261	=	0.893
4th Gear		1.000	=	0.656
5th Gear		0.821	=	...
Reverse Gear		3.325	=	2.437
Synchromesh syst. Gears 1-5		POSY	=	POSY
Final drive ratio		3.875	=	4.222
Limited slip differential		M	M	M
Lockup factor Load/Coast, %		40/40	=	=
Sportomatic transmission		925/15	925/16	...
Torque converter dia. (mm)		F&S 190	=	...
Converter stall rpm		1900	=	
Gear ratios				
1st Gear		2.400	=	
2nd Gear		1.428	=	
3rd Gear		0.926	=	
4th Gear		...	...	

Reverse Gear		1.81	=	
Synchromesh on fwd gears		POSY	=	
Final drive ratio		3.375	=	

Abbreviations:
M Optional equipment
S Standard equipment
F&S Manufacturer Fichtel & Sachs
POSY Porsche Blocking synchromesh system, molybdenum-coated synchro
rings

4. Steering, Suspension, Wheels, Brakes				
Front suspension				
Stabilizer bar dia.	(mm)	16	20	20
Steering ratio		17.87	=	=
Turning circle dia.	(m)	10.95	=	=
Rear suspension				
Stabilizer bar, man. trs.	(mm)	...	18	18
Brake system				
Brake booster dia.	(in.)	...	7	8
Master cylinder dia.	(mm)	20.64	=	23.81
Brake caliper piston dia.				
front	(mm)	48	=	=
rear	(mm)	38	=	=
Brake disc diameter				
front	(mm)	282.5	=	=
rear	(mm)	290	=	=
Brake disc thickness				
front	(mm)	20	=	=
rear	(mm)	20	=	=
Total eff. pad area	(cm^2)	257	=	=
Parking brake		Mechanical, acting on both rear wheels		
Brake drum diameter	(mm)	180	=	
Total pad area	(cm^2)	170	=	
Wheels and tires				
Standard tires front		185/70VR15	=	205/55VR16
on wheel size		6J x 15	6J x 15	7J x 16
Standard tires rear		185/70VR15	215/60VR15	225/50VR16
on wheel size		6J x 15	7J x 15	8J x 16
Space saver spare wheel		165-15 89P		
Tire pressure, front	(bar)	2.0	=	2.0
rear	(bar)	2.4	=	3.0
Space saver spare	(bar)	2.2	=	2.2

5. Body, interior equipment (Dimensions at empty weight)				
Length	(mm)	4291	=	=
Width	(mm)	1610	1652	1775
Height	(mm)	1320	=	=
Wheelbase	(mm)	2272	=	=
Track, front	(mm)	1369	=	1438
rear	(mm)	1354	1380	1511
Ground clearance at legal				
maximum weight	(mm)	120	=	=

9. Electrical system				
Generator output	(W/A)	980/70	=	=
Battery	(V/Ah)	12/66	=	=

Weights according to DIN 70020				
Empty weight	(kg)	1120	=	1195
Maximum permissible				
total weight	(kg)	1500	1449	1525
Permissible towing load				
unbraked	(kg)	480	=	none
braked	(kg)	800	=	none

Performance				
Maximum speed				
Manual trans.	(km/h)	>210	>230	>250
Acceleration 0...100 km/h				
Manual trans.	(s)	7.8	6.5	5.5
Standing-start kilometer				
Manual trans.	(s)	29.0	27.0	24.0

Abbreviations: > = greater than, < = less than

Model designation		911	911 Carrera	911 Turbo
Capacities				
Engine oil capacity 1*	(l)	13	=	=
Eng. Oil qty. w. SPM	(l)	+ 2	...	...
Oil change qty. 1*	(l)	10	=	=
Manual trans. 2*	(l)	3.0	=	3.7
Sportomatic 2*	(l)	2.5	...	...
Fuel tank capacity	(l)	80	=	=
Brake reservoir 6*	(l)	0.20	=	=

* Notes:
1* Approved motor oils: API SE/SF when combined with API SE/CC - SF/CC - SF/CD - SE/CD
Multigrade oils as approved by factory, (SAE 10 W/50 or 15 W/40 or 20 W/50).
Single grade oils are also approved. Summer SAE 30, Winter SAE 20.
2* Single-grade transmission oil SAE 90 to MIL-L 2105 B or API classification GL 5
6* Use only brake fluid meeting SAE J 1703 or DOT 3 or 4.
Abbreviations:
SPM Sportomatic

Model year 1978

Model designation		911 SC	911 Turbo
1. Engine			
Engine type, manual trans.		930/03	930/60
Bore	(mm)	95	97
Stroke	(mm)	70.4	74.4
Displacement	(cc)	2994	3299
Compression ratio		8.5:1	7.0:1
Power output	(kW/hp)	132/180	221/300
at rpm	(rpm)	5500	5500
Torque	(Nm)	265	412
at rpm	(rpm)	4200	4000
Specific output	(kW/l)	50	67
Maximum rpm	(rpm)	7000	7000
Engine weight	(kg)	200	230
2. Fuel system, Ignition, Settings			
Fuel supply		K-Jetronic	K-Jetronic
Fuel, Research Octane No.		91	98
Ignition system		BHKZ	BHKZ breakerless
Spark plugs, Bosch		W225T30	W280P21
Beru		225/14/3	225/14/3A
Spark plug gap	(mm)	0.8	0.8
Idle rpm	(rpm)	850...950	950...1050
Exhaust emission control		SLE+ZLP	SLE+ZLP
CO level	(%)	2.0...2.4	2.0...4.0

Abbreviations: BHKZ = Battery high voltage condenser ignition
SLE = Secondary air injection. ZLP = Air pump

Fuel economy to DIN 70 030	(l/100km)		
A. at steady 90 km/h		9.2	8.1
B. at steady 120 km/h		11.4	15.3
C. EC city cycle		17.3	20.0
3. Powertrain			
Clutch, pressure plate		G MFZ 225	G MFZ 240
Clutch disc		TD 225	GUD 240
Manual transmission type		915/62	930/34
Gear ratios			
1st Gear		3.181	2.250
2nd Gear		1.833	1.304
3rd Gear		1.261	0.893
4th Gear		1.000	0.625
5th Gear		0.785	...
Reverse Gear		3.325	2.437
Synchromesh syst. Gears 1-5		POSY	POSY
Final drive ratio		3.875	4.222

Model designation		911 SC	911 Turbo
Limited slip differential		M	M
Lockup factor Load/Coast, %		40/40	40/40
Sportomatic transmission		925/16	...
Torque converter dia.	(mm)	F&S 190	...
Converter stall rpm		1900	
Gear ratios			
1st Gear		2.400	
2nd Gear		1.428	
3rd Gear		0.926	
4th Gear		...	
Reverse Gear		1.81	
Synchromesh on fwd gears		POSY	
Final drive ratio		3.375	

Abbreviations:
M Optional equipment
S Standard equipment
F&S Manufacturer Fichtel & Sachs
POSY Porsche Blocking synchromesh system, molybdenum-coated synchro rings

4. Steering, Suspension, Wheels, Brakes			
Front suspension			
Stabilizer bar dia.	(mm)	20	20
Steering ratio		17.87	17.87
Turning circle dia.	(m)	10.95	10.95
Rear suspension			
Stabilizer bar. man. trans.	(mm)	18	18
Brake system			
Brake booster dia.	(in.)	7	8
Master cylinder dia.	(mm)	20.64	23.81
Brake caliper piston dia.			
front	(mm)	48	38+38
rear	(mm)	38	30+30
Brake disc diameter			
front	(mm)	282.5	304
rear	(mm)	290	309
Brake disc thickness			
front	(mm)	20.5	32
rear	(mm)	20	28
Total eff. pad area	(cm^2)	257	376
Parking brake		Mechanical, acting on both rear wheels	
Brake drum diameter	(mm)	180	=
Total pad area	(cm^2)	170	=
Wheels and tires			
Standard tires front		185/70VR15	205/55VR16
on wheel size		6J x 15	7J x 16
Standard tires rear		215/60VR15	225/50VR16
on wheel size		7J x 15	8J x 16
Space saver spare wheel		165-15 89P	=
Tire pressure, front	(bar)	2.0	2.0
rear	(bar)	2.4	3.0
Space saver spare	(bar)	2.2	2.2

5. Body, interior equipment (Dimensions at empty weight)			
Length	(mm)	4291	4291
Width	(mm)	1652	1775
Height	(mm)	1320	1310
Wheelbase	(mm)	2272	2272
Track, front	(mm)	1369 (1361)*	1432
rear	(mm)	1379 (1367)*	1501
Ground clearance at legal maximum weight	(mm)	120	120

* U.S. specifications in parentheses

9. Electrical system			
Generator output	(W/A)	980/70	=
Battery	(V/Ah)	12/66	=

Weights according to DIN 70020			
Empty weight	(kg)	1160	1300
Maximum permissible total weight	(kg)	1500	1680

For thirty years, the 911 has been unique, visually as well as below its sheet metal. This phantom view shows a 911 SC, with its 180 horsepower three-liter engine.

Model designation		911 SC	911 Turbo
Permissible towing load			
unbraked	(kg)	480	none
braked	(kg)	800	none
Performance			
Maximum speed			
Manual trans.	(km/h)	225	260
Acceleration 0...100 km/h			
Manual trans.	(s)	7.0	5.4
Standing-start kilometer			
Manual trans.	(s)	27.5	24.0
Capacities			
Engine oil capacity 1*	(l)	13	=
Eng. Oil qty. w. SPM	(l)	+ 2	...
Oil change qty. 1*	(l)	10	=
Manual trans. 2*	(l)	3.0	3.7
Sportomatic 2*	(l)	2.5	...
Fuel tank capacity	(l)	80	80
Brake reservoir 6*	(l)	0.20	0.20

* Notes:

1* Approved motor oils: API SE/SF when combined with API SE/CC - SF/CC - SF/CD - SE/CD
Multigrade oils as approved by factory, (SAE 10 W/50 or 15 W/40 or 20 W/50).

2* Single-grade transmission oil SAE 90 to MIL-L 2105 B or API classification GL 5

6* Use only brake fluid meeting SAE J 1703 or DOT 3 or 4.

Abbreviations:
SPM Sportomatic

Model year 1979

Model designation		911 SC	911 Turbo
1. Engine			
Engine type, manual trans.		930/03	930/60
Bore	(mm)	95	97
Stroke	(mm)	70.4	74.4
Displacement	(cc)	2994	3299
Compression ratio		8.5:1	7.0:1
Power output	(kW/hp)	132/180	221/300
at rpm	(rpm)	5500	5500
Torque	(Nm)	265	412
at rpm	(rpm)	4200	4000
Specific output	(kW/l)	50	67
Maximum rpm	(rpm)	7000	7000
Engine weight	(kg)	200	230
2. Fuel system, Ignition, Settings			
Fuel supply		K-Jetronic	K-Jetronic
Fuel, Research Octane No.		91	98
Ignition system		BHKZ	BHKZ breakerless
Spark plugs, Bosch		W225T30	W280P21
Beru		225/14/3	225/14/3A
Spark plug gap	(mm)	0.8	0.8
Idle rpm	(rpm)	850...950	950...1050
Exhaust system		SLE+ZLP	SLE+ZLP
CO level	(%)	2.0...2.4	2.0...4.0

Abbreviations:
BHKZ = Battery high voltage condenser ignition
SLE = Secondary air injection. ZLP = Air pump

Fuel economy to		
DIN 70 030 (l/100km)		
A. at steady 90 km/h	9.2	8.1
B. at steady 120 km/h	11.4	15.3
C. EC city cycle	17.3	20.0

3. Powertrain

	911 SC	911 Turbo
Clutch, pressure plate	G MFZ 225	G MFZ 240
Clutch disc	TD 225	GUD 240
Manual transmission type	915/62	930/34
Gear ratios		
1st Gear	3.181	2.250
2nd Gear	1.833	1.304
3rd Gear	1.261	0.893
4th Gear	1.000	0.625
5th Gear	0.785	...
Reverse Gear	3.325	2.437
Synchromesh syst. Gears 1-5	POSY	POSY
Final drive ratio	3.875	4.222
Limited slip differential	M	M
Lockup factor Load/Coast, %	40/40	40/40
Sportomatic transmission	925/16	...
Torque converter dia. (mm)	F&S 190	...
Converter stall rpm	1900	
Gear ratios		
1st Gear	2.400	
2nd Gear	1.428	
3rd Gear	0.926	
4th Gear	...	
Reverse Gear	1.81	
Synchromesh on fwd gears	POSY	
Final drive ratio	3.375	

Abbreviations:
M Optional equipment
S Standard equipment
F&S Manufacturer Fichtel & Sachs
POSY Porsche Blocking synchromesh system. molybdenum-coated synchro rings

4. Steering, Suspension, Wheels, Brakes

		911 SC	911 Turbo
Front suspension			
Stabilizer bar dia.	(mm)	20	20
Steering ratio		17.87	17.87
Turning circle dia.	(m)	10.95	10.95
Rear suspension			
Stabilizer bar, man. trans.	(mm)	18	18
Brake system			
Brake booster dia.	(in.)	7	8
Master cylinder dia.	(mm)	20.64	23.81
Brake caliper piston dia.			
front	(mm)	48	38+38
rear	(mm)	38	30+30
Brake disc diameter			
front	(mm)	282.5	304
rear	(mm)	290	309
Brake disc thickness			
front	(mm)	20.5	32
rear	(mm)	20	28
Total eff. pad area	(cm²)	257	376
Parking brake		Mechanical, acting on both rear wheels	
Brake drum diameter	(mm)	180	=
Total pad area	(cm²)	170	=
Wheels and tires			
Standard tires front		185/70VR15	205/55VR16
on wheel size		6J x 15	7J x 16
Standard tires rear		215/60VR15	225/50VR16
on wheel size		7J x 15	8J x 16
Space saver spare wheel		165-15 89P	=
Tire pressure, front	(bar)	2.0	2.0
rear	(bar)	2.4	3.0
Space saver spare	(bar)	2.2	2.2

5. Body, interior equipment (Dimensions at empty weight)

		911 SC	911 Turbo
Length	(mm)	4291	4291
Width	(mm)	1652	1775
Height	(mm)	1320	1310
Wheelbase	(mm)	2272	2272
Track, front	(mm)	1369 (1361)*	1432
rear	(mm)	1379 (1367)*	1501
Ground clearance at legal maximum weight	(mm)	120	120

* U.S. specifications in parentheses

9. Electrical system

		911 SC	911 Turbo
Generator output	(W/A)	990/70	=
Battery	(V/Ah)	12/66	=

Weights according to DIN 70020

		911 SC	911 Turbo
Empty weight	(kg)	1160	1300
Maximum permissible total weight	(kg)	1500	1680
Permissible towing load			
unbraked	(kg)	480	none
braked	(kg)	800	none

Performance

		911 SC	911 Turbo
Maximum speed			
Manual trans.	(km/h)	225	260
Acceleration 0...100 km/h			
Manual trans.	(s)	7.0	5.4
Standing-start kilometer			
Manual trans.	(s)	27.5	24.0

Capacities

		911 SC	911 Turbo
Engine oil capacity 1*	(l)	13	=
Eng. Oil qty. w. SPM	(l)	+ 2	...
Oil change qty. 1*	(l)	10	=
Manual trans. 2*	(l)	3.0	3.7
Sportomatic 2*	(l)	2.5	...
Fuel tank capacity	(l)	80	80
Brake reservoir 6*	(l)	0.20	0.20

* Notes:
1* Approved motor oils: API SE/SF when combined with API SE/CC - SF/CC - SF/CD - SE/CD
Multigrade oils approved by factory, (SAE 10 W/50 or 15 W/40 or 20 W/50)
2* Single-grade transmission oil SAE 90 to MIL-L 2105 B or API classification GL 5
6* Use only brake fluid meeting SAE J 1703 or DOT 3 or 4.
Abbreviations:
SPM Sportomatic

Model year 1980

Model designation	911 SC	911 Turbo

1. Engine

		911 SC	911 Turbo
Engine type, manual trans.		930/09	930/60
Bore	(mm)	95	97
Stroke	(mm)	70.4	74.4
Displacement	(cc)	2994	3299
Compression ratio		8.6:1	7.0:1
Power output	(kW/hp)	138/188	221/300
at rpm	(rpm)	5500	5500
Torque	(Nm)	265	412
at rpm	(rpm)	4200	4000
Specific output	(kW/l)	50	67
Maximum rpm	(rpm)	6500	7000
Engine weight	(kg)	190	230

2. Fuel system, Ignition, Settings

		911 SC	911 Turbo
Fuel supply		K-Jetronic	K-Jetronic
Fuel, Research Octane No.		91	98

Model designation		911 SC	911 Turbo
Ignition system		BHKZ	BHKZ breakerless
Spark plugs, Bosch		W260T2	W280P21
Beru		260/14/3	225/14/3A
Spark plug gap	(mm)	0.8	0.8
Idle rpm	(rpm)	850...950	950...1050
Exhaust emission control		SLE+ZLP	SLE+ZLP
CO level	(%)	2.0...2.4	2.0...4.0

Abbreviations:
BHKZ = Battery high voltage condenser ignition
SLE = Secondary air injection
ZLP = Air pump

Fuel economy to DIN 70 030	(l/100km)		
A. at steady 90 km/h		9.2	8.1
B. at steady 120 km/h		11.4	15.3
C. EC city cycle		17.3	20.0

3. Powertrain

		911 SC	911 Turbo
Clutch, pressure plate		G MFZ 225	G MFZ 240
Clutch disc		TD 225	GUD 240
Manual transmission type		915/62	930/34
Gear ratios			
1st Gear		3.181	2.250
2nd Gear		1.833	1.304
3rd Gear		1.261	0.893
4th Gear		1.000	0.625
5th Gear		0.785	...
Reverse Gear		3.325	2.437
Synchromesh syst. Gears 1-5		POSY	POSY
Final drive ratio		3.875	4.222
Limited slip differential		M	M
Lockup factor Load/Coast, %		40/40	40/40
Sportomatic transmission		925/16	...
Torque converter dia. (mm)		F&S 190	...
Converter stall rpm		1900	
Gear ratios			
1st Gear		2.400	
2nd Gear		1.428	
3rd Gear		0.926	
4th Gear		...	
Reverse Gear		1.81	
Synchromesh on fwd gears		POSY	
Final drive ratio		3.375	

Abbreviations:
M Optional equipment
S Standard equipment
F&S Manufacturer Fichtel & Sachs
POSY Porsche Blocking synchro system, molybdenum-coated synchro rings
BHKZ Battery high voltage condenser ignition

4. Steering, Suspension, Wheels, Brakes

		911 SC	911 Turbo
Front suspension			
Stabilizer bar dia.	(mm)	20	20
Steering ratio		17.87	17.87
Turning circle dia.	(m)	10.95	10.95
Rear suspension			
Stabilizer bar, man. trans.	(mm)	18	18
Brake system			
Brake booster dia.	(in.)	7	8
Master cylinder dia.	(mm)	20.64	23.81
Brake caliper piston dia.			
front	(mm)	48	38+38
rear	(mm)	38	30+30
Brake disc diameter			
front	(mm)	282.5	304
rear	(mm)	290	309
Brake disc thickness			
front	(mm)	20.5	32
rear	(mm)	20	28
Total eff. pad area	(cm²)	257	376
Parking brake		Mechanical, acting on both rear wheels	

Model designation		911 SC	911 Turbo
Brake drum diameter	(mm)	180	=
Total pad area	(cm²)	170	=
Wheels and tires			
Standard tires front		185/70VR15	205/55VR16
on wheel size		6J x 15	7J x 16
Standard tires rear		215/60VR15	225/50VR16
on wheel size		7J x 15	8J x 16
Space saver spare wheel		165-15 89P	=
Tire pressure, front	(bar)	2.0	2.0
rear	(bar)	2.4	3.0
Space saver spare	(bar)	2.2	2.2

5. Body, interior equipment (Dimensions at empty weight)

		911 SC	911 Turbo
Length	(mm)	4291	4291
Width	(mm)	1652	1775
Height	(mm)	1320	1310
Wheelbase	(mm)	2272	2272
Track, front	(mm)	1369 (1361)*	1432
rear	(mm)	1379 (1367)*	1501
Ground clearance at legal maximum weight	(mm)	120	120
* U.S. specifications in parentheses			

9. Electrical system

		911 SC	911 Turbo
Generator output	(W/A)	990/70	=
Battery	(V/Ah)	12/66	=

Weights according to DIN 70020

		911 SC	911 Turbo
Empty weight	(kg)	1160	1300
Maximum permissible total weight	(kg)	1500	1680
Permissible towing load			
unbraked	(kg)	480	none
braked	(kg)	800	none

Performance

		911 SC	911 Turbo
Maximum speed			
Manual trans.	(km/h)	225	260
Acceleration 0...100 km/h			
Manual trans.	(s)	7.0	5.4
Standing-start kilometer			
Manual trans.	(s)	27.5	24.0

Capacities

		911 SC	911 Turbo
Engine oil capacity 1*	(l)	13	=
Eng. Oil qty. w. SPM	(l)	+ 2	...
Oil change qty. 1*	(l)	10	=
Manual trans. 2*	(l)	3.0	3.7
Sportomatic 2*	(l)	2.5	...
Fuel tank capacity	(l)	80	80
Brake reservoir 6*	(l)	0.20	0.20

* Notes:
1* Approved motor oils: API SE/SF when combined with API SE/CC - SF/CC - SF/CD - SE/CD
Multigrade oils approved by factory, (SAE 10 W/50 or 15 W/40 or 20 W/50)
2* Single-grade transmission oil SAE 90 to MIL-L 2105 B or API classification GL 5
6* Use only brake fluid meeting SAE J 1703 or DOT 3 or 4.
Abbreviations:
SPM Sportomatic

Model year 1981

Model designation		911 SC	911 Turbo
1. Engine			
Engine type, manual trans.		930/10	930/66
Bore	(mm)	95	97
Stroke	(mm)	70.4	74.4
Displacement	(cc)	2994	3299
Compression ratio		9.8:1	7.0:1
Power output	(kW/hp)	150/204	221/300
at rpm	(rpm)	5900	5500

		911 SC	911 Turbo
Torque	(Nm)	267	412
at rpm	(rpm)	4300	4000
Specific output	(kW/l)	50.0	67
Maximum rpm	(rpm)	6800	7000
Engine weight	(kg)	190	245

2. Fuel system, Ignition, Settings

		911 SC	911 Turbo
Fuel supply		K-Jetronic	K-Jetronic
Fuel, Research Octane No.		98	98
Ignition system		BHKZ	BHKZ breakerless
Spark plugs, Bosch		WR 4 C1	W 3 DP
Beru		14/4 C1	...
Spark plug gap	(mm)	0.8	0.8
Idle rpm	(rpm)	800...950	900+-50
Exhaust emission control		SLE+ZLP	SLE+ZLP
CO level	(%)	1.0...2.0	1.5...2.5

Abbreviations:
BHKZ = Battery high voltage condenser ignition
SLE = Secondary air injection
ZLP = Air pump
Fuel economy to
EC standard (l/100km)

		911 SC	911 Turbo
A. at steady 90 km/h		8.0	8.1
B. at steady 120 km/h		9.7	15.3
C. EC city cycle		13.4	20.0

3. Powertrain

		911 SC	911 Turbo
Clutch, pressure plate		G MFZ 225	G MFZ 240
Clutch disc		TD 225	GUD 240
Manual transmission type		915/62	930/34
Gear ratios			
1st Gear		3.181	2.250
2nd Gear		1.833	1.304
3rd Gear		1.261	0.893
4th Gear		1.000	0.625
5th Gear		0.785	...
Reverse Gear		3.325	2.437
Synchromesh syst. Gears 1-5		POSY	POSY
Final drive ratio		3.875	4.222
Limited slip differential		M	M
Lockup factor Load/Coast, %		40/40	40/40

Abbreviations:
M Optional equipment
S Standard equipment
POSY Porsche Blocking synchromesh system, molybdenum-coated synchro rings

4. Steering, Suspension, Wheels, Brakes

		911 SC	911 Turbo
Front suspension			
Stabilizer bar dia.	(mm)	20	20
Steering ratio		17.87	17.87
Turning circle dia.	(m)	10.95	10.95
Rear suspension			
Stabilizer bar, man. trans.	(mm)	18	18
Brake system			
Brake booster dia.	(in.)	7	8
Master cylinder dia.	(mm)	20.64	23.81
Brake caliper piston dia.			
front	(mm)	48	38+38
rear	(mm)	38	30+30
Brake disc diameter			
front	(mm)	282.5	304
rear	(mm)	290	309
Brake disc thickness			
front	(mm)	24	32
rear	(mm)	24	28
Total eff. pad area	(cm²)	257	376
Parking brake		Mechanical, acting on both rear wheels	
Brake drum diameter	(mm)	180	=
Total pad area	(cm²)	170	=

Wheels and tires

		911 SC	911 Turbo
Standard tires front		185/70VR15	205/55VR16
on wheel size		6J x 15	7J x 16
Standard tires rear		215/60VR15	225/50VR16
on wheel size		7J x 15	8J x 16
Space saver spare wheel		165-15 89P	=
Tire pressure, front	(bar)	2.0	2.0
rear	(bar)	2.4	3.0
Space saver spare	(bar)	2.2	2.2

5. Body, interior equipment (Dimensions at empty weight)

		911 SC	911 Turbo
Length	(mm)	4291	4291
Width	(mm)	1652	1775
Height	(mm)	1320	1310
Wheelbase	(mm)	2272	2272
Track, front	(mm)	1369	1432
rear	(mm)	1379	1501
Ground clearance at legal maximum weight	(mm)	120	120

9. Electrical system

		911 SC	911 Turbo
Generator output	(W/A)	990/70	=
Battery	(V/Ah)	12/66	=

Weights according to DIN 70020

		911 SC	911 Turbo
Empty weight	(kg)	1160	1300
Maximum permissible total weight	(kg)	1500	1680
Permissible towing load			
unbraked	(kg)	480	none
braked	(kg)	800	none

Performance

		911 SC	911 Turbo
Maximum speed			
Manual trans.	(km/h)	235	260
Acceleration 0...100 km/h			
Manual trans.	(s)	6.8	5.4
Standing-start kilometer			
Manual trans.	(s)	26.8	24.0

Capacities

		911 SC	911 Turbo
Engine oil capacity 1*	(l)	13	=
Oil change qty. 1*	(l)	10	=
Manual trans. 2*	(l)	3.0	3.7
Fuel tank capacity	(l)	80	80
Brake reservoir 6*	(l)	0.20	0.20

* Notes:
1* Approved motor oils: API SE/SF when combined with API SE/CC - SF/CC - SF/CD - SE/CD
Multigrade oils as approved by factory.
2* Single-grade transmission oil SAE 90 to MIL-L 2105 B or API classification GL 5
6* Use only brake fluid meeting SAE J 1703 or DOT 3 or 4.

Model year 1982

Model designation		911 SC	911 Turbo

1. Engine

		911 SC	911 Turbo
Engine type, manual trans.		930/10	930/66
Bore	(mm)	95	97
Stroke	(mm)	70.4	74.4
Displacement	(cc)	2994	3299
Compression ratio		9.8:1	7.0:1
Power output	(kW/hp)	150/204	221/300
at rpm	(rpm)	5900	5500
Torque	(Nm)	267	412
at rpm	(rpm)	4300	4000
Specific output	(kW/l)	50.0	67
Maximum rpm	(rpm)	7000	7000
Engine weight	(kg)	190	245

Model designation		911 SC	911 Turbo
2. Fuel system, Ignition, Settings			
Fuel supply		K-Jetronic	K-Jetronic
Fuel, Research Octane No.		98	98
Ignition system		BHKZ	BHKZ
Spark plugs, Bosch		WR 4 C1	W 3 DP
Beru		14/4 C1	...
Spark plug gap	(mm)	0.8	0.8
Idle rpm	(rpm)	800...950	900+-50
Exhaust emission control		SLE+ZLP	SLE+ZLP
CO level	(%)	1.0...2.0	1.5...2.5

Abbreviations:
BHKZ = Battery high voltage condenser ignition
SLE = Secondary air injection.
ZLP = Air pump

Fuel economy to EC standard (l/100km)			
A. at steady 90 km/h		8.0	8.1
B. at steady 120 km/h		9.7	15.3
C. EC city cycle		13.4	20.0

3. Powertrain		911 SC	911 Turbo
Clutch, pressure plate		G MFZ 225	G MFZ 240
Clutch disc		TD 225	GUD 240
Manual transmission type		915/62	930/34
Gear ratios			
1st Gear		3.181	2.250
2nd Gear		1.833	1.304
3rd Gear		1.261	0.893
4th Gear		1.000	0.625
5th Gear		0.785	...
Reverse Gear		3.325	2.437
Synchromesh syst. Gears 1-5		POSY	POSY
Final drive ratio		3.875	4.222
Limited slip differential		M	M
Lockup factor Load/Coast, %		40/40	40/40

Abbreviations:
M Optional equipment
S Standard equipment
POSY Porsche Blocking synchro system, molybdenum-coated synchro rings

4. Steering, Suspension, Wheels, Brakes		911 SC	911 Turbo
Front suspension			
Stabilizer bar dia.	(mm)	20	20
Steering ratio		17.87	17.87
Turning circle dia.	(m)	10.95	10.95
Rear suspension			
Stabilizer bar, man. trans.	(mm)	18	18
Brake system			
Brake booster dia.	(in.)	7	8
Master cylinder dia.	(mm)	20.64	23.81
Brake caliper piston dia.			
front	(mm)	48	38+38
rear	(mm)	38	30+30
Brake disc diameter			
front	(mm)	282.5	304
rear	(mm)	290	309
Brake disc thickness			
front	(mm)	24	32
rear	(mm)	24	28
Total eff. pad area	(cm²)	257	376
Parking brake		Mechanical, acting on both rear wheels	
Brake drum diameter	(mm)	180	=
Total pad area	(cm²)	170	=
Wheels and tires			
Standard tires front		185/70VR15	205/55VR16
on wheel size		6J x 15	7J x 16
Standard tires rear		215/60VR15	225/50VR16
on wheel size		7J x 15	8J x 16
Space saver spare wheel		165-15 89P	=
Tire pressure, front	(bar)	2.0	2.0
rear	(bar)	2.4	3.0
Space saver spare	(bar)	2.2	2.2

Model designation		911 SC	911 Turbo
5. Body, interior equipment (Dimensions at empty weight)			
Length	(mm)	4291	4291
Width	(mm)	1652	1775
Height	(mm)	1320	1310
Wheelbase	(mm)	2272	2272
Track, front	(mm)	1369	1432
rear	(mm)	1379	1501
Ground clearance at legal maximum weight	(mm)	120	120
9. Electrical system			
Generator output	(W/A)	1050/75	=
Battery	(V/Ah)	12/66	=
Weights according to DIN 70020			
Empty weight	(kg)	1160	1300
Maximum permissible total weight	(kg)	1500	1680
Permissible towing load			
unbraked	(kg)	480	none
braked	(kg)	800	none
Performance			
Maximum speed			
Manual trans.	(km/h)	235	260
Acceleration 0...100 km/h			
Manual trans.	(s)	6.8	5.4
Standing-start kilometer			
Manual trans.	(s)	26.8	24.0
Capacities			
Engine oil capacity 1*	(l)	13	=
Oil change qty. 1*	(l)	10	=
Manual trans. 2*	(l)	3.0	3.7
Fuel tank capacity	(l)	80	80
Brake reservoir 6*	(l)	0.20	0.20

* Notes:
1* Approved motor oils: API SE/SF when combined with API SE/CC - SF/CC - SF/CD - SE/CD
Multigrade oils as approved by factory.
2* Single-grade transmission oil SAE 90 to MIL-L 2105 B or API classification GL 5
6* Use only brake fluid meeting SAE J 1703 or DOT 3 or 4.

Model year 1983

Model designation		911 SC	911 Turbo
1. Engine			
Engine type, manual trans.		930/10	930/66
Bore	(mm)	95	97
Stroke	(mm)	70.4	74.4
Displacement	(cc)	2994	3299
Compression ratio		9.8:1	7.0:1
Power output	(kW/hp)	150/204	221/300
at rpm	(rpm)	5900	5500
Torque	(Nm)	267	430
at rpm	(rpm)	4300	4000
Specific output	(kW/l)	50.0	67
Maximum rpm	(rpm)	7000	7200
Engine weight	(kg)	190	230
2. Fuel system, Ignition, Settings			
Fuel supply		K-Jetronic	K-Jetronic
Fuel, Research Octane No.		98	98
Ignition system		BHKZ	BHKZ breakerless
Spark plugs, Bosch		WR 4 C1	W 3 DP
Beru		14/4 CU	...
Spark plug gap	(mm)	0.8	0.8
Idle rpm	(rpm)	800...950	900+-50

		911 SC	911 Turbo
Exhaust emission control		SLE+ZLP	SLE+ZLP
CO level	(%)	1.0...1.5	1.5...2.5
Abbreviations:			
BHKZ = Battery high voltage condenser ignition			
SLE = Secondary air injection			
ZLP = Air pump			
Fuel economy to			
DIN 70 030	(l/100km)		
A. at steady 90 km/h		8.0	9.7
B. at steady 120 km/h		9.7	11.8
C. EC city cycle		13.4	15.5

3. Powertrain

		911 SC	911 Turbo
Clutch, pressure plate		G MFZ 225	G MFZ 240
Clutch disc		TD 225	GUD 240
Manual transmission type		915/62	930/34
Gear ratios			
1st Gear		3.181	2.250
2nd Gear		1.833	1.304
3rd Gear		1.261	0.893
4th Gear		1.000	0.625
5th Gear		0.785	...
Reverse Gear		3.325	2.437
Synchromesh syst. Gears 1-5		POSY	POSY
Final drive ratio		3.875	4.222
Limited slip differential		M	M
Lockup factor Load/Coast, %		40/40	40/40
Transmission weight			
including oil	(kg)	60	70.2
Abbreviations:			
M Optional equipment			
S Standard equipment			
POSY Porsche Blocking synchro system, molybdenum-coated synchro rings			

4. Steering, Suspension, Wheels, Brakes

		911 SC	911 Turbo
Front suspension			
Stabilizer bar dia.	(mm)	20	20
Steering ratio		17.87	17.8
Turning circle dia.	(m)	10.95	10.95
Rear suspension			
Stabilizer bar, man. trans.	(mm)	18	18
Brake system			
Brake booster dia.	(in.)	7	8
Master cylinder dia.	(mm)	20.64	23.81
Brake caliper piston dia.			
front	(mm)	48	38+38
rear	(mm)	42	30+30
Brake disc diameter			
front	(mm)	282.5	304
rear	(mm)	290	309
Brake disc thickness			
front	(mm)	24	32
rear	(mm)	24	28
Total eff. pad area	(cm²)	257	376
Parking brake		Mechanical, acting on both rear wheels	
Brake drum diameter	(mm)	180	=
Total pad area	(cm²)	170	=
Wheels and tires			
Standard tires front		185/70VR15	205/55VR16
on wheel size		6J x 15	7J x 16
Standard tires rear		215/60VR15	225/50VR16
on wheel size		7J x 15	8J x 16
Space saver spare wheel		165-15 89P	=
Tire pressure, front	(bar)	2.0	2.0
rear	(bar)	2.5	3.0
Space saver spare	(bar)	2.2	2.2

5. Body, interior equipment (Dimensions at empty weight)

		911 SC	911 Turbo
Length	(mm)	4291	4291
Width	(mm)	1652	1775
Height	(mm)	1320	1310
Wheelbase	(mm)	2272	2272

		911 SC	911 Turbo
Track, front	(mm)	1369	1432
rear	(mm)	1379	1501
Ground clearance at legal maximum weight	(mm)	120	120

9. Electrical system

		911 SC	911 Turbo
Generator output	(W/A)	1050/75	=
Battery	(V/Ah)	12/66	=

Weights according to DIN 70020

		911 SC	911 Turbo
Empty weight	(kg)	1160	1300
Maximum permissible total weight	(kg)	1500	1600
Permissible towing load			
unbraked	(kg)	480	none
braked	(kg)	800	none

Performance

		911 SC	911 Turbo
Maximum speed			
Manual trans.	(km/h)	235	260
Acceleration 0...100 km/h			
Manual trans.	(s)	6.8	5.4
Standing-start kilometer			
Manual trans.	(s)	26.8	24.0

Capacities

		911 SC	911 Turbo
Engine oil capacity 1*	(l)	13	=
Manual trans. 2*	(l)	3.1	3.7
Fuel tank capacity	(l)	80	80
Brake reservoir 6*	(l)	0.20	0.20

* Notes:
1* Approved motor oils: API SE/SF when combined with API SE/CC - SF/CC - SF/CD - SE/CD
Multigrade oils as approved by factory.
2* Single-grade transmission oil SAE 90 to MIL-L 2105 B or API classification GL 5
6* Use only brake fluid meeting SAE J 1703 or DOT 3 or 4.

Model year 1984

Model designation		911 Carrera	911 Turbo

1. Engine

		911 Carrera	911 Turbo
Engine type, manual trans.		930/20	930/66
Bore	(mm)	95	97
Stroke	(mm)	74.4	74.4
Displacement	(cc)	3164	3299
Compression ratio		10.3:1	7.0:1
Power output	(kW/hp)	170/231	221/300
at rpm	(rpm)	5900	5500
Torque	(Nm)	284	430
at rpm	(rpm)	4800	4000
Specific output	(kW/l)	53.7	67
Maximum rpm	(rpm)	6560	7200
Engine weight	(kg)	210	253

2. Fuel system, Ignition, Settings

		911 Carrera	911 Turbo
Fuel supply		DME	K-Jetronic
Fuel, Research Octane No		98	98
Ignition system		DME	BHKZ breakerless
Ignition		Single plug	Single plug
Spark plugs, Bosch		WR 4 CC	W 3 DP
Beru	14/4 CU	...	
Spark plug gap	(mm)	0.7	0.8
Idle rpm	(rpm)	880+-20	900+-50
Exhaust emission control		...	SLE+ZLP
CO level without catalyst, %		1.0...1.5	1.5...2.5
Abbreviations:			
BHKZ = Battery high voltage condenser ignition			

Model designation		911 Carrera	911 Turbo
SLE = Secondary air injection			
ZLP = Air pump			
Fuel economy to			
EC standard,	(l/100km)		
A. at steady 90 km/h		6.8	9.7
B. at steady 120 km/h		9.0	11.8
C. EC city cycle		13.6	15.5
Three-cycle average		9.8	12.3

3. Powertrain

		911 Carrera	911 Turbo
Clutch, pressure plate		G MFZ 225	G MFZ 240
Clutch disc		TD 225	GUD 240
Manual transmission type		915/67	930/34
Gear ratios			
1st Gear		3.181	2.250
2nd Gear		1.833	1.304
3rd Gear		1.261	0.829
4th Gear		0.965	0.625
5th Gear		0.7631	...
Reverse Gear		3.325	2.437
Synchromesh syst. Gears 1-5		POSY	POSY
Synchromesh on reverse		no	no
Final drive ratio		3,875	4.222
Limited slip differential		M	M
Lockup factor Load/Coast, %		40/40	40/40
Transmission weight			
including oil	(kg)	60	70.2

Abbreviations:
M Optional equipment
S Standard equipment
POSY Porsche Blocking synchromesh system, molybdenum-coated synchro rings
DME Digital Motor Electronics (Fuel injection + ignition)

4. Steering, Suspension, Wheels, Brakes

		911 Carrera	911 Turbo
Front suspension			
Stabilizer bar dia.	(mm)	20	20
Steering ratio		17.87	17.87
Turning circle dia.	(m)	10.95	10.95
Rear suspension			
Stabilizer bar, man.trans.	(mm)	18	18
Brake system			
Brake booster dia.	(in.)	8	8
Master cylinder dia.	(mm)	20.64	23.81
Brake caliper piston dia.			
front	(mm)	48	38+38
rear	(mm)	42	30+30
Brake disc diameter			
front	(mm)	282.5	304
rear	(mm)	290	309
Brake disc thickness			
front	(mm)	24	32
rear	(mm)	24	28
Total eff. pad area	(cm^2)	257	376
Parking brake		Mechanical, acting on both rear wheels	
Brake drum diameter	(mm)	180	=
Total pad area	(cm^2)	170	=
Wheels and tires			
Standard tires front		185/70VR15	205/55VR16
on wheel size		6J x 15	7J x 16
Wheel offset	(mm)		23.3
Standard tires rear		215/60VR15	225/50VR16
on wheel size		7J x 15	8J x 16
Space saver spare wheel		165-15 89P	=
Tire pressure, front	(bar)	2.0	2.0
rear	(bar)	2.5	3.0
Space saver spare	(bar)	2.2	2.2

5. Body, interior equipment (Dimensions at empty weight)

		911 Carrera	911 Turbo
Length	(mm)	4291	4291
Width	(mm)	1652	1775
Height	(mm)	1320	1310

Model designation		911 Carrera	911 Turbo
Wheelbase	(mm)	2272	2272
Track, front	(mm)	1372	1432
rear	(mm)	1380	1501
Ground clearance at legal			
maximum weight	(mm)	120	120

9. Electrical system

		911 Carrera	911 Turbo
Generator output	(W/A)	1260/90	=
Battery	(V/Ah)	12/66	=

Weights according to DIN 70020

		911 Carrera	911 Turbo
Empty weight	(kg)	1160	1300
Maximum permissible			
total weight	(kg)	1500	1680
Permissible towing load			
unbraked	(kg)	480	none
braked	(kg)	800	none

Performance

		911 Carrera	911 Turbo
Maximum speed			
Manual trans.	(km/h)	245	260
Acceleration 0...100 km/h			
Manual trans.	(s)	6.1	5.4
Standing-start kilometer			
Manual trans.	(s)	26.8	24.0

Capacities

		911 Carrera	911 Turbo
Engine oil capacity 1*	(l)	13	=
Manual trans. 2*	(l)	3.4	3.7
Fuel tank capacity	(l)	80	80
Brake reservoir 6*	(l)	0.20	0.20

* Notes:
1* Approved motor oils: API SE/SF when combined with API SE/CC - SF/CC - SF/CD - SE/CD
Multigrade oils as approved by factory.
2* Single-grade transmission oil SAE 90 to MIL-L 2105 B or API classification GL 5
6* Use only brake fluid meeting SAE J 1703 or DOT 3 or 4.

Model year 1985

Model designation		911 Carrera	911 Turbo

1. Engine

		911 Carrera	911 Turbo
Engine type, manual trans.		930/20	930/66
Bore	(mm)	95	97
Stroke	(mm)	74.4	74.4
Displacement	(cc)	3164	3299
Compression ratio		10.3:1	7.0:1
Power output	(kW/hp)	170/231	221/300
at rpm	(rpm)	5900	5500
Torque	(Nm)	284	430
at rpm	(rpm)	4800	4000
Specific output	(kW/l)	53.7	67
Maximum rpm	(rpm)	6560	7200
Engine weight	(kg)	219	253

2. Fuel system, Ignition, Settings

		911 Carrera	911 Turbo
Fuel supply		DME	K-Jetronic
Fuel, Research Octane No.		98	98
Ignition system		DME	BHKZ breakerless
Ignition		Single plug	Single plug
Spark plugs, Bosch		WR 4 CC	W 3 DP W 3 CP
Beru		...	...
Spark plug gap	(mm)	0.7	0.6
Idle rpm	(rpm)	880+-20	900+-50
Exhaust emission control		....	SLE+ZLP
CO level without catalyst %		1.0...1.5	1.5...2.5

Abbreviations:
DME = Digital Motor Electronics, (Fuel injection + ignition)

BHKZ = Battery high voltage condenser ignition
SLE = Secondary air injection.
ZLP = Air pump
Fuel economy to
EC standard (l/100km)

	911 Carrera	911 Turbo
A. at steady 90 km/h	6.8	9.7
B. at steady 120 km/h	9.0	11.8
C. EC city cycle	13.6	15.5
Three-cycle average	9.8	12.3

3. Powertrain

		911 Carrera	911 Turbo
Clutch, pressure plate		G MFZ 225	G MFZ 240
Clutch disc		TD 225	GUD 240
Manual transmission type		915/72	930/36
Gear ratios			
1st Gear		3.181	2.250
2nd Gear		1.833	1.304
3rd Gear		1.261	0.829
4th Gear		0.965	0.625
5th Gear		0.7631	...
Reverse Gear		3.325	2.437
Synchromesh syst. Gears 1-5		POSY	POSY
Synchromesh on reverse		no	no
Final drive ratio		3.875	4.222
Limited slip differential		M	M
Lockup factor Load/Coast, %		40/40	40/40
Transmission weight including oil	(kg)	60	70.2

Abbreviations:
M Optional equipment
S Standard equipment
POSY Porsche Blocking synchromesh system, molybdenum-coated synchro rings

4. Steering, Suspension, Wheels, Brakes

		911 Carrera	911 Turbo
Front suspension			
Stabilizer bar dia.	(mm)	20	22
Steering ratio		17.87	17.87
Turning circle dia.	(m)	10.95	10.95
Rear suspension			
Stabilizer bar. man.trans.	(mm)	18	20
Brake system			
Brake booster dia.	(in.)	8	8
Master cylinder dia.	(mm)	20.64	23.81
Brake caliper piston dia.			
front	(mm)	48	38+38
rear	(mm)	42	30+30
Brake disc diameter			
front	(mm)	282.5	304
rear	(mm)	290	309
Brake disc thickness			
front	(mm)	24	32
rear	(mm)	24	28
Total eff. pad area	(cm²)	258	344
Parking brake		Mechanical, acting on both rear wheels	
Brake drum diameter	(mm)	180	=
Total pad area	(cm²)	170	=
Wheels and tires			
Standard tires front		185/70VR15	205/55VR16
on wheel size		6J x 15	7J x 16
Wheel offset	(mm)		23.3
Standard tires rear		215/60VR15	225/45VR16
on wheel size		7J x 15	9J x 16
Space saver spare wheel		165-15 89P	=
Tire pressure, front	(bar)	2.0	2.0
rear	(bar)	2.5	3.0
Space saver spare	(bar)	2.5	2.5

5. Body, interior equipment (Dimensions at empty weight)

		911 Carrera	911 Turbo
Length	(mm)	4291	4291
Width	(mm)	1652	1775
Height	(mm)	1320	1310

		911 Carrera	911 Turbo
Wheelbase	(mm)	2272	=
Track, front	(mm)	1372	1432
rear	(mm)	1380	1501
Ground clearance at legal maximum weight	(mm)	120	120

9. Electrical system

		911 Carrera	911 Turbo
Generator output	(W/A)	1260/90	=
Battery	(V/Ah)	12/66	=

Weights according to DIN 70020

		911 Carrera	911 Turbo
Empty weight	(kg)	1160	1300
Maximum permissible total weight	(kg)	1500	1680
Permissible towing load			
unbraked	(kg)	480	none
braked	(kg)	800	none
Performance			
Maximum speed			
Manual trans.	(km/h)	245	260
Acceleration 0...100 km/h			
Manual trans.	(s)	6.1	5.4
Standing-start kilometer			
Manual trans.	(s)	26.8	24.0
Capacities			
Engine oil capacity 1*	(l)	13	=
Manual trans. 2*	(l)	3.4	3.7
Fuel tank capacity	(l)	80	80
Brake reservoir 6*	(l)	0.20	0.20

* Notes:
1* Approved motor oils: API SE/SF when combined with API SE/CC - SF/CC - SF/CD - SE/CD
Multigrade oils as approved by factory.
2* Single-grade transmission oil SAE 90 to MIL-L 2105 B or API classification GL 5
6* Use only brake fluid meeting SAE J 1703 or DOT 3 or 4.

Model year 1986

Model designation		911 Carrera	911 Turbo

1. Engine

		911 Carrera	911 Turbo
Engine type, manual trans.		930/20	930/66
Bore	(mm)	95	97
Stroke	(mm)	74.4	74.4
Displacement	(cc)	3164	3299
Compression ratio		10.3:1	7.0:1
Power output	(kW/hp)	170/231	221/300
at rpm	(rpm)	5900	5500
Torque	(Nm)	284	430
at rpm	(rpm)	4800	4000
Specific output	(kW/l)	53.7	67
Maximum rpm	(rpm)	6570	7200
Engine weight	(kg)	219	253

2. Fuel system, Ignition, Settings

		911 Carrera	911 Turbo
Fuel supply		DME	K-Jetronic
Fuel, Research Octane No.		98	98
Ignition system		DME	BHKZ breakerless
Ignition		Single plug	Single plug
Spark plugs, Bosch		WR 4 CC	W 3 DP
Beru		......	
Spark plug gap	(mm)	0.7	0.7
Knock sensor		no	no
Idle rpm	(rpm)	880	900+-50
Exhaust emission control.		...	SLE+ZLP
CO level without catalyst %		0.5...1.5	1.5...2.5
with catalyst %		0.4...0.8	...

Abbreviations:
DME = Digital Motor Electronics (Fuel injection + ignition)
BHKZ = Battery high voltage condenser ignition
SLE = Secondary air injection.
ZLP = Air pump
Fuel economy to
EC standard, manual trans.

	(l/100km)	911 Carrera	911 Turbo
A. at steady 90 km/h		6.8	9.7
B. at steady 120 km/h		9.0	11.8
C. EC city cycle		13.6	15.5
Three-cycle average		9.8	12.3

3. Powertrain

		911 Carrera	911 Turbo
Clutch, pressure plate		G MFZ 225	G MFZ 240
Clutch disc		TD 225	GUD 240
Manual transmission type		915/72	930/36
Gear ratios			
1st Gear		3.181	2.250
2nd Gear		1.833	1.304
3rd Gear		1.261	0.829
4th Gear		0.965	0.625
5th Gear		0.7631	...
Reverse Gear		3.325	2.437
Synchromesh syst. Gears 1-5		POSY	POSY
Synchromesh on reverse		no	no
Final drive ratio		3.325	4.222
Limited slip differential		M	M
Lockup factor Load/Coast, %		40/40	40/40
Transmission weight including oil	(kg)	60	70.2

Abbreviations:
M Optional equipment
S Standard equipment
POSY Porsche Blocking synchromesh system, molybdenum-coated synchro rings

4. Steering, Suspension, Wheels, Brakes

		911 Carrera	911 Turbo
Front suspension			
Stabilizer bar dia.	(mm)	22	22
Steering ratio		17.87	17.87
Turning circle dia.	(m)	10.95	10.95
Rear suspension			
Stabilizer bar, man. trans.	(mm)	21	20
Brake system			
Brake booster dia.	(in.)	8	8
Master cylinder dia.	(mm)	20.64	23.81
Brake caliper piston dia.			
front	(mm)	48	38+38
rear	(mm)	42	30+30
Brake disc diameter			
front	(mm)	282.5	304
rear	(mm)	290	309
Brake disc thickness			
front	(mm)	24	32
rear	(mm)	24	28
Total eff. pad area	(cm²)	258	344
Parking brake		Mechanical, acting on both rear wheels	
Brake drum diameter	(mm)	180	=
Total pad area	(cm²)	170	=
Wheels and tires			
Standard tires front		185/70VR15	205/55VR16
on wheel size		6J x 15	7J x 16
Wheel offset	(mm)		23.3
Standard tires rear		215/60VR15	245/45VR16
on wheel size		7J x 15	9J x 16
Wheel offset	(mm)		15
Space saver spare wheel		165-15 89P	=
Tire pressure, front	(bar)	2.0	2.0
rear	(bar)	2.5	3.0
Space saver spare	(bar)	2.5	2.5

5. Body, interior equipment (Dimensions at empty weight)

		911 Carrera	911 Turbo
Length	(mm)	4291	4291
Width	(mm)	1652	1775
Height	(mm)	1320	1310
Wheelbase	(mm)	2272	=
Track, front	(mm)	1372	1432
rear	(mm)	1380	1501
Ground clearance at legal maximum weight	(mm)	130	120

9. Electrical system

		911 Carrera	911 Turbo
Generator output	(W/A)	1260/90	=
Battery	(V/Ah)	12/66	=

Weights according to DIN 70020

		911 Carrera	911 Turbo
Empty weight	(kg)	1210	1335
Maximum permissible total weight	(kg)	1530	1680
Permissible towing load			
unbraked	(kg)	480	none
braked	(kg)	800	none

Performance

		911 Carrera	911 Turbo
Maximum speed			
Manual trans.	(km/h)	245	260
Acceleration 0...100 km/h			
Manual trans.	(s)	6.1	5.4
Standing-start kilometer			
Manual trans.	(s)	26.1	24.0
Capacities			
Engine oil capacity 1*	(l)	13	=
Manual trans. 2*	(l)	3.4	3.7
Front suspension 2*	(l)	...	...
Fuel tank capacity	(l)	85	85
Brake reservoir 6*	(l)	0.24	0.24
Refrigerant 4*	(g)	1350	1300
Compressor oil 5*	(ml)	120	120

* Notes:
1* Approved motor oils: API SE/SF when combined with API SE/CC - SF/CC - SF/CD - SE/CD
Multigrade oils as approved by factory.
2* Single-grade transmission oil SAE 90 to MIL-L 2105 B or API classification GL 5
4* Refrigerant R 12
5* Commercially available air conditioning compressor oil
6* Use only brake fluid meeting SAE J 1703 or DOT 3 or 4.

Model year 1987

Model designation		911 Carrera	911 Carrera CLUBSPORT	911 Turbo
1. Engine				
Engine type, manual trans.		930/20	=	930/66
Bore	(mm)	95	=	97
Stroke	(mm)	74.4	=	74.4
Displacement	(cc)	3164	=	3299
Compression ratio		10.3:1	=	7.0:1
Power output	(kW/hp)	170/231	=	221/300
at rpm	(rpm)	5900	=	5500
Torque	(Nm)	284	=	430
at rpm	(rpm)	4800	=	4000
Specific output	(kW/l)	53.7	=	67
Maximum rpm	(rpm)	6570	=	7200
Engine weight	(kg)	219	=	269
2. Fuel system, Ignition, Settings				
Fuel supply		DME	=	K-Jetronic
Fuel, Research Octane No.		98	=	98
Ignition system		DME	=	BHKZ breakerless

Model designation		911 Carrera	911 Carrera CLUBSPORT	911 Turbo
Ignition		Single plug	=	Single plug
Spark plugs, Bosch		WR 4 CK q	=	W 3 DP 0
Beru		...	=	...
Spark plug gap	(mm)	0.7	=	0.7
Knock sensor		no	no	no
Idle rpm	(rpm)	880	=	900+-50
Exhaust emission control		....	....	SLE+ZLP
CO level without catalyst, %		0.5...1.5	=	...
with catalyst %		0.4...0.8	=	...

Abbreviations:
DME = Digital Motor Electronics (Fuel injection + ignition)
BHKZ = Battery high voltage condenser ignition
SLE = Secondary air injection.
ZLP = Air pump
Fuel economy to
EC standard, manual trans.
(l/100km)

		911 Carrera		911 Turbo
A. at steady 90 km/h		6.8	=	9.7
B. at steady 120 km/h		9.0	=	11.8
C. EC city cycle		13.6	=	15.5
Three-cycle average		9.8	=	12.3

3. Powertrain

		911 Carrera		911 Turbo
Clutch, pressure plate		G MFZ 240	=	=
Clutch disc		GUD 240	=	=
Manual transmission type		G50/00	=	930/36
Gear ratios				
1st Gear		3.500	=	2.250
2nd Gear		2.059	=	1.304
3rd Gear		1.409	=	0.829
4th Gear		1.074	=	0.625
5th Gear		0.861	=	...
Reverse Gear		2.857	=	2.437
Synchromesh syst. Gears 1-5		VK	=	POSY
Synchromesh on reverse		VK	=	no
Final drive ratio		3.444	=	4.222
Limited slip differential		M	=	M
Lockup factor Load/Coast, %		40/40	=	40/40
Transmission weight				
including oil	(kg)	66	=	70.2

Abbreviations:
M   Optional equipment
S   Standard equipment
VK   Full cone synchromesh system with molybdenum-coated synchro rings
POSY   Porsche Blocking synchromesh system, molybdenum-coated synchro rings

4. Steering, Suspension, Wheels, Brakes

		911 Carrera		911 Turbo
Front suspension				
Stabilizer bar dia.	(mm)	22	=	22
Steering ratio		17.87	=	17.87
Turning circle dia.	(m)	10.95	=	10.95
Rear suspension				
Stabilizer bar, man. trs.	(mm)	21	=	18
Brake system				
Brake booster dia.	(in.)	8	=	8
Master cylinder dia.	(mm)	20.64	=	23.81
Brake pressure limit valve				
Activation pressure	(bar)	33	=	55
Reduction factor		0.46	=	0.46
Brake caliper piston dia.				
front	(mm)	48	=	38+38
rear	(mm)	42	=	30+30
Brake disc diameter				
front	(mm)	282.5	=	304
rear	(mm)	290	=	309
Brake disc thickness				
front	(mm)	24	=	32
rear	(mm)	24	=	28
Total eff. pad area	(cm^2)	258	=	344
Parking brake		Mechanical, acting on both rear wheels		
Brake drum diameter	(mm)	180	=	=

Model designation		911 Carrera	911 Carrera CLUBSPORT	911 Turbo
Total pad area	(cm^2)	170	=	=
Wheels and tires				
Standard tires front		185/70VR15	205/55ZR16	205/55VR16
on wheel size		6J x 15	7J x 16	7J x 16
Wheel offset	(mm)			23.3
Standard tires rear		215/60VR15	225/50ZR16	245/45VR16
on wheel size		7J x 15	8J x 16	9J x 16
Wheel offset	(mm)			15
Space saver spare wheel		165-15 89P	=	=
Tire pressure, front	(bar)	2.0	2.0	2.0
rear	(bar)	2.5	2.5	3.0
Space saver spare	(bar)	2.5	2.5	2.5

5. Body, interior equipment (Dimensions at empty weight)

		911 Carrera		911 Turbo
Length	(mm)	4291	=	4291
Width	(mm)	1652	=	1775
Height	(mm)	1320	=	1310
Wheelbase	(mm)	2272	=	2272
Track, front	(mm)	1398	=	1432
rear	(mm)	1405	=	1492
Ground clearance at legal				
maximum weight	(mm)	130	=	120
Approach angle, front	(deg.)	12.3	=	11.7
rear	(deg.)	13.9	=	14.0

9. Electrical system

		911 Carrera		911 Turbo
Generator output	(W/A)	1260/90	=	=
Battery	(V/Ah)	12/66	=	=

Weights according to DIN 70020

		911 Carrera	911 Carrera CLUBSPORT	911 Turbo
Empty weight	(kg)	1210	1160	1335
Maximum permissible				
total weight	(kg)	1530	1530	1680
Permissible towing load				
unbraked	(kg)	480	none	none
braked	(kg)	800	none	none

Performance

		911 Carrera	911 Carrera CLUBSPORT	911 Turbo
Maximum speed				
Manual trans.	(km/h)	245	=	260
Acceleration 0...100 km/h				
Manual trans.	(s)	6.1	5.9	5.2
Standing-start kilometer				
Manual trans.	(s)	26.1	25.9	24.0

Capacities

		911 Carrera		911 Turbo
Engine oil capacity 1*	(l)	13	=	=
Manual trans. 2*	(l)	3.4	=	3.7
Fuel tank capacity	(l)	85	=	=
Brake reservoir 6*	(l)	0.24	=	=
Refrigerant 4*	(g)	1350	=	1300
Compressor oil 5*	(ml)	120	=	=

* Notes:
1* Approved motor oils: API SE/SF when combined with API SE/CC - SF/CC - SF/CD - SE/CD
Multigrade oils as approved by factory.
2* Multigrade transmission oil 75 W 90 to MIL-L 2105 B or API classification GL 5
4* Refrigerant R 12
5* Commercially available air conditioning compressor oil
6* Use only brake fluid meeting SAE J 1703 or DOT 3 or 4.

Model year 1988

Model designation		911 Carrera	911 Turbo
1. Engine			
Engine type, manual trans.		930/20	930/66
Bore	(mm)	95	97
Stroke	(mm)	74.4	74.4
Displacement	(cc)	3164	3299
Compression ratio		10.3:1	7.0:1

Model designation		911 Carrera	911 Turbo
Power output	(kW/hp)	170/231	221/300
at rpm	(rpm)	5900	5500
Torque	(Nm)	284	430
at rpm	(rpm)	4800	4000
Specific output	(kW/l)	53.7	67
Maximum rpm	(rpm)	6570	7200
Engine weight	(kg)	219	269

2. Fuel system, Ignition, Settings

		911 Carrera	911 Turbo
Fuel supply		DME	K-Jetronic
Fuel, Research Octane No.		98	98
Ignition system		DME	BHKZ breakerless
Ignition		Single plug	Single plug
Spark plugs, Bosch		WR 4 CK	W 3 DP 0
Beru		...	...
Spark plug gap	(mm)	0.7	0.7
Knock sensor		no	no
Idle rpm	(rpm)	880	900+-50
Exhaust emission control		....	SLE+ZLP
CO level without catalyst %		0.5...1.5	1.5...2.5
with catalyst %		0.4...0.8	...

Abbreviations:
DME = Digital Motor Electronics (Fuel injection + ignition)
BHKZ = Battery high voltage condenser ignition
SLE = Secondary air injection. ZLP = Air pump
Fuel economy to
EC standard, manual trans.

	(l/100km)	911 Carrera	911 Turbo
A. at steady 90 km/h		7.9	10.7
B. at steady 120 km/h		9.8	13.0
C. EC city cycle		14.9	14.3
Three-cycle average		10.9	12.7

3. Powertrain

		911 Carrera	911 Turbo
Clutch, pressure plate		G MFZ 240	=
Clutch disc		GUD 240	=
Manual transmission type		G50/00	930/36
Gear ratios			
1st Gear		3.500	2.250
2nd Gear		2.059	1.304
3rd Gear		1.409	0.829
4th Gear		1.074	0.625
5th Gear		0.861	...
Reverse Gear		2.857	2.437
Synchromesh syst. Gears 1-5		VK	POSY
Synchromesh on reverse		VK	no
Final drive ratio		3.444	4.222
Limited slip differential		M	M
Lockup factor Load/Coast, %		40/40	40/40
Transmission weight including oil	(kg)	66	70.2

Abbreviations:
M Optional equipment
S Standard equipment
VK Full cone synchromesh system with molybdenum-coated synchro rings
POSY Porsche Blocking synchro system, molybdenum-coated synchro rings

4. Steering, Suspension, Wheels, Brakes

		911 Carrera	911 Turbo
Front suspension			
Stabilizer bar dia.	(mm)	22	22
Steering ratio		17.87	17.87
Turning circle dia.	(m)	10.95	10.95
Rear suspension			
Stabilizer bar, man. trans.	(mm)	21	18
Brake system			
Brake booster dia.	(in.)	8	8
Master cylinder dia.	(mm)	20.64	23.81
Brake pressure limit valve			
Activation pressure	(bar)	33	55
Reduction factor		0.46	0.46
Brake caliper piston dia.			
front	(mm)	48	38+38

		911 Carrera	911 Turbo
rear	(mm)	42	30+30
Brake disc diameter			
front	(mm)	282.5	304
rear	(mm)	290	309
Brake disc thickness			
front	(mm)	24	32
rear	(mm)	24	28
Total eff. pad area	(cm^2)	258	344
Parking brake		Mechanical, acting on both rear wheels	
Brake drum diameter	(mm)	180	=
Total pad area	(cm^2)	170	=
Wheels and tires			
Standard tires front		195/65VR15	205/55VR16
on wheel size		7J x 15	7J x 16
Wheel offset	(mm)		23.3
Standard tires rear		215/60VR15	245/45VR16
on wheel size		8J x 15	9J x 16
Wheel offset	(mm)		15
Space saver spare wheel		165-15 89P	=
Tire pressure, front	(bar)	2.0	2.0
rear	(bar)	2.5	3.0
Space saver spare	(bar)	2.5	2.5

5. Body, interior equipment (Dimensions at empty weight)

		911 Carrera	911 Turbo
Length	(mm)	4291	4291
Width	(mm)	1652	1775
Height	(mm)	1320	1310
Wheelbase	(mm)	2272	=
Track, front	(mm)	1398	1432
rear	(mm)	1405	1492
Ground clearance at legal maximum weight	(mm)	130	120
Approach angle, front	(deg.)	12.3	11.7
rear	(deg.)	13.9	14.0

9. Electrical system

		911 Carrera	911 Turbo
Generator output	(W/A)	1260/90	=
Battery	(V/Ah)	12/66	=

Weights according to DIN 70020

		911 Carrera	911 Turbo
Empty weight	(kg)	1210	1335
Maximum permissible total weight	(kg)	1530	1680
Permissible towing load			
unbraked	(kg)	480	none
braked	(kg)	800	none

Performance

		911 Carrera	911 Turbo
Maximum speed			
Manual trans.	(km/h)	245	260
Acceleration 0...100 km/h			
Manual trans.	(s)	6.1	5.2
Standing-start kilometer			
Manual trans.	(s)	26.1	24.0

Capacities

		911 Carrera	911 Turbo
Engine oil capacity 1*	(l)	13	=
Manual trans. 2*	(l)	3.4	3.7
Front suspension 2*	(l)	...	...
Fuel tank capacity	(l)	85	85
Brake reservoir 6*	(l)	0.24	0.24
Refrigerant 4*	(g)	1350	1300
Compressor oil 5*	(ml)	120	120

* Notes:
1* Approved motor oils: API SE/SF when combined with API SE/CC - SF/CC - SF/CD - SE/CD
Multigrade oils as approved by factory.
2* Multigrade transmission oil 75 W 90 to MIL-L 2105 B or API classification GL 5
4* Refrigerant R 12
5* Commercially available air conditioning compressor oil
6* Use only brake fluid meeting SAE J 1703 or DOT 3 or 4.

Model year 1989

Model designation		911 Carrera Speedster		Carrera 4	911 Turbo

1. Engine

		911 Carrera Speedster		Carrera 4	911 Turbo
Engine type, manual trans.		930/20 (930/25)		M64/01	930/66
Bore	(mm)	95	=	100	97
Stroke	(mm)	74.4	=	76.4	74.4
Displacement	(cc)	3164	=	3600	3299
Compression ratio		10.3:1 (9.5:1)		11.3:1	7.0:1
Power output	(kW/hp)	170/231 (160/217)		184/250	221/300
at rpm	(rpm)	5900		6100	5500
Torque	(Nm)	284 (265)		310	430
at rpm	(rpm)	4800		4800	4000
Specific output	(kW/l)	53.7 (50.6)		51.1	67
Maximum rpm	(rpm)	6570		6720	7200
Engine weight	(kg)	219	=	238	269
(Catalyst specifications in parentheses)					

2. Fuel system, Ignition, Settings

		911 Carrera Speedster		Carrera 4	911 Turbo
Fuel supply		DME	=	DME S	K Jetronic
Fuel, Research Octane No.		98 (95)	=	95	98
Ignition system		DME	=	DME	BHKZ breakerless
Ignition		Single plug	=	Dual plug	Single plug
Spark plugs, Bosch		WR 4 CK	=	FR 5 DTC	W 3 DP 0
Beru		...	...	...	...
Spark plug gap	(mm)	0.7	=	0.8	0.7
Knock sensor		no	no	yes	no
Idle rpm	(rpm)	880		880+-40	900+-50
Exhaust emission control		L sensor+Cat	L sensor+Cat	L sensor+Cat	SLE+ZLP
CO level without catalyst,%		0.5...1.5	=	0.5...1.0	1.5...2.5
with catalyst,%		0.4...0.8	=	0.4...1.2	...
Fuel economy to EC standard, manual trans. (l/100km)					
A. at steady 90 km/h		6.8 (7.9)	=	8.0	10.7
B. at steady 120 km/h		8.0 (9.8)	=	9.5	13.0
C. EC city cycle		13.6 (14.9)	=	17.9	14.3
Three-cycle average		9.8 (10.9)	=	11.8	12.7
(Catalyst specifications in parentheses)					

3. Powertrain

		911 Carrera Speedster		Carrera 4	911 Turbo
Clutch, pressure plate		G MFZ 240	=	=	=
Clutch disc		GUD 240	=	GUD 240	=
Manual transmission type		G50/00	G50/00	G64/00	G50/50
Gear ratios					
1st Gear		3.500	=	3.500	3.145
2nd Gear		2.059	=	2.118	1.789
3rd Gear		1.409	=	1.444	1.269
4th Gear		1.074	=	1.086	0.967
5th Gear		0.861	=	0.868	0.756
Reverse Gear		2.857	=	=	=
Synchromesh syst. Gears 1-5		VK	=	=	=
Synchromesh on reverse		VK	=	=	=
Final drive ratio		3.444	=	=	=
Limited slip differential		M	M	S	M
Lockup factor Load/Coast, %		40/40	40/40	variable 0...100	40/40
Transmission weight including oil	(kg)	66	=	79.65	70.2
Front differential	(kg)	...	...	22.65	...

Abbreviations:
M Optional equipment, S Standard equipment
VK = Full cone synchromesh system with molybdenum-coated synchro rings
BHKZ = Battery high voltage condenser ignition
DME = Digital Motor Electronics (Fuel injection + ignition)
DME S = Digital Motor Electronics with sequential fuel injection
SLE = Secondary air injection. ZLP = Air pump

4. Steering, Suspension, Wheels, Brakes

		911 Carrera Speedster		Carrera 4	911 Turbo
Front suspension					
Stabilizer bar dia.	(mm)	22	=	20	22
Steering ratio		17.87	=	18.48	17.87
Turning circle dia.	(m)	10.95	=	11.95	10.95

Model designation		911 Carrera Speedster		Carrera 4	911 Turb
Rear suspension					
Stabilizer bar, man. trans.	(mm)	21	=	20	18
Brake system					
Brake booster dia.	(in.)	8	=	hydr.	8
Master cylinder dia.	(mm)	20.64	=	23.81	=
Brake pressure limit valve					
Activation pressure	(bar)	33	=	55	...
Reduction factor		0.46	0.46	0.46	...
Brake caliper piston dia.					
front	(mm)	48	=	40+36	38+38
rear	(mm)	42	=	30+28	30+30
Brake disc diameter					
front	(mm)	282.5	=	298	304
rear	(mm)	290	=	299	309
Brake disc thickness					
front	(mm)	24	=	28	32
rear	(mm)	24	=	24	28
Total eff. pad area	(cm²)	258	=	344	344
Parking brake		Mechanical, acting on both rear wheels			
Brake drum diameter	(mm)	180	=	=	=
Total pad area	(cm²)	170	=	=	=
Wheels and tires					
Standard tires front		205/55ZR16	=	=	=
on wheel size		6J x 16 H2	=	7J x 16 H2	=
Wheel offset	(mm)	52		55	23.3
Standard tires rear		225/50ZR16	=	=	245/45ZR
on wheel size		8J x 16 H2	=	=	9J x 16
Wheel offset	(mm)	10.6	=	52	15
Space saver spare wheel		165-15 89P	=	=	=
Tire pressure, front	(bar)	2.0	2.0	2.5	2.0
rear	(bar)	2.5	2.5	3.0	3.0
Space saver spare	(bar)	2.5	2.5	2.5	2.5

5. Body, interior equipment (Dimensions at empty weight)

		911 Carrera Speedster		Carrera 4	911 Turb
Length	(mm)	4291		4250	4291
Width	(mm)	1652	=	1652	1775
Height	(mm)	1320	1220	1310	1310
Wheelbase	(mm)	2272	=	=	=
Track, front	(mm)	1380	=	=	=
rear	(mm)	1372	=	1380	1432
Ground clearance at legal maximum weight	(mm)	130	=	120	120
Approach angle, front	(deg.)	12.3	=	12.5	11.7
rear	(deg.)	13.9	=	12.0	14.0

9. Electrical system

		911 Carrera Speedster		Carrera 4	911 Turb
Generator output	(W/A)	1260/90	=	=	=
Battery	(V/Ah)	12/66	=	=	=

Weights according to DIN 70020

		911 Carrera Speedster		Carrera 4	911 Turb
Empty weight	(kg)	1210	1220	1450	1335
Maximum permissible total weight	(kg)	1530	=	1790	1680
Permissible towing load					
unbraked	(kg)	480	none	500	none
braked	(kg)	800	none	1200	none

Performance

		911 Carrera Speedster		Carrera 4	911 Turb
Max. speed, man. trans.	(km/h)	245 (240)	=	=	260
Acceleration 0...100 km/h					
Manual trans.	(s)	6.1 (6.3)	=	5.7	5.2
Standing-start kilometer					
Manual trans.	(s)	26.1	=	25.5	24.0
(Catalyst specifications in parentheses)					

Capacities

		911 Carrera Speedster		Carrera 4	911 Turb
Engine oil capacity 1*	(l)	13	=	11.5	=
Manual trans. 2*	(l)	3.4	=	3.6	3.7
Front suspension 2*	(l)	...	...	1.2	...
Fuel tank capacity	(l)	85	=	77	85
Brake reservoir 6*	(l)	0.24	=	0.75	0.34
Power steering fl. 3*	(l)	...	...	1.0	...
Refrigerant 4*	(g)	1350	=	930	1300
Compressor oil 5*	(ml)	120	=	100	120

Model year 1990

Model designation		Carrera 2	Carrera 4	Carrera 2 CUP
1. Engine				
Engine type, manual trans.		M64/01	M64/01	M30/
Tiptronic		M64/02	...	...
Bore	(mm)	100	100	100
Stroke	(mm)	76.4	76.4	76.4
Displacement	(cc)	3600	3600	3600
Compression ratio		11.3.1	11.3.1	11.3:1
Power output	(kW/hp)	184/250	184/250	195/265
at rpm	(rpm)	6100	6100	
Torque	(Nm)	310	310	
at rpm	(rpm)	4800	4800	
Specific output	(kW/l)	51.1	51.1	
Maximum rpm	(rpm)	6720	6720	6800
Engine weight	(kg)	238	238	238
2. Fuel system, Ignition, Settings				
Fuel supply		DME S	DME S	DME S
Fuel, Research Octane No.		95	95	95
Ignition system		DME	=	KFZ
Ignition		Dual plug	Dual plug	Dual plug
Spark plugs, Bosch		FR 5 DTC	=	=
Beru				
Spark plug gap	(mm)	0.7	=	0.6
Knock sensor		yes	yes	yes
Idle rpm	(rpm)	880+-40	=	
CO level without catalyst %		0.5...1.0	=	
with catalyst %		0.4...1.2	=	
Fuel economy to				
EC standard, manual trans.				
(l/100km)				
A. at steady 90 km/h		7.8	8.0	
B. at steady 120 km/h		9.7	9.5	
C. EC city cycle		17.1	17.9	
Three-cycle average		11.5	11.8	
With Tiptronic				
A. at steady 90 km/h		7.9	...	...
B. at steady 120 km/h		9.6	...	...
C. EC city cycle		17.1	...	...
Three-cycle average		11.4	...	...
3. Powertrain				
Dual-mass flywheel		Syst.F*	no	no
Clutch, pressure plate		G MFZ 240	=	=
Clutch disc		rigid 240	GUD 240	Sport
Manual transmission type		G50/03	G64/00	G50/
Gear ratios				
1st Gear		3.500	3.500	
2nd Gear		2.059	2.118	
3rd Gear		1.407	1.444	
4th Gear		1.086	1.086	
5th Gear		0.868	0.868	
Reverse Gear		2.857	=	=
Synchromesh syst. Gears 1-5		VK	=	=
Synchromesh on reverse		VK	=	=
Final drive ratio		3.444	3.444	3.444
Abbreviations:				
DME S = Digital Motor Electronics, sequential fuel injection				

Model designation		Carrera 2	Carrera 4	Carrera 2 CUP
KFZ = Map ignition, manifold pressure controlled				
Syst.F* = Dual-mass flywheel – System Freudenberg (rubber vibration dampers)				
Syst.LUK = Dual-mass flywheel – System LUK (steel spring vibration dampers)				
VK = Full cone synchromesh system with molybdenum-coated synchro rings				
Limited slip differential		M	S	S
Lockup factor Load/Coast, %		40/40	variable 0...100	40/40
Transmission weight				
including oil	(kg)	66	79.65	66
Front differential	(kg)	...	22.65	...
Tiptronic		A50/02	...	...
Torque converter dia.	(mm)	260	...	...
Converter stall rpm		2300 -400	...	...
Torque ratio		1.98:1	...	...
Gear ratios				
1st Gear		2.479	...	...
2nd Gear		1.479	...	...
3rd Gear		1.000	...	...
4th Gear		0.728	...	...
Reverse Gear		2.086	...	...
Intermediate shaft		1.100	...	...
Final drive ratio		3.667	...	...
Limited slip differential		no	...	...
Transmission weight with oil				
and ATF	(kg)	105	...	...
4. Steering, Suspension, Wheels, Brakes				
Front suspension				
Stabilizer bar dia.	(mm)	20	=	20
Steering ratio		18.48	=	=
Turning circle dia.	(m)	11.95	=	=
Rear suspension				
Stabilizer bar, man.trans.	(mm)	20	=	20
Tiptronic	(mm)	19	...	...
Brake system				
Power assist ratio		3.0:1	hydraulic	4.8:1
Master cylinder dia.	(mm)	20.64	23.81	23.81
Brake pressure limit valve				
Activation pressure	(bar)	45	55	45
Reduction factor		0.46	0.46	0.46
Brake caliper piston dia.				
front	(mm)	40+36	40+36	36+44
rear	(mm)	44	30+28	30+34
Brake disc diameter				
front	(mm)	298	298	322
rear	(mm)	299	299	299
Brake disc thickness				
front	(mm)	28	28	32
rear	(mm)	24	24	24
Total eff. pad area	(cm²)	284	344	422
Parking brake		Mechanical, acting on both rear wheels		
Brake drum diameter	(mm)	180	=	=
Total pad area	(cm²)	170	=	=
Wheels and tires				
Standard tires front		205/55ZR16	=	235/45ZR17
on wheel size		6J x 16 H2	=	8J x 17 H2
Wheel offset	(mm)	52	=	55
Standard tires rear		225/50ZR16	=	255/40ZR17
on wheel size		8J x 16 H2	=	9.5J x 17 H2
Wheel offset	(mm)	52	=	55
Space saver spare wheel		165-15 89P	=	165/70-16 89P
Tire pressure, front	(bar)	2.5	2.5	2.5
rear	(bar)	3.0	3.0	2.5
Space saver spare	(bar)	2.5	3.0	2.5
5. Body, interior equipment				
Dimensions at empty weight				
Length	(mm)	4250	=	=
Width	(mm)	1652	=	=

Model designation		Carrera 2	Carrera 4	Carrera 2 CUP
Height	(mm)	1310	=	
Wheelbase	(mm)	2272	=	=
Track, front	(mm)	1380	=	=
rear	(mm)	1374	=	=
Ground clearance at legal				
maximum weight	(mm)	115	120	115
Approach angle, front	(deg.)	11.5	=	
rear	(deg.)	12.5	=	

9. Electrical system

		Carrera 2	Carrera 4	Carrera 2 CUP
Generator output	(W/A)	1610/115	=	=
Battery	(V/Ah)	12/75	=	=

Weights according to DIN 70020

		Carrera 2	Carrera 4	Carrera 2 CUP
Empty weight with				
Manual trans.	(kg)	1350	1450	1220
Tiptronic	(kg)	1380	...	...
Maximum permissible total				
weight, manual trans	(kg)	1690	1790	1810
Tiptronic	(kg)	1720	...	...
Permissible towing load				
unbraked	(kg)	500	500	none
braked	(kg)	1200	1200	none

Performance

		Carrera 2	Carrera 4	Carrera 2 CUP
Maximum speed				
Manual trans.	(km/h)	260	260	
Tiptronic	(km/h)	256	...	...
Acceleration	0...100 km/h			
Manual trans.	(s)	5.7	5.7	
Tiptronic	(s)	6.6	...	...
Standing-start kilometer				
Manual trans.	(s)	25.2	25.5	
Tiptronic	(s)	26.2	...	...
Capacities				
Engine oil capacity 1*	(l)	11.5	=	=
Manual trans. 2*	(l)	3.6	3.8	3.6
Front suspension 2*	(l)	...	1.2	...
Automatic trans. 3*	(l)	9.0	...	...
Auto final drive 2*	(l)	0.9	...	...
Fuel tank capacity	(l)	77	=	=
Brake reservoir 6*	(l)	0.34	0.75	0.34
Power steering fl. 3*	(l)	1.0	1.0	1.0
Refrigerant 4*	(g)	930	=	...
Compressor oil 5*	(ml)	100	=	=

* Notes:

1* Approved motor oils: API SE/SF when combined with API SE/CC - SF/CC - SF/CD - SE/CD
Multigrade oils as approved by factory.
2* Multigrade transmission oil 75 W 90 to MIL-L 2105 B or API classification GL 5
3* ATF DEXRON II D
4* Refrigerant R 12
5* Commercially available air conditioning compressor oil
6* Use only brake fluid meeting SAE J 1703 or DOT 3 or 4.

Model year 1991

Model designation		Carrera 2	Carrera 4	911 Turbo
1. Engine				
Engine type, manual trans.		M64/01	M64/01	M30/69
Tiptronic		M64/02	...	
Bore	(mm)	100	100	97
Stroke	(mm)	76.4	76.4	74.4
Displacement	(cc)	3600	3600	3299
Compression ratio		11.3:1	11.3:1	7.0:1
Power output	(kW/hp)	184/250	184/250	235/320
at rpm	(rpm)	6100	6100	5750
Torque	(Nm)	310	310	450

Model designation		Carrera 2	Carrera 4	911 Turbo
at rpm	(rpm)	4800	4800	4500
Specific output	(kW/l)	51.1	51.1	71.2
Maximum rpm	(rpm)	6720	6720	6900
Engine weight	(kg)	238	238	275

2. Fuel system, Ignition, Settings

		Carrera 2	Carrera 4	911 Turbo
Fuel supply		DME S	DME S	K-Jetronic
Fuel, Research Octane No.		95	95	95
Ignition system		DME	=	KFZ
Ignition		Dual plug	Dual plug	Single plug
Spark plugs, Bosch		FR 5 DTC	=	WR 4 DPO
Beru				
Spark plug gap	(mm)	0.7	=	0.6
Knock sensor		yes	yes	no
Idle rpm	(rpm)	880+-40	=	1000 +-50
CO level without catalyst %		0.5...1.0	=	1+- 0.2
with catalyst %		0.4...1.2	=	1+- 0.2
Fuel economy to				
EC standard, Manual trans.				
(l/100km)				
A. at steady 90 km/h		7.8	8.0	8.5
B. at steady 120 km/h		9.7	9.5	10.4
C. EC city cycle		17.1	17.9	21.0
Three-cycle average		11.5	11.8	13.0
With Tiptronic				
A. at steady 90 km/h		7.9	...	...
B. at steady 120 km/h		9.6	...	...
C. EC city cycle		17.1	...	...
Three-cycle average		11.4	...	...

3. Powertrain

		Carrera 2	Carrera 4	911 Turbo
Dual-mass flywheel		Syst.F*	Syst.F*	Syst.LUK
Clutch, pressure plate		G MFZ 240	=	=
Clutch disc		rigid 240	rigid 240	rigid 240
Manual transmission type		G50/03	G64/00	G50/52
Gear ratios				
1st Gear		3.500	3.500	3.154
2nd Gear		2.059	2.118	1.789
3rd Gear		1.407	1.444	1.269
4th Gear		1.086	1.086	0.967
5th Gear		0.868	0.868	0.756
Reverse Gear		2.857	=	=
Synchromesh syst. Gears 1-5		VK	=	=
Synchromesh on reverse		VK	=	=
Final drive ratio		3.444	3.444	3.444

Abbreviations:
DME S = Digital Motor Electronics, sequential fuel injection
KFZ = Map ignition. manifold pressure controlled
Syst.F* = Dual-mass flywheel – System Freudenberg (rubber vibration dampers)
Syst.LUK = Dual-mass flywheel – System LUK (steel spring vibration dampers)
VK = Full cone synchromesh system with molybdenum-coated synchro rings

		Carrera 2	Carrera 4	911 Turbo
Limited slip differential		M	S	S
Lockup factor Load/Coast, %		40/40	variable 0...100	20/100
Transmission weight				
including oil	(kg)	66	79.65	71
Front differential	(kg)	...	22.65	...
Tiptronic		A50/02	...	...
Torque converter dia.	(mm)	260	...	...
Converter stall rpm		2300 -400	...	...
Torque ratio		1.98:1	...	...
Gear ratios				
1st Gear		2.479	...	...
2nd Gear		1.479	...	...
3rd Gear		1.000	...	...
4th Gear		0.728	...	...
Reverse Gear		2.086	...	...
Intermediate shaft		1.100	...	...
Final drive ratio		3.667	...	...
Limited slip differential		no	...	...
Transmission weight with oil				
and ATF	(kg)	105	...	...

Model designation		Carrera 2	Carrera 4	911 Turbo
4. Steering, Suspension, Wheels, Brakes				
Front suspension				
Stabilizer bar dia.	(mm)	20	=	21
Steering ratio		18.48	=	=
Turning circle dia.	(m)	11.95	=	11.45
Rear suspension				
Stabilizer bar, man. trs.	(mm)	20	=	22
Tiptronic	(mm)	19	...	...
Brake system				
Power assist ratio		3.0:1	hydraulic	4.8:1
Master cylinder dia.	(mm)	20.64	23.81	23.81
Brake pressure limit valve				
Activation pressure	(bar)	45	55	45
Reduction factor		0.46	0.46	0.46
Brake caliper piston dia.				
front	(mm)	40+36	40+36	36+44
rear	(mm)	44	30+28	30+34
Brake disc diameter				
rear	(mm)	299	299	299
Brake disc thickness				
front	(mm)	28	28	32
rear	(mm)	24	24	24
Total eff. pad area	(cm²)	284	344	422
Parking brake		Mechanical, acting on both rear wheels		
Brake drum diameter	(mm)	180	=	=
Total pad area	(cm²)	170	=	=
Wheels and tires				
Standard tires front		205/55ZR16	=	205/55ZR17
on wheel size		6J x 16 H2	=	7J x 17
Wheel offset	(mm)	52	=	55
Standard tires rear		225/50ZR16	=	255/40ZR17
on wheel size		8J x 16 H2	=	9J x 17
Wheel offset	(mm)	52	=	55
Space saver spare wheel		165/70-1692P		=
Tire pressure, front	(bar)	2.5	2.5	2.5
rear	(bar)	3.0	3.0	2.5
Space saver spare	(bar)	2.5	3.0	2.5
5. Body, interior equipment				
Dimensions at empty weight				
Length	(mm)	4250	=	4250
Width	(mm)	1652	=	1775
Height	(mm)	1310	=	1310
Wheelbase	(mm)	2272	=	=
Track, front	(mm)	1380	=	1442
rear	(mm)	1374	=	1499
Ground clearance at legal maximum weight	(mm)	115	120	115
Approach angle, front	(deg.)	11.5	=	11.5
rear	(deg.)	12.5	=	12.5

Model designation		Carrera 2	Carrera 4	911 Turbo
9. Electrical system				
Generator output	(W/A)	1610/115	=	=
Battery	(V/Ah)	12/75	=	=
Weights according to DIN 70020				
Empty weight with				
Manual trans.	(kg)	1350	1450	1470
Tiptronic	(kg)	1380	...	...
Maximum permissible total weight, manual trans.	(kg)	1690	1790	1810
Tiptronic	(kg)	1720	...	...
Permissible towing load				
unbraked	(kg)	500	500	none
braked	(kg)	1200	1200	none
Performance				
Maximum speed				
Manual trans.	(km/h)	260	260	270
Tiptronic	(km/h)	256	...	...
Acceleration 0...100 km/h				
Manual trans.	(s)	5.7	5.7	5.0
Tiptronic	(s)	6.6	...	...
Standing-start kilometer				
Manual trans.	(s)	25.2	25.5	24.3
Tiptronic	(s)	26.2	...	...
Capacities				
Engine oil capacity 1*	(l)	11.5	=	13
Manual trans. 2*	(l)	3.6	3.8	3.9
Front suspension 2*	(l)	...	1.2	...
Automatic trans. 3*	(l)	9.0	...	...
Auto final drive 2*	(l)	0.9	...	...
Fuel tank capacity	(l)	77	=	=
Brake reservoir 6*	(l)	0.34	0.75	0.34
Power steering fl. 3*	(l)	1.0	1.0	1.0
Refrigerant 4*	(g)	930	=	840
Compressor oil 5*	(ml)	100	=	140

* Notes:
1* Approved motor oils: API SE/SF when combined with API SE/CC - SF/CC - SF/CD - SE/CD
Multigrade oils as approved by factory.
2* Multigrade transmission oil 75 W 90 to MIL-L 2105 B or API classification GL 5
3* ATF DEXRON II D
4* Refrigerant R 12
5* Commercially available air conditioning compressor oil
6* Use only brake fluid meeting SAE J 1703 or DOT 3 or 4.

Model year 1992

Model designation		Carrera 2	Carrera 4	Carrera RS	RS America	911 Turbo	Turbo S	Turbo Look
1. Engine								
Engine type, manual trans.		M64/01	M64/01	M64/03	M64/01	M30/69	M30/69SL	M64/01
Tiptronic		M64/02	...	...	...	...	...	M64/02
Bore	(mm)	100	100	100	100	97	97	100
Stroke	(mm)	76.4	76.4	76.4	76.4	74.4	74.4	76.4
Displacement	(cc)	3600	3600	3600	3600	3299	3299	3600
Compression ratio		11.3:1	11.3:1	11.3:1	11.3:1	7.0:1	7.0:1	11.3:1
Power output	(kW/hp)	184/250	184/250	191/260	184/250	235/320	280/381	184/250
at rpm	(rpm)	6100	6100	6100	6100	5750	6000	6100
Torque	(Nm)	310	310	325	310	450	490	310
at rpm	(rpm)	4800	4800	4800	4800	4500	4800	4800
Specific output	(kW/l)	51.1	51.1	53.0	51.1	71.2	84.9	51.1
Maximum rpm	(rpm)	6720	6720	6720	6720	6900	6900	6720
Engine weight	(kg)	238	238	226	238	275	275	238

Model designation		Carrera 2	Carrera 4	Carrera RS	RS America	911 Turbo	Turbo S	Turbo Look
2. Fuel system, Ignition, Settings								
Fuel supply		DME S	DME S	DME S	DME S	K-Jetronic	K-Jetronic	DME S
Fuel, Research Octane No.		95	95	98	95	95	98	95
Ignition system		DME	=	=	=	KFZ	KFZ	DME
Ignition		Dual plug	Dual plug	Dual plug	Dual plug	Single plug	Single plug	Dual plug
Spark plugs, Bosch		FR 5 DTC	=	=	=	WR 4 DPO	WR4 DPO	FR5 DTC
Beru								
Spark plug gap	(mm)	0.7	=	=	=	0.6	0.6	0.7
Knock sensor		yes	yes	yes	yes	no	no	yes
Idle rpm	(rpm)	880+-40	=	=	=	1000 +-50	=	880+-40
CO level without catalyst	(%)	0.5...1.0	=	=	=	1+- 0.2	=	0.5...1.0
with catalyst	(%)	0.4...1.2	=	=	=	1+- 0.2	=	0.4...1.2
Fuel economy to								
EC standard, manual trans.	(l/100km)							
A. at steady 90 km/h		7.8	8.0	7.7	7.8	8.5	7.8	7.8
B. at steady 120 km/h		9.7	9.5	9.5	9.7	10.4	9.7	9.7
C. EC city cycle		17.1	17.9	15.7	17.1	21.0	17.1	17.1
Three-cycle average		11.5	11.8	11.0	11.5	13.3	11.5	11.5
With Tiptronic								
A. at steady 90 km/h		7.9	...	...	...	...	...	7.9
B. at steady 120 km/h		9.6	...	...	...	...	...	9.6
C. EC city cycle		17.1	...	...	...	...	...	17.1
Three-cycle average		11.4	...	...	...	...	...	11.4
3. Powertrain								
Dual-mass flywheel		Syst.F*	Syst.F*	no	Syst.F*	Syst.LUK	Syst.LUK	Syst.F*
Clutch, pressure plate		G MFZ 240	=	=	=	=	=	=
Clutch disc		rigid 240	rigid 240	spring 240	rigid 240	rigid 240	rigid 240	rigid 240
Manual transmission type		G50/03	G64/00	G50/10	G50/05	G50/52	G50/52	G50/03
Gear ratios								
1st Gear		3.500	3.500	3.154	3.500	3.154	3.154	3.500
2nd Gear		2.059	2.118	1.895	2.059	1.789	1.789	2.059
3rd Gear		1.407	1.444	1.407	1.407	1.269	1.269	1.407
4th Gear		1.086	1.086	1.086	1.086	0.967	0.967	1.086
5th Gear		0.868	0.868	0.868	0.868	0.756	0.756	0.868
Reverse Gear		2.857	=	=	=	=	=	=
Synchromesh syst. Gears 1-5		VK	=	=	=	=	=	=
Synchromesh on reverse		VK	=	=	=	=	=	=
Final drive ratio		3.444	3.444	3.444	3.333	3.444	3.444	3.444

Abbreviations:
DME S = Digital Motor Electronics, sequential fuel injection
KFZ = Map ignition, manifold pressure controlled
Syst.F* = Dual-mass flywheel – System Freudenberg (rubber vibration dampers)
Syst.LUK = Dual-mass flywheel – System LUK (steel spring vibration dampers)
VK = Full cone synchromesh system with molybdenum-coated synchro rings

		Carrera 2	Carrera 4	Carrera RS	RS America	911 Turbo	Turbo S	Turbo Look
Limited slip differential		M	S	S	M	S	S	M
Lockup factor Load/Coast, %		40/40	variable 0...100	20/100	40/40	20/100	20/100	40/40
Transmission weight								
including oil	(kg)	66	79.65	66	66	71	71	66
Front differential	(kg)	...	22.65	...	...	...	...	...
Tiptronic		A50/02	...	...	...	...	...	A50/02
Torque converter dia.	(mm)	260	...	...	...	...	...	260
Converter stall rpm		2300 -400	...	...	...	...	...	2300 -400
Torque ratio		1.98:1	...	...	...	...	...	...
Gear ratios								
1st Gear		2.479	...	...	...	...	...	2.479
2nd Gear		1.479	...	...	...	...	...	1.479
3rd Gear		1.000	...	...	...	...	...	1.000
4th Gear		0.728	...	...	...	...	...	0.728
Reverse Gear		2.086	...	...	...	...	...	2.086
Intermediate shaft		1.100	...	...	...	...	...	1.100
Final drive ratio		3.667	...	...	...	...	...	3.667
Limited slip differential		no	...	...	...	...	...	no
Transmission weight with oil								
and ATF	(kg)	105	...	...	...	...	...	105
4. Steering, Suspension, Wheels, Brakes								
Front suspension								
Stabilizer bar dia.	(mm)	20	=	24	20	21	21	21
Steering ratio		18.48	=	=	=	=	=	=
Turning circle dia.	(m)	11.95	=	=	=	11.45	=	11.95

Model designation		Carrera 2	Carrera 4	Carrera RS	RS America	911 Turbo	Turbo S	Turbo Look
Rear suspension								
Stabilizer bar, man. trans.	(mm)	20	=	18	20	22	22	22
Tiptronic	(mm)	19	...	...	...	...	...	21
Brake system								
Power assist ratio		3.0:1	hydraulic	3.6:1	3.0:1	4.8:1	=	4.8:1
Master cylinder dia.	(mm)	20.64	23.81	25.4	20.64	23.18	=	23.81
Brake pressure limit valve								
Activation pressure	(bar)	45	55	55	55	60	60	60
Reduction factor		0.46	0.46	0.46	0.46	0.46	0.46	0.46
Brake caliper piston dia.								
front	(mm)	40+36	40+36	36+44	40+36	36+44	36+44	44+36
rear	(mm)	44	30+28	30+34	44	30+34	30+34	30+34
Brake disc diameter								
front	(mm)	298	298	322	298	322	322	322
rear	(mm)	299	299	299	299	299	299	299
Brake disc thickness								
front	(mm)	28	28	32	28	32	32	32
rear	(mm)	24	24	24	24	28	28	28
Total eff. pad area	(cm^2)	284	344	284	284	422	422	422
Parking brake		Mechanical, acting on both rear wheels						
Brake drum diameter	(mm)	180	=	=	=	=	=	=
Total pad area	(cm^2)	170	=	=	=	=	=	=
Wheels and tires								
Standard tires front		205/55ZR16	=	205/50ZR17	205/50ZR17	=	235/40ZR18	205/50ZR17
on wheel size		6J x 16 H2	=	7 1/2J x 17AH	7J x 17 AH	=	8J x 18 H2	7J x 17 AH
Wheel offset	(mm)	52	=	55	55	55	52	55
Standard tires rear		225/50ZR16	=	255/40ZR17	255/40ZR17	=	265/35ZR18	255/40ZR17
on wheel size		8J x 16 H2	=	9J x 17 H2	8J x 17 AH	9J x 17 AH	10Jx18 H2	9J x 17 AH
Wheel offset	(mm)	52	=	55	52	55	55	55
Space saver spare wheel		165/70-1692P	=	=	=	=	=	=
Tire pressure, front	(bar)	2.5	2.5	2.5	2.5	2.5	2.5	2.5
rear	(bar)	3.0	3.0	2.5	2.5	2.5	2.5	2.5
Space saver spare	(bar)	2.5	3.0	2.5	2.5	2.5	2.5	2.5

5. Body, interior equipment

		Carrera 2	Carrera 4	Carrera RS	RS America	911 Turbo	Turbo S	Turbo Look
Dimensions at empty weight								
Length	(mm)	4250	=	4275	4275	4250	4250	4250
Width	(mm)	1652	=	=	=	1775	1775	1775
Height	(mm)	1310	=	1270	1310	1310	1270	1310
Wheelbase	(mm)	2272	=	=	=	=	=	=
Track, front	(mm)	1380	=	1379	1380	1493	1440	1434
rear	(mm)	1374	=	1380	1374	1499	1481	1493
Ground clearance at legal								
maximum weight	(mm)	115	120	92	115	115	115	115
Approach angle, front	(deg.)	11.5	=	=	12.5	11.5	11.5	11.5
rear	(deg.)	12.5	=	=	13.5	13.5	13	13.5

9. Electrical system

		Carrera 2	Carrera 4	Carrera RS	RS America	911 Turbo	Turbo S	Turbo Look
Generator output	(W/A)	1610/115	=	=	=	=	=	=
Battery	(V/Ah)	12/75	=	12/36	12/75	12/75	12/75	12/75

Weights according to DIN 70020

		Carrera 2	Carrera 4	Carrera RS	RS America	911 Turbo	Turbo S	Turbo Look
Empty weight with								
Manual transmission	(kg)	1350	1450	1220	1340	1470	1290	1420
Tiptronic	(kg)	1380	...	...	...	...	...	1450
Maximum permissible total								
weight, manual transmission	(kg)	1690	1790	1420	1520	1810	1510	1760
Tiptronic	(kg)	1720	...	...	...	...	...	1790
Permissible towing load								
unbraked	(kg)	500	500	none	none	none	none	none
braked	(kg)	1200	1200	none	none	none	none	none

Performance

		Carrera 2	Carrera 4	Carrera RS	RS America	911 Turbo	Turbo S	Turbo Look
Maximum speed								
Manual transmission	(km/h)	260	260	260	260	270	290	255
Tiptronic	(km/h)	256	...	...	...	...	...	251
Acceleration 0...100 km/h								
Manual transmission	(s)	5.7	5.7	5.3	5.7	5.0	4.66	5.7
Tiptronic	(s)	6.6	...	...	...	...	...	6.6
Standing-start kilometer								
Manual transmission	(s)	25.2	25.5	25.0	25.2	24.3	22.42	25.2
Tiptronic	(s)	26.2	...	...	...	...	...	26.2

Model designation		Carrera 2	Carrera 4	Carrera RS	RS America	911 Turbo	Turbo S	Turbo Look
Capacities								
Engine oil capacity 1*	(l)	11.5	=	=	=	13	13	11.5
Manual transmission 2*	(l)	3.6	3.8	3.6	3.6	3.7	3.7	3.6
Front suspension 2*	(l)	...	1.2	...	...	...	...	...
Automatic transmission 3*	(l)	9.0	...	...	...	...	...	9.0
Auto final drive 2*	(l)	0.9	...	...	...	...	...	0.9
Fuel tank capacity	(l)	77	=	=	=	=	92	77
Brake reservoir 6*	(l)	0.34	0.75	0.34	0.34	0.75	0.75	0.75
Power steering fluid 3*	(l)	1.0	1.0	...	...	1.0	1.0	1.0
Refrigerant 4*	(g)	930	=	...	930	100		930
Compressor oil 5*	(ml)	100	=	...	100	100	100	100

* Notes:
1* Approved motor oils: API SE/SF when combined with API SE/CC - SF/CC - SF/CD - SE/CD
Multigrade oils as approved by factory.
2* Multigrade transmission oil 75 W 90 to MIL-L 2105 B or API classification GL 5
3* ATF DEXRON II D
4* Refrigerant R 12
5* Commercially available air conditioning compressor oil
6* Use only brake fluid meeting SAE J 1703 or DOT 3 or 4

Model year 1993

Model designation		Carrera 2	Carrera 4	Turbo 3.6
1. Engine				
Engine type, manual trans.		M64/01	M64/01	M 64/50
Tiptronic		M64/02	...	...
Bore	(mm)	100	100	100
Stroke	(mm)	76.4	76.4	76.4
Displacement	(cc)	3600	3600	3600
Compression ratio		11.3:1	11.3:1	7.5:1
Power output	(kW/hp)	184/250	184/250	265/360
at rpm	(rpm)	6100	6100	5500
Torque	(Nm)	310	310	520
at rpm	(rpm)	4800	4800	4200
Specific output	(kW/l)	51.1	51.1	73.6
Maximum rpm	(rpm)	6720	6720	6600
Engine weight	(kg)	238	238	276
2. Fuel system, Ignition, Settings				
Fuel supply		DME S	DME S	K-Jetronic
Fuel, Research Octane No.		95	95	95
Ignition system		DME	=	KFZ
Ignition		Dual plug	Dual plug	Single plug
Spark plugs, Bosch		FR 5 DTC	=	FR 6 LDC
Beru		14Fr-5DTU	=	...
Spark plug gap	(mm)	0.7	=	0.8
Knock sensor		yes	yes	no
Idle rpm	(rpm)	880+-40	=	950+50
Exhaust emission control		Lambda sensor + 3-way metal catalyst		
CO level without catalyst %		0.5...1.0	=	1.0...1.4
with catalyst %		0.4...1.2	=	0.8...1.2
Fuel economy to				
EC standard, Manual trans.				
	(l/100km)			
A. at steady 90 km/h		7.8	8.0	8.3
B. at steady 120 km/h		9.7	9.5	10.5
C. EC city cycle		17.1	17.9	21.3
Three-cycle average		11.5	11.8	13.3
With Tiptronic				
A. at steady 90 km/h		7.9	...	...
B. at steady 120 km/h		9.6	...	...
C. EC city cycle		17.1	...	...
C. Three-cycle average		11.4	...	...
3. Powertrain				
Dual-mass flywheel		Syst.F*	Syst.F*	Syst.LUK
Clutch, pressure plate		G MFZ 240	=	=
Clutch disc		rigid 240	rigid 240	rigid 240

Model designation		Carrera 2	Carrera 4	Turbo 3.6
Manual transmission type		G50/03	G64/00	G50/52
Gear ratios				
1st Gear		3.500	3.500	3.154
2nd Gear		2.059	2.118	1.789
3rd Gear		1.407	1.444	1.269
4th Gear		1.086	1.086	0.967
5th Gear		0.868	0.868	0.756
Reverse Gear		2.857	=	=
Synchromesh syst. Gears 1-5		VK	=	=
Synchromesh on reverse		VK	=	=
Final drive ratio		3.444	3.444	3.444

Abbreviations:
DME S = Digital Motor Electronics, sequential fuel injection
KFZ = Map ignition, manifold pressure controlled
Syst.F* = Dual-mass flywheel – System Freudenberg (rubber vibration dampers)
Syst.LUK = Dual-mass flywheel – System LUK (steel spring vibration dampers)
VK = Full cone synchromesh system with molybdenum-coated synchro rings

		Carrera 2	Carrera 4	Turbo 3.6
Limited slip differential		M	S	S
Lockup factor Load/Coast. %		40/40	variable 0...100	20/100
Transmission weight				
including oil	(kg)	66	79.65	71
Front differential	(kg)	...	22.65	...
Tiptronic		A50/02	...	...
Torque converter dia.	(mm)	260	...	
Converter stall rpm		2300 -400	...	
Gear ratios				
1st Gear		2.479	...	
2nd Gear		1.479	...	
3rd Gear		1.000	...	
4th Gear		0.728	...	
Reverse Gear		2.086	...	
Intermediate shaft		1.100	...	
Final drive ratio		3.667	...	
Limited slip differential		no	...	
Transmission weight with oil				
and ATF	(kg)	105	...	
4. Steering, Suspension, Wheels, Brakes				
Front suspension				
Stabilizer bar dia.	(mm)	20	=	21
Steering ratio		18.48	=	18.48
Turning circle dia.	(m)	11.95	=	11.45
Rear suspension				
Stabilizer bar, man. trs.	(mm)	20	=	22
Tiptronic	(mm)	19	...	...

Model designation		Carrera 2	Carrera 4	Turbo 3.6
Brake system				
Power assist ratio		3.0:1	hydraulic	hydraulic
Master cylinder dia.	(mm)	20.64	23.81	23.81
Brake pressure limit valve				
Activation pressure	(bar)	45	55	60
Reduction factor		0.46	0.46	0.46
Brake caliper piston dia.				
front	(mm)	40+36	40+36	36+44
rear	(mm)	44	30+28	30+34
Brake disc diameter				
front	(mm)	298	298	322
rear	(mm)	299	299	299
Brake disc thickness				
front	(mm)	28	28	32
rear	(mm)	24	24	28
Total eff. pad area	(cm²)	284	344	474
Parking brake		Mechanical, acting on both rear wheels		
Brake drum diameter	(mm)	180	=	=
Total pad area	(cm²)	170	=	=
Wheels and tires				
Standard tires front		205/55ZR16	–	225/40ZR18
on wheel size		6J x 16 H2	=	8J x 18 H2
Wheel offset	(mm)	52	=	52
Standard tires rear		225/50ZR16	=	265/35ZR18
on wheel size		8J x 16 H2	=	10J x 18 H2
Wheel offset	(mm)	52	=	61
Space saver spare wheel		165/70-1692P	=	=
Tire pressure, front	(bar)	2.5	2.5	2.5
rear	(bar)	3.0	3.0	2.5
Space saver spare	(bar)	2.5	3.0	2.5

5. Body, interior equipment

		Carrera 2	Carrera 4	Turbo 3.6
Dimensions at empty weight				
Length	(mm)	4250	=	4275
Width	(mm)	1652	=	1775
Height	(mm)	1310	=	1290
Wheelbase	(mm)	2272	=	=
Track, front	(mm)	1380	=	1442
rear	(mm)	1374	=	1506
Ground clearance at legal				
maximum weight	(mm)	115	120	112
Approach angle, front	(deg.)	11.5	=	=
rear	(deg.)	12.5	=	=

9. Electrical system

		Carrera 2	Carrera 4	Turbo 3.6
Generator output	(W/A)	1610/115	=	=
Battery	(V/Ah)	12/75	=	=

Model designation		Carrera 2	Carrera 4	Turbo 3.6
Weights according to DIN 70020				
Empty weight with				
manual trans.	(kg)	1350	1450	1470
Tiptronic	(kg)	1380	...	...
Maximum permissible total				
weight, manual trans.	(kg)	1690	1790	1810
Tiptronic	(kg)	1720	...	...
Permissible towing load				
unbraked	(kg)	500	500	none
braked	(kg)	1200	1200	none
Performance				
Maximum speed				
Manual trans.	(km/h)	260	260	280
Tiptronic	(km/h)	256	...	...
Acceleration 0...100 km/h				
Manual trans.	(s)	5.7	5.7	4.8
Tiptronic	(s)	6.6	...	...
Standing-start kilometer				
Manual trans.	(s)	25.2	25.5	23.3
Tiptronic	(s)	26.2	...	...
Capacities				
Engine oil capacity 1*	(l)	11.5	=	12.0
Manual trans. 2*	(l)	3.6	3.8	3.9
Front suspension 2*	(l)	...	1.2	...
Automatic trans. 3*	(l)	9.0	...	...
Auto final drive 2*	(l)	0.9	...	...
Fuel tank capacity	(l)	77	=	92
Brake reservoir 6*	(l)	0.34	0.75	0.34
Power steering fl .3*	(l)	1.0	=	=
Refrigerant 4*	(g)	930	=	840
Compressor oil 5*	(ml)	100	=	140

* Notes:
1* Approved motor oils: API SE/SF when combined with API SE/CC - SF/CC - SF/CD - SE/CD
Multigrade oils as approved by factory.
2* Multigrade transmission oil 75 W 90 to MIL-L 2105 B or API classification GL 5
3* ATF DEXRON II D
4* Use only refrigerant R 134a (Porsche now uses HFC-free air conditioning refrigerant)
5* Commercially available air conditioning compressor oil
6* Use only brake fluid meeting DOT 4 Type 200
Abbreviations:
M Optional equipment
S Standard equipment

Model year 1994 (R Program)

Note: Due to introduction of the "new" Carrera (internal designation: Type 993), production of several 911 types ended during the 1994 model year. As of July, 1993, the Carrera 2 and 4, in coupe and Targa versions ceased production. The Carrera 2 Cabriolet and Speedster continued production until January 1994. The 30th anniversary model 911 continued until January 1994, with Turbo Look bodywork, special color "violametallic" and special interior trim. The 911 Turbo 3.6 also ceased production in January 1994, as the body plant could only build "new" Carrera bodies. This time period marks the production startup of Carrera Cup cars, Cabriolets and US market rear-drive "new Carreras."

Model designation		Carrera (993)	Carrera 2 Cabriolet	Carrera 2 SPEEDSTER	Carrera 4 Turbo Look*	Turbo 3.6
1. Engine						
Engine type, manual trans.		M64/05	M64/01	M64/01	M6/01	M 64/50
Tiptronic		M64/06	M64/02	M64/02	...	...
Bore	(mm)	100	100	100	100	100
Stroke	(mm)	76.4	76.4	76.4	76.4	76.4
Displacement	(cc)	3600	3600	3600	3600	3600
Compression ratio		11.3:1	11.3:1	11.3:1	11.3	7.5:1
Power output	(kW/hp)	200/272	184/250	184/250	184/250	265/360

Model designation		Carrera (993)	Carrera 2 Cabriolet	Carrera 2 SPEEDSTER	Carrera 4 Turbo Look*	Turbo 3.6
Specific output	(kW/l)	55.6	51.1	51.1	51.1	73.6
Maximum rpm	(rpm)	6700	6720	6720	6720	6600
Engine weight	(kg)	232	238	238	238	276

2. Fuel system, Ignition, Settings

		Carrera (993)	Carrera 2 Cabriolet	Carrera 2 SPEEDSTER	Carrera 4 Turbo Look*	Turbo 3.6
Fuel supply		DME S	DME S	DME S	DME S	K-Jetronic
Fuel,Research Octane No.		98	95	95	95	95
Ignition system		DME	DME	DME	DME	KFZ
Ignition		Dual plug	Dual plug	Dual plug	Dual plug	Single plug
Spark plugs, Bosch		FR 6 LDC	FR 5 DTC	=	=	FR 6 LDC
Beru		14Fr-5DTU	14FR-5DTU	=	=	...
Spark plug gap	(mm)	0.7	0.7	=	=	0.8
Knock sensor		yes	yes	yes	yes	no
Idle rpm	(rpm)	800+-40	880+-40	=	=	950+50
Exhaust emission control		Lambda sensor + 3-way metal catalyst				= + SLE+ZLP
CO level without catalyst	(%)	0.5...1.0	=	=	=	1.0...1.4
with catalyst	(%)	0.4...1.2	=	=	=	0.8...1.2
Fuel economy to						
EC standard, manual trans.	(l/100km)					
A. at steady 90 km/h		7.4	7.8	=	8.0	8.3
B. at steady 120 km/h		9.1	9.7	=	9.5	10.3
C. EC city cycle		17.9	17.1	=	17.9	21.3
Three-cycle average		11.4	11.5	=	11.8	13.3
With Tiptronic						
A. at steady 90 km/h		7.8	7.9	=	...	...
B. at steady 120 km/h		9.6	9.6	=	...	...
C. EC city cycle		17.2	17.1	=	...	...
Three-cycle average		11.5	11.4	=	...	...

Abbreviations:
Turbo Look* = Technical specifications based on Carrera 4 Turbo Look
DME S = Digital Motor Electronics, sequential fuel injection
KFZ = Map ignition, manifold pressure controlled
SLE = Secondary air injection
ZLP = Air pump
Syst.F* = Dual-mass flywheel – System Freudenberg (rubber vibration dampers)
Syst.LUK = Dual-mass flywheel – System LUK (steel spring vibration dampers)
VK = Full cone synchromesh system with molybdenum-coated synchro rings

3. Powertrain

		Carrera (993)	Carrera 2 Cabriolet	Carrera 2 SPEEDSTER	Carrera 4 Turbo Look*	Turbo 3.6
Dual-mass flywheel		Syst.F*	Syst.F*	Syst.F*	Syst.F*	Syst.LUK
Clutch, pressure plate		G MFZ 240	=	=	=	=
Clutch disc		rigid 240	=	=	=	=
Manual transmission type		G50/21	G50/03	=	G64/00	G50/52
Gear ratios						
1st Gear		3.818	3.500	=	3.500	3.154
2nd Gear		2.15	2.059	=	2.118	1.789
3rd Gear		1.56	1.407	=	1.444	1.269
4th Gear		1.242	1.086	=	1.086	0.967
5th Gear		1.027	0.868	=	0.868	0.756
6th Gear		0.820	...	...	...	...
Reverse Gear		2.857	=	=	=	=
Synchromesh on forward gears		VK	=	=	=	=
Synchromesh on reverse		VK	=	=	=	=
Final drive ratio		3.444	=	=	=	=
Limited slip differential		M	M	M	S	S
Lockup factor Load/Coast,%		25/65	40/40	40/40	variable 0...100	20/100
Transmission weight with oil	(kg)	66	=	=	79.65	71
Front differential	(kg)	...	...	...	22.65	...
Tiptronic		A50/04	A50/02	=	...	
Torque converter dia.	(mm)	260	=	=	...	
Converter stall rpm		2300 - 400	=	=	...	
Gear ratios						
1st Gear		2.479	=	=	...	
2nd Gear		1.479	=	=	...	
3rd Gear		1.000	=	=	...	
4th Gear		0.728	=	=	...	
Reverse Gear		2.086	=	=	...	
Intermediate shaft		1.100	=	=	...	
Final drive ratio		3.667	=	=	...	
Limited slip differential		no	no	no	...	
Trans. weight w/ oil and ATF	(kg)	105	=	=	...	

The power and the glory. The 3.3 liter Turbo powerplant needed every inch of available space in the engine bay. The shape of the rear spoiler had to be modified to carry the charge-air intercooler.

Model designation		Carrera (993)	Carrera 2 Cabriolet	Carrera 2 SPEEDSTER	Carrera 4 Turbo Look*	Turbo 3.6
4. Steering, Suspension, Wheels, Brakes						
Front suspension						
Stabilizer bar dia.	(mm)	21	20	=	21*	21
Steering ratio		16.48	18.48	=	=	18.48
Turning circle dia.	(m)	11.74	11.95	=	=	11.45
Rear suspension						
Stabilizer bar, man. trans.	(mm)	18	20	=	22*	22
Tiptronic	(mm)	18	19	...	...	...
Brake system						
Power assist ratio		3.15:1	3.0:1	=	4.8 hydraulic	=
Master cylinder dia.	(mm)	23.81	20.64	=	23.81	23.81
Brake pressure limit valve						
Activation pressure	(bar)	40	45	=	33*	60
Reduction factor		0.46	0.46	0.46	0.46	0.46
Brake caliper piston dia.						
front	(mm)	44+36	40+36	40+36	40+36	44+36
rear	(mm)	34+30	30+28	30+28	34+30	34+30
Brake disc diameter						
front	(mm)	304	298	298	298	322
rear	(mm)	299	299	299	299	299
Brake disc thickness						
front	(mm)	32	28	28	28	32
rear	(mm)	24	24	24	28	28
Total eff. pad area	(cm²)	422	284	284	344	474
Parking brake		Mechanical, acting on both rear wheels				
Brake drum diameter	(mm)	180	=	=	=	=
Total pad area	(cm²)	170	=	=	=	=

Abbreviations:
Turbo Look* = Technical specifications based on Carrera 4 Turbo Look

Model designation		Carrera (993)	Carrera 2 Cabriolet	Carrera 2 SPEEDSTER	Carrera 4 Turbo Look*	Turbo 3.6
Wheels and tires						
Standard tires front		205/55ZR16	205/55ZR16	205/50ZR17	205/50R17 98T	225/40ZR18
on wheel size		7J x 16	6J x 16 H2	7J x 17 AH	7J x 17	8J x 18 H2
Wheel offset	(mm)	55	52	55	55	52
Standard tires rear		245/45ZR16	225/50ZR16	255/40ZR17	225/45R17 90T	265/35ZR18
on wheel size		9J x 16	8J x 16 H2	8J x 17AH	8J x 17	10J x 18 H2
Wheel offset	(mm)	70	52	52	52	61
Space saver spare wheel		165/70-1692P	=	=	=	=
Tire pressure, front	(bar)	2.5	=	2.5	=	2.5
rear	(bar)	3.0	=	3.0	2.5	2.5
Space saver spare	(bar)	2.5	=	3.0	2.5	2.5
Dimensions at empty weight						
Length	(mm)	4245	4250	=	=	4275
Width	(mm)	1735	1652	=	1775	1775
Height	(mm)	1300	1310	1280	1290	1290
Wheelbase	(mm)	2272	2272	=	=	=
Track, front	(mm)	1405	1380	=	1434	1442
rear	(mm)	1444	1374	=	1499	1506
Ground clearance at legal maximum weight	(mm)	110	115	=	112	112
Approach angle, front	(deg.)	11	11.5	=	=	=
rear	(deg.)	12.5	=	=	13.5	=

9. Electrical system

Generator output	(W/A)	1610/115	=	=	=	=
Battery	(V/Ah)	12/75	=	=	=	=

Weights according to DIN 70020

Empty weight with						
Manual trans.	(kg)	1370	1350	1350	1500	1470
Tiptronic	(kg)	1395	1380	1380	...	...
Maximum permissible total						
Weight, manual trans.	(kg)	1710	1690	1600	1840	1810
Tiptronic	(kg)	1735	1720	1630	...	...
Permissible towing load						
unbraked	(kg)	none	500	none	500	none
braked	(kg)	none	1200	none	1200	none

Performance

Maximum speed						
Manual trans.	(km/h)	270	260	260	255	280
Tiptronic	(km/h)	265	256	256	...	...
Acceleration	0...100 km/h					
Manual trans.	(s)	5.6	5.7	5.7	5.7	4.8
Tiptronic	(s)	6.6	6.6	6.6	...	...
Standing-start kilometer						
Manual trans.	(s)	25.1	25.2	25.2	25.5	23.3
Tiptronic	(s)	25.9	26.2	26.2	...	...
Capacities						
Engine oil capacity 1*	(l)	11.5	=	=	=	12.0
Manual trans. 2*	(l)	3.6	=	=	3.8	3.9
Front suspension 2*	(l)	...	...	=	1.2	...
Automatic trans. 3*	(l)	9.0	=	=	...	...
Auto final drive 2*	(l)	0.9	0.9	=	...	...
Fuel tank capacity	(l)	71.5	77	=	=	92
Brake reservoir 6*	(l)	0.34	0.75	=	0.34	=
Power steering fl.3*	(l)	1.0	=	=	=	=
Refrigerant 4*	(g)	930	=	=	=	840
Compressor oil 5*	(ml)	100	=	=	=	140

* Notes:
1* Approved motor oils: API SE/SF when combined with API SE/CC - SF/CC - SF/CD - SE/CD
Multigrade oils as approved by factory
2* Multigrade transmission oil 75 W 90 to MIL-L 2105 B or API classification GL 5
3* ATF DEXRON II D
4* Use only refrigerant R 134a (Porsche now uses HFC-free air conditioning refrigerant)
5* Commercially available air conditioning compressor oil
6* Use only brake fluid meeting DOT 4 Type 200
Abbreviations:
Turbo Look = Technical specifications based on Carrera 4 Turbo Look
M Optional equipment
S Standard equipment

Chassis numbers

The key to the Porsche 911

The following list of chassis numbers and the more recent Vehicle Identification Numbers is taken directly from Porsche factory documentation. The sometimes altered number ranges for USA and Canadian vehicles are noteworthy. In these cases, some North American models, by virtue of later production startup date (compared to so-called "Rest of World" vehicles), are included with the following model year. As of 1970, a new numbering convention was introduced at Porsche. The sequential numbers at the end of the chassis or VIN number are assigned as follows: numbers ...0001 to ...0050 are for test vehicles, while numbers ...0051 through ...0060 are reserved for special vehicles. Each series of vehicle production actually begins with number ...0061.

Model Years 1965, 1966 and 1967

Composition of chassis numbers (six-digit)

Model year		Production time frame	Type	Model	Body Builder
1964:	300 001 ...300 232	Produced after Sept. 1964	911	Coupé	Porsche
1965:	300 233 ...303 390	Produced to July 1965	911	Coupé	Porsche
	350 001 ...351 970	Produced to July 1965	912	Coupé	Porsche
	450 001 ...454 470	Produced to July 1965	912	Coupé	Karmann
1966:	303 391 ...305 100	Aug. 1965 to July 1966	911	Coupé	Porsche
	351 971 ...353 000	Aug. 1965 to July 1966	912	Coupé	Porsche
	454 471 ...485 100	Aug. 1965 to July 1966	912	Coupé	Karmann
1967:	305 101 ...308 522	Aug. 1966 to July 1967	911	Coupé	Porsche
	305 101S ...308 523S	Aug. 1966 to July 1967	911S	Coupé	Porsche
	354 001 ...355 601	Aug. 1966 to July 1967	912	Coupé	Porsche
	458 101 ...463 204	Aug. 1966 to July 1967	912	Coupé	Karmann
	500 001 ...500 718	Aug. 1966 to July 1967	911	Targa	Porsche
	500 001S ...500 718S	Aug. 1966 to July 1967	911S	Targa	Porsche
	550 001 ...550 544	Aug. 1966 to July 1967	912	Targa	Porsche

Model Year 1968

Composition of chassis numbers (eight-digit)

11	8	2	0001 ... 9999
Vehicle	–	–	–
= all 911	Model year		
	8 = 1968	Version	
	7 = 1967	0 = Coupé S	Sequential number
	6 = 1966	1 = Coupé 911	
		3 = Coupé USA	
		5 = Targa S	
		6 = Targa L	
		7 = Targa T	
		8 = Targa USA	

Overview of chassis number ranges

11	8	0	0001 ... 1267	911 S Coupé
11	8	0	5001 ... 5449	911 L Coupé USA
11	8	1	0001 ... 0720	911 L Coupé
11	8	2	0001 ... 0928	911 T Coupé
11	8	2	5001 ... 5683	911 T Coupé Karm.
11	8	3	0001 ... 0473	911 Coupé USA
11	8	3	5001 ... 5742	911 Coupé Karmann
11	8	5	0001 ... 0442	911 S Targa
11	8	5	5001 ... 5134	911 L Targa USA
11	8	6	0001 ... 0307	911 L Targa
11	8	7	0001 ... 0521	911 T Targa
11	8	8	0001 ... 0268	911 Targa USA

Model Year 1969

Composition of chassis numbers (nine-digit)

11	9	2	0	0001 ... 9999
Vehicle	–	–	–	
11 = all 911	Model year	–		
	9 = 1969	Engine	–	
		1 = 911 T	Body	–
		2 = 911 E	0 = Coupé	Sequential number
		3 = 911 S	1 = Targa	
			2 = Karmann	

Overview of chassis number ranges

11	9	1	0	0001 ... 0343	911 T Coupé
11	9	1	2	0001 ... 3561	911 T Coupé Karmann
11	9	1	1	0001 ... 1282	911 T Targa
11	9	2	0	0001 ... 0954	911 E Coupé
11	9	2	2	0001 ... 1014	911 E Coupé Karmann
11	9	2	1	0001 ... 0858	911 E Targa
11	9	3	0	0001 ... 1492	911 S Coupé
11	9	3	1	0001 ... 0614	911 S Targa

Model Year 1970

Composition of chassis numbers (ten-digit)

911	0	2	0	0001 ... 9999
Vehicle	–	–	–	–
911 = all 911	Model year	–	–	–
	0 = 1970	Engine	–	–
	9 = 1969	1 = 911 T	Body	–
		2 = 911 E	0 = Coupé	Sequential number
		3 = 911 S	1 = Targa	
			2 = Karmann	

Overview of chassis number ranges

911	0	1	0	0001 ... 2418	911 T Coupé
911	0	1	1	0001 ... 2545	911 T Targa
911	0	1	2	0001 ... 4126	911 T Coupé Karmann
911	0	2	0	0001 ... 1304	911 E Coupé
911	0	2	1	0001 ... 0933	911 E Targa
911	0	2	2	0001 ... 0667	911 E Coupé Karmann
911	0	3	0	0001 ... 1744	911 S Coupé
911	0	3	1	0001 ... 0729	911 S Targa

Model Year 1971

Composition of chassis numbers (ten-digit)

911	1	2	0	0001 ... 9999
Vehicle	–	–	–	–
911 = all 911	Model year	–	–	–
	1 = 1971	Engine	–	–
	0 = 1970	1 = 911 T	Body	–
		2 = 911 E	0 = Coupé	Sequential number
		3 = 911 S	1 = Targa	
			2 = Karmann	

Overview of chassis number ranges

911	1	1	0	0001 ... 2583	911 T Coupé
911	1	1	1	0001 ... 3476	911 T Targa
911	1	1	2	0001 ... 1934	911 T Coupé Karmann
911	1	2	0	0001 ... 1088	911 E Coupé
911	1	2	1	0001 ... 0935	911 E Targa
911	1	3	0	0001 ... 1430	911 S Coupé
911	1	3	1	0001 ... 0788	911 S Targa

Model Year 1972

Composition of chassis numbers (ten-digit)

911	2	2	0	0001 ... 9999
Vehicle	–	–	–	–
911 = all 911	Model year	–	–	–
	2 = 1972	Engine	–	–
	1 = 1971	1 = 911 T	Body	–
		2 = 911 E	0 = Coupé	Sequential number
		3 = 911 S	1 = Targa	
		5 = 911 T Carbureted		

Overview of chassis number ranges

911	2	1	0	0001 ... 2931	911 T Coupé USA
911	2	1	1	0001 ... 1821	911 T Targa USA
911	2	2	0	0001 ... 1124	911 E Coupé
911	2	2	1	0001 ... 0861	911 E Targa
911	2	3	0	0001 ... 1750	911 S – E Coupé
911	2	3	1	0001 ... 0989	911 S – E Targa
911	2	5	0	0001 ... 1963	911 T Coupé
911	2	5	1	0001 ... 1523	911 T Targa

Model Year 1973
Composition of chassis numbers (ten-digit)

911	3	2	0	0001 ... 9999
Vehicle	–	–	–	–
911 = all 911	Model year	–	–	–
	3 = 1973	Engine	–	–
	2 = 1972	1 = 911 T	Body	–
		2 = 911 E	0 = Coupé	Sequential number
		3 = 911 S	1 = Targa	
		5 = 911 T Carburetor		
		6 = 911 Carrera		

Overview of chassis number ranges

911	3	1	0	0001 ... 1252	911 T Coupé USA
911	3	1	1	0001 ... 0781	911 T Targa USA
911	3	2	0	0001 ... 1366	911 E Coupé
911	3	2	1	0001 ... 1055	911 E Targa
911	3	3	0	0001 ... 1430	911 S Coupé
911	3	3	1	0001 ... 0925	911 S Targa
911	3	5	0	0001 ... 1875	911 T Coupé
911	3	5	1	0001 ... 1541	911 T Targa
911	3	6	0	0001 ... 1036	911 Carrera Coupe

Model Year 1974
Composition of chassis numbers (ten-digit)

911	4	2	0	0001 ... 9999
Vehicle	–	–	–	–
911 = all 911	Model year	–	–	–
	4 = 1974	Engine	–	–
	3 = 1973	1 = 911	Body	–
		3 = 911 S	0 = Coupé	Sequential number
		4 = Carrera	1 = Targa	
		USA		
		6 = Carrera		

Overview of chassis number ranges

911	4	1	0	0001 ... 4014	Rest of world 911 Coupé
911	4	1	1	0001 ... 3110	Rest of world 911 Targa
911	4	3	0	0001 ... 1359	Rest of world 911 S Coupé
911	4	3	1	0001 ... 0898	Rest of world 911 S Targa
911	4	4	0	0001 ... 0528	USA & California 911 Carrera Coupé
911	4	4	1	0001 ... 0246	USA & California 911 Carrera Targa
911	4	6	0	0001 ... 1036	Carrera Coupé
911	4	6	1	0001 ... 0433	Carrera Targa

Model Year 1975
Composition of chassis numbers (ten-digit)

911	5	2	0	0001 ... 9999
Vehicle	–	–	–	–
911 = all 911	Model year	–	–	–
930 = Turbo	5 = 1975	Engine	–	–
	4 = 1974	1 = 911	Body	–
		2 = 911 S	0 = Coupé	Sequential number
		USA	1 = Targa	
		3 = 911 S		
		4 = Carrera USA		
		6 = Carrera		
		7 = Turbo		

Overview of chassis number ranges

911	5	1	0	0001 ... 1238	Rest of world 911 Coupé
911	5	1	1	0001 ... 0998	Rest of world 911 Targa
911	5	2	0	0001 ... 2310	USA & California 911 S Coupé
911	5	2	1	0001 ... 1517	USA & California 911 S Targa
911	5	3	0	0001 ... 0385	Rest of world 911 S Coupé
911	5	3	1	0001 ... 0266	Rest of world 911 S Targa
911	5	4	0	0001 ... 0395	USA & California Carrera Coupé
911	5	4	1	0001 ... 0174	USA & California Carrera Targa
911	5	6	0	0001 ... 0518	Carrera Coupé
911	5	6	1	0001 ... 0197	Carrera Targa
930	5	7	0	0001 ... 0284	911 Turbo

Model Year 1976
Composition of chassis numbers (ten-digit)

911	6	2	0	0001 ... 9999
Vehicle	–	–	–	–
911 = all 911	Model year	–	–	–
930 = Turbo	6 = 1976	Engine	–	–
912 = 912E	5 = 1975	2 = 911 S	Body	–
		USA	0 = Coupe	Sequential number
		3 = 911	1 = Targa	
		6 = Carrera		
		7 = 911 Turbo		
		8 = 911 Turbo USA		

Overview of chassis number ranges

911	6	2	0	0001 ... 2079	USA & California 911 S Coupé
911	6	2	1	0001 ... 2175	USA & California 911 S Targa
911	6	3	0	0001 ... 1868	Rest of world 911 S Coupé
911	6	3	1	0001 ... 1576	Rest of world 911 S Targa
911	6	6	0	9001 ... 9123	Carrera Coupé
911	6	6	1	9001 ... 9030	Carrera Targa
930	6	7	0	0001 ... 0644	Rest of world 911 Turbo
930	6	8	0	0001 ... 0530	USA & California 911 Turbo
912	6	0	0	0001 ... 2099	912E

Model Year 1977
Composition of chassis numbers (ten-digit)

911	7	2	0	0001 ... 9999
Vehicle	–	–	–	–
911 = all 911	Model year	–	–	–
930 = Turbo	7 = 1977	Engine	–	–
	6 = 1976	2 = 911 S	Body	–
		USA	0 = Coupé	Sequential number
		3 = 911	1 = Targa	
		6 = Carrera		
		7 = 911 Turbo		
		8 = 911 Turbo USA		

Overview of chassis number ranges

911	7	2	0	0001 ... 3388	USA & California 911 S Coupé
911	7	2	1	0001 ... 2747	USA & California 911 S Targa
911	7	3	0	0001 ... 2449	Rest of world 911 S Coupé
911	7	3	1	0001 ... 1724	Rest of world 911 S Targa
911	7	6	0	0001 ... 1473	Carrera Coupé
911	7	6	1	0001 ... 0646	Carrera Targa
930	7	7	0	0001 ... 0695	Rest of world 911 Turbo
930	7	8	0	0001 ... 0727	USA & California 911 Turbo

Model Year 1978

Composition of chassis numbers (ten-digit)

911	8	3	0	0001 ... 9999
Vehicle	–	–	–	–
911 = all 911	Model year	–	–	–
930 = Turbo	8 = 1978	Engine	–	–
	7 = 1977	2 = 911 SC Body	–	
		USA 0 = Coupé	Sequential number	
		3 = 911 SC 1 = Targa		
		RoW		
		7 = 911 Turbo RoW		
		7 = 911 Turbo		
		8 = 911 Turbo USA		

Overview of chassis number ranges

911	8	2	0	0001 ... 2436	USA & California 911 SC Coupé
911	8	2	1	0001 ... 2579	USA & California 911 SC Targa
911	8	3	0	0001 ... 2438	Rest of world 911 SC Coupé
911	8	3	1	0001 ... 1729	Rest of world 911 SC Targa
911	8	3	0	9501 ... 9804	Japan 911 SC Coupé
911	8	6	1	9501 ... 9999**	Japan 911 SC Targa
930	8	7	0	0001 ... 0735	Rest of world 911 Turbo
930	8	8	0	9501 ... 9561	Japan 911 Turbo
930	8	8	8	0001 ... 0461	USA & California 911 Turbo

Model Year 1979

Composition of chassis numbers (ten-digit)

911	9	3	0	0001 ... 9999
Vehicle	–	–	–	–
911 = all 911	Model year	–	–	–
930 = Turbo	9 = 1979	Engine	–	–
	8 = 1978	2 = 911 SC Body	–	
		USA 0 = Coupé	Sequential number	
		3 = 911 SC 1 = Targa		
		RoW		
		7 = 911 Turbo RoW		
		8 = 911 Turbo USA		

Overview of chassis number ranges

911	9	2	0	0001 ... 2013	USA & California 911 SC Coupé
911	9	2	1	0001 ... 1965	USA & California 911 SC Targa
911	9	3	0	0001 ... 3319	Rest of world 911 SC Coupé
911	9	3	1	0001 ... 1874	Rest of world 911 SC Targa
911	9	3	0	9501 ... 9873	Japan 911 SC Coupé
911	9	6	1	9501 ... 9999**	Japan 911 SC Targa
930	9	7	0	0001 ... 0820	Rest of world 911 Turbo
930	9	8	0	9501 ... 9532	Japan 911 Turbo
930	9	8	8	0001 ... 1200	USA & California 911 Turbo

Model Year 1980

Note: Changes in the serial number system were required by new vehicle regulations in the European Community as well as the U.S. The goal of this international numbering convention is to create a system that will accommodate serial numbers of vehicles made over a thirty- year period. A seventeen-character serial number was created, which encodes manufacturer, country or plant of origin, vehicle type, vehicle specification and year of manufacture. Until the worldwide standard takes effect, the 1980 model year represents an interim solution, still given a ten-digit serial number.

Composition of chassis numbers (ten-digit)

91	A	0	1	3	0001 ... 9999
Vehicle	–	–	–	–	–
91 = all 911	Model year	–	–	–	–
93 = Turbo	A = 1980	Plant	–	–	–
	B = 1981		Model	–	–
			1 = 911	Engine version	–
			8 = 928	3 = RoW	Sequential number
			0 = 911 Turbo	4 = USA	
				7 = 911 Turbo	

Overview of chassis number ranges

91	A	0	1	3	0001 ... 4831	Rest of world & Japan	911 SC Coupé/Targa
91	A	0	1	4	0001 ... 4272	USA	911 SC Coupé/Targa
93	A	0	0	7	0001 ... 0840	Rest of world & Japan	911 Turbo

** these chassis numbers were not used

380

Model Year 1981

Note: As of the 1981 model year, all vehicles are identified by an internationally standardized 17-digit chassis number.

Serial numbers

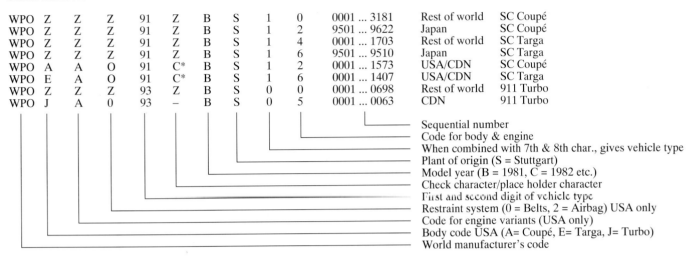

WPO	Z	Z	Z	91	Z	B	S	1	0	0001 ... 3181	Rest of world	SC Coupé
WPO	Z	Z	Z	91	Z	B	S	1	2	9501 ... 9622	Japan	SC Coupé
WPO	Z	Z	Z	91	Z	B	S	1	4	0001 ... 1703	Rest of world	SC Targa
WPO	Z	Z	Z	91	Z	B	S	1	6	9501 ... 9510	Japan	SC Targa
WPO	A	A	O	91	C*	B	S	1	2	0001 ... 1573	USA/CDN	SC Coupé
WPO	E	A	O	91	C*	B	S	1	6	0001 ... 1407	USA/CDN	SC Targa
WPO	Z	Z	Z	93	Z	B	S	0	0	0001 ... 0698	Rest of world	911 Turbo
WPO	J	A	0	93	–	B	S	0	5	0001 ... 0063	CDN	911 Turbo

Sequential number
Code for body & engine
When combined with 7th & 8th char., gives vehicle type
Plant of origin (S = Stuttgart)
Model year (B = 1981, C = 1982 etc.)
Check character/place holder character
First and second digit of vehicle type
Restraint system (0 = Belts, 2 = Airbag) USA only
Code for engine variants (USA only)
Body code USA (A= Coupé, E= Targa, J= Turbo)
World manufacturer's code

Model Year 1982
Serial numbers

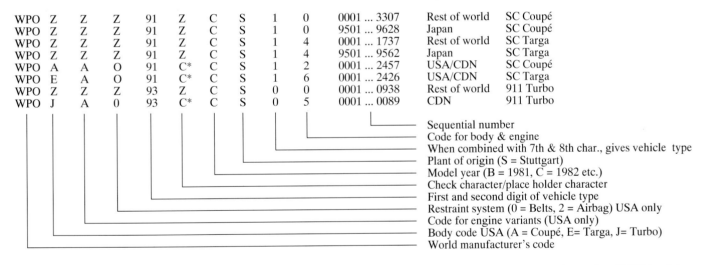

WPO	Z	Z	Z	91	Z	C	S	1	0	0001 ... 3307	Rest of world	SC Coupé
WPO	Z	Z	Z	91	Z	C	S	1	0	9501 ... 9628	Japan	SC Coupé
WPO	Z	Z	Z	91	Z	C	S	1	4	0001 ... 1737	Rest of world	SC Targa
WPO	Z	Z	Z	91	Z	C	S	1	4	9501 ... 9562	Japan	SC Targa
WPO	A	A	O	91	C*	C	S	1	2	0001 ... 2457	USA/CDN	SC Coupé
WPO	E	A	O	91	C*	C	S	1	6	0001 ... 2426	USA/CDN	SC Targa
WPO	Z	Z	Z	93	Z	C	S	0	0	0001 ... 0938	Rest of world	911 Turbo
WPO	J	A	0	93	C*	C	S	0	5	0001 ... 0089	CDN	911 Turbo

Sequential number
Code for body & engine
When combined with 7th & 8th char., gives vehicle type
Plant of origin (S = Stuttgart)
Model year (B = 1981, C = 1982 etc.)
Check character/place holder character
First and second digit of vehicle type
Restraint system (0 = Belts, 2 = Airbag) USA only
Code for engine variants (USA only)
Body code USA (A = Coupé, E= Targa, J= Turbo)
World manufacturer's code

C* = check character, could be 0 to 9 or X (USA only)
Z = filler character for rest of world vehicles

Model Year 1983

Serial numbers

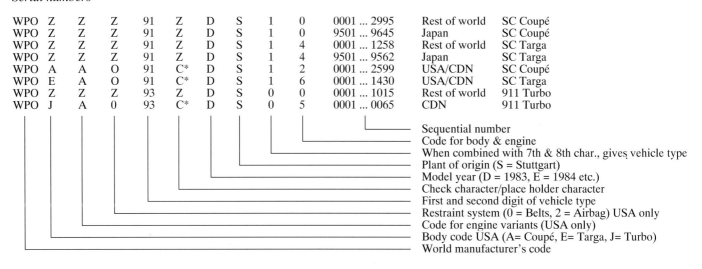

WPO	Z	Z	Z	91	Z	D	S	1	0	0001 ... 2995	Rest of world	SC Coupé
WPO	Z	Z	Z	91	Z	D	S	1	0	9501 ... 9645	Japan	SC Coupé
WPO	Z	Z	Z	91	Z	D	S	1	4	0001 ... 1258	Rest of world	SC Targa
WPO	Z	Z	Z	91	Z	D	S	1	4	9501 ... 9562	Japan	SC Targa
WPO	A	A	O	91	C*	D	S	1	2	0001 ... 2599	USA/CDN	SC Coupé
WPO	E	A	O	91	C*	D	S	1	6	0001 ... 1430	USA/CDN	SC Targa
WPO	Z	Z	Z	93	Z	D	S	0	0	0001 ... 1015	Rest of world	911 Turbo
WPO	J	A	0	93	C*	D	S	0	5	0001 ... 0065	CDN	911 Turbo

- Sequential number
- Code for body & engine
- When combined with 7th & 8th char., gives vehicle type
- Plant of origin (S = Stuttgart)
- Model year (D = 1983, E = 1984 etc.)
- Check character/place holder character
- First and second digit of vehicle type
- Restraint system (0 = Belts, 2 = Airbag) USA only
- Code for engine variants (USA only)
- Body code USA (A= Coupé, E= Targa, J= Turbo)
- World manufacturer's code

Model Year 1984

Serial numbers

WPO	Z	Z	Z	91	Z	E	S	1	0	0001 ... 4033	Rest of world	Carrera Coupé
WPO	Z	Z	Z	91	Z	E	S	1	0	9501 ... 9717	Japan	Carrera Coupé
WPO	Z	Z	Z	91	Z	E	S	1	4	0001 ... 1469	Rest of world	Carrera Targa
WPO	Z	Z	Z	91	Z	E	S	1	4	9501 ... 9564	Japan	Carrera Targa
WPO	Z	Z	Z	91	Z	E	S	1	5	0001 ... 1835	Rest of world	Carrera Cabriolet
WPO	Z	Z	Z	91	Z	E	S	1	5	9501 ... 9577	Japan	Carrera Cabriolet
WPO	A	B	O	91	C*	E	S	1	2	0001 ... 2282	USA/CDN	Carrera Coupé
WPO	E	B	O	91	C*	E	S	1	6	0001 ... 2260	USA/CDN	Carrera Targa
WPO	E	B	O	91	C*	E	S	1	7	0001 ... 1191	USA/CDN	Carrera Cabriolet
WPO	Z	Z	Z	93	Z	E	S	0	0	0001 ... 0804	Rest of world	911 Turbo
WPO	J	A	0	93	C*	E	S	0	5	0001 ... 0077	CDN	911 Turbo

- Sequential number
- Code for body & engine
- When combined with 7th & 8th char., gives vehicle type
- Plant of origin (S = Stuttgart)
- Model year (E = 1984, F = 1985 etc.)
- Check character/place holder character
- First and second digit of vehicle type
- Restraint system (0 = Belts, 2 = Airbag) USA only
- Code for engine variants (USA only)
- Body code USA (A= Coupé, E= Targa/Cabrio, J= Turbo)
- World manufacturer's code

C* = check character, could be 0 to 9 or X (USA only)
Z = filler character for rest of world vehicles

Model Year 1985

Serial numbers

										Serial range	Region	Model
WPO	Z	Z	Z	91	Z	F	S	1	0	0001 ... 3529	Rest of world	Carrera Coupé
WPO	Z	Z	Z	91	Z	F	S	1	0	9501 ... 9722	Japan	Carrera Coupé
WPO	Z	Z	Z	91	Z	F	S	1	4	0001 ... 1435	Rest of world	Carrera Targa
WPO	Z	Z	Z	91	Z	F	S	1	4	9501 ... 9564	Japan	Carrera Targa
WPO	Z	Z	Z	91	Z	F	S	1	5	0001 ... 1583	Rest of world	Carrera Cabriolet
WPO	Z	Z	Z	91	Z	F	S	1	5	9501 ... 9575	Japan	Carrera Cabriolet
WPO	A	B	O	91	C*	F	S	1	2	0001 ... 1959	USA/CDN	Carrera Coupé
WPO	E	B	O	91	C*	F	S	1	6	0001 ... 1942	USA/CDN	Carrera Targa
WPO	E	B	O	91	C*	F	S	1	7	0001 ... 1050	USA/CDN	Carrera Cabriolet
WPO	Z	Z	Z	93	Z	F	S	0	0	0001 ... 1063	Rest of world	911 Turbo
WPO	J	A	0	93	C*	F	S	0	5	0001 ... 0085	CDN	911 Turbo

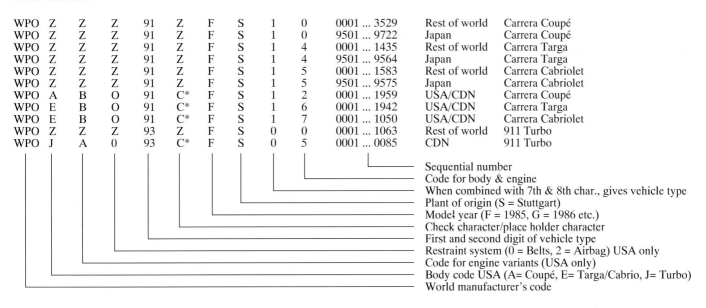

Sequential number
Code for body & engine
When combined with 7th & 8th char., gives vehicle type
Plant of origin (S = Stuttgart)
Model year (F = 1985, G = 1986 etc.)
Check character/place holder character
First and second digit of vehicle type
Restraint system (0 = Belts, 2 = Airbag) USA only
Code for engine variants (USA only)
Body code USA (A= Coupé, E= Targa/Cabrio, J= Turbo)
World manufacturer's code

Model Year 1986

Serial numbers

										Serial range	Region	Model
WPO	Z	Z	Z	91	Z	G	S	1	0	0001 ... 4031	Rest of world	Carrera Coupé
WPO	Z	Z	Z	91	Z	G	S	1	0	9501 ... 9733	Japan	Carrera Coupé
WPO	Z	Z	Z	91	Z	G	S	1	4	0001 ... 1758	Rest of world	Carrera Targa
WPO	Z	Z	Z	91	Z	G	S	1	4	9501 ... 9579	Japan	Carrera Targa
WPO	Z	Z	Z	91	Z	G	S	1	5	0001 ... 2358	Rest of world	Carrera Cabriolet
WPO	Z	Z	Z	91	Z	G	S	1	5	9501 ... 9580	Japan	Carrera Cabriolet
WPO	A	B	O	91	C*	G	S	1	2	0001 ... 2619	USA/CDN	Carrera Coupé
WPO	E	B	O	91	C*	G	S	1	6	0001 ... 1976	USA/CDN	Carrera Targa
WPO	E	B	O	91	C*	G	S	1	7	0001 ... 1986	USA/CDN	Carrera Cabriolet
WPO	Z	Z	Z	93	Z	G	S	0	0	0001 ... 1158	Rest of world	911 Turbo
WPO	J	A	O	93	C*	G	S	0	5	5001 ... 5088	CDN	911 Turbo
WPO	J	B	0	93	C*	G	S	0	5	0001 ... 1424	USA	911 Turbo

Sequential number
Code for body & engine
When combined with 7th & 8th char., gives vehicle type
Plant of origin (S = Stuttgart)
Model year (G = 1986, H = 1987 etc.)
Check character/place holder character
First and second digit of vehicle type
Restraint system (0 = Belts, 2 = Airbag) USA only
Code for engine variants (USA only)
Body code USA (A= Coupé, E= Targa/Cabrio, J= Turbo)
World manufacturer's code

C* = check character, could be 0 to 9 or X (USA only)
Z = filler character for rest of world vehicles

Model Year 1987

Note: as a result of the 8th revision of the German motor vehicle code, the term "chassis number" was altered in accordance with international regulations and renamed "vehicle identification number" (VIN number).

Vehicle Identification Numbers (VIN Numbers)

WPO	Z	Z	Z	91	Z	H	S	1	0	0001 ... 3381	Rest of world	Carrera Coupé
WPO	Z	Z	Z	91	Z	H	S	1	0	5001 ... 5081	Rest of world	Carrera Coupé (M637)
WPO	Z	Z	Z	91	Z	H	S	1	0	9501 ... 9808	Japan	Carrera Coupé
WPO	Z	Z	Z	91	Z	H	S	1	4	0001 ... 1354	Rest of world	Carrera Targa
WPO	Z	Z	Z	91	Z	H	S	1	4	9501 ... 9579	Japan	Carrera Targa
WPO	Z	Z	Z	91	Z	H	S	1	5	0001 ... 1464	Rest of world	Carrera Cabriolet
WPO	Z	Z	Z	91	Z	H	S	1	5	9501 ... 9585	Japan	Carrera Cabriolet
WPO	A	B	O	91	C*	H	S	1	2	0001 ... 2916	USA/CDN	Carrera Coupé
WPO	A	B	O	91	C*	H	S	1	2	5001 ... 5300	USA/CDN	Carrera Coupé (M637)
WPO	E	B	O	91	C*	H	S	1	6	0001 ... 2232	USA/CDN	Carrera Targa
WPO	E	B	O	91	C*	H	S	1	7	0001 ... 2653	USA/CDN	Carrera Cabriolet
WPO	Z	Z	Z	93	Z	H	S	0	0	0001 ... 0720	Rest of world	911 Turbo
WPO	J	A	O	93	C*	H	S	0	5	5001 ... 5088	CDN	911 Turbo
WPO	Z	Z	Z	93	Z	H	S	0	2	0001 ... 0142	Rest of world	911 Turbo Cabriolet
WPO	E	B	O	93	C*	H	S	0	7	0001 ... 0183	USA	911 Turbo Cabriolet
WPO	E	A	O	93	C*	H	S	0	7	5000 ... 7000 **	CDN	911 Turbo Cabriolet
WPO	Z	Z	Z	93	Z	H	S	0	1	0001 ... 0069	Rest of world	911 Turbo Targa
WPO	E	B	O	93	C*	H	S	0	6	0001 ... 0087	USA	911 Turbo Targa
WPO	E	A	O	93	C*	H	S	0	6	5001 ... 7000 **	CDN	911 Turbo Targa
WPO	Z	Z	Z	95	Z	H	S	9	0	0001 ... 0254	Worldwide	959 Coupé

- Sequential number
- Code for body & engine
- When combined with 7th & 8th char., gives vehicle type
- Plant of origin (S = Stuttgart)
- Model year (G = 1986, H = 1987 etc.)
- Check character/place holder character
- First and second digit of vehicle type
- Restraint system (0 = Belts, 2 = Airbag) USA only
- Code for engine variants (USA only)
- Body code USA (A= Coupé, E= Targa/Cabrio, J= Turbo)
- World manufacturer's code

Model Year 1988

Vehicle Identification Numbers (VIN Numbers)

WPO	Z	Z	Z	91	Z	J	S	1	0	0001 ... 3580	Rest of world	Carrera Coupé
WPO	Z	Z	Z	91	Z	J	S	1	0	5001 ... 5148	Rest of world	Carrera Coupé (M637)
WPO	Z	Z	Z	91	Z	J	S	1	0	9501 ... 9930	Japan	Carrera Coupé
WPO	Z	Z	Z	91	Z	J	S	1	4	0001 ... 1281	Rest of world	Carrera Targa
WPO	Z	Z	Z	91	Z	J	S	1	4	9501 ... 9586	Japan	Carrera Targa
WPO	Z	Z	Z	91	Z	J	S	1	5	0001 ... 1501	Rest of world	Carrera Cabriolet
WPO	Z	Z	Z	91	Z	J	S	1	5	9501 ... 9581	Japan	Carrera Cabriolet
WPO	A	B	O	91	C*	J	S	1	2	0001 ... 2066	USA/CDN	Carrera Coupé
WPO	A	B	O	91	C*	J	S	1	2	5001 ... 5082	USA/CDN	Carrera Coupé (M637)
WPO	E	B	O	91	C*	J	S	1	6	0001 ... 1500	USA/CDN	Carrera Targa
WPO	E	B	O	91	C*	J	S	1	7	0001 ... 2116	USA/CDN	Carrera Cabriolet
WPO	Z	Z	Z	93	Z	J	S	0	0	0001 ... 0677	Rest of world	911 Turbo
WPO	J	B	O	93	C*	J	S	0	5	0001 ... 0701	USA/CDN	911 Turbo
WPO	Z	Z	Z	93	Z	J	S	0	2	0001 ... 0242	Rest of world	911 Turbo Cabriolet
WPO	E	B	O	93	C*	J	S	0	7	0001 ... 0591	USA/CDN	911 Turbo Cabriolet
WPO	Z	Z	Z	93	Z	J	S	0	1	0001 ... 0136	Rest of world	911 Turbo Targa
WPO	Z	Z	Z	93	Z	J	S	0	6	0001 ... 0141	USA/CDN	911 Turbo Targa

- Sequential number
- Code for body & engine
- When combined with 7th & 8th char., gives vehicle type
- Plant of origin (S = Stuttgart)
- Model year (J = 1988, K = 1989 etc.)
- Check character/place holder character
- First and second digit of vehicle type
- Restraint system (0 = Belts, 2 = Airbag) USA only
- Code for engine variants (USA only)
- Body code USA (A= Coupé, E= Targa/Cabrio, J= Turbo)
- World manufacturer's code

C* = check character, could be 0 to 9 or X (USA only)
Z = filler character for rest of world vehicles
** these chassis numbers were not used

Model Year 1989
Vehicle Identification Numbers (VIN Numbers)

WPO	Z	Z	Z	91	Z	K	S	1	0	0001 ... 3532	Rest of world	Carrera Coupé
WPO	Z	Z	Z	91	Z	K	S	1	0	5001 ... 5300 **	Rest of world	Carrera Coupé (M637)
WPO	Z	Z	Z	91	Z	K	S	1	0	9501 ... 9999 **	Japan	Carrera Coupé
WPO	Z	Z	Z	91	Z	K	S	1	4	0001 ... 1063	Rest of world	Carrera Targa
WPO	Z	Z	Z	91	Z	K	S	1	4	9501 ... 9999 **	Japan	Carrera Targa
WPO	Z	Z	Z	91	Z	K	S	1	5	0001 ... 2787	Rest of world	Carrera Cabriolet
WPO	Z	Z	Z	91	Z	K	S	1	5	9501 ... 9999 **	Japan	Carrera Cabriolet
WPO	A	B	O	91	C*	K	S	1	2	0001 ... 5000	USA/CDN	Carrera Coupé
WPO	A	B	O	91	C*	K	S	1	2	5001 ... 5300 **	USA/CDN	Carrera Coupé (M637)
WPO	E	B	O	91	C*	K	S	1	6	0001 ... 0860	USA/CDN	Carrera Targa
WPO	E	B	O	91	C*	K	S	1	7	0001 ... 3829	USA/CDN	Carrera Cabriolet
WPO	Z	Z	Z	93	Z	K	S	0	0	0001 ... 0857	Rest of world	911 Turbo
WPO	J	B	O	93	C*	K	S	0	5	0001 ... 0639	USA/CDN	911 Turbo
WPO	Z	Z	Z	93	Z	K	S	0	2	0001 ... 0244	Rest of world	911 Turbo Cabriolet
WPO	E	B	O	93	C*	K	S	0	7	0001 ... 0600	USA/CDN	911 Turbo Cabriolet
WPO	Z	Z	Z	93	Z	K	S	0	1	0001 ... 0115	Rest of world	911 Turbo Targa

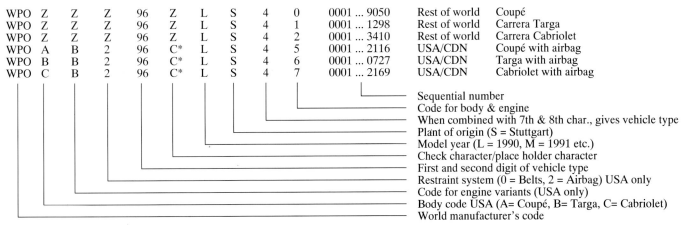

Sequential number
Code for body & engine
When combined with 7th & 8th char., gives vehicle type
Plant of origin (S = Stuttgart)
Model year (J = 1988, K = 1989 etc.)
Check character/place holder character
First and second digit of vehicle type
Restraint system (0 = Belts, 2 = Airbag) USA only
Code for engine variants (USA only)
Body code USA (A= Coupé, E= Targa/Cabrio, J= Turbo)
World manufacturer's code

Model Year 1990
Vehicle Identification Numbers (VIN Numbers)

WPO	Z	Z	Z	96	Z	L	S	4	0	0001 ... 9050	Rest of world	Coupé
WPO	Z	Z	Z	96	Z	L	S	4	1	0001 ... 1298	Rest of world	Carrera Targa
WPO	Z	Z	Z	96	Z	L	S	4	2	0001 ... 3410	Rest of world	Carrera Cabriolet
WPO	A	B	2	96	C*	L	S	4	5	0001 ... 2116	USA/CDN	Coupé with airbag
WPO	B	B	2	96	C*	L	S	4	6	0001 ... 0727	USA/CDN	Targa with airbag
WPO	C	B	2	96	C*	L	S	4	7	0001 ... 2169	USA/CDN	Cabriolet with airbag

Sequential number
Code for body & engine
When combined with 7th & 8th char., gives vehicle type
Plant of origin (S = Stuttgart)
Model year (L = 1990, M = 1991 etc.)
Check character/place holder character
First and second digit of vehicle type
Restraint system (0 = Belts, 2 = Airbag) USA only
Code for engine variants (USA only)
Body code USA (A= Coupé, B= Targa, C= Cabriolet)
World manufacturer's code

C* = check character, could be 0 to 9 or X (USA only)
Z = filler character for rest of world vehicles
** these chassis numbers were not used

Model Year 1991

Vehicle Identification Numbers (VIN Numbers)

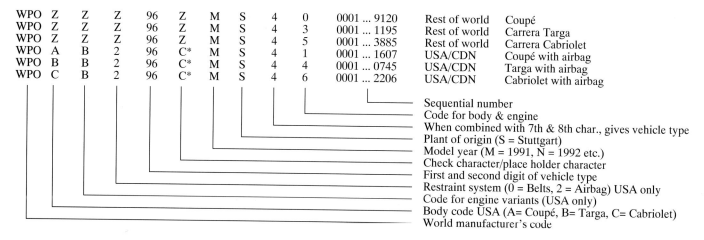

WPO	Z	Z	Z	96	Z	M	S	4	0	0001 ... 9120	Rest of world	Coupé
WPO	Z	Z	Z	96	Z	M	S	4	3	0001 ... 1195	Rest of world	Carrera Targa
WPO	Z	Z	Z	96	Z	M	S	4	5	0001 ... 3885	Rest of world	Carrera Cabriolet
WPO	A	B	2	96	C*	M	S	4	1	0001 ... 1607	USA/CDN	Coupé with airbag
WPO	B	B	2	96	C*	M	S	4	4	0001 ... 0745	USA/CDN	Targa with airbag
WPO	C	B	2	96	C*	M	S	4	6	0001 ... 2206	USA/CDN	Cabriolet with airbag

Sequential number
Code for body & engine
When combined with 7th & 8th char., gives vehicle type
Plant of origin (S = Stuttgart)
Model year (M = 1991, N = 1992 etc.)
Check character/place holder character
First and second digit of vehicle type
Restraint system (0 = Belts, 2 = Airbag) USA only
Code for engine variants (USA only)
Body code USA (A= Coupé, B= Targa, C= Cabriolet)
World manufacturer's code

Model Year 1992

Vehicle Identification Numbers (VIN Numbers)

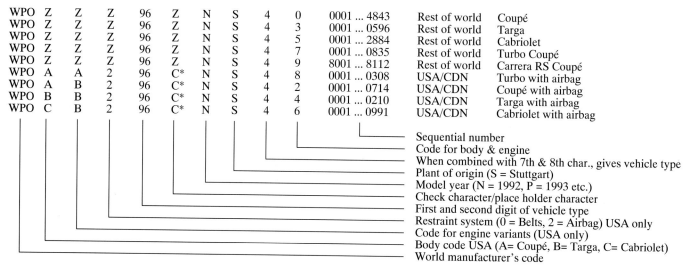

WPO	Z	Z	Z	96	Z	N	S	4	0	0001 ... 4843	Rest of world	Coupé
WPO	Z	Z	Z	96	Z	N	S	4	3	0001 ... 0596	Rest of world	Targa
WPO	Z	Z	Z	96	Z	N	S	4	5	0001 ... 2884	Rest of world	Cabriolet
WPO	Z	Z	Z	96	Z	N	S	4	7	0001 ... 0835	Rest of world	Turbo Coupé
WPO	Z	Z	Z	96	Z	N	S	4	9	8001 ... 8112	Rest of world	Carrera RS Coupé
WPO	A	A	2	96	C*	N	S	4	8	0001 ... 0308	USA/CDN	Turbo with airbag
WPO	A	B	2	96	C*	N	S	4	2	0001 ... 0714	USA/CDN	Coupé with airbag
WPO	B	B	2	96	C*	N	S	4	4	0001 ... 0210	USA/CDN	Targa with airbag
WPO	C	B	2	96	C*	N	S	4	6	0001 ... 0991	USA/CDN	Cabriolet with airbag

Sequential number
Code for body & engine
When combined with 7th & 8th char., gives vehicle type
Plant of origin (S = Stuttgart)
Model year (N = 1992, P = 1993 etc.)
Check character/place holder character
First and second digit of vehicle type
Restraint system (0 = Belts, 2 = Airbag) USA only
Code for engine variants (USA only)
Body code USA (A= Coupé, B= Targa, C= Cabriolet)
World manufacturer's code

C* = check character, could be 0 to 9 or X (USA only)
Z = filler character for rest of world vehicles

Model Year 1993

Note: U.S. market 1993 Turbo 3.6 build in calendar year 1993 are assigned 1994 VIN numbers.

Vehicle Identification Numbers (VIN Numbers)

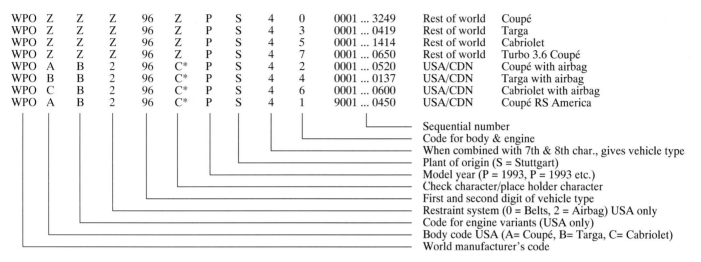

WPO	Z	Z	Z	96	Z	P	S	4	0	0001 ... 3249	Rest of world	Coupé
WPO	Z	Z	Z	96	Z	P	S	4	3	0001 ... 0419	Rest of world	Targa
WPO	Z	Z	Z	96	Z	P	S	4	5	0001 ... 1414	Rest of world	Cabriolet
WPO	Z	Z	Z	96	Z	P	S	4	7	0001 ... 0650	Rest of world	Turbo 3.6 Coupé
WPO	A	B	2	96	C*	P	S	4	2	0001 ... 0520	USA/CDN	Coupé with airbag
WPO	B	B	2	96	C*	P	S	4	4	0001 ... 0137	USA/CDN	Targa with airbag
WPO	C	B	2	96	C*	P	S	4	6	0001 ... 0600	USA/CDN	Cabriolet with airbag
WPO	A	B	2	96	C*	P	S	4	1	9001 ... 0450	USA/CDN	Coupé RS America

Sequential number
Code for body & engine
When combined with 7th & 8th char., gives vehicle type
Plant of origin (S = Stuttgart)
Model year (P = 1993, P = 1993 etc.)
Check character/place holder character
First and second digit of vehicle type
Restraint system (0 = Belts, 2 = Airbag) USA only
Code for engine variants (USA only)
Body code USA (A= Coupé, B= Targa, C= Cabriolet)
World manufacturer's code

Model Year 1994
Vehicle Identification Numbers (VIN Numbers)

WPO	Z	Z	Z	96	Z	R	S	4	0	0001 ... 0606	Rest of world	Coupé
WPO	Z	Z	Z	96	Z	R	S	4	5	0001 ... 0315	Rest of world	Cabriolet
WPO	Z	Z	Z	96	Z	R	S	4	5	5001 ... 5581	Rest of world	Speedster (964)
WPO	Z	Z	Z	96	Z	R	S	4	7	0001 ... 0471	Rest of world	Turbo 3.6 Coupé
WPO	A	B	2	96	C*	R	S	4	1	9001 ... 9144	USA/CDN	Coupé RS America
WPO	B	B	2	96	C*	R	S	4	2	0001 ... 0456	USA/CDN	Coupé
WPO	C	B	2	96	C*	R	S	4	4	0001 ... 9999 **	USA/CDN	Targa
WPO	C	B	2	96	C*	R	S	4	6	0001 ... 0283	USA/CDN	Cabriolet
WPO	C	B	2	96	C*	R	S	4	6	5001 ... 5469	USA/CDN	Speedster (964)
WPO	A	C	2	96	C*	R	S	4	8	0001 ... 0466	USA/CDN	Turbo 3.6
WPO	Z	Z	Z	99	Z	R	S	3	1	0001 ... 6412	Rest of world	Coupé ("new Carrera")
WPO	Z	Z	Z	99	Z	R	S	3	3	0001 ... 5850	Rest of world	Cabriolet ("new Carrera")
WPO	Z	Z	Z	99	Z	R	S	3	9	8001 ... 8100	Rest of world	Cup vehicle ("new Carrera")
WPO	A	B	2	99	C*	R	S	3	2	0001 ... 1453	USA/CDN	Coupé ("new Carrera")
WPO	C	B	2	99	C*	R	S	3	4	0001 ... 1224	USA/CDN	Cabriolet ("new Carrera")

Sequential number
Code for body & engine
When combined with 7th & 8th char., gives vehicle type
Plant of origin (S = Stuttgart)
Model year (P = 1993, P = 1993 etc.)
Check character/place holder character
First and second digit of vehicle type
Restraint system (0 = Belts, 2 = Airbag) USA only
Code for engine variants (USA only)
Body code USA (A= Coupé, B= Targa, C= Cabriolet)
World manufacturer's code

C* = check character, could be 0 to 9 or X (USA only)
Z = filler character for rest of world vehicles
** these chassis numbers were not used

Translated documents

Page 31

(Stamped) Received K.B.-A
Date: 17 Nov. 1961

```
I n t e r - o f f i c e   m e m o
====================================
```

Re: Type description, model T8

The T6 model is to be fitted with new bodywork, while retaining the present floorpan wherever possible; suspension, transmission and engine are to be carried over without modification.

The body is to reflect the following changes:

The model is to be a two-seater; the space formerly occupied by the rear seats, below the luggage space, is to be used by the fuel tank. This will result in a larger, more easily accessible front luggage area. In addition, the rear window is to form an openable hatch, which will also make the rear luggage area easily accessible from the outside. For ventilation, this rear hatch is to be slightly opened, which will eliminate the need for rear vent windows.

Spare tire location is to be improved if possible. Installation of a sliding roof is not planned. However, a cabriolet is to be developed in parallel to the coupe.

The body shape of the new type will be developed by the Styling Department, Herr Porsche jr. and documents to be provided to Reutter company.

Porsche will make Herr Schröder available to Reutter as co-worker and liaison between Porsche and Reutter. For this assignment, he will work under Herr Beierbach, who is responsible for this project.

Stuttgart, 10 Nov. 1961
To/pa

Distribution
Herr Porsche
Herr Kern
Herr Rabe
Herr W. Schmidt
Herr Komenda
Herr Schmid
Herr Porsche jr.
Reutter Co., 2x
File

Page 35

Draft

Brief description

of Porsche body, 901 Coupe.
Left hand drive version   Type 901

1. **Body shell:**   All-steel body with fixed roof, self-supporting unit body with floor pan. Single-piece monocoque structure from cowl to tail. Front fenders removable.

2. **Doors:**   All-steel doors, one door each left and right, hinged at front, latch at rear. Pushbutton-operated exterior door handles, lockable with same key. Interior actuation via push button on door lock strip. The main door lock is a knee lever action lock with locking wedge and door guide. Also installed are a hidden door stay with snubber, armrest acting as door pull, and below that an interior door release.

3. **Lids:**   Front and rear lids are fitted with inside-mounted hinges and are counterbalanced when opened. The installed locks can only be operated from inside the car, via cable pulls. (The front lid releases in the event of a broken pull cable).
The front lid is additionally secured against accidental opening.
The rear lid includes air inlet grilles.

4. **Windows:**   4.1 Single-piece, curved, panoramic laminated glass windshield, held by a rubber profile with metal trim strip.
4.2 The door glass consists of curved tempered glass and may be raised and lowered by means of a window winder mechanism. They are guided in a chrome plated brass frame fitted with a plush profile.
4.3 The vent windows in the door are made of tempered glass held in a chrome plated frame. A friction brake holds it in any position and is locked by a catch and safety.
4.4 The rear quarter windows are of curved tempered glass held in chrome plated frames.
4.5 The rear window is spherical, made of tempered glass, held by a rubber profile with metal trim strip.
-2-

5. Instrument panel:
The stressed instrument panel is welded in, and contains the mounting holes for instruments and controls as well as a storage compartment with locking lid. Top of instrument panel trimmed by a non-glare cover with padded rear edge.
The following are installed:
1 tachometer with oil temperature and oil pressure gauges, warning lights for battery charging and turn signals
1 speedometer with odometer and trip odometer, fuel level gauge with reserve warning light, high beam and parking brake warning lights, as well as marker light and fog light warning lights
1 light switch and rheostat for instrument panel lights
1 electric cigar lighter
1 glove compartment light with door contact switch
2 door contact switches for interior lights
1 control for fresh air vents
1 ashtray
1 passenger grab handle, next to storage compartment.
1 radio blanking plate (radio installation is customer option).

6. Electrical equipment
The wiring harness, including fusebox, relays, etc., is installed, ready to hook up. The components located in the instrument panel (see above) are connected, as well as connections to battery, starter, radio, fog lights and other electrical devices.
All lamps and headlights are fitted with bulbs.
Asymmetric "ES" headlights with low and high beams.
1 pair front turn signal/marker lights. Marker light may be turned on as parking light.
1 pair taillights; each light contains brake, tail and marker lights and reflectors (tail lights may be switched on as parking light.
1 starter-battery

On the steering column:
1 single-lever switch on left for turn signal, high/low beams and flashing high beams
1 single-lever switch on right for windshield wiper and washer operation
1 ignition/starter switch and steering column lock (with restart lockout), on right
1 push button for horn in steering wheel hub
2 license plate lights
1 tandem windshield wiper system, three selectable stages
1 pair high-volume horns (two-tone)
2 interior lights on left and right roof frame
1 windshield washer system
-3-

1 contact switch for parking brake warning light
1 backup light switch on transmission
1 trunk light with automatic contact switch

7. Heating and ventilation
The following interior heating and ventilation variations are planned:
7.1 Engine heat with temp. control by means of fresh air vented from engine cooling fan

7.2 Fresh air admitted from front by means of vent slots in cowl

The bare body shell is to be prepared for the installation of the engine heat system.
All channels, tubes, connecting holes etc. for installation of heating and ventilation are already present.

for Item 7.1
Warm engine air admitted to interior, windshield, rear window, and door windows via passages in longitudinals. The heat control is located on the center tunnel, ahead of the shift lever, and may be partially or fully opened as desired.
The passenger compartment warm air outlets may be partially or fully opened by means of slides on the longitudinals (left and right front).

for Item 7.2
To admit fresh air, vent slots are located in the cowl, ahead of the windshield. Mounted below the vents is an air funnel and water separator to remove water admitted with inlet air. Water drains out through a hose. Fresh air enters the passenger compartment only through a vent at the center of the windshield. The airflow can be adjusted by means of a flap in the water separator. Its control lever is located on the dashboard.

8. <u>Seats:</u> 2 front seats with forward folding, adjustable back rests (reclining seats). Passenger seat back rest secured against folding forward. Seats built on spring boxes, back rest with rubber springing. Two jump seats in rear, with divided back rest, which folds down to form luggage area.

9. <u>Luggage spaces:</u> The trunk is located under the front lid, and also contains the spare tire, battery and tool kit.
An additional luggage space is in the rear of the passenger compartment; folding down the rear seat backs forms a wide, flat luggage shelf.

-4-

- 4 -

10. <u>Bumpers:</u> The bumpers are attached at the front and rear by removable mounts, and fitted with light alloy trim strips and plastic inserts.
The rear bumper includes bumper guards.
Front horns are available as an option.
Bumpers painted in body color, inside and out.

11. <u>Trim:</u> 11.1 Traffic related trim items:
1 day-night inside rear view mirror
2 sun visors (passenger side w/ mirror)
1 outside rear view mirror (standard for domestic models, optional for export)

11.2 Trim and surfaces:
Trim strips for bumpers, door sills, windshield and rear window, as well as air inlet grille in light alloy with bright surface treatment.
Door and side window frames, vent window latches, window cranks, outside door handles, front lid handle, headlight trim rings, tail and brake light housings, outside and inside rear view mirrors of stainless steel (chrome plated mounts).
"PORSCHE" script gold plated.
Wiper arms and blades painted metallic silver.

12. <u>Floor covering:</u> Rubber mats ahead of the front seats, over the tunnel and in rear. Plywood boards on pedal bulkhead. Front trunk lined by a mat.

13. <u>Paint:</u> All body parts which will form hollow sections after completion of the body shell (longitudinal and transverse members, posts, pillars, roof members and hoops etc.) are to be painted with rust-preventive paint on those surfaces which will form the hollow sections, before spot welding; similarly, all spot welded seams must be protected against corrosion by means of spot weld paint, likewise the door skin and lid seams.

After assembly, the body shell is degreased and rust removed. All parts smoothed with lead must be treated to prevent later separation of primer. Primer will be baked on and then filler applied, the filler will be baked, sanded, then pre-coat applied and baked. This is also sanded, after which the cover coat is sprayed and baked. All seams which may admit water to the body must be sealed by body caulk before the cover coat is sprayed. The available colors are listed in the color combination sheets.

-5-

- 5 -

14. <u>Upholstery:</u> The side trim of the rear seat area, the rear wall, the doors and door pockets and arm rests/door pulls, left and right door posts, are trimmed with leatherette material identical to the side panels of the seats and the rear of the front seat backs.
The instrument panel trim and window sills are covered with leatherette. The headliner, door and window pillars, as well as the sun visors, are covered with leatherette (headliner perforated).
The sides of the passenger compartment, longitudinals, rear tunnel area and back of the jump seat backs are carpeted.
The colors and grades of upholstery materials, leatherette, carpets etc. are recorded on the color combination sheets.

15. <u>Accessories:</u> 1 key case with:
2 door keys
2 keys for ignition/starter switch
2 keys for glove compartment
1 Porsche touch-up paint bottle in car color
1 set body care instructions

16. <u>Sound deadener:</u>

16.1 <u>Spray application</u>
16.11 <u>Exterior parts</u>

Entire floor and frame, from nose to tail, including hollow spaces in front and rear suspension, all wheel wells and fenders, underside of front and rear outer panels with sound deadener.
Difficult to reach areas in nose and tail only sprayed or brushed with chassis paint.
Special fender reinforcement against rock impacts is not planned.
The entire body underside may be given a first coat of chassis paint, although this is not mandatory.

16.12 <u>Interior spaces</u>
Floor pan in passenger compartment, including front bulkhead and battery box wall, rear tunnel piece, rear wheel wells, firewall, rear seat pans, door pockets in front of the hinge posts left and right, one coat of sprayed on sound deadener (in car color as required).

Interior of doors precoated with one coat of chassis paint, one coat of sound deadener.
Front interior, transverse lock panel, wheel wells, fuel tank floor, front bulkhead, trunk floor and battery box one coat of sound deadener.

-6-

- 6 -

16.13 <u>Engine compartment</u>
All sides of engine compartment (front wall, side walls, rear wall, engine side sheet metal) two layers of sound deadener.

16.2 <u>Further sound deadening measures, with glued-in damping materials</u>
16.21 <u>Front compartment</u>
Trunk floor, bulkhead.

16.22 <u>Passenger compartment</u>
Pedal bulkhead, battery box wall, floor, sides of tunnel, kick panels, jump seats and luggage area floor. Also longitudinals, rear wheel wells, rear bulkhead and roof.

Prepared groove in hollow space between roof and rear bulkhead filled with foam during body assembly.

16.23 <u>Engine compartment</u>
Entire engine compartment including engine cover.

16.24 <u>Exterior parts</u>
Transmission floor, transmission hump (seat pans) and front door pillar.

16.3 <u>Transmission linkage cover at end of tunnel:</u>
Sound deadener glued to underside of cover, carpet on upper side.
For information regarding sound deadening materials, number of layers glued in etc. See parts list or drawing.

17. <u>Special equipment:</u>
A lid in the left front fender covers the fuel filler neck. The lid can only be opened by means of a cable pull from inside the car.

Page 36

<u>Technical Description</u>

<u>of Porsche T 8 chassis, Type 901</u>

<u>Front suspension:</u> Independent suspension. The wheels are attached to transverse members and struts, springing by adjustable torsion bars and strongly progressive rubber bump stops, damping by double acting shock absorbers in the struts. Maintenance free.

<u>Steering:</u> Light action rack and pinion steering with steering damper and "safety steering column."

<u>Rear suspension:</u> Independent suspension. The wheels are located by semi-trailing arms, sprung by torsion bars and strongly progressive rubber bump stops, and damped by long-stroke telescoping shock absorbers. Maintenance free.

<u>Brakes:</u> Service brakes: hydraulically operated disc brakes with automatic adjustment on all 4 wheels.
Parking brake: duo-servo brake acting on inner drum of the rear discs, activated by handle between front seats.

Tires:	Radial tires, 165 x 15.	
Transmission shifter:	Stick shift between front seats.	
General dimensions:	Track, front	1332 mm
	" rear	1310 mm
	Wheelbase	2204 mm
	Steering ratio	1 : 17
	Turns lock-to-lock	3 turns
	Turning circle	10 m

Stuttgart, 28 June 1963
KB-Hö//br

(signed)
Hönick

Page 38

(Stamped) Received K.B.-A
Date: 12 Nov. 1962

Distribution:
Herr Porsche
Herr Porsche jr.
Herr Tomala
Herr Rombold
Herr Reimspiess
Herr Komenda
Herr Linge
FV

I n t e r - o f f i c e   m e m o
===================================

Re: First test drive with 901 prototype on Friday, 9.11.1962

A. Basics
Outward visibility and seating position very good.
The vehicle is very maneuverable and has retained the character of a sports car. The handling characteristics resemble those of our T 8 predecessor with T 6 bodywork, i.e. the vehicle still oversteers too much and reacts too viciously to steering inputs, and is still not satisfactory in alternating curves. (Spring tuning not yet finalized, lack of new rear suspension).
Instruments are readily visible, seats are comfortable. Backup lights provide bright illumination and good light distribution.
Seen from the chase vehicle, the car appears strange from the rear. One has the impression that the rear window is trapezoidal, narrower at the back. The vehicle appears attractive and small.
The shrouding to hide engine and exhaust is also good, although the observation that the sound deadening mat on the engine sheet metal had already turned soft after the first short drive is probably related to poor cooling of the muffler by the slipstream.

B. Bodywork complaints
Doors rattle.
Windows rattle (temporary fitting).
Glove compartment door pops open.
Vehicle is loud overall (no sprayed-in sound deadener).
Windows fog heavily (is vent cross section adequate for winter service?)
Engine compartment light is visible through engine lid pad (other location possible?)
Why no symmetrical key for door and ignition lock?

C. Chassis complaints
Steering is slow and heavy in center position, yet vicious in corrective maneuvers. Some play on center.
Vehicle oversteers like Car 109.
Heating system smells.
Transmission howls.
Front suspension adjusted improperly, car has too little ground clearance.
Transverse tar strips on pavement come through, as if car is on rubber bump stops.
Front suspension bottoms.
Steering wheel not centered.
Tachometer probably reads too high.
Brake has extreme pedal changes; after several km without touching the brake, pedal goes to the floor. Pedal comes back after pumping.
- 2 -

- 2 -

D. Miscellaneous
Lights good, shifter good.
V max tunnel with obstruction 20.8 sec = 175 km/h. Tachometer indicates 6100 rpm.

E. Assembly program for 12. and 13.10.62
Correct steering wheel position.
Change glove box door latch.
Install floor board for passenger.
Check clearance between muffler and engine sheet metal (Temperature!)
Calibrate tachometer.
Remove transmission, install speedometer drive.
If tachometer cannot be corrected, additional installation of Hartmann & Braun equipment.

Record wheel deflection curves, measure frame elasticity and steering elasticity.
Correct front suspension settings.
Install parking brake.
Bleed and check brakes.

Stgt.-Zuffenhausen, 12.11.62
FV/Bo-scho

(Bott)

(Stamped) Received K.B.-A
Date: 16 Nov. 1962

Distribution:
Herr Porsche
Herr Porsche jr.
Herr Tomala
Herr Rombold
Herr Reimspiess
Herr Hönick
Herr Komenda
Herr Linge
FV

I n t e r - o f f i c e   m e m o
===================================

Re: Second test drive with 901 prototype on Wednesday, 14.11.1962

Outside air temperature + 6° C, dry roads.
Test drives between 21:00 and 22:00, winds calm.

Test results:

Standing start 2 km, average of both directions = 34.7 average speed 104 km/h. (Startup not entirely correct, the clutch jerks).

Maximum speed at tunnel = 188 km/h with brake power reading on meter of 88.7 hp.

At 6100 rpm, dropping to 6000, according to tachometer (calibration curve not yet available).
Speedometer indication at this speed is 197 km/h, speedometer reads 5% high.

Speedometer indication at 60 km/h = 60 km/h
                    at 120 km/h = 120 km/h
Deviation only at high speed.

Steering:
Even on driving off, the steering was not as lively as our production steering. During the drive, it got increasingly heavy, and after about 50 km, it had to be manually returned to center, even in tight curves.

Brakes:
The installed Girling brake with Girling master cylinder has pleasant pedal pressure, good braking action, and does not pull when braking from high speed. The pedal travel still varies greatly. During a maximum effort stop from 205 km/h, the brake pedal went to the floor. After 5 brake applications from 140 km/h to nearly a full stop, a loud noise, resulting from brake pads rubbing against the disc, was audible; this went away completely after about 2 km. Also, the brakes smoked heavily and smelled very strongly in the last two stops.

Tachometer:
At the beginning, the instrument functioned very well. The pointer was steady and did not run ahead to any discernible degree. After about 20 km, the pointer suddenly dropped to 0 and from time to time would operate again, with strong twitching. (Device not in order).

Engine:
The installed engine had a very poor idle (swinging between 800 and 100 rpm). Strong vibrations are transmitted to the car at idle. In contrast to good production engines, rpm dropped markedly on slight grades. The test drive was halted because the steering was so stiff that the car was no longer safe to operate.

- 2 -

- 2 -

Continuation of assembly program

1.)   Remove engine and deliver to MV.

2.)   Check clutch (jerks strongly).

3.)   Check Shore hardness of engine-transmission mounts.
       (Jerky clutch, strong noise transmission).

4.)   Check brakes
       Under full braking, both left wheels lock.
       The right wheels do not leave skid marks.
       Brake pedal hits hard when allowed to snap back.

5.)   Remove and check tachometer instrument.
       Attach calibration curve to instrument panel.

6.) Detach tie rods, check for friction in steering box and steering damper. If friction is excessive, remove steering box and fill with special grease.

7.) Install outside mirror per Studio instructions.

8.) Install passenger grab handle per Studio instructions.

9.) Check wheel alignment, correct steering wheel position.

10.) Operation of windshield washer and wiper is pleasant, column-mounted ignition lock, however, is difficult to reach; this is impossible.

11.) Prepare chassis elasticity and steering elasticity tests for Saturday.

Next test drive expected on Monday, 21.11.1962.

x) Parking brake is effective only when the hand lever is pulled with great force (unreasonable imposition for female drivers).

Stgt.-Zuffenhausen, 15.11.62
FV/Bo-scho
                                        (Bott)

Page 39

(Stamped) Received K.B.-A
Date: 29 Nov. 1962

Distribution:
Herr Porsche
Herr Porsche jr.
Herr Tomala
Herr Rombold
Herr Reimspiess
Herr Hönick
Herr Komenda
Herr Linge
MV
FV

I n t e r - o f f i c e   m e m o
==

Re: Third test drive with 901 prototype on Tuesday, 27.11.1962

Outside air temperature + 1° C, nearly calm wind.

Participants: Mssrs. Rombold, Spannagel, Bott.

Basic points:

Body
Passenger footrest should be flatter.
Vent windows cause loud wind noise.
Operation of vent windows is difficult as knurled knob does not provide enough grip.
Window has too much play in every open position.
Window crank is too difficult to turn, requires too many turns, window jams.
Glove compartment snubber is too weak.
Armrest on driver's door is very good, but too far back on passenger side.
Both armrests loose.
Backrest adjustment difficult to operate, rests against longitudinal.
Rear seat headroom/kneeroom seem smaller than on current production car.
Ignition switch very difficult to reach, see test report E 1055.
Heater control located too far forward and should be replaced by a simple lever.
Lack of contrast for instrument markings. Poor readability even at maximum illumination.
Storage area behind the rear seats should either be horizontal or be fitted with a ledge.
Rear seat backs must be fitted with locking arrangement.
Parking brake handle located too far forward.
Both sun visors have metal frames at their outside edges, which could result in injury in the event of an accident.

General criticisms:

Something between the steering wheel and steering box rubs when steering wheel is near center.
Right door rattles.
Strong draft through cigar lighter hole.
Low beams set too low.
Shifter is good, throws could be shorter.
Strong odor of exhaust under engine braking, more intense than in current production car.
Heater output is good.
Engine lid rattles. Trunk illumination does not work.
Ashtray is missing. Passenger grab handle is missing.
An undertray should be installed below the fuel tank.
Brake still exhibits extreme travel changes.

Stgt.-Zuffenhausen, 28.11.62
FV/Bo-scho
                                        (Bott)

Page 73

(Stamped) Received Techn. Direction
Date: 27 Aug. 1963

To all
Domestic General Distributorships   Stuttgart, 23 Aug. 1963

            41st IAA, Frankfurt/Main, Sept. 12 - 22, 1963

Dear Sirs,

Preparations are underway for this year's auto show. We will occupy the same location, i.e. Hall 1a, Stand 27.

We would like to bring a few items to your attention, items which might be of significance to a goal-oriented customer relations program.

1.   Exhibition items

We will display three vehicles from the 356 C model line, the Type 901 with 2-liter six-cylinder engine and the 1.7 liter Porsche industrial engine:

1.   Cabriolet C 75 (75 hp), enamel blue

2.   Coupe SC 95 (95 hp), togo brown

3.   Coupe Carrera 2000 GS, signal red

4.   Coupe Type 901, 2-liter six-cylinder engine, yellow (special color).

     This vehicle represents an extension of the 356 C model line. Important features include:
a)   New body, 120 mm longer wheelbase, resulting in greater interior space, considerably larger trunk space under the front lid.

                                        - 2 -

Page 78

(Stamped) Received Techn. Direction
Date: 13 July 1962

            Technical specifications — Engine Type 821/1

Type	Boxer
Number of cylinders	6
Cooling	Air
Bore	80 mm
Stroke	66 mm
Stroke/bore ratio	0.825
Displacement	1990.7 cc
Power output, Ne	130 hp
at rpm n	6500 rpm
brake mean effective pressure, bmep	9 kg/cm^2
max. torque	16.5 mkg
at engine rpm n	4600 rpm
brake mean effective pressure, bmep	10.4 kg/cm^2
specific output	65 hp/liter
compression ratio	9:1
connecting rod ratio	0.262
specific piston load	0.434 hp/cm^2
mean piston speed at 6500 rpm	14.3 m/sec
crankshaft	7 main bearings
camshaft	overhead, chain driven
electrical system	12 V

Page 82

Engine No.	Crankcase	Crankshaft	Pistons Cylinders	Heads	Timing	Camshaft	Carburetor	Test purpose	Mechanic	Type
1	Silumin old vers. oil passages 901	901	Ferral	821	1007 fixed	821 Normal 2	40 PICB	Temperature measurements	Dellin, 1 brake	821/1
2	Elektron case 821	821	Ferral	821	1007 fixed	821 Normal 2	40 floatless	Car T 8	Rapp, (Kolb)	821/1
3	Silumin old vers. oil passages 901	901	Ferral	821	1007 fixed	821 Normal 2	36 floatless	Intake manifold tests	Munding, Hahn	821/1
4	Silumin case vers. 821/901	901	Ferral	901	1008 fixed	821 Normal 2 adjustable		Cam tests	Herrmann, Himmelseher	901/1
5								Oil tests	Klieber Bartel	901/2
6								Chain tests	Enz, Binder, Ost	901/2
7								Cam train	1 mechanic	901/1 & 901/2

Page 220

Inter-office memo

To: Press Department   Deliver to: Herr von Hanstein
                              via Herr Piëch

issued 27.6.67
VF/Bo-kf

Re:

Marathon de la Route
Your memo dated 21.6.67

As I informed you verbally, we would like to prepare a vehicle for this event.

Body 911 R,
Sport-o-matic transmission with higher converter stall rpm,
Engine 911 with sport kit.

As crew for this vehicle, I propose drivers Elford, Herrmann, Neerpasch, all of whom are acquainted with the Sport-o-matic transmission after their drive to Sicily and practice [for the Targa Florio].

During the race, the road test department will provide a service crew consisting of 2 mechanics and 1 engineer (Sport-o-matic specialist). Of course, these people can also service the second Sport-o-matic vehicle. If you desire to have a timing crew, please inform me to that effect.

Alpine Trial
Your memo dated 21.6.67

Participation of an "R" is dependent on the return of our Mugello car in an undamaged condition.

(signed)
Bott

read by
Piëch

392